Tho.ᵗ Chubbuck, Eng.ʳ Springfield, Mass.

Engraved expressly for Holland's "Life of Lincoln".

A. Lincoln.

HOLLAND'S LIFE OF ABRAHAM LINCOLN

J. G. Holland

Introduction to the Bison Books Edition
by Allen C. Guelzo

UNIVERSITY OF NEBRASKA PRESS

LINCOLN AND LONDON

Introduction and index © 1998 by the University of Nebraska
Press

⊗ The paper in this book meets the minimum requirements of
American National Standard for Information Sciences—
Permanence of Paper for Printed Library Materials, ANSI
Z39.48-1984.

First Bison Books printing: 1998
Most recent printing indicated by the last digit below:
10   9   8   7   6   5   4   3   2   1

Library of Congress Cataloging-in-Publication Data
Holland, J. G. (Josiah Gilbert), 1819–1881.
[Life of Abraham Lincoln]
Holland's life of Abraham Lincoln / J. G. Holland; introduction
by Allen C. Guelzo.
p.   cm.
Originally published: Springfield, Mass.: Gurdon Bill, 1866.
Includes bibliographical references and index.
ISBN 0-8032-7303-7 (pbk.: alk. paper)
1. Lincoln, Abraham, 1809–1865.   2. Presidents—United
States—Biography.   I. Title.
E457.H729   1998
973.7′092—dc21
[B]
97-44474   CIP

Reprinted from the original 1866 edition by Gurdon Bill,
Springfield MA. As with the original, this Bison Books edition
begins chapter one on arabic page 17; no material has been
omitted.

TO

ANDREW JOHNSON,

TO WHOM PROVIDENCE HAS ASSIGNED THE COMPLETION

OF

ABRAHAM LINCOLN'S LABORS,

I DEDICATE

THIS RECORD OF

ABRAHAM LINCOLN'S LIFE:

WITH THE PRAYER

THAT HISTORY, WHICH WILL ASSOCIATE THEIR NAMES
FOREVER,

MAY BE ABLE TO FIND NO SEAM WHERE THEIR ADMINISTRATIONS
WERE JOINED,

AND

MARK NO CHANGE OF TEXTURE BY WHICH THEY MAY
BE CONTRASTED.

INTRODUCTION

Allen C. Guelzo

Published in 1866, Josiah Gilbert Holland's *Life of Abraham Lincoln* is, in a number of ways, the first great comprehensive Lincoln biography. Simply in terms of beating others to the line, Holland's *Life* leapt into print just ahead of Isaac Arnold's *The History of Abraham Lincoln and the Overthrow of American Slavery* and the book version of Francis Carpenter's *Six Months at the White House*, shortly before the completion of William Henry Herndon's sensational Springfield lecture series on Lincoln, and six years prior to Ward Hill Lamon's ghostwritten *Life of Abraham Lincoln*. Holland's *Life* also deserves pride of place among Lincoln biographies for turning away sharply from the pattern of the 1860 and 1864 campaign biographies by John Locke Scripps, Joseph Q. Howard, Joseph H. Barrett, and William Dean Howells, all of which were the initial model for the first postassassination Lincoln books. Unlike the campaign biographers, Holland saw no purpose in glorifying Lincoln's log-cabin origins, and he felt free to speculate on the complexities and ambiguities of Lincoln's character and Lincoln's religion. Above all, Holland's *Life* was the first to incorporate into a biography a substantial amount of direct interviews and correspondence with Lincoln's associates and relatives. Although James Q. Howard in 1860 (and later, William Thayer for *The Pioneer Boy* in 1863) interviewed several of Lincoln's early New Salem and Springfield acquaintances, Holland's interviews and letters produced a far larger cache of Lincoln recollections, all of which Holland used in creating the most substantial picture of Lincoln's early life then available.[1]

And yet, while Holland's *Life* sold well over 100,000 copies (and by subscription rather than through trade distribution) and brought Holland "more money than he probably ever dreamed of possessing during his early life," Holland's book has also been the Lincoln biography most consistently dismissed by modern Lincolnographers.[2] Benjamin P. Thomas condemned the "mawkish sentimentality of the book" and wrote Holland off as a "moralist" who did little more with Lincoln's life than dress it up as a self-improvement fable.[3] Even one of Holland's biographers characterized the *Life of Abraham Lincoln* as "hasty and partial" and admitted that "in recent years . . . few Lincoln bibliographers have bothered to list it at all."[4]

The reasons for this dismissal are complicated but not subtle. For one thing, Holland was working against the clock, and although the speed with which he turned out his *Life* is remarkable, it also guaranteed that he would run roughshod over complicated issues, neglect to introduce important characters, and leave a good deal of detail to the public memory of his readership. Much as he opened up new avenues of primary research into Lincoln's early life, he seems to have made no effort to interview Lincoln's immediate family, and Mary Todd Lincoln and her children appear only infrequently and in their public roles in Holland's *Life*. Holland's stature as a biographer was also undercut by his own instincts. Holland was, after all, a journalist—even his eulogists admitted that "his talent was pre-eminently journalistic" rather than literary—and it showed all too often when Holland put his political partisanship for Lincoln on display.[5] Although he promised in his preface not to write "a political or a military history of Mr. Lincoln's administration," it was politics which occupied most of his chapters on Lincoln's presidency, and a politics in which Lincoln was unapologetically the champion of "strength and moderation" and the opposition, whether from John Charles Frémont or Clement

Vallandigham, was "irresponsible" or "treasonable." Holland's authority was also weakened by his never having known Lincoln personally—never, in fact, having even met him— and his principal personal qualification for writing the book was a widely published eulogy on Lincoln that he had been called to deliver after the assassination.

But the factor that worked longest against Holland's long-term reputation was his position as an "outsider" to what would soon become a protective ring of Springfield "insiders" who had known Lincoln themselves and who treated Holland as an interloper. Holland was, after all, an easterner, and while he tried to draw many of Lincoln's professional acquaintances from his Springfield days into his book, too many of them were planning biographies or lectures or articles of their own to welcome Holland as a rival.[6] What was worse, Holland chose to promote Lincoln as "eminently a Christian president," which aroused the contempt of two of the most important "insiders," William Herndon and Ward Hill Lamon, neither of whom shared much of Holland's religious interest and both of whom were convinced that Lincoln was an "infidel" and even an "atheist." Despite the fact that Holland built more upon material given him by Herndon than any other source, and despite Herndon's original enthusiasm for Holland's work, Herndon was deeply opposed to any attempt to discover religious sensibilities in Lincoln, and when it became apparent shortly before Holland's *Life* was published that Holland intended to do exactly that, Herndon embarked on his own private campaign to condemn Holland's *Life* as "all bosh."[7]

And yet, even granting Holland's weakness for moralisms and journalistic slickness, his *Life* was a much greater accomplishment than Herndon wanted to admit. The measure of Holland's achievement becomes clearer when his *Life* is compared to the campaign biographies that preceded, rather than those that followed, him. Although at least thirteen campaign biographies of Lincoln had appeared for the 1860 presidential election alone, their coverage of Lincoln's formative years in the 1820s and 1830s was sparse and uninteresting, and most of them relied for their information on Lincoln's life before 1860 on two autobiographical sketches written by Lincoln, in 1859 for Jesse W. Fell and in 1860 for John Locke Scripps.[8] Joseph Barrett, for instance, published a campaign biography of Lincoln in 1860, reissued it with a review of Lincoln's first term as president, and then hurried a postassassination edition into print in the summer of 1865, but only 72 of its 842 pages were devoted to Lincoln's life before his election to Congress in 1846. In the same fashion, Henry Jarvis Raymond, the strongly pro-Lincoln editor of the *New York Times*, published an election-year *History of the Administration of President Lincoln* in May 1864, but only 50 pages were given over to biography and the rest went to assembling Lincoln's speeches, public letters, and other papers. The postassassination version of the *History* that Raymond brought out in 1865 as *Life and Public Services of Abraham Lincoln* greatly lengthened the overall narrative, to 801 pages, but the new material focused only on the war years. Holland, by contrast, devoted almost one-fifth of his narrative to Lincoln's life before the 1846 congressional election, and more than half the book was spent on the period before Lincoln's inauguration.

Much of what filled that first half was material on Lincoln's early life that was now appearing for the first time. Raymond had picked up a number of "early Lincoln" anecdotes for his *History*, including the tales of Lincoln's boyhood letter to pastor Elkin, the Crawford book story, the New Orleans flatboat account, and the trial of Duff Armstrong. But Holland included over thirty such "early Lincoln" stories, including the story of the turkey that young Lincoln shot from his father's cabin; being kicked by a horse at the mill; his accounting of the New Salem post office money from a sock; the pig in the road; swinging through a "scuttle" to defend Edward Dickinson Baker; and so on. Holland was able to retail these stories because he directly sought out a number of Lincoln acquaintances, including Stephen T. Logan, Horace White, Usher F. Linder, Orville Hickman Browning, Newton Bateman, George Boutwell, Dr.

Anson G. Henry, and Joshua Speed, and either interviewed them directly in Springfield or else solicited written reminiscences. Even more significant, advertisements that Holland took out in several Midwestern papers brought him into contact with the ring of Lincoln's collateral family, especially Augustus H. Chapman (who married the daughter of Lincoln's stepsister, Matilda Johnston), John Hanks (who had carried into the 1860 Illinois state Republican convention the split rails that gave Lincoln his campaign nickname), and the irrepressible Dennis Hanks (the illegitimate cousin who had grown up with Lincoln in Indiana). Above all, whether Herndon liked to admit it or not, Holland was the first to make use of Herndon's own testimony about Lincoln's early life. If Holland's *Life* was "all bosh," much of the "bosh" had come directly from Herndon.

This is not to say that Holland was incapable of dealing in "bosh" when he was so inclined. Born in Belchertown, Massachusetts, on 24 July 1819 as the youngest of Harrison and Anna Gilbert Holland's seven children, Josiah Gilbert Holland grew up in a household compounded of ultra-evangelical Calvinism and Micawberish poverty, and he spent virtually all of his life trying to get away from both. Ironically, in that respect, his early life was curiously similar to Lincoln's. Lincoln found his way out through wage labor, politics, and law; Holland tried to find his way out (since his parents were too poor to send him to Yale) through medicine, spending two quick terms in the Berkshire Medical College and learning most of his profession in the office of two Northampton, Massachusetts, doctors. He could not have made a worse mistake than choosing medicine: he went into practice with a fellow medical student in Springfield, Massachusetts, but he quickly turned out to be a failure as a physician, and by 1847 he was writing hack journalism just to make ends meet. Even there, he slipped badly. A small weekly that he founded in Springfield, the *Bay State Courier*, died unnoticed after six months. In desperation, he took a teaching job in Richmond, Virginia, in 1848, and then signed on as superintendent of schools in Vicksburg, Mississippi, where he found on arrival that it was up to him to organize the school system he was supposed to superintend. By May of 1849, he was back in Springfield.

But Springfield, Massachusetts, turned out to be the making of Holland, just as another Springfield had for Lincoln. Two weeks after returning from Mississippi, Holland was hired by Samuel Bowles, the owner and editor of the weekly *Springfield Republican*, which Bowles had taken up in 1844 as a Whig political organ (Bowles' first issue was an endorsement of Henry Clay's last futile campaign for the presidency). Bowles as editor and Holland as assistant editor amounted to the entire editorial staff, and virtually all the routine writing of the paper fell to Holland. But Holland thrived on it: after a year Bowles made him coeditor, after two more years Bowles made him part owner, and by 1853 the paper had been converted into the only daily in western Massachusetts. In 1854 Holland began serializing a *History of Western Massachusetts*, which was published in book form in 1855 and got him elected to the Massachusetts Historical Society. Even more, it gave him the raw material for his first turn at fiction, a historical romance entitled *The Bay-Path, A Tale of New England Colonial Life*, which began a highly lucrative march through sixteen editions. He gave up editing the *Republican*, but not his stake in the paper, and he now used the *Republican* as his platform for serializing what became his most popular production, a moral-advice book, *Timothy Titcomb's Letters to Young People* (1858). Two more novels followed by 1860, and thereafter Holland took to the lecture circuit.

It was his success as a lecturer which probably won Holland the invitation to deliver a eulogy on Lincoln at a mass meeting in the Springfield city hall on 19 April 1865, the Wednesday after Lincoln's death.[9] It was, as Holland's first biographer described it, "an oratorical triumph," and it moved Samuel Bowles to propose that Holland undertake a full-length Lincoln biography.[10] Holland wasted no time: even before Lincoln was buried, Holland had begun corresponding with John Locke Scripps, and exactly one month after delivering his Lincoln eulogy Holland was in Lincoln's Springfield, casually announcing that he was "engaged upon a new biography of President Lincoln" and "in search of original and authentic material for the work."[11] That search led him directly to William Henry Herndon, who shut down his office for two days to give Holland his own view of "the inner life of Mr. L." and an invaluable list of personal contacts for Holland to follow up.

Herndon seems to have taken an immediate liking to the suave New Englander. Herndon considered himself, in cultural terms, to be "turned *NewEnglandwards*," and Holland shared Herndon's interest in "the *subjective* Mr. Lincoln." It was probably Herndon who recounted to Holland the story that Lincoln had posed to Stephen Douglas his famous second question at Freeport, Illinois, because he hoped to sink Douglas's chances for the presidency in 1860, and it was probably also Herndon who told Holland that Lincoln's speeches against the Mexican War had cost him popular support in his home district and caused him to leave Congress without running for reelection. Both of these stories were of dubious accuracy, but Herndon believed them, and Holland could hardly have gotten them anywhere else in 1865. By the time Holland left Springfield, Herndon had become the most important, and most enthusiastic, direct source of information about Lincoln's pre-presidential life. "I regret," Herndon wrote him shortly afterwards, "that you could not have been with me 8 or 10 days consecutively."[12]

In fact, Holland was in Springfield only for a week before returning to New England.[13] But he held at least one major interview with Usher F. Linder and with Newton Bateman, the Illinois superintendent of public instruction and a Lincoln political ally, and perhaps also with Albert Hale, the minister of the Second (now Westminster) Presbyterian Church in Springfield, Stephen Logan, and Jesse K. Dubois. He also sent off a volley of requests for reminiscences, mostly from a long list of Lincoln acquaintances given him by Herndon. Not all of these contacts proved particularly encouraging. George Boutwell was only mildly interested in

Holland's project and glumly warned him that any effort to uncover fresh material on Lincoln's early years in Indiana's Spencer county was probably useless, since "all that is known of Mr. Lincoln in this County is rapidly going into tradition."[14] Others, like Anson Henry, were deliberately uncooperative. Henry refused to share the contents of any of Lincoln's letters to him because "their publication would only gratify a morbid curiosity," and he refused to make any further comment on Lincoln unless it was clear that "your undertaking meets with the approbation & approval of the family of Mr. Lincoln."[15]

But several other contacts rewarded Holland with pure biographical gold. Joshua Speed, who assured Holland that "till 1842, no two men were more intimate" than he and Lincoln, sent Holland copies of five key Lincoln letters (including the famous 24 August 1855 letter on slavery and Kansas, which Holland reprinted in full).[16] An advertisement in the *Cincinnati Advertiser* brought a response from Augustus H. Chapman, who dismissed the Barrett and Raymond biographies as the work of "hacks" and sent to Holland his own collection of "facts relating to Mr. Lincoln's early life, that of his Father and Mother, his sister and all of his ancestors." Even more important, Holland was able to recruit Erastus Wright, another Lincoln acquaintance in Springfield, to interview Dennis Hanks and John Hanks at the United States Sanitary Commission fair in Chicago in June 1865. Wright sent Holland a digest of the interviews (which Wright entitled "Biographical Sketches of Abraham Lincoln") in which Nancy Hanks Lincoln was identified as "Nancy Sparrow" and "Joseph Hanks niece," thus firing the first shot in a century-long controversy about Nancy Hanks Lincoln's possible illegitimacy.[17] Wright also interviewed James Short—the "Uncle Jimmy" Short of New Salem who had bought back Lincoln's surveying tools from the sheriff in 1835—and reported to Holland one of the earliest references (outside Herndon's collection of reminiscences) to yet another Lincoln controversy, the Ann Rutledge romance: "Lincoln boarded with said [James] Rutledge and was par-

tial towards his daughter, Miss Ann, an amiable young Lady
who took Sick and died, causing him much sorrow and un-
happiness."[18]

Holland seems to have gathered most of the interviews
and letters he wanted by the end of the summer of 1865,
and together with the Raymond, Barrett, and Scripps biographies, plus the appearance of Noah Brooks's "Personal Recollections of Abraham Lincoln" in the July 1865 issue of
Harper's Magazine and the serialization of Francis
Carpenter's "Six Months in the White House" in the *New
York Independent*, Holland was able swiftly to cobble together
his biography and have a prospectus ready for Samuel
Bowles to circulate to subscribers by December 1865. But
despite the book's sensational popularity when it was released early in 1866, Holland's *Life of Abraham Lincoln* made
itself into a critical target from the very first. Unlike Herndon
and the campaign biographers, Holland was unconvinced
that Lincoln's greatness had anything to do with his backcountry common-man origins (any more, of course, than
Holland wanted to concede any of his successes to his own
similarly hapless, pious origins). For Holland, what set Lincoln off from the ordinary was his drive to escape those origins, not to rely on them. Holland recognized that Lincoln
himself regarded his own origins as "common-place and
mean," and Holland consequently found little in Lincoln's
"primitive surroundings" worth romanticizing. "A good deal
of what is called 'the pioneer spirit,'" Holland sharply remarked, "is simply a spirit of shiftless discontent." Far from
being a man of the people, what distinguished the young
Lincoln in Holland's Whiggish eyes was that, "living among
the roughest of rough men, many of whom were addicted to
coarse vices," Lincoln had managed to avoid becoming like
them. "Not a circumstance of his life favored the development which he had reached," Holland grimly observed, "not
an influence around him ... which did not tend rather to
drag him down than lift him up."

Holland made no attempt "to disguise or conceal my own
personal partiality for Mr. Lincoln, and my thorough sym-

pathy with the political principles to which his life was devoted." And no wonder, since Holland and Lincoln were both Whigs who had scampered up the social ladder of the market revolution and were both Republicans who came to regard slavery as the ultimate contradiction of "the right to rise" in the market-driven economy which replaced the old Jeffersonian agrarianism championed by the Democrats. Holland rejoiced that Lincoln "was always a loyal party man" as a Whig, and his account of Lincoln's presidency gleefully stigmatized the northern Democratic opposition as "pestilent" and "malicious." He was merciless to George McClellan, who had commanded Lincoln's armies in 1862 and then ran against him for the presidency in 1864. "The whole history of McClellan's operations," Holland declared in a single damning litany, "is a history of magnificent preparations and promises, of fatal hesitations and procrastinations, of clamoring for more preparations, and justifications of hesitations and procrastinations, of government indulgence and forbearance, of military intrigues within the camp, of popular impatience and alarms, and of the waste of great means and golden opportunities." And Holland did not mind hinting broadly that McClellan "held a theory of his own as to the mode of conducting the war, and that independently of the government, he endeavored to pursue it"—which was as much as saying that McClellan, for political reasons, had tried to betray his country.

That Holland, like Lincoln, was more old Whig than new Republican also appeared from his applause of Lincoln's cautious approach to emancipation and Lincoln's reluctant clinging to schemes for colonization. "Sudden emancipation was never in accordance with Mr. Lincoln's judgement," Holland was convinced, "Nothing but the necessities of war would have induced him to decree it with relation to the slaves of any state." Holland took only scant notice of the Radical Republicans, and when he did, it was usually to wave them away as an ill-tempered distraction. "Many republicans suffered under private grievances," Holland sniffed. Frémont was "virtuous above his party, virtuous above Mr. Lincoln,"

Holland sardonically commented, and his failed 1864 presidential nomination was nothing more than "a damage to the national cause"; the Wade-Davis Manifesto was simply "an offensive paper."

And yet Holland heeded Herndon's warning that Lincoln "was not God—was man: he was not perfect."[19] Alongside the public Lincoln, Holland turned his attention onto the complexities and ambiguities of Lincoln's inner psyche. "He was not endowed with a hopeful temperament," Holland reported, "He had no force of self-esteem—no faith in himself that buoyed him up amid the contempt of the proud and prosperous." (Here was the beginning, along with Herndon's Springfield lecture in December 1865 on the "Analysis of the Character of Abraham Lincoln," of the image of Lincoln the melancholy, the Christ-like sufferer, the "marked and peculiar man.") Holland's Lincoln was, in fact, a bundle of psychological contradictions, at one moment "oppressed with a deep melancholy at times, weighed down by the great problems of his own life and of humanity at large," and the next capable of laughing "incontinently over incidents and stories that would hardly move any other man in his position to a smile." Much as Lincoln was able to rise above the crudeness of the frontier, he was also liable to slip back down into it at times, and Holland admitted that Lincoln was quite capable of "telling stories that it would not be proper to repeat in the presence of women. It is useless for Mr. Lincoln's biographers to ignore this habit, for it is notorious." Rather than being a starry-eyed idealist, Lincoln "was a man of practical expedients," even to the point where Lincoln "had the credit or the discredit, of being a cunning man" (although Holland promptly tried to redefine *cunning* as *ingenuity*). And yet Holland noted that Lincoln was also a man of ideas, whose habits of "mental absorption" were so great that "New Salem people . . . thought him crazy, because he passed his best friends in the street without seeing them."

This might have been quite enough in 1866 to have brought down on Holland the same storms of wrath for questioning Lincoln's character that followed after Herndon for his lectures later that same year. Instead, Holland brought down on himself the wrath of Herndon, and on a subject where Holland imagined he was paying Lincoln a compliment. Holland had been curious about Lincoln's religion after his first interview with Herndon, and although Herndon (as he later told Isaac Arnold) had simply shrugged the question off, Holland persisted. This was the first instance Holland had encountered of "insider" resistance to exposing awkward aspects of Lincoln's life to public gaze, and Herndon finally tried to bury the subject by telling Holland, "The less said the better." Then as now, this was not the best advice to give to a journalist, and Holland knowingly replied (at least as Herndon retailed the story) with a wink, "O never mind, I'll fix that." Indeed he did. Lincoln came off the pages of Holland's *Life* with a superimposed Christian halo. According to Holland, Lincoln had been taught the Christian faith at Nancy Hanks Lincoln's knee; he had come to a belief "in God, and in his personal supervision of the affairs of men" during the New Salem days; he had developed a "spirit of tender piety" after Gettysburg and Vicksburg; and he had governed an administration "which, in its policy and acts, expressed the convictions of a Christian people." Holland's Lincoln "grew more religious with every passing year of his official life," and "in all the great emergencies of his closing years, his reliance upon divine guidance and assistance was often extremely touching." The difficulty with this picture was that it clashed with a general suspicion in the public mind that Lincoln had never had any clear religious affiliations. He had attended, but never joined, churches; he had invoked the blessing of God but never specified *what* or *whose* God he was addressing; and he rebuffed efforts during the war for a constitutional amendment to give official national sanction to Christianity. Holland could not deny these suspicions, but he could tiptoe around them. It was true, Holland admitted, that Lincoln "always remained shy in the exposure of his religious experiences," but that was not the same as saying that he had never had any. This required Holland to introduce a sharp division between Lincoln's public life, where he remained religiously neutral, and his private life, where he practiced a Christianity as devout as anyone's. Political life, Holland explained, forced Lincoln to live "a double life." But this did not diminish for Holland the discovery that "Mr. Lincoln had, in his quiet way, found a path to the Christian stand-point—that he had found God, and rested on the eternal truth of God." He was, in the end, "a Christian president," a "true Christian, true man," and Holland was moved to conclude his biography with a hymn of gratitude "to that ministry of Providence and grace which endowed thee so richly, and bestowed thee upon the nation and mankind."

The other difficulty with Holland's Christianized Lincoln was Herndon, who was simply aghast when he read the "double life" explanation. "Mr. Lincoln had no idea of Christianity," Herndon angrily wrote to Holland in February 1866, "did not believe in it—was not a Christian—couldn't be from his very nature." The argument that Lincoln had somehow concealed his Christianity for political reasons suggested much too delicately that Lincoln was a hypocrite who would, for political advancement, say one thing while believing another. By the end of 1866, Holland had become almost unmentionable in Herndon's presence. "Do you suppose for an instant," Herndon erupted when one hapless correspondent asked him his opinion of Holland's account of Lincoln's religion, "that if Mr. Lincoln was really a converted man to the faith of three Gods, Revelation, Inspiration, Miraculous Conception, and their necessity, etc., as some of the Christian world pretend to believe of Mr. Lincoln, that he *would not have boldly said so and so acted like a deeply sincere man and an honest one fearlessly of that mob furor?*"[20]

But Holland never retracted his claims. When Ward Hill Lamon's *Life of Abraham Lincoln* appeared in 1872, built on Herndon's research materials and repeating Herndon's skepticism about Lincoln's "religion," Holland wrote a scorching review in *Scribner's Monthly* (which he was then editing) that reached out to knock both Lamon and Herndon on the head. "Mr. Herndon and Colonel Lamon may strive to demonstrate that he was nothing but a heathen, and a somewhat vulgar heathen, at the best . . . but the result of the attempted demonstration is injurious to no one half so much as to themselves."[21] And he insisted, Herndon and Lamon notwithstanding, that good reason existed for saying so: in the first place, not even Herndon could deny that Lincoln's state papers, from his farewell address in Springfield to the Second Inaugural, were shot through with religious references, and in ways and in sheer volume that departed markedly from Lincoln's Democratic predecessors. "No President had ever before asked the people, in a public address, to pray for him," Holland observed on Lincoln's Springfield farewell. "It sounded like the cant of the conventicle to ears unaccustomed to the language of piety from the lips of politicians . . . but it came from a heart surcharged with a sense of need, and strong in its belief that the Almighty listens to the prayers of men."

The clinching evidence for Holland's belief in Lincoln's sincere, if surreptitious, conversion to Christianity lay in an interview Holland held in May of 1865 with Newton Bateman, a devout evangelical Congregationalist who had been elected as Illinois's superintendent of public instruction in 1858, one of two Republican victors in the statewide elections that accompanied Lincoln's unsuccessful bid to unseat Stephen Douglas. Bateman certainly knew Lincoln well enough to speak with some degree of authority—he had first met Lincoln in Springfield in 1842, when he was only twenty years old, and Lincoln referred to him as "my little friend, the big schoolmaster of Illinois." More to the point, from June 1860 until January 1861, his office in the Illinois state capitol was next to an office temporarily lent to Lincoln as an election headquarters by the governor of Illinois. It was during those months (Bateman told Holland) that Lincoln would often look for relief from the crowds of wellwishers and interviewers by slipping through a connecting door into Bateman's office.

It was there, Bateman claimed, that Lincoln had asked Bateman to review with him a poll list that showed how

Springfield voters were expected to cast their votes in the upcoming presidential election. Finding that all but three of "twenty-three ministers, of different denominations" in Springfield were likely to vote against him, Lincoln sadly told Bateman that although he was "not a Christian—God knows I would be one—" he did not understand how Christian ministers could read their Bible and still vote, in effect, for the continuance of slavery. Bateman then told Holland that Lincoln had drawn "from his bosom a pocket New Testament" and protested, "I know there is a God, and that he hates injustice and slavery. . . . I know I am right because I know that liberty is right, for Christ teaches it, and Christ is God." The conversation then went on, according to Bateman, to dwell "much upon the necessity of faith in the Christian's God, as an element of successful statesmanship." Bateman wrote this out for Holland less than a month later on eight legal-sized sheets of paper and sent it to Holland with the half-qualification that "Mr. Lincoln's language made a vivid impression upon me, [and] while I do not claim that the above quotations are absolutely verbatim, I know that they are very nearly so, and the sentiments are exactly as he uttered them."[22] It was exactly what Holland needed to prove his point, and he printed Bateman's statement in the *Life* with only a few minor editorial changes.

The Bateman statement is the single most controversial aspect of the Holland *Life*, since so much of Holland's claims about this central aspect of Lincoln's inner life rest upon it. Herndon believed at first that "Bateman is a good man, but a mistaken one," and that Holland merely had to be warned against him; but when it became clear that Holland had bought the entire story, Herndon denounced both Bateman and Holland as charlatans.[23] "Holland's and Bateman's statement . . . I deem a farce," Herndon growled. "Bateman lied to Holland as Holland lies in his biography of Lincoln."[24] Others who knew Bateman tended to follow Herndon's judgment: Julian Sturtevant, who had known both Lincoln and Bateman, thought Bateman "naturally sly," and it is significant that on at least two other occasions when Bateman described his brief time as Lincoln's professional neighbor, no mention of the "Christ is God" conversation surfaced.[25] And more recently, Don and Virginia Fehrenbacher have rated Bateman's reminiscence as "dubious biographical material."[26]

Still, even the Fehrenbachers have conceded that "it is not inconceivable that Lincoln had some kind of discussion with Bateman in which he revealed more religious feeling than had been his custom." The months between his nomination for the presidency in May 1860 and his departure for Washington in February 1861 were months of unusually unbuttoned reflectiveness for the otherwise "shutmouthed" and "reticent" Lincoln, especially when old friends showed up to offer congratulations or encouragement. For instance: Isaac Cogdal's claim that Lincoln confessed he "did honestly and truly" love Ann Rutledge was vigorously debunked by James G. Randall as "artificial and made to order," but it has been revived as credible testimony by John Y. Simon; and the Cogdal interview, which Simon treats as an example of a rare moment of nostalgia on Lincoln's part, took place in the same period as Bateman's.[27] What is likely, therefore, is that Lincoln indeed had a conversation about religion with Bateman, and that it probably revolved around Lincoln's perceived incongruity between Christian teaching and the reluctance of Christian ministers to criticize slavery (an incongruity which Lincoln had earlier observed in the case of Frederick Augustus Ross's *Slavery Ordained of God* in 1857), and perhaps even about his own felt sense of helplessness at finding a way to be religious (which, again, Lincoln had also expressed as early as 1848). But Herndon was probably correct to observe that anything more than this was embroidery on Bateman's part. "The first part of the story is correct," Herndon unyieldingly declared, "that is, that Mr. Lincoln was not a Christian, but the second part, that is, that Christ was God is false."[28]

Oddly, by accepting Bateman's testimony at face value, Holland made more trouble for himself than he needed. If Bateman exaggerated Lincoln's Christianity, Herndon exaggerated Holland's "wink" and Holland's need to "fix that" into a deliberate plot to make Lincoln into a recommendation for orthodox evangelical Protestantism. Actually, Holland had nothing quite so relentless in view. Unlike Bateman, Holland was a liberal Congregationalist (Washington Gladden, the noted Social Gospeller, was one of the eulogists at his funeral) who was more interested in representing Lincoln as a decent Christian gentleman (as another way of indicating how successfully Lincoln had climbed from the muck of the backcountry) than in representing Lincoln as an evangelical convert. "Christianity, in the form of abstract statement and in the shape of a creed, has not any particular interest nor very much meaning," Holland wrote, in words more reminiscent of Lincoln than the ones Bateman used: "If they seem good and true and like Christ, it satisfies me, and nothing else does."[29] Nor did he press the subject of Lincoln's religion further. Apart from his hostile review of Lamon, Holland never returned to the Lincoln theme after the publication of the biography. He was a journalist, not a proselytizer, and within a year he had sold his partnership in the *Springfield Republican* and moved on to newer ventures. In November 1870 he launched *Scribner's Magazine*, which became the most successful literary monthly in the United States, and in 1872 moved permanently to New York City. He continued to turn out best-selling novels. In 1881 he was about to convert *Scribner's* into the *Century Magazine* when heart failure took his life. He was buried in Springfield, Massachusetts, three days later, on 15 October 1881.

But if Holland allowed his instinct to give "hurtless pleasure to multitudes" (as one New York obituary put it), he did no worse than Lamon and Herndon, whose biographies are plagued with irregularities of their own making, and who are forgiven largely because they at least had claims to knowing Lincoln, which Holland did not. In his pursuit of authentic material on Lincoln's early life, Holland partly followed but also partly blazed Herndon's path toward his own eventual *Lincoln* in 1889, and by turning attention away from the stress laid by Barrett and Raymond on the political Lincoln toward an "inner Lincoln," Holland injected a strong note of psychological realism in the midst of his political adulation of Lincoln. Benjamin Thomas once wrote of the Lincoln biographical literature that virtually all of it could be divided into the realist and the romantic; Mark E. Neely has more wisely revised that judgment to describe the two great traditions as a division between the public Lincoln (represented by Nicolay and Hay) and the private Lincoln.[30] In the latter tradition, the name that comes most easily to mind is Herndon. But before Herndon, there was Holland, and unwittingly or not, the broad stream of Lincoln biography that includes such widely separated work as Dwight Anderson, Charles Strozier, George Forgie, Michael Burlingame, William Barton, and Jesse Weik all find their first pattern in Josiah Holland's *Life of Abraham Lincoln*.

A sincere word of thanks belongs here to Michael Burlingame, Connecticut College, and Thomas Schwartz, Illinois State Historian, for their generous assistance, both in reading drafts of this introduction and in locating several important documents.

NOTES

1. Howard's interview notes with John Todd Stuart, William Green, William Butler, and others are reproduced in *The Lincoln Papers*, ed. David C. Mearns (New York, 1948), 1:150–59.

2. Edward Eggleston, "Josiah Gilbert Holland," *Century Magazine* 23 (December 1881): 165.

3. Benjamin P. Thomas, *Portrait for Posterity: Lincoln and His Biographers* (New Brunswick NJ, 1947), 16; see also Paul Angle, *A Shelf of Lincoln Books: A Critical Bibliography of Lincolniana* (New Brunswick NJ, 1946), 18–20, for a somewhat less dismissive evaluation.

4. Harry Houston Peckham, *Josiah Gilbert Holland in Relation to His Times* (Philadelphia, 1940), 64.

5. Eggleston, "Josiah Gilbert Holland," 167.

6. Merrill D. Peterson, *Lincoln in American Memory* (New York, 1994), 69–70.

7. Herndon to Lamon, 25 February 1870, in *The Hidden Lincoln: From the Letters and Papers of William H. Herndon*, ed. Emmanuel Hertz (New York, 1938), 68.

8. Lincoln, "To Jesse W. Fell, Enclosing Autobiography," 20 December 1859, and "Autobiography Written for John L. Scripps," in *Collected Works of Abraham Lincoln*, ed. Roy P. Basler (New Brunswick NJ, 1955), 3:511–12 and 4:60–67; and Roy P. Basler, introduction to *Life of Abraham Lincoln*, by John Locke Scripps (New York, 1968), 7–16.

9. *Eulogy on Abraham Lincoln, late President of the United States, pronounced at the City Hall, Springfield, Mass., April 19, 1865* (Springfield MA: Samuel Bowles, 1865).

10. Mrs. H. M. Plunkett, *Josiah Gilbert Holland* (New York, 1894), 48.

11. *Illinois State Journal*, 19 May 1865.

12. Herndon to Holland, 26 May 1865, Josiah Gilbert Holland Papers, New York Public Library; see also David Donald, *Lincoln's Herndon: A Biography* (New York, 1948), 169.

13. *Illinois State Journal*, 25 May 1865.

14. Boutwell to Holland, 28 June 1865, Holland Papers.

15. Henry to Holland, 16 June 1865, Holland Papers.

16. Speed to Holland, undated, Holland Papers.

17. Wright to Holland, 10 June 1865, Holland Papers.

18. Wright to Holland, 10 July 1865, Holland Papers. Wright must have interviewed Short no more than two weeks before Short provided Herndon with a similar description of the Rutledge romance; see Short to Herndon, 7 July 1865, in Herndon-Weik Papers, Library of Congress.

19. Herndon to Holland, 26 May 1865, Holland Papers.

20. Herndon, 3 December 1866, in *The Hidden Lincoln*, 45.

21. Thomas, *Portrait for Posterity*, 57–60.

22. Bateman to Holland, 19 June 1865, Holland Papers.

23. Herndon to Holland, 24 February 1866, Holland Papers.

24. Herndon to Lamon, 25 February 1870, in *The Hidden Lincoln*, 46, 68.

25. Sturtevant to William E. Barton, 8 March 1920, in the William E. Barton Papers, University of Chicago; Bateman interview manuscript, in the Ida M. Tarbell Papers, Allegheny College; see also Bateman's lecture *Abraham Lincoln: An Address* (Galesburg IL, 1899).

26. Fehrenbacher, *Recollected Words of Abraham Lincoln* (Stanford CA, 1996), 26.

27. Simon, "Abraham Lincoln and Ann Rutledge," *Journal of the Abraham Lincoln Association* 11 (spring 1990): 33.

28. Herndon, "Lincoln and Strangers," in *The Hidden Lincoln*, 404.

29. *A Memorial of Josiah Gilbert Holland* (New York, 1881), 12.

30. Mark E. Neely, "Abraham Lincoln," in *The American Civil War: A Handbook of Literature and Research*, ed. Steven E. Woodworth (Westport CT, 1996), 189–202.

PREFACE.

I HAVE undertaken to write a biography of Abraham Lincoln for the people; and, although they will be certain to learn what I have accomplished and what I have failed to accomplish in the book, I cannot consent to pass it into their hands without a statement of what I have aimed to do, and what I have not aimed to do, in its preparation. I am moved to this, partly by my wish that they may not be disappointed in the character of the effort, and partly by my desire that, in making up their judgment upon the work, they may have some reference to my intentions.

First, then, I have not aimed to write a History of the Rebellion. Second, I have not aimed to write a political or a military history of Mr. Lincoln's administration. Third, I have not aimed to present any considerable number of Mr. Lincoln's letters, speeches and state-papers. Fourth, I have not attempted to disguise or conceal my own personal partiality for Mr. Lincoln, and my thorough sympathy with the political principles to which his life was devoted. Though

unconscious of any partiality for a party, capable of blinding
my vision or distorting my judgment, I am aware that, at this
early day, when opinions are still sharply divided upon the
same questions concerning principles, policies and men, which
prevailed during Mr. Lincoln's active political life, it is impossible to utter any judgment which will not have a bearing upon the party politics of the time.   Thus, the only alternative
of writing according to personal partialities and personal convictions, has been writing without any partialities, and without any convictions.   I have chosen to be a man, rather than
a machine; and, if this shall subject me to the charge of writing in the interest of a party, I must take what comes of it.

I have tried to paint the character of Mr. Lincoln, and to
sketch his life, clinging closely to his side; giving attention to
cotemporaneous history no further than it has seemed necessary
to reveal his connection with public events; and re-producing
his letters, speeches and state-papers to no greater extent than
they were deemed requisite to illustrate his personal character,
to throw light upon specially interesting phases of his private
life and public career, to exhibit the style and scope of his
genius, and to expose his social, political and religious sentiments and opinions.   In pursuing this course, I have been
obliged to leave large masses of interesting material behind
me, and to condense into the briefest space what the more
general historian will dwell upon in detail.

From much of the history of Mr. Lincoln's public life, to
which his future biographers will have access, I have been
excluded.   The records and other evidences of his intimate

connection with all the events of the war for the preservation
of American nationality, are in the archives of the War Department; and they are there retained, only to be revealed
when the present generation shall have passed away. The
Life of Washington, even though it was written by a Marshall, with the abundant access to unpublished documents
which his position enabled him to command, or which it was
the policy of the government to afford him, waited half a
century for Irving, to give it symmetry and completeness.
The humbler biographers of Mr. Lincoln, though they satisfy
an immediate want, and gather much which would otherwise
be forever lost, can hardly hope to be more than tributaries
to that better and completer biography which the next, or
some succeeding generation, will be sure to produce and
possess.

I have no opportunity, except that which this page affords
me, to acknowledge my indebtedness to those who have assisted me in the collection of unpublished materials for this
volume. I have been indebted specially to William H. Herndon, Esq., of Springfield, Illinois, for many years Mr. Lincoln's
law partner, who has manifested, from the first, the kindest
interest in my book; to Newton Bateman, Esq., Superintendent of Public Instruction in Illinois; to James Q. Howard,
Esq., United States Consul at St. John, New Brunswick; to
Hon. John D. Defrees, Superintendent of Public Printing in
Washington; to Hon. Henry L. Dawes, of Massachusetts; to
Horace White, Esq., of the Chicago Tribune; to U. F. Linder,
Esq., of Chicago; to J. F. Speed, Esq., of Louisville, Ken-

tucky; to Judge S. T. Logan, Hon. Jesse K. Dubois, Rev. A. Hale, and Hon. Erastus Wright, old neighbors and friends of Mr. Lincoln in Illinois; to Rev. J. T. Duryea, of New York; and George H. Stuart, Esq., of Philadelphia. To these, and to the unnamed but not forgotten friends who have aided me, I return my hearty thanks.

Putnam's "Record of the Rebellion" has proved itself an inexhaustible fountain of valuable and interesting facts; and I have been much indebted to McPherson's History of the Rebellion, the best arranged and most complete collection of public documents relating to the war that has been published. I have freely consulted the campaign biographies of Messrs. Scripps, Raymond, and Barrett, to the excellence of which I bear cheerful testimony. Among other books that have been useful to me, are Nichols' "Story of the Great March," Coggeshall's "Journeys of Abraham Lincoln," Schalk's "Campaigns of 1862 and 1863," and Halsted's "Caucuses of 1860." Carpenter's "Reminiscences," published in the New York Independent, and an article by Noah Brooks in Harper's Magazine, have furnished me also with some very interesting materials.

.Hoping that the volume will be as pleasant, instructive and inspiring in the reading as it has been in the writing, I present it to my indulgent friends, the American people.

J. G. H.

SPRINGFIELD, MASS., November, 1865.

TABLE OF CONTENTS.

CHAPTER I.

BIRTH AND CHILDHOOD.

CHAPTER II.

YOUTH.

CHAPTER III.

EARLY MANHOOD.

CHAPTER IV.

THE BLACK HAWK WAR.

CHAPTER V.

CHARACTER OF MR. LINCOLN ON ENTERING PUBLIC LIFE.

CHAPTER VI.

MR. LINCOLN IN THE ILLINOIS LEGISLATURE.

CHAPTER VII.

MR. LINCOLN AS A LAWYER.

CHAPTER VIII.

MR. LINCOLN'S MARRIAGE.—THE CLAY CAMPAIGN.

CHAPTER IX.

MR. LINCOLN IN CONGRESS.—THE MEXICAN WAR.

CHAPTER XXV.

PRIVATE LIFE AT THE WHITE HOUSE.

CHAPTER XXVI.

SESSION OF CONGRESS, 1863-4.—SANITARY FAIRS.

CHAPTER XXVII.

PRESIDENTIAL CAMPAIGN OF 1864.—RE-ELECTION OF

MR. LINCOLN.

CHAPTER XXVIII.

MILITARY EVENTS OF 1864.—RE-INAUGURATION OF MR. LINCOLN.

CHAPTER XXIX.

MILITARY EVENTS OF 1865.—CLOSE OF THE WAR.

CHAPTER XXX.

THE ASSASSINATION.

T.D. Jones, Sculpt.   Thot Chubbuck Enge Springfield Mass

LIFE OF ABRAHAM LINCOLN.

CHAPTER I.

THE early life of ABRAHAM LINCOLN was a hard and humble backwoods and border life. As a boy and as a young man, he was not fond of wild sports and exciting adventures. It is doubtless true that the earlier years of many of his neighbors and companions would be more engaging to the pen of the biographer and the imagination of the reader, than his. His later career, his noble character, his association with the grandest and most important events of American history, have alone, or mainly, given significance and interest to his youthful experiences of hardship, the humble processes of his education, and his early struggles with the rough forces of nature among which he was born. The tree which rose so high, and spread its leaves so broadly, and bore such golden fruit, and then fell before the blast because it was so heavy and so high, has left its roots upturned into the same light that glorifies its branches, and discovered and made divine the soil from which it drew its nutriment.

When Mr. Lincoln was nominated for the presidency of the United States in 1860, it became desirable that a sketch of his life should be prepared and widely distributed; but, upon being applied to for materials for this sketch, by the gentleman who had undertaken to produce it,* he seemed oppressed

* J. L. Scripps, Esq., of Chicago.

with a sense of their tameness and lowliness, and the conviction that they could not be of the slightest interest to the American people. " My early history," said he, " is perfectly characterized by a single line of Gray's Elegy:

'The short and simple annals of the poor.'"

His judgment then was measurably just; but events have set it aside, and endowed the humble details that seemed to him so common-place and mean, with a profound and tender interest.

ABRAHAM LINCOLN was born in that part of Hardin County, Kentucky, now embraced by the lines of the recently formed county of Larue, on the 12th of February, 1809. A region more remarkably picturesque was at that time hardly to be found in all the newly-opened country of the West. Variegated and rolling in its surface, about two-thirds of it timbered and fertile, the remainder composed of barrens, supporting only black-jacks and post-oaks, and spreading into plains, or rising into knolls or knobs, and watered by beautiful and abundant streams, it was as attractive to the eye of the lover of nature as to the enterprise of the agriculturist and the passion of the hunter. Some of the knobs rising out of the barrens reach a considerable elevation, and are dignified by the name of mountains. " Shiny Mountain " is one of the most lovely of these, giving a view of the whole valley of the Nolin. A still larger knob is the " Blue Ball," from whose summit one may see, on a fair morning, the fog rising from the Ohio River, twenty miles away.

In a rude log cabin, planted among these scenes, the subject of this biography opened his eyes. The cabin was situated on or near Nolin Creek, about a mile and a half from Hodgenville, the present county seat of Larue County. Here he spent the first year or two of his childhood, when he removed to a cabin on Knob Creek, on the road from Bardstown, Kentucky, to Nashville, Tennessee; at a point three and a half miles south or southwest of Atherton's Ferry, (on the Rolling Fork,) and six miles from Hodgenville. It was in these two homes* that he spent the first seven years of his life ; but before saying anything of those years, it will be best to tell how his parents found their way into the wilderness, and to record what is known of his family history.

In 1769, Daniel Boone, at the head of a small and hardy party of adventurers, set out from his home on the Yadkin River, in South Carolina, to explore that part of Virginia which he then knew as "The Country of Kentucky." After participating in the most daring and dangerous adventures, and suffering almost incredible hardships, he returned, abundantly rewarded with peltry, in 1771. Two years after this, he undertook to remove his family to the region which had entirely captivated his imagination ; but it was not until 1775 that his purpose was accomplished. This brave and widely-renowned pioneer, with those who accompanied him and those who were attracted to the region by the reports which he had carried back to the Eastern settlements, lived a life of constant exposure to Indian warfare ; but danger seemed only to sharpen the spirit of adventure, and to attract rather than repel immigration.

Among those for whom "The Country of Kentucky" had its savage charms was Abraham Lincoln, the grandfather of the President, then living in Rockingham County, Virginia. Why he should have left the beautiful and fertile valley of the Shenandoah for the savage wilds West of him cannot be known, but he only repeated the mystery of pioneer life— the greed for something newer and wilder and more dangerous than that which surrounded him. His removal to Kentucky took place about 1780. Of the journey, we have no record ; but we know that at that date it must have been one of great hardship, as he was accompanied by a young and tender family. The spot upon which he built is not known,

---

*Mr. Lincoln, in the manuscript record of his life dictated to J. G. Nicolay, makes mention of but one home in Kentucky. Scripps' memoir, also gathered from Mr. Lincoln's lips, is silent on the subject; but Barrett's Campaign Life of Lincoln gives the statement circumstantially, and is probably correct.

though it is believed to have been somewhere on Floyd's Creek, in what is now Bullitt County. Hardly more of his history is preserved than that which relates to his death. In 1784, while at work in the field, at a distance from his cabin, he was stealthily approached by an Indian, and shot dead.

The care of five helpless children was, by this murder, thrown upon his widow. She subsequently removed to a place now embraced within the limits of Washington County, and there she reared, in such rude ways as necessity prescribed, her little brood. Three of these children, sons, were named in the order of their birth, Mordecai, Josiah and Thomas. The two daughters were named respectively Mary and Nancy. Mordecai remained in Kentucky until late in life, but a short time before his death, removed to Hancock County, Illinois, where several of his descendants still reside. Josiah, the second son, removed while a young man to what is now Harrison County, Indiana. Thomas, the third son, was the father of Abraham Lincoln, the illustrious subject of this biography. Mary Lincoln was married to Ralph Crume, and Nancy to William Brumfield. The descendants of these women still reside in Kentucky. All these children were probably born in Virginia,—Thomas, in 1778,—so that he was only about two years old when his father emigrated.

Tracing the family still further, we find that Abraham, the emigrant, had four brothers: Isaac, Jacob, John and Thomas. The descendants of Jacob and John are supposed to be still in Virginia. Isaac emigrated to the region where Virginia, North Carolina and Tennessee unite, and his descendants are there. Thomas went to Kentucky, probably later than his brother Abraham, where he lived many years, and where he died. His descendants went to Missouri.

Further back than this it is difficult to go. The most that is known, is, that the Lincolns of Rockingham County, Virginia, came, previous to 1752, from Berks County, Pennsylvania. Where the Lincolns of Berks County came from, no record has disclosed. They are believed to have been Quakers, but whether they were an original importation from Old England, under the auspices of William Penn, or a pioneer off-shoot from the Lincolns of New England, does not appear. There is the strongest presumptive evidence that the Pennsylvania and New England Lincolns were identical in their family blood. The argument for this identity rests mainly upon the coincidences which the Christian names of the two families present. Three Lincolns who came from Hingham, in England, and settled in Hingham, Massachusetts, between 1633 and 1637, bore the Christian name of Thomas. Another bore the name of Samuel, and he had three sons: Daniel, Mordecai and Thomas. Mordecai was the father of Mordecai, who was born in 1686. He was also the father of Abraham, born in 1689. About 1750, there were two Mordecai Lincolns in the town of Taunton.* Here we have the three names: Mordecai, Thomas and Abraham, in frequent and familiar family use. Passing to the Pennsylvania family, we find that among the taxable inhabitants of Exeter, Berks County, Pennsylvania, there were, soon after 1752, Mordecai and Abraham Lincoln; that Thomas Lincoln was living in Reading as early as 1757, and that Abraham Lincoln, of Berks County, was in various public offices in the state from 1782 to 1790.†

It has already been seen that these names have been perpetuated among the later generations of the Pennsylvania Lincolns, and that the three names—Abraham, Mordecai and Thomas—were all embraced in the family out of which the President sprang. The argument thus based upon the identity of favorite family names (and one of those quite an unusual name,) is very strong in establishing identity of blood, though, of course, it is not entirely conclusive. It is sufficient, certainly, in the absence of a reliable record, to make the theory plausible which transfers a Quaker from the unfriendly soil of Massachusetts to the paradise of Quakers in Pennsylvania. It is highly probable that an exceptional

*Rev. Elias Nason's Eulogy before the N. E. Historic-Geneological Society, at Boston, May 3, 1865.

†Rupp's History of Berks and Lebanon Counties, Pennsylvania.

Quaker among the Massachusetts Puritan family went, with other New Englanders, to Berks County in Pennsylvania, and that the blood which has given to New England a considerable number of most honorable names, has given to the nation one of the noblest that adorn its annals.

Thomas Lincoln, the father of the President, was made, by the early death of his father and the straitened circumstances of his mother, a wandering, laboring, ignorant boy. He grew up without any education. He really never learned anything of letters except those which composed his own name. This he could write clumsily, but legibly, and this he did write without any knowledge of the names and powers of the letters which composed it. While a lad not fully grown, he passed a year as a hired field hand on Wataga, a branch of the Holston River, in the employ of his Uncle Isaac. Without money or the opportunity to acquire it, all the early years of his life were passed in labor for others, at such wages as he could command, or in hunting the game with which the region abounded. It was not until he had reached his twenty-eighth year that he found it practicable to settle in life, and make for himself a home. He married Nancy Hanks, in 1806. She was born in Virginia, and was probably a relative of one of the early immigrants into Kentucky. He took her to the humble cabin he had prepared for her, already alluded to as the birth-place of the President, and within the first few years of her married life, she bore him three children. The first was a daughter named Sarah, who married when a child, and died many years ago, leaving no issue. The third was a son, (Thomas,) who died in infancy. The second was Abraham, who, born into the humblest abode, under the humblest circumstances, raised himself by the force of native gifts of heart and brain, and by the culture and power achieved by his own will and industry, under the blessing of a Providence which he always recognized, to sit in the highest place in the land, and to preside over the destinies of thirty millions of people.

From such materials as are readily accessible, let us paint a picture of the little family. Thomas Lincoln, the father, was a well built, sinewy man, about five feet ten and a half inches high, dressed in the humble garb which his poverty compelled and the rude art of the time and locality produced. Though a rover by habit and native tastes, he was not a man of enterprise. He was a good-natured man, a man of un-doubted integrity, but inefficient in making his way in the world, and improvident of the slender means at his command. He was a man, however, whom everybody loved, and who held the warm affection of his eminent son throughout his life. He attributed much of his hard fortune to his lack of education, and in one thing, at least, showed himself more wisely provident than the majority of his neighbors. He de-termined, at any possible sacrifice, to give his children the best education that the schools of the locality afforded.

Mrs. Lincoln, the mother, was evidently a woman out of place among those primitive surroundings. She was five feet, five inches high, a slender, pale, sad and sensitive woman, with much in her nature that was truly heroic, and much that shrank from the rude life around her. A great man never drew his infant life from a purer or more womanly bosom than her own; and Mr. Lincoln always looked back to her with an unspeakable affection. Long after her sensitive heart and weary hands had crumbled into dust, and had climbed to life again in forest flowers, he said to a friend, with tears in his eyes: " All that I am, or hope to be, I owe to my angel mother—blessings on her memory ! "

Here was the home and here were its occupants, all hum-ble, all miserably poor; yet it was a home of love and of virtue. Both father and mother were religious persons, and sought at the earliest moment to impress the minds of their children with religious truth. The mother, though not a ready writer, could read. Books were scarce, but occasion-ally an estray was caught and eagerly devoured. Abraham and his sister often sat at her feet to hear of scenes and deeds that roused their young imaginations, and fed their hungry minds.

Schools in Kentucky were, in those days, scarce and very

poor. Nothing more than instruction in the rudiments of education was attempted. Zachariah Riney was Abraham's first teacher. Riney was a Catholic, and though the Protestant children in his charge were commanded, or permitted, to retire when any of his peculiar religious ceremonies or exercises were in progress, Mr. Lincoln always entertained a pleasant and grateful memory of him. He began his attendance upon Mr. Riney's school when he was in his seventh year, but could hardly have continued it beyond a period of two or three months. His next teacher was Caleb Hazel, a fine young man, whose school he attended for about three months. The boy was diligent, and actually learned to write an intelligible letter during this period.

If the schools of the region were rude and irregular, its religious institutions were still more so. Public religious worship was observed in the neighborhood only at long intervals, and then under the charge of roving preachers, who, ranging over immense tracts of territory, and living on their horses and in the huts of the settlers, called the people together under trees or cabin-roofs, and spoke to them simply of the great truths of Christianity. The preachers themselves were peculiar persons, made so by the peculiarity of their circumstances and pursuits. For many years, Abraham Lincoln never saw a church; but he heard Parson Elkin preach. At intervals of several months, the good parson held meetings in the neighborhood. He was a Baptist, and Thomas and Nancy Lincoln were members of that communion. Abraham's first ideas of public speech were gathered from the simple addresses of this humble and devoted itinerant, and the boy gave evidence afterwards, as we shall see, that he remembered him with interest and affection.

When inefficient men become very uncomfortable, they are quite likely to try emigration as a remedy. A good deal of what is called "the pioneer spirit" is simply a spirit of shiftless discontent. Possibly there was something of this spirit in Thomas Lincoln. It is true, at least, that when Abraham was about seven years old, his father became possessed with the desire to sell his little home, and remove to another, in some fairer wilderness. It is probable, also, that he did not like to rear his children in Kentucky. He had been wise enough to appreciate the advantages of education to his children, and it is quite likely that he shrank from seeing them grow up in a community cursed with slavery. The state having outgrown, with marvelous rapidity, its ruder conditions, and become populous and powerful, was already the home of an institution which branded labor with disgrace, and made the position of the poor whites a hopeless one. He could see nothing in the future, for himself or his boy, but labor by the side of the negro, and degradation in his presence and companionship.

Mr. Lincoln himself never attributed his father's desire to remove from Kentucky to his dislike of slavery, as a principal motive. Kentucky, more than most of the new states, was cursed with defective land-titles. Daniel Boone himself, with hundreds of others who had shared with him the dangers of pioneer life, was dispossessed of nearly all his lands, after having lived upon them for years, and rendered them very valuable by improvements. It was mainly to this difficulty, of getting a valid title to land, that Abraham Lincoln attributed his father's desire and determination to remove to another state.

Thomas Lincoln found a purchaser, at last, for his home. He bartered it away for ten barrels of whisky and twenty dollars in money, the whole representing the sum of three hundred dollars, his price for the place.* After building a flat-boat and launching it upon the Rolling Fork, he loaded it with his stock of whisky, and all the heavier household wares of which he was possessed, pushed off alone, and floated safely down to the Ohio River. Here he met with an accident—a wreck, indeed. The flat-boat was upset, and two-thirds of his whisky and many of his housekeeping utensils and farming and other tools were lost. Meeting with assistance, his boat

* William M. Thayer's "Pioneer Boy," a singularly faithful statement of the early experiences of Abraham Lincoln.

was righted, and everything saved that it was found practicable to gather from the bottom of the river. Landing at Thompson's Ferry, he procured carriage for his goods about eighteen miles into Spencer County, Indiana, where, in almost an unbroken wilderness, he determined to settle. Leaving his goods in the care of a settler, he returned to Thompson's Ferry, and then, on foot, took as nearly as possible a bee-line for home, where he arrived in due time. It was probably during the absence of the father on his preliminary trip that the mother paid her last tribute of affection to the little one she had buried, by visiting its grave, in company with her living boy—an incident which he remembered with tender interest.

This voyage was made in the autumn of 1816, when Abraham was in his eighth year, and it was followed by the immediate removal of the whole family. The journey to the new home was made overland, upon three horses which carried in packs the bedding, wardrobe and all the lighter effects of the family. The humble cavalcade occupied seven days in the journey. At the end of it, the emigrants met with neighborly assistance in the erection of a dwelling, and were soon housed and ready to begin life anew.

It must not be inferred from the character of the material which Mr. Lincoln received, in principal, as the payment for his little homestead in Kentucky, and transferred to his new home in Indiana, that he was addicted to the vice of strong drink. In those days, alcoholic liquors were in general use among the settlers, not only as a beverage, but as a remedial agent in the treatment of the diseases peculiar to the new settlements of the West. The same liquors were used with the same freedom among all classes at the East, at that date, without a thought of evil. Mr. Lincoln supposed he was receiving a commodity which would be of great value to him in the new regions of Indiana, where distillation had not been attempted; and he doubtless found a ready market for the fraction of the cargo which he had saved from the river.

CHAPTER II.

THE point at which the Lincoln family settled in Indiana was not far from the present town of Gentryville. The campaign biographers of Abraham attribute to him some valuable service with the ax, both in building the cabin and in clearing the forest around it; but, at the age of seven, he could hardly have rendered much assistance in these offices. We are told that he had an ax; and there is no doubt that he learned at an early age to use it effectually. Indeed, his muscles were formed and hardened by this exercise, continued through all the years of his young manhood. It has already been stated that he had no taste for the sports of the forest; but he made an early shot, with a result that must have surprised him and his family. While yet a child, he saw through a crack in the cabin a flock of wild turkeys, feeding. He ventured to take down his father's rifle, and, firing through the crack, killed one of them. This was the largest game upon which he ever pulled trigger, his brilliant success having no power to excite in him the passion for hunting.

Among the most untoward circumstances, Thomas Lincoln embraced every opportunity to give Abraham an education. At different periods, all of them brief, he attended the neighborhood schools that were opened to him. Andrew Crawford taught one of these, a Mr. Sweeney another, and Azel W. Dorsey another, the last of whom lived to see his humble pupil a man of eminence, and to congratulate him upon his elevation. One year, however, would cover all the time spent by him with his two Kentucky teachers, and the three whose schools he attended in Indiana; and all the school education of his life was embraced by the limits of·this one year.

It is very difficult for any one bred in the older communities of the country to appreciate the extreme humility of border life, the meagerness and meanness of its household appointments, and the paucity of its stimulants to mental growth and social development. The bed in which the elder Lincolns, and, on very cold nights, the little Lincolns, slept, during their first years in Indiana, was one whose rudeness will give a key to the kind of life which they lived there. The head and one side of the bedstead were formed by an angle of the cabin itself. The bed-post standing out into the room was a single crotch, cut from the forest. Laid upon this crotch were the ends of two hickory sticks, whose other extremities were morticed into the logs, the two sides of the cabin and the two rails embracing a quadrilateral space of the required dimensions. This was bridged by slats "rived" from the forest log, and on the slats was laid a sack filled with dried leaves. This was, in reality, the bed of Thomas and Nancy Lincoln; and into it, when the skins hung at the cabin doorway did not keep out the cold, Abraham and his sister crept for the warmth which their still ruder couch upon the ground denied them.

The lot of the little family, already sadly dark, was rendered inexpressibly gloomy at an early day by an event which made a profound impression upon the mind of the boy—an impression that probably never wore away during all the eventful years that followed. His delicate mother bent to the dust under the burden of life which circumstances had imposed upon her. A quick consumption seized her, and her life went out in the flashing fevers of her disease. The boy and his sister were orphans, and the humble home in the wilderness was desolate. Her death occurred in 1818, scarcely two years after her removal to Indiana, and when Abraham was in his tenth year. They laid her to rest under the trees near the cabin, and, sitting on her grave, the little boy wept his irreparable loss. There were probably none but the simplest ceremonies at her burial, and neither father nor son was content to part with her without a formal Christian tribute to her worth and memory. Both thought of the good Parson Elkin whom they had left in Kentucky; and Abraham's skill in writing was brought into use in addressing to him a message. His imperfect penmanship had been acquired partly in the schools he had attended, and partly by practice in the sand and on the barks of trees—on anything and with any instrument by which letters might be formed.

Several months after Mrs. Lincoln died, Abraham wrote a letter to Parson Elkin, informing him of his mother's death, and begging him to come to Indiana, and preach her funeral sermon. It was a great favor that he thus asked of the poor preacher. It would require him to ride on horseback nearly a hundred miles through the wilderness; and it is something to be remembered to the humble itinerant's honor that he was willing to pay this tribute of respect to the woman who had so thoroughly honored him and his sacred office. He replied to Abraham's invitation, that he would preach the sermon on a certain future Sunday, and gave him liberty to notify the neighbors of the promised service.

As the appointed day approached, notice was given to the whole neighborhood, embracing every family within twenty miles. Neighbor carried the notice to neighbor. It was scattered from every little school. There was probably not a family that did not receive intelligence of the anxiously anticipated event.

On a bright Sabbath morning, the settlers of the region started for the cabin of the Lincolns; and, as they gathered in, they presented a picture worthy the pencil of the worthiest painter. Some came in carts of the rudest construction, their wheels consisting of sections of the huge boles of forest trees, and every other member the product of the ax and auger; some came on horseback, two or three upon a horse; others came in wagons drawn by oxen, and still others came on foot. Two hundred persons in all were assembled when Parson Elkin came out from the Lincoln cabin, accompanied by the little family, and proceeded to the tree under which the precious dust of a wife and mother was buried. The congregation, seated upon stumps and logs around the grave, received the preacher and the mourning family in a silence broken only by the songs of birds, and the murmur of insects, or the creaking cart of some late comer. Taking his stand at the foot of the grave, Parson Elkin lifted his voice in prayer and sacred song, and then preached a sermon. The occasion, the eager faces around him, and all the sweet influences of the morning, inspired him with an unusual fluency and fervor; and the flickering sunlight, as it glanced through the wind-parted leaves, caught many a tear upon the bronzed cheeks of his auditors, while father and son were overcome by the revival of their great grief. He spoke of the precious Christian woman who had gone with the warm praise which she deserved, and held her up as an example of true womanhood.

Those who knew the tender and reverent spirit of Abraham Lincoln later in life, will not doubt that he returned to his cabin-home deeply impressed by all that he had heard. It was the rounding up for him of the influences of a Christian mother's life and teachings. It recalled her sweet and patient example, her assiduous efforts to inspire him with pure and noble motives, her simple instructions in divine truth, her devoted love for him, and the motherly offices she had rendered him during all his tender years. His character was planted in this Christian mother's life. Its roots were fed by this Christian mother's love; and those who have wondered at the truthfulness and earnestness of his mature character, have only to remember that the tree was true to the soil from which it sprang.

Abraham, at an early day, became a reader. Every book upon which he could lay his hands he read. He became a writer also. The majority of the settlers around him were entirely illiterate, and when it became known that Mr. Lincoln's boy could write, his services were in frequent request by them in sending epistolary messages to their friends. In the composition of these letters his early habits of putting the thoughts of others as well as his own into language were formed. The exercise was, indeed, as good as a school to him; for there is no better discipline, for any mind, than that of giving definite expression to thought in language. Much of his subsequent power as a writer and speaker was undoubtedly traceable to this early discipline.

The books which Abraham had the early privilege of reading were the Bible, much of which he could repeat, Æsop's Fables, all of which he could repeat, Pilgrim's Progress, Weems' Life of Washington, and a Life of Henry Clay which his mother had managed to purchase for him. Subsequently he read the Life of Franklin and Ramsay's Life of Washington. In these books, read and re-read, he found meat for his hungry mind. The Holy Bible, Æsop and John Bunyan:—could three better books have been chosen for him from the richest library? For those who have witnessed the dissipating effects of many books upon the minds of modern children it is not hard to believe that Abraham's poverty of books was the wealth of his life. These three books did much to perfect that which his mother's teachings had begun, and to form a character which for quaint simplicity, earnestness, truthfulness and purity has never been surpassed among the historic personages of the world. The Life of Washington, while it gave to him a lofty example of patriotism, incidentally conveyed to his mind a general knowledge of American history; and the Life of Henry Clay spoke to him of a living man who had risen to political and professional eminence from circumstances almost as humble as his own. The latter book undoubtedly did much to excite his taste for politics, to kindle his ambition, and to make him a warm admirer and partizan of Henry Clay. Abraham must have been very young when he read Weems' Life of Washington, and we catch a glimpse of his precocity in the thoughts which it excited, as revealed by himself in a speech made to the New Jersey Senate, while on his way to Washington to assume the duties of the Presidency. Alluding to his early reading of this book, he says: " I remember all the accounts there given of the battle fields and struggles for the liberties of the country, and none fixed themselves upon my imagination so deeply as the struggle here at Trenton, New Jersey. * * * *I recollect thinking then, boy even though I was, that there must have been something more than common that those men struggled for.*" Even at this age, he was not only an interested reader of the story, but a student of motives.

Ramsay's Life of Washington was borrowed from his teacher, Andrew Crawford, and an anecdote connected with it illustrates Abraham's conscientiousness and characteristic honesty. The borrowed book was left unguardedly in an open window. A shower coming on, it was wet and nearly ruined. Abraham carried it to Mr. Crawford in great grief and alarm, and, after explaining the accident, offered to pay for the book in labor. Mr. Crawford accepted the proposal, and the lad "pulled fodder" three days to pay, not for the damages, but for the book itself, which thus became one of his own literary treasures.

In the autumn or early winter of 1819, somewhat more than a year after the death of Mrs. Lincoln, Abraham passed into the care of a step-mother. His father married and brought to his home in Indiana, Mrs. Sally Johnston, of Elizabethtown, Kentucky, undoubtedly one of his old acquaintances. She brought with her three children, the fruit of her previous marriage; but she faithfully fulfilled her assumed maternal duties to Thomas Lincoln's children. The two families grew up in harmony together, and the many kind offices which she performed for Abraham were gratefully returned then and in after years by him. She still survives, having seen her young charge rise to be her own ruler, and the ruler of the nation, and to fall amid expressions of grief from the whole civilized world.

As Abraham grew up, he became increasingly helpful in all the work of the farm, often going out to labor by the day for hire. Abundant evidence exists that he was regarded by the neighbors as being remarkable, in many respects, above the lads of his own age, with whom he associated. In physical strength and sundry athletic feats, he was the master of them all. Never quarrelsome or disposed to make an unpleasant show of his prowess, he was ready to help all who were in need of help, to do their errands, write their letters, and lighten their burdens.

An instance of his practical humanity at this early period of his life may be recorded. One evening, while returning from a "raising" in his wide neighborhood, with a number of companions, he discovered a straying horse, with saddle and bridle upon him. The horse was recognized as belonging to a man who was accustomed to excess in drink, and it was suspected at once that the owner was not far off. A short search only was necessary to confirm the suspicions of the young men. The poor drunkard was found in a perfectly helpless condition, upon the chilly ground. Abraham's companions urged the cowardly policy of leaving him to his fate, but young Lincoln would not hear to the proposition. At his request, the miserable sot was lifted to his shoulders, and he actually carried him eighty rods to the nearest house. Sending word to his father that he should not be back that night, with the reason for his absence, he attended and nursed the man until the morning, and had the pleasure of believing that he had saved his life.

That Abraham Lincoln was entirely content with the humdrum life he was living, or the prospects which it presented to him, is not probable. He had caught glimpses of a life of greater dignity and significance. Echoes from the great centers of civilization had reached his ears. When he was eighteen years old he conceived the project of building a little boat, and taking the produce of the Lincoln farm down the river to a market. He had learned the use of tools, and possessed considerable mechanical talent, as will appear in some other acts of his life. Of the voyage and its results we have no knowledge, but an incident occurred before starting which he related in later life to his Secretary of State, Mr. Seward, that made a very marked and pleasant impression upon his memory. As he stood at the landing, a steamer approached, coming down the river. At the same time two passengers came to the river's bank who wished to be taken out to the packet with their luggage. Looking among the boats at the landing, they singled out Abraham's, and asked him to scull them to the steamer. This he did, and after seeing them and their trunks on board, he had the pleasure of receiving upon the bottom of his boat, before he shoved off, a silver half dollar from each of his passengers. "I could scarcely believe my eyes," said Mr. Lincoln, in telling the story. "You may think it was a very little thing," continued he, "but it was a most important incident in my life. I could scarcely believe that I, a poor boy, had earned a dollar in less than a day. The world seemed wider and fairer before me. I was a more hopeful and confident being from that time."

A little incident occurred during these hard years in Indiana which illustrates the straits to which the settlers were subjected. At one time Abraham was obliged to take his grist upon the back of his father's horse, and go fifty miles to get it ground. The mill itself was very rude, and driven by horse-power. The customers were obliged to wait their turn, without reference to their distance from home, and then use their own horses to propel the machinery. On one occasion, Abraham, having arrived at his turn, fastened his mare to the lever, and was following her closely upon her rounds, when, urging her with a switch, and "clucking" to her in the usual way, he received a kick from her which prostrated him, and made him insensible. With the first instant of returning consciousness, he finished the cluck, which he had commenced when he received the kick, (a fact for the psychologist) and with the next he probably thought about getting home, where he arrived at last, battered, but ready for further service.

At the age of nineteen, Abraham made his second essay in navigation, and this time caught something more than a glimpse of the great world in which he was destined to play so important a part. A trading neighbor applied to him to take charge of a flat-boat and its cargo, and, in company with his own son, to take it to the sugar plantations near New Orleans. The entire business of the trip was placed in Abraham's hands. The fact tells its own story touching the young man's reputation for capacity and integrity. He had never made the trip, knew nothing of the journey, was unaccustomed to business transactions, had never been much upon the river; but his tact, ability and honesty were so far trusted that the trader was willing to risk his cargo and his son in his care.

The delight with which the youth swung loose from the shore upon his clumsy craft, with the prospect of a ride of eighteen hundred miles before him, and a vision of the great world of which he had read and thought so much, may be imagined. At this time, he had become a very tall and powerful young man. He had reached the remarkable height of six feet and four inches, a length of trunk and limb remarkable even among the tall race of pioneers to which he belonged.

The incidents of a trip like this were not likely to be exciting, but there were many social chats with settlers and hunters along the banks of the Ohio and Mississippi, and there was much hailing of similar craft afloat. Arriving at a sugar plantation somewhere between Natchez and New Orleans, the boat was pulled in, and tied to the shore for purposes of trade; and here an incident occurred which was sufficiently exciting, and one which, in the memory of recent events, reads somewhat strangely. Here seven negroes attacked the life of the future liberator of their race, and it is not improbable that some of them have lived to be emancipated by his proclamation. Night had fallen, and the two tired voyagers had lain down upon their hard bed for sleep. Hearing a noise on shore, Abraham shouted: "Who's there?" The noise continuing, and no voice replying, he sprang to his feet, and saw seven negroes, evidently bent on plunder. Abraham guessed the errand at once, and seizing a hand-spike, rushed toward them, and knocked one into the water the moment that he touched the boat. The second, third and fourth who leaped on board were served in the same rough way. Seeing that they were not likely to make headway in their thieving enterprise, the remainder turned to flee. Abraham and his companion growing excited and warm with their work, leaped on shore, and followed them. Both were too swift of foot for the negroes, and all of them received a severe pounding. They returned to their boat just as the others escaped from the water, but the latter fled into the darkness as fast as their feet could carry them. Abraham and his fellow in the fight were both injured, but not disabled. Not being armed, and unwilling to wait until the negroes had received reinforcements, they cut adrift, and floating down a mile or two, tied up to the bank again, and watched and waited for the morning.

The trip was brought at length to a successful end. The cargo, or "load," as they called it, was all disposed of for money, the boat itself sold for lumber, and the young men retraced the passage, partly, at least, on shore and on foot, occupying several weeks in the difficult and tedious journey.

Working thus for others, receiving only the humblest wages in return, reading every book upon which he could lay his hand, pursuing various studies in the intervals of toil with special attention to arithmetic, discharging his filial duties at home and upon his father's farm, picking up bits of information from neighbors and new-comers, growing in wisdom and practical sagacity, and achieving a place in the good will and respect of all with whom he came in contact, the thirteen years of his life in Indiana wore away. With a constitution as firm and flexible as whip-cord, he had arrived at his majority. The most that could be said of his education was that he could "read, write and cipher." He knew nothing of English grammar. He could not read a sentence in any tongue but his own; but all that he knew, he knew thoroughly. It had all been assimilated, and was a part not only of his inalienable possessions but of himself. While acquiring, he had learned to construct, organize, express. There was no part of his knowledge that was not an element of his practical power. He had not been made by any artificial process; he had grown. Holding within himself the germ of a great life, he had reached out his roots like the trees among which he was reared, and drawn into himself such nutriment as the soil afforded. His individuality was developed and nurtured by the process. He had become a man after God's pattern, and not a machine after man's pattern; he was a child of Nature and not a thing of art. And this was the secret of all his subsequent intellectual successes. He succeeded because he had himself and all his resources completely in hand; for he was not, and never became an educated man, in the common meaning of that phrase. He could train all his force upon any point, and it mattered little whether the direction was an accustomed one or otherwise.

It was a happy thing for the young man that, living among the roughest of rough men, many of whom were addicted to coarse vices, he never acquired a vice. There was no taint upon his moral character. No stimulant ever entered his lips, no profanity ever came forth from them, which defiled the man. Loving and telling a story better than any one around him, except his father, from whom he inherited the taste and talent, a great talker and a warm lover of social intercourse, good-natured under all circumstances, his honesty and truthfulness well known and thoroughly believed in, he was as popular throughout all the region where he lived as he became afterward throughout the nation.

CHAPTER III.

THOMAS LINCOLN had raised his little family; and the children of his wife were also grown to woman's and man's estate. There had indeed been three weddings in the family. Sarah Lincoln, the daughter, was married to Aaron Grigsby, a young man living in the vicinity, and two of Mrs. Lincoln's daughters had left the Lincoln cabin for new homes. The sister of Abraham had been married but a year, however, when she died, and thus a new grief was inflicted upon the sensitive heart of her brother. Her marriage occurred in 1822; and as she was born in 1808, she could have been only fourteen years old when she became a wife. It is not remarkable that the child found an early grave.

During the last two years of their residence in Indiana, a general discontent had seized upon the family concerning their location. The region at that day was an unhealthy one, and there could be no progress in agricultural pursuits without a great outlay of labor in clearing away the heavy timber which burdened all the fertile soil. At the same time, reports were rife of the superior qualities of the prairie lands of Illinois. There, by the sides of the water-courses, and in the edges of the timber, were almost illimitable farms that called for nothing but the plough and hoe to make them immediately productive. Dennis Hanks, a relative of the first Mrs. Lincoln, was sent to the new region to reconnoiter, and returned with a glowing account of the new country. It is probable that if Thomas Lincoln had been alone he would have remained at the old

Engraved expressly for Holland's "Life of Lincoln."

THE EARLY HOME
IN ILLINOIS.

home, but there was young life to be taken into the account. The new sons-in-law of Mrs. Lincoln, as well as Abraham, were doubtless averse to repeating the severe experiences of the father, and with fresh life and enterprise desired a new and more inviting field of operations.

Mr. Lincoln sold out his squatter's claim in Indiana, and, on the first of March, 1830, less than a month after Abraham had completed his twenty-first year, he started for the land of promise in company with his family and the sons-in-law and two daughters of his wife. Their journey was difficult and tedious in the extreme. They found the rivers swollen by the spring rains, and through such mud as only the rich soil of the West can produce, the ox-teams dragged the wagons, loaded with the entire personal effects of the emigrants. One of these teams was driven by Abraham. Taking a north-westerly course, they struck diagonally across the southern part of Indiana, making toward the central portion of Illinois. After a journey of two hundred miles, which they made in fifteen days, they entered Macon County in that state, and there halted. The elder Lincoln selected a spot on the north side of the Sangamon River, at the junction of the timber land and prairie, about ten miles westerly of Decatur. Here, Abraham assisted his father in building a log cabin, and in getting the family into a condition for comfortable life. The cabin, which still stands, was made of hewed timber, and near it were built a smoke-house and stable. All the tools they had to work with were a common ax, a broad ax, a hand-saw, and a "drawer knife." The doors and floor were made of puncheons and the gable ends of the structure boarded up with plank "rived" by Abraham's hand out of oak timber. The nails used—and they were very few—were all brought from their old home in Indiana. When the cabin and out-buildings were completed, Abraham set to work and helped to split rails enough to fence in a lot of ten acres, and built the fence. After breaking up the piece of inclosed prairie, and seeing it planted with corn, he turned over the new home to his father, and announced his intention to seek or make his

own fortune. He did not leave the region immediately, however, but worked for hire among the neighboring farmers,
picking up enough to keep himself clothed, and looking for
better chances. It is remembered that during this time he
broke up fifty acres of prairie with four yoke of oxen, and
that he spent most of the winter following in splitting rails
and chopping wood. No one seems to know who Mr. Lincoln
worked for during this first summer, but a little incident in the
pastoral labors of Rev. A. Hale of Springfield, Illinois, will
perhaps indicate his employer. There seems to be no room
for the incident afterwards in his life, and it is undoubtedly
associated with his first summer in Illinois. Mr. Hale, in May,
1861, went out about seven miles from his home to visit a sick
lady, and found there a Mrs. Brown who had come in as a
neighbor. Mr. Lincoln's name having been mentioned, Mrs.
Brown said: " Well, I remember Mr. Linken. He worked
with my old man thirty-four year ago, and made a crap.
We lived on the same farm where we live now, and he worked
all the season, and made a crap of corn, and the next winter
they hauled the crap all the way to Galena, and sold it for
two dollars and a half a bushel. At that time there was no
public houses, and travelers were obliged to stay at any house
along the road that could take them in. One evening a right
smart looking man rode up to the fence, and asked my old
man if he could get to stay over night. 'Well,' said Mr.
Brown, 'we can feed your crittur, and give you something
to eat, but we can't lodge you unless you can sleep on the
same bed with the hired man.' The man hesitated, and
asked 'Where is he?' 'Well,' said Mr. Brown, 'you can
come and see him.' So the man got down from his crittur,
and Mr. Brown took him around to where, in the shade of
the house, Mr. Lincoln lay his full length on the ground, with
an open book before him. 'There,' said Mr. Brown, pointing
at him, 'he is.' The stranger looked at him a minute, and
said, 'Well, I think he'll do,' and he staid and slept with the
President of the United States."

There are some mistakes in this story. Mr. Lincoln worked

for Mr. Taylor, who owned the farm, and boarded with Mr. Brown. There is an evident mistake in the date of the incident, for it puts Mr. Lincoln into Illinois three years or more before he removed from Indiana. Of the fact that he worked a summer, or part of a summer, on this farm, there is no doubt; and it is strongly probable that it was the first summer he spent in Illinois.

The expectation of the family to find a more healthy location than the one they had left was sadly disappointed. In the autumn of that year, all were afflicted with fever and ague. This was a new enemy, and they were much discouraged; but no steps for relief or removal could be taken then. They determined, however, to leave the county at the first opportunity. In the meantime, the winter descended, and it proved to be the severest season that had been known in the new state. It is still remembered for the enormous amount of snow that fell. In the following spring, the father left the Sangamon for a better locality in Coles County, where he lived long enough to see his son one of the foremost men of the new state, to receive from him many testimonials of filial affection, and to complete his seventy-third year. He died on the 17th day of January, 1851.

A man who used to work with Abraham occasionally during his first year in Illinois,* says that at that time he was the roughest looking person he ever saw. He was tall, angular and ungainly, and wore trousers made of flax and tow, cut tight at the ankle, and out at both knees. He was known to be very poor, but he was a welcome guest in every house in the neighborhood. This informant speaks of splitting rails with Abraham, and reveals some interesting facts concerning wages. Money was a commodity never reckoned upon. Abraham split rails to get clothing, and he made a bargain with Mrs. Nancy Miller to split four hundred rails for every yard of brown jeans, dyed with white walnut bark, that would be necessary to make him a pair of trousers. In these days he used to walk five, six and seven miles to his work.

* George Cluse.

He left home before his father removed to Coles County, but he did not cut entirely loose from the family until this removal. Then he was ready for any opening to business, and it soon came. During the winter of the deep snow, one Denton Offutt, a trader, who belonged in Lexington, Kentucky, applied to him, John D. Johnston, his stepmother's son, and John Hanks, a relative of his own mother, to take a flat-boat to New Orleans. Abraham had already made the trip, and was regarded as a desirable man for the service. A bargain was made, and the three men agreed to join Offutt at Springfield, the present capital of the state, as soon as the snow should be gone. The snow melted about the first of March, but the accumulation had been so great that the low country was heavily flooded. Finding they could not make the journey on foot, they purchased a large canoe, and proceeded along the Sangamon River in it. They found Offutt at Springfield, but learned that he had failed to buy a boat at Beardstown, as he had expected. As all were disappointed, they finally settled upon an arrangement by which young Lincoln, Hanks and Johnston were to build a boat on Sangamon River, at Sangamon town, about seven miles north-west of Springfield. For this work they were to receive twelve dollars a month each. When the boat was finished, (and every plank of it was sawed by hand with a whip-saw,) it was launched on the Sangamon, and floated to a point below New Salem, in Menard (then Sangamon) County, where a drove of hogs was to be taken on board. At this time, the hogs of the region ran wild, as they do now in portions of the border states. Some of them were savage, and all, after the manner of swine, were difficult to manage. They had, however, been gathered and penned, but not an inch could they be made to move toward the boat. All the ordinary resources were exhausted in the attempts to get them on board. There was but one alternative, and this Abraham adopted. He actually carried them on board, one by one. His long arms and great strength enabled him to grasp them as in a vise, and to transfer them rapidly from the shore to the boat. They then took the boat to New Orleans substantially on the original contract, though Hanks, finding that he would be obliged to be absent from his family longer than he expected, left the boat at St. Louis, and came back.

The voyage was successfully accomplished, and so great was the satisfaction of Lincoln's employer, that he immediately proposed to him a different and higher grade of employment. Offutt had a store at New Salem, and a mill. These he proposed to place in Abraham's care. His previous clerks, during his long absences, had not only cheated him, but, by their insolence and dissipated habits, had driven away his customers. Offutt met Lincoln on the previous winter an entire stranger, but, during a brief intercourse, he had become impressed with his capacity and honesty. So Abraham became a clerk in a pioneer " store." He had not many personal graces to exhibit there, but he at once became a center of attraction. Offutt's old customers came back, new ones were acquired, and all the business of the store was well performed.

It was while performing the duties of this new position that several incidents occurred which illustrated the young man's characteristics. He could not rest for an instant under the consciousness that he had, even unwittingly, defrauded anybody. On one occasion he sold a woman a little bill of goods amounting in value, by the reckoning, to two dollars and six and a quarter cents. He received the money, and the woman went away. On adding the items of the bill again, to make himself sure of correctness, he found that he had taken six and a quarter cents too much. It was night, and closing and locking the store, he started out on foot, a distance of two or three miles, for the house of his defrauded customer, and delivering over to her the sum whose possession had so much troubled him, went home satisfied. On another occasion, just as he was closing the store for the night, a woman entered, and asked for half a pound of tea. The tea was weighed out and paid for, and the store was left for the night. The next morning, Abraham entered to begin the duties of the day, when he discovered a four-ounce weight on the scales. He saw at once that he had made a mistake, and, shutting the store, he took a long walk before breakfast to deliver the remainder of the tea. These are very humble incidents, but they illustrate the man's perfect conscientiousness—his sensitive honesty—better perhaps than they would if they were of greater moment.

Another incident occurred in this store which illustrates other traits of his character. While showing goods to two or three women, a bully came in and began to talk in an offensive manner, using much profanity, and evidently wishing to provoke a quarrel. Lincoln leaned over the counter, and begged him, as ladies were present, not to indulge in such talk. The bully retorted that the opportunity had come for which he had long sought, and he would like to see the man who could hinder him from saying anything he might choose to say. Lincoln, still cool, told him that if he would wait until the ladies retired, he would hear what he had to say, and give him any satisfaction he desired. As soon as the women were gone, the man became furious. Lincoln heard his boasts and his abuse for a time, and finding that he was not to be put off without a fight, said—"Well, if you must be whipped, I suppose I may as well whip you as any other man." This was just what the bully had been seeking, he said, so out of doors they went, and Lincoln made short work with him. He threw him upon the ground, held him there as if he had been a child, and gathering some " smart-weed " which grew upon the spot, rubbed it into his face and eyes, until the fellow bellowed with pain. Lincoln did all this without a particle of anger, and when the job was finished, went immediately for water, washed his victim's face, and did everything he could to alleviate his distress. The upshot of the matter was that the man became his fast and life-long friend, and was a better man from that day. It was impossible then, and it always remained impossible, for Lincoln to cherish resentment or revenge

There lived at this time, in and around New Salem, a band of rollicking fellows or, more properly, roystering rowdies, known as "The Clary's Grove Boys." The special tie that united them was physical courage and prowess. These fellows, although they embraced in their number many men who have since become respectable and influential, were wild and rough beyond toleration in any community not made up like that which produced them. They pretended to be "regulators," and were the terror of all who did not acknowledge their rule; and their mode of securing allegiance was by flogging every man who failed to acknowledge it. They took it upon themselves to try the mettle of every new comer, and to learn the sort of stuff he was made of. Some one of their number was appointed to fight, wrestle, or run a foot-race, with each incoming stranger. Of course, Abraham Lincoln was obliged to pass the ordeal.

Perceiving that he was a man who would not easily be floored, they selected their champion, Jack Armstrong, and imposed upon him the task of laying Lincoln upon his back. There is no evidence that Lincoln was an unwilling party in the sport, for it was what he had always been accustomed to. The bout was entered upon, but Armstrong soon discovered that he had met with more than his match. The "Boys" were looking on, and, seeing that their champion was likely to get the worst of it, did after the manner of such irresponsible bands. They gathered around Lincoln, struck and disabled him, and then Armstrong, by "legging" him, got him down.

Most men would have been indignant, not to say furiously angry, under such foul treatment as this; but if Lincoln was either, he did not show it. Getting up in perfect good humor, he fell to laughing over his discomfiture, and joking about it. They had all calculated upon making him angry, and then they intended, with the amiable spirit which characterized the " Clary's Grove Boys," to give him a terrible drubbing. They were disappointed, and, in their admiration of him, immediately invited him to become one of the company. Strange as it may seem, this was the turning point, apparently, in Lincoln's life, a fact which will appear as our narrative progresses.

It was while young Lincoln was engaged in the duties of Offutt's store that he commenced the study of English grammar. There was not a text-book to be obtained in the neighborhood, but hearing that there was a copy of Kirkham's grammar in the possession of a person seven or eight miles distant, he walked to his house and succeeded in borrowing it. L. M. Green, a lawyer of Petersburg, in Menard County, says that every time he visited New Salem, at this period, Lincoln took him out upon a hill, and asked him to explain some point in Kirkham that had given him trouble. After having mastered the book, he remarked to a friend, that if that was what they called a science, he thought he could " subdue another." Mr. Green says that Mr. Lincoln's talk at this time showed that he was beginning to think of a great life, and a great destiny. Lincoln said to him, on one occasion, that all his family seemed to have good sense, but, somehow, none had ever become distinguished. He thought that perhaps he might become so. He had talked, he said, with men who had the reputation of being great men, but he could not see that they differed much from others. During this year, he was also much engaged with debating clubs, often walking six or seven miles to attend them. One of these clubs held its meetings at an old store-house in New Salem, and the first speech young Lincoln ever made was made there. He used to call the exercise " practicing polemics." As these clubs were composed principally of men of no education whatever, some of their " polemics " are remembered as the most laughable of farces. His favorite newspaper, at this time, was the Louisville Journal, a paper which he received regularly by mail, and paid for during a number of years when he had not money enough to dress decently. He liked its politics, and was particularly delighted with its wit and humor, of which he had the keenest appreciation. When out of the store, he was always busy in the pursuit of knowledge. One gentleman who met him during this period, says that the first time he saw him he was lying on a trundle-bed, covered with books and papers, and rocking a cradle with his foot. Of the amount of uncovered space between the extremities of his trousers and the top of his socks which this informant observed, there shall be no mention. The whole scene, however, was entirely characteristic—Lincoln reading and studying, and at the same time helping his landlady by quieting her child.

During the year that Lincoln was in Denton Offutt's store, that gentleman, whose business was somewhat widely and unwisely spread about the country, ceased to prosper in his finances, and finally failed. The store was shut up, the mill was closed, and Abraham Lincoln was out of business. The year had been one of great advances, in many respects. He had made new and valuable acquaintances, read many books, mastered the grammar of his own tongue, won multitudes of friends, and become ready for a step still further in advance. Those who could appreciate brains respected him, and those whose highest ideas of a man related to his muscles were devoted to him. Every one trusted him. It was while he was performing the duties of the store that he acquired the soubriquet " Honest Abe "—a characterization that he never dishonored, and an abbreviation that he never outgrew. He was judge, arbitrator, referee, umpire, authority, in all disputes, games and matches of man-flesh and horse-flesh; a pacificator in all quarrels; every body's friend; the best natured, the most sensible, the best informed, the most modest and unassuming, the kindest, gentlest, roughest, strongest, best young fellow in all New Salem and the region round about.

CHAPTER IV.

DURING the year that Lincoln was in the employ of Offutt, a series of Indian difficulties were in progress in the state. Black Hawk, a celebrated chief of the Sacs, a tribe that by the terms of a treaty entered into near the beginning of the century, were permanently removed to the western bank of the Mississippi, came down the river with three hundred of his own warriors, and a few allies from the Kickapoos and Pottawatomies, accompanied also by his women and children, and crossed to the eastern side with the avowed intention of taking possession of the old hunting grounds of the nation on the Rock River. As he was committing numerous outrages on the way, General Gaines, commanding the United States forces in that quarter, immediately marched a few companies of regulars to Rock Island, where he took up his position. Governor Reynolds seconded his efforts by sending to him several hundred volunteers, recruited in the northern and central portions of the state. Black Hawk, not being able to meet the force thus assembled, retreated, and, on receiving from General Gaines a threat to cross the river and chastise him on his own ground, sued for peace, and reaffirmed all the terms of the old treaty which confined him to the western shore of the Mississippi.

The old chief proved treacherous again, and showed in the spring of 1832 that his treaty was simply an expedient for gaining time, and raising a larger force. He gathered his warriors in large numbers, and crossed the river with the

intention, as he openly declared, of ascending the Rock River
to the territory of the Winnebagoes, among whom he doubtless hoped to receive reinforcements. Warned back by General Atkinson, then commanding the United States troops on
Rock Island, he returned a defiant message, and kept on. In
this threatening aspect of affairs, Governor Reynolds issued a
call for volunteers, and among the companies that immediately
responded was one from Menard County. Many of the volunteers were from New Salem and Clary's Grove, and Lincoln,
being out of business, was the first to enlist. The company
being full, they held a meeting at Richland for the election of
officers; and now the influence of the Clary's Grove Boys
was felt. Lincoln had completely won their hearts, and they
told him that he must be their captain. It was an office that
he did not aspire to, and one for which he felt that he had no
special fitness; but he consented to be a candidate. There
was but one other candidate for the office, (a Mr. Kirkpatrick,) and he was one of the most influential men in the
county. Previously, Kirkpatrick had been an employer of
Lincoln, and was so overbearing in his treatment of the
young man that the latter left him.

The simple mode of electing their captain, adopted by the
company, was by placing the candidates apart, and telling the
men to go and stand with the one they preferred. Lincoln
and his competitor took their positions, and then the word
was given. At least three out of every four went to Lincoln
at once. When it was seen by those who had ranged themselves with the other candidate that Lincoln was the choice
of the majority of the company, they left their places, one by
one, and came over to the successful side, until Lincoln's opponent in the friendly strife was left standing almost alone.
" I felt badly to see him cut so," says a witness of the scene.
Here was an opportunity for revenge. The humble laborer
was his employer's captain, but the opportunity was never
improved. Mr. Lincoln frequently confessed that no subsequent success of his life had given him half the satisfaction
that this election did. He had achieved public recognition;

4

and to one so humbly bred the distinction was inexpressibly delightful.

Captain Lincoln's company and several others formed in the vicinity, were ordered to rendezvous at Beardstown, on the Illinois River, and here for the first time he met the Hon. John T. Stuart, a gentleman who was destined to have an important influence upon his life. Stuart was a lawyer by profession, and commanded one of the Sangamon County companies. Captain Stuart was soon afterwards elected Major of a spy battalion, formed from some of these companies, and had the best opportunities to observe the merits of Captain Lincoln. He testifies that Lincoln was exceedingly popular among the soldiers, in consequence of his excellent care of the men in his command, his never-failing good nature, and his ability to tell more stories and better ones than any man in the service. He was popular also among these hardy men on account of his great physical strength. Wrestling was an every-day amusement, in which athletic game Lincoln had but one superior in the army. One Thompson was Lincoln's superior in "science," and vanquished everybody rather by superior skill than by superior muscular power.

On the 27th of April, the force at Beardstown moved. A few days of severe marching took the troops to the mouth of Rock River. It was there arranged with General Atkinson that they should proceed up the river to Prophetstown, where they were to await the arrival of the regulars. General Whiteside, in command of the volunteers, disregarding the arrangement for some reason, burnt the Prophet's village, and advanced up the stream forty miles further, to Dixon's Ferry. These marches were severe; but to men bred as Captain Lincoln had been, they were but the repetition of every-day hardships, under more exciting motives.

Before arriving at Dixon's Ferry, the army halted, and leaving behind their baggage-wagons, made a forced march upon the place. Arriving there, scouting parties were sent out to ascertain the position of the enemy. At this time they were joined by two battalions of mounted volunteers from

the region of Peoria, who, having a taste for a little fighting
on their own responsibility, had rashly engaged Black Hawk,
and had been chased in disorder from the field of their boyish
adventure, leaving eleven of their number behind them dead,—
an event which has passed into history with the title of "Stillman's Defeat." They came to General Whiteside panic-
stricken, and a council of war was immediately held which
resulted in the determination to march at once to the scene
of the disaster. A battle seemed imminent, but the wily savages had anticipated the movement, and not one was found.
They had pushed further up the river, and broken up into
predatory and foraging bands, one of which pounced upon a
settlement near Ottowa, murdered fifteen persons, and carried
two young women away captive.

General Whiteside, finding the enemy escaped, buried the
dead of the day before, returned to camp, and was soon joined
by General Atkinson with his troops and supplies. The
twenty-four hundred men thus brought together made a force
sufficiently large to annihilate Black Hawk's army, if they
could have brought the cunning warrior to a fight, but this
was impossible. Here a new trouble arose. The troops had
volunteered for a limited period, and, as their time had nearly
expired, and they were surfeited with hardship without glory,
they clamored to be discharged, and Governor Reynolds yielded to their demands. The danger still continuing, he issued
another call for volunteers. Captain Lincoln was among those
who had not had enough of the war. He had volunteered
for a purpose, and he did not intend to leave the service until
the purpose was accomplished. The Governor, in addition
to his general call for volunteers, asked for the formation of a
volunteer regiment from those just discharged. General
Whiteside himself immediately re-enlisted as a private, as did
also Captain Lincoln. Then followed a whole month of marching and maneuvering, without satisfactory results. There was
some fighting near Galena, and a skirmish at Burr-Oak Grove,
but there was not enough of excitement and success to keep
the restless spirits of the volunteers contented, and many of

them deserted.   Indeed, the force became reduced to one-half
of its original numbers.   Lincoln, however, remained true to
his obligations, although it was not his good fortune to participate in the engagements which brought the war to a speedy
close.   The Indians were overtaken at last by a force under
General Henry.   The pursuit had led them to the Wisconsin
River, and here the Indians were found in full retreat.   They
were charged upon, and driven in great confusion.   Sixty-
eight Indians were killed, a large number wounded, and at
last, just as the savages were crossing the Mississippi, the
battle of Bad-Ax was fought, which resulted in the capture
of Black Hawk himself, with nearly all his warriors.

The Black Hawk war was not a very remarkable affair.
It made no military reputations, but it was noteworthy in the
single fact that the two simplest, homeliest and truest men
engaged in it afterward became Presidents of the United
States, viz: General (then Colonel) Zachary Taylor, and
Abraham Lincoln.   Mr. Lincoln never spoke of it as anything
more than an interesting episode in his life, except upon one
occasion when he used it as an instrument for turning the
military pretensions of another into ridicule.   The friends of
General Cass, when that gentleman was a candidate for the
presidency, endeavored to endow him with a military reputation.   Mr. Lincoln, at that time a representative in Congress,
delivered a speech before the House, which, in its allusions to
General Cass, was exquisitely sarcastic and irresistibly humorous.   "By the way, Mr. Speaker," said Mr. Lincoln, "do
you know I am a military hero?   Yes, sir, in the days of the
Black Hawk war, I fought, bled and came away.   Speaking
of General Cass's career reminds me of my own.   I was not
at Stillman's Defeat, but I was about as near it as Cass to
Hull's surrender; and like him I saw the place very soon
afterward.   It is quite certain I did not break my sword, for
I had none to break; but I bent my musket pretty badly on
one occasion. * * * If General Cass went in advance of me
in picking whortleberries, I guess I surpassed him in charges
upon the wild onions.   If he saw any live, fighting Indians,

it was more than I did, but I had a good many bloody struggles
with the mosquitoes; and although I never fainted from loss
of blood, I can truly say I was often very hungry." Mr.
Lincoln then went on to say that if he should ever turn democrat, and be taken up as a candidate for the presidency by
the democratic party, he hoped they would not make fun of
him by attempting to make of him a military hero. He lived
to see himself the candidate of another party, and witnessed
a decided disposition on the part of his campaign biographers
to make a little political capital for him out of his connection
with the Black Hawk war—an attempt which must have appealed to his quick sense of the ludicrous, as well as recalled
the speech from which an extract has been quoted.

The soldiers from Sangamon County arrived home just ten
days before the state election, and Mr. Lincoln was immediately applied to for permission to place his name among the
candidates for the legislature. He was then but twenty-three
years old, had but just emerged from obscurity, and had been
but a short time a resident of the county. The application
was a great surprise to him. Indeed, aside from the evidence
of personal and neighborhood friendship which it afforded him,
the surprise could hardly have been a pleasant one, for his
political convictions had placed him among those who were in
almost a hopeless minority. Party feeling ran high between
the friends of General Jackson and Henry Clay, but the
friends of Mr. Clay had little power. Illinois was strongly
democratic and for many years remained so. His opponents
in the canvass were well known men, and had shown themselves and made their speeches throughout the county; yet
in Mr. Lincoln's own precinct he was voted for alike by political friend and foe. The official vote of the New Salem
precinct, as shown by the poll-book in the clerk's office at
Springfield, was, at this time, for Congress · Jonathan H.
Pugh 179, Joseph Duncan 97 ; while the vote for Abraham
Lincoln for the legislature was 277, or one more than the aggregate for both the candidates for Congress. This vote was
undoubtedly the result of the personal popularity acquired by

Lincoln during his brief military campaign. All his soldiers voted for him, and worked for his election wherever they had influence. But he was defeated on the general vote, and immediately looked about to find what there was for him to do.

It is interesting to recall the fact that at this time he seriously took into consideration the project of learning the blacksmith's trade. He was without means, and felt the immediate necessity of undertaking some business that would give him bread. It was while he was entertaining this project that an event occurred which, in his undetermined state of mind, seemed to open a way to success in another quarter. A man named Reuben Radford, the keeper of a small store in the village of New Salem, had somehow incurred the displeasure of the Clary's Grove Boys, who had exercised their "regulating" prerogatives by irregularly breaking in his windows. William G. Greene, a friend of young Lincoln, riding by Radford's store soon afterward, was hailed by him, and told that he intended to sell out. Mr. Greene went into the store, and, looking around, offered him at random four hundred dollars for his stock. The offer was immediately accepted. Lincoln happening in the next day, and being familiar with the value of the goods, Mr. Greene proposed to him to take an inventory of the stock, and see what sort of a bargain he had made. This he did, and it was found that the goods were worth six hundred dollars. Lincoln then made him an offer of a hundred and twenty-five dollars for his bargain, with the proposition that he and a man named Berry, as his partner, should take his (Greene's) place in the notes given to Radford. Mr. Greene agreed to the arrangement, but Radford declined it, except on condition that Greene would be their security, and this he at last assented to.

Berry proved to be a dissipated, trifling man, and the business soon became a wreck. Mr. Greene was obliged to go in and help Lincoln close it up, and not only do this but pay Radford's notes. All that young Lincoln won from the store was some very valuable experience, and the burden of a debt to Greene which, in his conversations with the latter, he always spoke of as "the national debt." But this national debt, unlike the majority of those which bear the title, was paid to the utmost farthing in after years. Six years afterwards, Mr. Greene, who knew nothing of the law in such cases, and had not troubled himself to inquire about it, and who had, in the meantime, removed to Tennessee, received notice from Mr. Lincoln that he was ready to pay him what he had paid for Berry—he, Lincoln, being legally bound to pay the liabilities of his partner.

About this time Mr. Lincoln was appointed postmaster by President Jackson. The office was too insignificant to be considered politically, and it was given to the young man because everybody liked him, and because he was the only man willing to take it who could make out the returns. He was exceedingly pleased with the appointment, because it gave him a chance to read every newspaper that was taken in the vicinity. He had never been able to get half the newspapers he wanted before, and the office gave him the prospect of a constant feast. Not wishing to be tied to the office, as it yielded him no revenue that would reward him for the confinement, he made a post-office of his hat. Whenever he went out, the letters were placed in his hat. When an anxious looker for a letter found the postmaster, he had found his office; and the public officer, taking off his hat, looked over his mail wherever the public might find him. He kept the office until it was discontinued, or removed to Petersburgh.

One of the most beautiful exhibitions of Mr. Lincoln's rigid honesty occurred in connection with the settlement of his accounts with the post-office department, several years afterwards. It was after he had become a lawyer, and had been a legislator. He had passed through a period of great poverty, had acquired his education in the law in the midst of many perplexities, inconveniences and hardships, and had met with temptations, such as few men could resist, to make a temporary use of any money he might have in his hands. One day, seated in the law office of his partner, the agent of the post-office department entered, and inquired if Abraham Lincoln was within. Mr. Lincoln responded to his name, and was informed that the agent had called to collect a balance due the department since the discontinuance of the New Salem office. A shade of perplexity passed over Mr. Lincoln's face, which did not escape the notice of friends who were present. One of them said at once : " Lincoln, if you are in want of money, let us help you." He made no reply, but suddenly rose, and pulled out from a pile of books a little old trunk, and, returning to the table, asked the agent how much the amount of his debt was. The sum was named, and then Mr. Lincoln opened the trunk, pulled out a little package of coin wrapped in a cotton rag, and counted out the exact sum, amounting to something more than seventeen dollars. After the agent had left the room, he remarked quietly that he never used any man's money but his own. Although this sum had been in his hands during all these years, he had never regarded it as available, even for any temporary purpose of his own.

The store having " winked out," to use his own expression, he was ready for something else, and it came from an unexpected quarter. John Calhoun, a resident of Springfield, and since notorious as President of the Lecompton Constitutional Convention, in Kansas, was the surveyor of Sangamon County. The constant influx of immigrants made his office a busy one, and, looking around for assistance, he fixed upon Lincoln, and deputed to him all his work in the immediate vicinity of New Salem. Lincoln had not the slightest knowledge of surveying, and but the slenderest acquaintance with the science upon which it was based. He would be obliged to fit himself for his work in the shortest possible time, and he did. Mr. Calhoun lent him a copy of Flint and Gibson, and after a brief period of study, he procured a compass and chain (the old settlers say that his first chain was a grape-vine,) and went at his work. The work procured bread, and, what seemed quite as essential to him, books ; for during all these months he was a close student, and a constant reader. Mr. Lincoln surveyed the present town of Petersburgh, and much of the adjacent territory. He pursued this business steadily fo𝑟 a year or more, and with such success that the accuracy of his surveys has never been called in question. One interruption must have occurred in his work, though it was brief. His compass and chain were attached and sold to pay a debt of Berry's, for which he was surety, but they were bought by a man named James Short, who immediately gave them back to him.

CHAPTER V.

HITHERTO the life of our subject has run in a single stream. His history thus far has related to his private career—to his birth, education, growth of mind and character, and personal struggles. Before entering upon that period of his life through which we are to trace a double current, a private and a public one, it will be proper to inquire what kind of a man he had become.

No man ever lived, probably, who was more a self-made man. than Abraham Lincoln. Not a circumstance of his life favored the development which he had reached. * He was self-moved to study under the most discouraging conditions. He had few teachers, few books, and no intellectual companions. His father could neither read nor write. His mother died when he was a child. He had none of those personal attractions which would naturally enlist the sympathies· and assistance of any refined men and women with whom he must occasionally have come in contact. He was miserably poor, and was compelled to labor among poor people to win his daily bread. There was not an influence around him except that left upon him by his "angel mother," which did not tend rather to drag him down than lift him up. He was not endowed with a hopeful temperament. He had no force·of self-esteem—no faith in himself that buoyed him up amid the contempt of the proud and prosperous. He was altogether a humble man—humble in condition, and humble in spirit. Yet, by the love of that which was good and great and true, and by the hunger and thirst of a noble nature, he was led to the acquisition of a practical education, and to the development of all those peculiar powers that were latent within him.

He was loyal to his convictions. There is no doubt that at this time he had begun to think of political life. He was, at least, thoroughly conversant with the politics of his own state and of the country. There was not a more diligent reader of political newspapers than he. He had become familiar with the position and history of the politicians and statesmen of the country, and must have been entirely aware of the unpopularity of those toward whom his judgment and sympathies led him. That he was then, and always remained, an ambitious man, there is no question; and with this fact in mind we can measure the sacrifice which adherence to his convictions cost him. His early love of Henry Clay has already been noticed; and this love for the great Kentuckian, though circumstances modified it somewhat, never ceased. He clung to him with the warmest affection through the most of his life, pronounced his eulogy when he died, and stood firmly by the principles which he represented. In a state overwhelmingly democratic, he took his position with the minority, and steadily adhered to the opposition against all the temptations to quick and certain success which desertion would bring him.

He was a marked and peculiar man. People talked about him. His studious habits, his greed for information, his thorough mastery of the difficulties of every new position in which he was placed, his intelligence touching all matters of public concern, his unwearying good nature, his skill in telling a story, his great athletic power, his quaint, odd ways, his uncouth appearance, all tended to bring him into sharp contrast with the dull mediocrity by which he was surrounded. Denton Offutt, his old employer in the store, said, in the extravagance of his admiration, that he knew more than any other man in the United States. The Governor of Indiana, one of Offutt's acquaintances, said, after having a conversation with Lincoln, that the young man "had talent enough in him to make a President." In every circle in which he found himself, whether refined or coarse, he was always the center of attraction. William G. Greene says that when he (Greene) was a member of Illinois college, he brought home with him, on a vacation, Richard Yates, the present Governor of the state, and some other boys, and, in order to entertain them, took them all up to see Lincoln. He found him in his usual position and at his usual occupation. He was flat on his back, on a cellar door, reading a newspaper. That was the manner in which a President of the United States and a Governor of Illinois became acquainted with one another. Mr. Greene says that Lincoln then could repeat the whole of Burns, and was a devoted student of Shakspeare. So the rough backwoodsman, self-educated, entertained the college boys, and was invited to dine with them on bread and milk. How he managed to upset his bowl of milk is not a matter of history, but the fact that he did so is, as is the further fact that Greene's mother, who loved Lincoln, tried to smooth over the accident, and relieve the young man's embarrassment.

Wherever he moved he found men and women to respect and love him. One man who knew him at that time says that "Lincoln had nothing, only plenty of friends." And these friends trusted him wholly, and were willing to be led by him. His unanimous election as Captain in the Black Hawk war, and the unanimous vote given him for the legislature by political friend and foe, wherever in the county he was known, illustrates his wonderful popularity. All the circumstances considered, it was probably without a precedent or parallel. When we remember that this popularity was achieved without any direct attempt to win it—that he flattered nobody, made no pretensions whatever, and was the plainest and poorest man in his precinct, we can appreciate something of the strength of his character and the beauty and purity of his life. He aroused no jealousies, for he was not selfish. He made no enemies, because he felt kindly toward every man. People were glad to see him rise, because it seemed just that he should rise. Indeed, all seemed glad to help him along.

He was a man of practical expedients. He always found some way to get out of difficulties, whether moral or mechanical, and was equally ingenious in his expedients for escaping or surmounting each variety. Governor Yates, in a speech at Springfield, before a meeting at which William G. Greene presided, quoted Mr. Greene as having said that the first time he ever saw Lincoln he was "in the Sangamon River, with his trousers rolled up five feet more. or less, trying to pilot a flat-boat over a mill-dam. The boat was so full of water that it was hard to manage. Lincoln got the prow over, and then, instead of waiting to bail the water out, bored a hole through the projecting part, and let it run out." Barring a little western extravagance in the statement of a measurement, the incident is truly recorded; and it illustrates more forcibly than words can describe the man's ingenuity in the quick invention of moral expedients, then and afterwards. His life had been a life of expedients. He had always been engaged in making the best of bad conditions and untoward circumstances, and in meeting and mastering emergencies. Among those who did not understand him, he had the credit or the discredit, of being a cunning man ; but cunning was not at all an element of his nature or character. He was simply ingenious; he was wonderfully ingenious; but he was not cunning. Cunning is, or tries to be, far-sighted; ingenuity disposes of occasions. Cunning contrives plots; ingenuity dissolves them. Cunning sets traps; ingenuity evades them. Cunning envelops its victims in difficulties; ingenuity helps them out of them. Cunning is the offspring of selfishness; ingenuity is the child or companion of practical wisdom. He took his boat safely over a great many mill-dams during his life, but always by an expedient.

He was a religious man. The fact may be stated without any reservation—with only an explanation. He believed in God, and in his personal supervision of the affairs of men. He believed himself to be under his control and guidance. He believed in the power and ultimate triumph of the right, through his belief in God. This unwavering faith in a Divine

Providence began at his mother's knee, and ran like a thread of gold through all the inner experiences of his life. His constant sense of human duty was one of the forms by which his faith manifested itself. His conscience took a broader grasp than the simple apprehension of right and wrong. He recognized an immediate relation between God and himself, in all the actions and passions of his life. He was not professedly a Christian—that is, he subscribed to no creed,—joined no organization of Christian disciples. He spoke little then, perhaps less than he did afterward, and always sparingly, of his religious belief and experiences; but that he had a deep religious life, sometimes imbued with superstition, there is no doubt. We guess at a mountain of marble by the outcropping ledges that hide their whiteness among the ferns.

At this period of his life he had not exhibited in any form that has been preserved, those logical and reasoning powers that so greatly distinguished him during his subsequent public career. The little clubs at and around New Salem where he "practiced polemics" kept no records, and have published no reports. The long talks in Offutt's store, on the flat-boat, on the farm and by the cabin fireside have not been preserved; but there is no doubt that the germ of the power was within him, and that the peculiarity of his education developed it into the remarkable and unique faculty which did much to distinguish him among the men of his generation. He had been from a child, in the habit of putting his thoughts into language. He wrote much, and to this fact is doubtless owing his clearness in statement. He could state with great exactness any fact within the range of his knowledge. His knowledge was not great, nor his vocabulary rich, but he could state the details of one by the use of the other with a precision that Daniel Webster never surpassed.

He was a childlike man. No public man of modern days has been fortunate enough to carry into his manhood so much of the directness, truthfulness and simplicity of childhood as distinguished him. He was exactly what he seemed. He was not awkward for a purpose, but because he could not help it. He did not dress shabbily to win votes, or excite comment, but partly because he was too poor to dress well, and partly because he had no love for dress, or taste in its arrangement. He was not honest because he thought honesty was "the best policy," but because honesty was with him "the natural way of living." With a modest estimate of his own powers, and a still humbler one of his acquisitions, he never assumed to be more or other than he was. A lie in any form seemed impossible to him. He could neither speak one nor act one, and in the light of this fact all the words and acts of his life are to be judged.

If this brief statement of his qualities and powers represents a wonderfully perfect character—so strangely pure and noble that it seems like the sketch of an enthusiast, it is not the writer's fault. Its materials are drawn from the lips of old friends who speak of him with tears—who loved him then as if he were their brother, and who worship his memory with a fond idolatry. It is drawn from such humble materials as composed his early history. He loved all, was kind to all, was without a vice of appetite or passion, was honest, was truthful, was simple, was unselfish, was religious, was intelligent and self-helpful, was all that a good man could desire in a son ready to enter life. We shall see how such a man with such a character entered life, and passed through it.

CHAPTER VI.

SEVERAL of the old acquaintances of Mr. Lincoln speak of his having studied law, or having begun the study of law, previous to 1834. He had doubtless thought of it, and had made it a subject of consideration among his friends. With a vague project of doing this at some time, he had bought a copy of Blackstone at an auction in Springfield, and had looked it over. This fact was enough to furnish a basis for the story; but by his own statement he did not begin the study of his profession until after he had been a member of the legislature.

Two years had passed away since his unsuccessful attempt to be elected a representative of Sangamon County. In the meantime, he had become known more widely. His duties as surveyor had brought him into contact with people in other localities. He had become a political speaker, and, although rather rough and slow and argumentative, was very popular. He had made a few speeches on the condition that the friends who persuaded him to try the experiment " would not laugh at him." They agreed to the condition, and found no occasion to depart from it.

In 1834, he became again a candidate for the legislature, and was elected by the highest vote cast for any candidate. Major John T. Stuart, whose name has been mentioned as an officer in the Black Hawk war, and whose acquaintance Lincoln made at Beardstown, was also elected. Major Stuart had already conceived the highest opinion of the young man, and seeing much of him during the canvass for the election, privately advised him to study law.   Stuart was himself engaged in a large and lucrative legal practice at Springfield. Lincoln said he was poor—that he had no money to buy books, or to live where books might be borrowed and used.   Major Stuart offered to lend him all he needed, and he decided to take the kind lawyer's advice, and accept his offer.   At the close of the canvass which resulted in his election, he walked to Springfield, borrowed "a load" of books of Stuart, and took them home with him to New Salem.   Here he began the study of law in good earnest, though with no preceptor. He studied while he had bread, and then started out on a surveying tour, to win the money that would buy more.   One who remembers his habits during this period says that he went, day after day, for weeks, and sat under an oak tree on a hill near New Salem and read, moving around to keep in the shade, as the sun moved.   He was so much absorbed that some people thought and said that he was crazy.   Not unfrequently he met and passed his best friends without noticing them.   The truth was that he had found the pursuit of his life, and had become very much in earnest.

During Lincoln's campaign, he possessed and rode a horse, to procure which he had quite likely sold his compass and chain, for, as soon as the canvass had closed, he sold a horse, and bought these instruments indispensable to him in the only pursuit by which he could make his living.   When the time for the assembling of the legislature approached, Lincoln dropped his law books, shouldered his pack, and, on foot, trudged to Vandalia, then the capital of the state, about a hundred miles, to make his entrance into public life.

His personal appearance at this time must have been something of an improvement upon former days.   A gentleman now living in Chicago, then a resident of Coles County,* met him at that time, or very soon afterwards, and says that he was dressed in plain mixed jeans, his coat being of the surtout fashion, which, at that day, and in that part of the country,

*U. F. Linder, Esq.

5

was a very reputable dress.   He speaks of him, also, as being
then extremely modest and retiring.   Colonel Jesse K. Dubois,
(one of the Sangamon County delegation,) and Lincoln were
the two youngest men in the House.   During this session,
Mr. Lincoln said very little, but learned much.   As he was
a novice in legislation, he left the talking to older and wiser
men.   James Semple, afterwards United States Senator, was
elected speaker, and by him Lincoln was assigned to the second
place on the committee on public accounts and expenditures.
The subject of controlling interest before the legislature has
no special interest in connection with Mr. Lincoln's life.   The
state was new, and very imperfectly developed.   A plan of
internal improvements was in agitation, special reference being
had to a loan for the benefit of the Illinois and Michigan Canal
Company, which had been incorporated in 1825.   The loan
bill was not carried at this session, though it was at a subsequent one.   Lincoln was constantly in his place, and faithful
in the performance of all the duties that were devolved upon
him.   When the session closed, he walked home as he came,
and resumed his law and his surveying.

    The canvass of 1836, which resulted in his re-election to
the legislature, was an unusually exciting one, and resulted in
the choice of a House which has probably never been equaled
in any state, in the whole history of the country, for its number of remarkable men.   As early as June 13th, of that
year, we find a letter in the Sangamon Journal, addressed by
Mr. Lincoln to the editor, beginning as follows: "In your
paper of last Saturday, I see a communication over the signature of 'Many Voters,' in which the candidates who are
announced in the Journal, are called upon to 'show their
hands.'   Agreed.   Here's mine."   He then goes on in his
characteristic way to "show his hand," which was that substantially of the new whig party.   It was during this canvass
that he made the most striking speech he had ever uttered,
and one that established his reputation as a first-class political
debater.   It has been spoken of, by some writers, as the first
speech he ever made ; but this is a mistake.   The opposing

candidates had met at Springfield, as is the custom in the western states, for a public discussion of the questions involved in the canvass; and a large number of citizens had gathered in the Court House to hear the speeches. Ninian W. Edwards, then a whig, led off, and was followed by Dr. Early, a sharp debater and a representative man among the democrats. Early bore down very heavily upon Edwards— so much so that the latter wanted the opportunity for an immediate rejoinder, but Lincoln took his turn upon the platform. Embarrassed at first, and speaking slowly, he began to lay down and fix his propositions. His auditors followed him with breathless attention, and saw him inclose his adversary in a wall of fact, and then weave over him a network of deductions so logically tight in all its meshes, that there was no escape for the victim. He forgot himself entirely, as he grew warm at his work. His audience applauded, and with ridicule and wit he riddled the man whom he had made helpless. Men who remember the speech allude particularly to the transformation which it wrought in Mr. Lincoln's appearance. The homely man was majestic, the plain, good-natured face was full of expression, the long, bent figure was straight as an arrow, and the kind and dreamy eyes flashed with the fire of true inspiration. His reputation was made, and from that day to the day of his death, he was recognized in Illinois as one of the most powerful orators in the state.

The Sangamon County delegation, consisting of nine representatives, was so remarkable for the physical altitude of its members that they were known as "The Long Nine:" Not a man of the number was less than six feet high, and Lincoln was the tallest of the nine, as he was the leading man intellectually, in and out of the House. Among those who composed the House, were General John A. McClernand, afterwards a member of Congress, Jesse K. Dubois, afterwards auditor of the state; James Semple, the speaker of this and the previous House, and subsequently United States Senator; Robert Smith, afterwards member of Congress; John Hogan, at present a member of Congress from St. Louis; General

James Shields, afterwards United States Senator; John De-
ment, who has since been treasurer of the state; Stephen A.
Douglas, whose subsequent public career is familiar to all;
Newton Cloud, president of the convention which framed the
present state constitution of Illinois; John J. Hardin, who fell
at Buena Vista; John Moore, afterwards Lieutenant Governor of the state; William A. Richardson, subsequently
United States Senator, and William McMurtny, who has
since been Lieutenant Governor of the state. This list does
not embrace all who had then, or who have since been distinguished, but it is large enough to show that Lincoln was,
during the term of this legislature, thrown into association
and often into antagonism with the brightest men of the new
state. It is enough, with this fact in mind, to say that he was
by them and by the people regarded as one of the leading men
in the House.

The principal measure with this legislature was the adoption
of a general system of public improvements. It was a great
object with the special friends of this measure to secure the
co-operation and support of the two senators and nine representatives from Sangamon County, but they firmly refused to
support the measure, unless the removal of the capital from
Vandalia to Springfield was made a part of the proposed system. So the measure for this removal passed through its
various stages in company with the internal improvement bill,
and both were enacted on the same day. The measure which
thus changed the location of the capital of the state to Springfield, brought great popularity to the members from Sangamon,
at least in their own home, and especially to Mr. Lincoln, who
was put forward on all occasions to do the important work in
securing it. When it is remembered that he had achieved his
position before the people and among the leading men of the
state at the early age of twenty-seven, it must be admitted
that the disadvantages under which he had labored had not
hindered him from doing what the best educated and most
favored would have been proud to do.

It was at this session that Mr. Lincoln met Stephen A.

Douglas for the first time. Mr. Douglas was then only twenty-three years old, and was the youngest man in the House. Mr. Lincoln, in speaking of the fact subsequently, said that Douglas was then "the least man he ever saw." He was not only very short but very slender. The two young men, who commenced their intellectual and political sparring during the session, could hardly have foreseen the struggle in which they were to engage in after years—a struggle which foreshadowed and even laid the basis of an epoch in the national history, and in the history of freedom and progress throughout the world.

This session of the legislature was notable for its connection with the beginning of Mr. Lincoln's anti-slavery history. It was at Vandalia, at this time, that Mr. Lincoln and Mr. Douglas marked out the course in which they were to walk— one to disappointment and a grave of unsatisfied hopes and baffled ambitions, the other to the realization of his highest dreams of achievement and renown, and a martyrdom that crowns his memory with an undying glory.

Illinois contained many immigrants from the border slave states. Its territory was joined to two of them; and there was a strong desire to live in harmony with neighbors quick to anger and resentment, and sensitive touching their "peculiar institution." The prevailing sentiment in the state was in favor of slavery, or in favor of slaveholders in the exercise of their legal and constitutional rights. There were, in fact, a few hundred slaves living in the state at that time, as appears by the census tables, but by what law is not apparent. The democratic party was unanimously pro-slavery, and whatever there may have been of anti-slavery sentiment among the whigs was practically of little account. The abolitionist was hated and despised by both parties alike, and the whigs deprecated and disowned the title with indignation. There was doubtless some anti-slavery sentiment among the whigs, but it was weak and timid. Both parties were strong in their professed regard for the Constitution, and neither party doubted that the Constitution protected the institution of American Slavery.

The agitation of the slavery question was just beginning to
create uneasiness among slaveholders and politicians; and during the winter the subject was broached in the legislature.
Resolutions were introduced of an extreme pro-slavery character, and the attempt was made to fix the stigma of abolitionism upon all who did not indorse them.   They were carried
through by the large democratic majority, and the opposition
to them was weak in numbers and weaker still in its positions.
We can judge something of its weakness when we learn that
only two men among all the whig members were found willing
to subscribe to a protest against these resolutions.   Abraham
Lincoln and Dan Stone, "representatives from the County of
Sangamon," entered upon the Journal of the House their
reasons for refusing to vote for these offensive resolutions, and
they were the only men in the state who had the manliness to
do it.   The points of the protest were these : that while "the
Congress of the United States has no power under the Constitution to interfere with the institution of slavery in the
different states," and that while "the promulgation of abolition
doctrines tends rather to increase than abate its evils," still, the
"institution of slavery is founded on both injustice and bad
policy," and Congress "has the power, under the Constitution,
to abolish slavery in the District of Columbia."   The latter
proposition was qualified by the statement that this power
"ought not to be exercised unless at the request of the people
of said District."   Certainly this protest was a moderate one,
and we may judge by it something of the character of the
resolutions which compelled its utterance.   We may judge
something also of the low grade of anti-slavery sentiment in
the whig party at that time, when only two men could be
found to sign so moderate and guarded a document as this.
Still, the refusal to sign may have been a matter of policy,
for which a good reason could be given.   It was something,
however, for two men to stand out, and protest that slavery
was a moral and political evil, over which Congress had power
upon the national territory.   It was the beginning of Mr.
Lincoln's anti-slavery record, and modest and moderate as it

was, and much as Mr. Lincoln afterwards accomplished for the abolition of slavery, he never became more extreme in his views than the words of this protest indicate. He never ceased to believe that Congress had no power under the Constitution to interfere with slavery in the different states. He never thought worse of slavery than that it was founded in injustice and bad policy. He never changed his belief touching the power of Congress over the institution of slavery in territory under the exclusive jurisdiction of the United States. This little protest, entered into with his brother representative, Dan Stone, was the outline of the platform upon which he stood, and fought out the great anti-slavery battle whose trophies were four million freedmen, and a nation redeemed to justice and humanity.

In the meantime, Mr. Lincoln had made no money. He had walked his hundred miles to Vandalia in 1836, as he did in 1834, and when the session closed he walked home again. A gentleman in Menard County remembers meeting him and a detachment of "The Long Nine" on their way home. They were all mounted except Lincoln, who had thus far kept up with them on foot. If he had money, he was hoarding it for more important purposes than that of saving leg-weariness and leather. The weather was raw, and Lincoln's clothing was none of the warmest. Complaining of being cold to one of his companions, this irreverent member of "The Long Nine" told his future President that it was no wonder he was cold—"there was so much of him on the ground." None of the party appreciated this homely joke at the expense of his feet (they were doubtless able to bear it) more thoroughly than Lincoln himself. We can imagine the cross-fires of wit and humor by which the way was enlivened during this cold and tedious journey. The scene was certainly a rude one, and seems more like a dream than a reality, when we remember that it occurred less than thirty years ago, in a state which now contains hardly less than a million and a half of people and three thousand miles of railway.

CHAPTER VII.

THE time had come with Mr. Lincoln for translation to a new sphere of life. By the scantiest means he had wrested from the hardest circumstances a development of his characteristic powers. He had acquired the rudiments of an English education. He had read several text books of the natural sciences, with special attention to geology, in the facts and laws of which he had become particularly intelligent. He had read law as well as he could without the assistance of preceptors. He had attended a few sessions of the courts held near him, and had become somewhat familiar with the practical application of legal processes. He had, from the most discouraging beginnings, grown to be a notable political debater. He had had experience in legislation, had received public recognition as a man of mark and power, had been accepted as one of the leaders of an intelligent and morally influential political party, and had fairly outgrown the humble conditions by which his life had hitherto been surrounded.

At this time he received from his Springfield friend, Major Stuart, a proposition to become his partner in the practice of the law. Mr. Lincoln's influence in securing the transfer of the capital from Vandalia to Springfield had already given him a favorable introduction to the people of the city; and on the 15th of April, 1837, he took up his abode there. He went to his new home with great self-distrust and with many misgivings concerning his future; but Springfield became his permanent home. He had been admitted to the bar during the autumn of 1836, and went to his work with the ambition to be something, and the determination to do something.

It must have been with something of regret that he turned his back upon New Salem, for he left behind him a town full of friends, who had watched his progress with the friendliest interest, aided him when he needed aid, and appreciated him. He left behind him all the stepping-stones by which he had mounted to the elevation he had reached—the old store-house where he had been a successful clerk, the old store-house where he had been an unsuccessful principal, the scenes of his wrestling-matches and foot-races, the lounging-places where he had sat and told stories with a post-office in his hat, the rough audience-rooms in which he had "practiced polemics," the places where he had had his rough encounters with the Clary's Grove Boys, and, last, the old oak tree whose shadow he had followed to keep his law text out of the sun. But these things could have touched him but little when placed by the side of a few cabin homes, presided over by noble women who, with womanly instinct, had detected the manliness of his nature, and had given him a home "for his company," as they kindly said, when he needed one in charity. He never forgot these women, and occasion afterward came to show the constancy of his gratitude and the faithfulness of his friendship. Arriving in Springfield he became a member of the family of Hon. William Butler, afterward treasurer of the state, and here came under influences which, to a man bred as he had been, were of the most desirable character.

Mr. Lincoln's business connection with Mr. Stuart must have been broken and brief, for he was still a member of the legislature, which was summoned to a special session on the July following his removal to Springfield, and Mr. Stuart, himself, was soon afterwards elected to, and took his seat in, Congress. Still, the connection was one of advantage to the young lawyer. Mr. Stuart's willingness to receive him as a partner was an indorsement of his powers and acquisitions that must have helped him to make a start in professional life. This life the people of Springfield, who gratefully remembered his services to them in the legislature, would not permit him to pursue without interruption. They kept him upon the legislative ticket in 1838, and he was re-elected. On the assembling of this legislature, Mr. Lincoln was at once recognized to be the foremost man on the whig side of the house, and was brought forward, without any dissent, as their candidate for speaker. The strength of this legislature was pretty evenly divided between the two parties. A great change, indeed, had occurred in the state. The financial crash of 1837 had prostrated industry and trade, and the people had, either justly or unjustly, held the dominant party responsible for the disasters from which they had suffered. Anti-slavery agitation had been voted down in Congress by the friends of Mr. Van Buren, who came into the presidential office during the previous year. All papers relating to slavery were, by solemn resolution of Congress, laid on the table without being debated, read, printed or referred. With financial ruin in the country, and a gag-law in Congress, the democratic party had a heavier load than it could carry. This was felt in Illinois, where the old democratic majority was very nearly destroyed. Colonel W. L. D. Ewing was the candidate of the democrats for speaker, in opposition to Mr. Lincoln, and was at last elected by a majority of one vote. Mr. Lincoln took a prominent part in all the debates of the session. Some of them were political, and were intended to have a bearing upon the next presidential election, and especially upon the politics of the state; but the most of them related to local and ephemeral affairs which will be of no interest to the general reader.

Allusion has already been made to Mr. Lincoln's ingenuity—his quickness at expedients. One of his modes of getting rid of troublesome friends, as well as troublesome enemies, was by telling a story. . He began these tactics early in life, and he grew to be wonderfully adept in them. If a man broached a subject which he did not wish to discuss, he told a story which changed the direction of the conversation. If he was called upon to answer a question, he answered it by telling a story. He had a story for everything—something had occurred at some place where he used to live, that illustrated every possible phase of every possible subject with which he might have connection. His faculty of finding or making a story to match every event in his history, and every event to which he bore any relation, was really marvelous. That he made, or adapted, some of his stories, there is no question. It is beyond belief that those which entered his mind left it no richer than they came. It is not to be supposed that he spent any time in elaborating them, but by some law of association every event that occurred suggested some story, and, almost by an involuntary process, his mind harmonized their discordant points, and the story was pronounced "pat," because it was made so before it was uttered. Every truth, or combination of truths, seemed immediately to clothe itself in a form of life, where he kept it for reference. His mind was full of stories; and the great facts of his life and history on entering his mind seemed to take up their abode in these stories, and if the garment did not fit them it was so modified that it did.

A good instance of the execution which he sometimes effected with a story occurred in the legislature. There was a troublesome member from Wabash County, who gloried particularly in being a "strict constructionist." He found something "unconstitutional" in every measure that was brought forward for discussion. He was a member of the Judiciary Committee, and was quite apt, after giving every measure a heavy pounding, to advocate its reference to this committee. No amount of sober argument could floor the member from Wabash. At last, he came to be considered a man to be silenced, and Mr. Lincoln was resorted to for an expedient by which this object might be accomplished. He soon afterwards honored the draft thus made upon him. A measure was brought forward in which Mr. Lincoln's constituents were interested, when the member from Wabash rose and discharged all his batteries upon its unconstitutional points. Mr. Lincoln then took the floor, and, with the quizzical expression of features which he could assume at will, and a mirthful twinkle in his gray eyes, said: "Mr. Speaker, the

attack of the member from Wabash on the constitutionality
of this measure reminds me of an old friend of mine. He's
a peculiar looking old fellow, with shaggy, overhanging eyebrows, and a pair of spectacles under them. (Everybody
turned to the member from Wabash, and recognized a personal
description.) One morning just after the old man got up, he
imagined, on looking out of his door, that he saw rather a
lively squirrel on a tree near his house. So he took down his
rifle, and fired at the squirrel, but the squirrel paid no attention to the shot. He loaded and fired again, and again, until,
at the thirteenth shot, he set down his gun impatiently, and
said to his boy, who was looking on, 'Boy, there's something
wrong about this rifle.' 'Rifle's all right, I know 'tis,' responded the boy, 'but where's your squirrel?' 'Don't you
see him, humped up about half way up the tree?' inquired
the old man, peering over his spectacles, and getting mystified.
'No, I don't,' responded the boy; and then turning and looking into his father's face, he exclaimed, 'I see your squirrel!
You've been firing at a louse on your eyebrow!'"

The story needed neither application nor explanation. The
House was in convulsions of laughter; for Mr. Lincoln's skill
in telling a story was not inferior to his appreciation of its
points and his power of adapting them to the case in hand.
It killed off the member from Wabash, who was very careful
afterwards not to provoke any allusion to his "eyebrows."

A man who practiced law in Illinois in the earlier years of
the state "rode the circuit," a proceeding of which the older
communities of the East know nothing. The state of Illinois,
for instance, is divided into a number of districts, each composed of a number of counties, of which a single judge, appointed or elected, as the case may be, for that purpose, makes
the circuit, holding courts at each county seat. Railroads
being scarce, the earlier circuit judges made their trips from
county to county on horseback, or in a gig; and, as lawyers
were not located in each county, all the prominent lawyers
living within the limits of the circuit made the tour of the
circuit with the judge. After the business of one county was

finished, the judge and all the lawyers mounted their horses or their gigs and pushed on to the next county-seat, and so repeated the process until the whole circuit was compassed; and this is what is known in the western states as "riding the circuit."

Mr. Lincoln rode the circuit; and it was upon these long and tedious trips that he established his reputation as one of the best lawyers in Illinois, and, in some respects, the superior of any lawyer in the state. It is doubtful whether he was ever regarded by his professional brethren as a well-read lawyer. Toward the latter part of his life, he had, by his own powers of generalization and deduction, become versed in the principles of law, and was coming to be recognized by the best lawyers as their peer; but his education was too defective at the first to make him anything better than what is called "a case lawyer." He studied his cases with great thoroughness, and was so uniformly successful in them that the people regarded him as having no equal. He had been engaged in practice but a short time when he was found habitually on one side or the other of every important case in the circuit. The writer remembers an instance in which many years ago, before he had risen to political eminence, he was pointed out to a stranger, by a citizen of Springfield, as "Abe Lincoln, the first lawyer of Illinois." He certainly enjoyed great reputation among the people.

Mr. Lincoln was a very weak lawyer when engaged by the weak side. This side he never took, if, by careful investigation of the case, he could avoid it. If a man went to him with the proposal to institute a suit, he examined carefully the man's grounds for the action. If these were good, he entered upon the case, and prosecuted it faithfully to the end. If the grounds were not good he would have nothing to do with the case. He invariably advised the applicant to dismiss the matter, telling him frankly that he had no case, and ought not to prosecute. Sometimes he was deceived. Sometimes he discovered, in the middle of a trial, by the revelation of a witness, that his client had lied to him. After the moment

that he was convinced that justice was opposed to him and
his client, he lost all his enthusiasm and all his courage. Indeed, he lost all interest in the case. His efforts for his client
after that moment were simply mechanical, for he would not
lie for any man, or strive to make the worse appear the better
reason for any man. He had a genuine interest in the establishment of justice between man and man. As a citizen, as a
lover of good order, as a man who believed in truth and justice, he was, by every instinct of his nature, opposed to the
success of villainy and the triumph of wrong, and he would
not sell himself to purposes of injustice and immorality. He
repeatedly refused to take fees on the wrong side of a case.
When his clients had practiced gross deception upon him, he
forsook their cases in mid-passage; and he always refused to
accept fees of those whom he advised not to prosecute. On
one occasion, while engaged upon an important case, he discovered that he was on the wrong side. His associate in the
case was immediately informed that he (Lincoln) would not
make the plea. The associate made it, and the case, much to
the surprise of Lincoln, was decided for his client. Perfectly
convinced that his client was wrong, he would not receive one
cent of the fee of nine hundred dollars which he paid. It is
not wonderful that one who knew him well spoke of him as
" perversely honest."

This " riding the circuit" was, in those early days, a peculiar business, and tended to develop peculiar traits of character. The long passages from court-house to court-house, the
stopping at cabins by the way to eat, or sleep, or feed the
horse, the evenings at the country taverns, the expedients resorted to to secure amusement, the petty, mean and shameful
cases that abounded, must have tended to make it a strange
business, and not altogether a pleasant one. These long passages while riding the circuit were seasons of reflection with
Mr. Lincoln. An amusing incident occurred in connection
with one of these journeys, which gives a pleasant glimpse
into the good lawyer's heart. He was riding by a deep
slough, in which, to his exceeding pain, he saw a pig strug-

gling, and with such faint efforts that it was evident that he could not extricate himself from the mud.   Mr. Lincoln looked at the pig and the mud which enveloped him, and then looked at some new clothes with which he had but a short time before enveloped himself.   Deciding against the claims of the pig, he rode on, but he could not get rid of the vision of the poor brute, and, at last, after riding two miles, he turned back, determined to rescue the animal at the expense of his new clothes. Arrived at the spot, he tied his horse, and coolly went to work to build of old rails a passage to the bottom of the hole. Descending on these rails, he seized the pig and dragged him out, but not without serious damage to the clothes he wore. Washing his hands in the nearest brook, and wiping them on the grass, he mounted his gig and rode along.   He then fell to examining the motive that sent him back to the release of the pig.   At the first thought, it seemed to be pure benevolence, but, at length, he came to the conclusion that it was selfishness, for he certainly went to the pig's relief in order (as he said to the friend to whom he related the incident,) to "take a pain out of his own mind."   This is certainly a new view of the nature of sympathy, and one which it will be well for the casuist to examine.

While Mr. Lincoln was not regarded by his professional associates as profoundly versed in the principles of law, he was looked upon by them as a very remarkable advocate. No man in Illinois had such power before a jury as he.   This was a fact universally admitted.   The elements of his power as an advocate were perfect lucidity of statement, great fairness in the treatment of both sides of a case, and the skill to conduct a common mind along the chain of his logic to his own conclusion.   In presenting a case to a jury, he invariably presented both sides of it.   After he had done this, there was really little more to be said, for he could state the points of his opponent better generally than his opponent could state them for himself.   The man who followed him usually found himself handling that which Mr. Lincoln had already reduced to chaff.   There was really no trick about this.   In the first place he would not take a case in which he did not believe he was on the side of justice. Believing that the right was with him, he felt that he could afford to give to the opposing counsel everything that he could claim, and still have material enough left for carrying his verdicts. His fairness was not only apparent but real, and the juries he addressed knew it to be so. He would stand before a jury and yield point after point that nearly every other lawyer would dispute under the same circumstances, so that, sometimes, his clients trembled with apprehension; and then, after he had given his opponent all he had claimed, and more than he had dared to claim, he would state his own side of the case with such power and clearness that that which had seemed strong against him was reduced to weakness, that which had seemed to be sound was proved to be specious, and that which had the appearance of being conclusive against him was plainly seen to be corroborative of his own positions on the question to be decided. Every juror was made to feel that Mr. Lincoln was an absolute aid to him in arriving at an intelligent and impartial verdict. The cunning lawyers thought that Mr. Lincoln was very cunning in all this—thought that his fairness was only apparent and assumed for a purpose—but it has already been stated that cunning was not an element of his nature. He had no interest in the establishment of anything but justice, and injustice, even if it favored him, could give him no satisfaction. The testimony of the lawyers who were obliged to try cases with him is that he was "a hard man to meet."

Coming from the people, and being perfectly familiar with the modes of thought and mental capacity of the men who generally composed his juries, he knew all their difficulties, knew just what language to address to them, what illustrations to use, and how to bring his arguments to bear upon their minds. This point is well illustrated by the details of a case in the Coles Circuit Court.

The controversy was about a colt, in which thirty-four witnesses swore that they had known the colt from its falling, and that it was the property of the plaintiff, while thirty swore that they had known the colt from its falling, and that it was the property of the defendant. It may be stated, at starting, that these witnesses were all honest, and that the mistake grew out of the exact resemblances which two colts bore to each other. One circumstance was proven by all the witnesses, or nearly all of them, viz: that the two claimants of the colt agreed to meet on a certain day with the two mares which were respectively claimed to be the dams of the colt, and permit the colt to decide which of the two he belonged to. The meeting occurred according to agreement, and, as it was a singular case and excited a good deal of popular interest, there were probably a hundred men assembled on their horses and mares, from far and near. Now the colt really belonged to the defendant in the case. It had strayed away and fallen into company with the plaintiff's horses. The plaintiff's colt had, at the same time, strayed away, and had not returned, and was not to be found. The moment the two mares were brought upon the ground, the defendant's mare and the colt gave signs of recognition. The colt went to its dam, and would not leave her. They fondled each other ; and, although the plaintiff brought his mare between them, and tried in various ways to divert the colt's attention, the colt would not be separated from its dam. It then followed her home, a distance of eight or ten miles, and, when within a mile or two of the stables, took a short cut to them in advance of its dam. The plaintiff had sued to recover the colt thus gone back to its owner.

In the presentation of this case to the jury, there were thirty-four witnesses on the side of the plaintiff, while the defendant had, on his side, only thirty witnesses : but he had on his side the colt itself and its dam—thirty-four men against thirty men and two brutes. Here was a case that was to be decided by the preponderance of evidence. All the witnesses were equally positive, and equally credible. Mr. Lincoln was on the side of the defendant, and contended that the voice of nature in the mare and colt ought to outweigh the testimony of a hundred men. The jury were all farmers, and all illiter-

6

ate men, and he took great pains to make them understand what was meant by the "preponderance of evidence." He said that in a civil suit, absolute certainty, or such certainty as would be required to convict a man of crime, was not essential. They must decide the case according to the impression which the evidence had produced upon their minds, and, if they felt puzzled at all, he would give them a test by which they could bring themselves to a just conclusion. "Now," said he, "if you were going to bet on this case, on which side would you be willing to risk a picayune? That side on which you would be willing to bet a picayune, is the side on which rests the preponderance of evidence in your minds. It is possible that you may not be right, but that is not the question. The question is as to where the preponderance of evidence lies, and you can judge exactly where it lies in your minds, by deciding as to which side you would be willing to bet on."

The jury understood this. There was no mystification about it. They had got hold of a test by which they could render an intelligent verdict. Mr. Lincoln saw into their minds, and knew exactly what they needed; and the moment they received it, he knew that his case was safe, as a quick verdict for the defendant proved it to be. In nothing connected with this case was the ingenuity of Mr. Lincoln more evident, perhaps, than in the insignificance of the sum which he placed in risk by the hypothetical wager. It was not a hundred dollars, or a thousand dollars, or even a dollar, but the smallest silver coin, to show to them that the verdict should go with the preponderance of evidence, even if the preponderance should be only a hair's weight.

If it was the habit of Mr. Lincoln to present both sides of his cases to the jury, it was, of course, his habit to study both sides with equal thoroughness. He was called slow in arriving at the points of a case. It is probably true that his mind was not one of the quickest in the processes of investigation. He certainly exercised great care in coming to his conclusions. It was then, in the days of his legal practice, his habit to argue against himself, and it always remained the habit of his life. He took special interest in the investigation of every point that could be made against him and his positions. This habit made his processes of investigation slower than those of other men, while the limited range of his legal education rendered it necessary that he should bestow more study upon his cases than better educated lawyers found it necessary to bestow.

One of the most even-tempered men that ever lived, Mr. Lincoln was the subject of great varieties of mood, and extremes of feeling. His constitution embraced remarkable contradictions. Oppressed with a deep melancholy at times, weighed down by the great problems of his own life and of humanity at large, assuming and carrying patiently the most important public burdens, he was as simple as a boy, took delight in the most trivial things, and with the subtlest and quickest sense of the ludicrous, laughed incontinently over incidents and stories that would hardly move any other man in his position to a smile. At one time, while riding the circuit with a friend, he entered into an exposition of his feelings touching what seemed to him the growing corruption of the world, in politics and morals. "Oh how hard it is," he exclaimed, "to die, and not to be able to leave the world any better for one's little life in it!" Here was a key to one cause of his depression, and an index to his aspirations. After this conversation and the ride were over, he probably arrived at a country tavern, and there spent the evening in telling stories to his brother lawyers, and in laughing over the most trifling incidents.

It will perhaps be as well, at this point of his history as elsewhere, to allude to his habit of telling stories that it would not be proper to repeat in the presence of women. It is useless for Mr. Lincoln's biographers to ignore this habit, for it was notorious. The whole West, if not the whole country, is full of these stories; and there is no doubt at all that he indulged in them with the same freedom that he did in those of a less exceptionable character. Good people are at a loss to account for this apparent love of impurity, in a man of such exalted aims, such deep truthfulness, such high aspirations. The matter is easily explained.

Those who have heard these stories will readily admit that they are the wittiest and most amusing of their kind, and, when they have admitted that, they have in their minds the only reason of Mr. Lincoln's indulgence in them. It was always the elements of wit and humor that captivated him. He was not an impure man in his life, or in his imaginations. For impurity's sake, he never uttered an impure word, or made an impure allusion, but, whenever he found anything humorous, ludicrous or witty, he could not resist the inclination to use it, whatever the incidents might be with which it was associated. Anything that was morally beautiful touched him to tears. He was equally sensitive to all that was heroic, beautiful, grand, sweet, ludicrous and grotesque in human life. He wept as readily over a tale of heroic self-devotion, as he laughed over a humorous story.

It is also to be said that the habit of telling these exceptionable stories was the habit of his profession, in his region of country, at the time he was engaged in practice there. He indulged in them no more than his brother lawyers, and he excelled them in his stories no more than he did in everything else. It is to be said, further, that there is something in the practice of the law that makes these stories more tolerable in the legal profession, even when the members of it are Christian men—men of pure morals and pure instincts—than in any other profession in the world. The legal profession brings men into constant association with impurity, with the details of cases of shame, with all the smut and dirt that can be raked from the haunts of vice, with all the particulars of prurient dalliance and bestial licentiousness. With this habitual—this professional—familiarity with impurity, it is not strange that the sense of propriety in language becomes deadened; and none know better than lawyers that there is in their profession, in the older parts of the country as well as in the newer, great laxity of speech, touching subjects which they would blush to introduce—which would cost them their self-respect and the respect of the community to introduce—among women. Mr. Lincoln was not a sinner in this thing above other men, equally pure and good in his profession. It is not a habit to be justified in any man. It is not a habit to be tolerated in any man who indulges in it to gratify simply his love of that which is beastly. In Mr. Lincoln's case, it is a habit to be explained and regretted. His whole life had been spent with people without refinement. His legal study and practice had rendered this class of subjects familiar. It was the habit of his professional brethren to tell these objectionable stories, and, even if his pure sensibilities sometimes rebelled—for he possessed and always maintained the profoundest respect for women—the wit and humor they contained over-tempted him.

One of the most beautiful traits of Mr. Lincoln was his considerate regard for the poor and obscure relatives he had left, plodding along in their humble ways of life. Wherever upon his circuit he found them, he always went to their dwellings, ate with them, and, when convenient, made their houses his home. He never assumed in their presence the slightest superiority to them, in the facts and conditions of his life. He gave them money when they needed and he possessed it. Countless times he was known to leave his companions at the village hotel, after a hard day's work in the court room, and spend the evening with these old friends and companions of his humbler days. On one occasion, when urged not to go, he replied, "Why, aunt's heart would be broken if I should leave town without calling upon her;" yet he was obliged to walk several miles to make the call.

A little fact in this connection will illustrate his ever-present desire to deal honestly and justly with men. He had always a partner in his professional life, and, when he went out upon the circuit, this partner was usually at home. While out, he frequently took up and disposed of cases that were never entered at the office. In these cases, after receiving his fees, he divided the money in his pocket book, labeling each sum (wrapped in a piece of paper,) that belonged to his partner, stating his name, and the case on which it was received. He could not be content to keep an account. He divided the money, so that if he, by any casualty, should fail of an opportunity to pay it over, there could be no dispute as to the exact amount that was his partner's due. This may seem trivial, nay, boyish, but it was like Mr. Lincoln. But we must set aside the professional man for a while, to notice other affairs which mingled in his life.

CHAPTER VIII.

THE "Sangamon Chief," as Mr. Lincoln had been popularly named, was placed upon the legislative ticket again in 1840, and re-elected. At a special session of the previous legislature, held during 1839, Vandalia as the capital of the state had been forsaken, and Springfield received the legislature and the archives and offices of the state government. Mr. Lincoln was in the legislature, and, at the same time, at home. The fact reconciled him to holding an office which he felt to be a disadvantage to his business, for he could attend upon his duties at the State House, and, at the same time, have a care that his professional interests were not entirely sacrificed. In the only session held by the legislature of 1840, no important business of general interest was transacted. The democratic preponderance in the state had been partially restored and was still maintained, and although Mr. Lincoln was again the first man on the whig side and the candidate for speaker, for which office he was supported by more than the strength of his party, he was defeated as he had been in 1838. This session finished up Mr. Lincoln's connection with the legislature of the state, for, although urged by the people to represent them again, considerations of a private nature made him peremptory in his refusal to be again a candidate. It is recorded, however, that he was re-elected in 1854, and that he resigned before taking his seat. The election was made against his will, for a larger political life was already dawning upon him.

It was about this time that a strange incident in his private life occurred—one, certainly, which was quite in discord with his principles and feelings.   A sharp, sarcastic poem appeared in the Sangamon Journal, edited at that time by Simeon Francis.   The poem had an evident allusion to James Shields, a young lawyer of Springfield, and since a United States Senator from Illinois.   General Shields was at that time hot-blooded and impulsive, and, instead of laughing off the matter, regarded it seriously, and demanded of Mr. Francis the author's name.   Mr. Francis knew at once what the demand meant, and sought to delay his answer.   He asked the young man for a day to consider whether he should reveal the name of his contributor or not.   The request was granted, when Mr. Francis went to work to ascertain how he could lift the responsibility of the publication from his own shoulders, as the writer of the poem was a lady.   On inquiry among the lady's friends, he ascertained that Mr. Lincoln was, at least, one of her admirers, and that he possibly bore a tenderer relation to her.   Accordingly he went to Mr. Lincoln, and told him that he was in trouble, and explained to him the cause of his difficulty.   It seemed certain that somebody would be obliged to fight a duel with Mr. Shields, or be branded by him as a coward; and Mr. Francis, though entirely responsible for the publication of a lady's poem shrank, in a very unworthy way, from the alternative.

As soon as Mr. Lincoln comprehended the case, and saw what Mr. Francis expected of him, he told the editor that if Mr. Shields should call again, and demand the author's name, to inform him that he, Lincoln, held himself responsible for the poem.   The result was just what was expected, at least by Mr. Francis.   Mr. Lincoln at once received a challenge and accepted it.   There must have existed in that part of the country, at that time, a state of feeling on this subject which cannot now be comprehended among the people of the North. With a natural aversion to all violence and bloodshed, with a moral sense that shrank from the barbaric arbitrament of the duel, with his whole soul at war with the policy which seeks to heal a wound of honor by the commission of a crime, he walked with his eyes wide open into this duel. It is possible that he imagined Mr. Shields did not mean a duel by his question, or that he would not fight a duel with him; but he certainly knew that he made himself liable to a challenge, and intended to accept it if it came. Gallantry was, of course, the moving power. The lady's name was to be protected, and the editor who had been imprudent enough to publish her poem relieved from all responsibility on her account.

Mr. Lincoln selected broad-swords as the weapons for the encounter, and immediately took instruction in the exercise of that arm, of Dr. E. H. Merriman, a physician of Springfield. The place of meeting was Bloody Island, a disputed or neutral territory on the Mississippi River, lying between Illinois and Missouri. The meeting took place according to appointment, but friends interfered, determined that on such foolish grounds no duel should be fought, and no blood shed. The parties were brought together, and a reconciliation easily effected. Mr. Lincoln felt afterwards that he could have done, under the circumstances, no less than he did. He stated to a friend, however, that he selected broad-swords because his arms were long. He had not the slightest intention of injuring Mr. Shields, and thought that the length of his arms would aid him in defending his own person.

This incident does not seem to have been remembered against Mr. Lincoln, by any class of the community in which he lived. It was certainly a boyish affair, and was probably regarded and forgotten as such. Even the excitements of a great political campaign, like that which resulted in his election to the presidency, did not call it from its slumbers, and the American people were spared a representation of Mr. Lincoln's atrocities as a duelist.

Mr. Lincoln's law partnership with Mr. Stuart was dissolved in 1840, when he immediately formed a business association with Judge S. T. Logan of Springfield, one of the ablest and most learned lawyers in the state. He entered upon this new partnership with a determination to devote his time more exclusively to business than he had done, but the people would not permit him to do so. He was called upon from all quarters to engage in the exciting political canvass of 1840, and made many speeches.

In 1842, having arrived at his thirty-third year, Mr. Lincoln married Miss Mary Todd, a daughter of Hon. Robert S. Todd of Lexington, Kentucky. The marriage took place in Springfield, where the lady had for several years resided, on the fourth of November of the year mentioned. It is probable that he married as early as the circumstances of his life permitted, for he had always loved the society of women, and possessed a nature that took profound delight in intimate female companionship. A letter written on the eighteenth of May following his marriage, to J. F. Speed, Esq., of Louisville, Kentucky, an early and a life-long personal friend, gives a pleasant glimpse of his domestic arrangements at this time. " We are not keeping house,",Mr. Lincoln says in this letter, " but boarding at the Globe Tavern, which is very well kept now by a widow lady of the name of Beck. Our rooms are the same Dr. Wallace occupied there, and boarding only costs four dollars a week. * * * I most heartily wish you and your Fanny will not fail to come. Just let us know the time, a week in advance, and we will have a room prepared for you, and we 'll all be merry together for a while." He seems to have been in excellent spirits, and to have been very hearty in the enjoyment of his new relation.

The private letters of Mr. Lincoln were charmingly natural and sincere, and there can be no harm in giving a passage from one written during these early years, as an illustration. Mr. Lincoln has been charged with having no strong personal attachments; but no one can read his private letters, written at any time during his life, without perceiving that his personal friendships were the sweetest sources of his happiness. To a particular friend, he wrote February 25th, 1842: " Yours of the sixteenth, announcing that Miss —— and you 'are no longer twain but one flesh,' reached me this morning. I have no way of telling you how much happiness I wish you both, though I believe you both can conceive it. I feel somewhat jealous of both of you now, for you will be so exclusively concerned for one another that I shall be forgotten entirely. My acquaintance with Miss —— (I call her thus lest you should think I am speaking of your mother,) was too short for me to reasonably hope to long be remembered by her; and still I am sure I shall not forget her soon. Try if you cannot remind her of that debt she owes me, and be sure you do not interfere to prevent her paying it.

"I regret to learn that you have resolved not to return to Illinois. I shall be very lonesome without you. How miserably things seem to be arranged in this world! If we have no friends we have no pleasure; and if we have them, we are sure to lose them, and be doubly pained by the loss. I did hope she and you would make your home here, yet I own I have no right to insist. You owe obligations to her ten thousand times more sacred than any you can owe to others, and in that light let them be respected and observed. It is natural that she should desire to remain with her relations and friends. As to friends, *she* could not need them anywhere;— she would have them in abundance here. Give my kind regards to Mr. —— and his family, particularly to Miss E. Also to your mother, brothers and sisters. Ask little E. D—— if she will ride to town with me if I come there again. And, finally, give —— a double reciprocation of all the love she sent me. Write me often, and believe me, yours forever, LINCOLN."

The kind feeling, the delicate playfulness, the considerate remembrance of all who were associated with the recipient of the missive, and the hearty, outspoken affection which this letter breathes, reveal a sound and true heart in the writer. It is true, indeed, that Mr. Lincoln had a friendly feeling toward everybody, and it is just as true that his personal friendships were as devoted and unselfish as those of a man of more exclusive feelings and more abounding prejudices.

Mr. Lincoln seems to have been thinking about a seat in Congress at this time. On the 24th of March, 1843, he wrote to his friend Speed: "We had a meeting of the whigs of the county here on last Monday, to appoint delegates to a district convention, and Baker* beat me, and got the delegation instructed to go for him. The meeting, in spite of my attempt to decline it, appointed me one of the delegates, so that, in getting Baker the nomination, I shall be 'fixed' a good deal like a fellow who is made groomsman to the man who has 'cut him out,' and is marrying his own dear gal."

In a subsequent letter, he writes: "In regard to the Congress matter here, you were right in supposing I would support the nominee. Neither Baker nor myself, however, will be the man, but Hardin." †

It was Mr. Lincoln's rule and habit to "support the nominee." He was always a loyal party man. In the ordinary use of the word, Mr. Lincoln was not, and never became, a reformer. He believed that a man, in order to effect anything, should work through organizations of men. In a eulogy upon Henry Clay which he delivered in 1852, occurs the following passage: "A free people, in times of peace and quiet, when pressed by no common danger, naturally divide into parties. At such times, the man who is not of either party, is not, cannot be, of any consequence. Mr. Clay, therefore, was of a party." Whether his position was sound or otherwise, he believed it was, and always acted upon it. With as true a love of freedom and progress as any man— with a regard for popular rights never surpassed by professional reformers—he was careful to go no faster, and no farther, than he could take his party with him, and no faster and no farther than was consistent with that party's permanent success. He would endanger nothing by precipitancy. His policy was to advance surely, even if he was obliged to proceed slowly. The policy which distinguished his presidential career was the policy of his life. It was adopted early, and he always followed it.

With Mr. Lincoln's modest estimate of his own services,

---

* Colonel Edward D. Baker, (afterwards United States Senator from Oregon,) who fell at Ball's Bluff.

† Colonel John J. Hardin, who fell at Buena Vista.

and with his friendly feelings toward all, it is not to be wondered at that he never made much money. It was not possible
for him to regard his clients simply in the light of business.
An unfortunate man was a subject of his sympathy, no matter
what his business relations to him might be. A Mr. Cogdal,
who related the incident to the writer, met with a financial
wreck in 1843. He employed Mr. Lincoln as his lawyer, and
at the close of the business, gave him a note to cover the regular lawyer's fees. He was soon afterwards blown up by an
accidental discharge of powder, and lost his hand. Meeting
Mr. Lincoln some time after the accident, on the steps of the
State House, the kind lawyer asked him how he was getting
along. "Badly enough," replied Mr. Cogdal, "I am both
broken up in business, and crippled." Then he added, "I have
been thinking about that note of yours." Mr. Lincoln, who
had probably known all about Mr. Cogdal's troubles, and had
prepared himself for the meeting, took out his pocket-book, and
saying with a laugh, "well, you needn't think any more about
it," handed him the note. Mr. Cogdal protesting, Mr. Lincoln
said "if you had the money, I would not take it," and hurried
away. At this same date, he was frankly writing about his
poverty to his friends, as a reason for not making them a visit,
and probably found it no easy task to take care of his family,
even when board at the Globe Tavern was "only four dollars
a week."

In the active discharge of the duties of his profession, in
the enjoyments of his new domestic life, and in the intrigues
of local politics, as betrayed in his letter to Mr. Speed, the
months passed away, and brought Mr. Lincoln to the great
political contest of 1844. Henry Clay, his political idol was
the candidate of the whig party for the presidency, and he
went into the canvass with his whole heart. As a candidate
for presidential elector, he canvassed the state of Illinois, and
afterwards went over into Indiana, and made a series of
speeches there. The result of this great campaign to Mr.
Clay and to the whig party was a sad disappointment. Probably no defeat of a great party ever brought to its members so

much personal sorrow as this. Mr. Clay had the power of exciting an enthusiastic affection for his person that few political men have enjoyed. The women of the country were as much interested in his election as their brothers and husbands were, and wept at his defeat as if he had been their best and most intimate friend. Mr. Lincoln was among the heartiest of these mourners; but, while the event rendered his great political exemplar a hopeless man politically, the canvass itself had raised Mr. Lincoln to the proudest hight he had occupied. He had greatly strengthened the whig organization in the state, and had established his reputation as one of the most powerful political debaters in the country. His exposition of the protective system of duties, which was the principal issue of the canvass, was elaborate and powerful. He had thoroughly mastered his subject, and his arguments are still remembered for the copiousness of their facts, and the closeness and soundness of their logic.

Mr. Clay's defeat was the more a matter of sorrow with Mr. Lincoln because it was, in a measure, unexpected. No personal defeat could have been more dispiriting to him thar this failure before the people of his political idol. He was not only disappointed but disgusted. With his strong convictions of the soundness of the principles of the whig party, and his belief in the almost immeasurable superiority of Mr. Clay over Mr. Polk, he doubtless had the same misgivings that have come to others, touching the capacity of the people for self-government, and realized the same distrust of the value of honors which could be so unworthily bestowed. It was to him a popular decision in the cause of political iniquity and bad government. It was not strange, therefore, in the first gush of his disappointment, that he made a new resolution to let politics alone, and attend more devotedly to the duties of his profession. But Mr. Lincoln's ambition, and Mr. Lincoln's friends, more powerful than his ambition, were not likely to permit this resolution to have a permanent influence upon his career.

Subsequently, Mr. Lincoln paid a personal visit to Mr.

Clay, and it is possible that he needed the influence of this visit to restore a healthy tone to his feelings, and to teach him that the person whom his imagination had transformed into a demigod was only a man, possessing the full measure of weaknesses common to men. In 1846, Mr. Lincoln learned that Mr. Clay had agreed to deliver a speech at Lexington, Kentucky, in favor of gradual emancipation. He had never seen the great Kentuckian, and this event seemed to give him an excuse for breaking away from his business, and satisfying his curiosity to look his demigod in the face, and hear the music of his eloquence. He accordingly went to Lexington, and arrived there in time to attend the meeting.

On returning to his home from this visit, he did not attempt to disguise his disappointment. The speech itself was written and read. It lacked entirely the spontaneity and fire which Mr. Lincoln had anticipated, and was not eloquent at all. At the close of the meeting Mr. Lincoln secured an introduction to the great orator, and as Mr. Clay knew what a friend to him Mr. Lincoln had been, he invited his admirer and partisan to Ashland. No invitation could have delighted Mr. Lincoln more, but the result of his private interview with Mr. Clay was no more satisfactory than that which followed the speech. Those who have known both men, will not wonder at this, for two men could hardly be more unlike in their motives and manners than the two thus brought together. One was a proud man; the other was a humble man. One was princely in his bearing; the other was lowly. One was distant and dignified; the other was as simple and teachable as a child. One received the deference of men as his due; the other received it with an uncomfortable sense of his unworthiness.

A friend of Mr. Lincoln, who had a long conversation with him after his return from Ashland, found that his old enthusiasm was gone. Mr. Lincoln said that though Mr. Clay was most polished in his manners, and very hospitable, he betrayed a consciousness of superiority that none could mistake. He felt that Mr. Clay did not regard him, or any other person in his presence, as, in any sense, on an equality with him. In short, he thought that Mr. Clay was overbearing and domineering, and that, while he was apparently kind, it was in that magnificent and patronizing way which made a sensitive man uncomfortable.

It is quite possible that Mr. Lincoln needed to experience this disappointment, and to be taught this lesson. It was, perhaps, the only instance in his life in which he had given his whole heart to a man without knowing him, or been carried away by his imagination into an unbounded zeal on behalf of a personal stranger. It made him more cautious in the bestowal of his love. He was, certainly, from that time forward, more careful to look on all sides of a man, and on all sides of a subject, before yielding to either his devotion, than ever before. If he became slow in moving, it was because he saw more than his own side of every case and question, and recognized, in advance, such obstacles as would be certain to impede his progress.

Much has been said of Mr. Lincoln's kindness, and many suppose that he was not brave—that his patient and universal love of men was inconsistent with those sterner qualities which are necessary to make, not only a true hero, but a true man. An incident occurred during the Clay campaign which shows how ill-founded this estimate of Mr. Lincoln is. On the occasion of a great mass convention at Springfield, U. F. Linder, Esq., now a resident of Chicago, and a man of rare eloquence, made a speech which seemed to rouse the enthusiasm of the assemblage to the highest pitch. The speech was very offensive to some of the democrats who were present—who, indeed, proposed to make a personal matter of it. Mr. Linder being called out again, in the course of the meeting, was considered in personal danger, if he should attempt to respond. At this juncture, Mr. Lincoln and Colonel Baker took their places by his side, and, when he finished, conducted him to his hotel. The ruffians knew both men, and prudently refrained from interfering with them. On a previous occasion, Mr. Lincoln had protected the person of Colonel Baker himself. Baker was speaking in a court-house, which had once been a store

house, and, and, on making some remarks that were offensive to
certain political rowdies in the crowd, they cried : " take him
off the stand." Immediate confusion ensued, and there was
an attempt to carry the demand into execution. Directly
over the speaker's head was an old scuttle, at which it appeared Mr. Lincoln had been listening to the speech. In an
instant, Mr. Lincoln's feet came through the scuttle, followed
by his tall and sinewy frame, and he was standing by Colonel
Baker's side. He raised his hand, and the assembly subsided
immediately into silence. " Gentlemen," said Mr. Lincoln,
" let us not disgrace the age and country in which we live.
This is a land where freedom of speech is guarantied. Mr.
Baker has a right to speak, and ought to be permitted to do
so. I am here to protect him, and no man shall take him
from this stand if I can prevent it." The suddenness of his
appearance, his perfect calmness and fairness, and the knowledge that he would do what he had promised to do, quieted
all disturbance, and the speaker concluded his remarks without difficulty.

Mr. Lincoln has already been spoken of as a strong party
man, and his thorough devotion to his party, on some occasions, though very rarely, led him into hasty expressions and
hasty actions, quite out of harmony with his usual self-poise
and good nature. A scene occurred in the room occupied by
Mr. Lincoln and his particular friend, Judge Davis, at Paris,
on one occasion, which illustrates this. There was present,
as a visitor, a young lawyer of the name of Constable, a gentleman of fine abilities, and at present a judge of the circuit
court. Mr. Constable was a whig, but had probably been
disappointed in some of his political aspirations, and did not
feel that the party had treated him fairly. He was in the
habit of speaking disparagingly of the policy of the party in
the treatment of its own friends, and particularly of its young
men, especially when he found whig leaders to listen to him.
On this occasion he charged the party with being "old fogy-
ish," and indifferent to rising men, while the democratic party
was lauded for the contrast which it presented in this partic-

7

ular. Mr. Lincoln felt the charge as keenly as if it had been
a personal one.   Indeed, his own experience disproved the
whole statement.   Constable went on, and charged the whig
party with ingratitude and neglect in his own case.   Mr. Lincoln stood with his coat off, shaving himself before his glass.
He had heard the charges without saying a word, but when
Mr. Constable alluded to himself, as having been badly treated,
he turned fiercely upon him, and said, "Mr. Constable, I understand you perfectly, and have noticed for some time back
that you have been slowly and cautiously picking your way
over to the democratic party."   Both men were angry, and it
required the efforts of all the others present to keep them from
fighting.   Mr. Lincoln seemed for a time, as one of the spectators of the scene remarks, to be "terribly willing."   Such
instances as this have been very rare in Mr. Lincoln's life, and
the fact that he was susceptible to the influence of such motives
renders his notorious equanimity of temper all the more creditable to him.   The matter was adjusted between him and Mr.
Constable, and, not long afterwards, the latter justified Mr.
Lincoln's interpretation of his motives, and was numbered
among the democrats.

CHAPTER IX.

THE political biographers of Mr. Lincoln have stated that in 1846 he was "induced to accept" the nomination for Congress from the Sangamon district. It has already been seen that he had aspirations for this place; and it is quite as well to adopt Mr. Lincoln's own frankness and directness, and say that the representatives of his wishes secured the nomination for him. As a party man, he had well earned any honor in the power of his party to bestow. As a man and a politician, his character was so sound and so truly noble that his nomination and election to Congress would be quite as honorable to his district as to him.

Having received the nomination, Mr. Lincoln did after the manner of Western nominees and "stumped" his district. He had abundant material for discussion. During the winter of 1845, Texas was admitted to the Union, and the war with Mexico was commenced. The tariff of 1842, constructed in accordance with the policy of the whig party, had been repealed. The country had a foreign war on its hands—a war which the whigs believed to have been unnecessarily begun, and unjustifiably carried on. It had received into the Union a new member in the interest of slavery. It had been greatly disturbed in its industrial interests by the subversion of the protective policy. The issues between the two parties then in the political field were positive and well defined. Mr. Lincoln's position on all the principal points at issue was that of the whig party, and the party had no reason to be ashamed of its western champion.

The eminent popularity of Mr. Lincoln in his own district was shown by the majority he received over that which it had given to Mr. Clay. Although he had made Mr. Clay's cause his own, and had advocated his election with an enthusiasm which no personal object could have excited in him, he received in his district a majority of one thousand five hundred and eleven votes to the nine hundred and fourteen majority which the district had given Mr. Clay in 1844. He undoubtedly was supported by more than the strength of his party, for his majority was unprecedented in the district, and has since had no parallel. It was not reached, on a much larger vote, by General Taylor in 1848. There is no question that this remarkable majority was the result of the popular faith in Mr. Lincoln's earnestness, conscientiousness and integrity.

He took his seat in the thirtieth Congress, December 6th, 1847, and was from the first entirely at home. He was no novice in politics or legislation. To the latter he had served a thorough apprenticeship in the Illinois legislature. To the study and discussion of the former, he had devoted perhaps the severest efforts of his life. He understood every phase of the great questions which agitated Congress and divided the people. Unlike many politicians who engage in the harangues of a political canvass, he had made himself the master of the subjects he discussed. He had been a debater, and not a declaimer. He had entertained a deeper interest in questions of public concern than he had felt in his own election; and he was at once recognized as the peer of his associates in the House. He derived considerable prominence from the fact that he was the only whig member from Illinois, a fact almost entirely due to his own presence and influence in the district which elected him.

It is noticeable here that Stephen A. Douglas took his seat in the Senate of the United States during this same session. They met first as representatives in the Illinois legislature. Mr. Douglas was the younger, the more adroit, the swifter in a political race. He had had with him the large democratic majority of the state, and had moulded it to his purposes. He had taken a step—perhaps many steps—in advance of Mr. Lincoln; but it seemed destined that the tallest man in the House and the shortest man in the Senate should keep in sight of each other, until the time should come when they should stand out before their own state and the country as the champions respectively of the antagonistic principles and policies which divided the American people.

It is interesting, at the close of a great rebellion, undertaken on behalf of slavery, to look back to this Congress, and see how, in the interests and associations of the old whig party, those men worked in harmony who have since been, or who, if they had lived would have been, so widely separated in feeling and action. John Quincy Adams voted on most questions with Robert Toombs; George Ashmun, afterwards president of the convention that nominated Mr. Lincoln for the presidency, with Alexander H. Stephens, afterwards vice-president of the Southern Confederacy; Jacob Collamer with Thomas Butler King, and Samuel F. Vinton with Henry W. Hilliard. History must record that the Mexican war was undertaken in the interest of human slavery; yet, touching the questions arising out of this war, and questions directly associated with or bearing upon it, these men of the old whig party acted together. The slaveholder then yielded to party what he has since denied to patriotism, and patriotism abandoned a party which held out to it a constant temptation to complicity with slavery.

Mr. Polk, at that time the President of the United States, was evidently anxious to justify the war which he had commenced against Mexico, and to vindicate his own action before the American people, if not before his own judgment and conscience. His messages to Congress were burdened with this effort; and Mr. Lincoln had hardly become wonted to his seat when he made an unsuccessful effort to bring the President to a statement of facts, upon which Congress and the country might either verify or falsify his broad and general asseverations. On

the twenty-second of December, he introduced a series of resolutions* which, had they been adopted, would have given the
President an opportunity to furnish the grounds of his allegations, and set himself right before the nation. These resolutions are remarkable for their definite statement of the points
actually at issue between the administration and the whig
party; but they found no advocates among Mr. Polk's friends.
Laid over under the rule, they were not called up again by Mr.
Lincoln himself, but they formed the thesis of a speech delivered by him on the following twelfth of January, in which
he fully expressed his views on the whole subject.

The opposition in this Congress were placed in a very difficult and perplexing position. They hated the war; they be-

---

* WHEREAS, The President of the United States, in his message of
May 11, 1846, has declared that "the Mexican Government not only refused to receive him [the envoy of the United States,] or listen to his
propositions, but, after a long continued series of menaces, has at last
invaded *our territory*, and shed the blood of our fellow citizens on *our
own soil:*"

And again, in his message of December 8, 1846, that "We had ample
cause of war against Mexico long before the breaking out of hostilities;
but even then we forbore to take redress into our own hands until
Mexico herself became the aggressor, by invading *our soil* in hostile
array, and shedding the blood of our citizens:"

And yet again, in his message of December 7, 1847, that "The Mexican Government refused even to hear the terms of adjustment which
he [our minister of peace] was authorized to propose, and finally, under
wholly unjustifiable pretexts, involved the two countries in war, by invading the territory of the State of Texas, striking the first blow, and
shedding the blood of our citizens on *our own soil:*" and,

WHEREAS, This House is desirous to obtain a full knowledge of all
the facts which go to establish whether the particular spot on which the
blood of our citizens was so shed was or was not at that time "*our own
soil:*" therefore,

Resolved by the House of Representatives, That the President of the
United States be respectfully requested to inform this house—

1st. Whether the spot on which the blood of our citizens was shed,
as in his messages declared, was or was not within the territory of
Spain, at least after the treaty of 1819, until the Mexican revolution.

2d. Whether that spot is or is not within the territory which was
wrested from Spain by the revolutionary Government of Mexico.

lieved it to have been unnecessarily begun by the act of the United States, and not by the act of Mexico; they were accused of being treacherous to the cause and honor of the country because they opposed the war in which the country was engaged; they felt obliged to vote supplies to the army because it would have been inhuman to do otherwise, yet this act was seized upon by the President to show that his position touching the war was sustained by them; they felt compelled to condemn the commander-in-chief of the armies, sitting in the White House, and to vote thanks to the generals who had successfully executed his orders in the field. Men picked their way through these difficulties according to the wisdom given to them. The opposition usually voted together, though there was more or less of division on minor points and matters of policy.

3d. Whether that spot is or is not within a settlement of people, which settlement has existed ever since long before the Texas revolution, and until its inhabitants fled before the approach of the United States army.

4th. Whether that settlement is or is not isolated from any and all other settlements by the Gulf and the Rio Grande on the south and west, and by wide uninhabited regions on the north and east.

5th. Whether the people of that settlement, or a majority of them, or any of them, have ever submitted themselves to the government or laws of Texas or of the United States, by consent or by compulsion, either by accepting office, or voting at elections, or paying tax, or serving on juries, or having process served upon them, or in any other way.

6th. Whether the people of that settlement did or did not flee from the approach of the United States army, leaving unprotected their homes and their growing crops, *before* the blood was shed, as in the messages stated; and whether the first blood, so shed, was or was not shed within the inclosure of one of the people who had thus fled from it.

7th. Whether our *citizens*, whose blood was shed, as in his messages declared, were or were not, at that time, armed officers and soldiers, sent into that settlement by the military order of the President, through the Secretary of War.

8th. Whether the military force of the United States was or was not so sent into that settlement after General Taylor had more than once intimated to the War Department that, in his opinion, no such movement was necessary to the defense or protection of Texas.

Mr. Hudson of Massachusetts introduced a resolution which covered essentially the question of abandoning the war—of restoring everything to the old status. Mr. Lincoln voted to lay this resolution on the table, and, when it came up for adoption, voted against it. The writer finds no record of the reasons for these votes. Whatever they may have been, they seemed good to him; and he took pains a few days afterward to show that they could not have grown out of any friendship to the war. Indeed, on the very day which saw these votes recorded, he had an opportunity to vote that the war " was unnecessarily and unconstitutionally begun by the President of the United States," in company with nearly all the whig members of the House, southern no less than northern. The same men voted thanks to General Taylor for his brilliant achievements in the war.

The speech of Mr. Lincoln on the twelfth of January, in committee of the whole House, was thoroughly characteristic of the author. Simple, direct, exact in its comprehension of the points at issue, without a superfluous word or sentence, as closely logical as if it were the work of a professor of dialectics, it was the equal if not the superior of any speech delivered during the session.

Mr. Lincoln spoke as follows:

" MR. CHAIRMAN: Some, if not all, of the gentlemen on the other side of the House, who have addressed the committee within the last two days, have spoken rather complainingly, if I have rightly understood them, of the vote given a week or ten days ago, declaring that the war with Mexico was unnecessarily and unconstitutionally commenced by the President. I admit that such a vote should not be given in mere party wantonness, and that the one given is justly censurable, if it have no other or better foundation. I am one of those who joined in that vote; and did so under my best impression of the *truth* of the case. How I got this impression, and how it may possibly be removed, I will now try to show. When the war began, it was my opinion that all those who, because of knowing too *little*, or because of knowing too *much*, could not conscientiously approve the conduct of the President (in the beginning of it), should, nevertheless, as good citizens and patriots, remain silent on that point, at least till the war should be ended. Some leading Democrats, including ex-President Van Buren, have taken this same view, as I understand them; and I adhered to it, and acted upon it, until since I took my seat here; and I think I should still adhere to it, were it not that the President and his friends will not allow it to be so. Besides the continual effort of the President to argue every silent vote given for supplies into an indorsement of the justice and wisdom of his conduct; besides that singularly candid paragraph in his late message, in which he tells us that Congress, with great unanimity (only two in the Senate and fourteen in the House dissenting) had declared that ' by the act of the Republic of Mexico a state of war exists between that Government and the United States,' when the same journals that informed him of this, also informed him that, when that declaration stood disconnected from the question of supplies, sixty-seven in the House, and not fourteen, merely, voted against it; besides this open attempt to prove by telling the *truth*, what he could not prove by telling the *whole truth*, demanding of all who will not submit to be misrepresented, in justice to themselves, to speak out; besides all this, one of my colleagues [Mr. Richardson], at a very early day in the session, brought in a set of resolutions, expressly indorsing the original justice of the war on the part of the President. Upon these resolutions, when they shall be put on their passage, I shall be *compelled* to vote; so that I can not be silent if I would. Seeing this, I went about preparing myself to give the vote understandingly, when it should come. I carefully examined the President's messages, to ascertain what he himself had said and proved upon the point. The result of this examination was to make the impression, that, taking for true all the President states as facts, he falls far short of proving his justification; and that the President would have gone further with his proof, if it had not been for the small matter that the *truth* would not permit him. Under the impression thus made I gave the vote before mentioned. I propose now to give, concisely, the process of the examination I made, and how I reached the conclusion I did.

" The President, in his first message of May, 1846, declares that the soil was *ours* on which hostilities were commenced by Mexico; and he repeats that declaration, almost in the same language, in each successive annual message—thus showing that he esteems that point a highly essential one. In the importance of that point I entirely agree with the President. To my judgment, it is the *very point* upon which he should be justified or condemned. In his message of December, 1846, it seems to have occurred to him, as is certainly true, that title, ownership to soil, or anything else, is not a simple fact, but is a conclusion following one or more simple facts; and that it was incumbent upon him to present the facts from which he concluded the soil was ours on which the first blood of the war was shed.

" Accordingly, a little below the middle of page twelve, in the message last referred to, he enters upon that task; forming an issue and introducing testimony, extending the whole to a little below the middle of page fourteen. Now, I propose to try to show that the whole of this—issue and evidence—is, from beginning to end, the sheerest deception. The issue, as he presents it, is in these words: ' But there are those who, conceding all this to be true, assume the ground that the true western boundary of Texas is the Nueces, instead of the Rio Grande; and that, therefore, in marching our army to the east bank of the latter river, we passed the Texan line, and invaded the territory of Mexico.' Now, this issue is made up of two affirmatives and no negative. The main deception of it is, that it assumes as true that *one* river or the *other* is necessarily the boundary, and cheats the superficial thinker entirely out of the idea that *possibly* the boundary is somewhere *between* the two, and not actually at either. A further deception is, that it will let in *evidence* which a true issue would exclude. A true issue, made by the President, would be about as follows; ' I say the soil *was ours* on which the first blood was shed; there are those who say it was not.'

"I now procéed to examine the President's evidence, as applicable to such an issue. When that evidence is analyzed, it is all included in the following propositions:

"1.   That the Rio Grande was the western boundary of Louisiana, as we purchased it of France in 1803.

"2.   That the Republic of Texas always *claimed* the Rio Grande as her western boundary.

"3.   That by various acts, she had claimed it *on paper.*

"4.   That Santa Anna, in his treaty with Texas, recognized the Rio Grande as her boundary.

"5.   That Texas *before*, and the United States *after*, annexation, had *exercised* jurisdiction *beyond* the Nueces, *between* the two rivers.

"6.   That our Congress *understood* the boundary of Texas to extend beyond the Nueces.

"Now for each of these in its turn:

"His first item is, that the Rio Grande was the western boundary of Louisiana, as we purchased it of France in 1803; and, seeming to expect this to be disputed, he argues over the amount of nearly a page to prove it true; at the end of which, he lets us know that, by the treaty of 1819, we sold to Spain the whole country, from the Rio Grande eastward to the Sabine. Now, admitting for the present, that the Rio Grande was the boundary of Louisiana, what, under heaven, had that to do with the *present* boundary between us and Mexico? How, Mr. Chairman, the line that once divided your land from mine can *still* be the boundary between us *after* I have sold my land to you, is, to me, beyond all comprehension. And how any man, with an honest purpose only of proving the truth, could ever have *thought* of introducing such a fact to prove such an issue, is equally incomprehensible. The outrage upon common *right*, of seizing as our own what we have once sold, merely because it *was* ours *before* we sold it, is only equaled by the outrage on common *sense* of any attempt to justify it.

"The President's next piece of evidence is, that 'The Republic of Texas always *claimed* this river (Rio Grande) as her western boundary.' That is not true, in fact. Texas *has* claimed it, but she has not *always* claimed it. There is, at least, one distinguished exception. Her State Constitution—the public's most solemn and well-considered act—that which may, without impropriety, be called her last will and testament, revoking all others—makes no such claim. But suppose she had always claimed it. Has not Mexico always claimed the contrary? So that there is but ·*claim* against *claim*, leaving nothing proved until we get back of the claims, and find which has the better *foundation*.

"Though not in the order in which the President presents his evidence, I now consider that class of his statements, which are, in substance, nothing more than that Texas has by various acts of her Convention and Congress, claimed the Rio Grande as her boundary—*on paper*. I mean here what he says about the fixing of the Rio Grande as her boundary, in her old Constitution (not her State Constitution,) about forming congressional districts, counties, etc. Now, all this is but naked *claim;* and what I have already said about claims is strictly applicable to this. If I should claim your land by word of mouth, that certainly would not make it mine; and if I were to claim it by a deed which I had made myself, and with which you had nothing to do, the claim would be quite the same in substance, or rather in utter nothingness.

• "I next consider the President's statement that Santa Anna, in his *treaty* with Texas, recognized the Rio Grande as the western boundary of Texas. Besides the position so often taken that Santa Anna, while a prisoner of war—a captive—could not bind Mexico by a treaty, which I deem conclusive; besides this, I wish to say something in relation to this treaty, so called by the President, with Santa Anna. If any man would like to be amused by a sight at that *little* thing, which the President calls by that *big* name, he can have it by turning to Niles' Register, volume 50, page 336. And if any one should suppose that Niles' Register is a curious repository of so mighty a document as a solemn treaty between nations, I can only say that I learned, to a tolerable degree of certainty, by inquiry at the State Department, that the President himself never saw it anywhere else. By the way, I believe I should not err if I were to declare, that during the first ten years of the existence of that document, it was never by anybody called a treaty; that it was never so called till the President, in his extremity, attempted, by so

calling it, to wring something from it in justification of himself in connection with the Mexican war. It has none of the distinguishing features of a treaty. It does not call itself a treaty. Santa Anna does
not therein assume to bind Mexico; he assumes only to act as President,
Commander-in-chief of the Mexican army and navy; stipulates that the
then present hostilities should cease, and that he would not *himself* take
up arms, nor *influence* the Mexican people to take up arms against Texas,
during the existence of the war of independence. He did not recognize
the independence of Texas; he did not assume to put an end to the war,
but clearly indicated his expectation of its continuance; he did not say
one word about boundary, and most probably never thought of it. It
is stipulated therein that the Mexican forces should evacuate the territory of Texas, *passing to the other side of the Rio Grande;* and in another
article it is stipulated, that to prevent collisions between the armies,
the Texan army should not approach nearer than within five leagues
—of *what* is not said—but clearly, from the object stated, it is of the
Rio Grande. Now, if this is a treaty recognizing the Rio Grande as the
boundary of Texas, it contains the singular feature of stipulating that
Texas shall not go within five leagues of *her own* boundary.

   "Next comes the evidence of Texas before annexation, and the
United States afterward, exercising jurisdiction beyond the Nueces, and
between the two rivers. This actual *exercise* of jurisdiction is the very
class or quality of evidence we want. It is excellent so far as it goes;
but does it go far enough? He tells us it went *beyond* the Nueces, but
he does not tell us it went *to* the Rio Grande. He tells us jurisdiction
was exercised *between* the two rivers, but he does not tell us it was exercised over *all* the territory between them. Some simple-minded people think it possible to cross one river and go beyond it, without going
all the way to the next; that jurisdiction may be exercised *between* two
rivers without covering *all* the country between them. I know a man,
not very unlike myself who exercises jurisdiction over a piece of land
between the Wabash and the Mississippi; and yet so far is this from
being *all* there is between those rivers, that it is just one hundred and
fifty-two feet long by fifty wide, and no part of it much within a hundred miles of either. He has a neighbor between him and the Mississippi—that is, just across the street, in that direction—whom, I am sure,
he could neither *persuade* nor *force* to give up his habitation; but which,
nevertheless, he could certainly annex, if it were to be done, by merely
standing on his own side of the street and claiming it, or even sitting
down and writing a deed for it.

   " But next, the President tells us, the Congress of the United States
understood the State of Texas they admitted into the Union to extend
beyond the Nueces. Well, I suppose they did—I certainly so understand
it—but how *far* beyond? That Congress did *not* understand it to ex-

tend clear to the Rio Grande, is quite certain by the fact of their joint resolutions for admission expressly leaving all questions of boundary to future adjustment. And, it may be added, that Texas herself is proved to have had the same understanding of it that our Congress had, by the fact of the exact conformity of her new Constitution to those resolutions.

"I am now through the whole of the President's evidence; and it is a singular fact, that if any one should declare the President sent the army into the midst of a settlement of Mexican people, who had never submitted, by consent or by force to the authority of Texas or of the United States, and that *there*, and *thereby*, the first blood of the war was shed, there is not one word in all the President has said which would either admit or deny the declaration. In this strange omission chiefly consists the deception of the President's evidence—an omission which, it does seem to me, could scarcely have occurred but by design. My way of living leads me 'to be about the courts of justice ; and there I have some times seen a good lawyer, struggling for his client's neck, in a desperate case, employing every artifice to work round, befog, and cover up with many words some position pressed upon him by the prosecution, which he *dared* not admit, and yet *could* not deny. Party bias may help to make it appear so; but, with all the allowance I can make for such bias, it still does appear to me that just such, and from just such necessity, are the President's struggles in this case.

"Some time after my colleague (Mr. Richardson) introduced the resolutions I have mentioned, I introduced a preamble, resolution, and interrogatories, intended to draw the President out, if possible, on this hitherto untrodden ground. To show their relevancy, I propose to state my understanding of the true rule for ascertaining the boundary between Texas and Mexico. It is, that *wherever* Texas was *exercising* jurisdiction was hers; and wherever Mexico was exercising jurisdiction was hers; and that whatever separated the actual exercise of jurisdiction of the one from that of the other, was the true boundary between them. If, as is probably true, Texas was exercising jurisdiction along the western bank of the Nueces, and Mexico was exercising it along the eastern bank of the Rio Grande, then *neither* river was the boundary, but the uninhabited country between the two was. The extent of our territory in that region depended not on any *treaty-fixed* boundary (for no treaty had attempted it), but on revolution. Any people anywhere, being inclined and having the power, have the *right* to rise up and shake off the existing government, and form a new one that suits them better. This is a most valuable, a most sacred right—a right which, we hope and believe, is to liberate the world. Nor is this right confined to cases in which the whole people of an existing government may choose to exercise it. Any portion of such people that *can* may revolutionize, and make their *own* of so much of the territory as they inhabit. **More** than this, a *majority* of any portion of such people may revolutionize, putting down a *minority*, intermingled with, or near about them, who may oppose their movements. Such minority was precisely the case of the Tories of our own Revolution. It is a quality of revolutions not to go by old lines, or old laws; but to break up both, and make new ones. As to the country now in question, we bought it of France in 1803, and sold it to Spain in 1819, according to the President's statement. After this, all Mexico, including Texas, revolutionized against Spain; and still later, Texas revolutionized against Mexico. In my view, just so far as she carried her revolution, by obtaining the *actual*, willing or unwilling submission of the people, *so far* the country was hers, and no further.

"Now, sir, for the purpose of obtaining the very best evidence as to whether Texas had actually carried her revolution to the place where the hostilities of the present war commenced, let the President answer the interrogatories I proposed, as before mentioned, or some other similar ones. Let him answer fully, fairly and candidly. Let him answer with *facts*, and not with arguments. Let him remember he sits where Washington sat: and, so remembering, let him answer as Washington would answer. As a nation *should* not, and the Almighty *will* not, be evaded, so let him attempt no evasion, no equivocation. And if, so answering, he can show that the soil was ours where the first blood of the war was shed—that it was not within an inhabited country, or, if within such, that the inhabitants had submitted themselves to the civil authority of Texas, or of the United States, and that the same is true of the site of Fort Brown—then I am with him for his justification. In that case, I shall be most happy to reverse the vote I gave the other day. I have a selfish motive for desiring that the President may do this; I expect to give some votes, in connection with the war, which, without his so doing, will be of doubtful propriety, in my own judgment, but which will be free from the doubt, if he does so. But if he *can not* or *will not* do this—if, on any pretense, or no pretense, he shall refuse or omit it— then I shall be fully convinced, of what I more than suspect already, that he is deeply conscious of being in the wrong; that he feels the blood of this war, like the blood of Abel, is crying to heaven against him; that he ordered General Taylor into the midst of a peaceful Mexican settlement, purposely to bring on a war; that originally having some strong motive—what I will not stop now to give my opinion concerning—to involve the two countries in a war, and trusting to escape scrutiny by fixing the public gaze upon the exceeding brightness of military glory—that attractive rainbow that rises in showers of blood— that serpent's eye that charms to destroy—he plunged into it, and has swept *on* and *on*, till, disappointed in his calculation of the ease with which Mexico might be subdued, he now finds himself he knows not where. How like the half insane mumbling of a fever dream is the whole war part of the late message! At one time telling us that Mexico has nothing whatever that we can get but territory; at another, showing us how we can support the war by levying contributions on Mexico. At one time urging the national honor, the security of the future, the prevention of foreign interference, and even the good of Mexico herself, as among the objects of the war; at another, telling us that, 'to reject indemnity by refusing to accept a cession of territory, would be to abandon all our just demands, and to wage the war, bearing all its expenses, *without a purpose or definite object.*' So, then, the national honor, security of the future, and everything but territorial indemnity, may be considered the *no purposes* and *indefinite* objects of the war! But having it now settled that territorial indemnity is the only object, we are urged to seize, by legislation here, all that he was content to take a few months ago, and the whole province of Lower California to boot, and to still carry on the war—to take *all* we are fighting for, and *still* fight on. Again, the President is resolved, under all circumstances, to have full territorial indemnity for the expenses of the war; but he forgets to tell us how we are to get the *excess* after those expenses shall have surpassed the value of the *whole* of the Mexican territory. So, again, he insists that the separate national existence of Mexico shall be maintained; but he does not tell us *how* this can be done after we shall have taken *all* her territory. Lest the questions I here suggest be considered speculative merely, let me be indulged a moment in trying to show they are not.

"The war has gone on some twenty months, for the expenses of which, together with an inconsiderable old score, the President now claims about one half of the Mexican territory, and that by far the better half, so far as concerns our ability to make anything out of it. It is comparatively uninhabited; so that we could establish land offices in it, and raise some money in that way. But the other half is already inhabited, as I understand it, tolerably densely for the nature of the country; and all its lands, or all that are valuable, already appropriated as private property. How, then, are we to make anything out of these lands with this incumbrance on them, or how remove the incumbrance? I suppose no one will say we should kill the · people, or drive them out, or make slaves of them, or even confiscate their property? How, then, can we make much out of this · part of the territory? If the prosecution of the war has, in expenses, already equaled the *better* half of the country, how long its future prosecution will be in equaling the less valuable half is not a *speculative* but a *practical* question, pressing closely upon us, and yet it is a question which the President seems never to have thought of.

"As to the mode of terminating the war and securing peace, the

President is equally wandering and indefinite. First, it is to be done by a more vigorous prosecution of the war in the vital parts of the enemy's country; and, after apparently talking himself tired on this point, the President drops down into a half despairing tone, and tells us that 'with a people distracted and divided by contending factions, and a government subject to constant changes, by successive revolutions, *the continued success of our arms may fail to obtain a satisfactory peace.*' Then he suggests the propriety of wheedling the Mexican people to desert the counsels of their own leaders, and, trusting in our protection, to set up a government from which we can secure a satisfactory peace, telling us that '*this may become the only mode of obtaining such a peace.* But soon he falls into doubt of this too, and then drops back on to the already half-abandoned ground of 'more vigorous prosecution.' All this shows that the President is in no wise satisfied with his own positions. First, he takes up one, and, in attempting to argue us into it, he argues himself *out* of it; then seizes another, and goes through the same process; and then, confused at being able to think of nothing new, he snatches up the old one again, which he has some time before cast off. His mind, tasked beyond its power, is running hither and thither, like some tortured creature on a burning surface, finding no position on which it can settle down and be at ease.

"Again, it is a singular omission in this message, that it nowhere intimates *when* the President expects the war to terminate. At its beginning, General Scott was, by this same President, driven into disfavor, if not disgrace, for intimating that peace could not be conquered in less than three or four months. But now at the end of about twenty months, during which time our arms have given us the most splendid successes—every department, and every part, land and water, officers and privates, regulars and volunteers, doing all that men could do, and hundreds of things which it had ever before been thought that men could *not* do; after all this, this same President gives us a long message without showing us that, *as to the end,* he has himself even an imaginary conception. As I have before said, he knows not where he is. He is a bewildered, confounded, and miserably-perplexed man. God grant he may be able to show that there is not something about his conscience more painful than all his mental perplexity."

With this speech on record, it is strange that the genuine literary abilities of the man were so long and so persistently ignored by literary people. There were men who voted for him for the presidency more than twelve years afterwards— twelve years of culture and development to him—who were surprised to find his messages grammatically constructed, and who suspected the intervention of a secretary whenever any touch of elegance appeared in his writings.

Mr. Lincoln had a position on the Committee on Post-offices and Post-roads, and, from the knowledge in his possession, felt called upon a few days previous to the speech on the war to expose a difficulty between the Postmaster-general and a transportation company, anxious to get the "Great Southern Mail" contract, and to get a better contract than the department had offered. The matter had excited some interest in Congress, and Mr. Lincoln showed a faithful study of the facts of the case in his speech and his freedom from any party feeling in the matter, by supporting the position of the Post-master-general.

On the 1st of June, 1848, the National Whig Convention met at Philadelphia to nominate a candidate for the presidency, and Mr. Lincoln was among its members. Mr. Polk, by his war with Mexico, had been engaged, much against his inclinations, in manufacturing available if not able candidates for his own place, two of whom afterwards achieved it. General Taylor had become a hero. The brilliancy of his victories and the modesty of his dispatches had awakened in his behalf the enthusiastic admiration of the American people, without distinction of party. He was claimed by the whigs as a member of that party, and regarded by them as the one man in the Union by whose popularity they might hope to win the power they coveted. The majority would doubtless have preferred Mr. Clay, but Mr. Clay had been their candidate, and had been beaten. Mr. Lincoln would have been glad to support Mr. Clay, it is not doubted, but he shared in the feeling of the majority concerning his "availability." It is possible that his visit to Mr. Clay, and its unsatisfactory results, already alluded to, had somewhat blunted his devotion and subdued his enthusiasm on behalf of the great chieftain. Certain it is that he was among those who believed that General Taylor and not Mr. Clay should be the nominee of his party.

Congress had continued its session into the summer, either for purposes of business, or with the design to control the nominating conventions, and do something to direct the campaign; and when the nominations were made it did according to its custom, and immediately commenced the campaign in a series of speeches. About two months after General Taylor was nominated, (July twenty-seventh,) Mr. Lincoln secured the floor, and made a speech concerning the points at issue between the two parties, and the merits of the respective candidates, General Cass having received the nomination of the democratic party. It was a telling, trenchant *talk*, rather than a speech—more like one of his stump orations in Illinois than like his previous efforts in the House. As a campaign harangue, touching the salient features of the principal questions in debate, and revealing the weak points of one candidate and the strong points of the other, it could not have been improved. Considered as a part of the business which he was sent to Washington to perform, it was execrable. He did what others did, and what his partisan supporters expected him to do; but his own sense of propriety must have suggested to him, or ought to have suggested to him if it did not, the indecency of the practice of president-making in Congress.

In the light of subsequent events, the speech contains some passages that are very curious and suggestive. In revealing the position and policy of General Taylor in 1848, he was unconsciously marking out his own in 1860 and 1864. General Taylor, in a letter to Mr. Allison, had said, "upon the subject of the tariff, the currency, the improvement of our great highways, rivers, lakes and harbors, the will of the people, as expressed through their representatives in Congress, ought to be respected and carried out by the executive." Mr. Lincoln, in remarking upon this, said: "The people say to General Taylor, 'if you are elected, shall we have a national bank?' He answers, 'Your will, gentlemen, not mine.' 'What about the tariff?' 'Say yourselves.' 'Shall our rivers and harbors be improved?' 'Just as you please. If you desire a bank, an alteration of the tariff, internal improvements, any or all, I will not hinder you; if you do not desire them, I will not attempt to force them on you. Send up your members of Congress from the various districts, with opinions according to your own, and if they are for these measures, or any of them, I shall have nothing to oppose; if they are not for them, I shall not, by any appliances whatever, attempt to dragoon them into their adoption.'" From this point Mr. Lincoln went on to show in what respect a president is a representative of the people. He said: "In a certain sense, and to a certain extent, he is a representative of the people. He is elected by them as Congress is. But can he, in the nature of things, know the wants of the people as well as three hundred other men coming from all the various localities of the nation? If so, where is the propriety of having a Congress?"

There is much in this exposition of General Taylor's position to remind us of that upon which the speaker himself subsequently stood, when invested with the powers of the chief magistracy.

Mr. Lincoln's dissection of General Cass' position upon the questions of the canvass, was effected with characteristic neatness and thoroughness. Alluding to the subject of internal improvements Mr. Lincoln said, "My internal improvement colleague (Mr. Wentworth) stated on this floor the other day that he was satisfied Cass was for improvements because that he had voted for all the bills that he (Wentworth) had. So far, so good. But Mr. Polk vetoed some of these very bills; the Baltimore Convention passed a set of resolutions among other things approving these vetoes, and Cass declares in his letter accepting the nomination that he has carefully read these resolutions, and that he adheres to them as firmly as he approves them cordially. In other words, General Cass voted for the bills, and thinks the President did right to veto them; and his friends here are amiable enough to consider him as being one side or the other, just as one or the other may correspond with their own respective inclinations. My colleague admits that the platform declares against the constitutionality of a general system of improvements, and that General Cass indorses the platform, but he still thinks General Cass is in favor of some sort of improvements. Well, what are they? As·he is against general objects, those he is for must be particular and local. Now this is taking the subject precisely by the wrong end. Particularity—expending the money of the whole people for an object which will benefit only a portion of them—is the greatest real objection to improvements, and has been so held by General Jackson, Mr. Polk, and all others, I believe, till now." Certainly this was a very logical exposition of General Cass on internal improvements; and the charge of double dealing or gross inconsistency which it involved was unanswerable.

Mr. Lincoln tried his powers of ridicule on General Cass on this occasion. One of his palpable hits has already been quoted in connection with the history of Mr. Lincoln's participation in the Black Hawk war, in which he draws a parallel between his own bloodless experiences and those of the democratic candidate. Quoting extracts to show how General Cass had vacillated in his action on the Wilmot Proviso, he added, "These extracts show that in 1846 General Cass was for the Proviso at once, that in March, 1847, he was still for it, but not just then; and that in December he was against it altogether. This is a true index to the whole man. When the question was raised in 1846, he was in a blustering hurry to take ground for it, * * * but soon he began to see glimpses of the great democratic ox-gad waving in his face, and to hear indistinctly, a voice saying, 'back! back, sir! back a little!' He shakes his head, and bats his eyes, and blunders back to his position of March, 1847; but still the gad waves, and the voice grows more distinct and sharper still—'back, sir! back, I say! further back!' and back he goes to the position of December, 1847; at which the gad is still, and the voice soothingly says—'so! stand still at that!'" The homely illustration, culled from his early experiences, was certainly forcible, if not elegant.

In this political canvass, the whigs found themselves nearly as much perplexed in the treatment of the Mexican war as they had been in Congress. They had selected as their candidate a man whose reputation had been made by the successful prosecution of a war which they had opposed. They were charged, of course, with inconsistency by their opponents, and were placed in the awkward position of being obliged to draw nice distinctions. It is possible that they deserved the embarrassment from which they suffered. General Taylor had, beyond dispute, been nominated because he was a military hero, and not because he had any natural or acquired fitness for the presidency. The war had made him; and the whigs had seized upon this product of the war as an instrument by which they might acquire power. Mr. Lincoln alluded to this in his speech, but showed that while the whigs had believed the war to be unnecessarily and unconstitutionally begun, they had voted supplies, and sent their men. "Through suffering and death," said he, "by disease and in battle, they have endured, and fought, and fallen with you. Clay and Webster each gave a son, never to be returned. From the state of my own residence, besides other worthy but less known whig names, we sent Marshall, Morrison, Baker and Hardin; they all fought, and one fell, and in the fall of that one we lost our best whig man. Nor were the whigs few in numbers, or laggard in the day of danger. In that fearful, bloody, breathless struggle at Buena Vista, where each man's hard task was to beat back five foes, or die himself, of the five high officers who perished, four were whigs." With an allusion to the distinction between the cause of the President in beginning the war, and the cause of the country after it was begun, Mr. Lincoln closed his speech.

During the time these presidential discussions were going on in Congress, Mr. Lincoln was in close communication with the whig leaders in Illinois, laying out the work of the canvass, and trying to convert the active men of the party to his own ideas of sound policy in the conduct of the campaign. Indeed, he began this work before General Taylor was nominated, under the evident conviction that he would be the candidate, and the strong desire that he should be. As early in the year as February twentieth, he wrote a letter to U. F. Linder, a prominent whig orator of Illinois, on this subject.

It betrays the perplexity to which more than one allusion has been made, of the whigs at the time. Mr. Lincoln says, in this letter, "In law, it is good policy to never plead what you need not, lest you oblige yourself to prove what you cannot. Reflect on this well before you proceed. The application I mean to make of this rule is that you should simply go for General Taylor, because you can take some democrats and lose no whigs; but if you go also for Mr. Polk, on the origin and mode of prosecuting the war, you will still take some democrats, but you will lose more whigs, so that, in the sum of the operation, you will be loser. This is, at least, my opinion; and if you will look around, I doubt if you do not discover such to be the fact among your own neighbors. Further than this: by justifying Mr. Polk's mode of prosecuting the war, you put yourself in opposition to General Taylor himself, for we all know he has declared for, and, in fact, originated, the defensive line policy."

In this letter, Mr. Lincoln talks like a politician (and he was one of the most acute that the country ever produced,) to a politician. It looks as if he were handling grave questions of state with reference only to party ends; but the letter does not represent him wholly. In a subsequent note to the same friend, in answer to the question whether "it would not be just as easy to elect General Taylor without opposing the war, as by opposing it," he replies: "the locofocos here will not let the whigs be silent, * * * so that they are compelled to speak, and their only option is whether they will, when they speak, tell the truth, or tell a foul, villainous and bloody falsehood." In this declaration, the politician sinks, and the man rises, and seems to be what he really is—honest and conscientious.

On the fourteenth day of August, the first session of the Thirtieth Congress came to a close, and the members went home to continue and complete the campaign which they had inaugurated at Washington. The session had been one of strong excitements, particular interest attaching to every important debate in consequence of its bearing upon the question of the presidency.   Mr. Lincoln had discharged his duties well—ably and conscientiously, at least.   He found to his regret that he had not entirely pleased his constituents in his course on the questions connected with the war.   It is probable that he could have secured a renomination had he himself been willing to risk the result.   That a man with his desire for public life would willingly retire from Congress at the end of a single term of service is not probable; and while it has been said that he peremptorily refused to be again considered a candidate, on account of his desire to engage more exclusively in the duties of his profession, it is not credible that this was his only motive.*   Indeed, there is evidence that he sought another office, in consequence of the fact that his professional business had suffered so severely by his absence that he would have been glad to quit it altogether.   He was in no hurry to return to it, certainly, for at the close of the session, he visited New England, and made a number of very effective campaign speeches, and then went home, and devoted his time to the canvass for the election of General Taylor until he had the satisfaction of witnessing the triumph of his candidate, and the national success of the party to whose fortunes he had been so long and so warmly devoted.

In his own district, Mr. Lincoln helped to give General Taylor a majority nearly equal to that by which he had been elected to Congress.   The general result of the election brought to him great satisfaction.   It justified his own judgment touching the candidate's availability, and promised a return to the policy which he believed essential to the welfare of the country. But little time was left between the close of the canvass and the commencement of the second session, so that Mr. Lincoln had no more than sufficient space for the transaction of his personal business at home, before he was obliged to take his departure again for Washington.

The second session of this Congress was comparatively a

* Mr. Scripps, in his campaign biography, says that his refusal to be again a candidate, was in accordance with an understanding with the leading whigs of his district before his election.

quiet one. Several months had elapsed since the treaty of
Guadalupe Hidalgo had ratified peace between the United
States and Mexico, the presidential campaign had transpired,
and the national political caldron had ceased to boil. Mr.
Lincoln carried into this session the anti-slavery record of an
anti-slavery whig. He had voted forty-two times for the
Wilmot Proviso, had stood firmly by John Quincy Adams
and Joshua R. Giddings on the right of petition, and was
recognized as a man who would do as much in opposition to
slavery as his constitutional obligations would permit him to
do. Early in the session, Mr. Gott of New York introduced
a resolution instructing the Committee on the District of Columbia to report a bill prohibiting the slave trade in the District. The language of the preamble upon which the resolution was based was very strong, and doubtless seemed to Mr.
Lincoln unnecessarily offensive ; and we find him voting with
the pro-slavery men of the House to lay it on the table, and
subsequently voting against its adoption. He had probably
been maturing a measure which he intended should cover the
same ground, in another way, and on the sixteenth of January
he introduced a substitute for this resolution, which had been
carried along under a motion to reconsider. It provided that
no person not within the District, and no person thereafter
born within the District, should be held to slavery within the
District, or held to slavery without its limits, while it provided
that those holding slaves in the slave states might bring them
in and take them out again, when visiting the District on
public business. It also provided for the emancipation of all
the slaves legally held within the District, at the will of their
masters, who could claim their full value at the hands of the
government, and that the act itself should be subject to the
approval of the voters of the District. The bill had also a
provision, " that the municipal authorities of Washington and
Georgetown, within their respective jurisdictional limits,"
should be " empowered and required to provide active and
efficient means to arrest and deliver up to their owners all
fugitive slaves escaping into said District."

If any evidence were needed to establish the fact that Mr. Lincoln regarded slaves as property under the Constitution, this bill would seem to furnish all that is desired. If he did not so regard them, this bill convicts him of friendliness rather than enmity to slavery. If he did not so regard them, his whole record relating to slavery was a record of duplicity. Mr. Lincoln's character as an anti-slavery man can have no consistency on any basis except that of his firm belief that slaves were recognized as property under the Constitution of the United States; and those who impute to him the opposite opinion, or action based upon the opposite opinion, inflict a wrong upon his memory.* He recognized slaves as property not only in Congress, but on the stump and even in his business. He was once employed by General Matteson of Bourbon County, Kentucky, who had brought five or six negroes into Coles County, Illinois, and worked them on a farm for two or three years, to get them out of the hands of the civil authorities, which had interfered to keep him from taking them back to Kentucky. Judge Wilson and Judge Treat, both of the Supreme Court, sat on the case, and decided against the claim of the slaveholder, as presented by Mr. Lincoln. It is remembered that he made a very poor plea, and exercised a good deal of research in presenting the authorities for and against, and that all his sympathies were on the side of the slaves, but such a man as Mr. Lincoln would never have consented to act on this case if he had not believed that slaves were recognized as property by the Constitution. It is true that in a speech delivered afterwards, during the famous Douglas campaign, he denied the statement made by the Supreme Court in the Dred Scott decision, that "the right of property in a slave is *distinctly and expressly affirmed* in the Constitution;" but there was to him, and there is in fact, a great difference between a distinct and express affirmation, and a real though it may be only a tacit recognition of property in a slave. Slavery was to him legally right and morally wrong.

---

* " His vote is recorded against the pretence that slaves were property under the Constitution."—*Charles Sumner's Eulogy at Boston, June* 1, 1865.

He was equally loyal to the Constitution and loving to his kind; and when the time came which gave him the privilege of striking off the fetters of the slave, in order to preserve his country and its Constitution, he did it, and counted the act the crowning one of his life.

Mr. Lincoln did not bring his bill forward without consultation. Mr. Seaton, of the National Intelligencer, is understood to have been most in his confidence; and Mr. Lincoln said, on presenting his bill to the House, that he was authorized to say that, of about fifteen of the leading citizens of the District to whom the proposition had been submitted, there was not one who did not give it his approval. A substitute for the bill was moved, and finally the whole subject was given up, and left to take its place among the unfinished business of the Congress. The reason for this is reported to have been Mr. Seaton's withdrawal from the support of the plan; and Mr. Seaton's withdrawal from the support of the plan is said to have been owing to the visits and expostulations of members of Congress from the slave states. Mr. Lincoln could hope to do nothing without the approval of the voters of the District, and to secure this approval he must secure the support of the National Intelligencer. That taken from his scheme, he took no further interest in pursuing it.

Mr. Lincoln had other occasions, during the session, to record his votes against slavery, in his own moderate way—always moved by his humanity and his love of that which was morally right, and withheld and controlled by his obligations to the Constitution and the law, as he apprehended those obligations.

The fourth of March brought his Congressional career to a close. While he had maintained a most respectable position in the House, there is no reason to believe that he made any great impression upon legislation, or upon the mind of the country. His highest honors were to be won in another field, for which his two years in the House were in part a preparation. After his return to Springfield, he found his practice dissipated. He saw that he should be obliged to begin again.

Business, for the time, had taken new channels, as it never fails to do in like cases.   The charms of the old life in Washington came back to him, and he was ready to take an office. He had a fancy that he would like to be Commissioner of the General Land Office, and Mr. Defrees, now the superintendent of public printing at Washington, and then the editor of the Indiana State Journal, wrote an extended article, urging his appointment, and published it in that newspaper.   The effort miscarried, very much to Mr. Lincoln's and the country's advantage; and Mr. Butterfield of Illinois secured the coveted place.   The unsuccessful application for this appointment was subsequently a theme of much merriment between Mr. Lincoln and his friends.

CHAPTER X.

On returning to his home, Mr. Lincoln entered upon the duties of his profession, and devoted himself to them through a series of years, less disturbed by diversions into state and national politics than he had been during any previous period of his business life. It was to him a time of rest, of reading, of social happiness and of professional prosperity. He was already a father, and took an almost unbounded pleasure in his children.* Their sweet young natures were to him a perpetual source of delight. He was never impatient with their petulance and restlessness, loved always to be with them, and took them into his heart with a fondness which was unspeakable. It was a fondness so tender and profound as to blind him to their imperfections, and to expel from him every particle of sternness in his management of them. It must be said that he had very little of what is called parental government. The most that he could say to any little rebel in his household was, " you break my heart, when you act like this ; " and the loving eyes and affectionate voice and sincere expres-

---

*Mr. Lincoln had four children, all sons, viz: Robert Todd, Edwards, who died in infancy, William, who died in Washington during Mr. Lincoln's presidency, and Thomas. The oldest and youngest survive. The latter became the pet of the White House, and is known to the country as " Tad." This nickname was conferred by his father who, while Thomas was an infant in arms, and without a name, playfully called him " Tadpole." This was abbreviated to the pet name which he will probably never outlive.

Engraved expressly for Holland's "Life of Lincoln".

HOME OF LINCOLN,
SPRINGFIELD, ILL.

sion of pain were usually enough to bring the culprit to his
senses and his obedience. A young man bred in Springfield
speaks of a vision that has clung to his memory very vividly,
of Mr. Lincoln as he appeared in those days. His way to
school led by the lawyer's door. On almost any fair summer
morning, he could find Mr. Lincoln on the sidewalk, in front
of his house, drawing a child backward and forward, in a
child's gig. Without hat or coat, and wearing a pair of rough
shoes, his hands behind him holding to the tongue of the gig,
and his tall form bent forward to accommodate himself to the
service, he paced up and down the walk, forgetful of everything around him, and intent only on some subject that absorbed his mind. The young man says he remembers won-
dering, in his boyish way, how so rough and plain a man
should happen to live in so respectable a house.

The habit of mental absorption—absent mindedness, as it is
called—was common with him always, but particularly during
the formative periods of his life. The New Salem people, it
will be remembered, thought him crazy, because he passed his
best friends in the street without seeing them. At the table,
in his own family, he often sat down without knowing or realizing where he was, and ate his food mechanically. When
he "came to himself," it was a trick with him to break the
silence by the quotation of some verse of poetry from a favorite author. It relieved the awkwardness of "the situation,"
served as a blind to the thoughts which had possessed him,
and started conversation in a channel that led as far as possible from the subject that he had set aside.

Mr. Lincoln's lack of early advantages and the limited
character of his education were constant subjects of regret
with him. His intercourse with members of Congress and
with the cultivated society of Washington had, without doubt,
made him feel his deficiencies more keenly than ever before.
There is no doubt that his successes were a constant surprise
to him. He felt that his acquisitions were very humble, and
that the estimate which the public placed upon him was, in
some respects, a blind and mistaken one. It was at this period

that he undertook to improve himself somewhat by attention to mathematics, and actually mastered the first six books of Euclid. In speaking of this new acquisition to a friend, he said that, in debates, he had frequently heard the word "demonstration" used, and he determined to ascertain for himself what it meant. After his mastery of geometry, he had no further uncertainty on the subject.

Allusion has been made to Mr. Lincoln's mechanical genius. That he had enough of this to make him a good mechanic, there is no doubt. With such rude tools as were at his command he had made cabins and flat-boats; and after his mind had become absorbed in public and professional affairs he often recurred to his mechanical dreams for amusement. One of his dreams took form, and he endeavored to make a practical matter of it. He had had experience in the early navigation of the Western rivers. One of the most serious hinderances to this navigation was low water, and the lodgment of the various craft on the shifting shoals and bars with which these rivers abound. He undertook to contrive an apparatus which, folded to the hull of a boat like a bellows, might be inflated on occasion, and, by its levity, lift it over any obstruction upon which it might rest. On this contrivance, illustrated by a model whittled out by himself, and now preserved in the patent office at Washington, he secured letters patent; but it is certain that the navigation of the Western rivers was not revolutionized by it.

Mr. Lincoln never made his profession lucrative to himself. It was very difficult for him to charge a heavy fee to anybody, and still more difficult for him to charge his friends anything at all for professional services. To a poor client, he was quite as apt to give money as to take it from him. He never encouraged the spirit of litigation. Henry McHenry, one of his old clients, says that he went to Mr. Lincoln with a case to prosecute, and that Mr. Lincoln refused to have anything to do with it, because he was not strictly in the right. "You can give the other party a great deal of trouble," said the lawyer, "and perhaps beat him, but you had better let the suit alone."

Mr. Lincoln had on hand a case for this same gentleman for three years, and took it through three courts to the Supreme Court, and charged him for his services only seventy-five dollars. His wants were not large. He had no expensive vices, took no delight in fine clothing, and had no strong desire to accumulate money. Indeed, after all his years of practice, which closed only with his election to the presidency, he had accumulated, as the sum total of all his gold and goods, only the estimated value of sixteen thousand dollars.

Some incidents illustrating his practice, and the motives which controlled him in it, may with propriety be stated here, although they are not all of them associated with this period of his life. An old woman of seventy-five years, the widow of a revolutionary pensioner, came tottering into his office one day, and, taking a seat, told him that a certain pension agent had charged her the exorbitant fee of two hundred dollars for collecting her claim. Mr. Lincoln was satisfied by her representations that she had been swindled, and finding that she was not a resident of the town, and that she was poor, gave her money, and set about the work of procuring restitution. He immediately entered suit against the agent to recover a portion of his ill-gotten money. The suit was entirely successful, and Mr. Lincoln's address to the jury before which the case was tried is remembered to have been peculiarly touching in its allusions to the poverty of the widow, and the patriotism of the husband she had sacrificed to secure the nation's independence. He had the gratification of paying back to her a hundred dollars, and sending her home rejoicing.

One afternoon an old negro woman came into the office of Lincoln & Herndon,* and told the story of her trouble, to which both lawyers listened. It appeared that she and her offspring were born slaves in Kentucky, and that her owner, one Hinkle, had brought the whole family into Illinois, and given them their freedom. Her son had gone down the Mississippi as a waiter or deck hand, on a steamboat. Arriv-

---

* William H. Herndon, who became Mr. Lincoln's partner after he dissolved his association with Judge Logan.

ing at New Orleans, he had imprudently gone ashore, and had been snatched up by the police, in accordance with the law then in force concerning free negroes from other states, and thrown into confinement. Subsequently, he was brought out, and tried. Of course he was fined, and, the boat having left, he was sold, or was in immediate danger of being sold, to pay his fine and the expenses. Mr. Lincoln was very much moved, and requested Mr. Herndon to go over to the State House, and inquire of Governor Bissell if there was not something that he could do to obtain possession of the negro. Mr. Herndon made the inquiry, and returned with the report that the Governor regretted to say that he had no legal or constitutional right to do anything in the premises. Mr. Lincoln rose to his feet in great excitement, and exclaimed, " By the Almighty, I 'll have that negro back soon, or I 'll have a twenty years' agitation in Illinois, until the Governor does have a legal and constitutional right to do something in the premises." He was saved from the latter alternative—at least in the direct form which he proposed. The lawyers sent money to a New Orleans correspondent—money of their own—who procured the negro, and returned him to his mother.

Mr. Lincoln's early athletic struggle with Jack Armstrong, the representative man of the " Clary's Grove Boys," will be remembered. From the moment of this struggle, which Jack agreed to call " a drawn battle," in consequence of his own foul play, they became strong friends. Jack would fight for Mr. Lincoln at any time, and would never hear him spoken against. Indeed, there were times when young Lincoln made Jack's cabin his home, and here Mrs. Armstrong, a most womanly person, learned to respect the rising man. There was no service to which she did not make her guest abundantly welcome, and he never ceased to feel the tenderest gratitude for her kindness. At length, her husband died, and she became dependent upon her sons. The oldest of these, while in attendance upon a camp-meeting, found himself involved in a melee, which resulted in the death of a young man; and young Armstrong was charged by one of his associates with striking the fatal blow. He was arrested, examined, and imprisoned to await his trial. The public mind was in a blaze of excitement, and interested parties fed the flame. Mr. Lincoln knew nothing of the merits of this case, that is certain. He only knew that his old friend Mrs. Armstrong was in sore trouble; and he sat down at once, and volunteered by letter to defend her son. His first act was to procure the postponement and a change of the place of the trial. There was too much fever in the minds of the immediate public to permit of fair treatment. When the trial came on, the case looked very hopeless to all but Mr. Lincoln, who had assured himself that the young man was not guilty. The evidence on behalf of the state being all in, and looking like a solid and consistent mass of testimony against the prisoner, Mr. Lincoln undertook the task of analyzing and destroying it, which he did in a manner that surprised every one. The principal witness testified that "by the aid of the brightly shining moon, he saw the prisoner inflict the death blow with a slung shot." Mr. Lincoln proved by the almanac that there was no moon shining at the time. The mass of testimony against the prisoner melted away, until "not guilty" was the verdict of every man present in the crowded court-room. There is, of course, no record of the plea made on this occasion, but it is remembered as one in which Mr. Lincoln made an appeal to the sympathies of the jury which quite surpassed his usual efforts of the kind, and melted all to tears. The jury were out but half an hour, when they returned with their verdict of "not guilty." The widow fainted in the arms of her son, who divided his attention between his services to her and his thanks to his deliverer. And thus the kind woman who cared for the poor young man, and showed herself a mother to him in his need, received the life of a son, saved from a cruel conspiracy, as her reward, from the hand of her grateful beneficiary.

The lawyers of Springfield, particularly those who had political aspirations, were afraid to undertake the defense of any one who had been engaged in helping off fugitive slaves. It was a very unpopular business in those days and in that lo-

9

cality; and few felt that they could afford to engage in it.
One who needed such aid went to Edward D. Baker, and
was refused defense distinctly and frankly, on the ground
that, as a political man, he could not afford it. The man applied to an ardent anti-slavery friend for advice. He spoke
of Mr. Lincoln, and said, "He's not afraid of an unpopular
case. When I go for a lawyer to defend an arrested fugitive
slave, other lawyers will refuse me, but if Mr. Lincoln is at
home, he will always take my case."

A sheep-grower sold a number of sheep at a stipulated av-
erage price. When he delivered the animals, he delivered
many lambs, or sheep too young to come fairly within the terms
of the contract. He was sued for damages by the injured
party, and Mr. Lincoln was his attorney. At the trial, the
facts as to the character of the sheep delivered were proved,
and several witnesses testified as to the usage by which all
under a certain age were regarded as lambs, and of inferior
value. Mr. Lincoln, on comprehending the facts, at once
changed his line of effort, and confined himself to ascertaining
the real number of inferior sheep delivered. On addressing
the jury, he said that from the facts proved they must give
a verdict against his client, and he only asked their scrutiny
as to the actual damage suffered.

In another case, Mr. Lincoln was conducting a suit against
a railroad company. Judgment having been given in his favor, and the court being about to allow the amount claimed
by him, deducting a proved and allowed offset, he rose and
stated that his opponents had not proved all that was justly
due them in offset; and proceeded to state and allow a further
sum against his client, which the court allowed in its judgment. His desire for the establishment of exact justice always
overcame his own selfish love of victory, as well as his partiality for his clients' feelings and interests.

These incidents sufficiently illustrate the humane feelings and
thorough honesty which Mr. Lincoln carried into the practice
of his profession, and, as allusion has already been made to
the high estimate placed by the people upon his ability as a

lawyer, it will be proper to record here the high opinion of his professional merits entertained by the most eminent representatives of the bar of Illinois. His death in 1865 was, in accordance with usage, made the subject of notice by the various courts of the state. The Supreme Court in session at Ottawa, received a series of resolutions from the bar, which were placed upon its records. Ex-Judge Caton, in presenting them, said, "He (Mr. Lincoln) understood the relations of things, and hence his deductions were rarely wrong, from any given state of facts. So he applied the principles of law to the transactions of men with great clearness and precision. He was a close reasoner. He reasoned by analogy, and enforced his views by apt illustration. His mode of speaking was generally of a plain and unimpassioned character, and yet, he was the author of some of the most beautiful and eloquent passages in our language, which, if collected, would form a valuable contribution to American literature. The most punctilious honor ever marked his professional and private life."

Judge Breese, in responding to the resolutions and the remarks of Judge Caton, was still more outspoken in his high opinion of Mr. Lincoln, as a lawyer. "For my single self," he said, "I have for a quarter of a century regarded Mr. Lincoln as the finest lawyer I ever knew, and of a professional bearing so high-toned and honorable as justly, and without derogating from the claims of others, entitling him to be presented to the profession as a model well worthy of the closest imitation." Judge Thomas Drummond of Chicago, representing the bar of that city, said, "I have no hesitation in saying that he was one of the ablest lawyers I have ever known." In addition, he said, "no intelligent man who ever watched Mr. Lincoln through a hard-contested case at the bar, questioned his great ability." Judge Drummond's picture of Mr. Lincoln at the bar, and his mode of speech and action is so graphic and so just that it deserves to be quoted:

"With a voice by no means pleasant, and, indeed, when excited, in its shrill tones, sometimes almost disagreeable; without any of the personal graces of the orator; without much in the outward man indicating superiority of intellect; without great quickness of perception—still, his mind was so vigorous, his comprehension so exact and clear, and his judgment so sure, that he easily mastered the intricacies of his profession, and became one of the ablest reasoners and most impressive speakers at our bar. With a probity of character known of all, with an intuitive insight into the human heart, with a clearness of statement which was itself an argument, with uncommon power and felicity of illustration,—often, it is true, of a plain and homely kind,—and with that sincerity and earnestness of manner which carried conviction, he was, perhaps, one of the most successful jury lawyers we have ever had in the state. He always tried a case fairly and honestly. He never intentionally misrepresented the evidence of a witness or the argument of an opponent. He met both squarely, and, if he could not explain the one or answer the other, substantially admitted it. He never misstated the law according to his own intelligent view of it."

These tributes to the professional excellence of Mr. Lincoln, by those best qualified to judge it, is all the more significant from the fact that it was rendered by those who, throughout his whole career, were opposed to him politically—by democrats and conservatives. Judge David Davis, of Bloomington, Illinois, a strong personal friend of Mr. Lincoln, in responding to resolutions presented by the bar of Indianapolis, said that "in all the elements that constitute the great lawyer, he (Mr. Lincoln) had few equals. He was great both at *Nisi Prius* and before an appellate tribunal. He seized the strong points of a case, and presented them with clearness and great compactness. A vein of humor never deserted him, and he was always able to chain the attention of court and jury when the cause was the most uninteresting, by the appropriateness of his anecdotes."

It was during this period of Mr. Lincoln's life that he was called upon to pronounce a eulogy upon Henry Clay. The death of this eminent statesman occurred in 1852, and the citizens of Springfield thought of no man so competent to do his memory justice as he who had through so many years been devoted to his interests and his political principles. The eulogy was pronounced in the State House, and was listened to by a large audience. The discourse, as it was printed in the city newspapers of the day, was by no means a remarkable one. It is remembered as a very dull one at its delivery, and was so regarded by Mr. Lincoln himself, who complained that he lacked the imagination necessary for a performance of that character. It is possible that the effect upon his mind of the old visit to Ashland was not entirely obliterated; for Mr. Lincoln was quite accustomed to find expression for any admiration that was really within him. The closing words of the eulogy, though hortatory in form, were prophetic in fact, and, in the light of subsequent events, have a touching interest. "Such a man," said he, "the times have demanded, and such in the Providence of God was given us. But he is gone. Let us strive to deserve, as far as mortals may, the continued care of Divine Providence, trusting that in future national emergencies he will not fail to provide us the instruments of safety and security." That Divine Providence which he so confidently trusted then, trusted him as the instrument for executing its own designs, in the greatest of national emergencies.

It is not to be supposed that during these years of quiet professional life Mr. Lincoln was entirely indifferent to the course of political affairs. Great national events were in progress, which must have impressed him profoundly. The slave states, conscious that power was departing from them, were desperate in their efforts and fruitful in their expedients to retain it. On the 9th of September, 1850, the free state of California was admitted to the Union. There was a double bitterness in this measure to those interested in the perpetuation of the influence of slavery in national affairs. The state was formed from territory on which the South had hoped to extend the area of their institution—which had been won from Mexico for that special purpose; and there was no slave state in readiness to be admitted with it, in accordance with southern policy and congressional usage. As an offset to this accession to the power of the free states, a series of concessions were exacted of them which excited great discontent among the people. The compromise measures of 1850, as they were called, did not satisfy either section. The South did not see in them the security they desired, and the North felt itself wronged and humiliated by them. Yet there was among the people of both sections a strong desire for peace. They had become weary with agitation, and readily fell in with the action of the two national conventions, which, in 1852, accepted these measures as a final settlement of the points of difference between the two sections of the country. It is easy, in looking back, to see how wretched a basis these measures furnished for peace between freedom and slavery; but the best men and the most patriotic men of the time found nothing better.

How far Mr. Lincoln shared in the desire that these measures should be the final settlement of the slavery question in the country, or believed it possible that they could be, is not known. Although he consented to stand on the Scott electoral ticket in 1852, he does not seem to have gone into the canvass with his characteristic earnestness. His party had committed him, in advance, to silence on the subject of slavery; and it was quite possible that he was willing to see how much could be done towards stifling what seemed to be a fruitless agitation. He made but few speeches, and these few made little impression. The defeat of General Scott and the election of General Pierce was in accordance with the popular expectation. Mr. Lincoln had not been diverted from his professional pursuits by the campaign, and for two years thereafter he found nothing in politics to call him from his business.

In 1854, a new political era opened. Events occurred of immeasurable influence upon the country; and an agitation of the slavery question was begun which was destined not to cease until slavery itself should be destroyed. Disregarding the pledges of peace and harmony, the party in the interest of slavery effected in Congress the abrogation of the Missouri Compromise of 1820—a compromise which was intended to shut slavery forever out of the north-west; and a bill organizing the territories of Kansas and Nebraska was enacted, which left them free to choose whether they would have slavery as an institution or not. The intention, without doubt, was to force slavery upon those territories—to make it impossible for them ever to become free states—as the subsequent exhibitions of "border ruffianism" in Kansas sufficiently testified. This great political iniquity aroused Mr. Lincoln as he had never before been aroused. It was at this time that he fully comprehended the fact that there was to be no peace on the slavery question until either freedom or slavery should triumph. He knew slavery to be wrong. He had always known and felt it to be so. He knew that he regarded the institution as the fathers of the republic had regarded it; but a new doctrine had been put forward. Slavery was right. Slavery was entitled to equal consideration with freedom. Slavery claimed the privilege of going wherever, into the national domain, it might choose to go. Slavery claimed national protection everywhere. Instead of remaining contentedly within the territory it occupied under the protection of the Constitution, it sought to extend itself indefinitely—to nationalize itself.

Judge Douglas of Illinois was the responsible author of what was called the Kansas-Nebraska bill—a bill which he based upon what he was pleased to denominate "popular sovereignty"—the right of the people of a territory to choose their own institutions; and between Judge Douglas and Mr. Lincoln was destined to be fought "the battle of the giants" on the questions that grew out of this great political crime. Mr. Lincoln's indignation was an index to the popular feeling all over the North. The men who, in good faith, had acquiesced in the compromise measures, though with great reluctance and only for the sake of peace—who had compelled themselves to silence by biting their lips—who had been forced into silence by their love of the Union whose existence the slave power had threatened—saw that they had been over-reached and foully wronged.

Mr. Douglas, on his return to his constituents, was met by a storm of indignation, so that when he first undertook to speak in vindication of himself he was not permitted to do so. He found that he had committed a great political blunder, even if he failed to comprehend the fact that he had been guilty of a criminal breach of faith. The first exhibitions of popular rage naturally passed away, so that the city which refused to hear him speak, now honors his dust as that of a great and powerful and famous man; but the city and the state have discarded his political principles; and the party which once honored him with so much confidence, remembers with regret—possibly with bitterness—that he was mainly responsible for its overthrow. Mr. Douglas, without doubt, foresaw what was coming, as the result of his political misdeeds, but he tried to avert the popular judgment. He spoke in various places in the state, but with little effect. Congress had adjourned early in August. His attempt to speak in Chicago was made on the first of September, and early in October, on the occasion of the State Fair, he found himself at Springfield.

The Fair had brought together a large number of representative men, from all parts of the state, many of whom had come for the purposes of political reunion and consultation. There was a great deal of political speaking, but the chief interest of the occasion centered in a discussion between Mr. Lincoln and Mr. Douglas. It had been many years since these two men had found themselves pitted against each other in debate, and during nearly all these years, Mr. Douglas had been in public life. He was a man known to the whole nation. He was the recognized leader of his party in Illinois, notwithstanding the fact that his course had driven many from his support. His experience in debate, his easy audacity and assurance, his great ability, his strong will, his unconquerable ambition, and his untiring industry, made him a most formidable antagonist. To say that his unlimited self-confidence, which not unfrequently made him arrogant and overbearing— at least, in appearance—assisted him in the work which he had before him, would be to insult the independent common sense of the people he addressed. Mr. Douglas entered into an exposition and defense of his principles and policy with the bearing of a man who had already conquered. His long and uninterrupted success had made him restive under inquisition, impatient of dispute, and defiant of opposition.

On the day following the speech of Mr. Douglas, Mr. Lincoln, who had listened to him, replied, and Mr. Douglas was among his auditors. The speech delivered on this occasion was one of the most powerful and eloquent efforts of his life. Mr. Lincoln began by saying that he wished to present nothing to the people but the truth, to which they were certainly entitled, and that, if Judge Douglas should detect him in saying anything untrue, he (Judge Douglas) would correct him. Mr. Douglas took license from this remark to interrupt him constantly, with the most unimportant questions, and in such a way as to show Mr. Lincoln that his only motive was to break him down. Finally, the speaker lost his patience, and said, " Gentlemen, I cannot afford to spend my time in quibbles. I take the responsibility of asserting the truth myself, relieving Judge Douglas from the necessity of his impertinent corrections." From this point, he was permitted to proceed uninterruptedly, until a speech occupying three hours and ten minutes was concluded. No report of this speech was made, and no judgment can be formed of it, except such as can be made up from the cotemporary newspaper accounts, the recollections of those who heard it, and its effect upon the politics of the state. The enthusiasm of the party press was unbounded, and was manifestly genuine. The Kansas-Nebraska bill was the subject of debate; and his exposure of its fallacies and iniquities was declared to be overwhelming. His whole heart was in his words. The Springfield Journal, in describing the speech and the occasion, says: " He quivered with feeling and emotion. The whole house was as still as death. He attacked the bill with unusual warmth and energy, and all felt that a man of strength was its enemy, and that he intended to blast it if he could by strong and manly efforts. He was most successful; and the house approved the glorious triumph of truth by loud and long-continued huzzas. Women waved their white handkerchiefs in token of woman's silent but heartfelt consent. * * * Mr. Lincoln exhibited Douglas in all the attitudes he could be placed in in a friendly debate. He exhibited the bill in all its aspects, to show its humbuggery and falsehoods, and when thus torn to rags, cut into slips, held up to the gaze of the vast crowd, a kind of scorn was visible upon the face of the crowd and upon the lips of the most eloquent speaker." The editor, in concluding his account, says: "At the conclusion of the speech, every man felt that it was unanswerable—that no human power could overthrow it, or trample it under foot. The long and repeated applause evinced the feelings of the crowd, and gave token of universal assent to Lincoln's whole argument; and every mind present did homage to the man who took captive the heart, and broke like a sun over the understanding."

The account of this speech in the Chicago Press and Tribune was not less enthusiastic in its praise, than the journal just quoted. After stating that, within the limits of a newspaper article, it would be impossible to give an idea of the strength of Mr. Lincoln's argument, and that it was by far the ablest effort of the campaign, he quotes the following passage directly from the speech, as remarkable in its power upon the audience: "My distinguished friend says it is an insult to the emigrants to Kansas and Nebraska to suppose they are not able to govern themselves. We must not slur over an argument of this kind because it happens to tickle the ear. It must be met and answered. I admit that the emigrant to Kansas and Nebraska is competent to govern himself, but (the speaker rising to his full hight,) *I deny his right to govern any other person without that person's consent.*" That touched the very marrow of the matter, and revealed the whole difference between him and Douglas. The crowd understood it. They saw through the iniquity of "popular sovereignty," and the Kansas-Nebraska bill, and the applause which followed showed their appreciation of the clearness and thoroughness with which the speaker had exposed it.

When Mr. Lincoln concluded his speech, Mr. Douglas hastily took the stand, and said that he had been abused, "though in a perfectly courteous manner." He spoke until the adjournment of the meeting for supper, but touched only slightly upon the great questions which Mr. Lincoln had handled with so much power. That he felt his effort to be a failure, is evident from subsequent events soon to be recounted. Before closing, he insisted on his right to resume his speech in the evening, but when evening came he did not resume, and did not choose to resume. The speech was never concluded.

The next meeting between the two party champions took place at Peoria, though not by pre-arrangement. Mr. Lincoln followed Mr. Douglas to Peoria, and challenged him there, as he had done at Springfield. At Peoria, Mr. Lincoln's triumph was even more marked than at Springfield, for his antagonist had lost something of his assurance. He was a wounded and weakened man, indeed. He had become conscious that he was not invulnerable. He had been a witness of Mr. Lincoln's power over the people; and it is quite possible that his faith in his own position had been shaken. It was noticed at Peoria that his manner was much modified, and that he betrayed a lack of confidence in himself, not at all usual with him. Here, as at Springfield, Mr. Lincoln occupied more than three hours in the delivery of his speech, and it came down upon Mr. Douglas so crushingly that the doughty debater did not even undertake to reply to it.

It is to be remembered that Mr. Lincoln, in his political speeches, resorted to none of the tricks common among what are called stump speakers. He was thoroughly in earnest and always closely argumentative. If he told stories, it was not to amuse a crowd, but to illustrate a point. The real questions at issue engaged his entire attention, and he never undertook to raise a false issue or to dodge a real one. Indeed, he seemed incapable of the tricks so often resorted to for the discomfiture of an opponent. Fortunately, the Peoria speech was reported, and we have an opportunity of forming an intelligent judgment of its character and its power. One passage will suffice to illustrate both. Mr. Douglas had urged that the people of Illinois had no interest in the question of slavery in the territories—that it concerned only the people of the territories. This was in accordance with his own feeling, when he declared that he did not care whether slavery was "voted up or voted down" in Kansas. Mr. Lincoln opposed this on the broad ground of humanity and the terms of the declaration of independence; but to bring the matter more directly home, and to show that the people of Illinois had a practical interest in the question of slavery in the territories, he said:

"By the Constitution, each state has two senators—each has a number of representatives in proportion to the number of its people, and each has a number of presidential electors, equal to the whole number of its representatives and senators together. But in ascertaining the number of the people for the purpose, five slaves are counted as being equal to three whites. The slaves do not vote; they are only counted, and so used as to swell the influence of the white people's votes. The practical effect of this is more aptly shown by a comparison of the states of South Carolina and Maine. South Carolina has six representatives and so has Maine; South Carolina has eight presidential electors and so has Maine. This is precise equality so far; and of course they are equal in senators, each having two. Thus, in the control of the government, they are equals precisely. But how are they in the number of their white people? Maine has 581,813, while South Carolina has 274,567. Maine has twice as many as South Carolina, and 32,679 over. Thus each white man in South Carolina is more than the double of any man in Maine. This is all because South Carolina, besides her free people, has 387,984 slaves. The South Carolinian has precisely the same advantage over the white man in every other free state as well as in Maine. He is more than the double of any one of us. The same advantage, but not to the same extent, is held by all the citizens of the slave states over those of the free; and it is an absolute truth, without an exception, that there is no voter in any slave state but who has more legal power in the government than any voter in any free state. There is no instance of exact equality; and the disadvantage is against us the whole chapter through. This principle, in the aggregate, gives the slave states in the present Congress twenty additional representatives—being seven more than the whole majority by which they passed the Nebraska bill.

"Now all this is manifestly unfair; yet I do not mention it to complain of it, in so far as it is already settled. It is in the Constitution, and I do not for that cause, or any other cause, propose to destroy, or alter, or disregard the Constitution. I stand to it fairly, fully and firmly. But when I am told that I must leave it altogether to other people to say whether new partners are to be bred up and brought into the firm, on the same degrading terms against me, I respectfully demur. I insist that whether I shall be a whole man or only the half of one in compari-son with others is a question in which I am somewhat concerned; and one which no other man can have a sacred right of deciding for me. If I am wrong in this—if it really be a sacred right of self-government in the man who shall go to Nebraska to decide whether he will be the equal of me or the double of me, then, after he shall have exercised that right, and thereby shall have reduced me to a still smaller fraction of a man than I already am, I should like for some gentleman deeply skilled in the mystery of 'sacred rights,' to provide himself with a microscope, and peep about and find out if he can what has become of my 'sacred rights.' They will surely be too small for detection by the naked eye.

"Finally, I insist that if there is anything that it is the duty of the whole people to never intrust to any hands but their own, that thing is the preservation and perpetuity of their own liberties and institutions. And if they shall think, as I do, that the extension of slavery endangers them more than any or all other causes, how recreant to themselves if they submit the question, and with it, the fate of their country, to a mere handful of men bent only on temporary self-interest!"

Mr. Douglas might well excuse himself from any attempt to answer this argument, or escape from its inevitable logic, for it was unanswerable.

It was naturally the wish of Mr. Lincoln to continue these discussions in other parts of the state. He felt that a revolu-tion of public opinion was in progress—that parties were breaking up, and that he had his opponent at a disadvantage. But Mr. Douglas had had enough for this time. He wished to withdraw his forces before they were destroyed. He had had a heavy skirmish, and been worsted. He shrank from a continuance of the fight. The great and decisive battle was to come.

At the close of the debate, the two combatants held a con-ference, the result of which has been variously reported. One authority* states that Mr. Douglas sent for Mr. Lincoln, and told him that if he would speak no more during the cam-paign, he (Douglas) would go home and remain silent during the same period, and that this arrangement was agreed upon and its terms fulfilled. That there was a conference on the subject sought by Mr. Douglas, there is no doubt; and there

* William H. Herndon, Mr. Lincoln's partner.

is no doubt that Mr. Lincoln promised not to challenge him again to debate during the canvass, but abundant evidence exists that Mr. Lincoln did not leave the field at all, but spoke in various parts of the state.

Owing very materially to Mr. Lincoln's efforts, a political revolution swept the state. The old stronghold of the democratic party fell before the onslaughts made upon it, and, for the first time since the democratic party was organized, the legislature of Illinois was in the hands of the opposition. Politics were in a transitional, not to say chaotic state. The opposition was made up of whigs, Americans, and anti-Nebraska democrats. Among the men elected was Mr. Lincoln himself, who had been put in nomination while absent, by his friends in the county. As has already been stated, he resigned before taking his seat. His election was effected without consultation with him, and entirely against his wishes.

The excitement attending the election of this legislature did not die out with the election, for the new body had the responsibility of electing a United States senator. The old whigs elected had not relinquished the hope that, by some means, their party, which had in reality been broken up by the southern whigs in Congress going over to the democrats on the vote for the repeal of the Missouri Compromise, would again be united, while the anti-Nebraska democrats declined to go over to the whigs, supposing that, by clinging together, they could force the regular democracy of the state to come upon their ground. Here were two strongly antagonistic interests that were in some way to be harmonized, in order to beat the nominee of the great body of the democrats who still acknowledged the lead of Judge Douglas. The anti-Nebraska democrats refused to go into a nominating caucus with the whigs, and three candidates were placed in the field. Mr. Lincoln was the nominee of the whigs, Lyman Trumbull of the anti-Nebraska democrats, and General James Shields of the democrats of the Douglas school. After a number of undecisive ballots in the legislature, the democrats having dropped their candidate and adopted Governor Joel A. Matteson—a gentleman who had not committed himself to either side of the great question—it became possible for the supporters of Mr. Lincoln and Mr. Trumbull to elect one of those gentlemen, by a union of their forces. That Mr. Lincoln was ambitious for the honors of this high office there is no question, but he had seen Governor Matteson come within three votes of an election, and perceived that there was actual danger of his triumph. At this juncture, he begged his friends to leave him, and go for Mr. Trumbull. They yielded to his urgent entreaties, though it is said that strong men among them actually wept when they consented to do so. The consequence was the election of Mr. Trumbull, to the great astonishment of the democrats, who did not believe it possible for the opposition to unite. Their triumph was due simply to the magnanimity of Mr. Lincoln and his devotion to principle. He had no reproaches for those anti-Nebraska democrats who had refused to go for him, although his arguments had done more than those of any other man to give them their power, and he cared far more for the triumph of political truth and honor than for his own elevation. Mr. Lincoln never had reason to regret his self-sacrifice, for, upon the organization of the republican party, all the opposition parties found themselves together, and Mr. Lincoln became their foremost man.

CHAPTER XI.

THE legitimate fruit of the Kansas-Nebraska bill had already begun to manifest itself in Kansas. Emigrants from the eastern states and from the north-west began to pour into the territory; and those who had intended that it should become a slave state saw that their scheme was in danger. Mr. Douglas may not have cared whether slavery was "voted up or voted down" in Kansas, but slaveholders themselves showed a strong preference for voting it up, and not only for voting it up, but of backing up their votes by any requisite amount of violence. An organization in Platte County, Missouri, declared its readiness, when called upon by the citizens of Kansas, to assist in removing any and all emigrants who go there under the auspices of any of the "Emigrant Aid Societies;" which societies, by the way, were supposed to be organizations operating in the free state interest. This was in July, 1854, the Kansas-Nebraska bill having been passed during the previous May. One B. F. Stringfellow was the secretary of the organization, and a fortnight later he introduced, at a meeting of the society, resolutions declaring in favor of extending slavery into Kansas. Almon H. Reeder was appointed Governor, and arrived in the territory during the following October. At two elections, held within the succeeding six months, the polls were entirely controlled by ruffians from the Missouri side of the border, and those disturbances were fully inaugurated which illustrated the desperate desire of slavery to extend its territory and its power, the hypocrisy of Mr. Douglas and his friends in the declaration that the people of the territory should be perfectly free to choose and form their institutions, and the shameful subserviency of the government at Washington to the interests of the barbarous institution.

This much of the history of Kansas, in order to a perfect appreciation of a private letter of Mr. Lincoln to his Kentucky friend, Mr. Speed:

"SPRINGFIELD, August 24, 1855.

"DEAR SPEED:—You know what a poor correspondent I am. Ever since I received your very agreeable letter of the twenty-second of May, I have been intending to write you in answer to it. You suggest that in political action now, you and I would differ. You know I dislike slavery, and you fully admit the abstract wrong of it. So far, there is no cause of difference. But you say that sooner than yield your legal right to the slave, especially at the bidding of those who are not themselves interested, you would see the Union dissolved. I am not aware that any one is bidding you yield that right—very certainly I am not. I leave that matter entirely to yourself. I also acknowledge your rights and my obligations under the Constitution, in regard to your slaves. I confess I hate to see the poor creatures hunted down, and caught and carried back to their stripes and unrequited toil; but I bite my lip, and keep quiet. In 1841, you and I had together a tedious, low-water trip on a steamboat from Louisville to St. Louis. You may remember, as I well do, that from Louisville to the mouth of the Ohio, there were on board ten or a dozen slaves, shackled together with irons. That sight was a continual torment to me, and I see something like it every time I touch the Ohio, or any other slave border. It is not fair for you to assume that I have no interest in a thing which has, and continually exercises, the power of making me miserable. You ought rather to appreciate how much the great body of the people of the North do crucify their feelings, in order to maintain their loyalty to the Constitution and the Union.

"I do oppose the extension of slavery, because my judgment and feelings so prompt me; and I am under no obligations to the contrary. If, for this, you and I must differ, differ we must. You say if you were President you would send an army, and hang the leaders of the Missouri outrages upon the Kansas elections; still, if Kansas fairly votes herself a slave state, she must be admitted, or the Union must be dissolved. But how if she votes herself a slave state unfairly—that is, by the very means for which you would hang men? Must she still be admitted, or

10

the Union dissolved ? That will be the phase of the question when it first becomes a practical one.*

" In your assumption that there may be a fair decision of the slavery question in Kansas, I plainly see you and I would differ about the Nebraska law. I look upon that enactment not as a law, but as a violence, from the beginning. It was conceived in violence, passed in violence, is maintained in violence, and is being executed in violence. I say it was conceived in violence, because the destruction of the Missouri Compromise under the Constitution was nothing less than violence. It was passed in violence, because it could not have passed at all but for the votes of many members in violent disregard of the known will of their constituents. It is maintained in violence, because the elections since clearly demand its repeal, and the demand is openly disregarded.

" You say men ought to be hung for the way they are executing that law ; and I say the way it is being executed is quite as good as any of its antecedents. It is being executed in the precise way which was intended from the first, else, why does no Nebraska man express astonishment or condemnation ? Poor Reeder has been the only man who has been silly enough to believe that anything like fairness was ever intended, and he has been bravely undeceived.

" That Kansas will form a slave constitution, and with it, will ask to be admitted into the Union, I take to be an already settled question, and so settled by the very means you so pointedly condemn. By every principle of law ever held by any court, North or South, every negro taken to Kansas is free ; and in utter disregard of this—in the spirit of violence merely—that beautiful legislature gravely passes a law to hang men who shall venture to inform a negro of his legal rights. This is the substance and real object of the law. If, like Haman, they should hang upon the gallows of their own building, I shall not be among the mourners for their fate.

" In my humble sphere, I shall advocate the restoration of the Missouri Compromise so long as Kansas remains a territory ; and when, by all these foul means it seeks to come into the Union as a slave state, I shall oppose it. I am very loth, in any case, to withhold my assent to the enjoyment of property acquired or located in good faith ; but I do not admit that good faith in taking a negro to Kansas, to be held in slavery, is a possibility with any man. Any man who has sense enough to be the controller of his own property, has too much sense to misunderstand the outrageous character of the whole Nebraska business.

"But I digress. In my opposition to the admission of Kansas, I shall have some company ; but we may be beaten. If we are, I shall not, on that account, attempt to dissolve the Union. I think it probable, how-

*This confident prediction was made two years before the Lecompton Constitution was framed.

ever, that we shall be beaten. Standing as a unit among yourselves, you can, directly, and indirectly, bribe enough of our men to carry the day—as you could on an open proposition to establish monarchy. Get hold of some man in the North whose position and ability are such that he can make the support of your measure—whatever it may be—a democratic party necessity, and the thing is done.

"Apropos of this, let me tell you an anecdote. Douglas introduced the Nebraska bill in January. In February, afterwards, there was a called session of the Illinois legislature. Of the one hundred members comprising the two branches of that body, about seventy were democrats. The latter held a caucus in which the Nebraska bill was talked of, if not formally discussed. It was thereby discovered that just three, and no more, were in favor of the measure. In a day or two, Douglas' orders came on to have resolutions passed, approving the bill, and they were passed by large majorities!!! The truth of this is vouched for by a bolting democratic member. The masses, too, democratic as well as, whig, were even more unanimous against it, but as soon as the party necessity of supporting it became apparent, the way the democracy began to see the wisdom and justice of it was perfectly astonishing.

"You say if Kansas fairly votes herself a free state, as a Christian you will rather rejoice at it. All decent slaveholders talk that way, and I do not doubt their candor. But they never vote that way. Although, in a private letter or conversation you will express your preference that Kansas shall be free, you would vote for no man for Congress who would say the same thing publicly. No such man could be elected, from any district, or any slave state. You think Stringfellow & Co. ought to be hung; and yet you will vote for the exact type and representation of Stringfellow. The slave-breeders and slave-traders are a small and detested class among you, and yet in politics they dictate the course of all of you, and are as completely your masters as you are the masters of your own negroes.

"You inquire where I now stand. That is a disputed point. I think I am a whig: but others say there are no whigs, and that I am an abolitionist. When I was in Washington, I voted for the Wilmot Proviso as good as forty times, and I never heard of any attempt to unwhig me for that. I now do no more than oppose the extension of slavery. I am not a Know-Nothing,—that is certain. How could I be? How can any one who abhors the oppression of the negroes be in favor of degrading classes of white people? Our progress in degeneracy appears to me to be pretty rapid. As a nation, we began by declaring that 'all men are created equal.' We now practically read it 'all men are created equal except negroes.' When the Know-Nothings get control, it will read, 'all men are created equal except negroes and foreigners and Catholics.' When it comes to that, I should prefer emigrating to some country where they make no pretense of loving liberty—to Russia for instance, where despotism can be taken pure, and without the base alloy of hypocrisy.

"Your friend forever,

"A. LINCOLN."

This letter, written with perfect freedom to an old personal friend attached to the interests of slavery in a slave state, gives with wonderful clearness the state of the slavery question at the time, and Mr. Lincoln's own views and feelings. Events justified the writer's judgment, and verified his predictions. Mr. Lincoln still considered himself a whig. The name was one he loved, and the old party associations were very precious to him. But he was passing through the weaning process, and was realizing more and more, with the passage of every month, that there could be no resuscitation of the dead or dying organization. The interests of slavery had severed from it forever that portion that had made it a powerful national party. It could not extend itself an inch south of Mason's and Dixon's line. The slavery question was the great question. Opposition to the extension and encroachments of slavery was sectional, and any party which exercised this opposition, however broad its views might be, was necessarily sectional. Mr. Lincoln's logical mind soon discovered this, and accordingly we find him, May 29th, 1856, attending a convention at Bloomington, of those who were opposed to the democratic party. Here, and with Mr. Lincoln's powerful assistance, the republican party of Illinois was organized, a platform adopted, a state ticket nominated, and delegates were appointed to the National Republican Convention in Philadelphia, which was to be held on the seventeenth of the following month.

There is no doubt that, from the date of this meeting, he felt himself more a free man in politics than ever before. His hatred of slavery had been constantly growing, and now he was the member of a party whose avowed purpose it was to resist the extension of slavery, and to shut it up in the territory where it held its only rights under the Constitution.

The speech which he made on this occasion was one of distinguished power and eloquence. Mr. Scripps, in the little sketch of his life to which an allusion has already been made in this volume, says: "Never was an audience more completely electrified by human eloquence. Again and again during the progress of its delivery, they sprang to their feet and upon the benches, and testified by long continued shouts and the waving of hats, how deeply the speaker had wrought upon their minds and hearts. It fused the mass of hitherto incongruous elements into perfect homogeneity, and from that day to the present they have worked together in harmonious and fraternal union.

Mr. Lincoln was now regarded, not only by the republicans of Illinois, but by all the western states, as their first man. Accordingly they presented his name to the national convention as their candidate for the vice-presidency. On the informal ballot, he received one hundred and ten votes to two hundred and fifty-nine for Mr. Dayton. This, of course, decided the matter against him, but the vote was a complimentary one, and was Mr. Lincoln's formal introduction to the nation. Mr. Lincoln labored with his accustomed zeal during the campaign for Fremont and Dayton, the republican nominees, and had the pleasure, at the end of the canvass, of finding the state revolutionized. Colonel William H. Bissell, the opposition candidate for Governor, was elected by a notable majority, although there were men enough who were not aware that the whig party was dead to give the electoral vote to Mr. Buchanan, through their support of Mr. Fillmore.

A little incident occurred during the campaign that illustrated Mr. Lincoln's readiness in turning a political point. He was making a speech at Charleston, Coles County, when a voice called out, "Mr. Lincoln, is it true that you entered this state barefoot, driving a yoke of oxen?" Mr. Lincoln paused for full half a minute, as if considering whether he should notice such cruel impertinence, and then said that he thought he could prove the fact by at least a dozen men in the crowd, any one of whom was more respectable than his questioner. But the question seemed to inspire him, and he went on to show what free institutions had done for himself, and to exhibit the evils of slavery to the white man wherever it existed, and asked if it was not natural that he should hate slavery, and agitate against it. "Yes," said he, "we will speak for freedom and against slavery, as long as the Constitution of our country guarantees free speech, until everywhere on this wide land, the sun shall shine and the rain shall fall and the wind shall blow upon no man who goes forth to unrequited toil."

From this time to the close of his life, he was almost entirely absorbed by political affairs. He still took charge of important cases in court, and practiced his profession at intervals; but he was regarded as a political man, and had many responsibilities thrown upon him by the new organization. During the summer succeeding the presidential canvass, and after Mr. Buchanan had taken his seat, Mr. Douglas was invited by the grand jury of the United States District Court for Southern Illinois, to deliver a speech at Springfield when the court was in session. In that speech, the senator showed the progress he had made in his departure from the doctrines of the fathers, by announcing that the framers of the Declaration of Independence, when they asserted that "all men are created equal," only meant to say that "British subjects on this continent were equal to British subjects born and residing in Great Britain." Mr. Lincoln was invited by a large number of citizens to reply to this speech, and did so. After showing in his own quiet and ingenious way the absurdity of this assumption of Judge Douglas, telling his auditors that, as they were preparing to celebrate the Fourth of July, and would read the Declaration, he would like to have them read it in Judge Douglas' way, viz: "We hold these truths to be self-evident, that all British subjects who were on this continent eighty-one years ago, were created equal to all British subjects born and then residing in Great Britain,"—he said: "And now I appeal to all—to democrats as well as others: are you really willing that the Declaration shall thus be frittered away?—thus left no more, at most, than an interesting memorial of the dead past?—thus shorn of its vitality and its practical value, and left without the germ or even the suggestion of the inalienable rights of man in it?" Then Mr. Lincoln added his opinion as to what the authors of the Declaration intended; and it has probably never been stated with a more catholic spirit, or in choicer terms:

"I think the authors of that notable instrument intended to include all men; but they did not intend to declare all men equal in all respects. They did not mean to say all were equal in color, size, intellect, moral developments, or social capacity. They defined with tolerable distinctness in what respects they did consider all men equal—equal in certain inalienable rights, among which are life, liberty and the pursuit of happiness. This they said and this they meant. They did not mean to assert the obvious untruth that all were then actually enjoying that equality, nor yet that they were about to confer it upon them. In fact, they had no power to confer such a boon. They meant simply to declare the right, so that the enforcement of it might follow as fast as circumstances should permit. They meant to set up a standard maxim for free society, which should be familiar to all and revered by all; constantly looked to, constantly labored for, and, even though never perfectly attained, constantly approximated, and thereby constantly spreading and deepening its influence, and augmenting the happiness and value of life to all people of all colors everywhere."

The project of making Kansas a slave state was in full progress. The event which Mr. Lincoln had so distinctly prophesied—the formation of a pro-slavery constitution by unfair means and alien agents—was in full view; and those who were interested in it did their best to prepare the minds of the people for it. Political morality seemed at its lowest ebb. A whole party was bowing to the behests of slavery, and those who were opposed to the institution and the power born of it had become stupefied in the presence of its bold assumptions and rapid advances. People had ceased to be surprised at any of its claims, and any exhibition of its spirit and policy. If Mr. Buchanan had any conscientious scruples, they were easily overborne, and he lent himself to the schemes of the plotters. A pro-slavery legislature was elected mainly by non-residents, at an election in which the free state men, who numbered three-fourths of the entire population, refused to participate, on account of illegality. This legislature, meeting at Lecompton, passed an act providing for the election of a convention to form a state constitution, preparatory to asking an admission into the Union. In the election of this convention, the free state men took no part, on the ground that the legislature which ordered it had no legal authority. About two thousand votes were cast, while the legal voters in the territory numbered more than ten thousand. The Lecompton Convention framed, of course, a pro-slavery constitution. It is not necessary to recount the means by which this constitution was subsequently overthrown, and one prohibiting slavery substituted in its place. It is sufficient for the present purpose to state that upon the promulgation of the constitution formed at Lecompton, Robert J. Walker, then Governor of Kansas, went immediately to Washington to remonstrate against its adoption by Congress, and that before he could reach the capitol it had received the approval of the President.

These facts have place here to give the basis of the political relations between Mr. Lincoln and Mr. Douglas; for they were approaching their great struggle. The senatorial term of Mr. Douglas was drawing to a close, and he wished to be indorsed by the people of Illinois, and returned to the Senate. The events of the previous year had shown him that a great political revolution was in progress, and that his seat was actually in danger. He saw what was going on in Kansas, and knew that the iniquities in progress there would be laid at his door. It was he who, in a time of peace, had opened the flood-gates of agitation. It was he who had given to the slave-power what it had not asked for, but could not consistently refuse. It was he who had gratuitously offered the slave-power the privilege of making territory forever set apart to freedom its own, if it could. He had divided his own party in his own state, and was losing his confidence as to his own political future. That he knew just what was coming in Kansas, and knew what the effect would be upon himself, is evident in the speech he made at Springfield, from Mr. Lincoln's reply to which a passage has already been quoted. In this he undertook to shift to the shoulders of the republican party the burden he felt to be pressing upon his own. Speaking of Kansas, he said: "The law under which her delegates are about to be elected is believed to be just and fair in all its objects and provisions. * * * If any portion of the inhabitants, acting under the advice of political leaders in distant states, shall choose to absent themselves from the polls, and withhold their votes with the view of leaving the free state democrats in the minority, and thus securing a pro-slavery constitution in opposition to the wishes of a majority of the people living under it, let the responsibility rest on those who, for partisan purposes, will sacrifice the principles they profess to cherish and promote. Upon them and upon the political party for whose benefit and under the direction of whose leaders they act, let the blame be visited of fastening upon the people of a new state institutions repugnant to their feelings and in violation of their wishes."

In a subsequent passage of this same speech, he amplifies these points, and both passages show that he knew the nature of the constitution that would be framed, knew that the free state men would not vote at all because they believed the movement was an illegal one, and knew that he and his party would be held responsible for the outrage. It is further to be said that, by his words on this occasion, he fully committed himself, in advance, to whatever the Lecompton Convention might do. "The present election law in Kansas is acknowledged to be fair and just," he says. "Kansas is about to speak for herself," he declares. By these words alone, he was morally committed to whatever might be the conclusions of the convention. This is to be remembered, for Mr. Douglas soon found that he could not shift the burden of the Kansas iniquity upon the opposition, and that his only hope of a re-election to the senate depended upon his taking issue with the administration on this very case, and becoming the champion of the anti-Lecompton men.

CHAPTER XII.

ONE of the most remarkable passages in Mr. Lincoln's history was his contest with Senator Douglas, in 1858, for the seat in the United States Senate which was soon to be vacated by the expiration of the term for which the latter was elected. Frequent allusion has been made to this already; but before proceeding to its description something further should be said of Mr. Douglas himself.

Mr. Douglas was but little more than twenty years of age when, in 1833, he entered Illinois. He was poor—penniless, indeed. The first money he earned in the state was as the clerk of an auction sale. His next essay was in teaching school. He began to practice law during the second year, and at the age of twenty-two was elected Attorney General of the state. He resigned this office in 1835, and was elected a member of the legislature. It was here that he and Abraham Lincoln met for the first time. In 1837, before he was twenty-five years old, he received the democratic nomination for Congress, and was only beaten by a majority of five votes. In 1840, he was appointed secretary of the state of Illinois, and in 1843 he was elected to Congress, and re-elected in 1844 and 1846. Before he took his seat under the last election, he was elected to the United States Senate; and his second term of service in this august body was about expiring at the present point of this history.

The career of Mr. Douglas had been one of almost uninterrupted political success. He was the recognized leader of the democratic party of Illinois, and had been known and felt as a positive power in national legislation. He had very decided opinions upon all the great questions passed upon by Congress, and, though not unfrequently at variance with the administrations he had himself assisted to place in power, his influence was great in whatever direction he might choose to exert it. He accomplished much in establishing and nourishing the prosperity of Illinois. No man did so much as Mr. Douglas for securing those magnificent grants of land which contributed to the development of his adopted state. To the material interests of Illinois, and the preservation of the power of the democratic party in that state, he was thoroughly devoted; and that party honored him with its entire confidence and almost unquestioning support. He was their first man; and they bestowed upon him, during his life, more honor than they ever gave to any other man living on their territory.

Mr. Lincoln had watched this man, with admiration for his tact and respect for his power with the people. He had seen him winning the highest honors in their gift, and, if he did not envy him, it was not because he was not ambitious. It was because nothing so mean as envy could have place in him. That he regarded Mr. Douglas as an unscrupulous man in the use of means for securing his ambitious ends, there is no doubt; and although he would have refused honor and office on the terms on which Mr. Douglas received them, he was much impressed by the dignities with which the Senator was invested, and felt that the power he held was a precious, aye, a priceless, possession.

From the original manuscript of one of Mr. Lincoln's speeches, these words are transferred to this biography: "Twenty-two years ago, Judge Douglas and I first became acquainted. We were both young then—he a trifle younger than I. Even then we were both ambitious,—I, perhaps, quite as much so as he. With me, the race of ambition has been a failure—a flat failure; with him, it has been one of splendid success. His name fills the nation, and is not unknown even in foreign lands. I affect no contempt for the high eminence he has reached. So reached that the oppressed of my species might have shared with me in the elevation, I would rather stand on that eminence than wear the richest crown that ever pressed a monarch's brow."

This extract touches the points of similarity between the two men, and their points of difference. Mr. Lincoln was far from insensible to the honors of Mr. Douglas' position; but he would not have them at the price Mr. Douglas had paid for them. The oppressed of his species had not shared with Mr. Douglas in his elevation. The slave had had none of his consideration; and he was in league with the slave's oppressor. It would not have been pleasant to Mr. Lincoln to wear the honors of Mr. Douglas, if, with them, he had been obliged to carry the responsibility of extending or giving latitude and lease to an institution which made chattels of men. Mr. Douglas looked upon slavery either with indifference or approval. He had publicly said that he did not care whether slavery was "voted up or voted down" in the territories. Mr. Lincoln regarded slavery as a great moral, social and political wrong. Here was the vital difference between the two, recognized as such by Mr. Lincoln himself.

After the adoption of the Lecompton Constitution in Kansas, Mr. Douglas having foreseen its character, and having virtually committed himself to it in advance—having, indeed, undertaken to make the republican party morally responsible for its existence and adoption, a change seems to have come over his opinions. Before he departed for Washington, to attend the session of 1857 and 1858, it was whispered that he was about to break with the administration on the Lecompton business. It is always pleasant to give men credit for the best motives; and those under which he acted may have been the best. To oppose that constitution was certainly not inconsistent with his pet doctrine "popular sovereignty" when taken by itself, for nothing was more easily demonstrable than the fact that that constitution was not the act and deed of the people of Kansas—that it was in no sense an expression of their will. While this is true, it is proper to remember that

Mr. Douglas was shrewd enough to see that he could not carry the burden of the Lecompton Constitution through the canvass for the senatorial prize, then imminent. The outrage was too flagrant to be ignored, and the facts too notorious to be disputed. He was also shrewd enough to see that his opposition to the Lecompton fraud would take from the republican party some of its best capital, and greatly distract the opposition in their efforts to defeat him.

During that session of Congress Mr. Douglas fought a gallant and manly fight against the administration on the Lecompton question, and, on that question, voted and labored with the republicans. It was a bold step. Without Mr. Douglas, it is easy to see that the Lecompton Constitution would have been impossible. He voluntarily threw open the territory to this outrage. Then he tried to kill his own legitimate child. He forsook the men whom he had led into the great iniquity. The republicans were grateful for his aid, and were naturally drawn to him in sympathy because, for his efforts on behalf of justice in Kansas, he had incurred the enmity of Mr. Buchanan, who was regarded as a most willing tool in the hands of the slave power.

The democratic state convention of Illinois assembled on the 21st of April, 1858, and endorsed Mr. Douglas in his position as an anti-Lecompton man. They placed a state ticket in the field, and engineered the canvass with such skill and vigor that the administration, through its office-holders, could make no headway against them. The power of Mr. Douglas over the politicians and masses in his own state, was never better illustrated than during this campaign, when all the patronage of the federal government could do nothing to defeat him. Before the close of the session, Mr. Douglas went home to look after his interests, and to prepare for the great campaign of his life.

A large number of republicans in the eastern states who had not known Mr. Douglas at home, and who had witnessed his bold and gallant fight with the administration and the slave-power in the senate, expressed the wish that their friends in

Illinois might find it in the line of their duty to aid in returning him to the senate. The republicans of Illinois, however, felt that they knew the man better, and that their duty did not lie in that direction at all. They urged that Mr. Douglas did not agree with them in a single point of doctrine—that he had differed with the administration merely on a question of fact, whether the Lecompton Constitution was the act and deed of the people of Kansas. They averred that he adhered to the outrageous decision of the Supreme Court in the Dred Scott case—that a negro cannot sue in a United States court, and that Congress cannot prohibit slavery in the territories—and that they dared not trust Mr. Douglas. To this it was replied that Mr. Douglas was coming over to the republican party as fast as he could carry his followers with him, and that his extraordinary hold upon the masses of the democratic party at the North would enable him to bring to the republican ranks a reinforcement which would prove irresistible at the approaching presidential election. The rejoinder of the Illinois republicans was that the probability of any sincere change of faith in Mr. Douglas was too remote and uncertain to warrant them in abandoning an organization which had been formed to advance a great and just cause, and which, once dissolved, could not be re-formed in time to render efficient service in the election of 1860. Quite a controversy grew out of the differences between the Illinois republicans and their eastern advisers, and no small degree of bitterness was engendered. The party in Illinois was nearly a unit in its views, but the controversy had undoubtedly the influence to loosen the hold of the organization upon some of its members. The effect was temporary, however, for the issues of the campaign were so thoroughly discussed, and the discussions themselves were so generally listened to, or read in the journals of the day, that it is doubtful whether Mr. Douglas gained any appreciable advantage from the controversy, or the sympathy of republicans in other states.

The republican state convention met at Springfield on the sixteenth of June, nearly two months after the assembling of the democratic convention. Aside from the senatorial question, there was but little interest in the proceedings. For state officers, only a treasurer and a superintendent of public instruction were to be nominated, and, besides these officers, only the members of a legislature were to be elected. Nearly six hundred delegates were present in the convention, and they, with their alternates, completed a round thousand of earnest men, gathered from all parts of the state. The fifth resolution adopted on this occasion covers the grand issue made with Judge Douglas.

" That while we deprecate all interference on the part of political organizations with the judiciary, if such action is limited to its appropriate sphere, yet we cannot refrain from expressing our condemnation of the principles and tendencies of the extra-judicial opinions of a majority of the Judges of the Supreme Court of the United States, in the matter of Dred Scott, wherein the political heresy is put forth that the federal constitution extends slavery into all the territories of the Republic, and so maintains it that neither Congress nor the people through the territorial legislature can by law abolish it. We hold that Congress possesses sovereign power over the territories, and has the right to govern and control them whilst they remain in a territorial condition, and that it is the duty of the general government to protect the territories from the curse of slavery, and to preserve the public domain for the occupation of free men and free labor; and we declare that no power on earth can carry and maintain slavery in the states against the will of their people and the provisions of their constitutions and laws; and we fully indorse the recent decision of the Supreme Court of our own state, which declares that property in persons is repugnant to the Constitution and laws of Illinois, and that all persons within its jurisdiction are presumed to be free, and that slavery, where it exists, is a municipal regulation, without any extra-territorial operation."

If there were men in the convention who had at first been affected by the representations of the republicans in the eastern states, the action of the democratic convention which met in April had restored their determination to stand by their party and its candidates. That convention had denounced the republicans, had indorsed the old democratic platform of the party adopted at Cincinnati in national convention, and, while it approved the course of Senator Douglas, failed to say one word in condemnation of the course and principles, or, rather, lack of principles, of Mr. Buchanan and his administration. The republican convention had hardly assembled before it was discovered that there was entire unanimity for Mr. Lincoln, as their nominee in opposition to Mr. Douglas. When a banner from Chicago was borne into the convention, inscribed with the words—" Cook County for Abraham Lincoln "—the whole convention rose to its feet, and gave three cheers for the candidate whom it was proposed to place in the field in opposition to the champion of " popular sovereignty." That the convention was embarrassed and doubtful as to results, there is no question. Mr. Douglas had the sympathy of many republicans abroad, he had attacked a hated administration with great vigor and persistence, he had the enmity of that administration, and, in the state, he had the advantage of an unjust apportionment of legislative districts, by which not less than ninety-three thousand people were virtually disfranchised.* Though it was not according to the wish of many of the members of the convention to make a formal nomination for the senate, yet, as Mr. Douglas had already declared that it was the intention to use Mr. Lincoln's name during the canvass, and to adopt another name in the legislature, the following resolution was brought forward, and unanimously adopted :

"That Hon. ABRAHAM LINCOLN is our first and only choice for United States Senator, to fill the vacancy about to be created by the expiration of Mr. Douglas' term of office."

The anxiety of the convention to see and hear their chosen man and champion was intense; and frequent calls were made for him during the day. That Mr. Lincoln expected the nomination, and had prepared himself for it, is evident. It was announced at length that he would address the members of the convention at the State House in the evening. During the day, he was busy in giving the finishing touches to his speech, which had been prepared with unusual care, every

* Scripps, p. 24.

sentence having been carefully weighed. He had put into it what he believed to be the real issues of the campaign, and had laid out in it the ground upon which he proposed to stand, and fight his battles. Before going to the hall, he entered his law office, where Mr. Herndon, his partner, was sitting, and turned the key against all intrusion. Taking out his manuscript, he read to Mr. Herndon the first paragraph of his speech, and asked him for his opinion of it. Mr. Herndon replied that it was all true, but he doubted whether it was good policy to give it utterance at that time. "That makes no difference," responded Mr. Lincoln. "It *is* the truth, and the nation is entitled to it." Then, alluding to a quotation which he had made from the Bible—"A house divided against itself cannot stand," he said that he wished to give an illustration familiar to all, "that he who reads may run." "The proposition is true," said Mr. Lincoln, "and has been true for six thousand years, and I will deliver it as it is written."

At eight o'clock, the hall of the House of Representatives was filled to its utmost capacity, and when Mr. Lincoln appeared he was received with the most tumultuous applause. The speech which he made on that occasion is so full of meaning, so fraught with prophecy, so keen in its analysis, so irresistible in its logic, so profoundly intelligent concerning the politics of the time, and, withal, so condensed in the expression of every part, that no proper idea can be given of it through any description or abbreviation. It must be given entire.

Mr. Lincoln said:

"If we could first know where we are, and whither we are tending, we could better judge what to do, and how to do it. We are now far into the fifth year, since a policy was initiated with the avowed object and confident promise of putting an end to slavery agitation. Under the operation of that policy, that agitation has not only not ceased, but has constantly augmented. In my opinion, it will not cease, until a crisis shall have been reached and passed. 'A house divided against itself cannot stand.' I believe this government cannot endure permanently half slave and half free. I do not expect the Union to be dissolved—I do not expect the house to fall—but I do expect it will cease to be divided. It will become all one thing, or all the other. Either

11

the opponents of slavery will arrest the further spread of it, and place it where the public mind shall rest in the belief that it is in the course of ultimate extinction; or its advocates will push it forward, till it shall become alike lawful in all the states, old as well as new—North as well as South.

"Have we no tendency to the latter condition?

"Let any one who doubts, carefully contemplate that now almost complete legal combination—piece of machinery, so to speak—compounded of the Nebraska doctrine, and the Dred Scott decision. Let him consider not only what work the machinery is adapted to do, and how well adapted; but also, let him study the history of its construction, and trace, if he can, or rather fail, if he can, to trace the evidences of design, and concert of action among its chief architects, from the beginning.

"The new year of 1854 found slavery excluded from more than half the states by State Constitutions, and from most of the national territory by Congressional prohibition. Four days later, commenced the struggle which ended in repealing that Congressional prohibition. This opened all the national territory to slavery, and was the first point gained.

"But, so far, Congress only had acted; and an indorsement by the people, real or apparent, was indispensable, to save the point already gained, and give chance for more.

"This necessity had not been overlooked; but had been provided for, as well as might be, in the notable argument of 'squatter sovereignty,' otherwise called 'sacred right of self-government,' which latter phrase, though expressive of the only rightful basis of any government, was so perverted in this attempted use of it as to amount to just this: That if any *one* man choose to enslave *another*, no *third* man shall be allowed to object. That argument was incorporated into the Nebraska bill itself, in the language which follows: 'It being the true intent and meaning of this act not to legislate slavery into any territory or state, nor to exclude it therefrom; but to leave the people thereof perfectly free to form and regulate their domestic institutions in their own way, subject only to the Constitution of the United States.' Then opened the roar of loose declamation in favor of 'squatter sovereignty,' and 'sacred right of self-government.' 'But,' said opposition members, 'let us amend the bill so as to expressly declare that the people of the territory may exclude slavery.' 'Not we,' said the friends of the measure; and down they voted the amendment.

"While the Nebraska bill was passing through Congress, a *law case* involving the question of a negro's freedom, by reason of his owner having voluntarily taken him first into a free state and then into a territory covered by the Congressional prohibition, and held him as a slave for a long time in each, was passing through the United States Circuit Court for the District of Missouri; and both Nebraska bill and lawsuit were brought to a decision in the same month of May, 1854. The negro's name was 'Dred Scott,' which name now designates the decision finally made in the case. Before the then next presidential election, the law case came to, and was argued in the Supreme Court of the United States: but the decision of it was deferred until after the election. Still, before the election. Senator Trumbull, on the floor of the Senate, requested the leading advocate of the Nebraska bill to state *his opinion* whether the people of a territory can constitutionally exclude slavery from their limits; and the latter answers. ' That is a question for the Supreme Court.'

" The election came. Mr. Buchanan was elected, and the indorsement, such as it was, secured. That was the second point gained. The indorsement, however, fell short of a clear popular majority by nearly four hundred thousand votes, and so, perhaps, was not overwhelmingly reliable and satisfactory. The outgoing President, in his last annual message, as impressively as possible echoed back upon the people the weight and authority of the indorsement. The Supreme Court met again; did not announce their decision, but ordered a re-argument. The presidential inauguration came, and still no decision of the court; but the incoming president in his inaugural address fervently exhorted the people to abide by the forthcoming decision, whatever it might be. Then, in a few days, came the decision.

" The reputed author of the Nebraska bill finds an early occasion to make a speech at this capital indorsing the Dred Scott decision, and vehemently denouncing all opposition to it. The new president, too, seizes the early occasion of the Silliman letter to indorse and strongly construe that decision, and to express his astonishment that any different view had ever been entertained!

" At length a squabble springs up between the president and the author of the Nebraska bill, on the mere question of *fact*, whether the Lecompton Constitution was or was not, in any just sense, made by the people of Kansas; and in that quarrel the latter declares that all he wants is a fair vote for the people, and that he cares not whether slavery be voted *down* or voted *up*. I do not understand his declaration that he cares not whether slavery be voted down or voted up to be intended by him other than as an apt definition of the policy he would impress upon the public mind—the principle for which he declares he has suffered so much, and is ready to suffer to the end. And well may he cling to that principle. If he has any parental feeling, well may he cling to it. That principle is the only shred left of his original Nebraska doctrine. Under the Dred Scott decision squatter sovereignty squatted out of existence, tumbled down like temporary scaffolding—like the mould at the foundry, served through one blast and fell back into loose sand—helped to carry an election, and then was kicked to the winds. His late joint struggle with the republicans, against the Lecompton Constitution, involves nothing of the original Nebraska doctrine. That struggle was made on a point—the right of a people to make their own constitution—upon which he and the republicans have never differed. .

"The several points of the Dred Scott decision, in connection with Senator Douglas' 'care not policy, constitute the piece of machinery, in its present state of advancement. This was the third point gained. The working points of that machinery are:

"First, That no negro slave, imported as such from Africa, and no descendant of such slave, can ever be a citizen of any state, in the sense of that term as used in the Constitution of the United States. This point is made in order to deprive the negro, in every possible event, of the benefit of that provision of the United States Constitution, which declares that 'The citizens of each state shall be entitled to all privileges and immunities of citizens in the several states.'

"Secondly, That 'subject to the Constitution of the United States,' neither Congress nor a territorial legislature can exclude slavery from any United States territory. This point is made in order that individual men may fill up the territories with slaves, without danger of losing them as property, and thus to enhance the chances of permanency to the institution through all the future.   •

"Thirdly, That whether the holding a negro in actual slavery in a free state, makes him free, as against the holder, the United States courts will not decide, but will leave to be decided by the courts of any slave state the negro may be forced into by the master. This point is made, not to be pressed immediately; but, if acquiesced in for awhile, and apparently indorsed by the people at an election, then to sustain the logical conclusion that what Dred Scott's master might lawfully do with Dred Scott, in the free state of Illinois, every other master may lawfully do with any other one, or one thousand slaves, in Illinois, or in any other free state.

"Auxiliary to all this, and working hand in hand with it, the Nebraska doctrine, or what is left of it, is to educate and mould public opinion, at least northern public opinion, not to care whether slavery is voted down or voted up. This shows exactly where we now are; and partially, also, whither we are tending.

"It will throw additional light on the latter, to go back, and run the mind over the string of historical facts already stated. Several things will now appear less dark and mysterious than they did when they were transpiring. The people were to be left 'perfectly free,' 'subject only to the Constitution.' What the Constitution had to do with it, outsiders could not then see. Plainly enough now, it was an exactly fitted niche, for the Dred Scott decision to afterward come in, and declare the perfect freedom of the people to be just no freedom at all. Why was the amendment, expressly declaring the right of the people, voted down? Plainly enough now: the adoption of it would have spoiled the niche for the Dred Scott decision. Why was the court decision held up? Why even a senator's individual opinion withheld, till after the presidential election? Plainly enough now: the speaking out then would have damaged the perfectly free argument upon which the election was to be carried. Why the out-going president's felicitation on the indorsement? Why the delay of a re-argument? Why the incoming president's advance exhortation in favor of the decision? These things look like the cautious patting and petting of a spirited horse preparatory to mounting him, when it is dreaded that he may give the rider a fall. And why the hasty after-indorsement of the decision by the president and others?

"We cannot absolutely know that all these exact adaptations are the result of preconcert. But when we see a lot of framed timbers, different portions of which we know have been gotten out at different times and places and by different workmen—Stephen, Franklin, Roger and James, for instance—and when we see these timbers joined together, and see they exactly make the frame of a house or a mill, all the tenons and mortices exactly fitting, and all the lengths and proportions of the different pieces exactly adapted to their respective places, and not a piece too many or too few—not omitting even scaffolding—or, if a single piece be lacking, we see the place in the frame exactly fitted and prepared yet to bring such piece in—in such a case, we find it impossible not to believe that Stephen and Franklin and Roger and James all understood one another from the beginning, and all worked upon a common plan or draft drawn up before the first blow was struck.

"It should not be overlooked that, by the Nebraska bill, the people of a *state* as well as territory, were to be left 'perfectly free,' 'subject only to the Constitution.' Why mention a state? They were legislating for territories, and not for or about states. Certainly the people of a state are and ought to be subject to the Constitution of the United States; but why is mention of this lugged into this merely territorial law? Why are the people of a territory and the people of a state therein lumped together, and their relation to the Constitution therein treated as being precisely the same? While the opinion of the court, by Chief Justice Taney, in the Dred Scott case, and the separate opinions of all the concurring judges, expressly declare that the Constitution of the United States neither permits Congress nor a territorial legislature to exclude slavery from any United States territory, they all omit to declare whether or not the same Constitution permits a state, or the people of a state, to exclude it. *Possibly*, this is a mere omission;

but who can be quite sure, if McLean or Curtis had sought to get into the opinion a declaration of unlimited power in the people of a state to exclude slavery from their limits, just as Chase and Mace sought to get such declaration, in behalf of the people of a territory, into the Nebraska bill;—I ask, who can be quite sure that it would not have been voted down in the one case as it had been in the other? The nearest approach to the point of declaring the power of a state over slavery, is made by Judge Nelson. He approaches it more than once, using the precise idea, and almost the language, too, of the Nebraska act. On one occasion, his exact language is, 'except in cases where the power is restrained by the Constitution of the United States, the law of the state is supreme over the subject of slavery within its jurisdiction.' In what cases the power of the states is so restrained by the United States Constitution, is left an open question, precisely as the same question as to the restraint on the power of the territories was left open in the Nebraska act. Put this and that together, and we have another nice little niche, which we may, ere long, see filled with another Supreme Court decision, declaring that the Constitution of the United States does not permit a *state* to exclude slavery from its limits. And this may especially be expected if the doctrine of 'care not whether slavery be voted down or voted up,' shall gain upon the public mind sufficiently to give promise that such a decision can be maintained when made.

"Such a decision is all that slavery now lacks of being alike lawful in all the states. Welcome, or unwelcome, such decision is probably coming, and will soon be upon us, unless the power of the present political dynasty shall be met and overthrown. We shall lie down pleasantly dreaming that the people of Missouri are on the verge of making their state free, and we shall awake to the reality instead, that the Supreme Court has made Illinois a slave state. To meet and overthrow the power of that dynasty, is the work now before all those who would prevent that consummation. That is what we have to do. How can we best do it?

"There are those who denounce us openly to their own friends, and yet whisper us softly that Senator Douglas is the aptest instrument there is with which to effect that object. They wish us to *infer* all, from the fact that he now has a little quarrel with the present head of the dynasty; and that he has regularly voted with us on a single point, upon which he and we have never differed. They remind us that he is a great man, and that the largest of us are very small ones. Let this be granted. But 'a living dog is better than a dead lion.' Judge Douglas, if not a dead lion, for this work, is at least a caged and toothless one. How can he oppose the advances of slavery? He don't care anything about it. His avowed mission is impressing the 'public heart' to *care nothing about it*. A leading Douglas democratic newspaper thinks Douglas' superior talent will be needed to resist the revival of the African slave trade. Does Douglas believe an effort to revive that trade is approaching? He has not said so. Does he really think so? But if it is, how can he resist it? For years he has labored to prove it a sacred right of white men to take negro slaves into the new territories. Can he possibly show that it is less a sacred right to buy them where they can be bought cheapest? And unquestionably they can be bought cheaper in Africa than in Virginia. He has done all in his power to reduce the whole question of slavery to one of a mere right of property; and as such, how can he oppose the foreign slave trade—how can he refuse that trade in that 'property' shall be 'perfectly free'—unless he does it as a protection to the home production? And as the home producers will probably not ask the protection, he will be wholly without a ground of opposition.

" Senator Douglas holds, we know, that a man may rightfully be wiser to-day than he was yesterday—that he may rightfully change when he finds himself wrong. But can we, for that reason, run ahead, and infer that he will make any particular change of which he himself has given no intimation? Can we safely base our action upon any such vague inference? Now, as ever, I wish not to misrepresent Judge Douglas' position, question his motives, or do aught that can be personally offensive to him. Whenever, if ever, he and we can come together on principle so that our cause may have assistance from his great ability, I hope to have interposed no adventitious obstacle. But clearly, he is not now with us—he does not pretend to be—he does not promise ever to be.

" Our cause, then, must be intrusted to, and conducted by, its own undoubted friends—those whose hands are free, whose hearts are in the work—who *do care* for the result. Two years ago the Republicans of the nation mustered over thirteen hundred thousand strong. We did this under the single impulse of resistance to a common danger, with every external circumstance against us. Of strange, discordant, and even hostile elements, we gathered from the four winds, and formed and fought the battle through, under the constant hot fire of a disciplined, proud and pampered enemy. Did we brave all then, to falter now?— now, when that same enemy is wavering, dissevered and belligerent? The result is not doubtful. We shall not fail—if we stand firm, we *shall not fail*. Wise counsels may accelerate, or mistakes delay it, but, sooner or later, the victory is sure to come."

The members of the convention carried away with them something to think about. There had been in Mr. Lincoln's speech no appeals to their partisan prejudices, no tricks to catch applause. He had appeared before them as an earnest, patriotic man, intent only on discussing, in the gravest and most candid manner, the most interesting and momentous political questions.

On the ninth of July, Mr. Douglas made a speech in Chicago. The reception he received was a magnificent one—one which might well have filled him with the gratification which he did not attempt to conceal—which, indeed, he took repeated occasion to express. In this speech he alluded to his efforts to crush the Lecompton fraud, and claimed that the republicans who had fought by his side had indorsed his popular sovereignty doctrine—the right of the people of a territory to form their own institutions.

He then took up the action of the republican convention at Springfield, and spoke at length of Mr. Lincoln and his speech. Of Mr. Lincoln, he said: "I take great pleasure in saying that I have known, personally and intimately, for about a quarter of a century, the worthy gentleman who has been nominated for my place, and I will say that I regard him as a kind, amiable and intelligent gentleman, a good citizen and an honorable opponent, and whatever issue I may have with him will be of principle and not of personalities." He then read from the opening paragraph of Mr. Lincoln's speech the words: "A house divided against itself cannot stand. I believe this government cannot endure permanently half slave and half free. I do not expect the Union to be dissolved. I do not expect the house to fall, but I do expect it to cease to be divided. It will become all one thing or all the other." The unfairness of his comments upon this simple statement of a conviction may be gathered from the construction which he put upon it in the words—"Mr. Lincoln advocates boldly and clearly a war of sections, a war of the North against the South, of the free states against the slave states, a war of extermination, to be continued relentlessly, until the one or the other shall be subdued, and all the states shall either become free or become slave."

Mr. Lincoln foresaw the approaching struggle between freedom and slavery and its inevitable result. He did not be-

lieve a dissolution of the Union possible, but he knew that
freedom and slavery were irreconcilable enemies. He knew
that slavery must die, or become national. He saw the determination of its friends to make it national, and he believed
that this attempt would succeed, or that, failing of success, it
would end in the universal abolition of slavery. Events have
entirely justified his most philosophical view of the subject.

The next point that Mr. Douglas endeavored to make was
as illegitimate as his previous one, viz: that Mr. Lincoln desired to reduce the states to a dead uniformity of interests and
institutions, contrary to the theory and policy of the fathers
of the republic. In order to do this, he was of course obliged
to ignore the fact that Mr. Lincoln had alluded to but one institution, and that, in its nature antagonistic with the principles
of the Declaration of Independence, and to recognize slavery
as having the same legitimate basis with the other institutions
of the country. Having construed Mr. Lincoln's position
unfairly, he logically drove to the unjust conclusion that when
the uniformity should be attained which Mr. Lincoln desired,
the government would have "converted these thirty-two sovereign, independent states, into one consolidated empire, with
the uniformity of disposition reigning triumphant throughout
the length and breadth of the land."

He next took up Mr. Lincoln's criticism of the Dred Scott
decision, and, by his treatment of it, fully vindicated the action of the Illinois republicans in their refusal to support him
in accordance with the wishes of their eastern friends. No
republican could consistently support a man who supported
that iniquitous and barbarous decision. If it is said that his
course on this question would have been changed by their
support, the case is still worse, for no man whose course could
be changed by such considerations would be worthy of the
support of any party. "I am opposed to this doctrine of Mr.
Lincoln," said Mr. Douglas, "by which he proposes to take
an appeal from the decision of the Supreme Court of the
United States upon this high constitutional question, to a republican caucus sitting in the country. * * * I respect the

decisions of that august tribunal; I shall always bow in deference to them. * * * I will sustain the judicial tribunals and
constituted authorities, in all matters within the pale of their
jurisdiction, as defined by the Constitution." Mr. Douglas did
not see fit to allude in this speech to Mr. Lincoln's charge that
the Dred Scott decision was a part of that building framed so
cunningly by "Stephen, Franklin, Roger and James," in which
was to be conserved the power of making slavery universal.

Mr. Douglas went farther than simply to indorse the Dred
Scott decision, and to declare his intention to sustain it. " I
am equally free," said he, " to say that the reason assigned by
Mr. Lincoln for resisting the decision of the Supreme Court
in the Dred Scott case does not, in itself, meet my approbation. * * * He says it is wrong, because it deprives the negro
of the benefit of that clause of the Constitution which says
that the citizens of one state shall enjoy all the privileges and
immunities of the citizens of the several states; in other
words, he thinks it wrong because it deprives the negro of
the privileges, immunities and rights of citizenship which
pertain, according to that decision, only to the white man.
I am free to say to you that, in my opinion, this government
of ours is founded on the white basis. It was made for the
white man, for the benefit of the white man, to be administered
by white men, in such manner as they should determine. It
is also true that a negro, an indian, or any other man of inferior race to a white man should be permitted to enjoy, and
humanity requires that he should have, all the rights, privileges and immunities which he is capable of exercising, consistent with the safety of society." What these rights should
be, was only legitimately to be determined by the states themselves, in Mr. Douglas' opinion. Illinois had decided for
herself what the black man's rights were in Illinois, and New
York and Maine had decided for themselves. By inference,
Kentucky had a right to say her negroes should be slaves,
Illinois that her negroes should not vote, New York that her
negroes might vote when qualified by property, and Maine
that the negro was equal at the polls to the white man.

These were the main points that Mr. Douglas made in his Chicago speech. Mr. Lincoln sat near him, on the platform, and heard the whole of it. Here, as elsewhere during the campaign which succeeded, he manifested his wonderful good nature under misrepresentation. There were incidents of this campaign which no man cast in the common mould could have passed through without yielding to the severest passions of indignation and anger. He was belied, abused, misrepresented; but he never betrayed a moment's irritation. That he smarted with a sense of wrong, there is abundant evidence; but he was never moved to a single act of resentment.

Mr. Lincoln had taken the speech all in, and, on the following evening, it was announced that he would reply to it. The greeting which he received when he took the stand was quite as enthusiastic as that which Mr. Douglas had met on the previous evening. He was introduced to the audience by Mr. C. L. Wilson of Chicago, and when he came forward, there was such a storm of long-continued applause that he was obliged to extend his hand in deprecation, before he could secure the silence necessary for proceeding. After disposing of some minor matters, he took up the points of Mr. Douglas' speech and treated them fully. Touching the comments upon his own declaration—" a house divided against itself cannot stand. I believe this government cannot endure permanently half slave and half free," &c., he said:

"I am not, in the first place, unaware that this Government has endured eighty-two years, half slave and half free. I know that. I am tolerably well acquainted with the history of the country, and I know that it has endured eighty-two years, half slave and half free. I *believe*—and that is what I meant to allude to there—I *believe* it has endured, because during all that time, until the introduction of the Nebraska bill, the public mind did rest all the time in the belief that slavery was in course of ultimate extinction. That was what gave us the rest that we had through that period of eighty-two years; at least, so I believe. I have always hated slavery, I think, as much as any abolitionist—I have been an old line whig—I have always hated it, but I have always been quiet about it until this new era of the introduction of the Nebraska bill began. I always believed that everybody was against it, and that it was in course of ultimate extinction.

" The adoption of the Constitution and its attendant history led the people to believe so; and such was the belief of the framers of the Constitution itself, else why did those old men, about the time of the adoption of the Constitution, decree that slavery should not go into the new territory, where it had not already gone? Why declare that within twenty years the African slave trade, by which slaves are supplied, might be cut off by Congress? Why were all these acts? I might enumerate more of these acts—but enough. What were they but a clear indication that the framers of the Constitution intended and expected the ultimate extinction of that institution? And now, when I say, as I said in my speech that Judge Douglas has quoted from—when I say that I think the opponents of slavery will resist the farther spread of it, and place it where the public mind shall rest with the belief that it is in course of ultimate extinction, I only mean to say that they will place it where the founders of this Government originally placed it.

" I have said a hundred times, and I have now no inclination to take it back, that I believe there is no right, and ought to be no inclination in the people of the free states to enter into the slave states, and interfere with the question of slavery at all. I have said that always; Judge Douglas has heard me say it—if not quite a hundred times, at least as good as a hundred times; and when it is said that I am in favor of interfering with slavery where it exists, I know it is unwarranted by anything I have ever *intended*, and, as I believe, by anything I have ever *said*. If, by any means, I have ever used language which could fairly be so construed (as, however, I believe I never have), I now correct it."

The next point touched upon was Judge Douglas' charge that Mr. Lincoln was in favor of reducing the institutions of all the states to uniformity:

" Now in relation to his inference that I am in favor of a general consolidation of all the local institutions of the various states. I will attend to that for a little while, and try to inquire, if I can, how on earth it could be that any man could draw such an inference from anything I said. I have said, very many times, in Judge Douglas' hearing, that no man believed more than I in the principle of self-government; that it lies at the bottom of all my ideas of just government, from beginning to end. I have denied that his use of that term applies properly. But for the thing itself, I deny that any man has ever gone ahead of me in his devotion to the principle, whatever he may have done in efficiency in advocating it. I think that I have said it in your hearing—that I believe each individual is naturally entitled to do as he pleases with himself and the fruit of his labor, so far as it in no wise interferes with any other man's rights—that each community, as a state, has a right to do exactly as it pleases with all the concerns within that state that interferes with the right of no other state, and that the general government, upon principle, has nó right to interfere with anything other than that general class of things that does concern the whole. I have said that at all times. I have said as illustrations, that I do not believe in the right of Illinois to interfere with the cranberry laws of Indiana, the oyster laws of Virginia, or the liquor laws of Maine. I have said these things over and over again, and I repeat them here as my sentiments.

"How is it, then, that Judge Douglas infers, because I hope to see slavery put where the public mind shall rest in the belief that it is in the course of ultimate extinction, that I am in favor of Illinois going over and interfering with the cranberry laws of Indiana? What can authorize him to draw any such inference? I suppose there might be one thing that at least enabled *him* to draw such an inference that would not be true with me or many others, that is, because he looks upon all this matter of slavery as an exceedingly little thing—this matter of keeping one-sixth of the population of the whole nation in a state of oppression and tyranny unequaled in the world. He looks upon it as being an exceedingly little thing—only equal to the question of the cranberry laws of Indiana—as something having no moral question in it—as something on a par with the question of whether a man shall pasture his land with cattle, or plant it with tobacco—so little and so small a thing, that he concludes, if I could desire that if anything should be done to bring about the ultimate extinction of that little thing, I must be in favor of bringing about an amalgamation of all the other little things in the Union. Now, it so happens—and there, I presume, is the foundation of this mistake—that the Judge thinks thus; and it so happens that there is a vast portion of the American people that do *not* look upon that matter as being this very little thing. They look upon it as a vast moral evil; they can prove it such by the writings of those who gave us the blessings of liberty which we enjoy, and that they so looked upon it, not as an evil merely confining itself to the states where it is situated; and while we agree that, by the Constitution we assented to, in the states where it exists we have no right to interfere with it, because it is in the Constitution; we are by both duty and inclination to stick by that Constitution, in all its letter and spirit, from beginning to end.

"So much then as to my disposition—my wish—to have all the state legislatures blotted out, and to have one consolidated government, and a uniformity of domestic regulations in all the states by which I suppose it is meant, if we raise corn here, we must make sugar-cane grow here too, and we must make those which grow North grow in the South. All this I suppose he understands I am in favor of doing. Now, so much for all this nonsense—for I must call it so. The Judge can have no issue with me on a question of establishing uniformity in the domestic regulations of the states."

Concerning the Dred Scott decision he said:

"I have expressed heretofore, and I now repeat, my opposition to the Dred Scott decision, but I should be allowed to state the nature of that opposition, and I ask your indulgence while I do so. What is fairly implied by the term Judge Douglas has used, 'resistance to the decision?' I do not resist it. If I wanted to take Dred Scott from his master, I would be interfering with property, and that terrible difficulty that Judge Douglas speaks of, of interfering with property would arise. But I am doing no such thing as that, but all that I am doing is refusing to obey it as a political rule. If I were in Congress, and a vote should come up on a question whether slavery should be prohibited in a new territory, in spite of the Dred Scott decision, I would vote that it should.

"That is what I would do. Judge Douglas said last night, that before the decision he might advance his opinion, and it might be contrary to the decision when it was made; but after it was made he would abide by it until it was reversed. Just so! We let this property abide by the decision, but we will try to reverse that decision. We will try to put it where Judge Douglas would not object, for he says he will obey it until it is reversed. Somebody has to reverse that decision, since it is made, and we mean to reverse it, and we mean to do it peaceably.

"What are the uses of decisions of courts? They have two uses. As rules of property they have two uses. First—they decide upon the question before the court. They decide in this case that Dred Scott is a slave. Nobody resists that. Not only that, but they say to everybody else, that persons standing just as Dred Scott stands, is as he is. That is, they say that when a question comes up upon another person, it will be so decided again, unless the court decides in another way, unless the court overrules its decision. Well, we mean to do what we can to have the court decide the other way. That is one thing we mean to try to do.

"The sacredness that Judge Douglas throws around this decision, is a degree of sacredness that has never been before thrown around any other decision. I have never heard of such a thing. Why, decisions apparently contrary to that decision, or that good lawyers thought were contrary to that decision, have been made by that very court before.

It is the first of its kind; it is an astonisher in legal history. It is a new wonder of the world. It is based upon falsehood in the main as to the facts—allegations of facts upon which it stands are not facts at all in many instances—and no decision made on any question—the first instance of a decision made under so many unfavorable circumstances—thus placed, has ever been held by the profession as law, and it has always needed confirmation before the lawyers regarded it as settled law. But Judge Douglas will have it that all hands must take this extraordinary decision, made under these extraordinary circumstances, and give their vote in Congress in accordance with it, yield to it and obey it in every possible sense. Circumstances alter cases. Do not gentlemen here remember the case of that same Supreme Court, some twenty-five or thirty years ago, deciding that a national bank was constitutional? I ask, if somebody does not remember that a national bank was declared to be constitutional? Such is the truth, whether it be remembered or not. The bank charter ran out, and a re-charter was granted by Congress. That re-charter was laid before General Jackson. It was urged upon him, when he denied the constitutionality of the bank that the Supreme Court had decided it was constitutional; and General Jackson then said that the Supreme Court had no right to lay down a rule to govern a co-ordinate branch of the Government, the members of which had sworn to support the Constitution—that each member had sworn to support that Constitution as he understood it. I will venture here to say, that I have heard Judge Douglas say that he approved of General Jackson for that act. What has now become of all his tirade about 'resistance to the Supreme Court?'"

There were some passages in this speech which illustrated Mr. Lincoln's readiness in "putting things" to the common apprehension. After having said that the much vaunted "popular sovereignty" which Mr. Douglas had put forth as his own invention was something which, when properly defined, the republicans had always accepted and acted upon, and that it came, not from Judge Douglas, but from the Declaration of Independence, which states that governments derive their just powers "from the consent of the governed," he alluded to the defeat of the Lecompton Constitution in Congress. He said that the republicans took ground against the Lecompton Constitution long before Judge Douglas did, and that he held in his hand a speech in which he urged the same reason against Douglas the year before that he (Douglas) was urging now. He went on:

"A little more, now, as to this matter of popular sovereignty and the Lecompton Constitution. The Lecompton Constitution, as the Judge tells us, was defeated. The defeat of it was a good thing, or it was not. He thinks the defeat of it was a good thing, and so do I, and we agree in that. Who defeated it?

"A voice—'Judge Douglas.'

"Mr. Lincoln—Yes, he furnished himself, and, if you suppose he furnished the other democrats that went with him, he furnished three votes, while the republicans furnished twenty. That is what he did to defeat It. In the House of Representatives he and his friends furnished some twenty votes and the republicans ninety odd. Now who was it that did the work?

"A voice—'Douglas.'

"Mr. Lincoln—Why, yes, Douglas did it. To be sure he did. Let us, however, put that proposition another way. The republicans could not have done it without Judge Douglas. Could he have done it without them? Which could have come the nearest to doing it without the other?"

The following point was so neatly made that it drew from the house three hearty cheers:

"We were often—more than once at least—in the course of Judge Douglas' speech last night, reminded that this government was made for white men—that he believed it was made for white men. Well, that is putting it into a shape in which no one wants to deny it; but the Judge then goes into his passion for drawing inferences that are not warranted. I protest, now and forever, against that counterfeit logic which presumes that because I do not want a negro woman for a slave, I do necessarily want her for a wife. My understanding is that I need not have her for either, but, as God made us separate, we can leave one another alone, and do one another much good thereby. There are white men enough to marry all the white women, and enough black men to marry all the black women, and in God's name let them be so married. The Judge regales us with the terrible enormities that take place by the mixture of races; that the inferior race bears the superior down. Why, Judge, if we do not let them get together in the territories they won't mix there."

And thus was opened the grand senatorial campaign of 1858. Mr. Douglas had not been present at Mr. Lincoln's speech, a fact which Mr. Lincoln regretted, and he soon took measures to secure his attendance. In the meantime, the campaign went on. Mr. Douglas spoke a week later at Bloomington, making much, as usual, of his doctrine of popular sovereignty, and of his rebellion against the administration on the Lecompton question. Mr. Lincoln's original Springfield speech came in for comment, particularly the two points which he criticised at Chicago. Mr. Lincoln was present on this occasion also, determined to find out the exact ground of his antagonist, that he might be able to meet him in the struggle which he had determined upon. On the day following his Bloomington speech, Mr. Douglas spoke at Springfield, as did also Mr. Lincoln, though not at the same meeting. Mr. Lincoln, in opening his speech, alluded to the disadvantages which the republicans of the state labored under in the unjust apportionment of the legislative districts, and particularly in the disparity that existed between the reputation and prospects of the senatorial candidates of the two parties. All the anxious politicians of the party of Mr. Douglas had been looking upon him as certain, at no distant day, to be the President of the United States. "They have seen," he said, "in his round, jolly, fruitful face, post-offices, land-offices, marshalships and cabinet appointments, charge-ships and foreign missions, bursting and sprouting out, in wonderful luxuriance, ready to be laid hold of by their greedy hands. And as they have been gazing upon this attractive picture so long, they cannot, in the little distraction that has taken place in the party, bring themselves to give up the charming hope; but with greedier anxiety they rush about him, sustain him, and give him marches, triumphal entries and receptions, beyond what, even in the days of his highest prosperity, they could have brought about in his favor. On the contrary, nobody has ever expected me to be president. In my poor, lean, lank face nobody has ever seen that any cabbages were sprouting out." The main body of the speech was devoted to the questions at issue between him and Judge Douglas, and does not contain matter of special interest beyond

12

what he had previously uttered upon the same points. He closed by reiterating the charge made in his speech of June seventeenth that Mr. Douglas was a party to the conspiracy for deceiving the people with the idea that the settlers of a territory could exclude slavery from their limits if they should choose to do so, and, at the same time, rendering it impossible for them to do so through the standing veto of the Dred Scott decision. The charge was a grave one, but Mr. Douglas had ignored it. Since it was made, he had not alluded to it at all. "On his own tacit admission," said Mr. Lincoln, "I renew the charge."

CHAPTER XIII.

Mr. Lincoln wanted closer work than Mr. Douglas had given him. He desired to address the same audiences with his antagonist, and to show to those whom he addressed the fallacy of his reasoning and the groundlessness of his charges. Accordingly, on the twenty-fourth of July, he dispatched the following note:—

"Hon. S. A. Douglas—My Dear Sir: Will it be agreeable to you to make an arrangement for you and myself to divide time, and address the same audiences the present canvass? Mr. Judd, who will hand you this, is authorized to receive your answer; and, if agreeable to you, to enter into the terms of such arrangement.

"Your obedient servant,   A. Lincoln."

To this Mr. Douglas replied, stating that recent events had interposed difficulties in the way of such an arrangement. In connection with the State Central Committee at Springfield, he had made a series of appointments extending over nearly the whole period that remained before the election, and the people of the various localities had been notified of the times and places of the meetings. The candidates for Congress, the legislature and other offices would desire to speak at these meetings, and thus all the time would be occupied. Then he proceeded to give, as a further reason for his refusal, that it was intended to bring out another candidate for United States senator, to divide the democratic vote for the benefit of Mr. Lincoln, and that he (the third candidate) would also claim a chance in the joint debates, so that he (said third candidate) and Mr. Lincoln would have the opening and closing speech in every instance. While, therefore, he declined the general invitation, he declared himself ready to make an arrangement for seven joint debates in the congressional districts respectively where they had not already spoken, and at the following places, viz: Freeport, Ottawa, Galesburg, Quincy, Alton, Jonesboro and Charleston. This letter was published in the Chicago Times, and read there by Mr. Lincoln before he received the autograph by mail.

To this letter Mr. Lincoln responded, denying, of course, the foolish charge of intended unfairness in bringing in a third candidate to divide the time to the disadvantage of Mr. Douglas, and agreeing to speak in the seven places mentioned. There is other matter in these letters* which thoroughly discovers the characteristics of the two writers, but it must be left behind.

Mr. Douglas replied to this second letter of Mr. Lincoln, designating the time and places of the debate as they follow:

Ottawa, LaSalle County, August 21st, 1858; Freeport, Stephenson County, August 27th; Jonesboro, Union County, September 15th; Charleston, Coles County, September 18th; Galesburg, Knox County, October 7th; Quincy, Adams County, October 13th; Alton, Madison County, October 15th.

The terms proposed in this letter and accepted in a subsequent note by Mr. Lincoln, were, that at Ottawa, Mr. Douglas should speak an hour, then Mr. Lincoln an hour and a half, Mr. Douglas having the closing speech of half an hour. At the next place, Mr. Lincoln should open and close in the same way, and so on, alternately, to the conclusion of the arrangement.

As about three weeks intervened between the date of this agreement for joint debates and the first appointment, both parties engaged zealously in their independent work. Mr.

---

*Political debates between Hon. Abraham Lincoln and Hon. Stephen A. Douglas, (Follett, Foster & Co.,) pages 64 and 65.

Lincoln began his canvass at Beardstown, the spot where, twenty-five years before, he had taken his military company for rendezvous before starting out for the Black Hawk war. After making a speech here, he went up the Illinois River to Havana and Bath in Mason County, to Lewistown and Canton in Fulton County, and to Peoria and Henry in Marshall County, making speeches at each place, and attracting immense audiences. Mr. Douglas was equally busy, and equally fortunate in attracting the people to listen to his utterances upon the great questions of the day. At Clinton, in DeWitt County, he found it no longer possible to pass in silence the charge of Mr. Lincoln that he had "left a niche in the Nebraska bill to receive the Dred Scott decision," which declared in effect, that a territorial legislature could not abolish slavery. Mr. Douglas here stated that his self-respect alone prevented him from calling this charge a falsehood. Subsequently, at Beardstown, he broke over his restraints, and called it "an infamous lie." To this Mr. Lincoln responded on a subsequent occasion as follows:

"I say to you, gentlemen, that it would be more to the purpose for Judge Douglas to say that he did not repeal the Missouri compromise; that he did not make slavery possible where it was impossible before; that he did not leave a niche in the Nebraska bill for the Dred Scott decision to rest in; that he did not vote-down a clause giving the people the right to exclude slavery if they wanted to; that he did not refuse to give his individual opinion whether a territorial legislature could exclude slavery; that he did not make a report to the senate in which he said that the rights of the people in this regard were held in abeyance, and could not be immediately exercised; that he did not make a hasty indorsement of the Dred Scott decision over at Springfield; that he does not now indorse that decision; that that decision does not take away from the territorial legislature the power to exclude slavery; and that he did not in the original Nebraska bill so couple the words 'state' and 'territory' together that what the Supreme Court has done in forcing open all the territories for slavery, it may yet do in forcing open all the states;—I say it would be vastly more to the point, for Judge Douglas to say he did not do some of these things, did not forge some of these links of overwhelming testimony, than to go to vociferating about the country that possibly he may be obliged to hint that somebody is a liar."

The first meeting of the series agreed upon was held at Ottawa according to appointment. A concourse of citizens estimated at twelve thousand had assembled. Mr. Douglas had the opening speech, and in this speech he resorted to an expedient for placing Mr. Lincoln on the defensive which was either very weak, or very wicked. He made a charge against Mr. Lincoln which, if he knew it to be false, was foul, and which, if he did not know to be true, was most impolitic. He charged that Mr. Lincoln, on the part of the whigs, and Mr. Trumbull, on the part of the democrats, entered into an arrangement in 1854, for the dissolution of the two parties, and the fusing of both in the republican party, for the purpose of giving Lincoln Shields' place in the Senate, and Trumbull, his (Douglas') own. Furthermore, that the parties met at Springfield in October of that year, and, in convention of their friends, laid down a platform of the principles upon which the new party was constructed. He then proceeded to read what he called "the most important and material resolutions of the abolition platform." What these resolutions were, will appear in Mr. Lincoln's replies to the questions which Mr. Douglas based upon them. His object in asking these questions was, as he said, in order that when he should "trot him (Lincoln) down" to lower Egypt (southern Illinois) he might put the same questions to him there.

The hearty reception which the audience gave to the principles of this platform as he pronounced them, did not please Mr. Douglas. He wished to see whether they would "bear transplanting from Ottawa to Jonesboro." "I have a right," said Mr. Douglas, "to an answer, for I quote from the platform of the republican party, made by himself (Lincoln) and others at the time that party was formed, and the bargain made by Mr. Lincoln to dissolve and kill the old whig party, and transfer its members, bound hand and foot, to the abolition party, under the direction of Giddings and Fred Douglass."

Mr. Douglas went on then to comment on Mr. Lincoln's Springfield speech, which had come to be known as "the house-divided-against-itself speech," and slid, as usual, into his talk about the inferiority of the negro.   Speaking of Mr. Lincoln and the " abolition orators," he said, " he and they maintain that negro equality is guarantied by the laws of God, and that it is asserted in the Declaration of Independence.   If they think so, of course they have a right to say so, and so vote.   I do not question Mr. Lincoln's conscientious belief that the negro was made his equal, and, hence, his brother; but for my own part, I do not regard the negro as my equal, and positively deny that he is my brother, or any kin to me whatever."

And here it may be said, because it will be impossible to describe with particularity all the speeches of the campaign, that the staple of the speeches of Mr. Douglas, as well as those of Mr. Lincoln, related to a very few points, which may be summed up in a brace of paragraphs.

Mr. Douglas did not believe in natural negro equality, and did believe that every state had the right to say just what rights she would confer upon the negro; that the people of every territory had a right to decide as to what their institutions should be, while he bowed, at the same time, to the Dred Scott decision, which declared that they had no right to abolish slavery; and that the country could endure half slave and half free as well for all coming time as it had for the previous eighty years, while slavery itself, to him, was a matter of indifference—an institution which might be "voted up or voted down," without any appeal to his preferences.

On the other hand, Mr. Lincoln placed himself on the broad ground of the Declaration of Independence, that *all* men are created equal, and are by heaven endowed with certain inalienable rights, such as life, liberty and the pursuit of happiness.   He recognized the negro as a man, coming within the broad sweep of this Declaration.   He believed thoroughly in Mr. Douglas' doctrine of popular sovereignty, without the Dred Scott qualification, which was a direct denial of the sovereignty; but he believed the abrogation of the Missouri compromise, which Mr. Douglas himself had effected, an unspeakable wrong, a foul breach of faith, by which it was rendered possible for the people of a territory to choose slavery, and by which the forcing of slavery upon them was rendered practicable. Furthermore, he saw in that "piece of machinery," made up of congressional legislation, Supreme Court decisions and executive and party connivance, an attempt to nationalize and perpetuate slavery, which he felt must logically ultimate in that result, or end in universal emancipation. Slavery, he believed, had lived by the side of freedom, and in partnership with it, simply because freedom had regarded itself as eternal, while it had regarded slavery as ephemeral. Thus the fathers regarded and treated slavery. They had curtailed its territory. They had forbidden the importation of slaves. All their arrangements looked to an early end of slavery; and Mr. Lincoln quoted the champions of slavery to sustain his views on this point. When the policy of the government changed, and it was proposed to nationalize slavery and make it perpetual—to confer upon it the same rights with freedom—nay, to make it impossible for freedom to abolish it—then he foresaw a conflict which could only end by its utter overthrow, or its universal prevalence. He did not believe the house would fall; he did believe that it would cease to be divided.

The seven joint debates rang their changes on these points, as they were held and maintained by the debaters. Mr. Douglas did not seem to be as fertile in thought and expression as his antagonist. He was more given to diversions, to the ordinary clap-trap of campaign speaking, to appeals to prejudices, to the springing of false issues, to quibbles and tricks. Mr. Lincoln, on the contrary, was in thorough earnest, and stuck with manly tenacity to the great questions he had in hand. He stripped every objectionable proposition and every specious argument of the disguises in which the ingenious language of Mr. Douglas had clothed them, and refused to be led away, by a hair's breadth, from the real, naked issues of the campaign.

In replying to Judge Douglas at Ottawa, he simply said that the story of his bargain with Mr. Trumbull was not true, and that he was so far from having had anything to do with the convention to which the Senator had alluded that he was attending court, off in Tazewell County, when it was held. That was all there was of Mr. Douglas' charges. They had not an inch of truth to stand upon; and it was discovered immediately after the debate that the resolutions which Mr. Douglas had quoted had not been passed in Springfield at all, by any convention, and that, although they had been uttered by a local convention in the town of Aurora, they were, for the purposes used, and under the circumstances, essentially a forgery, for which Mr. Douglas or his friends were guiltily responsible. The charge that Mr. Lincoln was in the convention, that he made a bargain with Mr. Trumbull, that he was responsible for a certain set of anti-slavery resolutions, and that the resolutions which he read were passed by the convention that was held at Springfield, was false in every particular. Did Mr. Douglas know it to be so? Perhaps the only reply that it is proper to make to this question is that he ought to have known it to be so.

In Mr. Lincoln's reply, he quoted from his Peoria speech made in 1854, to which allusion has been made in this history, to show his exact position on the subject of slavery in the states where it existed. He said in that speech that he had no prejudice against the southern people. They were just what we should be under their circumstances. "If slavery did not now exist among them, they would not introduce it. If it did now exist among us, we should not instantly give it up." He understood how difficult it was to get rid of slavery, and he did not blame them for not doing what he should not know how to do himself. He acknowledged his constitutional obligations, and went so far as to say that he would be willing to give them a law for reclaiming fugitives, provided a law could be made which would not be more likely to carry a free man into slavery than our ordinary criminal laws are to hang an innocent one. This, notwithstanding he hated slavery for the monstrous injustice of slavery itself, and for its disgrace to democratic institutions. But all these facts had no effect upon his mind when he came to consider the question of extending slavery over territory now free.   There was no more excuse, in his opinion, for permitting slavery to go into free territory, ·than for reviving the African slave-trade by law.   "The law which forbids the bringing a slave *from* Africa," said Mr. Lincoln, " and that which has so long forbidden the taking of them *to* Nebraska, can hardly be distinguished, on any moral principle."   The principal point urged against Judge Douglas in this speech touched his devotion to Supreme Court decisions.   A decision of this Court was to him a " Thus saith the Lord."   There was no appeal from it; and the next decision of this same Court, whatever it might be, was indorsed in advance.   It is simply for the Supreme Court to say that no *state* under the Constitution can exclude slavery, and he must bow to the decision, just as when it says no territory can thus exclude it.   Mr. Lincoln closed his remarks on this point by an *argumentum ad hominem*, equally characteristic and clever:

" The next decision, as much as this, will be a *Thus saith the Lord.* There is nothing that can divert or turn him away from this decision. It is nothing that I point out to him that his great prototype, General Jackson, did not believe in the binding force of decisions.   It is nothing to him that Jefferson did not so believe.   I have said that I have often heard him approve of Jackson's course in disregarding the decision of the Supreme Court pronouncing a national bank constitutional.   He says I did not hear him say so.   He denies the accuracy of my recollection. I say he ought to know better than I, but I will make no question about this thing, though it still seems to me that I heard him say it twenty times.   I will tell him though, that he now claims to stand on the Cincinnati platform, which affirms that Congress *cannot* charter a national bank, in the teeth of that old standing decision that Congress *can* charter a bank.   And I remind him of another piece of history on the question of respect for judicial decisions, and it is a piece of Illinois history, belonging to a time when the large party to which Judge Douglas belonged were displeased with a decision of the Supreme Court of Illinois, because they had decided that a Governor could not remove a Secretary of State.   You will find the whole story in Ford's History of Illinois; and I know that Judge Douglas will not deny that he was then in favor of overslaughing that decision by the mode of adding five new Judges, so as to vote down the four old ones.   Not only so, but it ended in *the Judge's sitting down on that very bench as one of the five new Judges to break down the four old ones.* It was in this way precisely that he got his title of Judge. Now, when the Judge tells me that men appointed conditionally to sit as members of a court, will have to be catechised beforehand upon some subject, I say, 'You know, Judge; you have tried it.' When he says a court of this kind will lose the confidence of all men, will be prostituted and disgraced by such a proceeding, I say, 'You know best, Judge; you have been through the mill.' But I cannot shake Judge Douglas' teeth loose from the Dred Scott decision. Like some obstinate animal (I mean no disrespect,) that will hang on when he has once got his teeth fixed; you may cut off a leg, or you may tear away an arm, still he will not relax his hold. And so I may point out to the Judge, and say that he is bespattered all over, from the beginning of his political life to the present time, with attacks upon judicial decisions—I may cut off limb after limb of his public record, and strive to wrench him from a single dictum of the court—yet I cannot divert him from it. He hangs, to the last, to the Dred Scott decision. These things show there is a purpose *strong as death and eternity* for which he adheres to this decision, and for which he will adhere to *all other decisions* of the same court."

At the close of the half hour which Mr. Douglas employed in his reply to Mr. Lincoln, the latter was literally borne away upon the shoulders of his friends, in a frenzy of enthusiasm, a fact to which Mr. Douglas made playful allusion a few days afterwards, in the statement that Mr. Lincoln was so much frightened that he had to be taken from the stand, and was laid up for seven days. Mr. Lincoln was too simple, too much in earnest, and too sensitive, to take this badinage gracefully. He really supposed there might be persons who would believe it, as appeared in a subsequent speech, in which he made it a matter of complaint.

At the Freeport meeting, Mr. Lincoln had the opening speech, and commenced by answering the interrogatories which Mr. Douglas had addressed to him at Ottawa, based upon the declarations of the Aurora resolutions. Mr. Douglas asked him if he stood pledged now to the same details of policy that he did in 1854—details which he drew from the resolutions he had read; and to his questions Mr. Lincoln made these replies, *seriatim :* that he was not then, and never had been pledged to the unconditional repeal of the fugitive slave law ;

that he was not then, and had never been, pledged against the admission of any more slave states; that he did not stand pledged against the admission of a new state into the Union with such a constitution as the people of that state may see fit to make; that he did not stand pledged to the abolition of slavery in the District of Columbia; that he did not stand pledged to the prohibition of the slave trade between the different states; and that he *was* pledged to a belief in the right and duty of Congress to prohibit slavery in all the United States territories. After saying that he had replied in terms to the Judge, and that he was not "pledged" to any of these principles or measures, he further said that he would not hang upon the form of the questions, but utter what he did think on all the subjects involved in them. He believed the southern people were entitled, under the Constitution, to a congressional fugitive slave law; said that he should be very sorry to see any more slave states applying for admission to the Union, and declared that he would not only be glad to see slavery abolished in the District of Columbia, but he believed that Congress had the constitutional power to abolish it there. Having answered Mr. Douglas' questions—these and the remainder—in accordance with opinions with which the reader is already familiar, he was ready to turn questioner, and give the Judge something to do, in the same line of effort. He had already consulted with his friends concerning the matter, and, in his conversation on the subject, had dropped an expression which showed that he was looking beyond the senatorial contest for the grand results of the discussion. In Mr. Lincoln's view the principal point of debate was Mr. Douglas' doctrine of popular sovereignty, in connection with the Dred Scott decision—the two things in his judgment being in direct antagonism, and being, in reality, a shameful fraud. This antagonism Mr. Lincoln proposed to present in the form of interrogatories, but his friends remonstrated. "If you put that question to him," they said, "he will perceive that an answer, giving practical force and effect to the Dred Scott decision in the territories, inevitably loses him the battle; and he will

therefore reply by offering the decision as an abstract principle, but denying its practical application." "But," said Mr.
Lincoln, "if he does that, he can never be President." His
friends replied, "that is not your lookout; you are after the
senatorship." "No, gentlemen," said he, "I am killing larger
game. The battle of 1860 is worth a hundred of this."*

Whether Mr. Lincoln then expected to be the republican
candidate for the presidency in 1860, there are no means of
judging; but that he intended the discussion to damage Mr.
Douglas' presidential prospects there is no doubt. So Mr.
Lincoln put his questions, which, in their order, were as they
follow:

"1. If the people of Kansas shall, by means entirely unobjectionable
in all other respects, adopt a state constitution, and ask admission into
the Union under it, before they have the requisite number of inhabitants according to the English bill—some ninety-three thousand—will
you vote to admit them?

"2. Can the people of a United States territory, in any lawful way,
against the wish of any citizen of the United States, exclude slavery
from its limits prior to the formation of a state constitution?

"3. If the Supreme Court of the United States shall decide that
states cannot exclude slavery from their limits, are you in favor of
acquiescing in, adopting and following such decision, as a rule of political action?

"4. Are you in favor of acquiring additional territory, in disregard
of how such acquisition may affect the nation on the slavery question?"

To the first question Mr. Douglas replied that he held it a
sound rule, of universal application, to require a territory to
contain the requisite population for a member of Congress,
before it is admitted as a state into the Union; but it having
been decided by Congress that Kansas had population enough
for a slave state, he held that she had enough for a free state.
His answer to the second question was in brief, this: "It
matters not what way the Supreme Court may hereafter decide, as to the abstract question whether slavery may or may
not go into a territory under the Constitution, the people have

* Scripps, p. 28.

the lawful means to introduce it, or exclude it as they please, for the reason that slavery cannot exist a day, or an hour, anywhere, unless it is supported by local police regulations. Those police regulations can only be established by the local legislature; and if the people are opposed to slavery, they will elect representatives to that body who will, by unfriendly legislation, effectually prevent the introduction of it into their midst." The third question he answered by stating that a decision of the Supreme Court that states could not exclude slavery from their limits, would "be an act of moral treason that no man on the bench would ever descend to." The thing in his view was simply impossible. This left the real question unanswered. Mr. Lincoln had not asked him whether the Supreme Court would or could make such a decision, but had inquired what he would do in the event that it should. To the fourth interrogatory he replied, "Whenever it becomes necessary, in our growth and progress, to acquire more terri- tory, I am in favor of it, without reference to the question of slavery; and when we have acquired it I will leave the people free to do as they please—either to make it slave or free terri- tory as they prefer."

To the answer to the second question Mr. Lincoln re- sponded by charging Mr. Douglas with changing his ground; and referred to the record to prove his charge. He referred to the inquiry made by Judge Trumbull of Judge Douglas in the United States Senate, on this very point, when the former asked the latter whether the people of a territory had the lawful power to exclude slavery, prior to the formation of a constitution. The Judge's reply then was that it was a ques- tion to be decided by the Supreme Court. The question has been decided by the Supreme Court, and now the Judge, by saying that the people can exclude slavery if they choose, virtually says that it is not a question for the Supreme Court but a question for the people. The proposition that "slavery cannot exist a day or an hour without local police regulations" is historically false, even in the case of Dred Scott himself, who was held in Minnesota territory not only without police regulations, but in the teeth of Congressional legislation, supposed to be valid at the time. The absurdity of adhering to the Dred Scott decision and maintaining popular sovereignty at the same time, he put into a single sentence in a subsequent speech, made in Ohio—a sentence which contained the whole argument. It was declaring, he said, "no less than that a thing may lawfully be driven away from a place where it has a lawful right to be."

It is impossible to follow to their conclusion this series of debates in the pages of this volume. Enough has been written to reveal the ground of the two antagonists, the merits of the questions they discussed and their modes of conducting debate. Into the side questions which sprang up on every fresh occasion, and which were connected with persons and local politics, it is not possible, and, perhaps, not desirable, to follow the debaters. They kept their appointments, and fulfilled the terms of their arrangement. They attracted to them immense crowds, wherever they appeared; and the whole nation looked on with an intense interest. There has never been a local canvass since the formation of the government which so attracted the attention of the politicians of other states as this. It was the key note of the coming presidential campaign. It was a thorough presentation of the issues upon which the next national battle was to be fought. The eyes of all the eastern states were turned to the west where young republicanism and old democracy were establishing the dividing lines of the two parties, and preparing the ground for the great struggle soon to be begun.

To say that Mr. Lincoln was the victor in this contest, morally and intellectually, is simply to record the judgment of the world. To say that he was victor in every way before the people of Illinois, it needs only to be recorded that he received a majority in the popular vote over Mr. Douglas of four thousand eighty-five. There is this to be said, however, in connection with these statements. Whatever the advantages of Mr. Douglas may have been, Mr. Lincoln had the great advantage of belonging to a new and aggressive party, which

had started freshly in the strife for power, and had not been
corrupted by power. It had not lived long enough to depart
from the principles of truth and justice in which it had its
birth. Standing on the ground that slavery was wrong and
that its perpetuation would be a calamity, and its diffusion
through new territory a crime, Mr. Lincoln not only felt,
but knew, that he was right. This made him strong. Mr.
Douglas was looking for the presidency, and knew that if he
should ever reach and grasp the prize before him, he must do
it through the aid of the slaveholding states. He knew that
he could only secure this support by a certain degree of
friendliness, or an entire indifference, to slavery. He intended
to ride into power on the back of popular sovereignty, giving
at least nominal equality to slavery and freedom in the territories, while, at the same time, endorsing the decision of the
Supreme Court as to what the exact rights of slavery were,
under the Constitution. His policy was not only that of the
democratic party of Illinois, but essentially that of the whole
North. He boasted of this on one occasion, upon which Mr.
Lincoln retorted the charge of sectionalism. Mr. Douglas
had been obliged to defer so much to the spirit of freedom
and to the rights of free labor in the territories—had been
obliged for fear of defeat to go so far from the original path
he had marked out for himself—that Mr. Lincoln called his
attention to the fact that his speeches would not pass current
south of the Ohio so readily as they had formerly done.
"Whatever may be the result of this ephemeral contest between Judge Douglas and myself," said he, "I see the day
rapidly approaching when his pill of 'sectionalism,' which he
has been thrusting down the throats of republicans for years
past, will be crowded down his own throat." It was undoubtedly the grand aim of Mr. Lincoln, throughout the whole
series of debates, to drive Mr. Douglas into such an open
declaration for slavery as to secure his defeat for the senatorial
office, or, failing in that, to compel him to such declarations
on behalf of freedom as would spoil him as a southern candidate for the presidency. "The battle of 1860 is worth a

hundred of this," Mr. Lincoln had said to his friends before the Freeport debate. He saw further than they. He was "killing larger game" than the senatorship, and he certainly did kill, or assist in killing, Judge Douglas, as a southern candidate for the presidency.

These debates of these two champions, respectively of the principles of the Declaration of Independence and of party policy, were published entire as a campaign document in the republican interest, when Mr. Lincoln was nominated for the presidency, without a word of comment, the people being left to form their own conclusions as to the merits of the controversy, and the relative ability of the men whom it represented.

It is in vain to look for any better presentation of the principles of the republican party, or a better definition of the issues which divided it from the democratic party of the time, than are to be found in these speeches of Mr. Lincoln. They cover the whole ground. They are clear, sound, logical, powerful and exhaustive; and, in connection with two or three speeches made afterwards in Ohio and New York, form the chief material on which his reputation as an orator and a debater must rest. The man who shall write the story of the great rebellion on behalf of human slavery must go back to these masterly speeches of an Illinois lawyer to find the clearest and most complete statement of those differences between the power of slavery and the spirit of freedom—the policy of slavery and the policy of freedom—which ended, after expenditures of uncounted treasure and unmeasured blood, in the final overthrow of the accursed institution.

Mr. Lincoln was beaten in his contest for the seat of Mr. Douglas in the Senate, in consequence of the unfair apportionment of the legislative districts. When it came to a ballot in the legislature, it was found that there were fourteen democrats to eleven republicans in the Senate, and forty democrats to thirty-five republicans in the House. This re-instated Mr. Douglas; and the champion of the republican party was defeated after a contest fought by him with wonderful power and persistence, with unfailing fairness, good nature and mag-

13

nanimity, and with a skill rarely if ever surpassed. He had visited every part of the state, made about sixty speeches, been received by the people everywhere with unbounded enthusiasm, had grown strong with every day's exercise, was conscious that he had worsted his antagonist in the intellectual struggle, and, when defeat came, he could not have been otherwise than disappointed. On being asked by a friend how he felt when the returns came in that insured his defeat, he replied that he felt, he supposed, very much like the stripling who had bruised his toe—"too badly to laugh and too big to cry." But the battle of 1860 was indeed worth a hundred of that, and to it, events will swiftly lead us.

CHAPTER XIV.

THE winter of 1858 and 1859 found Mr. Lincoln at leisure. His absorption in political pursuits had materially interfered with his professional business, although he retained all that he had the disposition to attend to. At this point occurred one of those strange diversions that were so characteristic of the man. He sat down and wrote, in the form of a lecture, a comprehensive history of inventions, beginning with the handiwork in brass and iron of Tubal Cain, and ending with the latest products of inventive art. This lecture he delivered at Springfield, and, in a single instance, in another city, but there the public delivery of it ceased. Whether he undertook this to detach his mind from subjects which had held it so long, or whether he did it to be able to meet the invitations that came to him from many quarters to address the winter lyceums, does not appear. The effort does not seem to have been a satisfactory one to himself, and it is easy to see that it was not likely to be particularly attractive to the lecture-going public. Reading lectures and delivering stump speeches are very different styles of effort; and the most effective political orators often surprise themselves as much as they do their audiences by their dryness and dreariness upon the platform of the lecturer. The facts of the matter are principally interesting as showing the natural drift of Mr. Lincoln's mind when diverted from professional and political pursuits.

This diversion was only temporary. Mr. Lincoln had become a political man. Whatever may have been his inclina-

tions at this time, he felt that he was in the hands of the party
to which he had just given the ripest and best efforts of his
life. He was a representative man, and was already regarded
by the great masses of the new party at the West as their
best man for the next presidential campaign. His senatorial
contest had done much to make his name known to the politicians of the nation. Political men everywhere had read his
masterly debates with Senator Douglas, and had given him his
position among the best politicians and most notable political
orators of the time. While this is true, it is also true that
east of the Alleghanies he was not much known among the
people. He had not been much in public office; and his field
of action and influence was so distant that they had heard but
little about him. If they had been told that within two years
Abraham Lincoln would be elected president of the United
States, three out of every four would have inquired who
Abraham Lincoln was. At the West all was different. Everybody knew "Old Abe." He was the people's friend—
the man of the people—the champion of freedom and free
labor—the man who had beaten the "little giant" in the popular vote of the democratic state of Illinois. His peculiarities were as well known to the people of the West as if he
had been the member of every man's family. To look upon
him was to look upon a lion. To shake hands with him or to
hear him speak, was a great privilege—a subject of self-grat-
ulation or neighborly boasting.

On the 17th of May, 1859, we find Mr. Lincoln answering
a letter addressed to him by Dr. Theodor Canisius, a German citizen of Illinois, who, with an eye to the future, inquired
concerning Mr. Lincoln's views of the constitutional provision
recently adopted in Massachusetts, in relation to naturalized
citizens, and whether he opposed or favored a fusion of the
republicans and other opposition elements in the approaching
campaign of 1860. Mr. Lincoln replied that, while he had
no right to advise the sovereign and independent state of
Massachusetts, concerning her policy, he would say that so
far as he understood the provision she had consummated, he

was against its adoption in Illinois, and in every other place where he had a right to oppose it. "As I understand the spirit of our institutions," said Mr. Lincoln, "it is designed to promote the elevation of men. I am, therefore, hostile to anything that tends to their debasement. It is well known that I deplore the depressed condition of the blacks, and it would, therefore, be very inconsistent for me to look with approval upon any measure that infringes upon the inalienable rights of white men, whether or not they are born in another land, or speak a different language from our own." As to the inquiry touching the fusion of all the opposition elements, he was in favor of it, if it could be done on republican principles, and upon no other condition. "A fusion upon any other platform," the letter proceeds, "would be as insane as unprincipled. It would thereby lose the whole North, while the common enemy would still have the support of the entire South. The question in relation to men is different. There are good and patriotic men and able statesmen in the South whom I would willingly support, if they would place themselves on republican ground; but I shall oppose the lowering of the republican-standard even by a hair's breadth."

It is to be remembered in this connection that Massachusetts was a representative republican state, and, regarding the ignorant foreign population, particularly of the eastern states, as holding the balance of power between the democratic and republican parties, which it never failed to exercise in the interest of the former and in the support of African slavery, had instituted measures which rendered naturalization a more difficult process. This embarrassed the republicans of the West, who were associated with a large and generally intelligent German population, with leanings toward the republican party rather than to the democratic. Hence this letter to Mr. Lincoln and his reply, which latter undoubtedly had its office in shaping public opinion, and in bringing the foreign population of the West into hearty sympathy with Mr. Lincoln himself.

It was during this year that the movement for making Mr.

Lincoln the republican candidate for the presidency took form. He was present as a spectator at the Illinois state republican convention held at Decatur on the tenth of May. When he entered the hall, he was greeted with such enthusiasm as few defeated men are favored with. There was no mistaking the high honor and warm affection in which the audience held him, and no doubting the fact that they regarded that which was nominally his defeat as a great triumph, whose fruits would not long be delayed. He had hardly taken his seat when Governor Oglesby of Decatur announced that an old democrat of Macon County desired to make a contribution to the convention. The offer being at once accepted, two old fence-rails were borne into the convention, gaudily decorated, and bearing the inscription: "ABRAHAM LINCOLN, the rail candidate for the presidency in 1860. Two rails from a lot of three thousand, made in 1830, by Thomas Hanks and Abe Lincoln—whose father was the first pioneer of Macon County."

The effect of this upon an audience already excited can be imagined by those only who have been familiar with the effect of similar melo-dramatic incidents under similar circumstances. The cheers were prolonged for fifteen minutes, or until the strength of the enthusiastic assembly was exhausted. Mr. Lincoln was called upon to explain the matter of the rails, which he did, repeating the story already in the reader's possession—the story of his first work in Illinois, when he helped to build a cabin for his father, and to fence in a field of corn.

It is the misfortune of great men who are candidates for office, that appeals must be made by them, or on their behalf, to the groundlings. It was a great misfortune to Mr. Lincoln that he was introduced to the nation as pre-eminently a rail-splitter, and that it was deemed necessary to his political fortunes that he should be called such. There is no question that the designation belittled him in the eyes of all people of education and culture, at home and abroad. And this, not because there was any prejudice among these people against labor, and not because they attached the slightest dishonor to Mr. Lincoln on account of his early poverty and humble pursuits. Splitting rails was in no way allied to the duties of the presidency. The ability to split rails did not add to moral or intellectual power. The fact that Mr. Lincoln had split rails did not increase his qualifications for office. Mr. Lincoln himself regretted that, while he was splitting these rails, he had not been in school or college. He felt that he should have been very much better fitted for the great duties that had been devolved upon him if, instead having devoted the best of his youth to splitting rails and other manual labor, he had enjoyed the advantages of a thorough education. The country took Mr. Lincoln at the estimate of his friends; and those friends thrust him before the country as a man whose grand achievement was the splitting of many rails. It took years for the country to learn that Mr. Lincoln was not a boor. It took years for them to unlearn what an unwise and boyish introduction of a great man to the public had taught them. It took years for them to comprehend the fact that in Mr. Lincoln the country had the wisest, truest, gentlest, noblest, most sagacious president who had occupied the chair of state since Washington retired from it. At this very period he said to Judge Drummond of Chicago, who had remarked to him that people were talking of him for the presidency: "It seems as if they ought to find somebody who knows more than I do." The rails and that which they symbolized were what troubled him, and, in his own judgment, detracted from his qualifications for the high office.

The latter part of 1859 and the first months of 1860 were broken by travel through various portions of the country, during which he delivered some of the best and most elaborate speeches of his life. He visited Kansas, and was received by her people with the honor due to one who had done brave battle for her freedom. On entering Leavenworth, although the weather was most inclement, he was met by a large procession of people, and escorted to his hotel, while a dense crowd gathered upon the sidewalks that lined the passage.

All the doors, windows, balconies and porticos were filled with men, women and children, anxious to catch a glimpse of the man whose speeches they had read, and of whom they had heard so much. The Leavenworth Register, in its notice of the occasion, said:—"never did man receive such honors at the hands of our people, and never did our people pay honors to a better man, or one who has been a truer friend of Kansas." Here he made a speech, and the following paragraph, selected from it, will show the state of political feeling at the time, and Mr. Lincoln's relation to it:

"But you democrats are for the Union; and you greatly fear the success of the republicans would destroy the Union. Why? Do the republicans declare against the Union? Nothing like it. .Your own statement of it is that if the black republicans elect a president, you 'wont stand it.' You will break up the Union. That will be your act, not ours. To justify it, you must show that our policy gives you just cause for such desperate action. Can you do that? When you attempt it, you will find that our policy is exactly the policy of the men who made the Union—nothing more, nothing less. Do you really think you are justified to break up the government rather than have it administered as it was by Washington? If you do, you are very unreasonable, and more reasonable men cannot and will not submit to you. While you elect presidents, we submit, neither breaking nor attempting to break up the Union. If we shall constitutionally elect a president, it will be our duty to see that you also submit. Old John Brown has been executed for treason against a state. We cannot object, even though he agreed with us in thinking slavery wrong. That cannot excuse violence, bloodshed and treason. It could avail him nothing that he might think himself right. So, if we constitutionally elect a president, and, therefore, you undertake to destroy the Union, it will be our duty to deal with you as old John Brown has been dealt with. We shall try to do our duty. We hope and believe that in no section will a majority so act as to render such extreme measures necessary."

In September, Mr. Lincoln paid a visit to Ohio, following Mr. Douglas, and made two speeches, one at Columbus and another at Cincinnati. These were the first occasions on which he had ever had the privilege of speaking to Ohio audiences, and the introductions to these speeches betrayed his diffidence. In Illinois the people knew and understood him.

He had won a reputation there, but, as he traveled eastward, he felt himself away from home. The names of Chase, Corwin and Wade were in his mind—eminent speakers, with whose voices the people of Ohio were familiar—and he felt that it would be difficult for him to establish his position as a political orator when brought into close comparison with them. His style of speech and mode of reasoning he knew to be his own; and he had misgivings touching their reception among those whose ideas of oratory were derived from other models. But these misgivings were groundless. His plainness, clearness, earnestness and thorough comprehension of the merits of his subject secured for him the honest admiration and esteem of all who heard him.

At Columbus, he devoted himself mainly to the discussion of a few points of an elaborate article that had previously appeared in Harper's Magazine, from the pen of Judge Douglas. In this article, the Senator had contrived to spread throughout the country his views touching the relations of slavery to the Constitution. It was the old talk of the senatorial campaign repeated with unimportant variations, though with some new illustrations. It was familiar ground with Mr. Lincoln; and, while his speech was a new one, it would convey but few new ideas to those who had read his speeches of the previous autumn. Mr. Douglas had preceded him at Cincinnati, and had alluded to him there. It was the battle of Illinois repeated upon the soil of Ohio. The contestants were the same—the questions upon which they took issue were the same. Popular sovereignty, the Dred Scott decision, the right and wrong of slavery, negro equality, the nationalization of slavery—these subjects, presented and illustrated in every possible way already, were again made the themes of discussion by these two men; and the people of Ohio gave them abundant audience. One of Mr. Lincoln's most effective points at Cincinnati was made upon the assumption that, being near the Kentucky border, some Kentuckians were present, to whom he addressed himself in an attempt to prove that they ought to nominate Judge Douglas at Charleston, as peculiarly

,the southern candidate for the presidency. He told them that Judge Douglas was the only man in the whole nation who gave them any hold of the free states; and then he proceeded to show that Mr. Douglas was as sincerely, and quite as wisely, for them, as they were for themselves. The points made in this part of the speech against his old antagonist were very ingenious and very damaging, so far as they related to his standing in Ohio, whatever effect they may have had upon the possible Kentuckians in the audience. After telling them that they must take Douglas under any circumstances or be defeated, and that it was possible, if they did take him, that they might be beaten, he told them what the opposition proposed to do with them in case it should be successful in the approaching presidential contest. The passage is worth quoting, as it is an embodiment of the policy he subsequently pursued when, the opposition having succeeded, he found himself endowed with the responsibilities of office, as well as a prophecy of the result of a collision then conditionally proposed.

"I will tell you, so far as I am authorized to speak for the opposition, what we mean to do with you. We mean to treat you, as near as we possibly can, as Washington, Jefferson and Madison treated you. We mean to leave you alone, and in no way to interfere with your institution; to abide by all and every compromise of the Constitution, and, in a word, coming back to the original proposition, to treat you, so far as degenerated men (if we have degenerated) may, according to the examples of those noble fathers—Washington, Jefferson and Madison. We mean to remember that you are as good as we; that there is no difference between us other than the difference of circumstances. We mean to recognize and bear in mind always that you have as good hearts in your bosoms as other people, or as we claim to have, and treat you accordingly. We mean to marry your girls when we have a chance—the white ones I mean—and I have the honor to inform you that I once did have a chance in that way.

"I have told you what we mean to do. I want to know, now, when that thing takes place, what you mean to do. I often hear it intimated that you mean to divide the Union whenever a republican or anything like it is elected president of the United States. [A voice—'That is so.'] 'That is so,' one of them says; I wonder if he is a Kentuckian?

[A voice—'He is a Douglas man.'] Well, then, I want to know what you are going to do with your half of it? Are you going to split the Ohio down through, and push your half off a piece? Or are you going to keep it right alongside of us outrageous fellows? Or are you going to build up a wall some way between your country and ours, by which that movable property of yours can't come over here any more, to the danger of your losing it? Do you think you can better yourselves on that subject, by leaving us here under no obligation whatever to return those specimens of your movable property that come hither? You have divided the Union because we would not do right with you, as you think, upon that subject; when we cease to be under obligations to do anything for you, how much better off do you think you will be? Will you make war upon us and kill us all? Why, gentlemen, I think you are as gallant and as brave men as live; that you can fight as bravely in a good cause, man for man, as any other people living; that you have shown yourselves capable of this upon various occasions; but man for man, you are not better than we are, and there are not so many of you as there are of us. You will never make much of a hand at whipping us. If we were fewer in numbers than you, I think that you could whip us; if we were equal it would likely be a drawn battle; but being inferior in numbers, you will make nothing by attempting to master us."

It is proper to say of Mr. Lincoln and Judge Douglas that no two men in the nation better apprehended the real nature of the struggle between the North and South than they. Mr. Douglas, so far back as the date of the abrogation of the Missouri Compromise, foresaw the coming conflict, and by that measure attempted to avert it. His bringing forward that measure at a time when the South did not demand it, could have been from no motive other than his wish to provide ground upon which the northern and southern democracy could stand together, in the presidential contest of 1860, when it was his expectation to be their candidate. Slavery was becoming discontented under the conviction that it was about to lose its power. It found itself either legally or practically shut out of the national domain. It is not at all improbable that the Senator knew something of the intrigues of those who were bent on disunion. It was then that he invented "popular sovereignty"—what he was accustomed to call his "great principle"—and there was indeed nothing foolish in the

tenacity with which he clung to it. It was his only ground
of hope for election to the presidency. He had no personal
responsibility for the Dred Scott decision. It was not for him
to say what the rights of slavery were among the people of
a territory; but he was willing to take the responsibility of
giving slavery and freedom the same rights. There was great
plausibility in his view, and he had little difficulty in carrying his party with him. It was a sort of neutral ground—
speciously it was catholic ground. His intention was to give
slavery a chance to enter territory then free,—territory forever
set apart to freedom. If he did not intend to give this chance,
his movement was without motive. On this chance, he intended, without doubt, to build up a claim upon southern
support; but he had a heavy load to carry, as events proved.
Mr. Lincoln was a thorn in his side. If he spoke in Illinois,
Mr. Lincoln challenged him to debate, and exposed his fallacies. If he went to Ohio, Mr. Lincoln followed close upon
his heels. If he betook himself to a New York publication,
Mr. Lincoln took measures practically to meet him there.

Mr. Lincoln's opportunity to meet his antagonist in the
press of New York came through an invitation to speak in
Brooklyn, at Mr. Beecher's church. This speech, which it was
finally concluded should be delivered at the Cooper Institute,
in New York, was by many regarded as the best he ever
made. It was the last elaborate speech of his life, and was
spread broadcast over the country by the press of the city.

Mr. Lincoln arrived in the great metropolis on the 25th of
February, 1860. He expected, as has been stated, to speak
at Mr. Beecher's church in Brooklyn, and had prepared his
address with some reference to the place. On learning that
he was expected to speak in New York, he said he must review his speech. He reached the Astor House on Saturday,
and spent the whole day in making such modifications of his
manuscript as seemed necessary, under the change of circumstances. On Sunday, he attended upon Mr. Beecher's preach-
ing, and seemed to take great satisfaction in the services.
When waited upon on Monday, by representative members

of the Republican Club, under whose auspices he was to appear, he was found encased in a new and badly wrinkled suit of black, which had evidently spent too much time in a small valise. He talked freely of the unbecoming dress, and, like a boy, expressed his surprise at finding himself in the great city. On being applied to for slips containing the speech of the evening, he showed that he was not familiar with the habit of eastern speakers of supplying such slips to the press in advance, and even expressed the doubt whether any of the papers would care to publish it entire. During the interview, he referred frequently to Mr. Douglas, and in so kind and cordial a manner that it was impossible to regard him as that gentleman's personal enemy in any sense.*

Being at leisure during the day, he accepted an invitation to ride about the city. Some of the more important streets were passed through, and a number of large establishments visited. At one place, he met an old acquaintance from Illinois, whom he addressed with an inquiry as to how he had fared since leaving the West. "I have made a hundred thousand dollars, and lost all," was his reply. Then turning questioner he said: "How is it with you, Mr. Lincoln?" "Oh very well," said he; "I have the cottage at Springfield, and about eight thousand dollars in money. If they make me vice-president with Seward, as some say they will, I hope I shall be able to increase it to twenty thousand; and that is as much as any man ought to want."

In a photographic establishment on Broadway, he met and was introduced to George Bancroft, the historian. The contrast which he presented in his person and manner to this gentleman was certainly not to his advantage; but his bluff, hearty way carried all before it. He informed Mr. Bancroft that he was on his way to Massachusetts where he had a son in college, who, if report were true, already knew much more than his father.

He was to speak at Cooper Institute that night, and having caught a glimpse of the great capital and of its gigantic in-

* R. C. McCormick, in the New York Evening Post.

terests and affairs, it is not strange that he should have been oppressed with a sense of his own insignificance. It was one of his peculiarities that, while he was the subject of the most exalted aspirations and ambitions, and the ready undertaker of the highest and most difficult tasks, he always bore about with him a sense of his imperfections, and experienced a sort of surprise at every success. Indeed, his triumphs became the subjects of his study. They really puzzled him; and frequent conversations with others betrayed his desire to find the secrets of his own power.

But Mr. Lincoln was not more curious concerning himself, or concerning the new scenes among which he found himself, than the people of New York were concerning him. There was a great and general curiosity to see and hear him; and when he entered the hall he found the platform covered with the republican leaders of the city, and of Brooklyn, and, in his audience, many ladies. The venerable William Cullen Bryant presided, and in introducing the speaker said: "It is a grateful office that I perform, in introducing to you an eminent citizen of the West, hitherto known to you only by reputation." There was nothing in the introduction, however, which pleased Mr. Lincoln so much as Mr. Bryant's statement in the next day's Evening Post, (of which he was the editor) that for the publication of such words of weight and wisdom as those of Mr. Lincoln, the pages of that journal were "indefinitely elastic."

Mr. Lincoln began his address in a low, monotonous tone, but gaining confidence in the respectful stillness, his tones, that had long been keyed to out-of-door efforts, rose in strength and gained in clearness, until every ear heard every word. His style of speech was so fresh, his mode of statement was so simple, his illustrations were so quaint and peculiar, that the audience eagerly drank in every sentence. The back-woods orator had found one of the most appreciative audiences he had ever addressed, and the audience gave abundant testimony that they were listening to the utterances of a master.

The speech which Mr. Lincoln made on this occasion must

have cost him much labor in the preparation. The historical study which it involved—study that led into unexplored fields, and fields very difficult of exploration—must have been very great; but it was intimate and complete. Gentlemen who afterward engaged in preparing the speech for circulation as a campaign document were much surprised by the amount of research that it required to be able to make the speech, and were very much wearied with the work of verifying its historical statements in detail. They were weeks in finding the works consulted by him.

As a text for the subject of his discourse, he took the words of Senator Douglas, uttered in a speech at Columbus, Ohio, the previous autumn, viz: " Our fathers when they framed the government under which we live, understood this question (the question of slavery) just as well, and even better, than we do now." To this statement the speaker agreed, so that he and the senator had a common starting point for discussion. The inquiry was, simply: what was the understanding those fathers had of the question mentioned? As questions preliminary to this inquiry he gave these: " what is the frame of government under which we live?" and " who were our fathers who framed the Constitution?" The frame of government is the Constitution itself, consisting of the original, framed in 1787, and twelve subsequent amendments, ten of which were framed in 1789. The thirty-nine men who framed the original Constitution are legitimately to be called the fathers, and these he took as " our fathers who framed the government under which we live." The question fully written out, which Senator Douglas thought these men understood better than we do, was: " Does the proper division of local from federal authority, or anything in the Constitution, forbid the federal government control as to slavery in our federal territories?"

From this point Mr. Lincoln went on to draw from the history of Congress every recorded act of these thirty-nine men on the question of slavery. Question after question upon which these men acted was stated in brief, and it was found that, of the thirty-nine fathers, twenty-one, a clear majority, so acted that they would be guilty of perjury if they did not believe that the federal government had power to control slavery in the territories.   Two voted against special measures, but in such a way as not to show whether they believed the government possessed this power or not.   Of the remaining sixteen, there is no record, but it is fair to conclude they had the same understanding with the majority, particularly as they included some of the most noted anti-slavery men of the time, among whom were Benjamin Franklin, Alexander Hamilton and Gouverneur Morris.

The historical argument was entirely unanswerable.   It was a solid and logical statement of facts and conclusions that no sane man would undertake to controvert.   The first third of the speech was devoted to this historical argument, and the remainder in about equal proportions to addresses to the southern people, and to the republicans.   His remarks addressed particularly to the South were in the kindest spirit, but they were charged with a force of argument and statement that is wonderful.   It is well that Mr. Lincoln be permitted to state his own attitude toward those to whom he was destined to come into such strange and momentous relations. He said:

"You say we are sectional.   We deny it.   That makes an issue; and the burden of proof is upon you.   You produce your proof; and what is it?   Why, that our party has no existence in your section—gets no votes in your section.   The fact is substantially true; but does it prove the issue?   If it does, then, in case we should, without change of principle, begin to get votes in your section, we should thereby cease to be sectional.   You cannot escape this conclusion; and yet, are you willing to abide by it?   If you are, you will probably soon find that we have ceased to be sectional, for we shall get votes in your section this very year.   You will then begin to discover, as the truth plainly is, that your proof does not touch the issue.   The fact that we get no votes in your section is a fact of your making, and not of ours.   And if there be fault in that fact, that fault is primarily yours, and remains so until you show that we repel you by some wrong principle or practice.   If we do repel you by any wrong principle or practice, the fault is ours· but this brings us to where you ought to have started—to a discussion

. of the right or wrong of our principle. If our principle, put in practice, would wrong your section for the benefit of ours, or for any other object, then our principle, and we with it, are sectional, and are justly opposed and denounced as such. Meet us, then, on the question of whether our principle, put in practice, would wrong your section; and so meet it as if it were possible that something may be said on our side. Do you accept the challenge? No? Then you really believe that the principle which our fathers, who framed the government under which we live, thought so clearly right as to adopt it, and indorse it again and again upon their official oaths, is, in fact, so clearly wrong as to demand your condemnation without a moment's consideration.

"Some of you delight to flaunt in our faces the warning against sectional parties given by Washington in his Farewell Address. Less than eight years before Washington gave that warning, he had, as President of the United States, approved and signed an act of Congress enforcing the prohibition of slavery in the Northwestern Territory, which act embodied the policy of the government upon that subject, up to and at the very moment he penned that warning; and about one year after he penned it he wrote Lafayette that he considered that prohibition a wise measure, expressing, in the same connection, his hope that we should some time have a confederacy of free states.

"Bearing this in mind, and seeing that sectionalism has since arisen upon this same subject, is that warning a weapon in your hands against us, or in our hands against you? Could Washington himself speak, would he cast the blame of that sectionalism upon us, who sustain his policy, or upon you, who repudiate it? We respect that warning of Washington, and we commend it to you, together with his example pointing to the right application of it.

"But you say you are conservative—eminently conservative—while we are revolutionary, destructive, or something of the sort. What is conservatism? Is it not adherence to the old and tried against the new and untried? We stick to, contend for, the identical old policy on the point in controversy which was adopted by our fathers who framed the government under which we live; while you, with one accord, reject, and scout, and spit upon that old policy, and insist upon substituting something new. True, you disagree among yourselves as to what that substitute shall be. You have considerable variety of new propositions and plans, but you are unanimous in rejecting and denouncing the old policy of the fathers. Some of you are for reviving the foreign slave-trade; some for a congressional slave-code for the territories; some for Congress forbidding the territories to prohibit slavery within their limits; some for maintaining slavery in the territories through the Judiciary; some for the gur-reat pur-rinciple' that, 'if one man would enslave another, no third man should object,' fantastically called 'popu-

14

lar sovereignty;' but never a man among you in favor of federal prohibition of slavery in federal territories, according to the practice of
our fathers who framed the government under which we live. Not one
of all your various plans can show a precedent or an advocate in the
century within which our government originated. Consider, then,
whether your claim of conservatism for yourselves, and your charge of
destructiveness against us, are based on the most clear and stable foundations.

"Again, you say we have made the slavery question more prominent
than it formerly was. We deny it. We admit that it is more prominent, but we deny that we made it so. It was not we, but you, who
discarded the old policy of the fathers. We resisted, and still resist,
your innovation; and thence comes the greater prominence of the
question. Would you have that question reduced to its former proportions? Go back to that old policy. What has been will be again,
under the same conditions. If you would have the peace of the old
times, re-adopt the precepts and policy of the old times."

Alluding to their threats to break up the Union if slavery
should be shut out of the territories, he said:

"In that supposed event, you say you will destroy the Union; and
then you say the great crime of having destroyed it will be upon us!
That is cool. A highwayman holds a pistol to my ear, and mutters
through his teeth: 'Stand and deliver, or I shall kill you, and then you
will be a murderer!' To be sure, what the robber demanded of me—
my money—was my own; and I had a clear right to keep it; but it was
no more my own than my vote is my own; and threat of death to me
to extort my money, and threat of destruction to the Union to extort
my vote, can scarcely be distinguished in principle."

Certainly this illustration disposed of the whole question as
to who would be responsible for the destruction of the Union,
under the circumstances stated.

His words to the republicans were words of profoundest
wisdom. He told them that nothing would satisfy the South
but to cease calling slavery wrong, and to join with them in
calling it right, and to do it thoroughly by acts as well as
words. "We must arrest and return their slaves with greedy
pleasure. We must pull down our free state constitutions.
The whole atmosphere must be disinfected from all taint of
opposition to slavery, before they will cease to believe that all

their troubles proceed from us." He continued: "I am quite aware they do not state their case precisely in this way. Most of them would probably say to us, 'let us alone, do nothing to us, and say what you please about slavery.' But we do let them alone—have never disturbed them—so that, after all, it is what we say that dissatisfies them. They will continue to accuse us of doing until we cease saying." After saying that we could not consistently deny the South in its most extreme demands, on any ground except the wrong of slavery, he put the case forcibly, as follows: "If slavery is right, all words, acts, laws and constitutions against it are themselves wrong, and should be silenced and swept away. If it is right, we cannot justly object to its nationality—its universality; if it is wrong, they cannot justly insist upon its extension, its enlargement. All they ask, we could readily grant if we thought slavery right; all we ask they could as readily grant if they thought slavery wrong. Their thinking it right and our thinking it wrong is the precise fact upon which depends the whole controversy." The closing paragraph is equally remarkable for its wit and wisdom—its pith and patriotism:

"Wrong as we think slavery is, we can yet afford to let it alone where it is, because that much is due to the necessity arising from its actual presence in the nation; but can we, while our votes will prevent it, allow it to spread into the national territories, and to overrun us here in these free states? If our sense of duty forbids this, then let us stand by our duty, fearlessly and effectively. Let us be diverted by none of those sophistical contrivances wherewith we are so industriously plied and belabored—contrivances such as groping for some middle ground between the right and the wrong, vain as the search for a man who should be neither a living man nor a dead man—such as a policy of 'don't care' on a question about which all true men do care—such as Union appeals beseeching true Union men to yield to disunionists, reversing the divine rule, and calling not the sinners, but the righteous to repentance—such as invocations to Washington, imploring men to unsay what Washington said, and undo what Washington did. Neither let us be slandered from our duty by false accusations against us, nor frightened from it by menaces of destruction to the Government, nor of dungeons to ourselves. Let us have faith that right makes might, and in that faith, let us, to the end, dare to do our duty, as we understand it."

The speech was, in the popular acceptation of the phrase, a great success.   Through all his passages of close and crowded reasoning, his audience followed him with an interest that produced the profoundest silence, and at every triumphant establishment of a point broke out into sudden and hearty applause.   Those who came from motives of curiosity went away thoughtful.   Many who had entered the hall in doubt as to their duty, went away with their path bright before them. Most of all were the New York politicians affected; and it is not to be doubted that the impressions of that evening left them convinced that if Mr. Seward, the man of their choice, should be set aside, as the republican candidate for the presidency, Mr. Lincoln, the favorite of the West, would be abundantly worthy of their support.

At the conclusion of the speech, a few friends took the speaker to the rooms of the Atheneum Club for supper.   Mr. Lincoln appreciated his success, and was in good humor over it.   He was as happy at the table as he was upon the platform—full of good humor, and abounding with jokes and pleasant stories.   Throwing off all reserve, and opening his heart like a boy, he talked long and late; and when he parted with his friends for the night they were as much charmed with the man as they had been instructed by his speech and entertained by his conversation.

The papers of the city were full of his address and with comments upon it the next day.   The Illinois lawyer was a lion.   Critics read the speech, and marveled at its pure and compact English, its felicity of statement and its faultless logic. It was read during the day not only by New York but by nearly all New England.

After the speech, he spent several days in New York, familiarizing himself with its wonders.   Some of his explorations he made alone, and on one occasion found his way into the Sunday School of the Five Points Mission.   The superintendent noticing his look of interest in the proceedings, invited him to speak to the children.   His remarks interested his young audience so much that on every attempt to stop they cried out "go on, oh! do go on!" None knew who he was, and as he turned to depart, the superintendent inquired his name. "Abraham Lincoln of Illinois," was the answer.

Invitations were received by Mr. Lincoln from many places in New England, to speak on political questions. On the fifth of March, he spoke at Hartford, in the city hall, and was escorted to the hall by the first company of "Wide-Awakes" ever organized in the country. This organization became universal throughout the free states, but was intended only for campaign service. He had an immense audience in Hartford, and produced a powerful impression. On the following day he was waited upon by a number of prominent citizens, and visited several objects of interest in the city, among which were the armories of Colt and Sharp. On the sixth of March, he spoke at New Haven, at Meriden on the seventh, at Woonsocket, Rhode Island, on the eighth, at Norwich, Connecticut, on the ninth, and at Bridgeport on the tenth. His speaking was always to immense audiences. Connecticut was that year carried by the republicans by about five hundred majority, against the most powerful efforts of the democrats—a fact which was due more to the speeches of Mr. Lincoln than to any other cause.

Some very interesting reminiscences of this trip were communicated to the public in 1864, by Rev. John P. Gulliver of Norwich, who listened to his address in that city.* On the morning following the speech, he met Mr. Lincoln upon a train of cars, and entered into conversation with him. In speaking of his speech, Mr. Gulliver remarked to Mr. Lincoln that he thought it the most remarkable one he ever heard. "Are you sincere in what you say?" inquired Mr. Lincoln. "I mean every word of it," replied the minister. "Indeed, sir," he continued, "I learned more of the art of public speaking last evening than I could from a whole course of lectures on rhetoric." Then Mr. Lincoln informed him of "a most extraordinary circumstance" that occurred at New Haven a few days previously. A professor of rhetoric in Yale College, he had

* New York Independent of September 1, 1864.

been told, came to hear him, took notes of his speech, and gave a lecture on it to his class the following day, and, not satisfied with that, followed him to Meriden the next evening, and heard him again for the same purpose. All this seemed to Mr. Lincoln to be "very extraordinary." He had been sufficiently astonished by his success at the West, but he had no expectation of any marked success at the East, particularly among literary and learned men. "Now," said Mr. Lincoln, "I should like very much to know what it was in my speech which you thought so remarkable, and which interested my friend the professor so much?" Mr. Gulliver's answer was: "The clearness of your statements, the unanswerable style of your reasoning, and, especially, your illustrations, which were romance and pathos and fun and logic all welded together."

After Mr. Gulliver had fully satisfied his curiosity by a further exposition of the politician's peculiar power, Mr. Lincoln said, "I am much obliged to you for this. I have been wishing for a long time to find some one who would make this analysis for me. It throws light on a subject which has been dark to me. I can understand very readily how such a power as you have ascribed to me will account for the effect which seems to be produced by my speeches. I hope you have not been too flattering in your estimate. Certainly I have had a most wonderful success for a man of my limited education." Then Mr. Gulliver inquired into the processes by which he had acquired his education, and was rewarded with many interesting details. When they were about to part, the minister said: "Mr. Lincoln, may I say one thing to you before we separate?" "Certainly; anything you please," was the response. "You have just spoken," said Mr. Gulliver, "of the tendency of political life in Washington to debase the moral convictions of our representatives there, by the admixture of considerations of mere political expediency. You have become, by the controversy with Mr. Douglas, one of our leaders in this great struggle with slavery, which is undoubtedly *the* struggle of the nation and the age. What I would like to say is this, and I say it with a full heart: *Be true to your principles, and we will be true to you, and God will be true to us all.*" Mr. Lincoln, touched by the earnestness of his interlocutor, took his hand in both of his own, and, with his face full of sympathetic light, exclaimed: "I say amen to that! amen to that!"

After visiting his son at Harvard College, making many acquaintances among the prominent men of New England, and looking with curious eyes upon New England scenes, and observing with his native shrewdness the characteristics of New England habits and manners, he turned his face homewards, spending a Sabbath in New York while on the way, and again attending Mr. Beecher's church.

One thing, at least, he had learned by this visit: that the people of the older states judge a man by the same rule that prevails on an Illinois prairie—by what he is, and what he can do, and not by the cloth he wears, the knowledge he has acquired, the wealth he possesses, or the blood that flows in his veins. He had been accepted as an honest, fresh, original and powerful man; and he went home gratified. Could he have made his visit longer, and been seen more generally by the people, it would not have been necessary for them to wait so long before knowing how great and good a man the providence of God had given to be their ruler.

CHAPTER XV.

THE frequent allusions in Mr. Lincoln's speeches to threats of secession on the part of the South, in the event of the success of the republican party, have already shown the reader that secession had become a matter of consideration and discussion among those interested in the perpetuation and nationalization of slavery. It was evident that the southern leaders were preparing the minds of their people for some desperate step, and that many of them desired, rather than deprecated, the election of a republican president. Many of them openly said that they should prefer the election of Mr. Seward or Mr. Lincoln to the election of Mr. Douglas, because then they should know exactly what they were to meet. The reason thus given was undoubtedly a fraud. They found themselves in desperate circumstances. All their schemes for the extension of slavery and the reinforcement of the slave power had miscarried. Kansas and California were lost to them. There was no hope for them in Nebraska or any of the new territories. The hope of acquiring Cuba was gone, and the fillibustering operations of Walker which they had patronized were failures. They knew of but one remedy— that which the great mischief-maker of South Carolina had pointed out to them many years before, viz: secession. It is doubtful whether they preferred secession to predominance in the nation, but, basing their policy on the doctrine of " state rights," their aim was to secede, and either to insist on a permanent separation, or by secession to coerce the government into the practical acknowledgment of their claims. There is no doubt that it was the policy of the shrewdest of the slavery-propagandists so to manage their party as to secure the election of a republican president. Overpowered in the nation, and hopeless of the future, they looked only for a plausible pretext for precipitating the execution of their scheme; and this could only be found in the election of a president professedly a foe to the extension of slavery.

"The Knights of the Golden Circle" were a band of secret conspirators organized in the interest of treason. The popular political leaders rose to the highest degrees in this order, and knew the whole plot, while the masses, many of whom had no real sympathy with secession, were kept in the dark, ready to be forced into measures that were in cunning and careful preparation. The Christian church of the whole South was the willing slave of this cabal. Preachers proclaimed the divine right of slavery and the doctrines of sedition from the pulpit. The press was an obedient instrument in their hands. There were traitors and plotters in the national government, industriously preparing the way for secession, and sapping the power of the government to prevent it. Mr. Cobb was squandering the national finances. Mr. Floyd, the secretary of war, was filling all the southern arsenals with arms at the expense of the government, and sending loyal officers to distant posts; and, although a northern man was at the head of the navy department, it was subsequently found, when ships were wanted, that they were very far from where they were wanted. These southern men, thus plotting, only waited for a pretext for springing their plot upon the people, and of course were not reluctant to make a pretext when opportunity offered.

This was the condition of affairs in the spring of 1860, a year which was to see a new president elected. Everybody felt that a severe political storm was ahead, though compara-tively few, either at the North or the South, knew what its character would be. The South blindly followed its leaders, without perfectly knowing whither it was to be led. The North had become accustomed to threats of dissolution of the

Union, and did not believe that those then rife would be better fulfilled than those which had preceded them. No one at the North, unless it may have been a few sympathetic politicians, had any faith in the earnestness of the pro-slavery schemers. The disruption of the government was regarded as an impossibility; and the Union-loving Yankee would not believe that there were any who would push their professed enmity to any practical exhibition.

Mr. Lincoln had scarcely returned to his home before the Democratic National Convention assembled at Charleston. This convention occurred on the twenty-third of April, and collected to itself all the plotters against the Union. That they met the northern members of the democratic party with any expectation to unite with them in a platform and the selection of a candidate, is not probable. Mr. Douglas, with his popular sovereignty, and Dred Scott decision, and "don't care" policy, offered them the only ground of Union. All saw this, and all were for or against Douglas. Douglas was the pivot of the convention. Everything turned on him. The northern men felt that nothing less than Douglas, who had fought the Lecompton fraud and the administration, and had been compelled to some concessions to freedom in order to win his seat in the senate, would do for them, while the South was determined to take no man who was not fairly and squarely a pro-slavery man, with a clean record, and to subscribe to no platform that did not accord to them fully the rights they claimed. The South would have only a "sound man," and would fight this time only "on principle." If it could not have honest victory, it wanted defeat. No "unfriendly legislation" should exclude slavery from the territories. They must have their property protected. Mr. Yancey was present as the leader of the "fire-eaters," and could probably have foretold the explosion of the convention. There is no doubt that he intended nothing else than this, and the convention did explode, and the old democratic party that had proved invincible on so many battle-fields was rent in twain. The southern members, by a large majority, withdrew and formed a "Constitutional Convention." The regular convention remained in session, and after fifty-seven unsuccessful ballotings, in which Mr. Douglas came near a nomination, they gave it up, and adjourned to meet in Baltimore on the eighteenth day of June, or two days after the appointed date of the Republican Convention at Chicago. The Constitutional Convention transacted no important business, and made no nomination, but adjourned to meet in Richmond on the second Monday in June.

The Charleston people were delighted with the results of the quarrel. The ladies, only a dozen of whom had been in attendance upon the regular convention, turned out and filled the hall of the seceders. All the smiles of all the beauty of Charleston were bestowed upon Mr. Yancey and his followers. They undoubtedly regarded this disruption of the party as insuring the pretext for disunion for which they so ardently wished.

The democratic host, as they retired in broken columns from Charleston, were jostled on the road by the members of another convention, on their way to Baltimore—the "National Constitutional Union Convention"—made up largely of old whigs who still dreamed that the party of their early love was in existence—that it was not dead, but sleeping. They met on the ninth of May—delegates from ten free states and eleven slave states. There is this to be said of this body of men—that they were in the main really anxious to save the Union, and that they had a juster appreciation of the dangers of the Union than the republicans, who were fond of ridiculing their fears. They passed a "conservative" resolution, declaring that they had no principles except "The Constitution of the country, the Union of the states, and the enforcement of the laws." The convention nominated John Bell of Tennessee for president, and Edward Everett of Massachusetts for vice-president, the former of whom, when secession came, went over to the disunionists, and the latter of whom devoted all his great influence and powers to the maintenance of the government, becoming at last a member of the republican party and the recipient of its honors.

Before entering upon an account of the Chicago Convention, it will be best to state, in brief, the result of the democratic split at Charleston. The Richmond Convention met and adjourned to await the doings of the Baltimore Convention, the members generally going to Baltimore. There they joined in an independent convention, making all the mischief possible, and nominating for president John C. Breckinridge, then vice-president of the United States, and since a Major General in the rebel army. The regular convention nominated Mr. Douglas, though he had begged them to sacrifice him rather than the party. The party, however, was already sacrificed; and he had had no small hand in the slaughter. The antagonism between the southern and northern sections of the democracy was irreconcilable. It was impossible for the two to agree upon a platform or a man who would carry either section of the country. Mr. Lincoln had his joke and his "little story" over the disruption of the democracy. He once knew, he said, a sound churchman of the name of Brown, who was the member of a very sober and pious committee having in charge the erection of a bridge over a dangerous and rapid river. Several architects failed, and at last Brown said he had a friend named Jones who had built several bridges, and could undoubtedly build that one. So Mr. Jones was called in. "Can you build this bridge?" inquired the committee. "Yes," replied Jones, "or any other. I could build a bridge to h—l if necessary." The committee were shocked, and Brown felt called upon to defend his friend. "I know Jones so well," said he, "and he is so honest a man, and so good an architect, that if he states soberly and positively that he can build a bridge to—to—the infernal regions, why, I believe it; but I feel bound to say that I have my doubts about the abutment on the other side." "So," said Mr. Lincoln, "when politicians told me that the northern and southern wings of the democracy could be harmonized, why, I believed them, of course, but I always had my doubts about the abutment on the other side."

Though the result of the Baltimore Convention was unknown at Chicago, it was foreseen, and it was believed that victory would come to the republican party with any respectable nominee. When the friends of Douglas left Baltimore, they left it with none but bitter feelings for those who had destroyed their party, and brought certain defeat to the man to whom they were strongly devoted. They felt that Mr. Douglas had deserved better treatment at the hands of the South than he had received, and saw, in the disruption of their party, the defeat of all their hopes.

The Republican Convention at Chicago assembled on the sixteenth of June. There was an immense crowd in attendance, casting into the shade entirely the assemblages at Charleston and Baltimore. Every hotel was crammed from basement to attic, even in that city of multitudinous and capacious hotels. It was calculated that fifteen hundred persons slept in the Tremont House alone. A huge building was erected for the sessions of the convention, which was called "The Wigwam;" and even this could not contain more than a fraction of the twenty-five thousand strangers who had assembled in the city, as delegates and interested observers.

Edward Bates, Judge McLean, Benjamin F. Wade, N. P. Banks, Abraham Lincoln, Simon Cameron, and William H. Seward, all had their partisans among outsiders and insiders; but it became evident very early that the contest was really between Mr. Seward and Mr. Lincoln. The chiefs of the party were all present, excepting, perhaps, those who imagined that they might possibly be made the recipients of the convention's favors.

Hon. George Ashmun of Massachusetts was elected to preside over the deliberations of the occasion. Canvassing, talking, prophesying, betting, declaiming, were actively in progress everywhere. On the morning of the seventeenth, Mr. Seward's friends made a demonstration in his favor, in the form of a procession, following a band of music and wearing badges. As they passed the Tremont House, they were greeted with tremendous cheers, the band playing "O, isn't he a darling?" Antagonisms were developed in every quarter. Pennsylvania, New Jersey and Indiana declared that if Mr. Seward should be nominated they could do nothing; Douglas would beat them ten to one. Illinois, devoted to Mr. Lincoln, joined in the cry, but the New Yorkers scouted the idea that Mr. Seward could not sweep with victory every northern state. The Lincoln men were quite as busy as the friends of Mr. Seward, and less noisy. Mr. Greeley telegraphed to the New York Tribune, on the evening of the seventeenth: "My conclusion, from all that I can gather, is, that the opposition to Governor Seward cannot concentrate on any candidate, and that he will be nominated;" and this, it must be remembered, was not in accordance with Mr. Greeley's wishes.

The platform upon which the party proposed to conduct the campaign was adopted on the second day. The action upon this showed that the party had not quite come to the standard of Mr. Lincoln, moderate as he had been. Hon. Joshua R. Giddings, one of the old enemies of slavery and the slave power, wished to introduce into the platform that part of the Declaration of Independence which asserts, as self-evident truths, "that all men are endowed by their Creator with certain inalienable rights, among which are those of life, liberty and the pursuit of happiness," and that governments are instituted among men to secure the enjoyment of these rights; but objections were made. The old man walked grieved and disgusted out of the wigwam, amid the protestations of the crowd. Mr. George W. Curtis, a New York delegate, made an appeal to the convention that was irresistible, and the declaration went in, and all felt the stronger and better for it. The utterances of Mr. Lincoln have already given us the substance of this platform. It contravened no right of slavery in the states, under the Constitution, denounced the subserviency of Mr. Buchanan's administration to a sectional interest and the dogma that the Constitution carried slavery into the territories and protected it there, declared that the normal condition of all the territory of the United States is that of freedom, and that a sound policy requires a protective tariff, &c., &c. It was the platform of the old whig party, repeated in most particulars, except that, in the matter of slavery, it introduced, not widely modified, the old platform of the "free soilers." The platform was adopted amid demonstrations of the wildest enthusiasm. An eye witness of the scene* says: "all the thousands of men in that enormous wigwam commenced swinging their hats, and cheering with intense enthusiasm; and the other thousands of ladies waved their handkerchiefs and clapped their hands. The roar that went up from that mass of ten thousand human beings is indescribable. Such a spectacle as was presented for some minutes has never before been witnessed at a convention. A herd of buffaloes or lions could not have made a more tremendous roaring."

The Seward men still carried a confident air on the third day. They had reason to do so. Their candidate was in many respects the greatest man in the party. He was a statesman of acknowledged eminence, and had been for many years the leading representative of the principles upon which the republican party stood. They were strong, too, in the convention; and they were sure to secure upon the first ballot more votes for their candidate than could be summoned to the support of any other man.

On the assembling of the convention, everybody was anxious to get at the decisive work, and, as a preliminary, the various candidates in the field were formally nominated by their friends. Mr. Evarts of New York nominated Mr. Seward, and Mr. Judd of Illinois named Abraham Lincoln. Afterwards, Mr. Dayton of New Jersey, Mr. Cameron of Pennsylvania, Mr. Chase of Ohio, Edward Bates of Missouri, and John McLean of Ohio, were formally nominated; but no enthusiasm was awakened by the mention of any names except those of Mr. Seward and Mr. Lincoln. Caleb B. Smith of Indiana seconded the nomination of Mr. Lincoln, as did also Mr. Delano of Ohio, while Carl Schurz of Wisconsin and

*M. Halstead, author of "Caucuses of 1860." Columbus: Follett, Foster & Co.

Mr. Blair of Michigan seconded the nomination of Mr. Seward. It was certain that one of these two men would be nominated. On every pronunciation of their names, their respective partisans raised their shouts, vieing with each other in the strength of their applause. The excitement of this mass of men at that time cannot be measured by those not there, or by men in their sober senses.

The ballot came. Maine gave nearly half her vote for Lincoln; New Hampshire, seven of her ten for Lincoln. Massachusetts was divided. New York voted solid for Mr. Seward, giving him her seventy votes. Virginia, which was expected also to vote solid for Mr. Seward, gave fourteen of her twenty-two votes for Lincoln. Indiana gave her twenty-six votes for Lincoln without a break. Thus the balloting went on, amid the most intense excitement, until the whole number of four hundred and sixty-five votes was cast. It was necessary to a choice that one candidate should have two hundred and thirty-three. William H. Seward had one hundred and seventy-three and a half, Abraham Lincoln one hundred and two, Edward Bates forty-eight, Simon Cameron fifty and a half, Salmon P. Chase forty-nine. The remaining forty-two votes were divided among John McLean, Benjamin F. Wade, William L. Dayton, John M. Reed, Jacob Collamer, Charles Sumner and John C. Fremont,—Reed, Sumner and Fremont having one each.

On the second ballot, the first gain for Lincoln was from New Hampshire. Then Vermont followed with her vote, which she had previously given to her senator, Mr. Collamer, as a compliment. Pennsylvania came next to his support, with the votes she had given to Cameron. On the whole ballot, he gained seventy-nine votes, and received one hundred and eighty-one; while Mr. Seward received one hundred and eighty-four and a half votes, having gained eleven. The announcement of the votes given to Mr. Seward and Mr. Lincoln was received by deafening applause by their respective partisans. Then came the third ballot. All felt that it was likely to be the decisive one, and the friends of Mr. Seward trembled for the result.   Hundreds of pencils were in operation, and before the result was announced it was whispered through the immense and excited mass of people that Abraham Lincoln had received two hundred and thirty-one and a half votes, only lacking one vote and a half of an election. Mr. Cartter of Ohio was up in an instant, to announce the change of four votes of Ohio from Mr. Chase to Mr. Lincoln. That finished the work.   The excitement had culminated. After a moment's pause, like the sudden and breathless stillness that precedes the hurricane, the storm of wild, uncontrollable and almost insane enthusiasm descended.   The scene surpassed description.   During all the ballotings, a man had been standing upon the roof, communicating the results to the outsiders, who, in surging masses, far outnumbered those who were packed into the wigwam.   To this man one of the secretaries shouted: "Fire the salute!   Abe Lincoln is nominated!"   Then, as the cheering inside died away, the roar began on the outside, and swelled up from the excited masses like the noise of many waters.   This the insiders heard, and to it they replied.   Thus deep called to deep with such a frenzy of sympathetic enthusiasm that even the thundering salute of cannon was unheard by many upon the platform.

When the multitudes became too tired to cheer more, the business of the convention proceeded.   Half a dozen men were on their feet announcing the change of votes of their states, swelling Mr. Lincoln's majority.   Missouri, Iowa, Kentucky, Minnesota, Virginia, California, Texas, District of Columbia, Kansas, Nebraska and Oregon insisted on casting unanimous votes for Mr. Lincoln, before the vote was declared. While these changes were going on, a photograph of the nominee was brought in and exhibited to the convention.   When the vote was declared, Mr. Evarts, on behalf of the New York delegation, expressed his grief that Mr. Seward had not been nominated, and then moved that the nomination of Mr. Lincoln should be made unanimous.   John A. Andrew of Massachusetts and Carl Schurz of Wisconsin seconded the motion, and it was carried.   Before the nomination of a vice-

15

president, the convention adjourned for dinner.   It is reported that such had been the excitement during the morning session that men who never tasted intoxicating liquors staggered like drunken men, on coming into the open air.   The nervous tension had been so great that, when it subsided, they were as flaccid and feeble as if they had but recently risen from a fever.

The excitement in the city only began as it subsided in the convention.   Mr. Lincoln was the favorite of Chicago and of Illinois—he was the people's idol.   Men shouted and sang, and did all sorts of foolish things in the incontinence of their joy.   After dinner the convention met again, and for the last time.   The simple business was the completion of the ticket by the nomination of a candidate for vice-president; and the result was the selection of Hannibal Hamlin of Maine.

The defeat of Mr. Seward was a sad blow to his friends. They had presented to the convention one of the prominent statesmen of the nation; and he had undoubtedly been slaughtered to satisfy the clamor for "availability."   The country at large did not know Mr. Lincoln in any capacity except that of a political debater; and many sections had no familiarity with his reputation, even in this character.   Mr. Seward, on the contrary, had been in public life for thirty years; and his name and fame were as common and as well established in the regard of the nation, as the name and fame of Henry Clay and Daniel Webster had been.   He was a man of great accomplishments, of wide experience, of large influence and surpassing ability—recognized as such abroad as well as at home.   Their disappointment is not to be wondered at, or blamed.   Mr. Lincoln had not been proved.   His capacity for public affairs had yet to be demonstrated; and he had been nominated over the head of Mr. Seward partly for this reason—the reason that he was a new man, and had no public record.   If events have proved that the choice between these two men was a fortunate one, they can hardly have proved that it was a wise one—that it was the result of an intelligent and honest choice between the two men.   It is pleasant to remember that Mr. Lincoln, when elected to the presidency, called to the first place in his cabinet the man whom the convention had set aside, and that the country had the advantage of his wise counsels throughout the darkest period and most difficult passage of its history.

As has been stated, the city of Chicago was wild with delight. One hundred guns were fired from the top of the Tremont House. Decorated and illuminated rails were around the newspaper offices. All the bars and drinking halls were crowded with men who were either worn out with excitement or mad with delight. From Chicago the news spread over the country, and the cannon's throat responded to the click of the telegraph from Maine to the Mississippi. The outgoing trains that night found bonfires blazing at every village, and excited crowds assembled to cheer the retiring delegates, most of whom were either too weak or too hoarse to respond.

In the little city of Springfield, in the heart of Illinois, two hundred miles from where those exciting events were in progress, sat Abraham Lincoln, in close and constant telegraphic communication with his friends in Chicago. He was apprised of the results of every ballot, and, with his home friends, sat in the Journal office receiving and commenting upon the dispatches. It was one of the decisive moments of his life—a moment on which hung his fate as a public man—his place in history. He fully appreciated the momentous results of the convention to himself and the nation, and foresaw the nature of the great struggle which his nomination and election would inaugurate. A moment, and he knew that he would either become the central man of a nation, or a cast-off politician whose ambition for the nation's highest honors would be forever blasted. At last, in the midst of intense and painful excitement, a messenger from the telegraph office entered with the decisive dispatch in his hand. Without handing it to any one, he took his way solemnly to the side of Mr. Lincoln, and said: "the convention has made a nomination, and Mr. Seward is——the second man on the list." Then he jumped upon the editorial table and shouted, "gentlemen, I propose three cheers for Abraham Lincoln, the next President of the United States;" and the call was boisterously responded to. He then handed the dispatch to Mr. Lincoln who read in silence, and then aloud, its contents. After the excitement had in a measure passed away from the little assembly, Mr. Lincoln rose, and remarking that there was "a little woman" on Eighth street who had some interest in the matter, pocketed the telegram and walked home.

As soon as the news reached Springfield, the citizens who had a personal affection for Mr. Lincoln which amounted almost to idolatry, responded with a hundred guns, and during the afternoon thronged his house to tender their congratulations and express their joy. In the evening, the State House was thrown open, and a most enthusiastic meeting held by the republicans. At its close, they marched in a body to the Lincoln mansion, and called for the nominee. Mr. Lincoln appeared, and after a brief, modest and hearty speech, invited as many as could get into the house to enter, the crowd responding that after the fourth of March they would give him a larger house. The people did not retire until a late hour, and then moved off reluctantly, leaving the excited household to their rest.

On the following day, which was Saturday, Mr. Ashmun, the president of the convention, at the head of a committee, visited Springfield to apprise Mr. Lincoln officially of his nomination. In order that the ceremony might be smoothly performed, the committee had an interview with Mr. Lincoln before the hour appointed for the formal call. They found him at a loss to know how to treat a present he had just received at the hands of some of his considerate Springfield friends. Knowing Mr. Lincoln's temperate or rather abstinent habits, and laboring under the impression that the visitors from Chicago would have wants beyond the power of cold water to satisfy, these friends had sent in sundry hampers of wines and liquors. These strange fluids troubled Mr. Lincoln; and he frankly confessed as much to the members of the committee. The chairman at once advised him to return the gift, and to offer no stimulants to his guests, as many would be present besides the committee. Thus relieved, he made ready for the reception of the company, according to his own ideas of hospitality. The evening came, and with it Mr. Ashmun and the committee and many others. Mr. Ashmun on being presented said:

"I have, sir, the honor, on behalf of the gentlemen who are present— a committee appointed by the republican convention recently assembled at Chicago—to discharge a most pleasant duty. We have come, sir, under a vote of instructions to that committee, to notify you that you have been selected by the convention of the republicans at Chicago for President of the United States. They instruct us, sir, to notify you of that selection ; and that committee deem it not only respectful to yourself, but appropriate to the important matter which they have in hand, that they should come in person, and present to you the authentic evidence of the action of that convention; and, sir, without any phrase which shall either be personally plauditory to yourself, or which shall have any reference to the principles involved in the questions which are connected with your nomination, I desire to present to you the letter which has been prepared, and which informs you of your nomination, and with it the platform, resolutions and sentiments which the convention adopted. Sir, at your convenience, we shall be glad to receive from you such a response as it may be your pleasure to give us."

Mr. Lincoln listened to the address with sad gravity. There was in his heart no exultation—no elation—only the pressure of a new and great responsibility. He paused thoughtfully for a moment, and then replied:

"Mr. Chairman, and Gentlemen of the Committee: I tender to you, and through you to the republican national convention, and all the people represented in it, my profoundest thanks for the high honor done me, which you now formally announce. Deeply and even painfully sensible of the great responsibility which is inseparable from this high honor—a responsibility which I could almost wish had fallen upon some one of the far more eminent and experienced statesmen whose distinguished names were before the convention—I shall, by your leave, consider more fully the resolutions of the convention denominated the platform, and, without any unnecessary or unreasonable delay, respond to you, Mr. Chairman, in writing, not doubting that the platform will be found satisfactory, and the nomination gratefully accepted. And now I will no longer defer the pleasure of taking you, and each of you, by the hand."

Judge Kelly of Pennsylvania, one of the committee, and a very tall man, looked at Mr. Lincoln, up and down, before it came his turn to take his hand, a scrutiny that had not escaped Mr. Lincoln's quick eye. So, when he took the hand of the Judge, he inquired: "what is your hight?" "six feet three," replied the Judge. "What is yours, Mr. Lincoln?" "Six feet four," responded Mr. Lincoln. "Then, sir," said the Judge, "Pennsylvania bows to Illinois. My dear man," he continued, "for years my heart has been aching for a president that I could look up to; and I've found him at last, in the land where we thought there were none but little giants."

The evening passed quickly away, and the committee retired with a very pleasant impression of the man in whose hands they had placed the standard of the party for a great and decisive campaign. Mr. Ashmun met the nominee as an old friend, with whom he had acted in Congress, when both were members of the old whig party; and the interview between them was one of peculiar interest. It is a strange coincidence that the man who received Mr. Lincoln's first spoken and written utterance as the standard bearer of the republican party, received the last word he ever wrote as President of the United States.

On the twenty-third of June, which occurred on the following week, Mr. Lincoln responded to the letter which Mr. Ashmun presented him as follows:

"Sir: I accept the nomination tendered me by the convention over which you presided, of which I am formally apprised in a letter of yourself and others, acting as a committee of the convention for that purpose. The declaration of principles and sentiments which accompanies your letter meets my approval, and it shall be my care not to violate it, or disregard it in any part. Imploring the assistance of Divine Providence, and with due regard to the views and feelings of all who were represented in the convention, to the rights of all the states and territories and people of the nation, to the inviolability of the Constitution and the perpetual union, harmony and prosperity of all, I am most happy to co-operate for the practical success of the principles declared by the convention.   Your obliged friend and fellow-citizen,

"ABRAHAM LINCOLN.

"Hon. GEORGE ASHMUN."

Thus was Abraham Lincoln placed before the nation as a candidate for the highest honor in its power to bestow. It had been a long and tedious passage to this point in his history. He was in the fifty-second year of his age. He had spent half of his years in what was literally a wilderness. Born in the humblest and remotest obscurity, subjected to the rudest toil in the meanest offices, gathering his acquisitions from the scantiest sources, achieving the development of his powers by means of his own institution, he had, with none of the tricks of the demagogue, with none of the aids of wealth and social influence, with none of the opportunities for exhibiting his powers which high official position bestows, against all the combinations of genius and eminence and interest, raised himself by force of manly excellence of heart and brain into national recognition, and had become the focal center of the affectionate interest and curious inquisition of thirty millions of people at home, and of multitudes throughout the civilized world.

CHAPTER XVI.

AND now began a new life, so unlike anything that Mr. Lincoln had hitherto experienced that he found himself altogether afloat as to the proprieties of his position. His nomination had not elevated or elated him; and he did not see why it should change his manners or his bearing toward anybody. He had been diminished in his own estimation—in some respects humbled and oppressed—by the great responsibilities placed upon him, rather than made important and great. He was the people's instrument, the people's servant, the people's creation. He could put on none of the airs of eminence; he could place no bars between himself and those who had honored him. None of his old heartiness and simplicity left him. Men who entered his house impressed with a sense of his new dignities, found him the same honest, affectionate, true-hearted and simple-minded Abraham Lincoln that he had always been. He answered his own bell, accompanied his visitors to the door when they retired, and felt all that interfered with his old homely and hearty habits of hospitality as a burden—almost an impertinence.

From this moment to the moment of his death he knew nothing of leisure. He was astonished to find how many friends he had. They thronged his house from every quarter of the country. Probably no candidate for presidential honors was ever so beset by place-seekers and lion-hunters as was Mr. Lincoln; for it is rare indeed that any man is nominated for the presidency with the same moral certainty of an election which attached to his prospects. It was almost universally believed, both at the North and the South, that he would be elected; and he was treated like a man who already had the reins of power in his hands.

Some of his friends who had witnessed his laborious way of receiving and dismissing his guests and visitors interposed with "Thomas," a colored servant who became very useful to him; but it was very hard and very unnatural for him to yield to another, and he a servant, the ministry of the courtesies which it was so much his delight to render; and he not unfrequently broke over the rules which his considerate advisers undertook to impose upon him. One thing was remarkable in these receptions—his attention to the humble and the poor. No poor, humble, scared man ever came into his house toward whom his heart did not at once go out with a gush of noble sympathy. To these he was always particularly attentive, and they were placed at ease at once. He took pains to show them that no change of circumstances could make him forget his early condition, or alienate his heart from those with whom he had shared the hardships and humilities of obscurity and poverty.

The interruption of family privacy and comfort by the constant throng of visitors at last became intolerable, and it was determined that Mr. Lincoln should hold his receptions elsewhere. Accordingly the Executive Chamber, a large fine room in the State House, was set apart for him; and in this room he met the public until, after his election, he departed for Washington. Here he met the millionaire and the menial, the priest and the politician, men, women and children, old friends and new friends, those who called for love and those who sought for office. From morning until night this was his business; and he performed it with conscientious care and the most unwearying patience.

As illustrative of the nature of many of his calls, a brace of incidents may be recorded as they were related to the writer by an eye-witness. Mr. Lincoln being seated in conversation with a gentleman one day, two raw, plainly dressed young

"Suckers" entered the room, and bashfully lingered near the door. As soon as he observed them, and apprehended their embarrassment, he rose and walked to them, saying, "How do you do, my good fellows? What can I do for you? Will you sit down?" The spokesman of the pair, the shorter of the two, declined to sit, and explained the object of the call thus: he had had a talk about the relative hight of Mr. Lincoln and his companion, and had asserted his belief that they were of exactly the same hight. He had come in to verify his judgment. Mr. Lincoln smiled, went and got his cane, and, placing the end of it upon the wall, said, "here, young man, come under here." The young man came under the cane, as Mr. Lincoln held it, and when it was perfectly adjusted to his hight, Mr. Lincoln said: "now come out and hold up the cane." This he did while Mr. Lincoln stepped under. Rubbing his head back and forth to see that it worked easily under the measurement, he stepped out, and declared to the sagacious fellow who was curiously looking on, that he had guessed with remarkable accuracy—that he and the young man were exactly of the same hight. Then he shook hands with them and sent them on their way. Mr. Lincoln would just as soon have thought of cutting off his right hand as he would have thought of turning those boys away with the impression that they had in any way insulted his dignity.

They had hardly disappeared when an old and modestly dressed woman made her appearance. She knew Mr. Lincoln, but Mr. Lincoln did not at first recognize her. Then she undertook to recall to his memory certain incidents connected with his rides upon the circuit—especially his dining at her house upon the road at different times. Then he remembered her and her home. Having fixed her own place in his recollection, she tried to recall to him a certain scanty dinner of bread and milk that he once ate at her house. He could not remember it—on the contrary, he only remembered that he had always fared well at her house. "Well," said she, "one day you came along after we had got through dinner, and we had eaten up everything, and I could give you nothing but a bowl of bread and milk; and you ate it; and when you got up you said it was good enough for the President of the United States." The good old woman, remembering the remark, had come in from the country, making a journey of eight or ten miles, to relate to Mr. Lincoln this incident, which, in her mind, had doubtless taken the form of prophesy. Mr. Lincoln placed the honest creature at her ease, chatted with her of old times, and dismissed her in the most happy and complacent frame of mind.

The interviews of this character were almost numberless, constantly intermingled with grave conversations with statesmen and politicians concerning the campaign in progress, and the condition and prospects of the country. The future was very dark. Threats of secession grew louder and deeper. Steps towards treason were bolder with every passing day. He knew the spirit of slavery. He had measured it in all the length and breadth of its malignity and treachery. He felt that he was entering upon a path full of danger, overshadowed all the way with doubt and fear. With this great care upon him—with the burden of a nation already taken upon his shoulders—he was often bowed down with the deepest despondency. He believed in his inmost soul that he was an instrument in the hands of God for the accomplishment of a great purpose. The power was above him, the workers were around him, the end was beyond him. In him, Providence, the people and the purpose of both met; and as a poor, weak, imperfect man, he felt humbled by the august presence, and crushed by the importance with which he had been endowed.

Of one thing Mr. Lincoln felt sure: that in the great struggle before him he ought to be supported by the Christian sentiment and the Christian influence of the nation. Nothing pained him more than the thought that a man professing the religion of Jesus Christ, and especially a man who taught the religion of Jesus Christ, should be opposed to him. He felt that every religious man—every man who believed in God, in the principles of everlasting justice, in truth and righteousness—should be opposed to slavery, and should support

and assist him in the struggle against inhumanity and oppression which he felt to be imminent. It was to him a great
mystery how those who preached the gospel to the poor, and
who, by their Divine Master, were sent to heal the broken-
hearted, to preach deliverance to the captives, and to set at
liberty those that were bruised, could be his opponents and
enemies.

Mr. Newton Bateman, Superintendent of Public Instruction
for the State of Illinois, occupied a room adjoining and opening
into the Executive Chamber. Frequently this door was open
during Mr. Lincoln's receptions; and throughout the seven
months or more of his occupation Mr. Bateman saw him
nearly every day. Often when Mr. Lincoln was tired he
closed his door against all intrusion, and called Mr. Bateman
into his room for a quiet talk. On one of these occasions
Mr. Lincoln took up a book containing a careful canvass of
the city of Springfield in which he lived, showing the candidate for whom each citizen had declared it his intention to
vote in the approaching election. Mr. Lincoln's friends had,
doubtless at his own request, placed the result of the canvass
in his hands. This was toward the close of October, and
only a few days before the election. Calling Mr. Bateman to a
seat at his side, having previously locked all the doors, he said:
"let us look over this book. I wish particularly to see how
the ministers of Springfield are going to vote." The leaves
were turned, one by one, and as the names were examined
Mr. Lincoln frequently asked if this one and that were not a
minister, or an elder, or the member of such or such a church,
and sadly expressed his surprise on receiving an affirmative
answer. In that manner they went through the book, and
then he closed it and sat silently and for some minutes regarding a memorandum in pencil which lay before him. At length
he turned to Mr. Bateman with a face full of sadness, and
said: ".Here are twenty-three ministers, of different denominations, and all of them are against me but three; and here
are a great many prominent members of the churches, a very
large majority of whom are against me. Mr. Bateman, I am

not a Christian—God knows I would be one—but I have carefully read the Bible, and I do not so understand this book;" and he drew from his bosom a pocket New Testament. "These men well know," he continued, "that I am for freedom in the territories, freedom everywhere as far as the Constitution and laws will permit, and that my opponents are for slavery. They know this, and yet, with this book in their hands, in the light of which human bondage cannot live a moment, they are going to vote against me. I do not understand it at all."

Here Mr. Lincoln paused—paused for long minutes, his features surcharged with emotion. Then he rose and walked up and down the room in the effort to retain or regain his self-possession. Stopping at last, he said, with a trembling voice and his cheeks wet with tears: "I know there is a God, and that He hates injustice and slavery. I see the storm coming, and I know that His hand is in it. If He has a place and work for me—and I think He has—I believe I am ready. I am nothing, but truth is everything. I know I am right because I know that liberty is right, for Christ teaches it, and Christ is God. I have told them that a house divided against itself cannot stand, and Christ and reason say the same; and they will find it so. Douglas don't care whether slavery is voted up or voted down, but God cares, and humanity cares, and I care; and with God's help I shall not fail. I may not see the end; but it will come, and I shall be vindicated; and these men will find that they have not read their Bibles aright."

Much of this was uttered as if he were speaking to himself, and with a sad and earnest solemnity of manner impossible to be described. After a pause, he resumed: "Does n't it appear strange that men can ignore the moral aspects of this contest? A revelation could not make it plainer to me that slavery or the government must be destroyed. The future would be something awful, as I look at it, but for this rock on which I stand" (alluding to the Testament which he still held in his hand,) "especially with the knowledge of how these ministers are going to vote. It seems as if God had borne with this thing (slavery) until the very teachers of religion have come to defend it from the Bible, and to claim for it a divine character and sanction; and now the cup of iniquity is full, and the vials of wrath will be poured out."

His last reference was to certain prominent clergymen in the South, Drs. Ross and Palmer among the number; and he went on to comment on the atrociousness and essential blasphemy of their attempts to defend American slavery from the Bible. After this the conversation was continued for a long time. Everything he said was of a peculiarly deep, tender and religious tone, and all was tinged with a touching melancholy. He repeatedly referred to his conviction that the day of wrath was at hand, and that he was to be an actor in the terrible struggle which would issue in the overthrow of slavery, though he might not live to see the end. He repeated many passages of the Bible, and seemed specially impressed with the solemn grandeur of portions of Revelation, describing the wrath of Almighty God. In the course of the conversation, he dwelt much upon the necessity of faith in the Christian's God, as an element of successful statesmanship, especially in times like those which were upon him, and said that it gave that calmness and tranquillity of mind, that assurance of ultimate success, which made a man firm and immovable amid the wildest excitements. After further reference to a belief in Divine Providence, and the fact of God in history, the conversation turned upon prayer. He freely stated his belief in the duty, privilege and efficacy of prayer, and intimated, in no unmistakable terms, that he had sought in that way the divine guidance and favor.

The effect of this conversation upon the mind of Mr. Bateman, a Christian gentleman whom Mr. Lincoln profoundly respected, was to convince him, that Mr. Lincoln had, in his quiet way, found a path to the Christian stand-point—that he had found God, and rested on the eternal truth of God. As the two men were about to separate, Mr. Bateman remarked: "I have not supposed that you were accustomed to think so much upon this class of subjects. Certainly your friends generally are ignorant of the sentiments you have expressed to me." He replied quickly: "I know they are.* I am obliged to appear different to them; but I think more on these subjects than upon all others, and I have done so for years; and I am willing that *you* should know it."

This remarkable conversation furnishes a golden link in the chain of Mr. Lincoln's history. It flashes a strong light upon the path he had already trod, and illuminates every page of his subsequent record. Men have wondered at his abounding charity, his love of men, his equanimity under the most distressing circumstances, his patience under insult and misrepresentation, his delicate consideration of the feelings of the humble, his apparent incapacity of resentment, his love of justice, his transparent simplicity, his truthfulness, his good will toward his enemies, his beautiful and unshaken faith in the triumph of the right. There was undoubtedly something in his natural constitution that favored the development of these qualities; but those best acquainted with human nature will hardly attribute the combination of excellencies which were exhibited in his character and life to the unaided forces of his constitution. The man who carried what he called "this rock" in his bosom, who prayed, who thought more of religious subjects than of all others, who had an undying faith in the providence of God, drew his life from the highest fountains.

It was one of the peculiarities of Mr. Lincoln to hide these religious experiences from the eyes of the world. In the same State House where this conversation occurred, there were men who imagined—who really believed—who freely said—that Mr. Lincoln had probably revealed himself with less restraint to them than to others—men who thought they knew him as they knew their bosom companions—who had never in their whole lives heard from his lips one word of all these religious convictions and experiences. They did not regard him as a religious man. They had never seen anything but the active lawyer, the keen politician, the jovial, fun-loving companion, in Mr. Lincoln. All this department of his life he had kept carefully hidden from them. Why he should say that he was obliged to appear differently to others does not appear; but the fact is a matter of history that he never exposed his own religious life to those who had no sympathy with it. It is doubtful whether the clergymen of Springfield knew anything of these experiences. Very few of them were in political sympathy with him; and it is evident that he could open his heart to no one except under the most favorable circumstances. The fountain from which gushed up so grand and good a life was kept carefully covered from the eyes of the world. Its possessor looked into it often, but the careless or curious crowd were never favored with the vision. There was much in his conduct that was simply a cover to these thoughts—an attempt to conceal them. It is more than probable that, on separating with Mr. Bateman on this occasion, he met some old friend, and, departing by a single bound from his tearful melancholy and his sublime religious passion, he told him some story, or indulged in some jest, that filled his own heart with mirthfulness, and awoke convulsions of laughter in him who heard it.

These sudden and wide transitions of feeling were common with him. He lived for years a double life—a deep and a shallow one. Oppressed with great responsibilities, absorbed by the most profound problems relating to his own spirit and destiny, brought into sympathetic relation with the woes of the world, and living much in the very depths of a sadness whose natural fountain had been deepened by the experience of his life, he found no relief except by direct and entire translation to that other channel of his life which lay among his shallowest emotions. His sense of the ludicrous and the grotesque, of the witty and the funny, was really something wonderful; and when this sense was appealed to by a story, or an incident, or a jest, he seemed to leave all his dignity aside, and give himself up to mirth with no more of self-restraint than if he were a boy of twelve years. He resorted to this channel of life for relief. It was here that he won

,strength for trial by forgetting trial. It was here that he restored the balance which sadness had destroyed. Such a nature and character seem full of contradictions; and a man who is subject to such transitions will always be a mystery to those who do not know him wholly. Thus no two men among his intimate friends will agree concerning him.

The writer has conversed with multitudes of men who claimed to know Mr. Lincoln intimately; yet there are not two of the whole number who agree in their estimate of him. The fact was that he rarely showed more than one aspect of himself to one man. He opened himself to men in different directions. It was rare that he exhibited what was religious in him; and he never did this at all, except when he found just the nature and character that were sympathetic with that aspect and element of his character. A great deal of his best, deepest, largest life he kept almost constantly from view, because he would not expose it to the eyes and apprehension of the careless multitude.

To illustrate the effect of the peculiarity of Mr. Lincoln's intercourse with men, it may be said that men who knew him through all his professional and political life have offered opinions as diametrically opposite as these, viz: that he was a very ambitious man, and that he was without a particle of ambition; that he was one of the saddest men that ever lived, and that he was one of the jolliest men that ever lived; that he was very religious, but that he was not a Christian; that he was a Christian, but did not know it; that he was so far from being a religious man or a Christian that "the less said upon that subject the better;" that he was the most cunning man in America, and that he had not a particle of cunning in him; that he had the strongest personal attachments, and that he had no personal attachments at all—only a general good feeling toward everybody; that he was a man of indomitable will, and that he was a man almost without a will; that he was a tyrant, and that he was the softest-hearted, most brotherly man that ever lived; that he was remarkable for his pure-mindedness, and that he was the foulest in his

16

jests and stories of any man in the country; that he was a witty man, and that he was only a retailer of the wit of others; that his apparent candor and fairness were only apparent, and that they were as real as his head and his hands; that he was a boor, and that he was in all essential respects a gentleman; that he was a leader of the people, and that he was always led by the people; that he was cool and impassive, and that he was susceptible of the strongest passions. It is only by tracing these separate streams of impression back to their fountain that we are able to arrive at anything like a competent comprehension of the man, or to learn why he came to be held in such various estimation. Men caught only separate aspects of his character—only the fragments that were called into exhibition by their own qualities.

Thus the months passed away until the election. His room was thronged by visitors from every portion of the Union, drawn to him by a great variety of motives; and to all he gave an open and cordial welcome. In the meantime his political opponents had virtually given up the contest. While they worked faithfully within their own organizations, they openly or secretly conceded his election. At the South no attempt was made to conceal the conviction that he would be the next President of the United States. Indeed, this was so entirely what they desired that they would have regarded the election of Mr. Douglas as a calamity, although it may well be doubted whether they would have been deterred from their disunion schemes by his election. They took pains to poison the public mind by every possible expedient. They identified the cause of the republicans with the John Brown raid into Virginia, with everything that was offensive to the pride of the South in Helper's "Impending Crisis," with "abolitionism" which was the most disgusting and dangerous sin in the proslavery catalogue of sins. It was all a lie. Not a republican was concerned in or approved of the John Brown invasion, for which Virginia had exacted the life of that stern old enthusiast.

Helper's book was a home production of the South; and the creed of the party had no item looking to the abolition of slavery. Not content with misrepresenting Mr. Lincoln's cause and principles, they traduced him and his associates upon the ticket. Mr. Lincoln was called the "Illinois ape," and this, not by the rabble, but by the leaders of public opinion; while Mr. Hamlin was actually believed by many southern people to be a mulatto, through the representations of presses and politicians. Every falsehood that could sting the southern mind to malignity and resentment against the North, and make detestable the man whom the North was about to elect to the presidency, was shamelessly uttered. The object, of course, was to fill the southern mind with bitterness against the North, to alienate the Union from its affections, to foster its pride, and to prepare it for the premeditated and prepared separation.

Mr. Lincoln saw the gathering storm, and felt that upon him it would expend its wildest fury; yet he cherished no resentment against these men or their section for all the wrongs they heaped upon him, and the woes they were bringing upon the country. He was only an instrument in the hands of a higher power. It was only the natural exhibition of the spirit of a system of wrong which was making its last terrible struggle for life. The hatred aroused in him passed over the heads of his enemies and fastened itself upon the institution which could make such demons of men. If he was an instrument in the hands of a higher power, they were instruments in the hands of a lower power, malignant but mighty indeed. He had charity, because he felt these men to be the victims of a false education—of a great mistake. He remembered that had he been bred as they had been, the probabilities were that he should sympathize with them.

Mr. Lincoln was what was called a wise candidate. He held his tongue. No abuse provoked him to utter a word in self-vindication. He had accepted the platform of the party and his record was before the country. So he calmly awaited the result.

On the sixth of November the election took place throughout the whole country, and the result was Mr. Lincoln's triumph, not by a majority of the votes cast, but by a handsome plurality. The popular vote for him was 1,857,610; while Stephen A. Douglas received 1,365,976 votes, John C. Breckinridge 847,953, and John Bell 590,631. In the electoral college Mr. Lincoln had 180 votes, Mr. Douglas receiving 12, Mr. Breckinridge 72, and Mr. Bell 39; and when, on the following thirteenth of February, in a joint session of both Houses of Congress, these votes were declared, it was the office of John C. Breckinridge himself, then Vice-President, to pronounce Mr. Lincoln the constitutionally elected President of the United States for four years from the succeeding fourth of March. And this man who, by going into the election as a candidate for the presidency, and declaring the result of the contest, had bound himself by every principle of honor to abide by the result, was a foul traitor at heart, and only left the chair he disgraced to become a leader in the armies of treason.

The result of the election was great popular rejoicing at the North, great exasperation at the South, great fear and trembling among compromisers of both sections, and a general conviction that the crisis so long threatened was actually upon the nation. Among the republicans there was this feeling: that they had fairly, on an open declaration of principles and policy, and strictly according to the provisions of the Constitution, elected a president; and that if, for this, the South was determined to make war, the contest might as well come first as last. They knew they had made no proposition and entertained no intention to interfere with slavery in the states where the Constitution protected it, that they had made no aggressions upon the institution, and had only endeavored to limit its spread into free territory. If this was cause of war, then they were ready for the fight. Feeling thus, and thus declaring themselves, they still did not generally believe there would be a war. They thought the matter would yet rise upon the wings of some convenient wind and be blown away.

Of course the man of all others chiefly concerned in the results of the election was intensely interested. The effect upon his nervous system, not altogether ephemeral, is well illustrated by an incident which he subsequently related to several of his friends, and which has found no better record, perhaps, than in an article from the pen of Major John Hay, one of his private secretaries in Washington, published in Harper's Magazine for July, 1865. Major Hay reports the incident as nearly as possible in Mr. Lincoln's own words.

"It was just after my election in 1860," said Mr. Lincoln, "when the news had been coming in thick and fast all day, and there had been a great ' hurrah boys !' so that I was well tired out and went home to rest, throwing myself upon a lounge in my chamber. Opposite to where I lay was a bureau with a swinging glass upon it ; and looking in that glass, I saw myself reflected nearly at full length ; but my face, I noticed, had two separate and distinct images, the tip of the nose of one being about three inches from the tip of the other. I was a little bothered, perhaps startled, and got up and looked in the glass, but the illusion vanished. On lying down again, I saw it a second time, plainer, if possible, than before ; and then I noticed that one of the faces was a little paler—say five shades—than the other. I got up and the thing melted away, and I went off, and, in the excitement of the hour forgot all about it,—nearly, but not quite, for the thing would once in a while come up, and give me a little pang as though something uncomfortable had happened. When I went home, I told my wife about it, and a few days after I tried the experiment again, when, sure enough, the thing came back again; but I never succeeded in bringing the ghost back after that, though I once tried very industriously to show it to my wife, who was worried about it somewhat. She thought it was ' a sign ' that I was to be elected to a second term of office, and that the paleness of one of the faces was an omen that I should not see life through the last term."

The President had good sense enough to regard the vision as an optical illusion, growing out of the excited condition of

his nervous system at the time; yet, with that tinge of superstition which clings to every sensitive and deeply thoughtful
man, in a world full of mysteries, he was so far affected by it
as to feel that "something uncomfortable had happened." In
the light of subsequent events, Mrs. Lincoln's prophetic interpretation of the vision has almost a startling interest.

Mr. Lincoln had become the most important man on the
continent. Parties were given in his honor, autograph hunters
beset him everywhere, and office-seekers met him on the right
hand and on the left. That he felt at home in this new life
is not probable, but he had the good sense to put on no airs,
and to undertake no change of his manners in meeting men
and women. From the day of his election to the day of his
death, he was the same unpretending man that he was when
he first entered Springfield to practice law. He had known
nothing of drawing-rooms in his youth, and he affected to
know nothing of them when every drawing-room of loyal
America would have swung wide its doors to welcome him.
It was noticed by the critical that he found great difficulty in
disposing of his hands and feet. It is quite possible that they
were hard to be disposed of, and that he succeeded with them
quite as well as he would if he had been a master of deport-
ment. If the hands were large, they had taken no bribes; if
his feet were heavy, they had outstripped the fleetest in the
race of ambition. If he could not win admiration for his
personal graces, he could win love for his personal goodness.

He visited Chicago after his election, and met with a magnificent welcome. One or two little incidents of this trip will
illustrate especially his consideration for children. He was
holding a reception at the Tremont House. A fond father
took in a little boy by the hand who was anxious to see the
new President. The moment the child entered the parlor door,
he, of his own motion, and quite to the surprise of his father,
took off his hat, and giving it a swing, cried, "Hurrah for
Lincoln!" There was a crowd, but as soon as Mr. Lincoln
could get hold of the little fellow, he lifted him in his hands,
and tossing him toward the ceiling laughingly shouted: "Hur-

rah for you!" To Mr. Lincoln it was evidently a refreshing episode in the dreary work of hand-shaking. At a party in Chicago, during this visit, he saw a little girl timidly approaching him. He called her to him, and asked her what she wished for. She replied that she wanted his name. Mr. Lincoln looked back into the room and said: "But here are other little girls—they would feel badly if I should give my name only to you." The little girl replied that there were eight of them in all. "Then," said Mr. Lincoln, "get me eight sheets of paper, and a pen and ink, and I will see what I can do for you." The paper was brought, and Mr. Lincoln sat down in the crowded drawing-room, and wrote a sentence upon each sheet, appending his name; and thus every little girl carried off her souvenir.

During all this period 'of waiting for office, Mr. Lincoln carried a calm exterior but events were transpiring in the nation that gave him the most intense anxiety, and filled every leisure hour with painful thought.

There were, of course, the usual efforts at cabinet making on the part of presses and politicians, and he was favored with copious advice. It has been publicly said that he really desired to put Mr. Stephens of Georgia, whom he had been somewhat intimate with in Congress, into his cabinet. The appointment was at least strongly urged upon him. The republicans were seeking for some policy by which the South could be silenced and held to its allegiance. Many republicans in Washington were inclined to compromise the slavery question on the popular sovereignty position. Others thought it would be well to put southerners into the cabinet, and the names of Stephens of Georgia and Scott of Virginia were mentioned. These facts a personal friend communicated to Mr. Lincoln, and under date of December eighteenth, he replied: "I am sorry any republican inclines to dally with popular sovereignty of any sort. It acknowledges that slavery has equal rights with liberty, and surrenders all we have contended for. Once fastened on us as a settled policy, fillibustering for all south of us and making slave states of it follow in spite of us, with an early supreme court decision holding our free state constitutions to be unconstitutional. Would Scott or Stephens go into the cabinet? And if yea, on what terms? Do they come to me? or I go to them? Or are we to lead off in open hostility to each other?"

In Mr. Lincoln, though the prospect was dark and the way dangerous, there was no disposition to compromise the principles of his life and his party, and no entertainment of the illusion that concord could come of discord in his cabinet. In the latter matter he kept his own counsel and awaited his own time.

CHAPTER XVII.

To appreciate the enormity of the rebellion of which Mr. Lincoln's election was made the pretext, by the southern leaders, it is never to be forgotten that the whole South, by becoming a party in the election, committed itself to the result. They were in all honor bound to abide by that result, whatever it might be. If the foes of Mr. Lincoln had refused to vote at all, they would have gone into the rebellion with a much cleaner record; but the first item of that record was a breach of personal honor on the part of every man who engaged in insurrection. Every member of both houses of Congress, every member of the cabinet, and every federal office-holder who turned against the government, was obliged, beyond this breach of personal honor to become a perjurer— to trample upon the solemn oath by virtue of which he held his office.

Allusion has already been made to the operations of the plotters in Mr. Buchanan's cabinet. Before the election, Floyd had, as has already been stated, sent one hundred and fifteen thousand muskets from northern armories to southern arsenals. General Scott had warned him of the danger to which the federal forts at the South were liable, and had advised that, as a precautionary measure, they should be garrisoned. To this warning the secret traitor paid no attention. Attorney General Black had given his official opinion that Congress had no right to carry on a war against any state. The President himself was only a weak instrument in the hands of the intriguers. He consented to have his hands tied; and if he made any protests they were weak and childish. More than anything else he longed to have them delay the execution of their schemes until he should be released from office.

South Carolina, the breeding bed of secession and the birth-place of the fatal State Rights Heresy, took the lead in the secession movement, and called a state convention to meet at Columbia on the seventeenth of December. On the tenth of November, four days after the election, a bill was introduced in the legislature of the state calling out ten thousand volunteers. The two senators from South Carolina, Chesnut and Hammond, resigned their seats, one on the tenth and the other on the eleventh of the same month. Robert Toombs, a Georgia senator, made a violent secession speech at Milledgeville in his own state, and this, notwithstanding the fact that he continued to hold his seat. Howell Cobb, the Secretary of the Treasury, resigned on the tenth of December, declaring his inability to relieve the treasury from the embarrassments into which he had purposely led it; and two days before the secession convention met in South Carolina the Secretary of War, Floyd, accepted the requisition of that state for her quota of United States arms for 1861. Meetings were held all over the South where treason was boldly plotted and promulgated, and the people were goaded to the adoption of the desperate expedients determined upon by the leaders. The South Carolina Secession Convention met at Columbia on the seventeenth of December, but, on account of the prevalence of the small pox there, adjourned to Charleston, where, on the twentieth, they formally passed an ordinance of separation, and declared "that the Union now (then) subsisting between South Carolina and other states under the name of the United States of America is hereby (was thereby) dissolved."

The passage of this ordinance filled the Charlestonians with delight, and, in the evening, in the presence of an immense crowd, the fatal instrument was signed and sealed; and Governor Pickens immediately issued a proclamation, declaring

South Carolina to be "a separate, free, sovereign and independent state." This was followed by the withdrawal of Messrs. McQueen, Boyd, Bonham and Ashmore from Congress, although their resignation was not recognized by the speaker, on the ground that such an act would be a recognition of the legitimacy of the action of the state.

Before the adjournment of the South Carolina Convention, resolutions were passed calling for a convention of the seceding states to be held at Montgomery, Alabama, for the purpose of forming a southern confederacy, and providing or suggesting a plan of operations and organization. The Congressional conspirators were active in Washington, and in constant communication with their respective states, urging on the work of national disintegration. On the eighth of January a caucus of southern senators at Washington counseled immediate secession; and at the national capital there was no influence that could, or would, withstand this reckless and rampant treason. As quickly as it could be done consistently with the safety of the cause of treason, Mississippi, Florida, Alabama, Georgia, Louisiana and Texas, followed the lead of South Carolina into secession. Forts and arsenals were seized in all the seceded states, the steamer Star of the West, sent to Charleston with reinforcements and supplies for Major Anderson, was driven out of the harbor, a southern confederacy was formed, with Jefferson Davis as president, and thus, by every necessary preliminary act, was the most terrible rebellion inaugurated that has ever reddened the pages of history. In cabinet meeting, the southern secretaries, still occupying places, were boldly demanding that the forts at Charleston should be evacuated; and Mr. Buchanan was too weak to take a position against them. But he had one man in his cabinet who was not afraid to speak the truth. Edwin M. Stanton who had been called to fill the office of attorney general on the retirement of Mr. Black, rose and said: "Mr. President, it is my duty, as your legal adviser, to say that you have no right to give up the property of the government, or abandon the soldiers of the United States to its enemies; and the course proposed by the Secretary of the Interior, if followed, is treason, and will involve you and all concerned in treason." For the first time in this cabinet treason had been called by its true name, and the men who were leading the President and the country to ruin were told to their faces the nature of their foul business. Floyd and Thompson, who had had everything their own way, sprang fiercely to their feet, while Mr. Holt, the Postmaster General, took his position by the side of Mr. Stanton; and Mr. Buchanan besought them with a senile whine to take their seats. Thus bolstered by Mr. Stanton the President determined not to withdraw Major Anderson. This act of Mr. Stanton was the first in Mr. Buchanan's administration that seemed to be based on a full comprehension of the nature of the situation; and it was a noble introduction to the great work he was destined to accomplish in the suppression of the rebellion.

These events occurring in rapid succession produced a profound impression at the North. The whole country was filled with feverish apprehension. A peace Congress took up its abode in Washington, with the notorious John Tyler for president. Measures of compromise were introduced into Congress and urged with great vigor. Those northern states that had passed "personal liberty bills," and other measures offensive to the South made haste to repeal them, that all possible pretexts for rebellion might be put out of the way. Every practicable attempt was made by the fearful and the faithless to compel such concessions to the slave power as would calm its ire, and obviate the necessity of armed collision. There were not wanting men in the North whose sympathies were with the traitors, and who would willingly and gladly have joined them in the attempt to revolutionize the government, by preventing Mr. Lincoln from taking his seat, and delivering over Washington and the government to the plotters. Indeed, many of the traitors openly declared that by secession they did not mean secession at all, but revolution. Commerce and manufactures begged for peace at the slaveholder's price, whatever it might be.

Washington itself was full of treason. It was the prevailing spirit of all the fashionable life of the national capital. All the governmental departments were crowded with it. It was the talk of the hotels. Loyalty was snubbed and dishonored. Maryland, though she had passed no ordinance of secession, was disloyal. The sympathies of the higher classes of Baltimore were all with the traitors. Thus secession was an accomplished fact, the forts and arsenals of the United States at the South were in the hands of the traitors, the northern arsenals were stripped, every available ship with the exception of two was beyond call, the confederate government was organized, the United States treasury was bankrupt, the whole South was seething with the excitement of treason, disloyalty reigned in every department of the government, southern sympathizers were scattered over the whole North, business was depressed, and a fearful looking-for of terrible days and terrible events had taken possession of those who still loved the Union, when Mr. Lincoln started on his journey to Washington, to assume the office to which he had been elected.

Silently, and with sad forebodings, had he waited in Springfield the opening of the storm. With an intense interest he had followed the development of the disunion scheme, and knowing the character of the southern leaders he appreciated the desperate nature of the struggle upon which he was entering.

On the 11th of February, 1861, Mr. Lincoln reluctantly bade adieu to the peaceful scenes of home and the grateful presence of his best personal friends, for the untried field of high official life. That he dreaded the change, and committed himself to it with the gravest forebodings, there is no question. Already had the threats of assassination reached his ears. It had been widely hinted by his enemies that his inauguration would never be permitted; and even if it should be, he knew that the most oppressive duties awaited him.

On his departure for the railroad station, he was accompanied by a large concourse of his neighbors and friends, the most of whom insisted on a parting shake of the hand. After passing through this trial, he appeared upon the platform of the car set apart for himself and his family and friends, and with the deepest feeling delivered to them his parting words.

"My friends," said he, "no one not in my position can appreciate the sadness I feel at this parting. To this people I owe all that I am. Here I have lived more than a quarter of a century. Here my children were born, and here one of them lies buried. I know not how soon I shall see you again. A duty devolves upon me which is greater, perhaps, than that which has devolved upon any other man since the days of Washington. He never would have succeeded except for the aid of Divine Providence, upon which he at all times relied. I feel that I cannot succeed without the same divine aid which sustained him, and on the same Almighty Being I place my reliance for support: and I hope you, my friends, will pray that I may receive that divine assistance without which I cannot succeed, but with which success is certain. Again, I bid you all an affectionate farewell."

This parting address was telegraphed to every part of the country, and was strangely misinterpreted. So little was the man's character understood that his simple and earnest request that his neighbors should pray for him was received by many as an evidence both of his weakness and his hypocrisy. No President had ever before asked the people, in a public address, to pray for him. It sounded like the cant of the conventicle to ears unaccustomed to the language of piety from the lips of politicians. The request was tossed about as a joke—"old Abe's last"—but it came from a heart surcharged with a sense of need, and strong in its belief that the Almighty listens to the prayers of men.

Mr. Lincoln had before him, on this journey, one of the most difficult tasks of his life. The country was very anxious to get some hint as to his policy. This hint he did not intend to give, until he should be obliged to give it officially. His task, then, of talking without saying anything, was not only a new one, but it was one for which he had no talent. He had never acquired, and could never acquire, the faculty of uttering graceful and acceptable nothings. Give him something to talk about, and he could talk. Give him a knotty point to argue, and he could argue; but to talk for the mere purpose of talk was beyond his power. To talk when it was his impulse and his policy to say nothing, was the hardest task of his life. Hence, there had never been a passage in his life in which he appeared to such a disadvantage as he did in the speeches made during this journey. He could win the profoundest admiration of the gifted and the learned at the Cooper Institute, but on the platform of a railroad car, or before an august committee of city magnates, he was as much at a loss as a school-boy would have been.

Mrs. Lincoln and her three boys were in the car as it rolled out of Springfield; and with them a number of Mr. Lincoln's old friends, Governor Yates, Ex-Governor Moore, Dr. W. M. Wallace, Hon. N. P. Judd, Hon. O. H. Browning, Judge David Davis and Colonel E. E. Ellsworth were of the number, as were also John M. Hay and J. G. Nicolay, afterwards Mr. Lincoln's private secretaries. The first point of destination was Indianapolis, but Mr. Lincoln was called out at various places on the route, to respond to the greetings of the crowds that had assembled at the way stations.

On arriving at Indianapolis, the party found the city entirely devoted for the time to the pleasant task of giving their elected chief magistrate a fitting reception. Business was suspended, flags were floating everywhere, and when, at five o'clock, the train rolled into the Union depot, a salute of thirty-four guns announced them and gave them greeting. Governor Morton addressed to Mr. Lincoln an earnest and hearty speech of welcome, and then the presidential party were escorted through the principal streets by a procession composed of both houses of the legislature, the municipal authorities, and the military and firemen. Arriving at the Bates House, Mr. Lincoln was called for, when he appeared, and made the following brief address:

"Fellow citizens of the State of Indiana: I am here to thank you much for this magnificent welcome, and still more for the very generous support given by your state to that political cause, which I think is the true and just cause of the whole country and the whole world. Solomon says 'there is a time to keep silence;' and when men wrangle by the mouth, with no certainty that they mean the same thing while using the same words, it perhaps were as well if they would keep silence. The words 'coercion' and 'invasion' are much used in these days, and often with some temper and hot blood. Let us make sure, if we can, that we do not misunderstand the meaning of those who use them. Let us get the exact definitions of these words, not from dictionaries, but from the men themselves, who certainly deprecate the things they would represent by the use of the words. What, then, is 'coercion?' What is 'invasion?' Would the marching of an army into South Carolina, without the consent of her people, and with hostile intent towards them, be invasion? I certainly think it would, and it would be 'coercion' also if the South Carolinians were forced to submit. But if the United States should merely hold and retake its own forts and other property, and collect the duties on foreign importations, or even withhold the mails from places where they were habitually violated, would any or all of these things be 'invasion' or 'coercion?' Do our professed lovers of the Union, who spitefully resolve that they will resist coercion and invasion, understand that such things as these, on the part of the United States, would be coercion or invasion of a state? If so, their idea of means to preserve the object of their great affection would seem to be exceedingly thin and airy. If sick, the little pills of the homœopathist would be much too large for it to swallow. In their view, the Union, as a family relation, would seem to be no regular marriage, but rather a sort of 'free-love' arrangement, to be maintained on passional attraction. By the way, in what consists the special sacredness of a state? I speak not of the position assigned to a state in the Union by the Constitution, for that is the bond we all recognize. That position, however, a state cannot carry out of the Union with it. I speak of that assumed primary right of a state to rule all which is less than itself, and to ruin all which is larger than itself. If a state and a county, in a given case, should be equal in extent of territory and equal in number of inhabitants, in what, as a matter of principle, is the state better than the county? Would an exchange of name be an exchange of rights? Upon what principle, upon what rightful principle, may a state, being no more than one-fiftieth part of the nation in soil and population, break up the nation, and then coerce a proportionably larger subdivision of itself in the most arbitrary way? What mysterious right to play tyrant is conferred on a district of country with its people, by merely calling it a state? Fellow-citizens, I am not asserting any thing. I am merely asking questions for you to consider. And now allow me to bid you farewell."

The unwillingness of Mr. Lincoln to speak on public questions at this time is evident enough from these remarks; but he could not resist the inclination to expose some of his ideas, touching certain words which were then in circulation, and they undoubtedly conveyed hints concerning his policy.

On the following day, Mr. Lincoln and his party started by a special train for Cincinnati. An immense crowd assembled, and cheered them as they moved off. The train was composed of four passenger cars, the third and fourth of which were occupied by the Cincinnati committee of reception, who greeted Mr. Lincoln at once—Judge Este on behalf of the citizens, and Major Dennis J. Yoohey on behalf of the Board of Common Council. Mr. Lincoln responded briefly. The first stop was at Shelbyville, where Mr. Lincoln was obliged to show himself to the enthusiastic assemblage, though, from the brevity of the stop, he could say nothing. At Greensburgh and Lawrenceburgh Mr. Lincoln made brief remarks to the crowds that had assembled. The wisest and most characteristic thing that he uttered at the latter place was in these words: "Let me tell you that if the people remain right, your public men can never betray you. If, in my brief term of office, I shall be wicked or foolish, if you remain right and true and honest you cannot be betrayed. My power is temporary and fleeting—yours as eternal as the principles of liberty. Cultivate and protect that sentiment, and your ambitious leaders will be reduced to the position of servants."

The train passed by the burial place of General Harrison who had occupied briefly the presidential chair, and here the family of the deceased patriot were assembled. Mr. Lincoln bowed his respects to the group and to the memory of his predecessor.

The twelfth day of February was remarkably sunny and cheerful, and a large concourse of citizens had assembled to give Mr. Lincoln greeting and to catch a glimpse of his face. All the streets leading to the railroad depot were thronged with people; and the windows and roofs and every perch from which a lookout could be obtained were occupied. It took a

17

large force of military and police to keep the way clear. A distant cannon announced the approach of the train, and then there went up from the multitude such a cheer as such a multitude alone can give. After some difficulty the party reached their carriages, and then the crowd went wild with enthusiasm, cheering the President and the Union, Mr. Lincoln rising in the carriage with uncovered head, and acknowledging the greetings that met him at every crossing. Mr. Lincoln's carriage was drawn by six white horses, and was surrounded by a detachment of police to keep off the crowd. Mayor Bishop occupied a seat by his side. All along the route of the procession houses were decorated with the national colors, and various devices for expressing personal and patriotic feeling. The Court House, Custom House, Catholic Institute, city buildings, newspaper offices, hotels, &c., were all gaily decorated. Banners, transparencies and patriotic emblems and mottoes were everywhere. At the Orphan Asylum, all the children came out and sang "Hail Columbia." Some incidents occurred that created special and peculiar interest, and some that excited no little amusement. A brawny German took a little girl in his arms, and carried her to the carriage, when she modestly presented to the President a single flower, which compliment he acknowledged by stooping and kissing the child. It was a small incident—a very pretty incident—but incidents like these depend for their effect upon the susceptibilities of the observers; and many of the excited multitude were touched to tears. One German devised a characteristic compliment. He took a seat upon a huge beer barrel, and, with a glass of its contents in his hand, addressed the President thus: "God be with you! Enforce the laws and save our country! Here's your health!" From the depot to the Burnet House, he rode through a dense mass of men, women and children, who took every mode of expressing their enthusiastic good will. It would have been impossible for Cincinnati to do more to receive an emperor or reward a conqueror.

The Burnet House was reached at five o'clock, and soon

afterwards Mr. Lincoln appeared upon the balcony. Mayor Bishop introduced him to the people and gave him a formal welcome "in the name of the people of all classes." Mr. Lincoln then replied:

"Mr. Mayor, Ladies and Gentlemen: Twenty-four hours ago, at the Capital of Indiana, I said to myself, 'I have never seen so many people assembled together in winter weather.' I am no longer able to say that. But it is what might reasonably have been expected—that this great city of Cincinnati would thus acquit herself on such an occasion. My friends, I am entirely overwhelmed by the magnificence of the reception which has been given, I will not say to me, but to the President elect of the United States of America. Most heartily do I thank you one and all for it. I am reminded by the address of your worthy Mayor, that this reception is given not by one political party; and even if I had not been so reminded by His Honor, I could not have failed to know the fact by the extent of the multitude I see before me now. I could not look upon this vast assemblage without being made aware that all parties were united in this reception. This is as it should be. It is as it should have been if Senator Douglas had been elected; it is as it should have been if Mr. Bell had been elected; as it should have been if Mr. Breckinridge had been elected; as it should ever be when any citizen of the United States is constitutionally elected President of the United States. Allow me to say that I think what has occurred here to-day could not have occurred in any other country on the face of the globe, without the influence of the free institutions which we have unceasingly enjoyed for three-quarters of a century. There is no country where the people can turn out and enjoy this day precisely as they please, save under the benign influence of the free institutions of our land. I hope that, although we have some threatening national difficulties now, while these free institutions shall continue to be in the enjoyment of millions of free people of the United States, we will see repeated every four years what we now witness. In a few short years I and every other individual man who is now living will pass away. I hope that our national difficulties will also pass away, and I hope we shall see in the streets of Cincinnati—good old Cincinnati—for centuries to come, once every four years, the people give such a reception as this to the constitutionally elected President of the whole United States. I hope you will all join in that reception, and that you shall also welcome your brethren across the river to participate in it. We will welcome them in every state in the Union, no matter where they are from. From away South, we shall extend to them a cordial good will, when our present differences shall have been forgotten and blown to the winds forever.

"I have-spoken but once before this in Cincinnati. That was a year previous to the late presidential election. On that occasion, in a playful manner but with sincere words, I addressed much of what I said to the Kentuckians. I gave my opinion that we as republicans would ultimately beat them as democrats, but that they could postpone that result longer by nominating Senator Douglas for the presidency than they could in any other way. They did not in the true sense of the word nominate Douglas, and the result has come certainly as soon as I expected. I also told them how I expected they would be treated after they should have been beaten; and I now wish to call or recall their attention to what I then said upon that subject. I then said: 'When we do, as we say, beat you, you perhaps will want to know what we will do with you. We mean to treat you as near as we possibly can as Washington, Jefferson and Madison treated you. We mean to leave you alone and in no way to interfere with your institutions, to abide by all and every compromise of the Constitution; and, in a word, coming back to the original proposition to treat you as far as degenerate men, if we have degenerated, may, according to the examples of those noble fathers Washington, Jefferson and Madison. We mean to remember that you are as good as we—that there is no difference between us— other than the difference of circumstances. We mean to recognize and bear in mind always that you have as good hearts in your bosoms as other people, or as good as we claim to have, and treat you accordingly.'

"Fellow-citizens of Kentucky, Friends, Brethren: May I call you such? In my new position I see no occasion and feel no inclination to retract a word of this. If it shall not be made good, be assured that the fault shall not be mine."

This little speech, remarkable for nothing so much as its thoroughly friendly feeling toward all classes and men of all opinions, was received with warm approval. Subsequently he was called upon by a procession of two thousand Germans, who, in their formal address, indicated a desire for some utterance touching his public policy. In his response, Mr. Lincoln begged to be excused from entering upon such an exposition. "I deem it due to myself and the whole country," said Mr. Lincoln, "in the present extraordinary condition of the country and of public opinion, that I should wait and see the last development of public opinion before I give my views, or express myself at the time of the inauguration. I hope at that time to be false to nothing you have been taught to expect of me."

On the morning of the thirteenth, the party started for Columbus, the capital of Ohio. The scenes of the previous day were repeated on the route, in the gathering of large crowds at all the intermediate stations. The reception in Columbus had been a fortnight in preparation, the legislature taking the initiative. At noon, on the thirteenth, it was calculated that five thousand strangers were in the city. As the time approached for the arrival of the train, the crowd around the depot became almost overwhelming. A thirty-four-gun salute announced the coming train, and as it drove slowly into the depot, the crowd called upon the President elect to show himself. He stepped out upon the platform of the rear car, and with head uncovered bowed his acknowledgments to the hearty greeting he received. On alighting and entering a carriage for the passage to the State House, the scenes at Cincinnati were re-enacted. Streets were full of people, the air was ringing with shouts and huzzas, and the same kind sun smiled upon all. He was received in the hall of the House of Representatives, and Governor Dennison introduced him to the Legislature. The President of the Senate responded in a speech of welcome which so concisely and happily conveyed the feelings of the people at that time, and so justly measured the nature and importance of the crisis, that it deserves record. He addressed Mr. Lincoln in the following words:

"Sir: On this day, and probably this very hour, the Congress of the United States will declare the verdict of the people, making you their President. It is my pleasurable duty, in behalf of the people of Ohio, speaking through this General Assembly, to welcome you to their Capital. Never in the history of this Government has such fearful responsibility rested upon the Chief Executive of the nation as will now devolve upon you. Never since the memorable time our patriotic fathers gave existence to the American Republic, have the people looked with such intensity of feeling to the inauguration and future policy of a President, as they do to yours. I need not assure you that the people of Ohio have full confidence in your ability and patriotism, and will respond to you in their loyalty to the Union and the Constitution. It would seem, sir, that the great problem of self-government is to be solved under your administration. All nations are deeply interested in its solution, and they wait with breathless anxiety to know whether this form of government, which has been the admiration of the world, is to be a failure or not. It is the earnest and united prayer of our people, that the same kind Providence which protected us in our colonial struggles, and has attended us thus far in our prosperity and greatness, will so imbue your mind with wisdom, that you may dispel the dark clouds that hang over our political horizon, and thereby secure the return of harmony and fraternal feeling to our now distracted and unhappy country. Again I bid you a cordial welcome to our Capital."

To this noble greeting Mr. Lincoln responded as follows:

"Gentlemen of the Senate and Citizens of Ohio: It is true, as has been said by the President of the Senate, that very great responsibility rests upon me in the position to which the votes of the American people have called me. I am deeply sensible of that weighty responsibility. I cannot but know, what you all know, that without a name—perhaps without a reason why I should have a name—there has fallen upon me a task such as did not rest upon the Father of his Country. And so feeling I cannot but turn and look for the support without which it will be impossible for me to perform that great task. I turn, then, and look to the American people, and to that God who has never forsaken them.

"Allusion has been made to the interest felt in relation to the policy of the new administration. In this I have received from some a degree of credit for having kept silence, from others some depreciation. I still think I was right. In the varying and repeatedly shifting scenes of the present, without a precedent which could enable me to judge from the past, it has seemed fitting that before speaking upon the difficulties of the country I should have gained a view of the whole field. To be sure, after all, I would be at liberty to modify and change the course of policy, as future events might make a change necessary.

"I have not maintained silence from any want of real anxiety. It is a good thing that there is no more than anxiety, for there is nothing going wrong. It is a consoling circumstance that when we look out there is nothing that really hurts anybody. We entertain different views upon political questions, but nobody is suffering anything. This is a most consoling circumstance, and from it I judge that all we want is time and patience, and a reliance on that God who has never forsaken this people."

The reporter for the Ohio State Journal, describing the incidents of the day, says that the impression produced by the President elect was most agreeable. "His great hight," he continues, "was conspicuous, even in that crowd of goodly men, and lifted him fully in view as he walked up the aisle. When he took the speaker's stand, a better opportunity was afforded to look at the man upon whom more hopes hang than upon any other living. At first, the kindness and amiability of his face strikes you; but as he speaks, the greatness and determination of his nature are apparent. Something in his manner, even more than in his words, told how deeply he was affected by the enthusiasm of the people; and when he appealed to them for encouragement and support, every heart responded with mute assurance of both. There was the simplicity of greatness in his unassuming and confiding manner, that won its way to instant admiration. He looked somewhat worn with travel and the fatigues of popularity, but warmed to the cordiality of his reception."

After the conclusion of the formalities in the hall, Mr. Lincoln went to the western steps of the Capitol, to say a word to the people. The address he made here consisted simply of commonplaces and phrases that had already become hackneyed. The hand-shaking that succeeded was something fearful. Every man in the crowd was anxious to wrench the hand of Abraham Lincoln. He finally gave both hands to the work, with great good nature. To quote one of the reports of the occasion: "people plunged at his arms with frantic enthusiasm, and all the infinite variety of shakes, from the wild and irrepressible pump-handle movement, to the dead grip, was executed upon the devoted dexter and sinister of the President. Some glanced at his face as they grasped his hand; others invoked the blessings of Heaven upon him; others affectionately gave him their last gasping assurance of devotion; others, bewildered and furious, with hats crushed over their eyes, seized his hands in a convulsive grasp, and passed on as if they had not the remotest idea who, what, or where they were." The President at last escaped, and took refuge in the Governor's residence, although he held a levee at the State House in the evening, where, in a more quiet way, he met many prominent citizens.

On the fourteenth, the presidential party left Columbus, for

Pittsburgh. The morning was rainy, but large numbers witnessed the departure of the train, and assembled at the stations along the route. At Steubenville, about five thousand people had assembled, and these Mr. Lincoln briefly addressed. The rain interfered very materially with the proposed reception at Pittsburgh, as did also the darkness, for it was night when the party arrived. At the Monongahela House, Mr. Lincoln addressed a large concourse of people in a few words of acknowledgment, and deferred his more formal remarks until the morning of the fifteenth. These latter were not charged with particular interest. They were rather an apology for not speaking at all, upon the great subject of which all wished to hear, than any exposition of opinion or policy upon any subject. A single paragraph showed that he still deemed a peaceful solution of the national difficulties possible:

"Notwithstanding the troubles across the river, there is really no crisis springing from anything in the Government itself. In plain words, there is really no crisis except an artificial one. What is there now to warrant the condition of affairs presented by our friends 'over the river?' Take even their own view of the questions involved, and there is nothing to justify the course which they are pursuing. I repeat it, then, there is no crisis, except such a one as may be gotten up at any time by turbulent men, aided by designing politicians. My advice, then, under such circumstances, is to keep cool. If the great American people will only keep their temper on both sides of the line, the trouble will come to an end, and the question which now distracts the country will be settled just as surely as all other difficulties of like character which have originated in this Government have been adjusted. Let the people on both sides keep their self-possession, and just as other clouds have cleared away in due time, so will this, and this great nation shall continue to prosper as heretofore."

The next place at which he was to be received was Cleveland, Ohio; and the party set out for this beautiful city in a hard shower of rain, that had not the power to dampen the enthusiasm of the Pittsburgh people who cheered their departing guests with great heartiness. There were the usual incidents along the road, and at four o'clock the train arrived at the Euclid Street Station of the Cleveland and Pittsburgh Railroad, where a very large escort waited to conduct Mr. Lincoln to the Weddell House. The President took his seat in a carriage drawn by four white horses. Notwithstanding the unpleasantness of the weather, Euclid Street was crowded from one end to the other, with persons who acted almost like wild men, in their anxiety to catch a glimpse of the President. Mr. I. U. Masters, the President of the City Council, made a formal speech of welcome, and was followed by Hon. Sherlock G. Andrews, who welcomed the guest of the occasion on behalf of the citizens' committee. Here, in his response, Mr. Lincoln repeated the substance of the remarks he made at Pittsburgh about the artificial nature of the crisis that was upon the country. "It was not argued up," he said, "and cannot, therefore, be argued down. Let it alone and it will go down of itself." In these remarks, and in all like these, he must have taken counsel of his hopes rather than his convictions; for in the same speech, while alluding to the grateful fact that his reception was by the citizens generally, without distinction of party, he said: "If all don't join now to save the good old ship of the Union this voyage, nobody will have a chance to pilot her on another voyage." There was a general reception and hand-shaking in the evening, and after the distinguished guest had become too tired for further honors, he was permitted to retire for the night.

Early the next morning the party took their leave, but they found many up and ready to get a parting glance of Mr. Lincoln, who, taking his seat in the rear car, appeared upon the platform as the train moved out of the depot, and bowed his farewell to the people who had so generously and cordially received him. His next public reception was at Buffalo, where he arrived late in the afternoon of the sixteenth, having received all along the route those testimonials of interest which had come to be as wearisome at last, as they were grateful at the first. On the arrival of the train at Buffalo, Mr. Lincoln was met by a very large concourse of citizens, with Ex-President Fillmore at their head. After being conducted to his hotel, the acting mayor gave him a formal welcome, to which Mr. Lincoln responded with hearty thanks, and such phrases of apology for not saying anything as had already become threadbare, and with his often repeated promise to say what the people wished to hear, when he should be called upon to do it officially.

From Buffalo, Mr. Lincoln and his party proceeded to Albany, receiving many demonstrations of respect from the beautiful cities along the route of three hundred miles. At Albany he was welcomed by Governor Morgan, to whom he made a brief response; and then he was conducted into the presence of the legislature, where he had another formal reception. To the speech addressed to him here, he made an unusually graceful and feeling response. He said:

"It is with feelings of great diffidence, and, I may say, feelings even of awe, perhaps greater than I have recently experienced, that I meet you here in this place. The history of this great state, the renown of its great men, who have stood in this chamber, and have spoken their thoughts, all crowd around my fancy, and incline me to shrink from an attempt to address you. Yet I have some confidence given me by the generous manner in which you have invited me, and the still more generous manner in which you have received me. You have invited me and received me without distinction of party. I could not for a moment suppose that this has been done in any considerable degree with any reference to my personal self. It is very much more grateful to me that this reception and the invitation preceding it were given to me as the representative of a free people than it could possibly have been were they but the evidence of devotion to me or to any one man.

"It is true that, while I hold myself, without mock-modesty, the humblest of all the individuals who have ever been elected President of the United States, I yet have a more difficult task to perform than any one of them has ever encountered. You have here generously tendered me the support, the united support, of the great Empire State. For this, in behalf of the nation—in behalf of the present and of the future of the nation—in behalf of the cause of civil liberty in all time to come—I most gratefully thank you. I do not propose now to enter upon any expressions as to the particular line of policy to be adopted with reference to the difficulties that stand before us, in the opening of the incoming administration. I deem that it is just to the country, to myself, to you, that I should see everything, hear everything, and have every light that can possibly be brought within my reach to aid me before I shall speak officially, in order that, when I do speak, I may have the best possible means of taking correct and true grounds. For this reason, I do not now announce anything in the way of policy for the new administration. When the time comes, according to the custom of the government, I shall speak, and speak as well as I am able for the good of the present and of the future of this country—for the good of the North and of the South—for the good of one and of the other, and of all sections of it. In the meantime, if we have patience, if we maintain our equanimity, though some may allow themselves to run off in a burst of passion, I still have confidence that the Almighty Ruler of the universe, through the instrumentality of this great and intelligent people, can and will bring us through this difficulty, as he has heretofore brought us through all preceding difficulties of the country. Relying upon this, and again thanking you, as I forever shall, in my heart, for this generous reception you have given me, I bid you farewell."

Mr. Lincoln was met at Albany by a delegation of the city government of New York, and started on the nineteenth for the great metropolis. He was not permitted to pass by Poughkeepsie without a formal welcome from the mayor of that city, to which he made a formal response. In this little speech there is a manifest improvement upon the earlier efforts of the route. Mr. Lincoln had found that there were things to talk about besides policy, and that it was better to yield himself up to the impulse of the moment than to be under the constant fear of saying some imprudent thing, concerning the character of the crisis and the policy of the incoming administration.

The reception at the city of New York was such as only New York can give. Places of business were generally closed, and the streets presented such crowds as only a city numbering a million of people can produce. Here he was formally received by Fernando Wood, then mayor of the city, to whose welcome he made the following response:

"Mr. Mayor:—It is with feelings of deep gratitude that I make my acknowledgments for the reception given me in the great commercial city of New York. I cannot but remember that this is done by a people who do not, by a majority, agree with me in political sentiment. It is the more grateful, because in this I see that, for the great principles of our Government, the people are almost unanimous. In regard to the difficulties that confront us at this time, and of which your Honor has thought fit to speak so becomingly and so justly, as I suppose, I can only say that I agree in the sentiments expressed. In my devotion to the Union, I hope I am behind no man in the nation. In the wisdom with which to conduct the affairs tending to the preservation of the Union, I fear that too great confidence may have been reposed in me; but I am sure that I bring a heart devoted to the work. There is nothing that could ever bring me to willingly consent to the destruction of this Union, under which not only the great commercial city of New York, but the whole country, acquired its greatness, except it be the purpose for which the Union itself was formed. I understand the ship to be made for the carrying and the preservation of the cargo, and so long as the ship can be saved with the cargo, it should never be abandoned, unless there appears no possibility of its preservation, and it must cease to exist, except at the risk of throwing overboard both freight and passengers. So long, then, as it is possible that the prosperity and the liberties of the people be preserved in this Union, it shall be my purpose at all times to use all my powers to aid in its perpetuation."

On the twentieth, Mr. Lincoln left New York for Philadelphia, visiting on the way both Houses of the New Jersey Legislature at Trenton. From the speech made before the Senate on this occasion, a quotation has been made in this volume, and the entire passage is worthy of record:

"I cannot but remember the place that New Jersey holds in our early history. In the early Revolutionary struggle, few of the states among the old thirteen had more of the battle-fields of the country within its limits than old New Jersey. May I be pardoned, if, upon this occasion, I mention, that away back in my childhood, the earliest days of my being able to read, I got hold of a small book, such a one as few of the younger members have ever seen, 'Weems' Life of Washington.' I remember all the accounts there given of the battle-fields and struggles for the liberties of the country, and none fixed themselves upon my imagination so deeply as the struggle here at Trenton, New Jersey. The crossing of the river—the contest with the Hessians—the great hardships endured at that time—all fixed themselves on my memory more than any single revolutionary event; and you all know, for you have all been boys, how these early impressions last longer than any others. I recollect thinking then, boy even though I was, that there must have been something more than common that those men struggled for. I am exceedingly anxious that that thing which they struggled for—that something even more than National Independence—that something that held out a great promise to all the people of the world to all time to come—I am exceedingly anxious that this Union, the Constitution, and the liberties of the people, shall be perpetuated in accordance with the original idea for which that struggle was made, and I shall be most happy indeed if I shall be an humble instrument in the hands of the Almighty, and of this, his almost chosen people, for perpetuating the object of that great struggle."

At Philadelphia Mr. Lincoln was received with great enthusiasm, and many demonstrations of popular regard. His formal welcome was given by the mayor of the city, but there was nothing in his response that calls for reproduction, except a single passage in which he hints at the possibility that he may never be permitted to take the presidential chair. Alluding to the popular desire to learn something definite concerning his policy, he said, "It were useless for me to speak of details of plans now; I shall speak officially next Monday week, *if ever*. If I should not speak then, it were useless for me to do so now."

He had been aware, ever since he left Springfield, that men were seeking for his life. An attempt was made to throw the train off the track that bore him out of Springfield; and at Cincinnati a hand grenade was found concealed upon the train. The fear excited by these hostile demonstrations was an indefinite one, but on his arrival at Philadelphia the plot was all unfolded to him.

Before Mr. Lincoln left home it was whispered about that he would never be permitted to pass through Baltimore alive; and a detective of great experience and skill was put to the task of ferreting out the conspiracy. He employed both men and women to assist him, and found that a conspiracy was indeed in existence, with an Italian refugee, a barber, at the head of it, who, assuming the name of "Orsini," indicated the part he expected to play in the plot.*

It was arranged, in case Mr. Lincoln should reach Baltimore safely, that, on a given signal, he should be shot by those

* For all the particulars of this attempt upon Mr. Lincoln's life the author is indebted to an article in the Albany Evening Journal.

who should gather in the guise of friends around his carriage, and that hand grenades should complete the work of destruction which the pistol had commenced. In the confusion thus produced, the guilty parties proposed to escape to a vessel in waiting, which would convey them to Mobile.

The detective and Mr. Lincoln reached Philadelphia nearly at the same time, and there the former submitted to a few of the President's friends the information he had secured. An interview between Mr. Lincoln and the detective was immediately arranged, which took place in the apartments of the former at the Continental Hotel. Mr. Lincoln having heard the officer's statement in detail, then informed him that he had promised to raise the American flag on Independence Hall the following morning—the morning of the anniversary of Washington's birthday—and that he had accepted an invitation to a reception by the Pennsylvania legislature in the afternoon of the same day. "Both of these engagements I will keep," said Mr. Lincoln, "if it costs me my life." For the rest, he authorized the detective to make such arrangements as he thought proper for his safe conduct to Washington.

In the meantime, General Scott and Senator Seward, both of whom were in Washington, learned from independent sources that Mr. Lincoln's life was in danger, and concurred in sending Mr. Frederick W. Seward to Philadelphia, to urge upon him the necessity of proceeding immediately to Washington in a quiet way. The messenger arrived late on Thursday night, after Mr. Lincoln had retired, and requested an audience. Mr. Lincoln's fears had already been aroused, and he was cautious, of course, in the matter of receiving a stranger. But satisfied that the messenger was indeed the son of Mr. Seward, he gave him audience. Nothing needed to be done, but to inform him of the plan entered into with the detective by which the President was to arrive in Washington early on Saturday morning, in advance of his family and party. This information was conveyed to Mr. Washburne of Illinois, among others, on Mr. Seward's return to Washington; and he was deputed to receive Mr. Lincoln at the depot on his arrival,

Such were the exciting events and disclosures of the day and night preceding Mr. Lincoln's appearance at Independence Hall, where he was formally received, and where he made the following address, one passage of which bears the burden of his apprehension:

"I am filled with deep emotion at finding myself standing here, in this place, where were collected the wisdom, the patriotism, the devotion to principle, from which sprang the institutions under which we live. You have kindly suggested to me that in my hands is the task of restoring peace to the present distracted condition of the country. I can say in return, sir, that all the political sentiments I entertain have been drawn, so far as I have been able to draw them, from the sentiments which originated and were given to the world from this hall. I have never had a feeling, politically, that did not spring from the sentiments embodied in the Declaration of Independence. I have often pondered over the dangers which were incurred by the men who assembled here, and framed and adopted that Declaration of Independence. I have pondered over the toils that were endured by the officers and soldiers of the army who achieved that independence. I have often inquired of myself what great principle or idea it was that kept this Confederacy so long together. It was not the mere matter of the separation of the colonies from the mother-land, but that sentiment in the Declaration of Independence which gave liberty, not alone to the people of this country, but, I hope, to the world for all future time. It was that which gave promise that in due time the weight would be lifted from the shoulders of all men. This is a sentiment embodied in the Declaration of Independence. Now, my friends, can this country be saved upon this basis? If it can, I will consider myself one of the happiest men in the world if I can help to save it. If it cannot be saved upon that principle, it will be truly awful. But if this country cannot be saved without giving up that principle, I was about to say I would rather be assassinated on this spot than surrender it. Now, in my view of the present aspect of affairs, there need be no bloodshed or war. There is no necessity for it. I am not in favor of such a course; and I may say, in advance, that there will be no bloodshed unless it be forced upon the Government, and then it will be compelled to act in self-defense."

At the conclusion of this speech, Mr. Lincoln was conducted to a platform outside, where he was publicly invited to raise the new flag. In responding to this invitation, he addressed a few words to the people, and then ran the flag up to the top of the staff, amid the cheers of a vast concourse of people. The ceremony was alike impressive to the principal actor and the multitude of observers. The great battles of Mr. Lincoln's life had been done for the principles of the Declaration of Independence. It was because he represented those principles, distinctively, that he had been elected to the presidency, that the slave-power was in active revolt, and that the friends of slavery were seeking for his life. It was certainly a remarkable occasion when he stood within the room where the Declaration was framed and signed, and pledged himself anew to its truths and principles, and then walked out into the presence of the people and ran up to its home the beautiful national ensign prepared for his hands.

At the conclusion of these ceremonies, Mr. Lincoln and his party left the city for Harrisburg, the capital of the state, where, in accordance with his promise, he visited both branches of the Pennsylvania legislature. The following were the more important passages in his response to the address of welcome:

"I thank you most sincerely for this reception, and the generous words in which support has been promised me upon this occasion. I thank your great Commonwealth for the overwhelming support it recently gave, not to me personally, but the cause, which I think a just one, in the late election. Allusion has been made to the fact—the interesting fact, perhaps we should say—that I, for the first time, appear at the capital of the great Commonwealth of Pennsylvania upon the birthday of the Father of his Country, in connection with that beloved anniversary connected with the history of this country. I have already gone through one exceedingly interesting scene this morning in the ceremonies at Philadelphia. Under the high conduct of gentlemen there, I was, for the first time, allowed the privilege of standing in Old Independence Hall, to have a few words addressed to me there, and opening up an opportunity of saying, with much regret, that I had not more time to express something of my own feelings, excited by the occasion—somewhat to harmonize and give shape to the feelings that had been really the feelings of my whole life.

"Besides this, our friends there had provided a magnificent flag of the country. They had arranged it so that I was given the honor of raising it to the head of its staff. And when it went up I was pleased that it went to its place by the strength of my own feeble arm; when, according to the arrangement, the cord was pulled, and it flaunted gloriously to the wind without an accident, in the bright glowing sunshine of the morning, I could not help hoping that there was in the entire success of that beautiful ceremony at least something of an omen of what is to come. Nor could I help feeling then, as I often have felt, that in the whole of that proceeding I was a very humble instrument. I had not provided the flag; I had not made the arrangements for elevating it to its place. I had applied but a very small portion of my feeble strength in raising it. In the whole transaction I was in the hands of the people who had arranged it; and if I can have the same generous co-operation of the people of the nation, I think the flag of our country may yet be kept flaunting gloriously.

"I recur for a moment to some words uttered at the hotel in regard to what has been said about the military support which the general government may expect from the Commonwealth of Pennsylvania in a proper emergency. To guard against any possible mistake do I recur to this. It is not with any pleasure that I contemplate the possibility that a necessity may arise in this country for the use of the military arm. While I am exceedingly gratified to see the manifestation upon your streets of your military force here, and exceedingly gratified at your promise here to use that force upon a proper emergency—while I make these acknowledgments, I desire to repeat, in order to preclude any possible misconstruction, that I do most sincerely hope that we shall have no use for them; that it will never become their duty to shed blood, and most especially never to shed fraternal blood. I promise that, so far as I may have wisdom to direct, if so painful a result shall in any wise be brought about, it shall be through no fault of mine."

It is proper to call renewed attention here to Mr. Lincoln's strong and ever present conviction that he was only a humble instrument in the hands of a higher power. He recognized the people as one of the higher powers which held him in service, and his illustration of his position, drawn from his office in raising the flag over Independence Hall, was extremely beautiful. We shall find this conviction deepening throughout the remainder of his life—the conviction that he was nothing—that he was of no consequence—save as an instrument, and that he had no rights and no mission except those which were deputed to him.

At the conclusion of the exercises of the day, Mr. Lincoln, who was known to be very weary, was permitted to pass undisturbed to his apartments in the Jones House. It was

18

popularly understood that he was to start for Washington the next morning; and the people of Harrisburg supposed they had taken only a temporary leave of him. He remained in his rooms until nearly six o'clock, when he passed into the street, entered a carriage unobserved, in company with Colonel Lamon, and was driven to a special train on the Pennsylvania Railroad, in waiting for him. As a measure of precaution, the telegraph wires were cut the moment he left Harrisburgh, so that, if his departure should be discovered, intelligence of it could not be communicated at a distance. At half past ten, the train arrived at Philadelphia, and here Mr. Lincoln was met by the detective, who had a carriage in readiness, in which the party were driven to the depot of the Philadelphia, Wilmington and Baltimore Railroad. At a quarter past eleven they arrived, and, very fortunately, found the regular train, which should have left at eleven, delayed. The party took berths in the sleeping car, and, without change of cars, passed directly through Baltimore to Washington, where Mr. Lincoln arrived at half past six o'clock in the morning, and found Mr. Washburne anxiously awaiting him. He was taken into a carriage, and in a few minutes he was talking over his adventures, with Senator Seward at Willard's Hotel.

Mr. Lincoln's family left Harrisburgh on the special train that had been intended for him, and as news of his safe arrival in Washington was already telegraphed over the country, no disturbance was made by the passage of the party through Baltimore. It was found that the number of original conspirators was about twenty, all of whose names were in possession of responsible parties. It was a bold plot, ingeniously foiled; but the detective through whose means the President's life had been saved, was not considered safe in Washington, and after a day or two was sent away. It should be added that the current story that Mr. Lincoln passed through Baltimore disguised in a "long military cloak and Scotch cap," is a pure fabrication, written by a man who hated Mr. Lincoln, and knew absolutely nothing of the event of which he wrote. Mr. Lincoln did not find it necessary to adopt any disguise.

It is a curious coincidence that Mr. Seward and his son who both were very active in the discovery of this plot, and in the measures for avoiding its consequences, were the only sharers in that violence which, at a later period, destroyed Mr. Lincoln's life. It is also a very suggestive fact, touching the responsibility of the southern leaders for Mr. Lincoln's assassination, that when a man of the name of Byrne was arrested in Richmond a year afterwards, for keeping a gambling house and for disloyalty to the confederate government, he was released on the testimony of Mr. Wigfall, who, to prove the man's truth to treason, swore that he was captain of the band that plotted to assassinate President Lincoln in Baltimore.

· The city of Washington was thrown into a flutter of excitement by this unexpected arrival. Mr. Lincoln's foes—and there were multitudes of them in Washington—ridiculed his fears, and his friends were equally angry and ashamed that the chosen chief of the nation should consent to sneak into his capital; but the latter, sooner or later, learned that he had taken the wiser course. It was, indeed, a very shameful thing that the President elect should have been obliged to do what he did, but so long as he was not responsible for it, the shame in no way attaches to him.

Mr. Lincoln went immediately into free conferences with his friends, visited both houses of Congress, and after a day he was waited upon by the Mayor and the municipal authorities, who gave him formal welcome to the city. In his brief reply, he took occasion to say that he thought much of the ill feeling existing between those living in free and slave states was owing to their failure to understand one another, and then assured the Mayor and his party that he did not then entertain, and had never entertained, any other than kindly feelings toward the South, that he had no disposition to treat the people of the South otherwise than as his own neighbors, and that he had no wish to withhold from them any of the benefits of the Constitution. On the second evening after his arrival, the Republican Association tendered him the courtesy of a serenade, which attracted a large crowd of friends and curious spectators. On being called out, he made much such an address as he had already made to the Mayor, closing with an expression of the conviction that when they should come to know each other better they would be better friends.

The days that preceded the inauguration were rapidly passing away. In the meantime, although General Scott had been busy and efficient in his military preparations for the occasion, many were fearful that scenes of violence would be enacted on that day, even should Mr. Lincoln be permitted to escape assassination in the meantime. It was a time of fearful uncertainty. The leading society of Washington hated Mr. Lincoln and the principles he represented. If it would be uncharitable to say that they would have rejoiced in his death, it is certainly true that they were in perfect sympathy with those who were plotting his destruction. His coming and remaining would be death to the social dominance of slavery in the national capital. This they felt; and nothing would have pleased them better than a revolution which would send Mr. Lincoln back to Illinois, and install Jefferson Davis in the White House. There was probably not one man in five in Washington at the time Mr. Lincoln entered the city who, in his heart, gave him welcome. It is not to be wondered at that his friends all over the country looked nervously forward to the fourth of March.

CHAPTER XVIII.

THE morning of the fourth of March broke beautifully clear, and it found General Scott and the Washington police in readiness for the day. The friends of Mr. Lincoln had gathered in from far and near, determined that he should be inaugurated. In the hearts of the surging crowds there was anxiety; but outside, all looked as usual on such occasions, with the single exception of an extraordinary display of soldiers. The public buildings, the schools and most of the places of business were closed during the day, and the stars and stripes were floating from every flag-staff. There was a great desire to hear Mr. Lincoln's inaugural; and, at an early hour, Pennsylvania Avenue was full of people, wending their way to the east front of the capitol, from which it was to be delivered.

At five minutes before twelve o'clock, Vice-President Breckinridge and Senator Foote escorted Mr. Hamlin, the Vice-President elect, into the Senate Chamber; and gave him a seat at the left of the chair. At twelve, Mr. Breckinridge announced the Senate adjourned without day, and then conducted Mr. Hamlin to the seat he had vacated. At this moment, the foreign diplomats, of whom there was a very large and brilliant representation, entered the chamber, and took the seats assigned to them. At a quarter before one o'clock, the Judges of the Supreme Court entered, with the venerable Chief Justice Taney at their head, each exchanging salutes with the new Vice-President, as they took their seats. At a quarter past one o'clock, an unusual stir and excitement announced the coming of the most important personage of the occasion. It was a relief to many to know that he was safely within the building; and those who were assembled in the hall regarded with the profoundest interest the entrance of President Buchanan and the President elect—the outgoing and the incoming man. A procession was then formed which passed to the platform erected for the ceremonies of the occasion, in the following order: Marshal of the District of Columbia, Judges of the Supreme Court and Sergeant-at-Arms, Senate Committee of Arrangements, President of the United States and President elect, Vice-President, Clerk of the Senate, Senators, Diplomatic Corps, heads of departments, Governors of states, and such others as were in the chamber. On arriving at the platform, Senator Baker of Oregon, whose name as one of Mr. Lincoln's old friends and political rivals in Illinois has been frequently mentioned in this volume, introduced Mr. Lincoln to the assembly. There was not a very hearty welcome given to the President, as he stepped forward to read his inaugural. His enemies were too many, and his friends too much in fear of exasperating them. The representative of American loyalty carried his burden alone. The inaugural was listened to with profound attention, every passage being vociferously cheered which contained any allusion to the Union, and none listening more carefully than Mr. Buchanan and Judge Taney, the latter of whom, with much agitation, administered the oath of office to Mr. Lincoln when his address was concluded.

Mr. Lincoln himself must have wondered at the strange conjunction of personages and events. The "Stephen" of his first speech in the old senatorial campaign was a defeated candidate for the presidency who then stood patriotically at his side, holding the hat of the republican President, which he had politely taken at the beginning of the inaugural address; "James" had just walked out of office to make room for him; "Franklin" had passed into comparative obscurity or something worse, and "Roger" had just administered to him the oath of office.

No thorough understanding of the moderate and conciliatory tone of the inaugural can be acquired without a perusal of the document itself. Its arguments were unanswerable, and its tone of respectful friendliness toward the South so marked that great pains were subsequently taken by the southern press to misrepresent it, and to counteract its effects. Mr. Lincoln said:

"FELLOW-CITIZENS OF THE UNITED STATES:—In compliance with a custom as old as the government itself, I appear before you to address you briefly, and to take, in your presence, the oath prescribed by the Constitution of the United States to be taken by the President before he enters on the execution of his office.

"I do not consider it necessary, at present, for me to discuss those matters of administration about which there is no special anxiety or excitement. Apprehension seems to exist among the people of the southern states, that, by the accession of a republican administration, their property and their peace and personal security are to be endangered. There has never been any reasonable cause for such apprehension. Indeed, the most ample evidence to the contrary has all the while existed, and been open to their inspection. It is found in nearly all the published speeches of him who now addresses you. I do but quote from one of those speeches, when I declare that 'I have no purpose, directly or indirectly, to interfere with the institution of slavery in the states where it exists.' I believe I have no lawful right to do so; and I have no inclination to do so. Those who nominated and elected me did so with the full knowledge that I had made this, and made many similar declarations, and had never recanted them. And, more than this, they placed in the platform, for my acceptance, and as a law to themselves and to me, the clear and emphatic resolution which I now read:

"'Resolved, That the maintenance inviolate of the rights of the states, and especially the right of each state to order and control its own domestic institutions according to its own judgment exclusively, is essential to that balance of power on which the perfection and endurance of our political fabric depend; and we denounce the lawless invasion by armed force of the soil of any state or territory, no matter under what pretext, as among the gravest of crimes.'

"I now reiterate these sentiments; and in doing so I only press upon the public attention the most conclusive evidence of which the case is susceptible, that the property, peace, and security of no section are to be in anywise endangered by the now incoming administration.

"I add, too, that all the protection which, consistently with the Constitution and the laws, can be given, will be cheerfully given to all the states when lawfully demanded, for whatever cause, as cheerfully to one section as to another.

" There is much controversy about the delivering up of fugitives from service or labor. The clause I now read is as plainly written in the Constitution as any other of its provisions:

"'No person held to service or labor in one state under the laws thereof, escaping into another, shall, in consequence of any law or regulation therein, be discharged from such service or labor, but shall be delivered up on claim of the party to whom such service or labor may be due.'

" It is scarcely questioned that this provision was intended by those who made it for the reclaiming of what we call fugitive slaves; and the intention of the lawgiver is the law.

" All members of Congress swear their support to the whole Constitution—to this provision as well as any other. To the proposition, then, that slaves whose cases come within the terms of this clause 'shall be delivered up,' their oaths are unanimous. Now, if they would make the effort in good temper, could they not, with nearly equal unanimity, frame and pass a law by means of which to keep good that unanimous oath?

" There is some difference of opinion whether this clause should be enforced by national or by state authority; but surely that difference is not a very material one. If the slave is to be surrendered, it can be of but little consequence to him or to others by which authority it is done; and should any one, in any case, be content that this oath shall go unkept on a merely unsubstantial controversy as to how it shall be kept?

" Again, in any law upon this subject, ought not all the safeguards of liberty known in civilized and humane jurisprudence to be introduced, so that a free man be not, in any case, surrendered as a slave? And might it not be well at the same time to provide by law for the enforcement of that clause in the Constitution which guarantees that 'the citizens of each state shall be entitled to all the privileges and immunities of citizens in the several states?'

" I take the official oath to-day with no mental reservations, and with no purpose to construe the Constitution or laws by any hypercritical rules; and while I do not choose now to specify particular acts of Congress as proper to be enforced, I do suggest that it will be much safer for all, both in official and private stations, to conform to and abide by all those acts which stand unrepealed, than to violate any of them, trusting to find impunity in having them held to be unconstitutional.

" It is seventy-two years since the first inauguration of a President under our national Constitution. During that period fifteen different and very distinguished citizens have in succession administered the executive branch of the government. They have conducted it through many perils, and generally with great success. Yet, with all this scope for precedent, I now enter upon the same task, for the brief constitutional term of four years, under great and peculiar difficulties.

"A disruption of the Federal Union, heretofore only menaced, is now formidably attempted. I hold that in the contemplation of universal law and of the Constitution, the union of these states is perpetual. Perpetuity is implied, if not expressed, in the fundamental law of all national governments. It is safe to assert that no government proper ever had a provision in its organic law for its own termination. Continue to execute all the express provisions of our national Constitution, and the Union will endure forever, it being impossible to destroy it except by some action not provided for in the instrument itself.

"Again, if the United States be not a government proper, but an association of states in the nature of a contract merely, can it, as a contract, be peaceably unmade by less than all the parties who made it? One party to a contract may violate it—break it, so to speak; but does it not require all to lawfully rescind it? Descending from these general principles, we find the proposition that in legal contemplation the Union is perpetual, confirmed by the history of the Union itself.

"The Union is much older than the Constitution. It was formed, in fact, by the Articles of Association in 1774. It was matured and continued in the Declaration of Independence in 1776. It was further matured, and the faith of all the then thirteen states expressly plighted and engaged that it should be perpetual, by the Articles of the Confederation, in 1778; and, finally, in 1787, one of the declared objects for ordaining and establishing the Constitution was to form a more perfect union. But if the destruction of the Union by one or by a part only of the states be lawfully possible, the Union is less perfect than before, the Constitution having lost the vital element of perpetuity.

"It follows from these views that no state, upon its own mere motion, can lawfully get out of the Union; that resolves and ordinances to that effect are legally void; and that acts of violence within any state or states against the authority of the United States are insurrectionary or revolutionary, according to circumstances.

"I therefore consider that, in view of the Constitution and the laws, the Union is unbroken, and, to the extent of my ability, I shall take care, as the Constitution itself expressly enjoins upon me, that the laws of the Union shall be faithfully executed in all the states. Doing this, which I deem to be only a simple duty on my part, I shall perfectly perform it, so far as is practicable, unless my rightful masters, the American people, shall withhold the requisition, or in some authoritative manner direct the contrary.

"I trust this will not be regarded as a menace, but only as the declared purpose of the Union that it will constitutionally defend and maintain itself.

"In doing this there need be no bloodshed or violence, and there shall be none unless it is forced upon the national authority.

"The power confided to me *will be used to hold, occupy, and possess the property and places belonging to the government,* and collect the duties and imposts; but beyond what may be necessary for these objects there will be no invasion, no using of force against or among the people anywhere.

"Where hostility to the United States shall be so great and so universal as to prevent competent resident citizens from holding federal offices, there will be no attempt to force obnoxious strangers among the people that object. While strict legal right may exist of the government to enforce the exercise of these offices, the attempt to do so would be so irritating, and so nearly impracticable withal, that I deem it best to forego for the time the uses of such offices.

"The mails, unless repelled, will continue to be furnished in all parts of the Union.

"So far as possible, the people everywhere shall have that sense of perfect security which is most favorable to calm thought and reflection.

"The course here indicated will be followed, unless current events and experience shall show a modification or change to be proper; and in every case and exigency my best discretion will be exercised according to the circumstances actually existing, and with a view and hope of a peaceful solution of the national troubles, and the restoration of fraternal sympathies and affections.

"That there are persons, in one section or another, who seek to destroy the Union at all events, and are glad of any pretext to do it, I will neither affirm nor deny. But if there be such, I need address no word to them.

"To those, however, who really love the Union, may I not speak, before entering upon so grave a matter as the destruction of our national fabric, with all its benefits, its memories, and its hopes? Would it not be well to ascertain why we do it? Will you hazard so desperate a step, while any portion of the ills you fly from have no real existence? Will you, while the certain ills you fly to are greater than all the real ones you fly from? Will you risk the commission of so fearful a mistake? All profess to be content in the Union if all constitutional rights can be maintained. Is it true, then, that any right, plainly written in the Constitution, has been denied? I think not. Happily the human mind is so constituted that no party can reach to the audacity of doing this.

"Think, if you can, of a single instance in which a plainly-written provision of the Constitution has ever been denied. If, by the mere force of numbers, a majority should deprive a minority of any clearly-written constitutional right, it might, in a moral point of view, justify revolution; it certainly would, if such right were a vital one. But such is not our case.

"All the vital rights of minorities and of individuals are so plainly assured to them by affirmations and negations, guaranties and prohibitions in the Constitution, that controversies never arise concerning them. But no organic law can ever be framed with a provision specifically applicable to every question which may occur in practical administration. No foresight can anticipate, nor any document of reasonable length contain, express provisions for all possible questions. Shall fugitives from labor be surrendered by national or by state authorities? The Constitution does not expressly say. Must Congress protect slavery in the territories? The Constitution does not expressly say. From questions of this class, spring all our constitutional controversies, and we divide upon them into majorities and minorities.

"If the minority will not acquiesce, the majority must, or the government must cease. There is no alternative for continuing the government but acquiescence on the one side or the other. If a minority in such a case will secede rather than acquiesce, they make a precedent, which, in turn, will ruin and divide them, for a minority of their own will secede from them whenever a majority refuses to be controlled by such a minority. For instance, why not any portion of a new confederacy, a year or two hence, arbitrarily secede again, precisely as portions of the present Union now claim to secede from it? All who cherish disunion sentiments are now being educated to the exact temper of doing this. Is there such perfect identity of interests among the states to compose a new Union as to produce harmony only, and prevent renewed secession? Plainly, the central idea of secession is the essence of anarchy.

"A majority held in restraint by constitutional check and limitation, and always changing easily with deliberate changes of popular opinions and sentiments, is the only true sovereign of a free people. Whoever rejects it, does, of necessity, fly to anarchy or to despotism. Unanimity is impossible; the rule of a minority, as a permanent arrangement, is wholly inadmissible. So that, rejecting the majority principle, anarchy or despotism, in some form, is all that is left.

"I do not forget the position assumed by some that constitutional questions are to be decided by the Supreme Court, nor do I deny that such decisions must be binding in any case upon the parties to a suit, as to the object of that suit, while they are also entitled to a very high respect and consideration in all parallel cases by all other departments of the government; and while it is obviously possible that such decision may be erroneous in any given case, still the evil effect following it, being limited to that particular case, with the chance that it may be overruled and never become a precedent for other cases, can better be borne than could the evils of a different practice.

"At the same time the candid citizen must confess that, if the policy of the government upon the vital question affecting the whole people is to be irrevocably fixed by the decisions of the Supreme Court, the instant they are made, as in ordinary litigation between parties in personal actions, the people will have ceased to be their own masters, unless having to that extent practically resigned their government into the hands of that eminent tribunal.

"Nor is there in this view any assault upon the court or the judges. It is a duty from which they may not shrink, to decide cases properly brought before them; and it is no fault of theirs if others seek to turn their decisions to political purposes. One section of our country believes slavery is right, and ought to be extended, while the other believes it is wrong, and ought not to be extended; and this is the only substantial dispute; and the fugitive slave clause of the Constitution and the law for the suppression of the foreign slave trade, are each as well enforced, perhaps, as any law can ever be in a community where the moral sense of the people imperfectly supports the law itself. The great body of the people abide by the dry legal obligation in both cases, and a few break over in each. This, I think, cannot be perfectly cured, and it would be worse, in both cases, after the separation of the sections, than before. The foreign slave trade, now imperfectly suppressed, would be ultimately revived, without restriction, in one section; while fugitive slaves, now only partially surrendered, would not be surrendered at all by the other.

"Physically speaking we can not separate; we can not remove our respective sections from each other, nor build an impassable wall between them. A husband and wife may be divorced, and go out of the presence and beyond the reach of each other, but the different parts of our country cannot do this. They can not but remain face to face; and intercourse, either amicable or hostile, must continue between them. Is it possible, then, to make that intercourse more advantageous or more satisfactory after separation than before? Can aliens make treaties easier than friends can make laws? Can treaties be more faithfully enforced between aliens than laws can among friends? Suppose you go to war, you cannot fight always; and when, after much loss on both sides, and no gain on either, you cease fighting, the identical questions as to terms of intercourse are again upon you.

"This country, with its institutions, belongs to the people who inhabit it. Whenever they shall grow weary of the existing government, they can exercise their constitutional right of amending, or their revolutionary right to dismember or overthrow it. I can not be ignorant of the fact that many worthy and patriotic citizens are desirous of having the national Constitution amended. While I make no recommendation of amendment, I fully recognize the full authority of the people over the whole subject, to be exercised in either of the modes prescribed in the instrument itself, and I should, under existing circumstances, favor rather than oppose a fair opportunity being afforded the people to act upon it.

"I will venture to add, that to me the convention mode seems preferable, in that it allows amendments to originate with the people themselves, instead of only permitting them to take or reject propositions originated by others not especially chosen for the purpose, and which might not be precisely such as they would wish either to accept or refuse. I understand that a proposed amendment to the Constitution (which amendment, however, I have not seen) has passed Congress, to the effect that the federal government shall never interfere with the domestic institutions of states, including that of persons held to service. To avoid misconstruction of what I have said, I depart from my purpose not to speak of particular amendments, so far as to say that, holding such a provison to now be implied constitutional law, I have no objection to its being made express and irrevocable.

"The chief magistrate derives all his authority from the people, and they have conferred none upon him to fix the terms for the separation of the states. The people themselves, also, can do this if they choose, but the executive, as such, has nothing to do with it. His duty is to administer the present government as it came to his hands, and to transmit it unimpaired by him to his successor. Why should there not be a patient confidence in the ultimate justice of the people? Is there any better or equal hope in the world? In our present differences is either party without faith of being in the right? If the Almighty Ruler of nations, with his eternal truth and justice, be on your side of the North, or on yours of the South, that truth and that justice will surely prevail by the judgment of this great tribunal, the American people. By the frame of the government under which we live, this same people have wisely given their public servants but little power for mischief, and have with equal wisdom provided for the return of that little to their own hands at very short intervals. While the people retain their virtue and vigilance, no administration, by any extreme wickedness or folly, can very seriously injure the government in the short space of four years.

"My countrymen, one and all, think calmly and well upon this whole subject. Nothing valuable can be lost by taking time.

"If there be an object to hurry any of you, in hot haste, to a step which you would never take deliberately, that object will be frustrated by taking time: but no good object can be frustrated by it.

"Such of you as are now dissatisfied still have the old Constitution unimpaired, and, on the sensitive point, the laws of your own framing under it; while the new administration will have no immediate power, if it would, to change either.

"If it were admitted that you who are dissatisfied hold the right side in the dispute, there is still no single reason for precipitate action. Intelligence, patriotism, Christianity, and a firm reliance on Him who has never yet forsaken this favored land, are still competent to adjust, in the best way, all our present difficulties.

"In your hands, my dissatisfied fellow-countrymen, and not in mine, is the momentous issue of civil war. The government will not assail you.

"You can have no conflict without being yourselves the aggressors. You have no oath registered in Heaven to destroy the government; while I shall have the most solemn one to 'preserve, protect, and defend' it.

"I am loth to close. We are not enemies, but friends. We must not be enemies. Though passion may have strained, it must not break our bonds of affection.

"The mystic cords of memory, stretching from every battle-field and patriot grave to every living heart and hearthstone all over this broad land, will yet swell the chorus of the Union, when again touched, as surely they will be, by the better angels of our nature."

The address delivered and the oath administered, the august ceremonies of the occasion were concluded; and, passing back through the Senate Chamber, the President was escorted to the White House, where Mr. Buchanan took leave of him, and where the people were received by him in large numbers. Mr. Lincoln, on being asked whether he felt frightened while delivering his address, in consequence of the threats of assassination, replied that he had frequently experienced greater fear in addressing a dozen western men on the subject of temperance. Of one thing the "fire-eaters" were assured by the address, viz: that if a war was to be inaugurated, they would be obliged to fire the first gun. Mr. Lincoln had pledged himself to take no step of even doubtful propriety. He proposed simply to possess and hold the property of the United States.

And now began the great work of Mr. Lincoln's life. The humble boy, reared in a log cabin, was the great man, occupying the proudest place in the nation, in the most perilous period of that nation's existence. He was in the White House as God's and the people's instrument, to work for both.

His first duty was the formal designation of a cabinet, for undoubtedly his choice of secretaries was essentially settled in his own mind before he left home. The highest position was offered to Mr. Seward, the first statesman in the republican party, and the equal if not the superior of any in the country. Concerning the filling of the office of Secretary of State, it is believed that Mr. Lincoln had no hesitation. Mr. Seward was his first and last choice. With equal promptitude he decided to call Edward Bates of Missouri to the office of Attorney General. Simon Cameron of Pennsylvania was known to be an aspirant for cabinet honors; and, it is believed, would have accepted the post of Secretary of the Treasury with more alacrity than he did that of Secretary of War, to which Mr. Lincoln called him. Salmon P. Chase of Ohio, who shared with Mr. Seward the highest regards of the republican party and the confidence of the country, was appointed to the Treasury. The men thus brought into the government were all prominent candidates for the presidency at Chicago, and on the first ballot received an aggregate of three hundred and twenty-one votes of the four hundred and sixty-five cast. The great majority of the party thus had the expression of their first choice for the presidency honored by Mr. Lincoln in a remarkable degree. Gideon Welles of Connecticut was appointed Secretary of the Navy. Caleb B. Smith of Indiana, an old personal friend of Mr. Lincoln, and for many years a distinguished politician of the West, was offered the Portfolio of the Interior, and accepted it; and Montgomery Blair of Maryland was appointed Postmaster General.

Thus furnished with his secretaries, another most important work opened before him—the clearing the departments of the sympathizers with treason. This was indeed a Herculean task. Treason was everywhere. Every department was infected. The men had been manipulated so long by treasonable hands—had been moulded into such thorough sympathy with the rebellion—and had so imbibed its treacherous spirit, that no measure could be discussed or adopted by the new administration that was not reported to the rebels by some clerk or confidant. The government was betrayed every day by its own agents. Not a step could be taken by Mr. Lincoln, in any direction, that some spy in the departments, or some traitor in his confidence, did not report to his enemies.

There were certain things that Mr. Lincoln specially endeavored to do in his inaugural address, and in all the preliminary work of his administration. He endeavored to show that the rebellion was without an adequate cause—to show this first to his own people, and then to the governments and peoples on the other side of the Atlantic. He endeavored to leave no way untried that promised to procure or preserve an honorable peace. He endeavored so to manage affairs that whenever open hostilities should come, they should be begun by the rebels and not by the government. He intended to preserve for himself and for the government a clean record. He intended to bear with the rebellion just so long as it confined itself to paper—nay, further than this—to bear with it to the silent sufferance of many practical indignities. He did not mean to unsheath a sword, or fire a gun, until the rebellion absolutely compelled him to do so. Yet, while waiting the development of events, he was very busily engaged in clearing the government for action. Many of the revelations and movements of the first few weeks would doubtless be startling, even to-day, but the time has not yet come for their exposure.

Mr. Lincoln found not only the departments corrupt and unreliable, but he found the public mind abroad thoroughly poisoned against him, and fully in sympathy with the secessionists. Perhaps a majority of the representatives of the government in Europe were in the secrets of the seceders, and, in company with many who had gone from the southern states to shape public opinion to the interests of treason, were doing everything in their power to injure the government which had honored them. The places thus disgraced and made instruments in the hands of treason were to be filled by loyal men; and a set of influences were to be put in motion which should secure respect for the government, and a sound understanding of the merits of the controversy between the government and slavery. To fill these places was not an easy task, but it was done quickly and, in the main, wisely.

It is proper here to give an explanation of Mr. Lincoln's pacific policy, at this time. Great fault was subsequently found with him by the extremists among his northern friends, for his deference to the border states; and a full understanding of his policy, as it related to these states, cannot be had without going back to this period when it was initiated. There were fifteen slave states, which those engaged in the rebellion hoped to lead or to force into secession. At the time of the inauguration, only seven of these fifteen—less than a majority—had revolted. The cotton states alone had followed the lead of South Carolina out of the Union. Several weeks had passed since a state had seceded; and unless other states could be dragooned into the movement, the rebellion would be practically a failure from the start. Such a confederacy could not hope to live a year, and would be obliged to find its way back into the Union upon some terms. In the meantime, two or three conventions in the border states, delegated freshly from the people, had voted distinctly and decidedly not to secede. The affairs of the confederacy were really in a very precarious condition when Mr. Lincoln came into power. The rebel government was making very much more bluster than progress.

It became Mr. Lincoln's policy so to conduct affairs as to strengthen the Union feeling in the border states, and to give utterance to no sentiment and to do no deed which should drive these states toward the confederacy. He saw that if he could hold these states, there could not be a very serious war; for the first condition of success to the rebel cause was its general adoption by the border slave states. To hold these states by every means that did not bring absolute disgrace upon the government was his object. He must do nothing that would weaken the hands of Union men. The difficult position of these Union men he fully comprehended and considered. Of course, he had a hard path to pursue; and it is not strange that those more hasty than himself should sometimes think he was loitering by the way, or was making it

19

more tortuous than was either necessary or expedient. It is doubtful whether the politicians of New England ever gave Mr. Lincoln the credit which was his due for retaining in the Union those slave states which never left their allegiance. An early and decided war policy would have been morally certain to drive every slave state into the confederacy, except Maryland and Delaware, and they would only have been retained by force.

The confederacy found that it must make progress or die. The rebel Congress passed a measure for the organization of an army, on the ninth of March, and on the twelfth two confederate commissioners—Mr. Forsyth of Alabama and Mr. Crawford of Georgia—presented themselves at the State Department at Washington for the purpose of making a treaty with the United States. They knew, of course, that they could not be received officially, and that they ought to be arrested for treason. The President would not recognize them, but sent to them a copy of his Inaugural, as the embodiment of the views of the government. The commissioners hung about Washington for a month, learning what they could, and in daily communication with the traitors who still haunted the confidence of the heads of the government. Mr. Seward's reply to them, on the eighth of April, was delayed at their own request until that time, and when it came they probably knew what its contents and character would be. In order to give secession a new impetus, they wished, in some way, to throw the responsibility of beginning war upon the Washington authorities, and to make it appear that they had exhausted all peaceable measures for an adjustment of the difficulties.

In the meantime, Lieutenant Talbot, on behalf of Mr. Lincoln, was having interviews with Governor Pickens of South Carolina and with General Beauregard, in command of the confederate forces there, in which he informed them that provisions would be sent to Fort Sumter peaceably if possible,—otherwise by force. This was communicated to L. P. Walker, then rebel Secretary of War. Before Talbot had made his communication, Beauregard had informed Major Anderson, in command of Fort Sumter, that he must have no further intercourse with Charleston; and Talbot himself was refused permission to visit that gallant and faithful officer.

These were very dark days with Mr. Lincoln. The rebels were determined to wrest from him a pretext for war—determined to make him take a step which could be made to appear to be the first step. At the same time, he was making rapid preparations for war, all of which must be kept secret from friends, that they might not exasperate foes. The loyal press became impatient with his apparent inactivity, and under the inspiration of this press the loyal masses became uneasy. Under these circumstances, there were not wanting disloyal men in the North, who became bold in the entertainment of schemes for a revolution. Mr. Douglas himself did not support the administration, although he had publicly declared for coercion. He could not forget his hatred of the republican party; and was ready for almost any scheme for its destruction. He wished to organize a great compromise party, which would consent to the reconstruction of the Union, with slavery recognized and protected in all its departments. Until the first overt act of war had been committed, he brought no aid to the government.

While Mr. Lincoln's friends were clamoring for a policy—as if he had not a very decided one—and his foes north and south were busy with their schemes for the destruction of himself, his party and his country, he was performing the most exhausting labors. He was thronged with office-seekers, to whose claims he gave his personal attention. He was holding protracted cabinet meetings. He was in almost hourly intercourse with prominent men from every section of the country. All these labors he was performing with the con- · sciousness that his nominal friends were doubtful, that seven states were in open revolt, and that a majority throughout the Union had not the slightest sympathy with him.

There was distraction, also, in his counsels. Loyal men, burning with patriotic indignation, were demanding that Fort Sumter should be reinforced and provisioned, while the veteran Lieutenant General was advising its abandonment as a military necessity. The wisdom of Mr. Lincoln's waiting became evident at a day not too long delayed. Fort Pickens, which the rebels had not taken, was quietly reinforced, and when the vessels which carried the relief were dispatched, Mr. Lincoln gave official information to General Beauregard that provisions were to be sent to Major Anderson in Fort Sumter, by an unarmed vessel. He was determined that no hostile act on the part of the government should commence the war, for which both sides were preparing; although an act of open war had already transpired in Charleston harbor, for which the rebel forces were responsible. The steamer Star of the West, loaded with troops and provisions for Major Anderson, was fired upon and driven out of the harbor two months before the expiration of Mr. Buchanan's term of office. The supplying the garrison with food was an act of humanity, and not an act of war, except as it might be so construed.

Beauregard laid this last intelligence before his Secretary of War, and under special instructions, on the twelfth of April, he demanded the surrender of Fort Sumter. He was ready to make the demand, and to back it by force. The city of Charleston was full of troops, and, for months, batteries had been in course of construction, with the special purpose of compelling the surrender of the fort. Major Anderson had seen these batteries going up, day after day, without the liberty to fire a gun. He declined to surrender. He was called upon to state when he would evacuate the fort. He replied that on the fifteenth he would do so, should he not meantime receive controlling instructions from the government, or additional supplies. The response which he received was that the confederate batteries would open on Fort Sumter in one hour from the date of the message. The date of the message was "April 12, 1861, 3:30 A. M." Beauregard was true to his word. At half past four, the batteries opened upon the fort, which, after a long and terrible bombardment, and a gallant though comparatively feeble defense by a small and half-starved garrison, was surrendered the following day.

This was practically the initial act of war. Mr. Lincoln, by his determined forbearance, had thrown the *onus* of its commencement upon the rebel government. Never by word, or deed, or declared or concealed intention, had he wronged the South, or denied its rights under the Constitution. By no hostile act had he provoked war. From the time he had first opened his lips as President of the United States, he had breathed none but pacific words. He had claimed the least that he could claim for the government, and still preserve a show of right and power. Upon the heads of the conspirators rested every particle of responsibility for the beginning of the war, and the train of horrors that followed. The rebellion was conceived in perjury, brought forth in violence, cradled in ignorance, and reared upon spoil. It never had an apology for existence that will be entertained for a moment at the bar of history. It never was anything from its birth to its death but a crime—a crime against Christianity, against patriotism, against humanity, against civilization, against progress, against personal and political honor, against the people who were forced to support it, against the people who voluntarily put it down, and against that God to whom it blasphemously appealed for justification, and arrogantly prayed for success.

The fall of Sumter was the resurrection of patriotism. The North needed just this. Such a universal burst of patriotic indignation as ran over the North under the influence of this insult to the national flag has never been witnessed. It swept away all party lines as if it had been flame and they had been flax. No combination of moral influences could thus have united in one feeling and purpose the elements which the fire from those batteries welded into a burning union. All disloyalty was silenced. Compromise was a word that had no significance. "Coercion"—a word which had had a fearful meaning among the timid—lost its terrors. There was a universal desire, all over the North, to avenge the foul insult. It was worth a life-time of indifference or discord to feel and to see a nation thus once more united in thought and purpose, and to realize that underneath all divisions of party and sect, and deeper down than selfish interest and personal prejudice, there was a love of country which made us a nation.

Now was the time for Mr. Lincoln to act. Up to this date he had had no basis for action in the popular feeling. If he had raised an army, that would have been an act of hostility—that would have been a threat of "coercion." A thousand northern presses would have pounced upon him as a provoker of war. On the fifteenth of April he issued a proclamation, calling upon the loyal states for seventy-five thousand men to protect the national capital, and suppress such combinations as had been made to resist the inforcement of the laws of the United States. "I appeal" said Mr. Lincoln, in this proclamation, "to all loyal citizens to favor, facilitate and aid this effort to maintain the honor, the integrity and existence of our national Union, and the perpetuity of popular government, and to redress the wrongs already long enough endured." The first service, he stated, to which the forces thus called for would be subjected would be to repossess the forts, places and property taken from the Union by the rebels. By the same proclamation he convened both Houses of Congress to assemble on the fourth of July.

The utterance of this proclamation was so clearly a necessity, and was so directly a response to the uprising of the people, that not a voice was raised against it. It was received with no small degree of excitement, but it was a healthy excitement. It was a necessity; and loyal men everywhere felt that the great struggle between slavery and the country was upon them. "Better that it should be settled by us than by our children," said men, everywhere; and in their self-devotion they were encouraged by their mothers, sisters and wives. The South knew that war must come, and they were prepared. Nearly all the southern forts were already in their hands. They had robbed the northern arsenals through the miscreant Floyd. They had cut off the payment of all debts due the North. They had ransacked the mails, so that the government could have no communication with its friends and forces. They had been instructing officers for years, and drilling troops for months. They knew that there were not arms enough in the North to furnish an army competent to overcome them. When, therefore, Mr. Lincoln called for his seventy-five thousand men, they met the proclamation with a howl of derision.

Massachusetts was the first state to respond to the call for troops. Governor Andrew, a devoted friend of the administration, acted as promptly then in the support of the government as he afterwards labored with efficient persistence in the destruction of the rebellion; but the credit of having the troops ready for motion and action was due mainly to the foresight of Governor N. P. Banks, afterwards a Major General in the federal service. He was Governor Andrew's predecessor; and three years before the breaking out of the rebellion declared, when rallied on his devotion to the military, that the troops would be called upon within a few years to suppress a slaveholders' rebellion. The prediction seemed very wild then, and probably would never have been recalled but for its exact fulfillment. The troops which he had made ready, Governor Andrew, coming after him, promptly dispatched.

The moral effect of the marching of the Massachusetts Sixth was very great. The hearts of the people were stirred all along their route by the most powerful emotions. They were fed and applauded at every considerable station. Women thronged around the cars, bringing to them their Bibles and other gifts, and giving them their tearful blessing. New York city was much impressed by their sturdy march through the great metropolis. It was a new sensation. Men forgot their counting-rooms and ware-houses, and gave themselves up to the emotions excited by so prompt and gallant an exhibition of patriotism. But the tramp of the Sixth awoke the young men everywhere to deeds of emulation. Within forty-eight hours after this regiment left Boston, two more regiments had been made ready, and were dispatched. On its way through Baltimore, the Sixth Regiment was attacked by a mob, carrying a secession flag, and several of its members killed and wounded. This outrage added new fuel to the fire.

The North was growing angry. The idea that a loyal regiment could not pass through a nominally loyal city, on its way to protect the national capital, without fighting its way through, aroused a storm of indignation that swept over the whole of loyal America.

Governor Hicks of Maryland and Mayor Brown of Baltimore were frightened. They did not wish to have any more troops taken through Baltimore. Mr. Lincoln assured them that he made no point of bringing troops through that city, and that he left the matter with General Scott, who had said in his presence that the troops might be marched around Baltimore. By this arrangement a collision with the people of Baltimore would be avoided, unless they should go out of the way to seek it. "Now and ever," said Mr. Lincoln, in closing a note to these gentlemen, "I shall do all in my power for peace, consistently with the maintenance of the government."

Governor Hicks wished the quarrel between the North and South referred to Lord Lyons, the British minister, for arbitration. To this Mr. Seward, speaking for the President, made a most admirable reply, stating that whatever noble sentiments, once prevalent in Maryland, had been obliterated, the President would be hopeful, nevertheless, that there is one that would forever remain there and everywhere. That sentiment is that no domestic contention whatever, that may arise among the parties of this republic, ought, in any case, to be referred to any foreign arbitrament—least of all to the arbitrament of a foreign monarchy."

Governor Hicks occupied, without doubt, a difficult position. Out of ninety-two thousand votes cast at the presidential election, only a little more than two thousand had been cast for Mr. Lincoln. More than forty-two thousand votes had been given for Mr. Breckinridge, and almost an equal number for John Bell. Maryland was a southern slave-holding state, and the sympathies of four persons in every five were with the rebellion. His people threatened him, while the government would have its troops, and insisted that they should pass through Maryland.

After the passage of the Massachusetts Sixth, the mob had control. They burnt the bridges north of Baltimore, so as to cut off the means of access to the city; and then, against the protests of the governor, the troops were forwarded by way of Annapolis.

Four days after Mr. Lincoln's call for troops—on the day of the bloody passage of the Massachusetts Sixth through Baltimore—he issued a proclamation declaring a blockade of the ports of South Carolina, Georgia, Alabama, Florida, Mississippi, Louisiana and Texas. This call for troops and the establishment of a blockade were the preliminaries of one of the most remarkable wars that have occurred in the history of the human race—a war which, for the number of men involved, the amount of spaces traversed, of coast line blockaded, of material consumed and results achieved, surpasses all the wars of history.

The South had calculated upon the disloyalty of Maryland. Nay, more, it had calculated on the assistance of a large party at the North. It did not intend to be confined in its warlike operations to its own territory. Northern politicians, and among them ex-President Pierce, had told them it would not be. It expected to take and hold Washington, and to banish the government; and Maryland had an important part to play in the drama. Jefferson Davis had openly declared that the North and not the South should be the field of battle. The rebel Secretary of War said publicly in Montgomery that while no man could tell where the war would end, he would prophesy that the flag which then flaunted the breeze at Montgomery would float over the dome of the old capitol at Washington before the first of May; and that it "might float eventually over Fanueil Hall itself." To make good these predictions, the rebel government organized and sent toward Virginia, a force of 20,000 men, calculating upon the secession of Virginia which had not then joined the confederacy, and which, left to the popular choice, never would have taken that fatal step.

The attitude of the two governments at this period presented a strong contrast—a most instructive contrast to all who are curious to mark the respective degrees of responsibility attaching to them for the war which followed. The confederate forces, or the state forces in the confederate interest, had seized and occupied nearly every fort, arsenal and dock-yard belonging to the United States, upon the southern territory. The rebel government had opened its batteries upon United States vessels, and had bombarded and captured Fort Sumter. It had issued letters of marque to distress our commerce. It was engaged in the attempt to force every border slave state into the support of its schemes. It was pushing its soldiers northward for a war of aggression; and its highest representatives were publicly boasting that their flag would soon float over the capitol at Washington, and that the war should not be carried on upon confederate soil. The attitude of the rebel government was that of direct, bitter, determined, aggressive hostility.

Virginia at this time was holding a state convention which, to the dismay and vexation of the rebel leaders, was controlled by a large majority of Union men. Nothing is more demonstrable than that the choice of Virginia was to remain in the Union. These delegates were chosen as Union men; yet every possible influence was brought to bear upon them to cajole or coerce them into disunion. Threats, misrepresentations, promises of power, social proscription, appeals to personal and sectional interest, everything that treasonable ingenuity could suggest were resorted to to urge the laggard state into the vortex of secession. The fall of Sumter, the inaugural of President Lincoln and the failure of the confederate commissioners to secure a treaty were used in different ways to inflame southern pride, and loosen the love of the loyal members from the old Union. The President's Inaugural had been so misconstrued as to convey the idea that his policy was one of coercion; and the convention sent a committee to Mr. Lincoln, commissioned to ask him to communicate to the convention the policy which the federal executive intended to pursue, in regard to the confederate states, complaining that great and injurious uncertainty prevailed in the public mind in regard to this policy.

To this request Mr. Lincoln gave a formal answer; and in this answer appears the contrast to which attention has been called. He expressed his regret and mortification that, after having stated his position and policy as plainly as he was able to state it in his inaugural address, there should be any uncertainty on the subject. "As I then and therein said,". the reply proceeds, "'the power confided in me will be used to hold, occupy and possess property and places belonging to the government, and to collect duties and imposts; but, beyond what is necessary for these objects, there will be no invasion, no using of force against, or among, people anywhere.'" Fort Sumter, he declared it his purpose to repossess, with all the other places seized from the government, and to the best of his ability he should repel force by force. In consequence of the attack on Sumter, it was possible that he should cause the withdrawal of the mails from the states which claimed to have seceded. He closed by reiterating the claim of the government upon the military posts and property which had been seized, and by stating that, whatever else he might do for the purpose, he should not "attempt to collect the duties and imposts by any armed invasion of any part of the country," not meaning by that, however, to cut himself off from the liberty to land a force necessary to relieve a fort upon the border of the country.

On one side was rampant treason and a policy of aggressive war; on the other, patient forbearance, and the most considerate care not to take any step not absolutely necessary to the maintenance of the indisputable rights of the government. No man in the United States who pretended to be loyal could find fault with Mr. Lincoln for claiming too much, or being harsh with those "erring sisters" who, it was believed by many, might be gently led back to their allegiance

On the seventeenth of April, Virginia went out of the Union by a convention vote of eighty-eight to fifty-five; and on the twenty-first of May the confederate capital was transferred to Richmond. Thenceforth Virginia went straight toward desolation. Its "sacred soil" was from that hour devoted to trenches, fortifications, battle-fields, military roads, camps and graves.

The conciliatory policy of Mr. Lincoln had threatened the ruin of the confederacy; but the confederacy made war, and then appealed to the border states for sympathy and help. Governor Pickens of South Carolina telegraphed the fall of Sumter to the Governor of Virginia, and appealed to Virginia to know what she was going to do. This was the policy—to precipitate war, and then appeal to sectional pride and interest for sectional assistance. The first practical show of sectional feeling on the part of the border states was contained in the angry and insulting responses which they returned to Mr. Lincoln's call for troops. These responses exhibited the sympathies of their Governors, at least. Tennessee, North Carolina and Arkansas followed Virginia out of the Union, and thus the confederate cause made the gain it sought.

At the North and West the response to the President's call for soldiers was rendered with enthusiastic alacrity, the states vieing with each other in the office of raising, fitting out and dispatching troops. Money was offered to the government by millions, and the President found that he had a basis for a policy in the national feeling. After a week of great anxiety, Washington was relieved; and while troops from the North were rushing southward, a still larger number from the South were pushing northward in preparation for the grand struggle.

One of the most encouraging incidents of this opening chapter of the war was a visit of Mr. Douglas to Mr. Lincoln, in which the former gave to the latter the assurance of his sympathy and support in the war for the preservation of the Union. It is to be remembered that Mr. Douglas was an ambitious man, that he was a strong party man, that he had battled for power with all the persistence of a strong and determined nature, and that he was a sadly disappointed man. The person with whom he had had his hardest fights occupied the chair to which he had for many years aspired.

On Sunday, the fourteenth of April, all Washington was alive with excitement under the effect of the news of the fall of Sumter. Secessionists could not conceal their joy, and the loyal were equally sad and indignant. Churches were forsaken, and the opening of the war was the only topic of thought and conversation. Under these circumstances, Hon. George Ashmun of Massachusetts, who was personally on the most friendly terms with Mr. Lincoln and Mr. Douglas, called on the latter in the evening, to obtain from him some public declaration that should help the government in its extremity. He found the Senator surrounded by political friends, who were soon dismissed, and then, for an hour, the two men discussed the relations of Mr. Douglas to the administration. The first impulse of the Senator was against Mr. Ashmun's wishes, who desired him to go to the President at once, and tell him he would sustain him in all the needful measures which the exigency demanded. His reply was: "Mr. Lincoln has dealt hardly with me, in removing some of my friends from office, and I don't know as he wants my advice or aid." Mr. Ashmun remarked that he had probably followed democratic precedents in making removals, but that the present question was above party, and that it was now in the power of Mr. Douglas to render such a service to his country as would not only give him a title to its lasting gratitude, but would show that in the hour of his country's need he could trample all party considerations and resentments under feet. At this juncture, Mrs. Douglas came in, and gave the whole weight of her affectionate influence in the direction in which Mr. Ashmun was endeavoring to lead him. He could not withstand the influence of his friend, his wife, and that better nature to which they appealed. He gave up all his enmity, all his resentment, cast every unworthy sentiment and selfish feeling behind him, and cordially declared his willingness to go to Mr. Lincoln, and offer him his earnest and hearty support.

It was nearly dark when the two gentlemen started for the President's house. Mr. Lincoln was alone, and on learning their errand gave them a most cordial welcome. For once, the life-long antagonists were united in heart and purpose. Mr. Lincoln took up the proclamation, calling for seventy-five thousand troops, which he had determined to issue the next day, and read it. When he had finished, Mr. Douglas rose from his chair and said: "Mr. President, I cordially concur in every word of that document, except that instead of the call for seventy-five thousand men I would make it two hundred thousand. You do not know the dishonest purposes of those men as well as I do." Then he asked the President and Mr. Ashmun to look at a map of the United States which hung at one end of the room. On this he pointed out, in detail, the principal strategic points which should be at once strengthened for the coming contest. Among the more prominent of these were Fortress Monroe, Washington, Harper's Ferry and Cairo. He then enlarged upon the firm, warlike course which should be pursued, while Mr. Lincoln listened with earnest interest, and the two old foes parted that night thorough friends, perfectly united in a patriotic purpose.

After leaving the President, Mr. Ashmun said to Mr. Douglas: "You have done justice to your own reputation and to the President; and the country must know it. The proclamation will go by telegraph all over the country in the morning, and the account of this interview must go with it. I shall send it, either in my own language or yours. I prefer that you should give your own version." Mr. Douglas said he would write it; and so the dispatch went with the message wherever the telegraph would carry it, confirming the wavering of his own party, and helping to raise the tide of loyal feeling, among all parties and classes, to its flood. The dispatch, the original of which Mr. Ashmun still retains, was as follows:

"Mr. Douglas called on the President this evening, and had an interesting conversation on the present condition of the country. The substance of the conversation was that while Mr. Douglas was unalterably opposed to the administration on all its political issues, he was prepared to sustain the President in the exercise of all his constitutional functions to preserve the Union, and maintain the government and defend the federal capital. A firm policy and prompt action were necessary. The capital of our country was in danger and must be defended at all hazards, and at any expense of men or money. He spoke of the present and future without reference to the past."

The writer of the life of Mr. Lincoln and the chronicler of the rebellion will find few more delightful tasks than that of recording the unwearied devotion of Mr. Douglas to the cause of his country during the brief remainder of his life. He was done with his dreams of power, done with the thought that compromise would save the country, and done, for the time at least, with schemes for party aggrandizement. Six days after his interview with Mr. Lincoln he was on his way home, and at Bellair, Ohio, he was called out to make a speech. All parties received him with the greatest enthusiasm, and every word he uttered had the genuine ring of patriotism. Subsequently he addressed the legislature of Illinois, at Springfield, and his own fellow-citizens at Chicago. The old party talk and the old party policy were all forgotten, and only the sturdy, enthusiastic patriot spoke. In one of the last letters he ever wrote he said: "We should never forget that a man cannot be a true democrat unless he is a loyal patriot." In May he became sick, and on the third of June he died. In the low delirium that attended his disease he talked of nothing but his country, and almost his last coherent words were shaped to a wish for its honor and prosperity, through the defeat and dispersion of its enemies.

Mr. Lincoln felt his death as a calamity. He had been of great service to him in unveiling the designs of the rebels, and in bringing to the support of the government an element which a word from him at a favorable moment would have alienated. He freely said that he regarded Mr. Douglas as one of his best and most valuable friends.

To those who are curious in marking strange coincidences, it will be interesting to remember that just four years to an hour after Mr. Douglas parted with Mr. Lincoln, at the close of the interview that has been described, Mr. Lincoln was slain by an assassin. Both died with a common purpose uppermost in their minds, one in the threatening morning of the rebellion, and the other when its sun had just set in blood; and both sleep in the dust of that magnificent state almost every rod of which, within a quarter of a century, had echoed to their contending voices as they expounded their principles to the people.

CHAPTER XIX.

THE emergency which the rebellion forced upon the government found that government no less prepared to meet it than it found the loyal people of the country wanting in military knowledge and experience. The people were so eager to furnish men and supplies that they at once became impatient for results. No one among them seemed to doubt that the rebellion might be crushed in a few months, at most. They did not comprehend the almost infinite detail of a war. Patience was a virtue which it took four years to teach them; and when every man connected with the government was making all the efforts possible to forward the preparations for the struggle, the popular press—meaning well, but much misapprehending the difficulties of the situation—were already finding fault with the tardiness of operations. They had apparently forgotten how long it took to bring the Mexican war to a successful termination;—indeed, they stood in a very different relation to this war from that which they had held toward the Mexican war. That was a war of the government against another power; this was a war of their own, against domestic traitors who sought to overthrow the government. Every loyal man had a direct interest in the war; and he judged every movement and every delay as if it were his own private enterprise. There were inconveniences in this; but, in this universal personal interest, lay the secret of those four years of popular devotion to the war which so astonished the observers of other lands, and made ultimate victory, under Providence, a certainty from the first.

This popular impatience was, during the first two or three years of the war, one of the serious difficulties with which the administration had to deal. It had its advantages in holding to vigilance and industry all who were in responsible positions, but it had disadvantages in sometimes compelling precipitancy of action, and in breeding in the administration the idea that the people were to be managed like children whose food should be carefully prepared in the departments whenever it was administered, or carefully withheld when their stomachs were not able to receive it. This idea of the people was not born in the White House. Mr. Lincoln had a profound respect for the people, and never had any sympathy with efforts which aimed to make them instruments in the hands of the government, or which ignored the fact that they were the source of all his power.

During the latter part of April, certain important military operations were effected. Washington, the safety of which was the first consideration, was relieved from immediate danger; Fortress Monroe, commanding the water gateway of Virginia, was reinforced and held; the government works at Harper's Ferry were blown up and burned by Lieutenant Jones, in command of a company of regulars, moved by the intelligence of an advance of a large confederate force; Cairo, Illinois, an important strategic point at the confluence of the Ohio and the Mississippi rivers, had been occupied by government forces, and the blockade was extended so as to embrace the states of Virginia and North Carolina. Then began organization. On the twenty-seventh of April, Adjutant General Thomas made the following announcement of new military departments: First, The military department of Washington, including the District of Columbia, according to its original boundary, Fort Washington and the adjacent country, and the state of Maryland as far as Bladensburgh, to be under the charge of Colonel Mansfield, with head-quarters at Washington. Second, The department of Annapolis, head-quarters at that city, and including the country for twenty miles on either side of the railroad between Annapolis and

Washington, under command of General B. F. Butler, of the Massachusetts volunteers. Third, The department of Pennsylvania, including that state, Delaware and all of Maryland not included in the other departments already mentioned, and with Major General Patterson in command. The extension of the department of Washington to the old limits of the district was for the purpose of including territory absolutely necessary for the defense of the capital.

On the following tenth of May, another department was added to this list, including the states of Ohio, Indiana and Illinois, under the charge of General George B. McClellan. The object of this department was to maintain a defensive line on the Ohio River from Wheeling to Cairo.

On the twenty-ninth of April, Jefferson Davis convened his Congress at Montgomery, and sent them a message which was intended to be a justification of himself, and his cause, before the country and the world. It was a document of rare ability, in its plausible presentation of the favorite southern doctrine of state rights, and its rehearsal of the pretended wrongs which the South had suffered at the hands of the North. It must have made a profound impression upon the great multitude of minds ready to receive it among his own people, and upon statesmen abroad who, from the first opening of the American difficulties, manifested 'a strange ignorance of the genius and structure of American institutions.

It is interesting to notice here the attempt on the part, both of Mr. Lincoln and Mr. Davis, to argue the rightfulness of their respective positions, in a great number of their state papers. Mr. Lincoln's old intellectual struggle with Mr. Douglas had ceased, and Jefferson Davis was now his antagonist— a man of higher culture and deeper character.

Mr. Davis, in his message, assumed the role of the wronged party. Notwithstanding the fact that he had seized all the property of the United States upon which he could lay his hands, and had, by bombardment, compelled the surrender of Fort Sumter, he tried to shift the burden of opening the war upon Mr. Lincoln, whose call for troops, weeks after a confederate army was on its feet and actively gathering numbers, was the pretended cause of the convening of the rebel Congress. In this very message, indeed, he announces that there were already nineteen thousand men in different forts, and that sixteen thousand were on their way to Virginia.

In the doctrine of state rights was the only justification of the rebellion; and it was necessary that Mr. Davis should labor to establish it. With him, a state was greater than the United States. The state was sovereign, and the Union was essentially subject. Whenever, therefore, any state should have a plausible pretext for dissolving its union with other states, it had a right to do so. Mr. Davis did not stop to consider that he could not establish a government on any such basis as this, and that the doctrine of state rights would, in the end, be just as fatal to his confederacy as he was endeavoring to make it to the United States. On the other hand, Mr. Lincoln held the Union sovereign and the state subject. A state had no right to coerce a nation into dissolution, any more than a county had a right to force a state into dissolution. He maintained that the United States were a nation, one and indivisible, and that any attempt to dissolve it on the part of a state, or a combination of states, was treason. Here was where the Union and the new confederacy separated. The confederacy was a logical result of the doctrine of state rights, and its destruction, by all the power of the federal government, was the logical necessity of its contravention. Mr. Lincoln believed that a nation had a fundamental right to live, and that the United States were a nation. Mr. Davis believed that the United States were not a nation—or, if one—that it held its only right to live at the will of any state that might choose to exercise it.

On the third of May, Mr. Lincoln found it necessary to call for forty-two thousand additional volunteers, to serve for three years, unless sooner discharged, and for an aggregate of twenty-two thousand seven hundred and fourteen men for different classes of service in the regular army. An additional call for eighteen thousand men to serve in the navy was also made in the same proclamation. The country gave quick response to this call, and the demand for army volunteers was soon answered to excess.

The area of operations was rapidly spreading. Secessionists in and around St. Louis, Missouri, were plotting for the seizure of the arsenal in that city, but Captain (afterward General) Lyon promptly thwarted the scheme, and secured the arms for the government forces. A secession camp, forming in the same city, was captured, and many within it taken prisoners. The Governor of Missouri was disloyal, and did what he could to throw that state into the hands of the rebels; and General Harney, for a short time in command of the military department of the West, so far aided his schemes as to agree with Sterling Price that the whole duty of maintaining order in the state should be intrusted to the state authorities. Harney was removed, and General Lyon put in his place, with a force for which he found abundant employment, and at the head of which he afterwards fell—one of the first and costliest sacrifices of the war.

During all the first part of May, a secession flag floated over a building in Alexandria, in sight of the capitol at Washington; the rebel forces were gathering at Manassas Junction, and rebel troops held Harper's Ferry. On the twenty-second of May, General Butler took command of the new department of the South, with head-quarters at Fortress Monroe. Five days afterward, he issued his famous order declaring slaves "contraband of war." The phrase imbodied a new idea, which was the germ of a new policy, as well as the basis of a new name for the freed negro. General Butler had under command here about twelve thousand men. Confederate troops were already gathering and fortifying in the vicinity, and on the tenth of June occurred the first considerable battle of the war at Big Bethel. It was a badly managed affair on the part of the Union forces; and, in the excited and expectant state of the public mind, produced a degree of discouragement in the country quite disproportioned to the importance of its results. Here fell Major Winthrop, a young

man of great bravery and rare literary ability. The troops
fought well, but were badly handled. Enough was learned,
however, of the bravery of the Yankee, to give prophecy of
fine results when the art of war should be better learned.

These comparatively small and widely separated movements
were but ripples shot out into the coves and reaches of treason
from the tidal sweep of the loyal armies, crowding southward
to dash against the grand front of the rebellion. The government had no lack of men; but it suffered sadly for the want
of arms to put into their hands. But they were armed in one
way and another—some of them very poorly. The impatient
people could not know how poorly, because it would expose
the weakness of the government to the enemy; so they clamored for a movement, and it was made. On the twenty-fourth
of May, General Mansfield began his passage into Virginia.
The gallant and lamented Colonel Ellsworth was sent with
his regiment of Zouaves to Alexandria; and troops to the
number of thirteen thousand were moved across the river,
and set to work in the erection of forts for the defense of
Washington. Colonel Ellsworth, on landing at Alexandria,
without resistance, went personally to the Marshall House,
kept by James Jackson, and mounting to the top, pulled down
the secession flag with which Jackson had for weeks been insulting the authorities at Washington. On descending, the
owner shot him dead, and was in turn immediately shot dead
by a private named Brownell, who accompanied his Colonel.

It is interesting to remember the profound impression which
the death of this young and enthusiastic officer produced upon
the country. He was among the first the nation gave to the
war, and his name, with those of Greble and Winthrop, who
fell at Big Bethel, and Lyon who afterward fell in Missouri,
were embalmed in the fresh sensibilities of the people, and remain there, fixed and fragrant, while thousands of those since
fallen have found only weary and sickened hearts to rest in,
or memories too sadly crowded with precious names to give
them room. Ellsworth's death affected Mr. Lincoln with peculiar sorrow. He had known the young man well. At one

time, Ellsworth was a student in Lincoln & Herndon's office; and he accompanied Mr. Lincoln on his journey to Washington. The body of the young martyr was borne sadly back to Washington, and was received into the White House itself, where the funeral took place, Mr. Lincoln himself assuming the position of chief mourner.

After the accumulation of a large army on the Virginia side of the Potomac, it was determined to push forward the forces then under the command of Major General McDowell, for a battle with the rebel army which had been gathered at Manassas. For this battle each side had been preparing with great industry. The enemy had withdrawn his forces from the occupation of Harper's Ferry, and that important point had passed into federal control. From every quarter he gathered in his troops, or held them within easy call, and waited for the attack. It began on the nineteenth, and ended on the twenty-first of July, in a most terrible rout of the Union forces. The whole army upon which the President and the people had rested such strong hope and expectation was broken in pieces, and came flying back toward Washington, panic-stricken, worn out, disorganized and utterly demoralized. They had fought bravely and well; but they were not above influences that have affected armies since time began, and they yielded to fears which made them uncontrollable.

The loss of this battle, fought under the pressure of popular impatience, cost the country a fearful amount of sacrifice. It greatly encouraged the rebels, their sympathizers abroad sent up a shout of triumph, and the loyal masses were put to such a test of their patriotism and determined bravery as they had never been subjected to. The work had all to be done again, under the most discouraging circumstances; but when the case was reviewed, reason was found for gratitude that it had been no worse. Washington, at the close of the battle at Bull Run, was at the mercy of the rebels. It was well that they did not know this, or that, if they knew it, they were not in a condition to push on, and occupy what must have fallen into their hands.

Among all the millions to whom this event brought sorrow, there was not one who suffered so keenly as the tender-hearted and patient man who, walking back and forth between the White House and the War Department, felt the great burden of it all upon his own shoulders. He had need of the full exercise of his abounding faith in Providence to sustain him in that dark and perilous hour. He could not but feel that peace had been put far away by the result of the battle; but he learned afterwards that Providence had wise and beneficent designs in that result. Peace conquered then, would have been peace with the cause of the war retained. Peace then would have left four million slaves in bondage. Peace then would have left the "house divided against itself" still, with the possibility of an indefinite extension of slavery. It was not so to be. A thousand plagues were yet to come before the public mind would be ready to let the bondman go.

Soon after the original movement into Virginia, the Post-master-general suspended all postal service in the seceded states; and at this time active movements commenced in General McClellan's department. Under the auspices of Governor Magoffin of Kentucky—one of the governors who had sent back an insulting response to the President's original call for troops—his Inspector-general Buckner organized a force in Kentucky, which was watched with much anxiety by the loyal people on the other side of the Ohio, because it was believed to be intended for the rebel service. Buckner visited General McClellan at Cincinnati on the eighth of June, and on the twenty-second of that month he reported to Governor Magoffin the terms of a convention into which he had entered with the federal general. Briefly he reported that General McClellan stipulated that Kentucky should be regarded by the United States as neutral territory, even though southern troops should occupy it. In such a case, the United States should call upon Kentucky to remove such troops, and if she should fail to do so within a reasonable time, then the General claimed the same right of occupation accorded to the southern troops, and promised to withdraw so soon as those troops should be expelled. Whether this was a true statement of the agreement or not, General McClellan did nothing inconsistent with it, although he afterwards denied Buckner's statement of the results of the consultation. The occupation and defense of important points upon the bank of the river opposite Cincinnati were abandoned, and, in a letter to Mr. Crittenden, he disclaimed all responsibility for the intrusion of a body of General Prentiss' men, who had landed on the Kentucky shore and brought away a secession flag. The General, it was evident, did not comprehend the character of the rebellion, or he failed to recognize the fact that in such a struggle there could be no such thing as the neutrality which Kentucky was professedly desirous to maintain.

The tenderness of the government, as well as of the generals it had appointed, toward slavery, is worthy of note at this juncture. Mr. Lincoln had always taken great pains to show that he respected the legal rights of slavery under the Constitution. The republicans, in national convention and in Congress, had done the same. The three democratic generals it had placed in command—Butler, Patterson and McClellan—went a step further, and promised in advance that they would not only not interfere with slavery, but would assist the rebels in putting down a slave insurrection. General Butler, of the three, experienced a healthy reaction from this devotion to slavery at an early day.

Western Virginia was loyal, and, on the seventeenth of June, in convention at Wheeling, repudiated the ordinance of secession passed by the state convention, and promptly inaugurated a new state government, with Francis H. Pierpoint for Governor. This was the first step toward "reconstruction," and it was taken under the direct sanction of Mr. Lincoln. The doctrine of secession thus early returned to plague the inventors. Rebel forces and rebel sympathizers were of course in Western Virginia; and a campaign was inaugurated there, early in June, for the expulsion of these forces from the territory. General Rosecrans and General Thomas A. Morris had this campaign in hand, and, on the twenty-third of June,

General McClellan arrived. On the tenth of July, a skirmish was had with the rebels at Laurel Hill, and two days later the battle of Rich Mountain was fought, which resulted in the defeat and surrender of the rebel Colonel Pegram, with a thousand men. This did not compass the successes of the day. General Garnett who was bringing supports to General Pegram was pursued, his forces routed, and himself killed. This temporarily cleaned out the enemy from Western Virginia. General McClellan's dispatch to the war department announcing this very grateful victory was direct, spirited and well written, and immediately attracted the attention of the country. These successes in Western Virginia, together with the Napoleonic manner of their announcement, paved the way to that wonderful popular confidence which was afterward accorded to the commanding general, although he had very little to do in planning the campaign in which they were won, or the battles by which they were secured.

Congress, according to the proclamation of the President, had assembled on the fourth of July, and was of course in session when the successes in Western Virginia were achieved, as well as when the rout of the army at Bull Run occurred. Indeed, the presence of the members at Washington added to the pressure which precipitated the movement that resulted so disastrously. Some of the members went out to see the fight. One of these was taken prisoner, and others took such a lesson in retreating as to cure them of all curiosity concerning battles and battle-fields forever.

On the meeting of Congress, the President communicated a message which was received with profound interest, both by Congress and the whole country. The opening portions of the document were strictly historical of the events of the rebellion up to the date of its utterance; and as the most of these events have already found record in these pages, their reproduction is not necessary.

By opening fire upon Sumter, when it had not "a gun in sight, or in expectancy, to return their fire, save only the few in the fort sent to that harbor years before for their own protection," he declared that the rebels had forced upon the country the distinct issue—*immediate dissolution or blood.* "And this issue," the message proceeds, "embraces more than the fate of these United States. It presents to the whole family of man the question whether a constitutional republic or democracy—a government of the people by the same people—can or cannot maintain its territorial integrity, against its own domestic foes. It presents the question whether discontented individuals, too few in numbers to control administration according to organic law in any case, can always, upon the pretences made in this case, or on any other pretences, or arbitrarily, without any pretence, break up their government, and thus practically put an end to free government upon the earth. It forces us to ask, 'Is there in all republics, this inherent and fatal weakness?' 'Must a government, of necessity, be too strong for the liberties of its own people, or too weak to maintain its own existence?'"

The attempt of some of the border states to maintain a sort of armed neutrality—as illustrated in the case of Kentucky—the arming of those states to keep the forces on either side from passing over their territory—he declared would be disunion completed, if for a moment entertained. It would be building "an impassable wall along the line of separation, and yet, not quite an impassable one, for, under the guise of neutrality, it would tie the hands of Union men, and freely pass supplies from among them to the insurrectionists, which it could not do as an open enemy. At a stroke it would take all the trouble off the hands of secession, except only what proceeds from the external blockade."

Soon after the first call for militia, liberty was given to the commanding general to suspend the privilege of the writ of *habeas corpus* in certain cases, or "to arrest and detain without resort to the ordinary processes of law such individuals as he might deem dangerous to the public safety." Although this liberty was indulged very sparingly, there were not wanting men unfriendly to the administration who made it the subject of factious complaint. This fact Mr. Lincoln noticed, and this was his defense:

"The whole of the laws which were required to be faithfully executed were being resisted, and failing of execution, in nearly one-third of the states. · Must they be allowed to finally fail of execution, even had it been perfectly clear that by the use of the means necessary to their execution some single law, made in such extreme tenderness of the citizen's liberty, that, practically, it relieves more of the guilty than the innocent, should, to a very limited extent, be violated? To state the question more directly: are all the laws but one to go unexecuted, and the government itself go to pieces, lest that one be violated? Even in such a case, would not the official oath be broken, if the government should be overthrown when it was believed that disregarding the single law would tend to preserve it? But it was not believed that this question was presented. It was not believed that any law was violated. The provision of the Constitution that 'the privilege of the writ of *habeas corpus* shall not be suspended, unless, when in cases of rebellion or invasion, the public safety may require it,' is equivalent to a provision—is a provision—that such privilege may be suspended when, in case of rebellion or invasion, the public safety does require it. It was decided that we have a case of rebellion, and that the public safety does require the qualified suspension of the privilege of the writ, which was authorized to be made. Now it is insisted that Congress, and not the Executive, is invested with this power. But the Constitution itself is silent as to which or who is to exercise this power; and as the provision was plainly made for a dangerous emergency, it cannot be believed the framers of the instrument intended that, in every case, the danger should run its course until Congress could be called together, the very assembling of which might be prevented, as was intended in this case by the rebellion."

After recommending that Congress make the contest a short and decisive one, by placing at the control of the government four hundred thousand men and four hundred million dollars, and stating that a right result at that time would be worth more to the world than ten times the men and ten times the money, Mr. Lincoln took up the doctrine of state rights, state sovereignty, the right of secession, &c., and argued against it at length, doubtless as a reply to the message of Mr. Davis, and to place before the world, whose governments and peoples were sitting in judgment on the case, the grounds of the national struggle with the rebellion. The passage is too important to be abbreviated:

"It might seem, at first thought, to be of little difference whether the present movement at the South be called "secession," or "rebellion." The movers, however, will understand the difference. At the beginning, they knew they could never raise their treason to any respectable magnitude by any name which implies violation of law. They knew their people possessed as much of moral sense, as much of devotion to law and order, and as much pride in, and reverence for the history and government of their common country, as any other civilized and patriotic people. They knew they could make no advancement directly in the teeth of these strong and noble sentiments. Accordingly, they commenced by an insidious debauching of the public mind. They invented an ingenious sophism, which, if conceded, was followed by perfectly logical steps, through all the incidents, to the complete destruction of the Union. The sophism itself is, that any state of the Union may, consistently with the national Constitution, and therefore lawfully and peacefully, withdraw from the Union without the consent of the Union, or of any other state. The little disguise that the supposed right is to be exercised only for just cause, themselves to be the sole judges of its justice, is too thin to merit any notice.

"With rebellion thus sugar-coated they have been drugging the public mind of their section for more than thirty years, and until at length they have brought many good men to a willingness to take up arms against the government the day after some assemblage of men have enacted the farcical pretence of taking their state out of the Union, who could have been brought to no such thing the day before.

"This sophism derives much, perhaps the whole, of its currency from the assumption that there is some omnipotent and sacred supremacy pertaining to a state—to each state of our Federal Union. Our states have neither more nor less power than that reserved to them in the Union by the Constitution—no one of them ever having been a state out of the Union. The original ones passed into the Union even before they cast off their British colonial dependence; and the new ones each came into the Union directly from a condition of dependence, excepting Texas. And even Texas, in its temporary independence, was never designated a state. The new ones only took the designation of states on coming into the Union, while that name was first adopted by the old ones in and by the Declaration of Independence. Therein the "United Colonies" were declared to be "free and independent states;" but, even then, the object plainly was not to declare their independence of one another, or of the Union, but directly the contrary, as their mutual pledge and their mutual action before, at the time, and afterwards, abundantly show. The express plighting of faith by each and all of the original thirteen in the Articles of Confederation, two years later, that the Union shall be perpetual, is most conclusive. Having never been states, either in substance or in name, outside of the Union, whence this magical omnipotence of "state rights," asserting a claim of power to lawfully destroy the Union itself? Much is said about the "sovereignty" of the states; but the word even is not in the national Constitution; nor, as is believed, in any of the state constitutions. What is "sovereignty" in the political sense of the term? Would it be far wrong to define it "a political community without a political superior?" Tested by this, no one of our states except Texas, ever was a sovereignty. And even Texas gave up the character on coming into the Union; by which act she acknowledged the Constitution of the United States and the laws and treaties of the United States made in pursuance of the Constitution, to be for her the supreme law of the land. The states have their *status* in the Union, and they have no other legal *status*. If they break from this, they can only do so against law and by revolution. The Union, and not themselves, separately, procured their independence and their liberty. By conquest or purchase the Union gave each of them whatever of independence or liberty it has. The Union is older than any of the states, and, in fact, it created them as states. Originally some dependent colonies made the Union, and, in turn, the Union threw off their old dependence for them, and made them states, such as they are. Not one of them ever had a state constitution independent of the Union. Of course, it is not forgotten that all the new states framed their constitutions before they entered the Union; nevertheless dependent upon, and preparatory to, coming into the Union.

"Unquestionably the states have the powers and rights reserved to them in and by the national Constitution: but among these, surely, are not included all conceivable powers, however mischievous or destructive; but, at most, such only as were known in the world, at the time, as governmental powers; and, certainly, a power to destroy the Government itself had never been known as a governmental—as a merely administrative power. This relative matter of national power and state rights, as a principle, is no other than the principle of generality and locality. Whatever concerns the whole should be confided to the whole—to the general government; while whatever concerns only the state should be left exclusively to the state. This is all there is of original principle about it. Whether the national Constitution in defining boundaries between the two has applied the principle with exact accuracy, is not to be questioned. We are all bound by that defining, without question.

"What is now combated, is the position that secession is consistent with the Constitution—is lawful and peaceful. It is not contended that there is any express law for it; and nothing should ever be implied as law which leads to unjust or absurd consequences. The nation purchased with money the countries out of which several of these states were formed; is it just that they shall go off without leave and without refunding? The nation paid very large sums (in the aggregate, I believe, nearly a hundred millions) to relieve Florida of the aboriginal tribes; is it just that she shall now be off without consent, or without making any return? The nation is now in debt for money applied to the benefit of these so-called seceding states in common with the rest; is it just either that creditors shall go unpaid, or the remaining states pay the whole? A part of the present national debt was contracted to pay the old debts of Texas; is it just that she shall leave and pay no part of this herself?

"Again, if one state may secede, so may another; and when all shall have seceded, none is left to pay the debts. Is this quite just to creditors? Did we notify them of this sage view of ours when we borrowed their money? If we now recognize this doctrine by allowing the seceders to go in peace, it is difficult to see what we can do if others choose to go, or to extort terms upon which they will promise to remain.

"The seceders insist that our Constitution admits of secession. They have assumed to make a national constitution of their own, in which, of necessity, they have either discarded or retained the right of secession, as they insist it exists in ours. If they have discarded it, they thereby admit that on principle it ought not to exist in ours; if they have retained it, by their own construction of ours they show that, to be consistent, they must secede from one another whenever they shall find it the easiest way of settling their debts, or effecting any other selfish or unjust object. The principle itself is one of disintegration, and upon which no government can possibly endure.

"If all the states save one should assert the power to drive that one out of the Union, it is presumed the whole class of seceder politicians would at once deny the power, and denounce the act as the greatest outrage upon state rights. But suppose that precisely the same act, instead of being called 'driving the one out,' should be called 'the seceding of the others from that one,' it would be exactly what the seceders claim to do, unless, indeed, they make the point that the one, because it is a minority, may rightfully do what the others, because they are a majority, may not rightfully do. These politicians are subtle, and profound on the rights of minorities. They are not partial to that power which made the Constitution, and speaks from the preamble, calling itself 'We, the people.'"

The popular government of the United States, Mr. Lincoln said, had been called an experiment. Two points of the ex-

periment had already been settled; the government had been
established, and it had been administered. One point remained
to be established: its successful maintenance against a formidable internal attempt to overthrow it. It remained to be demonstrated to the world that those who could fairly carry an
election could also suppress a rebellion—"that ballots are the
rightful and peaceful successors to bullets, and that when ballots have fairly and constitutionally decided, there can be no
successful appeal back to bullets—that there can be no successful appeal, except to ballots themselves, at succeeding
elections." Another justification of the war in which he was
engaged he found in that article of the Constitution which
provides that "the United States shall guarantee to every
state in this Union a republican form of government." If a
state might lawfully go out of the Union, it might also, having
gone out, discard the republican form of government, "so that
to prevent its going out is an indispensable means to the end
of maintaining the guarantee mentioned; and when an end is
lawful and obligatory, the indispensable means to it are also
lawful and obligatory."

Congress was ready to do all that the President desired,
and even more. Instead of four hundred million dollars, they
placed at his disposal five hundred millions, and instead of
confining his levy of troops to four hundred thousand, they
gave him liberty to call out half a million. They also legal-
ized all the steps he had thus far taken for the suppression
of the rebellion, and labored in all ways to strengthen his
hands and encourage his heart. These measures were passed
in the presence, and against the protest, of secessionists, who
still held their places in both houses of Congress. Burnett
of Kentucky and Reid and Norton of Missouri, in the House,
afterwards proved their treason by engaging directly in the
rebellion. Breckinridge and Powell of Kentucky and Polk
and Johnson of Missouri, in the Senate, were known at the
time to be anything but loyal. And they had sympathizers
who, under any other government, would have been arrested
and held, if not treated with still greater severity. Vallan-

digham of Ohio was afterwards sent into the rebel lines for treason, and it is undoubtedly true that Kennedy of Maryland, Bayard of Delaware, Bright of Indiana, and Ben Wood of New York had personal reason for feeling that he had been very harshly used. Yet it was best that these men should be where they were, to bicker and bite, and illustrate the spirit of that incorporate infamy—a slaveholders' rebellion. Such toleration illustrated alike the strength and moderation of the government. Some of these men were permitted to rise in the places they had justly forfeited, and, with perjured lips, to talk treason—to complain of arbitrary arrests when they were suffered to go and come, and scheme and brawl with perfect liberty, in the streets of the national capital.

There was plenty of treasonable talk in Congress, but no treasonable action. The party friends of the government were in a majority, and they were aided by numbers of loyal democrats. The schemes of finance recommended by Mr. Chase, the Secretary of the Treasury, were adopted essentially as recommended, a moderate confiscation act was passed, and a resolution adopted by the House—introduced by Mr. Crittenden of Kentucky—that the war had been forced upon the country by the disunionists of the southern states, then in revolt against the constitutional government and in arms around the capital: that Congress, banishing all feeling of passion or resentment, would recollect only its duty to the whole country: that the war was not waged on the part of the government in the spirit of oppression, nor for any purpose of conquest or subjugation, nor purpose of overthrowing or interfering with the rights or established institutions of the states; but to defend and maintain the supremacy of the Constitution, and to preserve the Union, with all the dignities, equality and rights of the several states unimpaired: and that as soon as those objects were accomplished, the war ought to cease. During the session, Mr. Trumbull of Illinois introduced a bill in the Senate to emancipate all the slaves in the rebel states. This was a prophecy and a threat of what would come as the reward of rebel contumacy.

The session closed on the sixth day of August, having lasted but little more than a month. The President found himself abundantly supported, and the means in his hands for carrying on the great contest.

The message of Mr. Lincoln to this extra session of Congress, taken with his inaugural, did much to overcome the unpleasant impressions produced by the speeches he made on his way to Washington. There is no question that those speeches seriously damaged him, and shook the confidence of the country in his ability. The inaugural and the message had the old ring in them, and betrayed something of those qualities which had originally attracted the country to him.

It is true, however, that he did not spend much time in writing his messages. His later efforts in this line did not bear always so many marks of painstaking as the first. He had a great aversion to what he called "machine writing," and always used the fewest words possible to express his meaning. Mr. Defrees, the public printer, an intimate personal friend of Mr. Lincoln, testifies that he made the fewest corrections in his proof of any man he ever knew. He knew nothing of the rules of punctuation, yet the manuscripts of very few of our public men are as well punctuated as his uniformly were, though his use of commas was excessive.

Mr. Defrees, being on easy terms with Mr. Lincoln, took it upon him to suggest with relation to his first message that he was not preparing a campaign document, or delivering a stump speech in Illinois, but constructing an important state paper, that would go down historically to all coming time; and that, therefore, he did not consider the phrase, "sugar-coated," which he had introduced, as entirely a becoming and dignified one. "Well, Defrees," said Mr. Lincoln, good naturedly, "if you think the time will ever come when the people will not understand what "sugar-coated" means, I 'll alter it; otherwise, I think I 'll let it go." To make people understand exactly what he meant, was his grand aim. Beyond that, he had not the slightest ambition to go.

To close this chapter, it only remains to record the relief

of Major General McDowell, a worthy but unfortunate officer, and the appointment of General McClellan to the command of the army of the Potomac.   The country had been attracted to McClellan by his dispatches from Western Virginia. General Scott favored him, and to him was accordingly assigned the work of re-organizing the shattered army.   The public hope was ready to cling somewhere, and the public heart gave itself to McClellan with an enthusiastic devotion rarely accorded to any man.   His pictures were in all the windows of the shops, and on all the center tables of all the drawing-rooms in the land.   If he had done but little before to merit this confidence—if he did but little afterwards to justify it—he, at least, served at that time to give faith to the people, and furnish a rallying point for their patriotic service. For three months, under his faithful and assiduous supervision, the organization of troops went on, until he had at his command a magnificent army which needed only to be properly led to be victorious.

CHAPTER XX.

THE victory of the rebels at Bull Run was singularly barren of material results to them. It did not encourage the disloyal masses of the country more than it filled with new determination the loyal people who opposed them. They were as badly punished as the troops they had defeated, and could take no advantage of their victory; and they failed to bring nearer the day of foreign recognition for which they were laboring and longing.

This matter of foreign recognition was a very important one to Mr. Davis and his confederates. That he expected it, and had reason to expect it, there is no question. Hostilities had hardly opened when the British and French governments, acting in concert, recognized the government established at Montgomery as a belligerent power. If this was not a pledge of friendliness, and a promise of recognition, nothing could have been, for the proceeding was unprecedented. The United States was a power in friendly intercourse with these two great powers of Europe, through complete diplomatic relations. Without a word of warning, without a victory on the part of the insurgents, without a confederate fleet afloat, with only a half of the slave states in insurrection, these two governments, with the most indecent haste, gave their moral support to the enemies of the United States by recognizing a portion of its people engaged in an insurrection which the government had not yet undertaken to suppress—as a belligerent power, with just the same rights on land and sea as if they were an established government.

But for the decided position assumed by Mr. Lincoln, through his accomplished Secretary, Mr. Seward, the rebel government would certainly have had an early and full recognition. England and France were, without doubt, very friendly to the United States; but they would have been friendlier to two governments than to one. In his instructions to Mr. Charles Francis Adams, on his departure to represent the government at the court of St. James, Mr. Seward said:

"If, as the President does not at all apprehend, you shall unhappily find Her Majesty's government tolerating the application of the so-called seceding states, or wavering about it, you will not leave them to suppose, for a moment, that they can grant that application, and remain the friends of the United States. You may even assure them promptly, in that case, that, if they determine to recognize, they may, at the same time, prepare to enter into an alliance with the enemies of this republic. You alone will represent your country at London, and you will represent the whole of it there. When you are asked to divide that duty with others, diplomatic relations between the government of Great Britain and this government will be suspended, and will remain so until it shall be seen which of the two is most strongly intrenched in the confidence of their respective nations and of mankind."

Against the recognition of the rebels as a belligerent power, Mr. Adams was directed to make a decided and energetic protest; and when, on the fifteenth of June, the representatives of England and France at Washington applied to Mr. Seward for the privilege of reading to him certain instructions they had received from their governments, he declined to hear them officially until he had had the privilege of reading them privately. This privilege was accorded to him; and then he declined to receive any official notice of the documents. Four days afterwards, he wrote a letter to Mr. Adams, informing him of the nature of the instructions, which were prefaced by a statement of the decision of the British government that this country was divided into two belligerent parties, of which the government represented one; and that the government of Great Britain proposed to assume the attitude of a neutral between them.

Touching this decision, Mr. Seward said that the government of the United States could not debate it with the government of Her Majesty—much less consent to receive the announcement of a decision thus derogating from the sovereignty of the United States—a decision at which it had arrived without conferring with us upon the question. "The United States" said Mr. Seward, "are still solely and exclusively sovereign, within the territories they have lawfully acquired and long possessed, as they have always been. They are living under the obligations of the law of nations and of treaties with Great Britain, just the same now as heretofore; they are, of course, the friend of Great Britain; and they insist that Great Britain shall remain their friend now, just as she has hitherto been. Great Britain, by virtue of these relations, is a stranger to parties and sections in this country, whether they are loyal to the United States or not; and Great Britain can neither rightfully qualify the sovereignty of the United States, nor concede nor recognize any rights or interests or power, of any party, state or section, in contravention to the unbroken sovereignty of the federal Union. What is now seen in this country is the occurrence, by no means peculiar, but frequent in all countries, more frequent in Great Britain than here, of an armed insurrection, engaged in attempting to overthrow the regularly constituted and established government. But these incidents by no means constitute a state of war, impairing the sovereignty of the government, creating belligerent sections, and entitling foreign states to intervene or to act as neutrals between them, or in any other way to cast off their lawful obligations to the nation thus, for the moment, disturbed. Any other principle than this would be to resolve government everywhere into a thing of accident and caprice, and ultimately all human society into a state of perpetual war."

Instructions corresponding with these were sent to our representatives at the French and other European courts. These governments were plainly given to understand that our government considered the difficulty with the slaveholding states to be exclusively its own—that it was purely a domestic rebellion, which it proposed to extinguish by its own power, and one in which foreign governments had no right to intermeddle. Our ministers were told by Mr. Seward that they could not be too decided or explicit in making known to the governments at which they represented us, that there was not then, and would not be, any idea existing in the government of suffering a dissolution of the Union to take place, in any way whatever.

Throughout all the war that followed, England and France maintained their most unjustifiable and cruel recognition of the belligerent rights of the rebels—unjustifiable, because it was an unfriendly act toward a friendly power, on behalf of a rebellion whose forces were still unorganized, and whose suppression the government had hardly entered upon; and cruel, because it encouraged the rebels to persevere in a war which could only end in defeat to them, and which was so prolonged that it made a desolation of their whole country. There is probably nothing more morally certain than that the expectation of full recognition by England and France, on the part of Mr. Davis and his people, helped to continue the struggle of the rebellion with the government, until tens of thousands of loyal and disloyal lives were needlessly sacrificed. The act was unfriendly to this government; it was a cruelty to the hapless insurgents it deceived, for the promise it contained was never redeemed, and would have accomplished nothing if it had been; and it was a great blunder, from which those blundering governments have retreated, amid the jeers of the nations of the world, and the shuffling apologies of their own people. This sympathy with the rebellion on the part of these foreign governments is something not to be forgotten, because we are to measure by it the magnanimity of Mr. Lincoln in the treatment of international questions arising afterwards. This sympathy is to-day denied; it was then ·blatant and bellicose. An American could not pass through England without insult; he could not speak for the national cause in England without a mob. England, or all of England that had a voice, rejoiced in rebel successes and federal defeats, and garbled and qualified all the news which favored the prospects of national success. Whatever may be the professions of England now, no true American can forget that all the influence she dared to give in favor of the rebellion was given, beginning promptly at the start; and that her position rendered the task of subduing the rebellion doubly severe. Whatever may be the professions of her people now, no true American will forget the insults that were heaped upon his countrymen abroad whenever an allusion was made to the national difficulties, and heaped upon the country by the issues of a press that represented the British people, and persistently misrepresented our own. It was not, of course, to be expected that monarchies would be friendly to the great prosperity of democracies, or that they would give them their open sympathy and co-operation in difficulty; but the latter should be spared receiving the hypocrisies of the former as courtesies; and, after having been compelled to drink of gall for four years, should be permitted to remember that it was gall, and to make the best of it, without being persistently assured that it was honey.

The opening of the war found Colonel John C. Fremont in Europe; and he, with a large number of loyal Americans, hastened home to give their services to their country. Colonel Fremont, defeated as the republican candidate for the presidency four years before the election of Mr. Lincoln, had had military experience, and was recognized as a popular man, who would rally to his command, at the West, large numbers of soldiers, especially among the German population of the region. He received the appointment of Major-General, and on the same day (July 25th,) that General McClellan arrived in Washington to take command of the Army of the Potomac, he arrived at St. Louis, and entered upon the command of the Department of the West, to which he had been assigned.

Before General Fremont arrived at St. Louis, a battle was

fought on Wilson's Creek by General Lyon and General Sigel, with a large force under the command of Ben McCulloch.   It was the second considerable battle of the war, and resulted in the death of General Lyon himself, and the final orderly retreat of the federal forces under Sigel.   General Lyon had inflicted, with his little force of six thousand men, such injury upon McCulloch's twenty-two thousand, that the latter could not pursue; and, on the whole, there was no special discouragement as the result of the defeat.

General Fremont's name had a great charm for the western masses, and especially for the Germans; and volunteers in large numbers sought service under him.   His campaign, upon the organization of which he entered with great energy, contemplated not only the restoration of order in Missouri, but the reclaiming the control of the Mississippi River.   For this latter object, he organized a gun-boat service, which was destined to play a very important part in the operations associated with the western inland waters.

Missouri was in a condition of most unhappy disorder.   It was a border slave state, containing many disunionists of its own, and abounding with secession emissaries from other states, determined to carry it over to the confederacy.   Brother was arrayed against brother.   Neighborhoods were distressed with deadly feuds.   Murders were of every-day occurrence on every hand, and outrages of every kind were rife.   The civil administration of the state was altogether unreliable; and on the thirty-first of August, General Fremont issued a proclamation declaring martial law, defining the lines of the army of occupation, and threatening with death by the bullet all who should be found within those lines with arms in their hands.   Furthermore, the real and personal property of all persons in the state who should take up arms against the United States was declared confiscated to the public use, and their slaves, if they had any, were declared free men.

This proclamation produced a strong effect upon the public mind.   The proclaiming of freedom to the slaves of rebels struck the popular chord, particularly among thoroughly loyal men in the free states. Of course, it maddened all the sympathizers with the rebellion, infuriated the rebels themselves, and perplexed those loyal men who had upon their hands the task of so conducting affairs as to hold to their allegiance the border slave states which had not seceded.

Mr. Lincoln did not approve some features of General Fremont's proclamation. As soon as he read it, he wrote, under date of September second, to the General, that there were two points in it which gave him anxiety. The first was, that, if he should shoot a man according to his proclamation, "the confederates would certainly shoot our best men in their hands in retaliation, and so, man for man, indefinitely." He therefore ordered him to allow no man to be shot under the proclamation without first having his (the President's) approbation or consent. The second cause of anxiety was that the paragraph relating to the confiscation of property and the liberation of slaves of traitorous owners would alarm Unionists at the South, and perhaps ruin the fair prospect of saving Kentucky to the Union. He, therefore, wished General Fremont, as of his own motion, so to modify his proclamation as to make it conformable to the confiscation act just passed by the extra session of Congress, which only freed such slaves as were engaged in the rebel service. Mr. Lincoln did not wish to interfere with General Fremont, or unreasonably to curtail his authority, although he had assumed an unwarrantable responsibility in taking so important a step without consultation or notice. Congress had had that very matter in hand, and had embodied its opinion in an act. To this act he wished to have the General conform his proclamation, and that was all he desired. The wisdom of his criticism of the first point was proved by a document issued by the rebel Jeff Thompson on the same day he wrote it. "Jeff Thompson, Brigadier General of the first military district of Missouri," acting under the state government, did "most solemnly promise" that for every soldier of the state guard, "or soldier of our allies, the armies of the confederate States," who should be put to death under the proclamation, he would "*hang, draw and quarter a minion of Abraham Lincoln.*"

General Fremont received the President's letter respectfully, and replied to it September eighth, stating the difficulties under which he labored, with communication with the government so difficult, and the development of perplexing events so rapid in the department under his command. As to the part of his proclamation concerning the slaves, he wished the President openly to order the change desired, as, if he should do it of his own motion, it would imply that he thought himself wrong, and that he had acted without the reflection which the gravity of the point demanded. This the President did, in a dispatch under date of September eleventh, in the words: "It is therefore ordered that the said clause of said proclamation be so modified, held, and construed, as to conform to, and not to transcend, the provisions on the same subject contained in the act of Congress entitled, 'An act to confiscate property used for insurrectionary purposes,' approved August 6, 1861; and that such act be published at length with this order." Before this order had been received, or on the day following its date, General Fremont, though acquainted with the President's wishes, manumitted two slaves of Thomas L. Snead of St. Louis, in accordance with the terms of his proclamation.

Although Mr. Lincoln desired General Fremont so to modify his proclamation as to make it accordant with the act of Congress approved August sixth, it is hardly to be supposed that he did it solely out of respect to that act. Congressional acts that were passed under certain circumstances, could not be regarded as binding the hands of the executive under all circumstances; and when, in a state of war, circumstances were widely changing with the passage of every day, they would be a poor rule of military action. If he had believed that the time had come for the measure of liberating the slaves of rebels by proclamation, the act of Congress would not have stood in his way. This act was an embodiment of his policy at that time, and he used it for his immediate purpose.

The day after he gave his modifying order, he received a letter from Hon. Joseph Holt of Kentucky, in which that gentleman spoke of the alarm and condemnation with which the Union-loving citizens of that state had read the proclamation, and begged him to modify it by an order such as he had already issued. Judge Holt concluded his letter by saying: "The magnitude of the interest at stake, and my extreme desire that by no misapprehension of your sentiments or purposes shall the power and fervor of the loyalty of Kentucky be at this moment abated or chilled, must be my apology for the frankness with which I have addressed you."

Complications in the personal relations of General Fremont and Colonel F. P. Blair, under whose personal and family influence General Fremont had received his position, occurred at an early day. Colonel Blair doubtless thought that he had not sufficient weight in the General's counsels, and the General, doubtless, exercised his right, in choosing his own counselors. Whether he followed the advice of others, or was guided by his own judgment and impulses, he conducted himself quite as much after the manner of an eastern satrap as a republican commander. The public found it difficult to get at him, he kept around him a large retinue, and dispensed patronage and contracts with a right royal hand. The most there is to be said of the matter, is, that it was his way. Power was in his hands, a great work was before him, great personal popularity attended him, and the sudden elevation was not without its effect upon him. Colonel Blair, who was the gallant commander of the First Missouri Volunteers, stood in a peculiar relation to him, and was not, by virtue of that relation, and by reason of a high and worthily won political and social position, to be lightly put aside. He came down upon his superior with a series of charges which covered a long catalogue of sins:—neglect of duty, unofficerlike conduct, disobedience of orders, conduct unbecoming a gentleman, extravagance and the waste of the public moneys, and despotic and tyrannical conduct. Among the specifications were Fremont's alleged failure to repair at once to St. Louis to enter upon his

duties; his neglecting to reinforce Lyon and Mulligan; his
suffering Brigadier-General Hurlburt, "a common drunkard,"
to continue in command; his refusal to see people who sought
his presence on matters of urgent business; his violation of
the presidential order in the matter of his proclamation and
the manumissions under it; his persistency in keeping disrepu-
table persons in his employ; and his unjust suppression of the
St. Louis Evening News. General Fremont had no better
opinion of Colonel Blair than Blair had of him, and placed
him under arrest for alluding disrespectfully to superior officers.
ᴠ It was a very unhappy quarrel, and it is quite likely that
there was blame upon both sides, though it occurred between
men equally devoted to the sacred cause of saving the country
to freedom and justice. It is not necessary to believe, with
the enemies of General Fremont, that he found the country
going to pieces, and intended to place himself at the head of
a huge north-western fraction; nor, with the enemies of Colonel Blair, that he was offended with his General because he
could not have as good a chance at stealing from the government as was believed to be accorded to some of the General's
California friends. Both were loyal men, both were anti-
slavery men—Colonel Blair being quite the equal of General
Fremont in this respect—and both wished to serve their country. Mr. Lincoln always gave to each the credit due to his
motives, and so far refused to mingle in the general quarrel
that grew out of the difficulty, that he kept the good-will of
both sides, and compelled them to settle their own differences.

On the sixth of September, General Grant, under General
Fremont's command, occupied Paducah, Kentucky, at the
mouth of the Tennessee River. Price and Jackson were
raising a formidable army for service in Missouri, and, on the
twelfth of September, compelled the surrender of Colonel
Mulligan and his forces at Lexington. General Fremont at
length took the field in person. On the eighth of October
he left Jefferson City for Sedalia. As he advanced with his
forces, Price retreated, until it was widely reported that he
would give battle to the national forces at Springfield. Just

as Fremont was making ready to engage the enemy, he was overtaken by an order relieving him of his command. He was succeeded by General Hunter; but Hunter's command was brief, and was transferred at an early day to General Halleck.

General Fremont was relieved of his command by the President not because of his proclamation, not because he hated slavery, and not because he believed him corrupt or vindictive or disloyal. He relieved him simply because he believed that the interests of the country, all things considered, would be subserved by relieving him and putting another man in his place. The matter was the cause of great excitement in Missouri, and of much complaint among the radical anti-slavery men of the country: but the imputations sought to be cast upon the President were not fastened to him; and did not, four years later, when Fremont himself became a candidate for the presidency, prevent the warmest anti-slavery men from giving Mr. Lincoln their support.

The federal army under General Hunter retreated without a battle; and thus the campaign, inaugurated with great show and immense expense, was a flat failure.

In the meantime, General Rosecrans finished up the work in Western Virginia that General McClellan had prematurely declared, accomplished, and the army of the Potomac, under the latter General, was swelling in numbers, and active in organization and discipline. General McClellan's popularity with the army was very great. They felt his organizing hand, and regarded him with the proudest confidence. The country, however, was becoming impatient with him. He would spare no men for any outside enterprises, and still rolled up the numbers of his cumbersome forces, though good roads lay in front, and pleasant weather invited to action. On the twenty-ninth of August, General Butler, acting with a naval force under Commodore Stringham, took possession of the Hatteras forts, with a force which he had raised independently for the expedition. This gave great satisfaction to the country, and helped to keep up the popular courage under the depressing influence of delay on the part of the army of the Potomac.

In the month of August, Munson's Hill, within view of the capitol, was occupied by the rebel forces; and, though they were not strong in numbers, and took but limited pains to intrench themselves, they remained there undisturbed until nearly the last of September, when they left of their own accord.   On the twenty-first of October, there occurred a disastrous battle and blunder at Ball's Bluff.   It was a sad failure to fulfill the promise of a magnificent preparation for action. The country was disappointed and indignant.   The number killed, drowned, wounded and captured was eleven hundred— full half that went into the action.   Here Colonel Baker, the President's friend, fell; and, although General McClellan, in his report of the affair, said that, "situated as their troops were—cut off alike from retreat or reinforcements—five thousand against one thousand seven hundred—it was not possible that the issue could have been successful," the unmilitary mind will still inquire why, with an immense army but a few miles away, they were left or placed where reinforcement and retreat were alike impossible?

General Scott did not like the looks or management of military affairs, and felt that his place was becoming unpleasant.   Only a few days after the affair at Ball's Bluff, he made known to Mr. Lincoln his desire to be released from all active duties, in consequence of his increasing physical infirmity.   In a letter dated November first, the President acceded to his request, and added: "The American people will hear with sadness and deep emotion that General Scott has withdrawn from the active control of the army, while the President and the unanimous Cabinet express their own and the nation's sympathy in his personal affliction, and their profound sense of the important public services rendered by him to his country, during his long and brilliant public career, among which will ever be gratefully distinguished his faithful devotion to the Constitution, the Union and the flag, when assailed by parricidal rebellion."   To do all possible honor to the noble veteran who had stood by the country when so many army officers had gone over to the rebellion under the appeal of sectional friendship—an appeal made to him with all the persuasions that in-genuity could devise—the President and his entire Cabinet waited upon him at his residence; and there, with his Secretaries around him, Mr. Lincoln read to him his letter. It was a grand moment in the old man's life. "This honor overwhelms me," he responded. "It overpays all services I have attempted to render to my country. If I had any claims before, they are all obliterated by this expression of approval by the President, with the unanimous support of the Cabinet. I know the President and this Cabinet well—I know that the country has placed its interests in this trying crisis in safe keeping. Their councils are wise; their labors are untiring as they are loyal, and their course is the right one."

Thus, after fifty-three years of service in the armies of his country, General Scott went into his nobly earned retirement, with the blessing of his government and the blessing of his country upon his venerable head; and it is one of the sweetest satisfactions of both to remember that he lived to see his country's enemies vanquished, and to hear of those who taunted him with faithlessness to his sectional friends, humbly seeking pardon of the government which they had outraged, and which he had so loyally supported.

On General Scott's retirement, General McClellan held the highest rank in the army, and was intrusted with the chief command.

During the month of November, the Union forces achieved several important and encouraging successes. South Carolina was invaded by an expedition under the joint command of General T. W. Sherman and Commodore Dupont, the latter of whom achieved a brilliant naval victory in Port Royal Harbor. Generals Grant and McClernand, with a force of three thousand five hundred men, attacked a rebel camp in Missouri under General Polk, captured twelve guns, burned their camp, and took baggage, horses and many prisoners. The rebels were afterwards reinforced, and compelled the Union forces to return to their transports. Notwithstanding the fact that the rebels claimed a victory, the results were substantially with their assailants. General Buckner, with whom McClellan was alleged to have made his treaty of neutrality, had thrown off his neutral mask, and was gathering an army of rebels in Kentucky, co-operating with General Bragg who was invading the state with the determination to force it into secession. To meet and repel this invasion, General W. T. Sherman advanced with a large force to Bowling Green, while General Nelson, on his left, gained a decisive victory over the rebels under Colonel Williams. The various operations of the Union forces broke up the rebel project of subjugation, and re-invigorated the efforts of the Union men to hold the state to its loyalty. General Halleck was appointed to the command of the army of the West, and General Buell took General W. T. Sherman's command in Kentucky.

The question of slavery was an ever-present one during all the operations of the year. The instructions given by the War Department to General Butler on the eighth of August, were based upon "the desire of the President that all existing rights in all the states should be respected and maintained;" yet it was declared that " the rights dependent on the laws of the states within which military operations are conducted must necessarily be subordinate to the military exigencies created by the insurrection, if not wholly forfeited by the treasonable conduct of the parties claiming them." The difficulty of settling the claims of loyal masters was such that it was recommended to receive all fugitives, keep a record of them, and set them to work. Congress, the Secretary of War believed, would provide for the repayment of loyal masters. On the departure of General T. W. Sherman on his expedition to Port Royal, Mr. Cameron referred him to the letter to General Butler on this subject. He was directed to receive the services of any persons, whether fugitives from labor or not, who should offer them to the national government. These fugitives might be organized into "squads, companies, or otherwise," though that liberty was not intended to mean a general arming of them for military service. Loyal masters were

22

to be assured, meantime, that Congress would provide for them a just compensation for services thus lost to them. The time for emancipation had not come, in the opinion of the government. That Mr. Lincoln desired it, none can doubt; but he had undertaken to save the Union under the Constitution—to save the Union while preserving inviolate all the rights of all the states. He so understood the oath by which he was invested with power. Whatever might be his hatred of slavery—and it was the intensest passion of his life—he could only interfere with it as a military necessity—an essential means of saving the Union.

CHAPTER XXI.

EARLY in November, an event occurred which gave to our relations with England a very threatening aspect—an event which aroused the ire of the British people to a feverish pitch, encouraged the rebels, and filled with uneasiness the friends of the government. Although the blockade, under the energetic measures of the government, had become something very different from a blockade on paper, there were still many ports in the southern states which carried on a large contraband commerce, through the agency of blockade-runners, the majority of which were owned in England, and navigated by British seamen. The capture of the Hatteras forts and of the defenses of Port Royal Harbor had shut two of these ports; but Charleston, notwithstanding all the efforts of the blockading fleet, continued to receive numbers of foreign vessels, and to dispatch them in safety. On the twelfth of October, the steamship Theodora shot out of that harbor, with two notorious rebels on board, James M. Mason and John Slidell, both perjured senators of the United States, and accredited by the Davis government respectively to the governments of England and France. They went to get recognition for their government. They went as enemies of the United States.

Proceeding to Cuba, these emissaries took passage from Havana on the seventh of November, on the British mail steamer Trent, bound immediately for St. Thomas. On the following day, the Trent was hailed by the United States frigate San Jacinto, Captain Wilkes, who directed a shot

across her bows to bring her to.   Then two officers and
twenty men, more or less, put off from the San Jacinto,
boarded the Trent, and, after a search, took out Mr. Mason
and Mr. Slidell and their two secretaries, and, by force, against
the protest of the Trent's officers, bore them to their vessel.
These rebel emissaries Captain Wilkes brought to the United
States, and they were lodged in Fort Warren.

The excitement which this affair produced in both countries
was intense, and but little favorable to its calm consideration.
It was unquestionably a doubtful proceeding, and cool British
blood came up to a boiling heat wherever in England or her
provinces the intelligence of the affair was published.   The
news found the loyal people of America smarting under a
sense of the injustice of the relation which England had assumed toward their struggle, and sensitive to the insults which
their people had received from the British press and public.
America came to care less for England afterward; but then
she was sensitive in every fiber to her opinion, her lack of
sympathy, and her covert aid to the rebellion.   To the American public the news of this capture was most grateful.   They
felt that whatever the laws of nations might be—and in these
they were but little versed—it was morally right that these
men should be in their power, and that it was morally wrong
that any other power should have our traitors under its protection.   So they greeted the event with huzzas, and made
a hero of the impulsive Captain Wilkes, who, though a most
loyal and excellent person, was possessed by a zeal that sometimes surpassed his discretion.

The effect of this capture was, of course, foreseen by the
government; and on the thirtieth of November Mr. Seward
communicated to Mr. Adams, our minister in England, a
statement of the facts, with the assurance that Captain Wilkes
had acted without any instructions from the government, and
that our government was prepared to discuss the matter in a
friendly spirit, so soon as the position of the British government should be made known.   Earl Russell wrote under the
same date to Lord Lyons, rehearsing his understanding of the

facts of the case, and saying that his government was "willing to believe that the naval officer who committed the aggression was not acting in compliance with any authority from his government," because the government of the United States "must be fully aware that the British government could not allow such an affront to the national honor to pass without full reparation." The minister expressed the hope that the United States would, of its own motion, release the commissioners, and make an apology.

This was a very sensible and neighborly dispatch, but Earl Russell seems to have been subjected afterward to a pressure that changed his feelings and sharpened his policy, for, in a subsequent note, he transformed his polite dispatch into an insulting ultimatum. Lord Lyons was directed to wait seven days after having made his demand for reparation; and then, in case no answer should be given, or any other answer should be given than a full compliance with the terms of the demand, he should pack up the archives of the legation, and return to London, bringing his archives with him. Usually an ultimatum comes at the end of a long series of negotiations—after all the resources of diplomacy are exhausted—after there is plainly seen to be a warlike, or unreasonable, or contumacious spirit on the part of the power from which redress is sought. Earl Russell gave Mr. Lincoln his ultimatum at the start. It was an insult—a threat. It was uttered to gratify the warlike feeling of the British people. There is no question that they desired war; and when the British people are mentioned in this connection, those are meant who, in print and speech, represent them and assume to speak for them. War with America was looked upon in England as probable. Measures were taken to prepare for it. Indeed, many of the London journals regarded war as inevitable; and when the peaceful nature of Mr. Seward's first dispatches were known, the Morning Post hastened to publish in large type an official contradiction of the news. "The war will be terrible," said the London journals. "It will begin by a recognition of the South, by the alliance of the South, by the assured triumph of the South." That was the precise point. War was wanted by the people, that their cherished desire for the disruption of the Republic might be fulfilled; and they were disappointed when they found that even an impertinent ultimatum could not bring it.

If British statesmen sympathized with these views and feelings;—and some of them did,—it showed how poorly informed they were; for there was never anything in the difficulty, from the first, to give either government alarm. The British people found that there was a government at Washington,—calm, dignified and intelligent, not under the control of the mob at all, and showing, in the cool independence of its action, its entire freedom from the misdirected passions of the people. Only in the early approval of the Secretary of the Navy and of the lower House of Congress, awarded to Captain Wilkes, was there anything to give the British government cause of alarm, or ground of serious complaint; and the news of these ill-advised indorsements reached England after the tempest of passion had been spent.

On the twenty-sixth of December Mr. Seward addressed a note to Lord Lyons, in which he elaborately discussed all the questions growing out of the case. The paper was one of great moderation, and consummate ability—indeed, one of the finest to which he ever gave utterance. It was a profound lesson in the law of nations, which could not be read without benefit by statesmen everywhere. By it the British government learned that there were two sides to the case, and that there was something to be said upon the side of Captain Wilkes; for in it he argued most ingeniously, if not in all instances decisively, that Messrs. Mason and Slidell and their dispatches were contraband of war, that Captain Wilkes might lawfully stop and search the Trent for contraband persons and dispatches, and that he had the right to capture the persons presumed to have contraband dispatches. He did not, however, exercise the right of capture in the manner allowed and recognized by the laws of nations, as understood and practically entertained by the American government. "If I decide this case in favor of my own government," said Mr. Seward, "I must disavow its most cherished principles, and reverse and forever abandon its essential policy. If I maintain those principles and adhere to that policy, I must surrender the case itself." He therefore declared that the persons held in military custody in Fort Warren would be "cheerfully liberated." Mr. Seward could not forbear to say that, if the safety of the Union required their detention, they would have been detained; to draw a contrast between the action of our government and that of Great Britain under similar circumstances; and to indulge in the irony that "the claim of the British government is not made in a discourteous manner."

Earl Russell was satisfied with the "reparation." The prisoners were released, peace between the two nations was kept, the war feeling subsided, disunion sympathizers all over Europe were disgusted with Mr. Seward's pusillanimity, and at the South there was no attempt to disguise the disappointment felt at the result. The hopes excited in the South by the difficulty are well expressed in the language of Pollard's "History of the First Year of the War," which says: "Providence was declared to be in our favor; the incident of the Trent was looked upon almost as a special dispensation; and it was said in fond imagination that on its deck and in the trough of the weltering Atlantic the key of the blockade had at last been lost." The same author continues: "The surrender was an exhibition of meanness and cowardice unparalleled in the political history of the civilized world." Patriots may well be content with a decision which brought grief to their enemies everywhere, and raised the whole nation in the respect of Christendom.

On the second day of December, Congress met in regular session, and on the following day Mr. Lincoln sent in his annual message. The message opened with an allusion to the attitude of foreign governments, and a statement of the fact that, should those governments be controlled only by material considerations, they would find that the quickest and best way out of the embarrassments of commerce consequent upon the

American difficulties, would be rather through the maintenance, than the destruction, of the Union. It was undoubtedly with reference to the excitement then existing concerning the Trent affair that he penned the sentence: "Since, however, it is apparent that here, as in every other state, foreign dangers necessarily attend domestic difficulties, I recommend that adequate and ample measures be adopted for maintaining the public defenses on every side."

The message announced the financial measures of the government to have been very successful; recommended a re-organization of the Supreme Court, the machinery of which the country had outgrown; suggested a codification or digest of the statutes of Congress, so as to reduce the six thousand pages upon which they were printed to the measure of a volume; indicated his wish that the Court of Claims should have power to make its decisions final, with only the right of appeal on questions of law to the Supreme Court; asked for increased attention on the part of Congress to the interests of agriculture; expressed his gratification with the success of efforts for the suppression of the African slave trade; and broached a plan for colonizing such slaves as had been freed by the operation of the confiscation act, passed on the previous sixth of August, on territory to be acquired. The progress made by the federal armies, and by his own careful and moderate management of affairs in the border states, is shown in the following passage:

"The last ray of hope for preserving the Union peaceably, expired at the assault upon Fort Sumter; and a general review of what has occurred since may not be unprofitable. What was painfully uncertain then, is much better defined and more distinct now; and the progress of events is plainly in the right direction. The insurgents confidently claimed a strong support from north of Mason and Dixon's line; and the friends of the Union were not free from apprehension on the point. This, however, was soon settled definitely, and on the right side. South of the line, noble little Delaware led off right from the first. Maryland was made to seem against the Union. Our soldiers were assaulted, bridges were burned, and railroads torn up within her limits; and we were many days, at one time, without the ability to bring a single regiment over her soil to the capital. Now her bridges and railroads are repaired and open to the Government; she already gives seven regiments to the cause of the Union, and none to the enemy; and her people, at a regular election, have sustained the Union by a larger majority and a larger aggregate vote than they ever before gave to any candidate or any question. Kentucky, too, for some time in doubt, is now decidedly and, I think, unchangeably ranged on the side of the Union. Missouri is comparatively quiet, and, I believe, can not again be overrun by the insurrectionists. These three states of Maryland, Kentucky and Missouri, neither of which would promise a single soldier at first, have now an aggregate of not less than forty thousand in the field for the Union; while of their citizens, certainly not more than a third of that number, and they of doubtful whereabouts and doubtful existence, are in arms against it. After a somewhat bloody struggle of months, winter closes on the Union people of Western Virginia, leaving them masters of their own country.

"An insurgent force of about fifteen hundred, for months dominating the narrow peninsular region constituting the counties of Accomac and Northampton, and known as the Eastern Shore of Virginia, together with some contiguous parts of Maryland, have laid down their arms; and the people there have renewed their allegiance to, and accepted the protection of the old flag. This leaves no armed insurrectionist north of the Potomac, or east of the Chesapeake.

"Also, we have obtained a footing at each of the isolated points on the southern coast, of Hatteras, Port Royal, Tybee Island near Savannah, and Ship Island; and we likewise have some general accounts of popular movements in behalf of the Union in North Carolina and Tennessee.

"These things demonstrate that the cause of the Union is advancing steadily and certainly southward."

In the development of the insurrection, Mr. Lincoln detected a growing enmity to the first principle of popular government—the rights of the people. In the grave and well considered public documents of the rebels he found labored arguments to prove that "large control of the people in government is the source of all political evil. Monarchy itself," he adds, "is sometimes hinted at as a possible refuge from the power of the people." Proceeding from this, Mr. Lincoln said:

"It is not needed, nor fitting here, that a general argument should be made in favor of popular institutions; but there is one point, with its connections, not so hackneyed as most others, to which I ask a brief attention. It is the effort to place capital on an equal footing with, if not above, labor, in the structure of the government. It is assumed that labor is available only in connection with capital; that nobody labors unless somebody else, owning capital, somehow by the use of it induces him to labor. This assumed, it is next considered whether it is best that capital shall hire laborers, and thus induce them to work by their own consent, or buy them, and drive them to it without their consent. Having proceeded so far, it is naturally concluded that all laborers are either hired laborers or what we call slaves. And further, it is assumed that whoever is once a hired laborer, is fixed in that condition for life.

"Now, there is no such relation between capital and labor as assumed; nor is there any such thing as a free man being fixed for life in the condition of a hired laborer. Both these assumptions are false, and all inferences from them are groundless.

"Labor is prior to and independent of capital. Capital is only the fruit of labor, and could never have existed if labor had not first existed. Labor is the superior of capital, and deserves much the higher consideration. Capital has its rights, which are as worthy of protection as any other rights. Nor is it denied that there is, and probably always will be, a relation between labor and capital, producing mutual benefits. The error is in assuming that the whole labor of the community exists within that relation. A few men own capital, and those few avoid labor themselves, and, with their capital, hire or buy another few to labor for them. A large majority belong to neither class—neither work for others, nor have others working for them. In most of the southern states, a majority of the whole people of all colors are neither slaves nor masters; while in the northern, a large majority are neither hirers nor hired. Men, with their families—wives, sons, and daughters—work for themselves, on their farms, in their houses, and in their shops, taking the whole product to themselves, and asking no favors of capital on the one hand, nor of hired laborers or slaves on the other. It is not forgotten that a considerable number of persons mingle their own labor with capital—that is, they labor with their own hands, and also buy or hire others to labor for them; but this is only a mixed, and not a distinct class. No principle stated is disturbed by the existence of this mixed class.

"Again: as has already been said, there is not of necessity any such thing as the free hired laborer being fixed to that condition for life. Many independent men everywhere in these states, a few years back in their lives, were hired laborers. The prudent, penniless beginner in the world, labors for wages awhile, saves a surplus with which to buy tools or land for himself, then labors on his own account another while, and at length hires another new beginner to help him. This is the just and generous and prosperous system, which opens the way to all, gives hope to all, and consequent energy and progress, and improvement of condition to all. No men living are more worthy to be trusted than those who toil up from poverty—none less inclined to take or touch aught which they have not honestly earned. Let them beware of surrendering a political power which they already possess, and which, if surrendered, will surely be used to close the door of advancement against such as they, and to fix new disabilities and burdens upon them, till all of liberty shall be lost."

Aside from the bills passed for sustaining the war, and sustaining the President in his mode of and means for suppressing the rebellion, very little important action was taken by this session of Congress, that did not relate to slavery. The question of "arbitrary arrests," of which the enemies of the President made loud complaint, came up, and Mr. Lincoln was sustained in the House by a vote of one hundred and eight to twenty-six. A provision was made for the issue of legal-tender notes, for increasing the internal revenue, and establishing a basis for the payment of interest on loans, in accordance with the policy of Mr. Chase, the distinguished Secretary of the Treasury; and a confiscation act was passed, more stringent than its predecessor.

We now enter upon a review of that series of measures and movements which culminated in the overthrow of slavery; and, as Mr. Lincoln has been assailed on one side for being too slow, and on the other for being too precipitate, these movements and measures deserve careful consideration.

If there is one thing that stands out more prominently than any other in Mr. Lincoln's history, it is his regard for the Constitution and the laws. Especially was this the case in relation to that clause of the Constitution which protected slavery, and all the laws by which the relation of master and slave was preserved. This was not attributable to his love of slavery, for he hated it; but it was because that on this point only was he suspected, and on this point only was there any sensitiveness in the nation. He voluntarily and frequently declared that he considered the slaveholders entitled to a fugitive slave law. By the Constitution he was determined to stand; yet there is evidence that from the first he considered emancipation to be the logical result of persistence in rebellion. As the rebellion progressed, and the rebels themselves had forfeited all right to constitutional protection for their peculiar institution, he felt himself still withheld from meddling with slavery by any sweeping measure, for, in the four border states—Maryland, Delaware, Kentucky and Missouri—which had not seceded, the government had many friends, whose hands he felt it his duty to strengthen by every possible means. He saw the time of emancipation coming, but he wished to save them; and this was the principal reason for his delay. How faithfully he endeavored to do this, and with how little avail, will appear in the narrative. Amid the attacks of bitter political foes, and the reproaches of well-meaning but impatient friends, he had a difficult path to pursue.

Following Mr. Lincoln's lead, Mr. Seward had announced to foreign governments that no change in the institutions of the South was contemplated. General McClellan had abundant reason in the President's position for assuring the people of Virginia, as he did, that he contemplated nothing of the kind. But the people were becoming discontented with this mild policy, and Congress obeyed their voice by an early tabling of the Crittenden resolution, which had satisfied that body at their session in July.

Mr. Lincoln was quick to see the tendency of the public mind, and began at once to shape his measures for the result which could not long be delayed. On the sixth of March, he sent a message to Congress, recommending the passage of a joint resolution which should be substantially as follows:

"Resolved: That the United States ought to co-operate with any state which may gradually adopt abolishment of slavery, giving to such state pecuniary aid, to be used by such state in its discretion, to compensate for inconveniences, public and private, produced by such change of system."

"If the proposition contained in the resolution does not meet the approval of Congress and the country," added Mr. Lincoln, "there is an end; but if it does command such approval, I deem it of importance that the states and people immediately interested should be at once distinctly notified of the fact, so that they may begin to consider whether to accept or reject it." It was Mr. Lincoln's opinion that one ot the severest blows the rebellion could receive would be the abolition of slavery in the border states. To deprive the rebels of the hope of securing the still loyal slave states, he believed would be substantially to end the rebellion. If these states should abolish slavery, it would in effect be saying to the confederacy, "We will join you under no circumstances." He believed that gradual was better than sudden emancipation; and that, as a war measure, the government would make the scheme of compensation a paying one. Still true to his old tenderness on the subject of national interference with slavery, he took pains to show that his plan threw the whole matter into the hands of the states themselves.

There was kindly warning to his friends in the border slave states, in these words:

"In the annual message of last December, I thought fit to say—'The Union must be preserved; and hence all indispensable means must be employed.' I said this not hastily, but deliberately. War has been made, and continues to be, an indispensable means to this end. A practical re-acknowledgment of the national authority would render the war unnecessary, and it would at once cease. If, however, resistance continues, the war must also continue; and it is impossible to foresee all the incidents which may attend, and all the ruin which may follow it. Such as may seem indispensable, or may obviously promise great efficiency toward ending the struggle, must and will come. The proposition now made (though an offer only), I hope it may be esteemed no offense to ask whether the pecuniary consideration tendered would not be of more value to the states and private persons concerned, than are the institutions and property in it, in the present aspect of affairs.

"While it is true that the adoption of the proposed resolution would be merely initiatory, and not within itself a practical measure, it is recommended in the hope that it would soon lead to important practical results. In full view of my great responsibility to God and my country, I earnestly beg the attention of Congress and the people to the subject."

It took no special degree of sagacity to learn what this passage meant; but those for whom this thoughtful measure was intended, though the resolution went through both

Houses of Congress, and stood as a pledge of compensation for emancipation, turned their backs upon it. Only a very few members from the border states voted for it. But the President could not let the matter stop there. He saw that emancipation would surely come as a war measure; and that these slave states that had stood by him through much difficulty, would lose, in that event, that which the Constitution recognized as their property.

Before the close of the session, he invited the senators and representatives from those states to a conference, at the Executive Mansion. It was early in July; and, while Congress had been talking and acting, McClellan had been fighting with very unsatisfactory results. The nation was depressed by reverses; and Mr. Lincoln wished to give these men and the people they represented another chance to escape from the loss which he felt must soon befall them. Having convened them, he read to them this carefully prepared address, in which he argued his own case and theirs, and appealed to them to save themselves and the country:

"Gentlemen—After the adjournment of Congress, now near, I shall have no opportunity of seeing you for several months. Believing that you of the border states hold more power for good than any other equal number of members, I feel it a duty which I cannot justifiably waive, to make this appeal to you.

"I intend no reproach or complaint when I assure you that, in my opinion, if you all had voted for the resolution in the gradual emancipation message of last March, the war would now be substantially ended. And the plan therein proposed is yet one of the most potent and swift means of ending it. Let the states which are in rebellion see definitely and certainly that in no event will the states you represent ever join their proposed confederacy, and they cannot much longer maintain the contest. But you cannot divest them of their hope to ultimately have you with them, as long as you show a determination to perpetuate the institution within your own states. Beat them at elections, as you have overwhelmingly done, and, nothing daunted, they still claim you as their own. You and I know what the lever of their power is. Break that lever before their faces, and they can shake you no more forever.

"Most of you have treated me with kindness and consideration; and I trust you will not now think I improperly touch what is exclusively your own, when, for the sake of the whole country, I ask, can you, for your states, do better than to take the course I urge? Discarding punctilio and maxims adapted to more manageable times, and looking only to the unprecedentedly stern facts of our case, can you do better in any possible event? You prefer that the constitutional relation of the states to the nation shall be practically restored without disturbance of the institution: and if this were done, my whole duty, in this respect, under the Constitution and my oath of office, would be performed. But it is not done, and we are trying to accomplish it by war. The incidents of the war cannot be avoided. If the war continues long, as it must if the object be not sooner attained, the institution in your states will be extinguished by mere friction and abrasion—by the mere incidents of the war. It will be gone, and you will have nothing valuable in lieu of it. Much of its value is gone already. How much better for you and for your people, to take the step which at once shortens the war, and secures substantial compensation for that which is sure to be wholly lost in any other event! How much better to thus save the money which else we sink forever in the war! How much better to do it while we can, lest the war ere long render us pecuniarily unable to do it! How much better for you, as seller, and the nation, as buyer, to sell out and buy out that without which the war never could have been, than to sink both the thing to be sold and the price of it in cutting one another's throats!

"I do not speak of emancipation at once, but of a decision at once to emancipate gradually. Room in South America for colonization can be obtained cheaply, and in abundance; and, when numbers shall be large enough to be company and encouragement for one another, the freed people will not be so reluctant to go.

"I am pressed with a difficulty not yet mentioned—one which threatens division among those who, united, are none too strong. An instance of it is known to you. General Hunter is an honest man. He was, and I hope still is, my friend. I valued him none the less for his agreeing with me in the general wish that all men everywhere could be free. He proclaimed all men free within certain states, and I repudiated the proclamation. He expected more good and less harm from the measure than I could believe would follow. Yet, in repudiating it, I gave dissatisfaction, if not offense, to many whose support the country cannot afford to lose. And this is not the end of it. The pressure in this direction is still upon me, and is increasing. By conceding what I now ask, you can relieve me, and, much more, can relieve the country in this important point.

"Upon these considerations I have again begged your attention to the message of March last. Before leaving the capital, consider and discuss it among yourselves. You are patriots and statesmen, and as such I pray you consider this proposition; and at the least commend it to the consideration of your states and people. As you would perpetuate popular government for the best people in the world, I beseech you that you do in nowise omit this. Our common country is in great peril, demanding the loftiest views and boldest action to bring a speedy relief. Once relieved, its form of government is saved to the world; its beloved history and cherished memories are vindicated; and its happy future fully assured, and rendered inconceivably grand. To you, more than to any others, the privilege is given to assure that happiness and swell that grandeur, and to link your own names therewith forever."

What Mr. Lincoln said in this paper, touching the dissatisfaction with which his revocation of General Hunter's order of emancipation had been received, was true. People were tired of the governmental protection of slavery in the rebel states; and they had reason to be. Mr. Lincoln felt all this, but he could not forsake his friends, until he had tried every means to save them. In his revocation of General Hunter's order, one of the most beautiful and touching appeals that man ever penned, occurs—an appeal which the mistaken men before him had already had the opportunity of reading. In that paper, after quoting the resolution which Congress had passed pledging the country to compensation for emancipation, he said:

" To the people of those states I now earnestly appeal. I do not argue—I beseech you to make the argument for yourselves. You cannot, if you would, be blind to the signs of the times. I beg of you a calm and enlarged consideration of them, ranging, if it may be, far above personal and partisan politics. This proposal makes common cause for a common object, casting no reproaches upon any. It acts not the Pharisee. The changes it contemplates would come gently as the dews of Heaven, not rending nor wrecking anything. Will you not embrace it? So much good has not been done by one effort in all past time, as, in the providence of God, it is now your high privilege to do. May the vast future not have to lament that you have neglected it."

Still forbearing, still arguing, still beseeching, Mr. Lincoln stood before these border-state legislators, for whose sake he was suffering sharp reproach in the house of his best friends; but they were unmoved. They could not read the signs of the times. Only nine of the twenty-nine who responded gave words of friendliness and approval. If, since then, they have found themselves and their friends in distress through the destruction of their property, they can have no reproaches to cast upon the patient man who so faithfully besought them to save themselves while there was an opportunity.

Two acts were passed by this session which respectively called out a message from the President. The confiscation act, to which allusion has already been made, touched a subject on which he had peculiar views. It would be difficult to express in the English language the basis of the right of Congress to free the slaves of rebels, in clearer and more unanswerable tones than Mr. Lincoln used when he wrote: "It is startling to say that Congress can free a slave within a state, and yet, were it said that the ownership of the slave had first been transferred to the nation, and that Congress had then liberated him, the difficulty would vanish; and this is the real case. The traitor against the general government forfeits his slave, at least as justly as he does any other property; and he forfeits both to the government against which he offends. The government, so far as there can be ownership, owns the forfeited slaves; and the question for Congress, in regard to them, is,—Shall they be made free, or sold to new masters? I see no objection to Congress deciding in advance that they should be free." The argument of a whole volume would not make the subject clearer.

The other act abolished slavery in the District of Columbia, and he merely pointed out an oversight in the bill, expressing at the same time his gratification that it recognized the two principles of colonization and compensation. It must have been with peculiar satisfaction that he thus completed a work which he began while he was a member of Congress himself, many years before.

Late in the session, Mr. Lincoln sent to Congress the draft of a bill for the compensation of any state that might abolish slavery within its limits; which, although it was referred to a committee, was not acted upon, as there appeared no disposition on the part of the border states to respond to the action which Congress had already taken.

Meantime, and especially after the enactment of the confiscation bill, presses and people maintained their clamor for a sweeping proclamation of emancipation. The clamor took a direct and definite form in a letter addressed by Horace Greeley, through the New York Tribune. The letter was severe in its terms, and intemperate in spirit. Any President who had occupied the office previous to Mr. Lincoln, would have passed over such a letter in silence, however much it might have annoyed or pained him. Mr. Lincoln, however, never thought of his dignity, and saw no reason why the President of the United States should not appear in a newspaper, as well as other men. He accordingly replied to Mr. Greeley, under date of August twenty-second, in a letter which, for conciseness and lucidity, may well be regarded as a model, whether the position assumed in it was sound or otherwise. Mr. Lincoln wrote as follows:

"Hon. Horace Greeley,. Dear Sir: I have just read yours of the nineteenth instant, addressed to myself through the New York *Tribune.*

"If there be in it any statements or assumptions of fact which I may know to be erroneous, I do not now and here controvert them.

"If there be any inferences which I may believe to be falsely drawn, I do not now and here argue against them.

"If there be perceptible in it an impatient and dictatorial tone, I waive it in deference to an old friend whose heart I have always supposed to be right.

"As to the policy I 'seem to be pursuing,' as you say, I have not meant to leave any one in doubt. I would save the Union. I would save it in the shortest way under the Constitution.

"The sooner the national authority can be restored, the nearer the Union will be—the Union as it was.

"If there be those who would not save the Union unless they could at the same time save slavery, I do not agree with them.

"If there be those who would not save the Union unless they could at the same time destroy slavery, I do not agree with them.

"My paramount object is to save the Union, and not either to save or destroy slavery.

"If I could save the Union without freeing any slave, I would do it; if I could save it by freeing all the slaves, I would do it; and if I could do it by freeing some and leaving others alone, I would also do that.

"What I do about slavery and the coloured race, I do because I believe it helps to save this Union; and what I forbear, I forbear because I do not believe it would help to save the Union.

"I shall do less whenever I shall believe what I am doing hurts the cause, and I shall do more whenever I believe doing more will help the cause.

"I shall try to correct errors when shown to be errors, and I shall adopt new views so fast as they shall appear to be true views.

"I have here stated my purpose according to my views of official duty, and I intend no modification of my oft-expressed personal wish that all men everywhere could be free.

"Yours,   A. LINCOLN."

Mr. Lincoln was anxious to take no steps which he should be obliged to retrace through the lack of popular support, and at this time he was carefully measuring the public opinion on the subject of emancipation. A part of the preliminary work he had accomplished. He had performed with the tenderest and most assiduous fidelity all his duty toward the border slave states. He had warned them, besought them, advised them, to get out of the way of an event which he felt certain would come. He knew that the institution of slavery would not be worth a straw, in any state, after it should be destroyed in the rebel states. But they turned a deaf ear to his warnings and entreaties; and in this manner, if not in the manner desired, took themselves out of his way.

His letter to Horace Greeley was, without doubt, intended to prepare the mind of the country for emancipation, and to exhibit the principles and exigencies by which he should be controlled in proclaiming it. He was clearing away obstacles, and preparing his ground; and, in connection with events which wait for record, the time for action came at last.

Mr. Cameron was not very successful in the administration of the affairs of his bureau. It is no derogation to his ability as a statesman to say that, for the discharge of the duties of the war office, at the time he occupied it, he had no eminent fitness. It was not the office he would have chosen for himself. He had immense and almost countless contracts at his disposal, and could give to them but little personal care. That

he was overreached, under the circumstances, was almost a
matter of course, and many of his contracts were very bad
ones.   Congress, after his resignation, censured him for his
loose way of doing business, in intrusting Alexander Cummings of New York with the expenditure of large sums of
money without restriction; but Mr. Lincoln, by a special
message, assumed all the responsibility of Mr. Cummings'
appointment to this duty and responsibility.   Mr. Cameron
resigned his position on the 11th of January, 1862; and Mr.
Lincoln showed what he thought of the charges of fraud
against him, by appointing him minister to Russia.   Nevertheless, it was to be said of him that Mr. Chase found it difficult
to raise money while he remained to make contracts.   He resigned while the House was busy with overhauling his affairs;
and it occurred that he sent in his resignation on the same day
on which Mr. Dawes of Massachusetts was making a powerful speech against him, and on which the special committee
on government contracts made a report severely condemning
his operations.

Mr. Lincoln appointed Edwin M. Stanton of Ohio to the
office thus vacated.   Mr. Stanton was a democrat, and had
been a member of Mr. Buchanan's cabinet—was, indeed, the
first one in that cabinet to protest against the downright treason into which it was drifting.   He was a man of indomitable
energy, devoted loyalty and thorough honesty.   Contractors
could not manipulate him, and traitors could not deceive him.
Impulsive, perhaps, but true; willful, it is possible, but placa-
ble; impatient, but persistent and efficient,—he became, at
once, one of the most marked and important of the members of
the cabinet.   Mr. Lincoln loved him and believed in him from
first to last.   When inquired of concerning the reasons for
his appointment, Mr. Lincoln said he rather wished, at first,
to appoint a man from one of the border states, but he knew
the New England people would object; and then, again, it
would have given him great satisfaction to appoint a man
from New England, but that would displease the border states.
On the whole, he thought he had better take a man from some
intervening territory; "and, to tell you the truth, gentlemen,"

said he, "I don't believe Stanton knows where he belongs himself." The gentlemen proceeding to discuss Mr. Stanton's impulsiveness, Mr. Lincoln said: "Well, we may have to treat him as they are sometimes obliged to treat a Methodist minister I know of out west. He gets wrought up to so high a pitch of excitement in his prayers and exhortations, that they are obliged to put bricks into his pockets to keep him down. We may be obliged to serve Stanton the same way, but I guess we'll let him jump awhile first."

The country has sometimes thought the time for bricks had come; but, on the whole, the leaders of the rebellion have had greatest cause of complaint. Mr. Stanton's place in history will be a proud one.

Malcontents, who felt that everything went wrong because there was something wrong in the cabinet, were much encouraged by the change that had been made, and personally and by letter urged Mr. Lincoln to make further changes. A number of them called upon him to insist on changes that they considered absolutely necessary. Mr. Lincoln heard them through, and then, with his peculiar smile, said, "Gentlemen, the case reminds me of a story of an old friend of mine out in Illinois. His homestead was very much infested with those little black and white animals that we needn't call by name; and, after losing his patience with them, he determined to sally out and inflict upon them a general slaughter. He took gun, clubs and dogs, and at it he went, but stopped after killing one, and returned home. When his neighbors asked him why he had not fulfilled his threat of killing all there were on his place, he replied that his experience with the one he had killed was such that he thought he had better stop where he was."

This story was told with no disrespect to Mr. Cameron, or to the other members of his cabinet, for he honored them all; but it was told to get rid of his troublesome advisers. They went away forgetting that they had failed to make any impression on the President—forgetting that they had failed in their errand utterly—and laughing over the story by which the President had dismissed them.

CHAPTER XXII.

A CIVILIAN, ignorant of the art of war, can only judge a military man by what he accomplishes in the long run by his policy and action; and it is difficult for such a judge to perceive what General McClellan accomplished, with his magnificent army of a hundred and sixty thousand as good soldiers as ever the sun shone upon—well drilled, well fed, well clothed and well armed—but to scatter and wear out that army, volunteer general advice to a government that was presumed to be competent to the management of its own affairs, and win the doubtful honor of becoming the favorite of men who, from the first, opposed the war, and threw all possible obstacles in the way of its successful prosecution. The whole history of McClellan's operations is a history of magnificent preparations and promises, of fatal hesitations and procrastinations, of clamoring for more preparations, and justifications of hesitations and procrastinations, of government indulgence and forbearance, of military intrigues within the camp, of popular impatience and alarms, and of the waste of great means and golden opportunities. Even the opportunity of becoming "the hero of Antietam" came to General McClellan through his culpable remissness in permitting the enemy to cross the Potomac; and this victory lost all its value by his failure to gather its fruits.

When General McClellan assumed command, he found waiting for him fifty thousand men, more or less, in and around Washington. He assumed command during the last days of July; and, within a period of less than three months, that army was raised to a force of more than a hundred and fifty thousand men, with five hundred pieces of artillery. The people gave him more men than any one commander was ever known to handle effectively in the field; and the government lavishly bestowed upon his army all the material of war. The unfortunate matter of Ball's Bluff, which occurred on the twenty-second of October, has already found record. This was the first return for the fresh means that the government had placed at the commanding General's disposal. The Potomac was blockaded by a small force of rebels, and both the President and Secretary of War felt that there was no necessity for permitting this vexatious and humiliating blockade to continue. They tried to induce McClellan to aid in this business; and, at one time in October, he agreed to send four thousand men to co-operate with a naval force for this purpose; but he falsified his promise, on the ground that his engineers told him that so large a force could not be landed. It did not matter that the department assumed the responsibility of landing the troops. It did not matter, even, that he made another promise to send the troops. They were never sent, the second refusal being based upon his fear of bringing on a general engagement, which was exactly what ought to have been brought on. Captain Craven of the navy, with whom these troops were to co-operate, threw up his command in disgust, and the rebels never were driven away from the Potomac. They kept this grand highway closed until the following spring, and then retired of their own accord, and at leisure.

The confidence in General McClellan on the part of the government and the country generally was at this time unbounded; and he could not appear among his soldiers without such demonstrations of enthusiastic affection as few commanders have ever received. On the first of November he succeeded General Scott in the command of all the armies of the Union, still retaining personal command of the Army of the Potomac; but he seemed to be unable to move. Cautious, hesitating, always finding fresh obstacles to a movement, he permitted the golden days of autumn to pass away. In the meantime, the government was urging him to do something, as the rebel forces were massing in his front, and the country was clamorous for action. Instead of holding the commanding General responsible for these delays, the country blamed the government, and manifested its dissatisfaction by its votes in the fall elections.

All that autumn passed away, and not a blow was struck. The Potomac was closed to government war vessels and transports, by a few batteries which the over-cautious General was afraid to touch.

Mr. Lincoln was determined to break the spell which seemed to hold the General's mind; and, on the twenty-seventh of January, he issued an order that on the twenty-second day of February, 1862, there should be a general movement of the land and naval forces of the United States, against the insurgent armies—especially the army at and about Fortress Monroe, the army of the Potomac, the army of Western Virginia, the army near Mumfordsville, Kentucky, the army and flotilla at Cairo, and a naval force in the gulf of Mexico. He further declared "that the heads of departments, and especially the Secretaries of War and of the Navy, with all their subordinates, and the General-in-Chief with all other commanders and subordinates of land and naval forces, will severally be held to their strict and full responsibilities for prompt execution of this order." On the thirty-first of January— four days afterward—he issued another order, specially to the army of the Potomac, to engage, on or before the twenty-second of February, in the attempt to seize upon and occupy a point upon the railroad south-west of Manassas Junction, the details of the movement to be in the hands of the Commander-in-Chief.

To this last order of the President, General McClellan replied in a long letter to the Secretary of War. He objected to the President's plan, that the roads would be bad at the season proposed; and wished to substitute a plan of his own, which had in its favor a better soil for the moving of troops.

He wished to move by the Lower Rappahannock, making Urbana his base. He would throw upon the new line from one hundred and ten thousand to one hundred and forty thousand troops, according to circumstances, hoping to use the latter number, by bringing such fresh troops into Washington as would protect the capital. He "respectfully but firmly" advised that he might be permitted to make this substitution of his own for the President's plan. So firm was he that he was willing to say: "I will stake my life, my reputation, on the result,—more than that, I will stake on it the success of our cause." His judgment, he declared, was against the movement on Manassas. On the third of February, Mr. Lincoln addressed a note to the General on this difference of opinion, which ought to have shown him that his superior was a competent adviser and a keen critic:

"My dear Sir:—You and I have distinct and different plans for a movement of the army of the Potomac; yours to be done by the Chesapeake, up the Rappahannock, to Urbana, and across land to the terminus of the railroad on the York River; mine to move directly to a point on the railroad south-west of Manassas. If you will give satisfactory answers to the following questions, I shall gladly yield my plans to yours:

"1. Does not your plan involve a greatly larger expenditure of time and money than mine?

"2. Wherein is a victory more certain by your plan than mine?

"3. Wherein is a victory more valuable by your plan than mine?

"4. In fact, would it not be less valuable in this: that it would break no great line of the enemy's communications, while mine would?

"5. In case of disaster, would not a retreat be more difficult by your plan than mine?"

General McClellan replied to this through the Secretary of War, after his fashion; but the President was not convinced, and finally agreed to submit the two plans to a council of twelve officers. This council, eight to four, decided in favor of the General's plan. The President acquiesced; but the rebels rendered both plans useless by withdrawing from Manassas on the ninth of March to the other side of the Rappahannock—which date will be seen to be two weeks later than the date fixed for the advance of all the armies by the President.

On the eighth of March, the President ordered General McClellan to organize that part of his army which he proposed to engage in active operations, into four Army Corps, to be commanded respectively by General McDowell, General Sumner, General Heintzelman and General Keyes; and directed the order to be executed with such dispatch as not to delay operations already determined on—alluding to the movement by the Chesapeake and Rappahannock. On the same day, he issued another order: that no change of base should take place without leaving in and about Washington such an army as should make the city secure; that no more than two army corps should move before the Potomac should be cleared of rebel batteries; and that the movement should begin as early as the eighteenth of March.

On the next day, as has already been stated, the enemy retired unsuspected and undisturbed from his defenses; and then General McClellan moved forward, not to pursue, according to his own authority, but to give his troops some exercise, and a taste of the march and bivouac, before more active operations. On the fifteenth, the army moved back to Alexandria.

On the eleventh of March, General McClellan was relieved from the command of other military departments, because he had personally taken the field. Major-General Halleck received the command of the department of the Mississippi, and General Fremont that of the mountain department. On the thirteenth, a council of war decided that, as the enemy had retreated behind the Rappahannock, the new base of operations should be Fortress Monroe, on certain conditions which touched the neutralization of the power of the Merrimac, (an iron plated rebel vessel which had already destroyed the frigates Cumberland and Congress, and been beaten back by the Monitor,) means of transportation, and naval auxiliaries sufficient to silence the batteries on York River. On the same day, Mr. Stanton wrote to General McClellan, stating that the

President saw no objection to the plan, but directing that such a force should be left at Manassas Junction as would make it entirely certain that the enemy should not repossess it, that Washington should be left secure, and that, whatever place might be chosen as the new base, the army should move *at once* in pursuit of the enemy, by some route.

The President was impatient for action. Not a blow had been struck. Back from the Potomac blockade, and back from Manassas, the enemy had been permitted to retire without the loss of a man or a gun.

On the thirty-first of March, Mr. Lincoln ordered Blenker's division from the army of the Potomac to join General Fremont, who had importuned him for a larger force, and who was supported in his request by exacting friends. In a note to General McClellan, he said,—"I write this to assure you that I did so with great pain, understanding that you would wish it otherwise. If you could know the full pressure of the case, I am confident that you would justify it." General Banks, who had been ordered to cover Washington by occupying Manassas, was ordered on the first of April to force General Jackson back from Winchester.

Transportation had already been provided by the War Department for moving the troops to any new base that might be determined on, and General McClellan was not obliged to wait. On the first of April, there were under his command, by the official report of the Adjutant-general, 146,255 men in the four corps, with regular infantry and cavalry and other troops to raise the number to 158,419. In all the orders given by the President concerning the movements of this army, there was one condition that he insisted upon, viz, that troops should be left sufficient to protect Washington; and by General McClellan's order only twenty thousand effective men were to be left with General Wadsworth, the military governor of the District. The force was much smaller than was necessary, according to General McClellan's previous calculations; and General Wadsworth was so much impressed with its inadequacy that he called the attention of the war department to the subject. The letter was referred to Adjutant-general Thomas and General E. A. Hitchcock, whose decision was embodied in the words: "In view of the opinion expressed by the council of the commanders of army corps, of the force necessary for the capital, though not numerically stated, and of the force represented by General McClellan as left for that purpose, we are of opinion that the requirement of the President that this city shall be left entirely secure, not only in the opinion of the General-in-chief, but that of the commanders of all the army corps also, has not been fully complied with." In the meantime, General McClellan had gone forward to Fortress Monroe, and all but two corps of the troops had left for the new base. When, therefore, Generals Thomas and Hitchcock made their report, and the President saw that Washington was about to be left without sufficient defense, he directed the Secretary of War to order that one of the two corps not then embarked should remain in front of Washington, and that the other corps should go forward as speedily as possible. This was under date of April third. The first corps, under General McDowell, was designated for this protective service, numbering 38,454 men. Two new military departments were at once erected—the Department of the Rappahannock, under General McDowell, and the Department of the Shenandoah, lying between the mountain department and the Blue Ridge, under General Banks.

General McClellan pushed a portion of his troops toward Yorktown at once—toward a line of intrenchments held by the enemy, stretching across the Peninsula. On the fifth of April he wrote to the President, dating his letter "Near Yorktown," and stating that the enemy were in large force in his front, and that they apparently intended to make a determined resistance. At that time, the rebel force at that point, according to subsequent reports by the rebels themselves, did not exceed ten thousand men. No one doubts now that General McClellan's cautiousness betrayed his judgment, and that a strong and well-directed attack would have swept the rebels out of their works.

In this letter, he began his long-continued complaint of inadequate force. He begged the President to reconsider his order detaching the first corps from his command, as it was his opinion that he should have to fight all the available force of the rebels, not far from the place where he was writing. If he could not have the whole corps, he begged for Franklin and his division. On the sixth, Mr. Stanton replied that Sumner's troops were on the way to him, that Franklin's division was on the advance to Manassas, and that there were no means of transportation to send it forward in time for service in his operations. "All in the power of the government," added the Secretary, "shall be done to sustain you, as occasion may require."

Another day passed away; and, on the date of Mr. Stanton's dispatch, General McClellan wrote again, begging for Franklin's division, complaining that he had no sufficient transportation, and stating that the order forming new departments deprived him of the power of ordering up wagons and troops, absolutely necessary for his advance on Richmond. He requested that the material he had prepared and necessarily left behind, with wagon trains, ammunition; and Woodbury's brigade, might be subject to his order. Mr. Lincoln immediately telegraphed him that his order for forwarding what he had demanded, including Woodbury's brigade, was not, and would not be interfered with, informing him at the same time that he had then more than one hundred thousand troops with him, independent of those under General Wool's command. Mr. Lincoln closed his dispatch with the words: "I think you had better break the enemy's line from Yorktown to Warwick River at once. They will probably use time as advantageously as you can."

Mr. Lincoln, like the whole country, was convinced that there was no such force behind those works as the fears of the General had counted there; and it is now humiliating to learn from the official report of the rebel commander Magruder, that, "with five thousand men, exclusive of the garrisons, we (they) stopped and held in check over one hundred thousand of the enemy." At Gloucester, Yorktown and Mulberry Island, he was obliged to put garrisons amounting to six thousand men, and he had only five thousand men   to defend a line of thirteen miles. With a hundred thousand men at his back, General McClellan went to work with shovels to begin a regular siege. On the ninth of April, Mr. Lincoln wrote him a letter which is so full of wise counsel, kind criticism, and personal good-will, that it deserves record here:

"My Dear Sir—Your dispatches, complaining that you are not properly sustained, while they do not offend me, do pain me very much.

"Blenker's division was withdrawn from you before you left here; and you know the pressure under which I did it, and, as I thought, acquiesced in it—certainly not without reluctance.

"After you left, I ascertained that less than twenty thousand unorganized men, without a single field battery, were all you designed to be left for the defence of Washington and Manassas Junction; and part of this even was to go to General Hooker's old position. General Banks' corps, once designed for Manassas Junction, was diverted and tied up on the line of Winchester and Strasburg, and could not leave it without again exposing the upper Potomac and the Baltimore and Ohio Railroad. This presented, or would present, when McDowell and Sumner should be gone, a great temptation to the enemy to turn back from the Rappahannock and sack Washington. My implicit order that Washington should, by the judgment of all the commanders of army corps, be left entirely secure, had been neglected. It was precisely this that drove me to detain McDowell.

"I do not forget that I was satisfied with your arrangement to leave Banks at Manassas Junction: but, when that arrangement was broken up, and nothing was substituted for it, of course I was constrained to substitute something for it myself. And allow me to ask, do you really think I should permit the line from Richmond, *via* Manassas Junction, to this city, to be entirely open, except what resistance could be presented by less than twenty thousand unorganized troops? This is a question which the country will not allow me to evade.

"There is a curious mystery about the number of troops now with you. When I telegraphed you on the sixth, saying you had over a hundred thousand with you, I had just obtained from the Secretary of War a statement taken, as he said, from your own returns, making one hundred and eight thousand then with you and *en route* to you. You now say you will have but eighty-five thousand when all *en route* to you shall have reached you. How can the discrepancy of twenty-three thousand be accounted for?

"As to General Wool's command, I understand it is doing for you precisely what a like number of your own would have to do if that command was away.

"I suppose the whole force which has gone forward for you is with you by this time. And, if so, I think it is the precise time for you to strike a blow. By delay, the enemy will relatively gain upon you—that is, he will gain faster by fortifications and reinforcements than you can by reinforcements alone. And once more let me tell you, it is indispensable to you that you strike a blow. I am powerless to help this. You will do me the justice to remember I always insisted that going down the bay in search of a field, instead of fighting at or near Manassas, was only shifting, and not surmounting, a difficulty; that we would find the same enemy, and the same or equal intrenchments, at either place. The country will not fail to note—is now noting—that the present hesitation to move upon an intrenched enemy is but the story of Manassas repeated.

"I beg to assure you that I have never written to you or spoken to you in greater kindness of feeling than now, nor with a fuller purpose to sustain you, so far as, in my most anxious judgment, I consistently can. But you must act.

Yours, very truly,   A. LINCOLN.

The President yielded to McClellan, and sent General Franklin to him, with his division; and General McClellan thanked him for his kindness and consideration, adding, "I now understand the matter which I did not before." Certainly his misunderstanding of the matter had not been the result of any lack of effort on the part of the President to make him understand it. Through the whole month in which the great army lay before Yorktown, the President and War Department were fed with dispatches of the most encouraging character. General McClellan was leaving nothing undone to enable him to attack without delay; after receiving reinforcements, he was "confident of results;" he was soon to be "at them;" there was to be "not a moment's unnecessary delay;" he was "getting up the heavy guns, mortars and ammunition quite rapidly;" there were heavy rains, and horrid roads, but he was "making progress all the time." He was making progress in the concentration of troops, certainly, for, on the thirtieth of April, he had, by Adjutant-general

Townsend's report, 130,378 men, of whom 112,392 were reck-oned effective. At this time, he called upon the department for Parrott guns; and, on the first of May, the President wrote him: "Your call for Parrott guns from Washington alarms me—chiefly because it argues indefinite procrastina-tion. Is anything to be done?"

There was something to be done, but the enemy did it. After the absolute waste of a month's time, opportunities, and resources of strength and material, the rebels quietly evacu-ated their position, and retired up the Peninsula. It was the old story of great preparations to fight, and no fighting—no weakening of the enemy. General McClellan thought the success brilliant, if we may judge by his dispatches. It was the costly victory of an engineer. He telegraphed to Mr. Stanton, on the fourth, that he held the entire line of the en-emy's works; that he had thrown all his cavalry and horse artillery, supported by infantry, in pursuit; that no time should be lost, and that he should "push the enemy to the wall." The enemy retired to his second line of works at Williams-burgh without pushing, and took his position behind the wall. Here was fought the battle of Williamsburgh, which McClel-lan designated in his final report as "one of the most brilliant engagements of the war." He bestows the highest praise upon General Hancock, though Hooker had fought with equal gallantry, and encountered greater losses. All did their duty; and when, between four and five o'clock in the afternoon, General McClellan arrived upon the ground (the battle hav-ing commenced early in the morning,) he did his duty, and helped materially toward a favorable result of the action. On the next morning, there was no enemy; and, owing to the bad roads, the lack of food, and the exhaustion of the troops, there could be no immediate pursuit.

On the seventh of May, General Franklin landed at West Point with his division, further up the peninsula, supported by the divisions of Sedgwick, Porter and Richardson. The rebels were obliged to attack, to give the retreating columns from Williamsburgh time and opportunity to pass; but, after a battle of six hours they were repulsed, though not until they had accomplished their object.

General McClellan did not like the organization of the army into corps. The measure did not originate with him, and the men appointed to their command were not men of his choosing. He did not believe in fighting the battle of Williamsburgh. The three corps-commanders, Sumner, Heintzelman and Keyes, were all on the ground; and were regarded by the commanding General as indiscreet in commencing the attack, and incompetent in its conduct.

At this time, Mr. Lincoln, Mr. Stanton and Mr. Chase were all on a visit to Fortress Monroe; and, on the ninth of May, General McClellan took occasion to write to the Secretary of War, asking permission to re-organize the army corps. He wished to return to the organization by divisions, or to be authorized to relieve incompetent commanders of army corps. To give force to his request, he declared in his note that, had he been half an hour later on the field, the army would have been routed, and would have lost everything. He declared that he found on the field "the utmost confusion and incompetency," and added that "at least a thousand lives were really sacrificed by the organization into corps." Mr. Stanton replied that the President, who would write him privately, would give him liberty to suspend the corps organization temporarily, or until further orders. Mr. Lincoln wrote privately, and wrote a very frank and honest letter, dated at Fortress Monroe, of which these were the essential paragraphs:

"I have just assisted the Secretary of War in forming the part of a dispatch to you, relating to army corps, which dispatch, of course, will have reached you long before this will. I wish to say a few words to you privately on this subject. I ordered the army corps organization not only on the unanimous opinion of the twelve Generals of division, but also on the unanimous opinion of every *military man* I could get an opinion from, and every modern military book, yourself only excepted. Of course I did not on my own judgment pretend to understand the subject. I now think it indispensable for you to know how your struggle against it is received in quarters which we cannot entirely disregard. It is looked upon as merely an effort to pamper one or two pets, and to

24

persecute and degrade their supposed rivals. I have had no word from Sumner, Heintzelman and Keyes. The commanders of these corps are of course the three highest officers with you, but I am constantly told that you have no consultation or communication with them, that you consult and communicate with nobody but Fitz John Porter, and perhaps General Franklin. I do not say these complaints are true or just; but, at all events, it is proper you should know of their existence. Do the commanders of corps disobey your orders in anything?

"Are you strong enough, even with my help, to set your foot upon the neck of Sumner, Heintzelman and Keyes, all at once? This is a practical and very serious question to you."

After the receipt of this private letter, General McClellan concluded not to make the change which seemed so essential; but he created two new corps, or "provisional corps," which he placed respectively under the command of Fitz John Porter and General Franklin, the men whom Mr. Lincoln had mentioned as his favorites.

Leaving the army to make its way toward Richmond, events take us back to Fortress Monroe for a brief space, where the Washington dignitaries were consulting and watching the progress of affairs. Nothing could be done on the James River, on account of the presence of the formidable Merrimac; and, in the meantime, Norfolk was held by the rebels. It was desirable to take Norfolk; and an expedition was fitted out at Fortress Monroe, under command of General Wool, for that purpose. To show how this was done, and, at the same time, to illustrate the free and easy manner in which the President dealt with his officers, we shall let Mr. Lincoln tell his own "little story." In a subsequent conversation with Major General Garfield, he said: "By the way, Garfield, do you know that Chase, Stanton, General Wool and I had a campaign of our own? We went down to Fortress Monroe in Chase's revenue cutter, and consulted with Admiral Goldsborough on the feasibility of taking Norfolk by landing on the North shore and making a march of eight miles. The Admiral said there was no landing on that shore, and we should have to double the cape, and approach the place from the south side, which would be a long journey, and a difficult one. I asked him if he had ever tried to find a landing, and he replied that he had not. I then told him a story of a fellow in Illinois who had studied law, but had never tried a case. He was sued, and, not having confidence in his ability to manage his own case, employed a lawyer to manage it for him. He had only a confused idea of the meaning of law terms, but was anxious to make a display of learning, and, on the trial, constantly made suggestions to his lawyer, who paid but little attention to him. At last, fearing that his lawyer was not handling the opposing counsel very well, he lost all his patience; and, springing to his feet, cried out, 'Why don't you go at him with a *capias* or a *surre-butter* or something, and not stand there like a confounded old *nudum-pactum?*' 'Now, Admiral,' said I, 'if you don't know that there is no landing on the North shore, I want you to find out.'"

Continuing his narrative, Mr. Lincoln said: "The Admiral took the hint; and, taking Chase and Wool along, with a company or two of marines, he went on a voyage of discovery, and Stanton and I remained at Fortress Monroe. That night we went to bed, but not to sleep, for we were very anxious for the fate of the expedition. About two o'clock the next morning, I heard the heavy tread of Wool ascending the stairs. I went out into the parlor and found Stanton hugging Wool in the most enthusiastic manner, as he announced that he had found a landing, and had captured Norfolk."

Thus Norfolk came into our possession on the ninth of May; and on the eleventh the Merrimac was blown up by command of her own officers, releasing our navy from its long durance, though its passage up the James was repulsed by a heavy battery at Drury's Bluff.

General McClellan was still busy with his dispatches. Of the nature of these dispatches, we can judge by the replies of the President. Under date of May fifteenth, the latter writes: "I have done all I could, and can, to sustain you. I hoped that the opening of James River, and putting Wool and Burnside in communication with an open road to Richmond, or to you, had effected something in that direction." For five days our army lay at Williamsburgh, on account of bad roads, which roads the rebel army found it convenient to pass with sufficient rapidity to place themselves within the outer defenses of Richmond, a distance of nearly forty miles. They were, at least, all across the Chickahominy River.

Head-quarters reached White House on the sixteenth. Two days previously, the General had written the President that he could bring only eighty thousand men into the field, and that he wanted every man the government could send him. Mr. Stanton wrote him on the eighteenth that the President was unwilling to uncover the capital entirely, but desired that he would extend his right wing to the north of Richmond, so that McDowell could communicate with him by his left wing. "At your earnest call for reinforcements," said Mr Stanton, "he is sent forward to co-operate in the reduction of Richmond, but charged, in attempting this, not to uncover the city of Washington." General McClellan seemed to have no idea that the capital was in danger, and replied to this that he wished McDowell to join him by water. He feared that he could not join him overland in season for the coming battle, and complained that McDowell was not put more directly under his command. On the twenty-fourth of May, the President wrote, saying that McDowell and Shields would move for him on the following Monday, Shields' troops being too much worn to march earlier; and that they had so weakened their line already that Banks, in the Shenandoah valley, was in peril, and had met with a serious loss. On the same day, Mr. Lincoln was obliged, in order to save the capital, to suspend McDowell's movement toward McClellan; for the rebel General Jackson had begun a desperate push for Harper's Ferry. Against this action of the President, McClellan protested; and, on the twenty-fifth, the former wrote him a note, giving a full statement of the situation:

"Your dispatch received. General Banks was at Strasburg with about six thousand men, Shields having been taken from him to swell a column for McDowell to aid you at Richmond, and the rest of his force scattered at various places. On the twenty-third, a force of seven-thousand to ten thousand fell upon one regiment and two companies guarding the bridge at Front Royal, destroying it entirely; crossed the Shenandoah, and on the twenty-fourth, yesterday, pushed on to get north of Banks on the road to Winchester General Banks ran a race with them, beating them into Winchester yesterday evening This morning a battle ensued between the two forces, in which General Banks was beaten back into full retreat toward Martinsburg, and probably is broken up into a total rout. Geary, on the Manassas Gap Railroad, just now reports that Jackson is now near Front Royal with ten thousand troops, following up and supporting, as I understand, the force now pursuing Banks. Also, that another force of ten thousand is near Orleans, following on in the same direction. Stripped bare, as we are here, I will do all we can to prevent them crossing the Potomac at Harper's Ferry or above. McDowell has about twenty thousand of his forces moving back to the vicinity of Front Royal; and Fremont, who was at Franklin, is moving to Harrisonburg: both these movements intended to get in the enemy's rear.

" One more of McDowell's brigades is ordered through here to Harper's Ferry; the rest of his forces remain for the present at Fredericksburg. We are sending such regiments and dribs from here and Baltimore as we can spare to Harper's Ferry, supplying their places in some sort, calling in militia from the adjacent states. We also have eighteen cannon on the road to Harper's Ferry, of which arm there is not one at that point. This is now our situation.

"*If McDowell's force was now beyond our reach, we should be entirely helpless. Apprehension of something like this, and no unwillingness to sustain you, has always been my reason for withholding McDowell's forces from you.*

" Please understand this, and do the best you can with the forces you have."

A few hours after this dispatch was sent, the President sent another, stating that the enemy was driving General Banks' before him, and was threatening Leesburgh and Geary on the Manassas Gap Railroad; that the movement looked like a general and concerted one—such an one as he would not make if he were acting on the purpose of a very desperate defense of Richmond; and that, if McClellan did not at once attack that capital, he would probably have to give up the job, and come to the defense of Washington.

This dispatch moved the General. General Fitz John Porter was sent to attack a rebel force near Hanover Court-

House, which he did with favorable results. General Mc-Clellan described it as a perfect rout of the enemy, at which the President wrote a dispatch, stating his gratification, but expressing his surprise that the Richmond and Fredericksburg Railroad was not seized again. On the twenty-sixth, Mr. Lincoln informed General McClellan that Banks was safe at Williamsport. Still the General wanted troops sent to him by water, still he wanted more troops, and still the President assured him, again and again, that he was doing and would do for him everything he could do, consistently with the safety of Washington.

A movement was commenced on the twenty-fifth to cross the Chickahominy; and, on the thirtieth and thirty-first, a battle was fought, which resulted in such a repulse of the rebels, and such heavy losses to them as greatly to alarm Richmond, and impress upon the city the belief that an immediate and fatal pursuit would be made by the federal forces. After the engagement, General McClellan crossed the river, but found the roads so bad that artillery could not be handled, and that pursuit was impossible; although the rebels had found it convenient to get back, and expected to be pursued. The following day, General Heintzelman sent a reconnoitering party within four miles of Richmond, without finding an enemy. Informed of this, General McClellan ordered the force to fall back to its old position: and on the same day wrote to Washington that he only waited for the river to fall, to cross over the rest of his army, and make a general attack; and that the *morale* of his army was such that he could venture much, not fearing the odds against him.

McClellan had met great losses by battle and disease; and the government did what it could for him, by placing under his command the troops at Fortress Monroe, and by sending to him McCall's division of McDowell's corps. On the seventh of June, the General wrote to the Secretary of War that he should be ready to move as soon as McCall should reach him, and McCall reached him on the tenth. On that day, he had caught a rumor that Beauregard had reinforced the rebels in Richmond; and then he wanted some of Halleck's army in Tennessee sent to him. The Secretary assured him that Beauregard and his army were not in Richmond, but that Halleck would be urged to comply with the request, so far as he could do so with safety. The particular friends of McClellan were busy at this time with suspicions and reports that the President and Secretary of War were trying to sacrifice him; and, to put an extinguisher on this, Mr. Stanton wrote: "Be assured, General, that there never has been a moment when my desire has been otherwise than to aid you with my whole heart, mind and strength, since the hour we first met; and, whatever others may say, for their own purposes, you have never had, and never can have, any one more truly your friend, or more anxious to support you, or more joyful than I shall be at the success which I have no doubt will soon be achieved by your arms."

With a long series of dispatches in which General McClellan quarrels with the relations which General McDowell's troops held to his command, it is not necessary to burden these pages. The President wished to hold on to McDowell's troops, and still have them assist McClellan. He had sent McCall's division by water; but these were directed to be posted so that they could unite with the corps coming by land, and to be kept under McDowell. McClellan saw in this arrangement only ambition on the part of McDowell; and, in one of his dispatches, wrote the government: "If I cannot fully control all his troops, I want none of them, but would prefer to fight the battle with what I have, and let others be responsible for the results," which was equivalent to saying that he would rather be whipped without McDowell's troops, under the circumstances, than be victorious with them.

On the twenty-first, the General sent a dispatch to the President, saying that ten thousand men had been sent from Richmond to reinforce Jackson. Mr. Lincoln informed him of the confirmation of the news, and told him that it was as good to him as a reinforcement of an equal number.

Thus the time passed away, while his army was wasting

with disease in the Chickahominy swamps, and he, with every fresh dispatch, was just "about to move." He had lain there a month; and the rebels thought it was time for him to move in the other direction. He saw the preparations, and, anticipating a defeat, he wrote to inform the government that the rebel force before him was two hundred thousand strong, and that, in case of a disaster, the responsibility could not be thrown on his shoulders. This kind of talk troubled Mr. Lincoln. "I give you all I can," said he, "and act on the presumption that you will do the best you can with what you have; while you continue, ungenerously, I think, to assume that I could give you more if I would." At this very moment, as it appears by McClellan's report, he had ordered supplies to a point on the James River, to which he expected to retreat. On the afternoon of the twenty-sixth, the extreme right of the army was attacked; and, from that time until the army had wheeled back to the James River, there was no rest. They fell back, fighting every day, inflicting terrible losses on the enemy, and receiving sad punishment themselves. The General's pen was busy still, as it might be, for he took no part in the engagements. If he had ten thousand fresh troops, he could take Richmond, he thought; but, as it was, he could only cover his retreat. He was not responsible for the result; he must have more troops. "If I save this army now," said he to the Secretary of War, "I tell you plainly that I owe no thanks to you, or to any persons in Washington; you have done your best to sacrifice this army." Was ever such petulance, such insolence, borne with such patience before? The President wrote him: "Save your army at all events." The President would not blame him. "We protected Washington," said he, "and the enemy concentrated on you. Had we stripped Washington, he would have been upon us before the troops sent could have got to you. Less than a week ago, you notified us that reinforcements were leaving Richmond to come in front of us. It is the nature of the case, and neither you nor the government is to blame." General McClellan called upon the President for a reinforcement of fifty thousand troops, to which Mr. Lincoln replied: "When you ask for fifty thousand men to be promptly sent to you, you surely labor under some gross mistake of fact. Recently, you sent papers showing your disposal of forces made last spring, for the defense of Washington, and advising a return to that plan. I find it included, in and about Washington, seventy-five thousand men. Now, please be assured that I have not men enough to fill that very plan by fifteen thousand." Further on he says: "I have not, outside of your army, seventy-five thousand men east of the mountains. Thus the idea of sending you fifty thousand men, or any other considerable forces promptly, is simply absurd." He closed by assuring him that he did not blame him for his disasters, asking that he would be equally generous toward the government, and adjuring him to save his army. It was absolutely impossible for the government to send reinforcements at once, to enable McClellan to assume the offensive. On the seventh of July, the General, who seems to have had a *penchant* for giving general advice to the government, found time to write a long letter to Mr. Lincoln, telling him that he thought the war should not look to the "subjugation of the people of any state, *in any event*." He would have no political execution of persons, no confiscation, and no forcible abolition of slavery; though it appears that he did not object to the practical abolition of slavery upon military necessity, and by military means. "A declaration of radical views, especially upon slavery, will rapidly disintegrate our present armies," said the General: but he did not seem to produce a profound impression upon the mind of the Executive.

The President determined to ascertain, by personal inspection, the condition of the army; and, on the eighth, visited General McClellan at Harrison's Landing. At this time it was understood that the enemy was organizing his forces for an advance on Washington. It was the opinion of Mr. Lincoln, and of the corps commanders, that the army should repair to Washington, but General McClellan was against it. The army, he declared, ought not to be withdrawn. It ought to be promptly reinforced, and thrown again upon Richmond. He wanted the whole of General Burnside's command in North Carolina to help him. He dreaded the effects of a retreat upon the *morale* of his army, although he had just tried it, and declared, in a dispatch of the eleventh, that the army was in "fine spirits."

On the thirteenth, the President wrote him that one hundred and sixty thousand men had gone with his army to the Peninsula, and that, when he was with him, a few days before, he was informed that only eighty-six thousand remained, leaving seventy-three thousand five hundred to be accounted for. After making all allowances for deaths, wounds and sickness, fifty thousand men were still absent. General McClellan replied that 38,250 men were absent by authority. Here was a reinforcement at command worth having. Why did the General let them go? Why did he not call them back?

It was determined at last to withdraw the army from the Peninsula, and the order found McClellan still protesting. "The true defense of Washington" was just where he was. He received the order to remove his sick on the second of August; but it was not until the twenty-third that General Franklin's corps started from Fortress Monroe, and not until the twenty-sixth that McClellan himself arrived at Alexandria. On the following day, he was ordered to take the entire direction of the forwarding of the troops from Alexandria to assist General Pope, who, two months before, had taken the consolidated commands of McDowell and Fremont, the latter retiring at his own request, and being replaced by Sigel. That portion of the army of the Potomac which arrived before McClellan, pushed off at once to reinforce Pope; but not a man that came afterwards took any part in those battles by which that General was driven back upon Washington. The dispatches by which he was urged, ordered, almost besought, to forward troops to the assistance of Pope, would fill several pages of this volume; and, when we know how promptly troops went forward before his arrival, it is impossible to find in his

miserable excuses for inaction anything but a disposition to
embarrass Pope, and deprive him of success.   It is a hard judgment, and a sad one to render; but it must be rendered, or
the conclusion is inevitable that the General was either incompetent to comprehend the emergency or afraid to meet it.
It is impossible to find an apology for his failure to act in this
great necessity, that would not damage his reputation as a
military man.

The triumphant rebels moved up the Potomac with the evident intention of crossing and invading Maryland.   No time
was to be lost.   Under the representation that the army of
the Potomac would serve under no commander but Mc-
Clellan, General Pope was relieved, and the former placed in
command of all the troops.   On the fourth of September, he
commenced moving into Maryland for the purpose of expelling
the rebel forces.   Washington was in a panic, and the whole
country was in a condition of the most feverish excitement.
Still he called for reinforcements.   He wanted to uncover
Washington again, and said that, "even if Washington should
be taken," it "would not bear comparison with the ruin and
disaster that would follow a single defeat of this army."
When that same army was fighting under Pope, it did not,
apparently, impress him in that way at all.

The battle of South Mountain was fought on the fourteenth,
and, on the seventeenth, the battle of Antietam.   The rebels'
were whipped, and recrossed the Potomac, broken and dis-
heartened.   General McClellan did not pursue, owing to the
condition of his army, one whole corps of which (Fitz John
Porter's) had not been in the action at all; and, as if the habit
of calling for reinforcements had become chronic, renewed his
application for more troops.   There he remained, with no
effort to follow up his victory.   The President was impatient,
but, to be sure that he did no injustice to the General, he visited the army in person, to ascertain what its real condition
was.   The result was an order, issued on the sixth, for the
army to move across the Potomac, and give battle to the enemy, or drive him south.   The President promised him thirty

thousand new men, if he would move across the river between the enemy and Washington.   If he would prefer to move up the Shenandoah valley, he could only spare him fifteeen thousand.   Then General McClellan began to make inquiries, and call for shoes and other supplies; but he did not begin to move. A few days afterward, the rebel General Stuart made a raid into Pennsylvania, with a large cavalry force, keeping General McClellan busy, and calling forth from him the confident statement that the daring raiders would be bagged; but they went completely around the army, and escaped in safety.   A note written to the General by Mr. Lincoln, on the thirteenth, so well illustrates the situation at the moment, and, at the same time, betrays so fully his knowledge of affairs and the intelligence of his military criticisms, that it must be given entire:

"My Dear Sir—You remember my speaking to you of what I called your over-cautiousness.   Are you not over-cautious when you assume that you can not do what the enemy is constantly doing?   Should you not claim to be at least his equal in prowess, and act upon the claim?

"As I understand, you telegraphed General Halleck that you can not subsist your army at Winchester, unless the railroad from Harper's Ferry to that point be put in working order.   But the enemy does now subsist his army at Winchester, at a distance nearly twice as great from railroad transportation as you would have to do, without the railroad last named.   He now wagons from Culpepper Court-House, which is just about twice as far as you would have to do from Harper's Ferry.   He is certainly not more than half as well provided with wagons as you are.   I certainly should be pleased for you to have the advantage of the railroad from Harper's Ferry to Winchester; but it wastes all the remainder of autumn to give it to you, and, in fact, ignores the question of *time*, which can not and must not be ignored.

"Again, one of the standard maxims of war, as you know, is, "to operate upon the enemy's communications as much as possible without exposing your own."   You seem to act as if this applies *against* you, but can not apply in your *favor*.   Change positions with the enemy, and think you not he would break your communication with Richmond within the next twenty-four hours?   You dread his going into Pennsylvania.   But, if he does so in full force, he gives up his communications to you absolutely, and you have nothing to do but to follow and ruin him; if he does so with less than full force, fall upon and beat what is left behind all the easier.

" Exclusive of the water line, you are now nearer Richmond than the enemy is by the route that you *can* and he *must* take. Why can you not reach there before him, unless you admit that he is more than your equal on a march? His route is the arc of a circle, while yours is the chord. The roads are as good on yours as on his.

" You know I desired, but did not order you, to cross the Potomac below, instead of above, the Shenandoah and Blue Ridge. My idea was, that this would at once menace the enemy's communications, which I would seize if he would permit. If he should move northward, I would follow him closely, holding his communications. If he should prevent our seizing his communications, and move toward Richmond, I would press closely to him, fight him if a favorable opportunity should present, and at least try to beat him to Richmond on the inside track. I say 'try;' if we never try, we shall never succeed. If he make a stand at Winchester, moving neither north nor south, I would fight him there, on the idea that, if we cannot beat him when he bears the wastage of coming to us, we never can when we bear the wastage of going to him. This proposition is a simple truth, and is too important to be lost sight of for a moment. In coming to us, he tenders us an advantage which we should not waive. We should not so operate as to merely drive. him away. As we must beat him somewhere, or fail finally, we can do it, if at all, easier near to us than far away. If we cannot beat the enemy where he now is, we never can, he again being within the intrenchments of Richmond. Recurring to the idea of going to Richmond on the inside track, the facility of supplying from the side away from the enemy is remarkable; as it were, by the different spokes of a wheel, extending from the hub toward the rim;—and this whether you move directly by the chord, or on the inside arc, hugging the Blue Ridge more closely. The chord-line, as you see, carries you by Aldie, Haymarket, and Fredericksburg, and you see how turnpikes, railroads, and finally the Potomac by Acquia Creek, meet you at all points from Washington. The same, only the lines lengthened a little, if you press closer to the Blue Ridge part of the way. The gaps through the Blue Ridge I understand to be about the following distances from Harper's Ferry, to wit: Vestal's, five miles; Gregory's, thirteen; Snicker's, eighteen; Ashby's, twenty-eight; Manassas, thirty-eight; Chester, forty-five; and Thornton's, fifty-three. I should think it preferable to take the route nearest the enemy, disabling him to make an important move without your knowledge, and compelling him to keep his forces together for dread of you. The gaps would enable you to attack if you should wish. For a great part of the way you would be practically between the enemy and both Washington and Richmond, enabling us to spare you the greatest number of troops from here. When, at length, running to Richmond ahead of him enables him to move this way, if he does so, turn and attack him in the rear. But I think he should be engaged long before such point is reached. It is all easy if our troops march as well as the enemy, and it is unmanly to say they cannot do it. This letter is in no sense an order."

Still the government urged the General forward, and still he had excuses for not going forward. His horses were fatigued, and had the sore tongue, he said; and the President could not forbear asking him what his horses had done since Antietam that would fatigue anything. The General did not like what the President said about his cavalry, and called out another note from Mr. Lincoln, who, under date of October twenty-sixth, wrote him that if he had done any injustice he deeply regretted it. He added: "To be told, after five weeks' total inactivity of the army, and during which period we had sent to that army every fresh horse we possibly could, amounting in the whole to 7,918, that the cavalry horses were too much fatigued to move, presented a very cheerless, almost hopeless prospect for the future." On the fifth of November, the army had crossed—just a month after the order to cross was given;—and, of course, the rebels had made all the needful preparations, either for battle or retreat.

But patience at Washington, tried long, and terribly tried, had become exhausted; and, on the same day on which the General announced the army all across the Potomac, an order arrived relieving him of his command.

Military men will judge this remarkable campaign in the light of their own science; but the civilian will read its history by the light of its results, and by the light of those later magnificent operations of Thomas in Tennessee,—of Sheridan in the Shenandoah valley and near Richmond,—of Sherman's march from Chattanooga through the heart of the rebellion and up the Atlantic coast, with cities falling before and on either side of him as if swept by a tornado,—and of Grant before Vicksburg, or in the Wilderness and at Richmond, capturing whole armies, and finishing up a war so weakly begun. In the light of these operations, the campaign of McClellan looks like the work of a boy or the play of a man.

With General McClellan's motives, the writer has no desire to deal. That he became the favorite of men whose heart was not in the war, may well be considered his misfortune. That he became the representative of the party opposed to the administration in its general policy, on all subjects, was not inconsistent with his desire and determination to do his whole military duty. That he entertained and acted upon the determination to injure the administration for political purposes, there is very little evidence; and there is absolutely no evidence that the administration, through any jealousy of him, withheld its support from him, that he might be ruined and put out of its way. Such a supposition cannot live a moment in the light of Mr. Lincoln's life. If there is one fact in McClellan's campaign that stands out with peculiar prominence, it is that both Mr. Lincoln and Mr. Stanton sent him every man they could spare, consistently with the safety of the capital, by the General's own showing at first, and by the showing of events at last. On one side, we see the presumptuous volunteering of general political and military advice, the unreasonable call for reinforcements when assured again and again that he had every man that could be given him, expostulations against government orders, quarreling with government arrangements, absolute criminations of the government, unaccountable hesitations and boyish inefficiency; while, on the other, there were almost unbroken respectfulness, patience and toleration, ardent desire for the best results, constant urgency to action, constant sacrifice of personal feeling and opinion, and a patent wish to do everything practicable or possible to give the commanding General everything he wanted.

That General McClellan loved power, is evident; and it is just as evident that it was not pleasant to him to share it with any one; but, on the whole, there is no evidence that he was not a good, well-meaning, and patriotic man. The difficulty was that he was great mainly in his infirmities. He was not a great man, nor a great general. He was a good organizer of military force, and a good engineer; he was a good theorizer,

and wrote good English; he had that quality of personal mag-
netism which drew the hearts of his soldiers to him; but he
was not a man of action, of expedients, of quick judgment,
of dash and daring, of great, heroic deeds. He was never
ready. There were many evidences that he held a theory of
his own as to the mode of conducting the war, and that, independently of the government, he endeavored to pursue it;
but, even if he did, his failure must always be regarded as
mainly due to constitutional peculiarities for which he was not
responsible.

This chapter should be concluded here, but space must be
taken for a very brief record of the immediately succeeding
fortunes of the army of the Potomac, and a hurried chronicle
of the other military events of the year. On the retirement
of General McClellan, General Burnside was placed in command of the army of the Potomac; and, at the same time, the
rebel army commenced falling back upon Richmond. On the
fourteenth, the army left its camps, and marched for Fredericksburg, arriving there at about the same time with the rebel
army. Burnside was obliged to wait for his pontoons, and
is was not until the twelfth of December that he was ready to
cross. Only a feeble resistance was made to his passage, but
it was a worse than fruitless procedure. The attempt to
carry the hills was a failure, and he was obliged to withdraw
his army, with a loss of from ten thousand to twelve thousand
men. This gave a sad finishing up to the year's sad business,
with this ill-starred army.

The opening of the campaign of 1862 found the government with a newly created navy at its command. Mr. Welles,
though reputed inefficient, had accomplished what no other
man had ever done in an equal space of time. Not only were
the southern ports efficiently blockaded, but materials for formidable naval expeditions were prepared. General Burnside,
at the head of an expedition, captured Roanoke Island on the
eighth of February, with three thousand prisoners; and subsequently engaged in other successful movements on the coast
and up the rivers of North Carolina. On the nineteenth of

June, Charleston was attacked, without success. In the latter part of April, Forts Jackson and St. Philip, below New Orleans, were assalled by the fleet under Commodore Farragut, and so far disalbed that they were passed. As a consequence, New Orleans fell into our hands, all the rebel troops fleeing the city. This affair was equally brilliant in its execution and important in its results, and encouraged the government as much as it distressed and discouraged its foes. Fort Pulaski, guarding the entrance to Savannah, was also taken, and that port effectually shut up.

While these much desired, though hardly expected, successes attended the operations at the mouth of the Mississippi, events of equal importance were in progress on its tributaries. At the West movements were on a gigantic scale. The capture of Forts Henry and Donelson on the Cumberland River drew the enemy out of Bowling Green and Nashville, and gave us Columbus. General Price was driven out of Missouri. Island Number Ten and Forts Pillow and Randolph all fell into our hands, and then our forces occupied Memphis. A combination of all the rebel armies at Corinth surprised our troops at Pittsburg Landing, under General Grant, on the morning of April sixth, with overwhelming numbers, and drove them back to the protection of our gunboats; but on the following day, through the opportune arrival of General Buell, with his forces, the rebels were pushed back into retreat, with terrible losses, leaving our victorious army almost as badly punished as themselves. The victory was so decided that Mr. Lincoln was moved to issue a Proclamation of Thanksgiving, in which he also recognized the other victories that have been chronicled. The people were called upon to "render thanks to our Heavenly Father for these inestimable blessings," and were also desired to "implore spiritual consolation in behalf of all those who have been brought into affliction by the casualties and calamities of civil war."

The rebels fell back to Corinth, and, remaining there a few days, retired to Grenada. A powerful effort of General Bragg to invade Kentucky, made later in the season, for the purpose

25

mainly of gathering reinforcements, encouraging the secession spirit, and collecting supplies, was a failure, in nearly every point; and, after a battle at Terryville, he retreated. General Rosecrans was attacked at Corinth by a powerful confederate force, but he repulsed the rebels with great loss. At the very last of the year, there was a severe fight at Murfreesboro which resulted favorably to our arms; and the new year of 1863 found a great advance made toward the entire redemption of Kentucky, Tennessee and Missouri, from the presence of rebel armies and the prevalence of rebel influence.

CHAPTER XXIII.

WHILE these operations, pursued upon a most gigantic scale, for crushing the rebellion and defending the national existence were in progress, Mr. Lincoln was taking every opportunity, personally and through his generals, to assure the people of the South that he meant them no ill. No father ever dealt more considerately and carefully with erring children than he did with those who had determined to break up the government. On the twenty-fifth of July, he issued a proclamation, in pursuance of a section in the confiscation act, passed by Congress a few days previously, warning all persons to cease participating in the rebellion, and adjuring them to return to their allegiance to the government, on pain of the forfeitures and seizures provided by the act.

There had been men—and there continued to be throughout the war—who believed, or pretended to believe, that peace and Union could be won without war—that friendly negotiation would settle everything. There never was any basis for these fancies, except in rebel desires to embarrass the government, or in party policy among those opposed to the administration, or in the hearts of simple men who believed that reason and common sense had a place in the counsels of the rebel leaders. From the beginning of the rebellion to the end, there was not a time in which peace could have been procured, short of an acknowledgment of the independence of the confederate rebel states, as events have proved. Mr. Lincoln understood this, and understood better than the country generally the desperate men with whom he had to deal; yet he never repelled those who thought they had found some way to peace besides the bloody way. Late in 1862, a period which showed decided advantages won by the Union forces, regarded as a whole, Fernando Wood, the man who, as Mayor of New York, had advocated the separate secession of that metropolis and its erection into a free city, wrote Mr. Lincoln a letter, stating that, on the twenty-fifth of November, he was reliably advised that "The southern states would send representatives to the next Congress," provided that a full and general amnesty should permit them to do so. Mr. Wood urged his point with ardent professions of loyalty, and with arguments drawn from Mr. Lincoln's inaugural; but Mr. Lincoln passed by his arguments and exhortations, and, in a reply dated December twelfth, said that the most important part of his (Wood's) letter related to the alleged fact that men from the South were ready to appear in Congress, on the terms stated. "I strongly suspect your information will prove to be groundless," said Mr. Lincoln; "nevertheless, I thank you for communicating it to me. Understanding the phrase in the paragraph above quoted, 'the southern states would send representatives to the next Congress,' to be substantially the same as that 'the people of the southern states would cease resistance, and would re-inaugurate, submit to, and maintain, the national authority, within the limits of such states, under the Constitution of the United States,' I say that in such case the war would cease on the part of the United States, and that if, within a reasonable time, a full and general amnesty were necessary to such an end, it would not be withheld."

Mr. Wood thought the President ought to make an effort to verify his (Wood's) statement, by permitting a correspondence to take place between the rebels, and gentlemen "whose former political and social relations with the leaders of the southern revolt" would make them good media for the purpose, the correspondence all to be submitted to Mr. Lincoln. The latter, however, knew Mr. Wood, and knew that he bore no good-will to him, or his administration, or the country; and he told him that he did not think it would do any good to communicate what he had said to the South, either formally or informally, for they already knew it. Neither did he think it the time to stop military operations for negotiations. If Mr. Wood had any positive information, he should be glad to get it; and such information might be more valuable before the first of January than after it. At this, Mr. Wood was filled with "profound regret;" and proceeded to read Mr. Lincoln a solemn lecture on his Constitutional obligations, which, doubtless, made a profound impression upon the mind of the President, as he was not known, in a single instance, to be unmindful of those obligations afterwards. The kernel of this nut was in the words: "Your emancipation proclamation told of punishment. Let another be issued, speaking the language of mercy, and breathing the spirit of conciliation." Mr. Wood was interposing on behalf of his southern friends, to prevent a final proclamation of emancipation; and he knew this was to come on the first of January, and that Mr. Lincoln's allusion to that date was a gentle hint to him that the executive purposes were undisturbed and that he was understood.

But we are getting ahead of great events which were destined to have a radical influence upon the war, upon the sentiments and sympathies of Christendom, upon the social institutions of the country, and the destinies of a race. Mr. Wood's allusion to the emancipation proclamation touched a document and an event of immeasurable importance; and to these we now turn our attention.

Mr. Lincoln had tried faithfully, in accordance with his oath of office and his repeated professions, to save the Union without disturbing a single institution which lived under it. He had warned the insurgent states of a measure touching slavery that their contumacy would render necessary. He had besought the border slave states to take themselves out of the way of that impending measure. He had braved the criminations and the impatience of his friends for his tenderness toward an institution which the Constitution protected. He had been accused of being under the pro-slavery influence of the border states; yet, during all this time, he had entertained the emancipation of the slaves as a measure which would be almost sure to come in time, and which he had determined should come just so soon as it could be justified to his own conscience and to history, as a military necessity. In no other event could he take this step, consistently with his oath.

Emancipation was a measure of ineffable moment, and one which dwelt in Mr. Lincoln's thoughts by day and by night. By his own subsequent revelations, it was a measure which, upon his knees, he had presented to his Maker. The events of the Peninsular campaign were connected in his mind with the tenacity with which he held to the unchristian institution. He sought not only for the people's will upon the subject, but the will of God; and there is no question that he regarded the misfortunes of the army of the Potomac as providentially connected with the relations of the government to the great curse which was the motive of the rebellion.

Fortunately, we have the record of Mr. Lincoln's reasoning upon the subject, in a letter which he wrote to Mr. A. G. Hodges of Frankfort, Kentucky, April 4th, 1864. Mr. Hodges had previously had a conversation with him, and had requested him to put into writing the substance of his remarks. The President complied; and, to show that he had acted in his emancipation policy purely upon military necessity, stated that, although he was naturally anti-slavery, and could not remember when he did not think and feel that slavery was wrong, he never understood that the presidency conferred upon him any right to act upon that judgment and feeling. He understood that his oath of office forbade the practical indulgence of his abstract moral hatred of slavery. He had declared that, many times, in many ways. But he shall say the rest in his own language:

"I did understand, however, that very oath to preserve the Constitution to the best of my ability, imposed upon me the duty of preserving, by every indispensable means, that government—that nation of which that Constitution was the organic law. Was it possible to lose the nation and yet preserve the Constitution? By general law, life *and* limb must be protected; yet often a limb must be amputated to save a life, but a life is never wisely given to save a limb. I felt that measures, otherwise unconstitutional, might become lawful by becoming indispensable to the preservation of the Constitution through the preservation of the nation. Right or wrong, I assumed this ground, and now avow it. I could not feel that, to the best of my ability, I had even tried to preserve the Constitution, if, to preserve slavery, or any minor matter, I should permit the wreck of government, country, and Constitution altogether. When, early in the war, General Fremont attempted military emancipation, I forbade it, because I did not then think it an indispensable necessity. When, a little later, General Cameron, then Secretary of War, suggested the arming of the blacks, I objected, because I did not yet think it an indispensable necessity.* When, still later, General Hunter attempted military emancipation, I again forbade it, because I did not yet think the indispensable necessity had come. When, in March and May and July, 1862, I made earnest and successive appeals to the border states to favor compensated emancipation, I believed the indispensable necessity for military emancipation and arming the blacks would come, unless averted by that measure. They declined the proposition; and I was, in my best judgment, driven to the alternative of either surrendering the Union, and with it the Constitution, or of laying strong hand upon the colored element. I chose the latter."

With Mr. Lincoln's statement of the results of his action, which completes the letter, we have nothing at present to do. We have thus the political and military reasons for proclaiming emancipation in Mr. Lincoln's own language; and we are scarcely less fortunate in a record of his personal struggles and feelings, made by Mr. F. B. Carpenter, who had the privilege of frequent intimate conversations with Mr. Lincoln, while he was employed at the White House, upon his picture commemorative of a scene in the event itself.

It was mid-summer in 1862, when, things having gone on

---

* This allusion is to a passage of Mr. Cameron's annual report, which he had sent off to the press for publication without receiving Mr. Lincoln's approval. The publication of the objectionable paragraph was suppressed by telegraph from Washington, while the fact that Mr. Cameron ventured upon such an act without consulting the President, occasioned him great annoyance and vexation.

from bad to worse, he felt that he must "change his tactics or lose his game." So, without consulting his cabinet, or giving them any knowledge of what he was doing, he prepared the original draft of the Proclamation. Now it should be remembered, in order to understand Mr. Lincoln's peculiarity of arguing against his own conclusions, until his time should come for uttering them, that this was before the date of his letter to Horace Greeley, already given to the reader, in which he gives no hint of his determination, but only lays out the ground upon which he should make it. It was also previous to a visit which he received from a body of Chicago clergymen, who called to urge upon him the emancipation policy. The proclamation was all written; and it was a full month after its utterance had been determined on in Cabinet meeting, when he told these clergymen: "I do not want to issue a document that the whole world will see must necessarily be inoperative, like the Pope's bull against the comet." He wished them, however, not to misunderstand him. He had simply indicated some of the difficulties that had stood in his way; but he had not decided against a proclamation of liberty to the slaves. "Whatever shall appear to be God's will," said he, "I will do." Throughout this affair, and indeed in all the great affairs in which he took part, he followed the old practice of his legal career, of arguing his opponent's side of the question—often for the simple purpose, evidently, of winning support for his own convictions.

Sometime during the last of July, or the first part of August, he called a cabinet meeting. None of the members knew the occasion of the meeting, and for some time they were unable to ascertain, for there was a delay. What was its cause? Here was an august body of men. All the cabinet were present excepting Mr. Blair, who came in afterwards. Mr. Lincoln had before him a document which he knew was to perpetuate his name to all futurity,—a document which involved the liberty of four millions of human beings then living, and of untold millions then unborn,—which changed the policy of the government and the course and character of the war,—which revolutionized the social institutions of more than a third of the nation,—which brought all the governments of Christendom into new relations to the rebellion,—and which involved Mr. Lincoln's recognition of the will of the Divine Ruler of the universe. It was the supreme moment of his life. Did he feel it to be so? He did; and he took his own way of showing it. He took down from a shelf a copy of "Artemus Ward—His Book," and read an entire chapter of that literary harlequin's drollery, giving himself up to laughter the most hearty, until some of the dignified personages around him were far more pained than amused. Little did those men understand the pressure of the occasion upon Mr. Lincoln's mind, and the necessity of this diversion.

A member of this noble and notable group has said that, on closing the trifling volume, the whole tone and manner of the President changed instantaneously; and, rising to a grandeur of demeanor that inspired in all a profound respect, akin to awe, he announced to them the object of the meeting. He had written a proclamation of emancipation, and had determined to issue it. He had not called them together to ask their advice on the general question, because he had determined it for himself. He wished to inform them of his purpose, and to receive such suggestions upon minor points as they might be moved to make. Mr. Chase wished the language stronger with reference to arming the blacks. Mr. Blair deprecated the policy, because it would cost the administration the fall elections; but nothing was said which the President had not anticipated, until Mr. Seward said: "Mr. President, I approve of the proclamation, but I question the expediency of its issue at this juncture. The depression of the public mind consequent upon our repeated reverses is so great that I fear the effect of so important a step. It may be viewed as the last measure of an exhausted government— a cry for help—the government stretching forth its hands to Ethiopia, instead of Ethiopia stretching forth her hands to the government—our last shriek on the retreat." He further advised Mr. Lincoln to postpone the measure until it could be given to the country supported by military success, rather than after the greatest disasters of the war.

Mr. Lincoln admitted the force of the suggestion, and so the matter was suspended for a brief period. This was before General Pope's retreat upon Washington, and the invasion of Maryland; and during all these disasters the proclamation waited, though it was occasionally taken out and retouched. At last came the battle of Antietam, and the news of national success met Mr. Lincoln at the Soldier's Home. There he immediately wrote the second draft of the preliminary proclamation, and came back to Washington on Saturday of that week, and held a cabinet meeting, at which he declared that the time for the enunciation of the emancipation policy could no longer be delayed. Public sentiment, he thought, would sustain it; many of his warmest friends and supporters demanded it; "and," said Mr. Lincoln, in a low and reverent tone, "I have promised my God that I will do it." These last words were hardly heard by any one but Mr. Chase, who sat nearest to him. Mr. Chase inquired: "Did I understand you correctly, Mr. President?" Mr. Lincoln replied: "I made a solemn vow before God that, if General Lee should be driven back from Pennsylvania, I would crown the result by the declaration of freedom to the slaves."

This statement was made by Mr. Chase to Mr. Carpenter, and does not differ materially from one communicated to the writer by Hon. George S. Boutwell of Massachusetts. Mr. Boutwell, then in Washington, determined in October to visit Massachusetts, and take a part in the state canvass; and previous to his departure he called upon Mr. Lincoln. In the course of the interview, he told the President that an active leader of the People's Party in Massachusetts had asserted, in a public speech, that Mr. Lincoln was frightened into issuing the emancipation proclamation, by the meeting of loyal governors at Altoona, Pennsylvania, which had occurred during the summer. "Now," said the President, dropping into a chair, as if he meant to be at ease, "I can tell you just how that was. When Lee came over the river, I made a resolve that when McClellan should drive him back,—and I expected he would do it some time or other,—I would send the proclamation after him. I worked upon it, and got it pretty much prepared. The battle of Antietam was fought on Wednesday, but I could not find out till Saturday whether we had really won a victory or not. It was then too late to issue the proclamation that week, and I dressed it over a little on Sunday, and Monday I gave it to them. The fact is, I never thought of the meeting of the governors at Altoona, and I can hardly remember that I knew anything about it."

On Monday, the 22d of September, 1862, the proclamation was issued. Even from this sweeping measure he had left an opportunity to escape. It was only a preliminary proclamation. It only declared free the slaves of those states and those sections of states which should be in rebellion on the 1st of January, 1863, leaving to every rebel state an opportunity to save its pet institution by becoming loyal, and doing what it could to save the Union:

"I, ABRAHAM LINCOLN, President of the United States of America, and Commander-in-Chief of the army and navy thereof, do hereby proclaim and declare that hereafter, as heretofore, the war will be prosecuted for the object of practically restoring the constitutional relation between the United States and each of the states, and the people thereof, in which states that relation is or may be suspended or disturbed.

"That it is my purpose, upon the next meeting of Congress, to again recommend the adoption of a practical measure tendering pecuniary aid to the free acceptance or rejection of all slave states so-called, the people whereof may not then be in rebellion against the United States, and which states may then have voluntarily adopted, or thereafter may voluntarily adopt, immediate or gradual abolishment of slavery within their respective limits; and that the effort to colonize persons of African descent, with their consent, upon this continent or elsewhere, with the previously obtained consent of the governments existing there, will be continued.

"That on the first day of January, in the year of our Lord one thousand eight hundred and sixty-three, all persons held as slaves within any state, or designated part of a state, the people whereof shall then be in rebellion against the United States, shall be then, thenceforward, and forever free; and the Executive Government of the United States, including the military and naval authority thereof, will recognize and maintain the freedom of such persons, and will do no act or acts to repress such persons, or any of them, in any efforts they may make for their actual freedom.

"That the Executive will, on the first day of January aforesaid, by proclamation, designate the states and parts of states, if any, in which the people thereof respectively shall then be in rebellion against the United States; and the fact that any state, or the people thereof, shall on that day be in good faith represented in the Congress of the United States, by members chosen thereto at elections wherein a majority of the qualified voters of such state shall have participated, shall, in the absence of strong countervailing testimony, be deemed conclusive evidence that such state, and the people thereof, are not then in rebellion against the United States.

"That attention is hereby called to an act of Congress entitled 'An Act to make an additional Article of War,' approved March 13th, 1862, and which act is in the words and figures following:

"'Be it enacted by the Senate and House of Representatives of the United States of America in Congress assembled, That hereafter the following shall be promulgated as an additional article of war for the government of the army of the United States, and shall be obeyed and observed as such:

"'ARTICLE—All officers or persons in the military or naval service of the United States are prohibited from employing any of the forces under their respective commands for the purpose of returning fugitives from service or labor who may have escaped from any persons to whom such service or labor is claimed to be due; and any officer who shall be found guilty by a court-martial of violating this article shall be dismissed from the service.'

"'SEC. 2. And be it further enacted, That this act shall take effect from and after its passage.'

"Also, to the ninth and tenth sections of an act entitled 'An Act to suppress Insurrection, to punish Treason and Rebellion, to seize and confiscate Property of Rebels, and for other purposes,' approved July 16th, 1862, and which sections are in the words and figures following:

"'SEC. 9. And be it further enacted, That all slaves of persons who shall hereafter be engaged in rebellion against the government of the United States, or who shall in any way give aid or comfort thereto, escaping from such persons and taking refuge within the lines of the army; and all slaves captured from such persons, or deserted by them, and coming under the control of the government of the United States; and all slaves of such persons found on [or] being within any place occupied by rebel forces and afterwards occupied by forces of the United States, shall be deemed captives of war, and shall be forever free of their servitude, and not again held as slaves.

"'SEC. 10. *And be it further enacted,* That no slave escaping into any state, territory, or the District of Columbia, from any other state, shall be delivered up, or in any way impeded or hindered of his liberty, except for crime, or some offense against the laws, unless the person claiming said fugitive shall first make oath that the person to whom the labor or service of such fugitive is alleged to be due is his lawful owner, and has not borne arms against the United States in the present rebellion, nor in any way given aid and comfort thereto; and no person engaged in the military or naval service of the United States shall, under any pretense whatever, assume to decide on the validity of the claim of any person to the service or labor of any other person, or surrender up any such person to the claimant, on pain of being dismissed from the service.'

"And I do hereby enjoin upon and order all persons engaged in the military and naval service of the United States to observe, obey, and enforce, within their respective spheres of service, the act and sections above recited.

"And the Executive will in due time recommend that all citizens of the United States who shall have remained loyal thereto throughout the rebellion, shall (upon the restoration of the constitutional relation between the United States and their respective states and people, if that relation shall have been suspended or disturbed) be compensated for all losses by acts of the United States, including the loss of slaves.

"In witness whereof, I have hereunto set my hand, and caused the seal of the United States to be affixed.

"Done at the city of Washington, this tenth day of April, in the year
    of our Lord one thousand eight hundred and sixty-two, and of
[L. S.] the Independence of the United States the eighty-seventh.

"ABRAHAM LINCOLN.

"By the President:
"WM. H. SEWARD, *Secretary of State.*"

In the cabinet meeting held previous to the issue of the proclamation, Mr. Lincoln had concluded the reading of the third paragraph, when Mr. Seward interrupted him by saying: "Mr. President, I think that you should insert after the word, 'recognize,' the words, 'and maintain.'" The President replied that he had fully considered the import of the expression, and that it was not his way to promise more than he was sure he could perform; and he was not prepared to say that he thought he was able to "maintain" this. Mr. Seward insisted that the ground should be taken, and the words finally went in.

The proclamation was received with profound interest by the whole country. The radical anti-slavery men were delighted, conservative politicians shrugged their shoulders doubtfully, and the lovers of the peculiar institution gnashed their teeth. It is very doubtful whether it affected the fall elections so much adversely to Mr. Lincoln, as the fact that he was ignorantly or maliciously held responsible for the blunders of McClellan's campaign. If it affected them at all unfavorably, its influence in that direction soon ceased; and the proclamation became his tower of strength in the sight of his own people and the peoples of the world.

Two days after the issue of the proclamation, a large body of men assembled before the White House with music, and called for the President. He appeared, and addressed to them a few words of thanks for their courtesy, and, in alluding to the proclamation, said: "What I did, I did after a very full deliberation, and under a heavy and solemn sense of responsibility. I can only trust in God I have made no mistake." After two years of experience he was enabled to say: "As affairs have turned, it is the central act of my administration, and the great event of the nineteenth century."

It will be remembered that General McClellan had warned Mr. Lincoln against the effect of a general policy of emancipation upon his army. He thought that such a policy would cause its disintegration. It certainly became a theme of angry discussion;—so much so that, on the seventh of October, the General felt called upon to issue an order reminding officers and soldiers of their relations and their duties to the civil authorities. It was an admirable order, and evidently well intended. "Discussion by officers and soldiers concerning public measures, determined upon and declared by the government," said he, "when carried beyond the ordinary temperate and respectful expression of opinion, tends greatly to impair and destroy the discipline and efficiency of the troops, by substituting the spirit of political faction, for the firm, steady, and earnest support of the authority of the government, which is the highest duty of the American soldier." If there was any fault to be found with the order, it was connected with the time of its promulgation. It was issued the day after Mr. Lincoln left the army, which, it will be remembered, he visited while it rested from the battle of Antietam. General McClellan had learned something during that visit. He had learned that, notwithstanding Mr. Lincoln's proclamation, he was held in strong and enthusiastic affection by the army. For nearly a week, he mingled with the weary officers and soldiers, meeting the heartiest reception everywhere. A general officer who was with the President on the trip, said: "I watched closely to see if, in any division, or regiment, I could find symptoms of dissatisfaction, or could hear an allusion to the proclamation. I found none. I heard only words of praise."

It was undoubtedly the aim of traitors outside of the army, and of their sympathizers within, to alienate the army from the President and the government; but they failed. One Major Key came down from the army to Washington, with the story that our Generals did not push the advantages they had won, because it was not considered desirable to crush the rebellion at once, if, indeed, at all; but so to manage affairs as to secure a compromise as the result of a prolonged war. It is quite probable that he had heard this talk among the leading officers, as he declared he had. One thing was evident—that he agreed with their policy; and, telling Mr. Lincoln plainly so to his face, he was at once removed from the service. The example served an excellent purpose; and, with McClellan's order, and the effect of Mr. Lincoln's personal visit, brought the disloyal and factious elements of the army into their proper relations to the government and its policy.

On the 1st of January, 1863, the final proclamation of emancipation was issued, and the great act was complete. It was as follows:

"Whereas, on the twenty-second day of September, in the year of our Lord one thousand eight hundred and sixty-two, a proclamation was issued by the President of the United States, containing, among other things, the following, to wit:

"'That on the first day of January, in the year of our Lord one thousand eight hundred and sixty-three, all persons held as slaves within any state or designated part of a state, the people whereof shall then be in rebellion against the United States, shall be then, thenceforward, and forever free; and the Executive government of the United States, including the military and naval authority thereof, will recognize and maintain the freedom of such persons, and will do no act or acts to repress such persons, or any of them, in any efforts they may make for their actual freedom.

"'That the Executive will, on the first day of January aforesaid, by proclamation, designate the states and parts of states, if any, in which the people thereof respectively shall then be in rebellion against the United States; and the fact that any state or the people thereof shall on that day be in good faith represented in the Congress of the United States, by members chosen thereto at elections wherein a majority of the qualified voters of such state shall have participated, shall, in the absence of strong countervailing testimony, be deemed conclusive evidence that such state, and the people thereof, are not then in rebellion against the United States.'

"Now, therefore, I, ABRAHAM LINCOLN, President of the United States, by virtue of the power in me vested as Commander-in-Chief of the army and navy of the United States in time of actual armed rebellion against the authority and government of the United States, and as a fit and necessary war measure for suppressing said rebellion, do, on this first day of January, in the year of our Lord one thousand eight hundred and sixty-three, and in accordance with my purpose so to do, publicly proclaimed for the full period of one hundred days from the day first above mentioned, order and designate, as the states and parts of states wherein the people thereof respectively are this day in rebellion against the United States, the following, to wit:

"Arkansas, Texas, Louisiana (except the parishes of St. Bernard, Plaquemine, Jefferson, St. John, St. Charles, St. James, Ascension, Assumption, Terre Bonne, Lafourche, St. Marie, St. Martin and Orleans, including the city of New Orleans), Mississippi, Alabama, Florida, Georgia, South Carolina, North Carolina, and Virginia (except the forty-eight counties designated as West Virginia, and also the counties of Berkely, Accomac, Northampton, Elizabeth City, York, Princess Anne, and Norfolk, including the cities of Norfolk and Portsmouth), and which excepted parts are for the present left precisely as if this proclamation were not issued.

"And, by virtue of the power and for the purpose aforesaid, I do order and declare that all persons held as slaves within said designated

States and parts of States, are, and henceforward shall be free; and that the Executive Government of the United States, including the military and naval authorities thereof, will recognize and maintain the freedom of said persons.

" And I hereby enjoin upon the people so declared to be free, to abstain from all violence, unless in necessary self-defense; and I recommend to them, that in all cases, when allowed, they labor faithfully for reasonable wages.

" And I further declare and make known that such persons of suitable condition will be received into the armed service of the United States, to garrison forts, positions, stations and other places, and to man vessels of all sorts in said service.

" And upon this act, sincerely believed to be an act of justice, warranted by the Constitution, upon military necessity, I invoke the considerate judgment of mankind, and the gracious favor of Almighty God.

" In testimony whereof, I have hereunto set my name, and caused the seal of the United States to be affixed.

" Done at the city of Washington, this first day of January, in the year of our Lord one thousand eight hundred and sixty-three, and of [L. S.] the Independence of the United States the eighty-seventh.

" ABRAHAM LINCOLN.

" By the President:
" WILLIAM H. SEWARD, *Secretary of State.*"

A single paragraph in this proclamation was written by Secretary Chase. He had himself prepared a proclamation, which embodied his views, and had submitted it to Mr. Lincoln. Mr. Lincoln selected from it this sentence: " And upon this act, believed to be an act of justice warranted by the Constitution [upon military necessity,] I invoke the considerate judgment of mankind and the gracious favor of Almighty God; " and adopted it, interpolating only the words between brackets. It is an illustration of Mr. Lincoln's freedom from vanity, first that he adopted the words at all, notwithstanding their dignity and beauty; and, second, that he freely told of the circumstance, so that it found publicity through his own revelations.

On the twenty-fourth of September, two days after the issue of the preliminary proclamation, Mr. Lincoln gave utterance to a proclamation suspending the writ of *habeas corpus.* Proceeding from the fact that the ordinary processes of law were not sufficient to restrain disloyal persons from hindering the execution of a draft of militia which had been ordered, discouraging enlistments, and giving aid and comfort in various ways to the insurrection, he declared the writ of *habeas corpus* suspended, touching all persons who should be arrested, confined, or sentenced by court martial, for these offenses. The measure created great dissatisfaction, particularly among those who were not in favor of the war, and those who were anxious to make political headway against the administration. There was an outcry against "military despotism," against the "abridgment of the right of free speech," against the "suppression of the liberty of the press," etc. etc.; the freedom with which these strictures were made, without attracting the slightest notice of the government, refuting the charges as rapidly as they were uttered.

At the succeeding session of Congress, these complaints had immediate expression; and the proclamation was furiously attacked at once. Resolutions were introduced, censuring the "arbitrary arrest" of persons in the loyal states; and the suspension of the writ of *habeas corpus* was vehemently denounced. It appeared by these demonstrations that the public liberty was endangered, and that the Constitution was subverted. It is possible that some of those engaged in this outcry were honest in their fears and denunciations; but some of them were notorious sympathizers with the rebels, and were doing, and had done everything in their power to aid the rebellion. Nothing was more notorious than that the country abounded with spies and informers, and men who discouraged enlistments, and counseled resistance to a draft. Congress, however, was on the side of the government, and passed a bill sustaining the President, and indemnifying him and all who acted under him in the execution of his policy. It is quite possible that injustice was done in some of these "arbitrary arrests"—it would be strange, indeed, if it were otherwise—but the prophets of the degeneracy of the government into a military despotism have their answer now, in the peaceful and ready return to the old status.

There was one vice of the army that gave Mr. Lincoln great pain; and that was the unnecessary disregard of the Sabbath. Armies, of course, cannot always be good Sabbath-keepers; but he saw in them a disposition to do work on that day not at all necessary, and to engage in sports quite in dissonance with its spirit. So, on the sixteenth of November, he issued a circular letter upon the subject, in which he told the soldiers that "the importance for man and beast of the prescribed weekly rest, the sacred rights of Christian soldiers and sailors, a becoming deference to the best sentiment of a Christian people, and a due regard for the Divine Will, demand that Sunday labor in the army and navy be reduced to the measure of strict necessity." He continued: "The discipline and character of the national forces should not suffer, nor the cause they defend be imperiled, by the profanation of the day, or the name of the Most High." The letter shows how closely he had associated the will of the Most High with the national cause, and how profound was his reverence for the institutions of Christianity.

This chapter, and the record of the events of the year, cannot be better closed, perhaps, than by an incident which shows that, in Mr. Lincoln's greatest necessity for popular support, he disdained, with all the strength of his old sense of justice and fairness, any trick for gaining that support. After New Orleans was taken, and a certain portion of the state reclaimed and held by military power, movements were commenced for the representation of the state in Congress. Mr. Lincoln was charged with conniving with this movement, and with intending to secure members of Congress from Louisiana, elected under military pressure, who would assist in maintaining his policy, and make a show of the returning loyalty of the state. On the twenty-first of November, he wrote to G. F. Shepley, the military governor of Louisiana, as follows:

"Dear Sir—Dr. Kennedy, bearer of this, has some apprehension that Federal officers, not citizens of Louisiana, may be set up as candidates for Congress in that state. In my view, there could be no possible object in such an election.   We do not particularly need members of Congress from those states to enable us to get along with legislation here.   What we do want is the conclusive evidence that respectable citizens of Louisiana are willing to be members of Congress, and to swear support to the Constitution; and that other respectable citizens there are willing to vote for them and send them.   To send a parcel of northern men here as representatives, elected as would be understood (and perhaps really so), at the point of the bayonet, would be disgraceful and outrageous; and, were I a member of Congress here, I would vote against admitting any such man to a seat."

CHAPTER XXIV.

The events of 1863, legislative, military, and personal as they relate to Mr. Lincoln, must receive only a brief and condensed review. It will have been noticed, by several incidents that have been recorded in this narrative, and by sundry papers of Mr. Lincoln, that, during the whole of his presidency thus far, he had indulged in projects of colonization of the freed blacks. Congress had so far regarded his suggestions as to place at his disposal a sum of money for experiments in colonization. In August, 1862, he called to the Executive Mansion a representative company of negroes whom he familiarly addressed on the subject, freely telling them of the disadvantages under which they labored, expressing his convictions that they suffered much by living in association with the whites, and uttering his conviction that the whites suffered by living with them, even when they were free. His wish was to have them colonized at some point in Central America; and he promised to spend some of the money intrusted to him, if they would join in sufficient numbers to make an experiment.

In his message delivered to Congress on the opening of the session of 1862–63, he called up the subject again; and communicated information of the measures he had taken, for effecting his wishes, and securing to the blacks the benefits of the congressional provision. He had had correspondence with some of the Spanish-American republics, and they had protested against the reception of black colonies. He had declined to move any colonists forward, under the circumstances, and

should still desist, unless they could be protected.   Liberia
and Hayti were the only countries to which they could go,
with the certainty of immediate adoption as citizens; and the
blacks manifested a strange indisposition to emigrate to those
countries.

This dream of colonization, in which Mr. Lincoln so be-
nevolently indulged, was destined to fail of even partial realization.   He loved the negro too well to wish him to remain
where the prejudices of race would shut him out from the full
recognition of his manhood.   He not only wanted him free,
but he wanted him located where he might receive all the
rights of citizenship, and where he could live—self-respectful
and independent—in the society of his equals and his race.
It was a matter of pitying wonder with him that the negro
should love to live with a race that abused him, and held him
at so low a value in the scale of humanity.

All the closing portion of this message was devoted to an
earnest discussion of the scheme of compensated emancipation.   Notwithstanding he had issued his preliminary proclamation of freedom to the slaves of rebels, and expected soon
to complete that work; and notwithstanding his conviction
that slavery could not long survive this proclamation, even in
the loyal slave states, he never forgot that neither over
slavery in these states, the Constitution nor the necessities of
war gave him any control.   One thing he did forget, viz:
that these states had uniformly turned their backs upon all
his earnest and kindly efforts to save them from a loss which
he was certain must ultimately fall upon them.

With the exposition of his views upon this subject, Mr. Lincoln submitted the draft of a resolution embodying his policy.
This resolution proposed certain articles as amendments to the
Constitution of the United States, to be acted upon by the legislatures or conventions of the several states.   These articles,
by being adopted by the legislatures of three-fourths of the
states, should become valid, and be held as parts of the Constitution.   They provided that every slave state which should
voluntarily abolish the slave system at any date previous to

the year 1900, should receive a specified compensation. Slaves who should be freed by the chances of war should remain free, though loyal masters should receive compensation for them. The closing article provided that Congress might "appropriate money, and otherwise provide for colonizing free colored persons, with their own consent, at any place or places without the United States."

Sudden emancipation was never in accordance with Mr. Lincoln's judgment. Nothing but the necessities of war would have induced him to decree it with relation to the slaves of any state. His thought was, that, by giving every state the opportunity to terminate slavery in its own way, within a period of thirty-seven years, the institution could be removed without a shock to the prosperity and the social institutions of the whites, and without bringing to the blacks a freedom which many of them, at least, would not know how to use. The stress of feeling under which he urged this measure, is sufficiently exhibited by the closing paragraph of the message: "Fellow citizens,"—thus reads the passage—"We cannot escape history. We of this Congress, and this Administration, will be remembered in spite of ourselves. No personal significance or insignificance can spare one or another of us. The fiery trial through which we pass will light us down in honor or dishonor to the latest generation. We say that we are for the Union. The world will not forget that we say this. We know how to save the Union. The world knows we know how to save it. * * * In giving freedom to the slave, we assure freedom to the free—honorable alike in what we give and what we preserve. We shall nobly save or meanly lose the last, best hope of earth. Other means may suceeed; this could not, cannot, fail. The way is plain, peaceful, generous, just—a way which, if followed, the world will forever applaud, and God must forever bless."

Allusion has been made, in the preceding chapter, to the action of this session, on the subject of arbitrary arrests; and the subject does not need to be recalled further than to say that the discussion which it excited fully illustrated the political antagonisms which, prevalent among the people, were brought into thorough exposition by their representatives. In the precise degree in which the members of both houses sympathized with treason, or were exercised by their party feelings against the general policy of the government toward the rebellion, did they oppose the suspension of the writ of *habeas corpus.* The same rule held good, with rare exceptions, with relation to the discussion of a project for arming the blacks. There were some friends of the government from the border states who were very timid and doubtful about the adoption of this measure: but the majority of the House agreed to it; and the Senate would undoubtedly have done the same, had not the committee to which the matter was referred reported that the President already had the power to call persons of African descent into the military and naval service, by an act passed during the previous session.

The same antagonisms were exhibited concerning a measure for enrolling and drafting the militia of the different states, so that each state should be compelled to contribute its equitable quota, the troops when raised to be under the control of the President. The absolute necessity of this measure was attributable partly to the stage at which the war had arrived— when the surplus population was all in the army, and it was essential to draw upon the vital resources of the country— and partly to party feeling and party policy. Either through the failure of McClellan's campaign, or the effect of the emancipation proclamation, or the influence of both together, the administration had received a rebuke through the autumn elections of 1862. This had greatly encouraged the opposition, who, as opponents of the war, or as most unreliable friends of the President's war policy, so conducted their counsels that the government became fearful concerning its ability to raise men for the campaign of 1863. Just in proportion to the treasonable sympathies of the members of the Senate and the House, did they oppose the measure. The bill was finally passed and approved; and it became an efficient instrument in the hands of the government for prosecuting the war.

It contained provisions for procuring substitutes, for exemption by the payment of three hundred dollars, a clause defining the conditions of exemption, &c.

Much of the session was devoted to a discussion of measures of finance, which ended in giving the Secretary of the Treasury leave to borrow nine hundred millions of dollars, bearing six per cent interest, payable in not less than ten nor more than forty years. The Secretary was authorized to issue four hundred millions in treasury notes bearing interest, and a hundred and fifty millions without interest. To meet the immediate necessities of the army and navy, especially as they related to debts due the soldiers and sailors, authority was given for the issue of one hundred millions of treasury notes, before the leading measures of finance were perfected.

The latter measure was signed by the President at once, in order that the soldiers and marines might have their due; but he took occasion, in a special message, to express his regret that it had been found necessary to make so large an additional issue of United States notes, at a time when the combined circulation of those notes and the notes of the suspended banks had advanced the prices of everything beyond real values, augmenting the cost of living, to the injury of labor, and the cost of supplies, to the injury of the country. "It seems very plain," he said, "that continued issues of United States notes, without any check to the issues of suspended banks, and without adequate provision for the raising of money by loans, and for funding the issues, so as to keep them within due limits, must soon produce disastrous consequences." He had already, in his annual message, advocated the national bank system for the production of a uniform currency, secured by the pledge of United States bonds, thus increasing the demand for the bonds. A bill for the object desired was passed by small majorities, and approved. It was a doubtful measure, and touched a great many selfish and corporate interests, carrying more or less of disturbance into the various financial systems of the states; but the country has had no reason to find fault with its results.

Two events during the session marked the beginning of those reconstructive measures which were destined eventually to embrace all the members of the old Union. Western Virginia, loyal from the first, was admitted into the Union as a state; and two representatives from Louisiana were admitted to the House, under the representation, on the part of the committee to which their application was referred, that they had been elected in accordance with the constitutional conditions and provisions of that state.

When Congress adjourned, it left the Executive strong in all the powers and prerogatives necessary for the successful prosecution of the war. The president's hands were strengthened by competent financial provisions, by the confirmation of his power to arrest and hold suspicious and inimical persons, and by authority to levy upon the militia of the states for such force as might be necessary to effect the purposes of the government. His efforts for measures of compensated emancipation failed. A single measure concerning Missouri miscarried through the failure of the House to confirm the action of the Senate.

On the twenty-second of November, 1862, two months after Mr. Lincoln issued his proclamation suspending the privilege of the writ of *habeas corpus*, the opponents of the government became so quiet that an order was issued from the War Department, discharging from further military restraint all those persons who had been arrested for discouraging volunteer enlistments, opposing the draft, or otherwise giving aid and comfort to the enemy, in all states where the draft had been effected, or the quota of volunteers and militia had been furnished. The order also released persons held in military custody who had been arrested for disloyalty by the military governors of rebel states, on giving their parole to do no act of hostility against the United States. They had the liberty to live under military surveillance; or to go to the rebel states, not to return until after the war, or until they should be permitted to do so by the President. The suspension of the writ, and the acts which accompanied it, accomplished their object temporarily; but, at the close of the session of Congress, in March, the more malicious of the malcontents began their foul work again. Undoubtedly the country was tired of the war; and many of the weaker and more unreasoning classes, finding themselves more than ever in the hands of the government by the legislation of the winter, lent willing ears to disloyal politicians. Agitation against the war was revived. The people were called upon to mark the great sacrifices they had already uselessly made; the war was declared to be a failure, and peace as far off as ever; and the country was adjured to demand a cessation of the coercive policy.

Among the most pestilent of these sympathizers with traitors, was Clement L. Vallandigham of Ohio—a person who, as member of Congress, stump politician and private citizen, had opposed the war from the start. In Congress, he had steadily voted against every measure instituted by the government for maintaining the integrity of the nation and putting down the rebellion. Not a step did the President take, in the execution of his purpose, that Vallandigham did not dispute. Indeed, he offered in the House resolutions of censure for those early acts of the President in calling out a military force, by which alone Washington was saved from capture. His language in the House had been so bitter and disloyal that the feelings of every friend of the government had been outraged. Going home from Congress, where he had been engaged in his foul work, he entered upon a canvass of his district, denouncing the government, and maligning its motives. The tendency of his malicious utterances was to weaken the hands of the Executive in its great work of subduing the insurrection, and to give aid and comfort to the national enemies.

General Burnside, then in command of the Department of the Ohio, issued an order (Number 38,) announcing that thereafter all persons found within the federal lines who should commit acts for the benefit of the enemy would be tried as spies or traitors; and, if convicted, would suffer death. This order, the demagogue publicly denounced; and then he

called upon the people to resist its execution.   General Burnside arrested him at once, and ordered him to be tried by court-
martial at Cincinnati.   On the fifth of May, the day following his arrest, he applied to the United States Circuit Court
for a writ of *habeas corpus;* and, after an elaborate argument
from his counsel, and the reading of a long letter from General Burnside giving the reasons for his arrest, Judge Leavitt
decided against his application, giving his opinion that "The
legality of the arrest depends upon the extent of the necessity
for making it; and that was to be determined by the military
commander."   Judge Leavitt dealt with the case nobly.
"Those who live under the protection and enjoy the blessings
of our benignant government," said he, "must learn that they
cannot stab its vitals with impunity.   If they remain with us,
while they are not of us, they must be subject to such a course
of dealing as the great law of self-preservation prescribes and
will enforce."   Further, he said: "I confess I am but little
moved by the eloquent appeals of those who, while they in-
dignantly denounce violation of personal liberty, look with no
horror upon a despotism as unmitigated as the world has ever
witnessed."

On the following day, Vallandigham had his trial, was convicted, and was sentenced to confinement in some fortress of
the United States, to be designated by General Burnside, who
approved the finding of the court, and designated Fort Warren
as his prison.   The President, however, modified the sentence,
and directed that the convict should be sent within the rebel
lines, among the people which he held in such cordial sympathy, with the direction that he should not return until after
the termination of the war.   The man thus sent to his own
found safe conduct through the rebel states, and managed to
reach Canada, from whose territory he subsequently emerged,
without waiting for the termination of the war, and without
saying to the President, "By your leave."

There were numbers of men in the loyal states who were
quite as guilty as Mr. Vallandigham, even if less bold than
he.   These took alarm.   If Mr. Vallandigham could be ar-

rested and sent within the rebel lines for abusing the motives and acts of the government, who, that sympathized with Mr. Vallandigham, was safe? It was a natural and pertinent inquiry. So they began to hold public meetings, to denounce the government, and to call upon the President to reconsider his act in Vallandigham's case. Governor Seymour of New York was powerfully exercised in the matter, and wrote a very spirited letter to one of these meetings held in Albany, on the sixteenth of May. If the Ohio demagogue used treasonable language, it is hard to see why the New York governor did not. The sanction of the act by which Vallandigham was sent among his friends, by President and people, was, in his opinion, not only despotism but revolution. He almost copied the language of the convict himself. Mr. Vallandigham had said that the government was aiming not to restore the Union, but to crush out liberty. Governor Seymour said: "The action of the administration will determine, in the minds of more than one half of the people in the loyal states, whether this war is waged to put down rebellion in the South, or destroy free institutions at the North."

This meeting and others of the same kind, held in the leading cities of the Union, denounced arbitrary arrests and the suspension of the writ of *habeas corpus*, protested against Vallandigham's sentence, and called upon the President to recall their injured friend and protégé. A month after Vallandigham was banished, the Democratic State Convention of Ohio met, and, by almost a unanimous vote, nominated him as their candidate for governor, and Senator Pugh, his legal counsel, as their candidate for lieutenant governor. They also sent a committee to Washington to demand of the President the recall of their candidate. The letter which they bore was answered at length by the President; and he gave the supporters of Mr. Vallandigham a very plain talk. He told them what he believed to be the facts touching Mr. Vallandigham's words and influence, in opposition to those means which the government deemed indispensable to its own preservation, and then said: "Your own attitude, therefore, encourages desertion, resistance to the draft, and the like, because it teaches those who incline to desert and to escape the draft, to believe it is your purpose to protect them." He told them, however, that the proceedings in Mr. Vallandigham's case were "for prevention, not for punishment—an injunction to stay an injury;"— and that the modification of General Burnside's order was made as a less disagreeable mode to Mr. Vallandigham himself of securing the desired prevention.

It is hardly to be doubted that Mr. Lincoln would never, of his own motion, have arrested the greatly over-rated subject of these discussions. He had talked as badly in Washington as he had in Ohio, and lost no opportunity to abuse the President himself; but Mr. Lincoln very severely let him alone. When, therefore, he clandestinely returned, a year afterwards, and fulminated his threats against the government, in case he should be arrested in any way except by officers of the civil tribunals, he was permitted to say what he pleased. The people of Ohio had already decided against him by a majority of one hundred thousand votes; and he had lost his power for harm, except where he might choose to bestow his friendship.

To the resolutions passed by the Albany meeting of which Hon. Erastus Corning was president, Mr. Lincoln made an elaborate reply. This was his favorite field. He had got hold of a case to argue; and its importance, in his apprehension, may be judged by the fact that he spent more time and exhausted more pains upon this paper than upon any other written during his administration, messages included. It was intended to be the full and exhaustive vindication of his policy, upon the subjects it covered, before the American people; and the American people so regarded it. No headway could be made against it, and no serious and candid attempt was made to answer it.

These pages will not give space to the entire document, or even a review of the argument; but some of its illustrations may be cited as giving its drift and style. In arguing the necessity of the arrest of those who were known to be traitors, but who had committed no overt act of treason, he said: "General John C. Breckinridge, General Robert E. Lee, General Joseph E. Johnston, General John B. Magruder, General William B. Preston, General Simon B. Buckner, and Commodore Franklin Buchanan, now occupying the very highest places in the. rebel war service, were all within the power of the government since the war began, and were nearly as well known to be traitors then as now. Unquestionably, if we had seized and held them, the insurgent cause would be much weaker. But no one of them had committed any crime defined in the law. Every one of them, if arrested, would have been discharged on *habeas corpus*, were the writ allowed to operate. In view of these and similar cases, I think the time not unlikely to come when I shall be blamed for having made too few arrests, rather than too many."

Certainly here was a case in point; and it is hard to see why reasoning that applies so well to those men would not apply as well to those still in the power of the government, who had notoriously so opposed the war as to hinder that government from conquering the traitors named. Mr. Vallandigham "was not arrested," he said, "because he was damaging the political prospects of the administration, or the personal interests of the commanding general; but because he was damaging the army, upon the existence and vigor of which the life of the nation depends." Furthermore: "Must I shoot a simple-minded soldier-boy, who deserts, while I must not touch a hair of a wily agitator who induces him to desert? I think that, in such a case, to silence the agitator and save the boy, is not only constitutional, but withal a great mercy."

The Albany meeting had spoken to Mr. Lincoln as "democrats." To this aspect of the matter he paid his addresses. He would have preferred to meet them on the higher platform of "American citizens," at such a time; but, since he was denied this privilege, he comforted himself with the reflection that all democrats did not. believe with them. General Burnside, who arrested Mr. Vallandigham, was a democrat. Judge Leavitt, who refused to release him on the writ of *habeas corpus*, was also a democrat who received his mantle from the hands of Jackson himself; and speaking of Jackson reminded him of an incident in point: "After the battle of New Orleans, and while the fact that the treaty of peace had been concluded was well known in the city, but before official knowledge of it had arrived, General Jackson still maintained martial or military law. Now that it could be said the war was over, the clamor against martial law, which had existed from the first, grew more furious. Among other things, a Mr. Louiallier published a denunciatory newspaper article. General Jackson arrested him. A lawyer by the name of Morel procured the United States Judge Hall to issue a writ of *habeas corpus* to relieve Mr. Louiallier. General Jackson arrested both the lawyer and the Judge. A Mr. Hollander ventured to say of some part of the matter that it was a 'dirty trick.' General Jackson arrested him. When the officer undertook to serve the writ of *habeas corpus*, General Jackson took it from him, and sent him away with a copy. Holding the Judge in custody a few days, the General sent him beyond the limits of his encampment, and set him at liberty, with an order to remain until the ratification of peace should be regularly announced, or until the British should have left the southern coast. A day or two more elapsed, the ratification of a treaty of peace was regularly announced, and the Judge and others were fully liberated. A few days more, and the Judge called General Jackson into court, and fined him one thousand dollars for having arrested him and the others named. The General paid the fine, and there the matter rested for nearly thirty years, when Congress refunded principal and interest."

Mr. Lincoln could not avoid adding that Senator Douglas, then a member of the House, was a prominent advocate of this democratic measure; and remarking: "First, that we had the same constitution then as now; second, that we then had a case of invasion, and now we have a case of rebellion; and, third, that the permanent right of the people to public discussion, the liberty of speech and of the press, the trial by jury, the law of evidence, and the *habeas corpus*, suffered no detriment whatever by that conduct of General Jackson, or its subsequent approval by the American Congress."

To obviate an objection made to the course of the administration, in permitting the privilege of the writ of *habeas corpus* to be suspended at the pleasure of the heads of military departments, thus delegating the authority, Mr. Lincoln, by proclamation on the fifteenth day of September, suspended the writ throughout the United States.

Under the enrollment act, passed March third, a draft of militia was ordered for July, and was effected without serious disturbance, except in a single instance, in the city of New York. Great efforts had been made by interested politicians, during the spring and summer, to make certain provisions of the act odious to the people, especially to the lower and more unreasoning classes. The clause exempting from conscription on the payment of three hundred dollars, was represented to be intended for the benefit of the rich; and the bad passions of the mob were wrought upon in various ways. The first day of the draft in New York, July eleventh, though attended with some excitement, witnessed no outbreak or violent opposition: but the Sunday that intervened between that day and the resumption of the draft on the thirteenth, afforded an opportunity for organization: and, when the fateful wheels started again, one of them was seized by a mob, and destroyed; and the building which contained it was fired. For four days thereafter, New York was under the reign of riot. The troops were all away, having been called upon to resist the invasion of Maryland and Pennsylvania. During this fearful period, the most fiendish outrages were visited upon the harmless black population of the city, houses belonging to prominent supporters of the government were sacked and burned, and plunder became the one ruling passion of all the worst inhabitants of the city. Those who had led on the mob, as a demonstration against the draft, soon found that

27

they could not direct the whirlwind, and that the passions they had aroused were altogether beyond their control. Women and children of the lowest classes gave free rein to their thievish impulses; and, after a single day of riot, the draft was forgotten in the greed for spoil. The disgraceful proceedings were not stayed until the return of the regiments that had been sent away.

The Governor of New York, friendly neither to the administration nor to the draft, asked for a postponement of the measure of conscription until volunteering could be tried; and he complained of certain inequalities of the government requisitions in certain districts of the state. Mr. Lincoln replied, temporarily yielding the point in relation to four districts, and promising a careful re-enrollment, but saying that the draft must be proceeded with. The Governor wished for delay, also, in order that the constitutionality of the draft law might be tried. Mr. Lincoln replied that he should be willing to facilitate the bringing of the law before the Supreme Court, but he could not consent to lose the time. "We are contending," said he, "with an enemy who, as I understand, drives every able-bodied man he can reach into his ranks, very much as a butcher drives bullocks into a slaughter-pen. No time is wasted, no argument is used. This produces an army which will soon turn upon our now victorious soldiers, already in the field, if they shall not be sustained by recruits as they should be. It produces an army with a rapidity not to be matched on our side, if we first waste time to re-experiment with the volunteer system, already deemed by Congress, and palpably, in fact, so far exhausted as to be inadequate; and then more time to obtain a court decision as to whether a law is constitutional which requires a part of those not now in the service to go to the aid of those already in it; and still more time to determine with absolute certainty that we get those who are to go in the precisely legal proportion to those who are not to go." The Governor was still in trouble about the inequality of the quotas in the districts, and regretted that the President would not suspend the draft. The

President understood his duty, and did not misunderstand Governor Seymour; and the draft was resumed and peacefully consummated, through measures of protection instituted by the war department.

The popularity of Mr. Lincoln and his administration had entirely recovered from whatever depressing influence the emancipation policy had occasioned, and from the effects of the Peninsular campaign. His determined pursuit of duty, whatever the consequences might be to himself, won him friends among his enemies. The spring elections of 1863 showed a reaction from those of the previous autumn, and the fall elections confirmed his growing popularity. The elections in New York were a direct and decided indorsement of the draft in that state, and, in the same degree, a condemnation of those who had opposed it. Ohio decided Mr. Vallandigham's case by giving a tremendous majority on the side of the government. Pennsylvania re-elected Governor Curtin by an unexpected majority; and the same successes occurred in every state, with the single exception of New Jersey. To Mr. Lincoln, who watched the indications of the public feeling and opinion with constant anxiety, these events brought great relief and encouragement. The South had been watching for outbreaks, and its northern friends had been prophesying them. The South had been expecting the growth of a peace party, and its northern friends had endeavored to bring one into the field; but the fall elections of 1863 crushed the rebel expectations; and the whole North was regarded by the traitors as bound to the fortunes of that horrible tyrant— that blood-thirsty boor—Abraham Lincoln. In the meantime, Mr. Lincoln had made great progress in the esteem of foreign governments and foreign peoples, of which he received abundant testimonials.

Early in the year, the working men of Manchester, England, sent him a letter, to which he gave a grateful and cordial reply. They, although greatly suffering in consequence of the war, sent him their sympathy; and in his reply, he said to them: "It has been often and studiously represented that the attempt to overthrow this government, which was built upon the foundation of human rights, and to substitute for it one which should rest exclusively upon the basis of human slavery, was likely to obtain the favor of Europe. Through the action of our disloyal citizens, the working men of Europe have been subjected to severe trial, for the purpose of forcing their sanction to that attempt. Under these circumstances, I cannot but regard your decisive utterances upon the question as an instance of sublime Christian heroism, which has not been surpassed in any age, or in any country. * * * I do not doubt that the sentiments you have expressed will be sustained by your great nation; and, on the other hand, I have no hesitation in assuring you that they will excite admiration, esteem, and the most reciprocal feelings of friendship among the American people."

In a letter written August twenty-sixth, to James C. Conkling, in reply to an invitation to attend a mass meeting of "unconditional Union men," to be held at his old home in Springfield, Illinois, it is evident that Mr. Lincoln was hopeful and confident of results. In this letter he treated again of the subject of emancipation; and handled the clamorer for peace, the enemies of the Emancipation Proclamation, and the advocates of compromise, with most admirable skill. The closing paragraphs are peculiarly keen, clear and sparkling:

"You say that you will not fight to free negroes. Some of them seem willing to fight for you; but no matter. Fight you, then, exclusively to save the Union. I issued the Proclamation on purpose to aid you in saving the Union. Whenever you shall have conquered all resistance to the Union, if I shall urge you to continue fighting, it will be an apt time then for you to declare you will not fight to free negroes. I thought that, in your struggle for the Union, to whatever extent the negroes should cease helping the enemy, to that extent it weakened the enemy in his resistance to you. Do you think differently? I thought that whatever negroes can be got to do as soldiers, leaves just so much less for white soldiers to do in saving the Union. Does it appear otherwise to you? But negroes, like other people, act upon motives. Why should they do anything for us, if we will do nothing for them? If they stake their lives for us, they must be prompted by the strongest motive, even the promise of freedom. And the promise, being made, must be kept.

"The signs look better   The Father of Waters again goes unvexed to the sea. Thanks to the great Northwest for it; nor yet wholly to them. Three hundred miles up they met New England, Empire, Keystone, and Jersey, hewing their way right and left. The sunny South, too, in more colors than one, also lent a helping hand. On the spot, their part of the history was jotted down in black and white. The job was a great national one; and let none be slighted who bore an honorable part in it. And while those who have cleared the great river may well be proud, even that is not all. It is hard to say that anything has been more bravely and well done than at Antietam, Murfreesboro, Gettysburg, and on many fields of less note. Nor must Uncle Sam's webfeet be forgotten. . At all the watery margins they have been present, not only on the deep sea, the broad bay, and the rapid river, but also up the narrow, muddy bayou, and wherever the ground was a little damp they have been and made their tracks. Thanks to all. For the great Republic—for the principle it lives by and keeps alive—for man's vast future—thanks to all.

"Peace does not appear so distant as it did. I hope it will come soon, and come to stay; and so come as to be worth the keeping in all future time. It will then have been proved that among freemen there can be no successful appeal from the ballot to the bullet, and that they who take such appeal are sure to lose their case and pay the cost. And there will be some black men who can remember that with silent tongue, and clinched teeth, and steady eye, and well-poised bayonet, they have helped mankind on to this great consummation; while I fear there will be some white ones unable to forget that with malignant heart and deceitful speech they have striven to hinder it."

The military events of the year were of great importance, and, on the whole, well calculated to give hope, not only to Mr. Lincoln, but to the loyal people of the whole country. After the battle of Fredericksburg, in December, 1862, the army of the Potomac did nothing for several months. Late in April—General Burnside having meantime been relieved, and General Hooker placed in command—a movement was made across the river, and the battle of Chancellorsville was fought, which resulted in the retreat of our army, and a loss of eighteen thousand men. It was a sad beginning of the year's operations, and was followed by the invasion of Maryland and Pennsylvania by the whole of General Lee's forces.

The invasion took place in June; and it was accomplished so quickly, so easily, and by so great a force, that the whole country became terribly excited. The President issued a proclamation calling for one hundred thousand militia to assist in driving back the foe. The army under Hooker crossed the Potomac at about the same time with the army of Lee, and both entered Maryland together. Here General Hooker was relieved, and General Meade placed in command, who, finding the enemy advancing toward and into Pennsylvania, pushed forward with his army to dispute the movement. On the first of July, the battle of Gettysburg in Pennsylvania began; and it raged with terrific energy for three days. It was one of the most brilliant and terrible battles of the war. On the fifth of July, the enemy, who had been terribly punished, and saw that his invasion was a failure, retreated, and was pursued by our weary forces back to the old position on the Rappahannock. At the close of the fighting on the third, it was evident that the enemy was whipped; and the President announced the fact on the fourth, by a dispatch sent over the whole country, stating that the news was such as to cover the army with the highest honor, and to promise a great success to the cause of the Union. With characteristic reverence, he closed by expressing his desire that on that day—the anniversary of the national independence—"He whose will, not ours, should ever be done, be everywhere remembered, and reverenced with profoundest gratitude." Our losses in this battle, in killed, wounded and missing, amounted to twenty-three thousand men, while those of the enemy were much greater, leaving, indeed, fourteen thousand prisoners in our hands. The state of Pennsylvania, with considerate liberality, subsequently purchased a piece of land adjoining the cemetery of the town, where much severe fighting took place, as a burial ground for the loyal dead of the great battle. This place was dedicated on the succeeding nineteenth of November, in the presence of Mr. Lincoln and his cabinet, Hon. Edward Everett delivering the formal address of the occasion. The brief remarks of Mr. Lincoln, though brought into immediate comparison with the elaborate eloquence of the venerable Massachusetts orator, were very effective, and betrayed a degree of literary ability quite unexpected to those who had read only his formal state papers. He said:

"Fourscore and seven years ago our fathers brought forth upon this continent a new nation, conceived in liberty, and dedicated to the proposition that all men are created equal. Now we are engaged in a great civil war, testing whether that nation, or any nation so conceived and so dedicated, can long endure. We are met on a great battle-field of that war. We have come to dedicate a portion of that field as a final resting-place for those who here gave their lives that that nation might live. It is altogether fitting and proper that we should do this. But in a larger sense we cannot dedicate, we cannot consecrate, we cannot hallow this ground. The brave men, living and dead, who struggled here, have consecrated it far above our power to add or detract. The world will little note, nor long remember, what we say here; but it can never forget what they did here. It is for us, the living, rather to be dedicated here to the unfinished work which they who fought here have thus far so nobly advanced. It is rather for us to be here dedicated to the great task remaining before us, that from these honored dead we take increased devotion to that cause for which they gave the last full measure of devotion; that we here highly resolve that these dead shall not have died in vain; that this nation, under God, shall have a new birth of freedom, and that the government of the people, by the people, and for the people, shall not perish from the earth."

Did Mr. Everett say more or better in all his pages than Mr. Lincoln said in these lines? Yet they were written after he left Washington, and during a brief interval of leisure.

The Fourth of July was further rendered memorable by the surrender of the city of Vicksburg—the stronghold of the Mississippi River—by General Pemberton to General Grant, with all his defenses and his army of thirty thousand men. After various unsuccessful operations, beginning with the year, contemplating the capture of this city, General Grant ran by the batteries with his transports, and landed far down the river, to attempt the approach of the city from the rear. Fighting all the way, and winning every battle, he reached Jackson, and then advanced westward, directly upon the doomed town. General Pemberton, in the endeavor to dispute his progress, lost at Baker's Creek four thousand men and twenty-nine pieces of artillery. On the banks of the Big Black, the enemy gave battle again, and was again defeated, with a loss of nearly three thousand men, and seventeen pieces of artillery. Then Pemberton fell back behind his defenses, which he did not leave till, on the national anniversary, he and his army marched forth as prisoners of war, leaving behind them more than two hundred cannon, and seventy thousand stand of small-arms. Four days later, Port Hudson, which had been closely besieged by an army advancing from the south, under General Banks, surrendered with seven thousand prisoners and fifty cannon.

Thus was the confederacy cut in twain; and from that hour its cause was doomed. Not a life was lost afterwards that was not lost in the destruction and defense of a hopeless cause. "The Father of Waters," wrote Mr. Lincoln, in glad and poetic mood, to Mr. Conkling, "again goes unvexed to the sea." It was a great event, and one which might well fill the heart of the President with exultation.

These victories gave great encouragement to the loyal people of the country; and, from the day of their occurrence, there was but little doubt among them of the final triumph of the national cause. In Washington, there were great rejoicings; and of course there was a popular call upon Mr. Lincoln, who, in response to a serenade, came out, and made a brief speech. These calls were not occasions in which he delighted, and it was honest and characteristic for him to say, in beginning: "I am very glad indeed to see you to-night, and yet I will not say I thank you for this call; but I do most sincerely thank Almighty God for the occasion on which you have called."

Another very characteristic utterance of Mr. Lincoln, in connection with these events, was a letter written to General Grant, July thirteenth, in which he took occasion to acknowledge that results had confirmed the General's judgment rather than his own:

"My Dear General: I do not remember that you and I ever met personally. I write this now as a grateful acknowledgment for the almost inestimable service you have done the country. I write to say a word further. When you first reached the vicinity of Vicksburg, I thought you should do what you finally did—march the troops across the neck, run the batteries with the transports, and thus go below; and I never had any faith, except a general hope that you knew better than I, that the Yazoo Pass expedition and the like could succeed. When you got below, and took Port Gibson, Grand Gulf, and vicinity, I thought you should go down the river and join General Banks; and when you turned northward, east of the Big Black, I feared it was a mistake. I wish now to make the personal acknowledgment that you were right and I was wrong."

The President's praise of General Grant was the voice of the country. The capture of Vicksburg, with its preliminary battles, was the work of a great general, and one of the most brilliant feats in the history of war. The country felt that it had one man, at least, who was not only thoroughly in earnest, but who was the master of his profession.

The operations in the west were pursued with various fortunes during the year; but with final results wholly in our favor. On the fifth of January, a battle occurred at Murfreesboro, which ended in the federal occupation of the place, and the falling back of the enemy to Tullahoma, where he entrenched himself. On the twenty-fifth of June, General Rosecrans advanced, and made an attack, driving Bragg and his army back in confusion. Pursuit was made as far as practicable, and Bragg kept up his retreat until he reached Chattanooga. Rosecrans came up with him August twenty-first, and then Bragg retired again, but, after receiving reinforcements, turned, and, on September nineteenth, made an attack upon our army. The engagement was a desperate one, inflicting severe losses upon the federal forces; but the rebels gained no permanent advantages. Burnside at Knoxville had been ordered to join Rosecrans, but had failed to do so, and, after the battle, Longstreet's corps of the rebel army was sent against him, while the enemy held his main force at or near Chattanooga. On the twenty-fifth of November, General Grant, who, having finished up his Vicksburg job, had assumed command, attacked Bragg, and utterly routed him, crowding him back into Georgia. Then Grant paid his respects to Longstreet, who was besieging Knoxville, and that General made safe his retreat into Virginia.

Mr. Lincoln, who had prayed for all these successes, referred them directly and at once to the favor of God. His announcement of the federal success at Gettysburg was accompanied by a call upon the people to remember and reverence Him with profoundest gratitude. After the fall of Vicksburg, he publicly thanked Almighty God for the event. On the fifteenth of July, he issued a proclamation, setting apart the sixth day of August to be observed as a day for national thanksgiving, praise and prayer: inviting the people to "render the homage due to the Divine Majesty, for the wonderful things he has done in the nation's behalf: and invoke the influences of his Holy Spirit to subdue the anger which has produced and so long sustained a needless and cruel rebellion; to change the hearts of the insurgents; to guide the counsels of the government with wisdom adequate to so great a national emergency; and to visit with tender care and consolation, throughout the length and breadth of our land, all those who, through the vicissitudes of marches, voyages, battles and sieges, have been brought to suffer in mind, body, or estate; and, finally, to lead the whole nation through paths of repentance and submission to the Divine Will, back to the perfect enjoyment of union and fraternal peace." On the third of October he issued another proclamation of thanksgiving, setting apart the last Thursday of November as the day to be observed. The spirit of tender piety which this document breathed in every part, could only have come from a heart surcharged with that spirit. Still again, having heard of the retreat of the insurgent forces from East Tennessee, he issued a dispatch on the seventh of December, recommending all loyal people, on the receipt of the information, to assemble at their places of worship, "and render special homage and gratitude to Almighty God for this great advancement of the national cause."

One of the most vexatious events of the year, to Mr. Lincoln, was the quarrel among his friends in Missouri, dating as far back as the removal of General Fremont, and not frowned upon by that General at its inception. An order of General Halleck, who succeeded General Hunter in Missouri, excluding fugitive slaves from his lines, though issued only for military reasons, helped on the discord. Then came discussions and action concerning emancipation, the parties dividing on the issue of gradual or immediate emancipation; and this was followed, or accompanied, by disagreement between the commander of the federal forces and Governor Gamble, controlling the state troops, raised originally as auxiliary to the government. General Curtis, who was in command of the department, was removed because he and Governor Gamble could not agree, and not because he had done any wrong; and General Schofield was put in his place. This offended Governor Gamble's enemies, and they remonstrated. Mr. Lincoln, in a note written at this time, said: "It is very painful to me that you, in Missouri, cannot or will not settle your factional quarrel among yourselves. I have been tormented with it beyond endurance for a month, by both sides. Neither side pays the least respect to my appeals to your reason."

General Fremont's friends wanted him recalled, and desired him to be military governor, setting Governor Gamble aside. Deputations, committees, and independent partisans visited Washington to "torment" the President still more. Each carried back a report, and made the most of it, to feed the quarrel. During the summer of 1863, the public feeling came up to fever heat. Gradual emancipationists were denounced as traitors by the radical emancipation party, which claimed to represent the only loyal elements of the state; and, of course, gradual emancipationists retorted the charge, and assumed the claim. On the fifth of October, the President wrote a long letter, reviewing the whole case, in his own frank and lucid way. He also sent a letter of instruction to General Schofield, in which he directed him so to use his power as "to compel the excited people there to let one another alone." Neither the letter nor the instructions produced

the slightest effect in quieting the political agitation, or soften-
ing the personal feeling which accompanied it. The department was subsequently placed under the command of General
Rosecrans; and the quarrel itself died out, or ceased to attract
public and presidential attention.   In the President's letter to
General Schofield, at the time of his appointment, he said to
him: "If both factions or neither abuse you, you will probably be about right.   Beware of being assailed by one and
praised by the other."   Judged by his own rule in this case,
the President was as nearly right as he could be, for both sides
abused him thoroughly.   Let it be said, however, to their
credit, that, at the succeeding presidential election, both supported him, and contributed to his triumph.

CHAPTER XXV.

THE pen has been so busy with the record of the great national events with which Mr. Lincoln was directly concerned, that no space has been found for entering the White House, and witnessing the kind of life that was lived there. The closing paragraphs of the last chapter will give an intimation of some of the perplexities that attended Mr. Lincoln's daily experience. More than any of his predecessors was he regarded as the father of his people. He was so accessible that they came to him with all their troubles, from the representatives of the factions in Missouri, to the old woman who applied to him to have a sum of money reserved from the wages of a clerk in one of the departments, that he might pay her bill for board. Every man seemed to think that Mr. Lincoln could settle his little difficulty, or provide for his little want, whatever it might be. It was the story of his younger life re-enacted. He had always been a reconciler of difficulties between men; and he remarked, while in the presidential chair, that it seemed as if he was regarded as a police justice, before whom all the petty troubles of men were brought for adjustment.

In one matter—and that an important one—he differed from all who had preceded him in his office. Such an affair as a genuine cabinet consultation hardly occurred during his administration. His heads of departments were heads of departments indeed. He intended that they should do the work of their special office, and that they should be held responsible for it. The affairs of state were managed by Mr. Seward, and not by Mr. Lincoln. The Treasury was almost as much in the hands of Mr. Chase, during his occupation of office, as if he were irresponsible to the head of the government. The same fact held concerning all the other secretaries. He was more intimate with the Secretary of War, probably, than with any other member of the cabinet, because operations in the field were the leading affairs of interest and importance; and it is probable, also, that his influence was more felt in the war office than in any other of the departments. Mr. Chase has said that he never attended a meeting of the cabinet without taking with him the figures that showed the exact condition of the Treasury at the time, and that, during the whole of his official life, he was not once called upon to show these figures. Mr. Lincoln contented himself with such knowledge as he gained in a general way concerning the affairs entrusted to him. The tenacity with which he clung to his chosen advisers and official family, throughout all the attempts of politicians and the public to unseat them, was remarkable; and illustrated not only the faithfulness of his friendship but the inflexibleness of his will.

If any action was ever taken by one of his secretaries that seemed to him ill-advised, he did not hesitate to interfere; but, sitting in his place, and performing what seemed to him to be his special duties, he intended that his associates in the government should sit in their places, and perform their duties; and he left them free to win such honor as they could, by the administration of the affairs of their respective departments.

The first three years of the war, with all their excitements, responsibilities and anxieties, produced a powerful effect upon his physical constitution. He entered the White House, a healthy man, with a frame of iron; and, without indulgence in a single debilitating vice, he became a feeble man, weary and worn beyond the reach of rest. The tired feeling very rarely left him. His relief was in story-telling, in books of humor, in theatrical representations, and in music. A lady who was, for a time, a member of his family, related to the writer an incident touching his love of music and its effect upon him.   One evening he was prevailed upon to attend the opera.   He was very tired, and quite inclined to remain at home; but, at the close of the evening's entertainment, he declared himself so much rested that he felt as if he could go home and work a month.   Simple heart-songs pleased him, however, much more than the elaborate music of the opera. The poetry of Burns, and the class of verse to which it belonged, were subjects of his special admiration; and the music that was their fitting expression was to him the most delightful of all.

With the soldiers who were fighting the battles of the country, he had the deepest sympathy.   Whenever he was congratulated upon a success in the field, he never failed to allude gratefully to the noble men who had won it.   The trials of these men—their sacrifices of comfort and health, of limb and life—touched him with a sympathy that really sapped the foundations of his constitution.   They were constantly in his thoughts; and not a battle was fought to whose sacrifices his own vitality did not contribute.   He admired the fighting man, and looked upon him as, in one sense, his superior.   Although he did not plead guilty to the weakness of moral cowardice, he felt that the battle-field was a fearful place, from which, unaided by its special inspirations, he should run.   Indeed, Mr. Lincoln did not give himself credit for the physical courage which he really possessed, though he had probably grown timid with his failing strength.

This sympathy with the soldiers he manifested in many ways, and in none more than in his treatment of their offenses against military law.   In a letter to the author, a personal friend of the President says: "I called on him one day in the early part of the war.   He had just written a pardon for a young man who had been sentenced to be shot, for sleeping at his post, as a sentinel.   He remarked as he read it to me: 'I could not think of going into eternity with the blood of the poor young man on my skirts.'   Then he added: 'It is not to be wondered at that a boy, raised on a farm, probably in the habit of going to bed at dark, should, when required to watch, fall asleep; and I cannot consent to shoot him for such an act.'" This story, with its moral, is made complete by Rev. Newman Hall of London, who, in a sermon preached after and upon Mr. Lincoln's death, says that the dead body of this youth was found among the slain on the field of Fredericksburg, wearing next his heart a photograph of his preserver, beneath which the grateful fellow had written, "God bless President Lincoln!" From the same sermon, another anecdote is gleaned, of a similar character, which is evidently authentic. An officer of the army, in conversation with the preacher, said: "The first week of my command, there were twenty-four deserters sentenced by court martial to be shot, and the warrants for their execution were sent to the President to be signed. He refused. I went to Washington, and had an interview. I said: 'Mr. President, unless these men are made an example of, the army itself is in danger. Mercy to the few is cruelty to the many.' He replied: 'Mr. General, there are already too many weeping widows in the United States. For God's sake, do n't ask me to add to the number, for I won't do it.'"

Whole chapters might be occupied by the record of such incidents as these. The woe that the war brought upon the people kept his sympathetic heart always bleeding. One of the last acts of his official life was the granting of a pardon for a military offense. A friend from Illinois called to plead for the life of a neighbor—a soldier who was on his way with his regiment through Washington, and, falling out of the ranks, entered a drinking saloon, was overcome with liquor, and failed to join his regiment before it left the city. He was arrested for desertion, and sentenced to be shot. The soldier's friend found Mr. Lincoln with a table before him literally covered with documents, which were all to be signed by him. There was not room enough on the table to hold the paper for a pardon. Mr. Lincoln heard the explanation of the case, and remarked: "Well, I think the boy can do us more good above ground than under ground;" and then he proceeded to another table to write his pardon. Afterwards, laughingly regarding the table from which the mass of papers had driven him, he said: "By the way, do you know how the Patagonians eat oysters? They open them, and throw the shells out of the window, till the pile gets higher than the house, and then they move!" He could not omit his "little story," even in a case of life and death.

There never lived a man more considerate of human weakness than Abraham Lincoln. He always found so many apologies for the sins of others that he could cherish no resentments against them, even when those sins were maliciously committed against himself. When his friends went to him with the remarks of ill-natured and inimical persons, he preferred not to have them repeated, and turned off his indignant informers with a story, or the remark: "I guess we won't talk about that now." He never read the public abuse of himself in the newspapers; and of one of the most virulent attacks upon him he simply remarked that it was "ill-timed." Of one of his bitter political enemies, he said: "I've been told that insanity is hereditary in his family, and I think we will admit the plea in his case." Charity, pity, mercy, sympathy—these were virtues which reigned in the White House during Mr. Lincoln's occupation of it.

Yet Mr. Lincoln could be severe. Toward crimes resulting from sudden anger, or untoward circumstances and sharp temptations,—the long catalogue of vices growing out of human weakness,—toward these, he was always lenient; but toward a cool, calculating crime against the race, or any member of it, from ambitious or mercenary motives, he was severe. The systematic, heartless oppression of one man by another man, always aroused his indignation to the highest pitch. An incident occurred soon after his inauguration which forcibly illustrates this point. Hon. John B. Alley of Lynn, Massachusetts, was made the bearer to the President of a petition for pardon, by a person confined in the Newburyport jail for being engaged in the slave-trade. He had been sentenced to five years' imprisonment, and the payment of a fine of one

28

thousand dollars. The petition was accompanied by a letter to Mr. Alley, in which the prisoner acknowledged his guilt and the justice of his sentence. He was very penitent,—at least, on paper,—and had received the full measure of his punishment, so far as it related to the term of his imprisonment; but he was still held because he could not pay his fine. Mr. Alley read the letter to the President, who was much moved by its pathetic appeals; and when he had himself read the petition, he looked up, and said: "My friend, that is a very touching appeal to our feelings. You know my weakness is to be, if possible, too easily moved by appeals for mercy, and, if this man were guilty of the foulest murder that the arm of man could perpetrate, I might forgive him on such an appeal; but the man who could go to Africa, and rob her of her children, and sell them into interminable bondage, with no other motive than that which is furnished by dollars and cents, is so much worse than the most depraved murderer, that he can never receive pardon at my hands. No! He may rot in jail before he shall have liberty by any act of mine." A sudden crime, committed under strong temptation, was venial in his eyes, on evidence of repentance; but the calculating, mercenary crime of man-stealing and man-selling, with all the cruelties that are essential accompaniments of the business, could win from him, as an officer of the people, no pardon.

Two ladies, wives of rebel officers imprisoned on Johnson's Island, applied for their release, with great importunity, one of them urging that her husband was a very religious man. As he granted their request, he said to the lady who had testified to her husband's religion: "You say your husband is a religious man: tell him, when you meet him, that I say I am not much of a judge of religion; but that, in my opinion, the religion that sets men to rebel and fight against their government, because, as they think, that government does not sufficiently help some men to eat their bread in the sweat of other men's faces, is not the sort of religion upon which men can get to heaven."

Certainly Mr. Lincoln's religion was very different from

this. It was one which sympathized with all human sorrow; which lifted, so far as it had the power, the burden from the oppressed; which let the prisoner go free; and which called daily for supplies of strength and wisdom from the divine fountains. He grew more religious with every passing year of his official life. The tender piety that breathed in some of his later state papers is unexampled in any of the utterances of his predecessors. In all the great emergencies of his closing years, his reliance upon divine guidance and assistance was often extremely touching. "I have been driven many times to my knees," he once remarked, "by the overwhelming conviction that I had no where else to go. My own wisdom and that of all about me seemed insufficient for that day." On another occasion, when told that he was daily remembered in the prayers of those who prayed, he said that he had been a good deal helped by the thought; and then he added with much solemnity: "I should be the most presumptuous blockhead upon this footstool, if I for one day thought that I could discharge the duties which have come upon me since I came into this place, without the aid and enlightenment of One who is wiser and stronger than all others." He felt, he said, that he should leave Washington a better man if not a wiser, from having learned what a very poor sort of man he was. He always remained shy in the exposure of his religious experiences, but those around him caught golden glimpses of a beautiful Christian character. With failing strength and constant weariness, the even temper of the man sometimes gave way, while his frequent experience of the faithlessness and cupidity of men made him at last distrustful of those who approached him.

In February, 1862, Mr. Lincoln was visited by severe affliction in the death of his beautiful son Willie, and the extreme sickness of Thomas, familiarly called "Tad." This was a new burden; and the visitation which, in his firm faith in Providence, he regarded as providential, was also inexplicable. Why should he, with so many burdens upon him, and with such necessity for solace in his home and his affections, be brought into so tender a trial? It was to him a trial of faith, indeed. A Christian lady of Massachusetts, who was officiating as nurse in one of the hospitals, came in to attend the sick children. She reports that Mr. Lincoln watched with her about the bedside of the sick ones, and that he often walked the room, saying sadly: "This is the hardest trial of my life; why is it? Why is it?" In the course of conversations with her, he questioned her concerning her situation. She told him she was a widow, and that her husband and two children were in Heaven; and added that she saw the hand of God in it all, and that she had never loved him so much before as she had since her affliction. "How is that brought about?" inquired Mr. Lincoln. "Simply by trusting in God, and feeling that he does all things well," she replied. "Did you submit fully under the first loss?" he asked. "No," she answered, "not wholly; but, as blow came upon blow, and all was taken, I could and did submit, and was very happy." He responded: "I am glad to hear you say that. Your experience will help me to bear my afflictions."

On being assured that many Christians were praying for him on the morning of the funeral, he wiped away the tears that sprang in his eyes, and said: "I am glad to hear that. I want them to pray for me. I need their prayers." As he was going out to the burial, the good lady expressed her sympathy with him. He thanked her gently, and said: "I will try to go to God with my sorrows." A few days afterward, she asked him if he could trust God. He replied: "I think I can, and I will try. I wish I had that childlike faith you speak of, and I trust He will give it to me." And then he spoke of his mother, whom so many years before he had committed to the dust among the wilds of Indiana. In this hour of his great trial, the memory of her who had held him upon her bosom, and soothed his childish griefs, came back to him with tenderest recollections. "I remember her prayers," said he, "and they have always followed me. They have clung to me all my life."

This lady was with the President on subsequent occasions.

After the second defeat at Bull Run, he appeared very much distressed about the number of killed and wounded, and said: "I have done the best I could. I have asked God to guide me, and now I must leave the event with him." On another occasion, having been made acquainted with the fact that a great battle was in progress, at a distant but important point, he came into the room where the lady was engaged in nursing a member of the family, looking worn and haggard, and saying that he was so anxious that he could eat nothing. The possibility of defeat depressed him greatly; but the lady told him he must trust, and that he could at least pray. "Yes," said he, and taking up a Bible, he started for his room. Could all the people of the nation have overheard the earnest petition that went up from that inner chamber, as it reached the ears of the nurse, they would have fallen upon their knees with tearful and reverential sympathy. At one o'clock in the afternoon, a telegram reached him announcing a Union victory; and then he came directly to the room, his face beaming with joy, saying: "Good news! Good news! The victory is ours, and God is good." "Nothing like prayer," suggested the pious lady, who traced a direct connection between the event and the prayer which preceded it." "Yes there is," he replied—"praise:—prayer and praise." The good lady who communicates these incidents closes them with the words: "I do believe he was a true Christian, though he had very little confidence in himself."

Mr. Lincoln always manifested a strong interest in the peculiar work of the Christian Commission in the army, and attended the important meetings of that body at Washington. His official and personal approval of the plan of this charity was one of the greatest encouragements of those engaged in the work. In the early part of 1864, a meeting of the commission was held, at which Mr. Lincoln was a deeply interested spectator. He was particularly moved on this occasion by the remarks of Chaplain McCabe, just released from Libby prison, at Richmond, who described, in a graphic manner, the scene among the prisoners on the reception of the news of the national victory at Gettysburg, as they took up Mrs. Howe's spirited lyric, beginning with the line,

"Mine eyes have seen the glory of the coming of the Lord,

and made the prison walls rock with the melody. The Chaplain sang it to the meeting, and Mr. Lincoln requested its repetition. That was a song that he could appreciate; and it stirred him like a trumpet.

At another of these meetings, he was greatly interested and amused by a story told by General Fisk of Missouri. The General had begun his military life as a Colonel; and, when he raised his regiment in Missouri, he proposed to his men that he should do all the swearing of the regiment. They assented; and for months no instance was known of the violation of the promise. The Colonel had a teamster named John Todd, who, as roads were not always the best, had some difficulty in commanding his temper and his tongue. John happened to be driving a mule-team through a series of mud-holes a little worse than usual, when, unable to restrain himself any longer, he burst forth into a volley of energetic oaths. The Colonel took notice of the offense, and brought John to an account. "John," said he, "didn't you promise to let me do all the swearing of the regiment?" "Yes, I did, Colonel," he replied, "but the fact was the swearing had to be done then, or not at all, and you weren't there to do it."

Mr. Lincoln enjoyed this story quite as much as he did the singing of the previous occasion, and gave himself up to laughter the most boisterous. The next morning, General Fisk attended the reception at the White House; and saw, waiting in the ante-room, a poor old man from Tennessee. Sitting down beside him, he inquired his errand; and learned that he had been waiting three or four days to get an audience, and that on his seeing Mr. Lincoln probably depended the life of his son, who was under sentence of death for some military offense. General Fisk wrote his case in outline on a card, and sent it in, with a special request that the President would see the man. In a moment, the order came; and past senators, governors and generals, waiting impatiently, the old man went into the President's presence.   He showed Mr. Lincoln his papers; and he, on taking them, said he would look into the case, and give him the result on the following day. The old man, in an agony of apprehension, looked up into the President's sympathetic face, and actually cried out: "To-morrow may be too late!   My son is under sentence of death! The decision ought to be made now!" and the streaming tears told how much he was moved.   "Come," said Mr. Lincoln, "wait a bit, and I'll tell you a story;" and then he told the old man General Fisk's story about the swearing driver; and, as he told it, the old man forgot his boy, and both the President and his listener had a hearty laugh together at its conclusion.   Then he wrote a few words which the old man read, and in which he found new occasion for tears; but the tears were tears of joy, for the words saved the life of his son.

Only a few months before Mr. Lincoln died, he was waited upon at the White House by about two hundred members of the commission, who had been holding their annual meeting. The chairman of the commission, George H. Stuart, addressed a few words to Mr. Lincoln, speaking of the debt which the country owed him.   "My friends," said Mr. Lincoln in reply, "you owe me no gratitude for what I have done: and I—" and here he hesitated, and the long arm came through the air awkwardly, as if he might be misunderstood in what he was going to say;—"and I, I may say, owe you no gratitude for what you have done; just as, in a sense, we owe no gratitude to the men who have fought our battles for us.   I trust that this has all been for us a work of duty;" and at the mention of that word, the homely, sad face was irradiated with the light of a divine emotion.   Looking around for encouragement into the faces of the eager group, he then proceeded in the simplest words to say that all gratitude was due to the Great Giver of all good.   At the close of his remarks, Mr. Stuart, who cared as little for precedent as Mr. Lincoln himself, asked him if he had any objection, then and there, to a word of prayer.   Quietly, but very cordially, as if he were grateful for the suggestion, he assented; and Bishop Janes offered in the East Room a brief and fervent petition. It was a memorable scene, which must always be reverted to with interest by every Christian patriot.

On another occasion, when a number of the members of the commission were holding an interview with the President, Rev. J. T. Duryea of New York referred to the trust that they were encouraged to repose in the Providence of God, and to the fact that appeal was so constantly made to it in the prayers of Christian people that even children were taught to pray for the President in their simple morning and evening petitions. "If it were not for my firm belief in an over-ruling Providence," responded Mr. Lincoln, "it would be difficult for me, in the midst of such complications of affairs, to keep my reason on its seat. But I am confident that the Almighty has his plans, and will work them out; and, whether we see it or not, they will be the wisest and best for us. I have always taken counsel of him, and referred to him my plans, and have never adopted a course of proceeding without being assured, as far as I could be, of his approbation. To be sure, he has not conformed to my desires, or else we should have been out of our trouble long ago. On the other hand, his will does not seem to agree with the wish of our enemy over there (pointing across the Potomac). He stands the judge between us, and we ought to be willing to accept his decisions. We have reason to anticipate that it will be favorable to us, for our cause is right." It was during this interview that the fact was privately communicated to a member of the commission, that Mr. Lincoln was in the habit of spending an early hour each day in prayer.

It was during this interview, also, that, on some allusion being made to the unfriendly personal criticisms of the press, he said: "It has been asserted that we are conducting the present administration in the interest of a party, to secure a re-election. It is said that appointments in the army are made with this view, and that the removals are intended to put promising rivals out of the way. Now, if any man shows himself to be able to save the country, he shall have my hearty support. If he wants to be president, he ought to be, and I will help him. The charge is absurd. What matters it who is chosen the next president, if there is to be no next presidency? What matters it who is appointed pilot for the next voyage, if the ship is going down this voyage?" When allusion was made to the carping spirit of some of the professed friends of the government, who, distinguishing between the administration and the government, condemned the former while pretending to defend the latter, he said: "There is an important sense in which the government is distinct from the administration. One is perpetual, the other is temporary and changeable. A man may be loyal to his government, and yet oppose the peculiar principles and methods of the administration. I should regret to see the day in which the people should cease to express intelligent, honest, generous criticism upon the policy of their rulers. It is true, however, that, in time of great peril, the distinction ought not to be so strongly urged; for then criticism may be regarded by the enemy as opposition, and may weaken the wisest and best efforts for the public safety. If there ever was such a time, it seems to me it is now."

An illustration of Mr. Lincoln's interest in the efforts of religious men, is found in his treatment of a case brought before him by Rev. Mr. Duryea, whose name has already been mentioned. Colonel Loomis, commandant at Fort Columbus, on Governor's Island, was to be removed because he had passed the legal limit of age for active service. His religious influence was so powerful that the Chaplain of the post appealed to Mr. Duryea to use his influence for the good officer's retention in the service. Accordingly, appeal was made to the President for that object, purely on religious grounds. "What does Mr. Duryea know of military matters?" inquired Mr. Lincoln, with a smile, of the bearer of his petition. "Nothing," replied the gentleman; "and he makes no request on military considerations. The record of Colonel Loomis for fifty years, in the War Department, will furnish these. He asks simply to retain the influence of a man whose Christian character is pure and consistent, who sustains religious exercises at the fort, leads a weekly prayer-meeting, and teaches a Bible class in the Sabbath School." Mr. Lincoln replied: "That is his highest possible recommendation. Take this petition to the Secretary of War, with my approval." The result was the retention of Colonel Loomis at his post, until his services were needed in important court-martial business.

Mr. Lincoln's habits at the White House were as simple as they were at his old home in Illinois. He never alluded to himself as "President," or as occupying "the Presidency." His office, he always designated as "this place." "Call me Lincoln," said he to a friend,—"Mr. President" had become so very tiresome to him. "If you see a newsboy down the street, send him up this way," said he to a passenger, as he stood waiting for the morning news at his gate. Friends cautioned him against exposing himself so openly in the midst of enemies; but he never heeded them. He frequently walked the streets at night, entirely unprotected; and he felt any check upon his free movements as a great annoyance. He delighted to see his familiar western friends; and he gave them always a cordial welcome. He met them on the old footing, and fell at once into the accustomed habits of talk and story-telling. An old acquaintance, with his wife, visited Washington. Mr. and Mrs. Lincoln proposed to these friends a ride in the presidential carriage. It should be stated, in advance, that the two men had probably never seen each other with gloves on in their lives, unless when they were used as protection from the cold. The question of each—Mr. Lincoln at the White House, and his friend at the hotel—was, whether he should wear gloves. Of course, the ladies urged gloves; but Mr. Lincoln only put his in his pocket, to be used or not, according to circumstances. When the presidential party arrived at the hotel, to take in their friends, they found the gentleman, overcome by his wife's persuasions, very handsomely gloved. The moment he took his seat, he began to draw off the clinging kids, while Mr. Lincoln began to draw his on. "No! no!

no!" protested his friend, tugging at his gloves; "It is none
of my doings: put up your gloves, Mr. Lincoln." So the
two old friends were on even and easy terms, and had their
ride after their old fashion.

Let us look a little deeper into this life in the White House.
The writer has before him a private letter written by a lady
of great intelligence and the keenest powers of observation,
from which he has the liberty to draw some most interesting
materials, illustrative of Mr. Lincoln's mode of dealing with
men and women, and with the questions which were presented
to him for decision. They will illustrate as well his weakness as his strength; and show, better than any direct statement, how the duties of his position had worn upon his nerves
and his temper. The lady was the widow of one who had
died while serving the soldiers of the state of which he was
the Governor; and she had taken up his work of charity, and
pursued it from the time of his death.

The lady says she was received by Mr. Lincoln after a
brief delay. He was alone, in a medium-sized, office-like
room, with no elegance around him, and no elegance in him.
He was plainly clad in a suit of black, that fitted him poorly;
and was sitting in a folded-up sort of way, in his arm-chair.
At his side stood a high writing-desk and table combined;
under his feet was a simple straw matting; and around him
were sofas and chairs, covered with green worsted. Nothing
more unpretending could be imagined. As she entered, his
head was bent forward, his chin resting on his breast, and his
hand holding the letter she had sent in. He made a feint
of rising; and, looking out from under his eyebrows, said
inquiringly: "Mrs. ——?" Hastening forward, she replied:
"Yes, and I am very glad to see you, Mr. Lincoln." He
took her hand, and "hoped she was well," but gave no smile
of welcome. She had come on business which interfered
with his policy and plans; and she anxiously read his face,
full of its lines of care and thought, and almost stern in
its expression. He motioned her to a chair; and, while he was
reading her letter, she continued the perusal of his features.

After he had finished, he looked up, ran his fingers through his slightly silvered brown hair, and with an air of sad severity said: "Madam, this matter of northern hospitals has been talked of a great deal, and I thought it was settled; but it seems this is not the case. What have you got to say about it?" "Simply this," she replied, "that many soldiers, sick in our western army on the Mississippi, must have northern air, or die. There are thousands of graves along the Mississippi and Yazoo, for which the government is responsible—ignorantly, undoubtedly; but this ignorance must not continue. If you will permit these men to come North, you, will have ten men in one year where you have got one now."

Mr. Lincoln could not see the logic of this. Shrugging his shoulders, and smiling in his peculiar, quizzical way, he said: "If your reasoning were correct, your argument would be a good one. I don't see how sending one sick man North is going to give us ten well ones." The lady replied: "You understand me, I think." "Yes, yes," said he, "I understand you; but if they go North they will desert, and where is the difference?" Her reply was: "Dead men cannot fight, and they may not desert." "A fine way to decimate the army!" exclaimed the President. "We should never get a man back—not one—not one." "Pardon me," responded the lady, "but I believe you are mistaken. You do not understand our people. They are as true and as loyal to the government as yourself. The loyalty is among the common soldiers, and they are the chief sufferers." Almost contemptuously Mr. Lincoln replied: "This is your opinion!"

The reader will see in this exhibition of petulance, evidence that the President was conscious of being undermined in his predeterminations. "Mrs. ——," said he, earnestly, "How many men of the army of the Potomac do you suppose the government was paying at the battle of Antietam? and how many men do you suppose could be got for active service at that time?" She replied: "I know nothing of the army of the Potomac, except that it has made some noble sacrifices."

"Well, but give a guess," persisted the President. "Indeed, I cannot," was her answer. He threw himself awkwardly around in his chair, with one leg over the arm, and spoke slowly: "This war might have been finished at that time, if every man had been in his place who was able to be there; but they were scattered here and there over the North—some on furloughs, and in one way and another gone, so that, out of one hundred and seventy thousand men, whom the government was paying, only eighty-three thousand could be got for action. The consequences, you know, proved nearly disastrous." The President paused for a response, and it came. "It was very sad; but the delinquents were certainly not in northern hospitals, nor were they deserters from northern hospitals, for we have had none: so your argument is not against them."

The President appreciated this logic thoroughly, and replied: "Well, well; you go and call on the Secretary of War, and see what he says." He then took the lady's letter, and wrote on the back: "Admit Mrs. —— at once. Listen to what she says. She is a lady of intelligence, and talks sense. A. Lincoln." "May I return to you, Mr. Lincoln?" she inquired. "Certainly," said he, gently; and then the lady found her way to Mr. Stanton's office, and was listened to and treated with great respectfulness and kindness. She was told by the Secretary that he had sent the Surgeon-general to New Orleans, with directions to come up the river, and visit all the hospitals. Mrs. —— had no faith in these inspections, and told him so—told him, further, that no good to the western soldiers had ever resulted from them. She also indicated what she believed to be the reasons for the favorable reports from the southern hospitals, that had uniformly been made. "I believe," said she, "that it is because the medical authorities know that the heads of departments are opposed to establishing hospitals so far from army lines, and report accordingly. I wish this could be over-ruled. Can nothing be done?" "Nothing until the Surgeon-general returns," he replied. Personally, he expressed himself in favor of hospitals in every northern state, but he had to be guided by the medical authorities.

She bade him "good morning," and returned to the President. No one was waiting, and at the invitation of the messenger she passed directly into the President's room. She found a gentleman engaged in conversation with the President, but neither noticed her entrance. Taking a seat at a distance from the two gentlemen, she waited her opportunity. The visitor handed a paper to Mr. Lincoln. He looked it over carelessly, and said: "Yes, that is a sufficient indorsement for anybody: what do you want?" The reply was not heard; but the promotion of some person in the army was strongly urged. She heard the sarcastic words from the applicant: "I see there are no vacancies among the Brigadiers, from the fact that so many Colonels are commanding brigades."

At this, the President threw himself forward in his chair in such a way as to expose to the lady the most curious, comical expression of features imaginable. He was looking the man squarely in the face; and, with one hand softly patting the other, and the funny look pervading every line of his countenance, he said: "My friend, let me tell you something about that. You are a farmer, I believe; if not, you will understand me. Suppose you had a large cattle-yard, full of all sorts of cattle—cows, oxen and bulls,—and you kept killing and selling and disposing of your cows and oxen, in one way and another, taking good care of your bulls. By and by you would find out that you had nothing but a yard full of old bulls, good for nothing under heaven. Now it will be just so with the army, if I don't stop making Brigadier-generals."

The man was answered, and he tried to laugh; but the effort was a feeble one. Mr. Lincoln laughed, however, enough for both parties. He laughed all over, and laughed his visitor out of the room.

The lady stepped forward; and, as Mr. Lincoln motioned her to a chair, he inquired what the Secretary of War had said to her. She gave him a full account of the interview, and added: "I have nowhere to go but to you." He replied,

"Mr. Stanton knows there is an acting Surgeon-general here, and that Hammond will not return these two months. I will see the Secretary of War myself, to-night; and you may come again in the morning." He then dismissed her in the kindest manner and with the kindest words.

No reader can doubt that from this moment he had determined to grant the lady her request; and this is to be remembered in the reading of the interviews which followed; for in these interviews occurred a strange exhibition of his *penchant* for arguing against and opposing his own conclusions—in this case almost with temper—certainly not in the most amiable manner.

In the morning, the lady returned, full of hope, expecting to be greeted by the same genial face and cordial manner with which Mr. Lincoln had dismissed her. The President raised his eyes as she entered his room, said "good morning," and pointed to a chair. He was evidently annoyed at something which had occurred during some previous conversation of the morning, and waited for her to speak. She waited for him. "Well?" said he, after a minute of delay. "Well?" replied his visitor. He looked up under his eyebrows, a little startled, and inquired: "Have you nothing to say?" "Nothing," she replied, "until I hear your decision. Have you decided? You know you bade me come this morning." "No, I have not decided; and I believe this idea of northern hospitals is a great humbug, and I am tired of hearing about it." The lady pitied him in his weak and irritable mood, and said: "I regret to add a feather's weight to your already overwhelming care and responsibility. I would rather have stayed at home." With a feeble smile, he responded: "I wish you had." She was earnest, and replied: "Nothing would have given me greater pleasure, sir; but a keen sense of duty to this government, justice and mercy to its most loyal supporters, and regard for your honor and position, made me come. The people cannot understand why their husbands, fathers and sons are left to die, when, with proper care and attention, they ought to live, and yet do good service for their conntry. Mr. Lincoln, I do believe you will yet be grateful for my coming. I do not come to plead for the lives of criminals, nor for the lives of deserters; but I plead for the lives of those who were the first to hasten to the support of this government, who helped to place you where you are—for men who have done all they could; and now, when flesh and nerve and muscle are gone, who still pray for your life, and the life of the republic. They scarcely ask for that for which I plead. They expect to sacrifice their lives for their country. I know that, if they could come North, they could live, and be well, strong men again,—at least, many of them. I say I know, because I was sick among them last spring, surrounded by every comfort, with the best of care, and determined to get well. I grew weaker and weaker, day by day, until, not being under military law, my friends brought me North. I recovered entirely by breathing northern air."

While she was so earnestly speaking, Mr. Lincoln's expression of face changed often, but he did not take his eyes from her. He was evidently distressed, for he was convinced that she was speaking the truth. His face contracted almost painfully as he said: "You assume to know more than I do." The tears almost came in the lady's eyes as she replied: "Pardon me, Mr. Lincoln, I intend no disrespect; but it is because of this knowledge, and because I do know what you do not know, that I come to you. If you had known what I know, and had not already ordered what I ask, I should know that an appeal to you would be in vain; but I believe in you. I believe the people have not trusted you in vain. The question only is—do you believe me, or not? If you believe in me, you will give us hospitals; if not—well."

"You assume to know more than surgeons do," said Mr. Lincoln, sharply. "Oh no," she replied; "I could not perform an amputation nearly so well as some of them do. But this is true: I do not come here for your favor. I am no aspirant for military favor or promotion. While it would be the pride of my life to command your respect and confidence, still, even this I can waive to gain my object—waive for the time. You will do me justice, some time. Now the medical authorities know as well as you and I do, that you are opposed to establishing northern hospitals; and they report to please you. They desire your favor. I come to you from no casual tour of inspection, having passed rapidly through the general hospitals, with a cigar in my mouth and a ratan in my hand, talking to the surgeon in charge of the price of cotton, and abusing our generals in the army for not knowing and performing their duty better, and finally coming into the open air with a long-drawn breath as though I had just escaped suffocation, and complacently saying to the surgeon: 'A very fine hospital you have here, Sir. The boys seem to be doing very well. A little more attention to ventilation is desirable, perhaps.' It is not thus that I have visited hospitals. For eight long months—from early morning until late at night, sometimes—I have visited the regimental and general hospitals on the Mississippi, from Quincy to Vicksburg; and I come to you from the cots of men who have died, and who might have lived if you had permitted it. This is hard to say, but it is true."

While she was speaking the last sentences, Mr. Lincoln's brow had become severely contracted; and a pained, hard expression had settled upon his whole face. Then he sharply asked her how many men her state had sent to the field. She replied: "about fifty thousand." "That means," he responded, "that she has about twenty thousand now." With an unpleasant voice and manner he continued: "You need not look so sober; they are not all dead." The veins filled in his face painfully, and one across his forehead was fearfully large and blue. Then, with an impatient movement of his whole frame, he said: "I have a good mind to dismiss them all from the service, and have no more trouble with them."

The lady was astonished, as she might well be, for she knew that he was not in earnest. They sat looking at one another in silence. He had become very pale, and at last she broke the silence by saying: "They have been faithful to the government; they have been faithful to you; they will still be

29

loyal to the government, do what you will with them. But, if you will grant my petition, you will be glad as long as you live. The prayers of grateful hearts will give you strength in the hour of trial, and strong and willing arms will return to fight your battles."

The President bowed his head; and, with a look of sadness which it is impossible for language to describe, said: "*I shall never be glad any more.*" All severity had passed away from his face, and he seemed looking inward and backward, and appeared unconscious of the fact that he was not alone. The great burdens he had borne, the terrible anxieties and perplexities that had poisoned his life at the fountain, and the peaceful scenes he had forever left behind, swept across his memory; and then the thought that it was possible that he had erred in judgment, and done injustice to the noble men who had fought the nation's battles, brought back all his childlike tenderness.

The lady heard his mournful utterances, and said: "Oh! do not say so, Mr. Lincoln, for who will have so much reason to rejoice as yourself, when the government shall be restored— as it will be?"

"I know—I know," he said, pressing a hand on either side; "but the springs of life are wearing away, and I shall not last." She asked him if he felt that his great cares were injuring his health. "No," he replied; "not directly, perhaps." She asked him if he slept well. He never was a good sleeper, he replied, and of course slept now less than ever before. Then, with earnestness, he said: "The people do not yet comprehend the magnitude of this rebellion, and will be a long time before the end."

The lady, feeling that she had occupied too much of his time, rose to take her leave; and, as she did so, said: "Have you decided upon your answer to me?" "No," he replied, "come to-morrow morning:—stop, it is cabinet-meeting to-morrow. Yes, come at twelve o'clock; there is not much for the cabinet to do, to-morrow." Then he bade his visitor a cordial good morning, and she retired.

The next morning, the lady found that her interview had prostrated her; but at twelve o'clock she was at the White House. The President sent her word that the cabinet would adjourn soon, and that she must wait. For three long hours she waited, receiving occasional messages from Mr. Lincoln, to the effect that the cabinet would soon adjourn, and he would then see her. She was in distress, expecting defeat. She walked the room, and gazed at the maps, and, at last, she heard the sound of feet. The cabinet had adjourned. Mr. Lincoln did not send for her, but came shuffling into the room, rubbing his hands, and saying: " My dear Madam, I am sorry I have kept you waiting so long, but we have this moment adjourned." " My waiting is no matter," she replied, " but you must be very tired, and we will not talk to-night." Bidding her to a seat, she having risen as he entered, he sat down at her side, and quietly remarked: " I only wish to say to you that an order which is equivalent to the granting of a hospital in your state, has been issued from the War Department, nearly twenty-four hours."

The lady could make no reply, except through the tears that sprang at once. Mr. Lincoln looked on, and enjoyed it. When, at last, she could command her voice, she said: " God bless you!" Then, as doubts came, touching the nature of the order, she said earnestly: " Do you mean, really and truly, that we are going to have a hospital now?" With a look full of benevolence and tenderness,—such a look as rarely illuminates any face,—he said: " I do most certainly hope so;" and then he told her to come on the following morning, and he would give her a copy of the order. But his visitor was too much affected to talk; and perceiving this, he kindly changed the subject, asking her to look at a map which hung in the room, representing the great battle-grounds of Europe. " It is a very fine map," said he; " see—here is Waterloo, here are all the battle-fields about the Crimea." Then, suddenly turning to the lady, he said: " I'm afraid you will not like it so well, when I tell you who executed it." She replied: " It is a great work, whoever executed it. Who was it, Mr.

President?" "McClellan," he answered, and added: "He certainly did do *this* well. He did it while he was at West Point."

The next morning sick with the excitement through which she had passed, the lady was at the White House again. She found more than fifty persons waiting for an audience; so she sent in her name, and said she would call again. The messenger said he thought the President would see her, and she had better be seated. Soon afterward, he informed her that the President would see her. As she passed in, she heard the words from one of the waiting throng: "She has been here six days; and, what is more, she is going to win." As she entered, Mr. Lincoln smiled pleasantly, drew a chair to his side, and said: "Come here, and sit down." As she did so, he handed her a copy of the coveted order. She thanked him, and apologized for not being more promptly at the house; she had been sick all night. "Did joy make you sick?" he inquired. "I suppose," he added, "you would have been mad if I had said 'no.'" She replied: "No, Mr. Lincoln, I should have been neither angry nor sick." "What would you have done?" he inquired. "I should have been here at nine o'clock this morning." "Well," said he, laughing, "I think I have acted wisely then." Then he turned suddenly, and looked into her face as he said: "Don't you ever get angry?" She replied that she never did when she had an important object to attain. Further conversation occurred as to the naming of the hospital, when the lady rose, and said: "You will not wish to see me again." "I did not say that, and I shall not say it," said the President. "You have been very kind to me, and I am very grateful for it," said his visitor. He looked up at her from under his eyebrows, in his peculiar way, and said: "You almost think I am handsome, don't you?" His face was full of benevolence, and his countenance lighted by a cordial smile; and it is not strange that the lady exclaimed: "You are perfectly lovely to me *now*, Mr. Lincoln." The President colored a little, and laughed a good deal, at the impulsive response, and reached out his hand to bid her farewell. She took it reverently, bowed her head upon it, and, bowing, prayed: "God bless you, Abraham Lincoln!" Then she turned, heard his "good bye," and was gone.

"I shall never be glad any more!" The young men of his people were slain. His enemies were seeking his life. With a heart that beat kindly toward every human being, his motives were maligned, and his good name was contemned; greedy politicians and ambitious officers were about him, pushing forward their selfish schemes; he had daily experience of the faithlessness of men; and "this great trouble," as he was accustomed to call the war, was always on his mind and heart. He could not sleep; and, such was the character of the impression he had received from all his toils and cares, that he felt he could never be glad any more.

In Mr. Lincoln's senatorial campaign, and during the course of his debates with Mr. Douglas, it will be remembered that he was not once betrayed into a loss of temper. He was misrepresented and abused in every way, in order to break down his good nature; but, from the first to the last, he did not utter an angry or an impatient word. Then he was well—in the full strength of a hardy constitution. The interview just narrated has shown how much he had become changed by bearing the burdens of office. When he saw that his visitor was not only overthrowing his theory but the policy he had based upon it, and felt either that he was, or that he might be, in the wrong, he became peevish and querulous. This was very unlike Mr. Lincoln in health. He was one of the most generous of men in his dealings; but weakness and weariness made him on this, and on some other occasions, childish and petulant. Exhibitions of this character, which occurred during the last two years of his life, are all referable to the prostrated and irritable condition of his nervous system, resulting from excessive labor, mental suffering, and loss of sleep.

The interview with the lady will show, too, how universal and how minute were his cares. This case was only one among ten thousand cases that came to him for decision. It was a great thing to her, and of itself made her sick. It lasted with her a week. It concerned the establishment of a hospital, simply. With him, the burden never was laid aside. He bore hundreds of matters upon his mind, all as important as this; and felt pressing upon his shoulders the interests of freedom, the future of a wonderful nation, and the destiny of a race; while he wielded as instruments for the accomplish ment of his purposes a great government, and an army com posed of the flower of the national life. It was killing him. There was always one tired spot in him that was not reached by rest.

Throughout the rebellion, Mr. Lincoln was the recipient of many attentions from the various bodies which constitute the Christian church of America. There was hardly a denomination that did not take occasion to express itself upon the war, and the great questions of humanity which it involved. They visited Mr. Lincoln at the White House; they approached him with addresses and resolutions; and the majority of them called forth from him either spoken or written responses. Representatives of foreign religious and philanthropic organizations mingled their voices with these. Expressions of personal sympathy, declarations of loyalty and devotion to the national cause, recommendations of policy, counsels, prayers, encouragements,—all poured in, in almost bewildering profusion, and of themselves became a burden. McPherson's History of the Rebellion gives forty-seven large and finely printed pages, consisting entirely of records of the action of the northern churches upon the rebellion; and the results of this action were communicated to the President in a way to draw from him either grateful acknowledgments, or responses that related to their subject matter.

The wear and tear of brain and nerve were often manifested in a deep melancholy, to which he had a natural tendency. "Whichever way it ends," said he to Mrs. Stowe, the authoress, alluding to the war, "I have the impression that I shall not last long after it is over." Hon. Schuyler Colfax met him one morning, after having received bad news which had not been made public. He had neither slept nor breakfasted, and exclaimed: "How willingly would I exchange places to-day with the soldier who sleeps on the ground in the army of the Potomac!" During the doubts and disasters of 1862, a member of Congress called on him for conversation. Mr. Lincoln began to tell a trifling story. "Mr. President," said the Congressman, rising, "I did not come here this morning to hear stories. It is too serious a time." The smile fled from Mr. Lincoln's face, as he replied: "A., sit down. I respect you as an earnest and sincere man. You cannot be more anxious than I am constantly; and I say to you now, that, if it were not for this occasional vent, I should die." To another he said: "I feel a presentiment that I shall not outlast the rebellion. When it is over, my work will be done." Of this presentiment he made no secret, but spoke of it to many of his friends.

Thus sad and weary, working early and late, full of the consciousness that God was working through him for the accomplishment of great ends, praying daily for strength and guidance, with a heart full of warm charity toward his foes, and open with sympathy toward the poor and the suffering, this Christian President sat humbly in his high seat, and did his duty. It is with genuine pain that the writer is compelled to leave behind, unrecorded, save in the floating literature of the day, multiplied instances which illustrate his tender-heartedness, his pity, his over-ruling sense of justice, his patience under insult, his loveliness of spirit, his devotion to humanity, his regard for the poor and the despised, his truthfulness, his simplicity, and the long list of manly virtues which distinguished his character and his career. They would of themselves fill a volume.

Mr. Lincoln's character was one which will grow. It will become the basis of an ideal man. It was so pure, and so unselfish, and so rich in its materials, that fine imaginations will spring from it, to blossom and bear fruit through all the centuries. This element was found in Washington, whose human weaknesses seem to have faded entirely from memory, leaving him a demi-god; and it will be found in Mr. Lincoln in a still more remarkable degree. The black race have already crowned him. With the black man, and particularly the black freed man, Mr. Lincoln's name is the saintliest which he pronounces, and the noblest he can conceive. To the emancipated, he is more than man—a being scarcely second to the Lord Jesus Christ himself. That old, white-headed negro who undertook to tell what "Massa Linkum" was to his dark-minded brethren, imbodied the vague conceptions of his race, in the words: "Massa Linkum, he ebery whar; he know ebery ting; he walk de earf like de Lord." He was to these men the incarnation of power and goodness; and his memory will live in the hearts of this unfortunate and oppressed race while it shall exist upon the earth.

CHAPTER XXVI.

On the 9th of December, 1863, Mr. Lincoln sent in his annual message to Congress, which had assembled on the seventh. It represented the country as holding satisfactory relations with foreign powers; spoke favorably of the establishment of an international telegraph across the Atlantic; referred to the movements abroad for emigration to this country, to fill the demand for labor in every field of industry; stated that the operations of the Treasury Department had been successfully conducted during the year; and gave a general historical account of the operations of the army and navy. Eleven months had passed since the final proclamation of emancipation was issued; and Mr. Lincoln took up the matter to see what progress had been made under its operations. The policy of emancipation and of the employment of black soldiers had changed the aspect of affairs; and, though it was immediately followed by dark and doubtful days, the results had vindicated its wisdom. The rebel borders had been pressed still further back; the rebel territory had been divided by the opening of the Mississippi; Tennessee and Arkansas had been substantially cleared of insurgent control; and, in these states, influential citizens were declaring openly for emancipation. Maryland and Missouri, neither of which states, three years previously, would tolerate any restraint upon the extension of slavery into new territories, were disputing only as to the best mode of removing it from their own limits. Of those who were slaves at the beginning of the rebellion, full one hundred thousand were in the military service of the United States, and about one-half of them were bearing arms in the ranks. No servile insurrection, or tendency to violence or cruelty, had marked the measures of emancipation and the arming of the blacks. The tone of public feeling abroad had improved under the influence of the policy, while the government had been encouraged and supported by elections at home. The new reckoning showed that the crisis which threatened to divide the friends of the Union was passed.

The message treated with considerable detail a question which had, from the first, been one of great importance, and which, it was seen, would grow more important with the progress of events. On the day previous to the delivery of the message, he had issued a proclamation of amnesty, to all those engaged in the rebellion who should take an oath to support, protect, and defend the Constitution of the United States, and the Union of the states under it, with the acts of Congress passed during the rebellion, and the proclamations of the President concerning slaves. This proclamation made certain exceptions of persons in the civil and military service of the rebel government, and of persons who had left the civil and military service of the United States to aid in the rebellion. It further declared that whenever, in any of the rebel states, a number of persons, not less than one-tenth of the qualified voters, should take this oath, and establish a state government which should be republican, it should be recognized as the true government of the state. These were the principal provisions of the proclamation; and to them the President called congressional attention.

He had issued it, he said, "looking to the present and the future, and with reference to a resumption of the national authority in the states wherein that authority had been suspended." He had given the form of an oath; but no man was coerced to take it. Men were only promised pardon in case they should voluntarily take it. Amnesty was offered, so that, if, in any of the rebel states, a state government should be set up, in the mode prescribed, it should be recognized and guaranteed by the United States, and protected against invasion and domestic violence.   The following passage is his justification for prescribing the peculiar oath which he had made the condition of pardon:

"An attempt to guarantee and protect a revived state government, constructed in whole or in preponderating part from the very element against whose hostility and violence it is to be protected, is simply absurd.   There must be a test by which to separate the opposing elements, so as to build only from the sound; and that test is a sufficiently liberal one which accepts as sound whoever will make a sworn recantation of his former unsoundness.   But, if it be proper to require, as a test of admission to the political body, an oath of allegiance to the Constitution of the United States and to the Union under it, why also to the laws and proclamations in regard to slavery?   Those laws and proclamations were enacted, and put forth, for the purpose of aiding in the suppression of the rebellion.   To give them their fullest effect, there had to be a pledge for their maintenance.   In my judgment, they have aided and will further aid the cause for which they were intended.   To now abandon them, would be not only to relinquish a lever of power, but would also be a cruel and an astounding breach of faith.   I may add, at this point, that while I remain in my present position, I shall not attempt to retract, or modify, the Emancipation Proclamation; nor shall I return to slavery any person who is free by the terms of that proclamation, or by any of the acts of Congress.

"For these and other reasons, it is thought best that support of these measures shall be included in the oath; and it is believed that the Executive may lawfully claim it, in return for pardon and restoration of forfeited rights, which he has a clear constitutional power to withhold altogether, or grant upon the terms which he shall deem wisest for the public interest.   It should be observed, also, that this part of the oath is subject to the modifying and abrogating power of legislation and supreme judicial decision."

This proclamation was issued as a rallying point for those loyal or penitent elements which were believed to exist in many of the insurgent states, and which, in the confusion of plans for reconstruction, were lying dormant, and without practical advantage to the states themselves and to the government.   He believed his plan of reconstruction would save labor, and avoid great confusion.   On the 24th of March, 1864, he issued a supplementary and explanatory

proclamation, defining more carefully the cases in which rebels were to be pardoned, and the manner in which they were
to avail themselves of the benefits of the amnesty. He shut
out many from the benefits of the proclamation, though he
excluded none from personal application to the President for
clemency.

The action of Congress during this session was not of notable importance. Important subjects were discussed at length;
but they were not embodied in measures, or, rather, the measures sought to be enacted were not successfully carried
through. A bill for the establishment of a Bureau of Freedmen's Affairs passed the House, but failed in the Senate; while
a resolution to submit to a vote of the states an amendment
of the Constitution, permanently prohibiting the existence of
slavery in the states and territories of the Union, was passed
by the Senate, but rejected by the House. The fugitive slave
law—one of those compromise measures which were to silence
the anti-slavery agitation forever, and be a final settlement of
the slavery question—was repealed, with surprising ease and
unanimity. A heated debate occurred upon a resolution
introduced by Speaker Colfax, for the expulsion from the
House of Alexander Long of Ohio, for declaring himself in
favor of recognizing the rebel confederacy. A two-thirds
vote being necessary for the purpose of the resolution, and
this vote not being obtainable, the mover contented himself
with a substitute, declaring Mr. Long an unworthy member
of the House. During the discussion of the resolution, Mr.
Harris of Maryland thanked God that the South had not yet
been brought into subjection, and prayed God that it might
not be; and straightway a resolution was introduced for his
expulsion, which failed of passage by lack of the requisite
two-thirds vote. He was, however, "severely censured;"
and, although no extreme measures were effected in these
cases, the debate had a healthy influence, in defining the boundaries of legitimate debate on the great questions which agitated the country.

An outcropping of the Missouri imbroglio showed itself

above the surface during the session. General F. P. Blair resigned his seat in the House, and resumed his place in the army, at the close of a discussion introduced by one of his colleagues, who charged him with improprieties in the administration of affairs in his department. Although he cleared himself of the charges, the House called upon the President for an explanation of his restoration to command. The President gave them a reply at length, and frankly stated all the circumstances of the case. The two facts which the letter and all the correspondence in the case reveal most prominently, were, that Mr. Lincoln had a strong personal friendship for General Blair, and a firm belief in his anti-slavery principles and sentiments; and that he wished him to be where he could do the government the most good in the prosecution of the war. Mr. Lincoln's representation of the case was, that General Blair and General Schenck of Ohio, having been elected to Congress, were permitted to resign their commissions, and take their seats, with the distinct verbal understanding with the President and the Secretary of War that they might, at their pleasure, withdraw their resignations, leave their places in the House, and return to the field. It is apparent that Mr. Lincoln wished for General Blair's aid in the organization of the House, and, after that, in the field, if he could be most useful to the government there. The arrangement seems to have been a little irregular, though entered upon with the best motives. It was one of Mr. Lincoln's short cuts out of the labyrinth of "red tape," in which it was always difficult for him to walk. In a letter which he wrote to Montgomery Blair, he revealed one of the motives which actuated him in making the arrangement. "It will relieve him (the General) from a dangerous position, or a misunderstanding," said he, "as I think he is in danger of being permanently separated from those with whom only he can ever have a real sympathy—the sincere opponents of slavery."

A measure which time has proved to be of great importance was the restoration of the grade of Lieutenant-general, with reference to investing General Grant with the chief command of the armies of the United States. His appointment to this office, by the President, was an expression of the popular confidence in his devotion to the national cause, and his transcendent ability as a military man. In presenting him with his commission, Mr. Lincoln took occasion to say: "The expression of the nation's approbation of what you have already done, and its reliance on you for what remains to do, in the existing struggle, is now presented with this commission, constituting you Lieutenant-general of the armies of the United States." The modest General made a fitting response: "I feel the full weight of the responsibilities now devolving on me ; and I know that, if they are met, it will be due to those armies, and above all to the favor of that Providence which leads both nations and men." Fit officer with fit superior! Two simpler-hearted, truer men than President Lincoln and Lieutenant-general Grant, have not been produced by the republic; and, in their hands, unweakened by selfish ambition, and entirely consecrated to the work of saving the country, the cause of nationality, freedom, and humanity was destined to a glorious triumph. The victories of both had been victories of character. Not brilliant gifts, but a noble spirit had made the President a mighty man. Neither the courage of the brute nor the dash of the cavalier had made General Grant a great soldier; but a devoted purpose and a will of iron had crowned him with the name and enrobed him with the prestige of the greatest general living.

An incident occurred on the 18th of April, 1864, which forcibly illustrated the progress, not only of events, but of ideas. A grand fair, for the benefit of the United States Sanitary Commission, the original and leading charity established to mitigate the immediate horrors of war, was held in Baltimore; and one of the attractions was the presence and the voice of President Lincoln. Three years had introduced and confirmed great changes. Three years before this occasion, he was obliged to pass through the city in the night, to escape assassination. Three years before, the Massachusetts Sixth, hastening to the protection of Washington, had left some of their members dead in the streets. Three years before, the whole city was seething with treason. Now, gold was pouring into the treasury of the great charity which had been established to aid the soldiers of the Union; and the President was welcomed to the city with grateful gladness.

There was a large crowd, and, in the anxiety to get a glimpse of Mr. Lincoln and to hear his voice, great confusion; but enough of his remarks have been preserved to give an idea of their drift and spirit. "Calling it to mind that we are in Baltimore," said he, "we cannot fail to note that the world moves. Looking upon the many people I see assembled here, to serve as they best may the soldiers of the Union, it occurs to me that three years ago those soldiers could not pass through Baltimore. I would say, blessings upon the men who have wrought these changes, and the women who have assisted them!" These allusions to the changes in Baltimore were heartily applauded by the Baltimoreans; and, when he proceeded to the mention of changes which had been wrought upon the institution of slavery, the applause was still more hearty and enthusiastic. Maryland had practically abolished the institution; and the President thanked her for what she had done and what she was doing.

A month or two later, the President attended another fair of the Sanitary Commission at Philadelphia. Of course, these movements were not entered upon to gratify a love of excitement or a desire for display, but to manifest his friendliness to the beneficent purposes of the commission. Here a grand supper was given; and, in response to a toast, Mr. Lincoln made a brief speech. Opening with an allusion to the terrors and burdens of war, he spoke of the two great associations which had done so much to relieve the soldier, in the field and in the hospital, and paid a grateful tribute to the ministry of woman in the great work of alleviating the suffering of the army. Speaking of the generous outpouring of means for sustaining these charities, he said: "They are voluntary contributions, giving proof that the national resources are not at all exhausted, and that the national patriotism will sustain us through all." Here, as always and everywhere, the war was uppermost in his mind. "It is a pertinent question," said he, "When is the war to end? I do not wish to name a day when it will end, lest the end should not come at the given time. We accepted the war, and did not begin it. We accepted it for an object, and, when that object is accomplished, the war will end; and I hope to God it will never end until that object is accomplished. We are going through with our task, so far as I am concerned, if it takes us three years longer. I have not been in the habit of making predictions, but I am almost tempted now to hazard one. It is, that Grant is this evening in a position, with Meade and Hancock of Pennsylvania, whence he can never be dislodged by the enemy, until Richmond is taken." Events that wait to be recounted verified the President's prediction.

A fair for the benefit of the soldiers, held at the Patent Office, in Washington, called out Mr. Lincoln as an interested visitor; and he was not permitted to retire without giving a word to those in attendance. "In this extraordinary war," said he, "extraordinary developments have manifested themselves, such as have not been seen in former wars; and among these manifestations nothing has been more remarkable than these fairs for the relief of suffering soldiers and their families. And the chief agents in these fairs are the women of America. I am not accustomed to the use of language of eulogy; I have never studied the art of paying compliments to women; but I must say that if all that has been said by orators and poets, since the creation of the world, in praise of women, were applied to the women of America, it would not do them justice for their conduct during this war. I will close by saying, God bless the women of America!"

The government was pledged to the protection of its black soldiers. The President felt that the matter involved many difficulties, for the government was not always able to·protect them. When these soldiers were shown no quarter in battle, or when, as prisoners, they were killed or enslaved by the infuriated and unscrupulous foe, he who could not prevent his white soldiers from starving to death in rebel prisons, could hardly protect the colored soldiers from the indignities which rebel policy and rebel spite inflicted upon them. But he did what he could. As early as July 30th, 1863, he issued an order declaring that: "The government of the United States will give the same protection to all its soldiers; and, if the enemy shall sell or enslave any one, because of his color, the offense shall be punished by retaliation upon the enemy's prisoners in our possession." Proceeding, he definitely ordered, "that for every soldier of the United States killed in violation of the laws of war, a rebel soldier should (shall) be executed; and for every one enslaved by the enemy, or sold into slavery, a rebel soldier should (shall) be placed at hard labor on the public works, and continued at such labor until the other should (shall) be released, or receive such treatment as was (is, or may be) due to a prisoner of war." This matter of retaliation was brought up during Mr. Lincoln's speech at the Baltimore Fair, to which allusion has been made in this chapter. He had just heard the rumor of the massacre of black soldiers and white officers at Fort Pillow. His mind was full of the horrible event; and, as his custom was, he spoke of that which interested him most. The public thought the government was not doing its whole duty in this matter. For the measure which put the black man into the war, he declared himself responsible to the American people, the future historian, and, above all, to God; and he declared that the black soldier ought to have, and should have, the same protection given to the white soldier. His closing words were:

"It is an error to say that the government is not acting in this matter. The government has no direct evidence to confirm the reports in existence relative to this massacre, but I believe the facts in relation to it to be as stated. When the government does know the facts from official sources, and they prove to substantiate the reports, retribution will be surely given. What is reported, I think, will make a clear case. If it is not true, then all such stories are to be considered as false. If proved to be true, when the matter shall be thoroughly examined, what

30

shape is to be given to the retribution? Can we take the man who was captured at Vicksburg, and shoot him for the victim of this massacre? If it should happen that it was the act of only one man, what course is to be pursued then? It is a matter requiring careful examination and deliberation; and, if it shall be substantiated by sufficient evidence, all may rest assured that retribution will be had."

And now we leave these minor matters, for the consideration of great and decisive events, concerning alike the life of Mr. Lincoln and the life of the nation.

CHAPTER XXVII.

THE year 1864 was distinguished by two grand campaigns: one, political; the other, military: and, as the latter did not terminate with the year, it is well, perhaps, to give the former the precedence in the record. After four years, marked by mighty changes in the nation, the year of the presidential election had come again. It came in with doubt and darkness. The country was feeling the distresses of the war, and was wincing under the drafts made upon its vital and financial resources. Call after call for men had been made. Draft after draft had been enforced. Taxation brought home the burden to every man's door; and still no end appeared. Still the rebel confederacy seemed full of vitality; still it commanded immense resources of men and material; still its spirit and its words were uncompromising and defiant. During four years of administration, Mr. Lincoln had made many enemies, among those who had originally supported him; and the democratic party were not scrupulous in the use of means to bring him into disrepute with the people. Many republicans suffered under private grievances. Their counsels had not been sufficiently followed; their friends had not been properly served. Some thought Mr. Lincoln had been too fast and too severe in his measures; others thought that he had been too slow. All this was to have been expected; and it may well be imagined that no decision as to the true policy of the republican party, in its nominations, could have been made, without an exhibition of all the elements of discord.

That this period had been anticipated by friends and ene-

mies abroad as one of the most terrible tests to which the republican institutions of the country had been or could be subjected, was evident.   We were called upon in the very heat
of civil war—that war involving questions upon which even
the loyal portion of the country was almost evenly divided—
to elect a president for four years.   With immense armies in
the field and immense navies afloat,—with fresh drafts for
troops threatened or in progress,—with discord among the
friends of the government and the foes of the rebellion,—and
with a watchful opposition, skilled in party warfare, taking advantage of every mistake of the government and every success of its enemies, to push its own fortunes in the strife for
power,—it is not strange that cool observers looked doubtfully
upon the result, as it related to the power of a republican
government to take care of itself, and maintain its hold upon
the nation and its place among the governments of the world.
How well the people behaved in this startling emergency, the
calm discussions of the presidential campaign, the solemn and
conscientious manner of the people at the polls, the triumph
of the national arms, and the present peace and stability of
the country, bear witness.

   Mr. Chase, the distinguished Secretary of the Treasury,
had his friends, and they were many and powerful.   General
Fremont had also his friends, who felt that he had not been
well treated by the administration, and who were anxious for
a diversion in his favor.   Although both of these gentlemen
had strong adherents among the politicians, and although
either of them would have been cordially supported by the
people under favorable circumstances, it was abundantly evident that the great masses of the people were in favor of Mr.
Lincoln.   He had had experience, and had grown wise under
its influence.   His unobtrusive character and his unbending
honesty had won their confidence; and, although the future
looked dark, they were conscious that progress had been made
toward the destruction of the rebellion, and that, if the policy
of war should be pursued, it would inevitably ultimate in the
national success.   They were convinced, also, that the way to

a permanent peace was through war. Under these circumstances, they were reluctant to change leaders and rulers. The result was, that, at an early day, Mr. Chase withdrew his name from the list of candidates, and left much of the disaffected element afloat.

Outside of the republican and democratic parties, there was no organization; and, to institute one, an irresponsible call was issued, for a convention to be held at Cleveland, Ohio, on the thirty-first of May. The call represented that the public liberties were in danger, and declared for the "one-term principle," by which Mr. Lincoln should be set aside, however efficiently he might have served the government. The regular convention of the republican party, which was to be held at Baltimore on the eighth of June, was denounced in the call, as failing to answer the conditions of a truly national convention, in consequence of its proximity to "administrative influence."

The people recognized this call to be simply what it, in reality, was—an anti-Lincoln demonstration; and paid no attention to it, except in one or two instances. The Germans of Missouri did something by way of indorsement; as did also a few radicals elsewhere, who had really never been members of the republican party proper.

The convention was held at the appointed time; and it brought together an insignificant number of politicians, self-appointed to their seats in the convention. It was, in no sense, the offspring of the popular feeling or conviction; and its action found no response in the popular heart. Fremont's name formed the rallying point of the convention. Wendell Phillips and Frederick Douglass sent letters to it. Mrs. E. Cady Stanton approved of the convention in a letter. John Cochrane presided, and was honored with the nomination for Vice-president, on the ticket with General Fremont. The platform adopted dealt briefly with generalities, condemning no person save by implication, and containing no vital element which had not already been appropriated by the mass of republicans throughout the nation. Although the convention was organized and engineered to bring an influence to bear upon the Baltimore Convention, it failed to have influence anywhere.

The saddest feature of the whole movement was General Fremont's connivance with it, when he could not but see that its only influence would be to divide the friends of the government; and the eagerness with which he accepted his nomination. He opened his letter of acceptance by speaking of the convention as an assemblage of the "representatives of the people," when he ought to have known that they were nothing of the kind. General Fremont, it is to be remembered here, was the republican candidate for the presidency eight years before, receiving the honor of every republican vote. The party had once been beaten with him for its standard-bearer; and, if he had been thoroughly magnanimous, he would have remembered it. At the opening of the war, Mr. Lincoln had given him the highest military commission he had it in his power to bestow; and, after his Missouri failure, he had created a department for him. In this, he had not won distinguished honor; and, when, at last, he was subordinated to another General, to meet the conditions of a great emergency, he threw up his position on a point of etiquette, and retired from his command. Mr. Lincoln had found it very difficult to please the General, or to satisfy his friends. The President was supposed to be jealous of him; and, if the readers of the life of Mr. Lincoln are not already convinced that such jealousy could have no place in him, no present attempt to vindicate his motives will avail. The truth was that Mr. Lincoln entertained none but the kindliest feelings toward him, though it is doubtful whether he had great confidence in his administrative and military ability. General Fremont knew, of course, that the little band of men gathered at Cleveland did not represent the republican party; and he knew that the republican party loved Mr. Lincoln. The party had been true to General Fremont, even if they had been disappointed in him. When he undertook to stab the official reputation of the President, he was engaged in the attempt to ruin the chosen man of the republican party. "Had Mr. Lincoln remained faithful to the principles he was elected to defend, no schism could have been created, and no contest could have been possible," said the General in his letter. Had the people decided that Mr. Lincoln was faithless to the principles he was chosen to defend? Had the republican party so decided? "The ordinary rights secured under the Constitution and laws of the country have been violated," continued the General. He charged the administration with managing the war for personal ends, with "incapacity and selfishness," with "disregard of constitutional rights," with "violation of personal liberty and the liberty of the press," and with "feebleness and want of principle." Among the objects of the convention itself, he recognized the effort "to arouse the attention of the people" to certain alleged facts, which he had enumerated; "and to bring them to realize that, while we are saturating southern soil with the best blood of the country, in the name of liberty, we have really parted with it at home." His own preference, he declared: would be to aid in the election of some one, other than Mr. Lincoln, who might be nominated at Baltimore, "But if Mr. Lincoln should be nominated," said he, "as I believe it would be fatal to the country to indorse a policy and renew a power which has cost us the lives of thousands of men, and needlessly put the country on the road to bankruptcy, there will be no other alternative but to organize against him every element of conscientious opposition, with the view to prevent the misfortune of his re-election."

General Fremont, virtuous above his party, virtuous above Mr. Lincoln, quick to see encroachments upon the rights of the people in advance of the people themselves, ready to find personal motives in the management of the war by the administration, and himself, of course, acting solely upon principle, failed to be appreciated by those whose good he so tenderly sought. The republican party gave him no response, other than at once and forever to count him out of its confidence and affections. Convention, platform, and candidates were early counted among political lumber; and whether the General at last withdrew from the field as a matter of principle, or from personal considerations, does not appear. He withdrew his name from the list of candidates before the people in September, after it became evident to everybody that his position was a damage to the national cause, administering a parting thrust at Mr. Lincoln in the words: "In respect to Mr. Lincoln, I continue to hold exactly the sentiments contained in my letter of acceptance. I consider that his administration has been politically and financially a failure, and that its necessary continuance is a cause of regret for the country." General Fremont, an old favorite of the republican party, and a man who virtually claimed to be a better republican than the majority of his party, said this, and said it with a purpose, or, wantonly, without a purpose, when he knew that the alternative of Mr. Lincoln's election was the election of General McClellan, on a peace platform, supported by such patriots as Fernando Wood and Clement L. Vallandigham.

Four days before the date appointed for the assembling of the Baltimore Convention, a meeting was held in New York to do honor to General Grant. The General had not then concluded the war, and had not, in fact, met with decisive successes with the army of the Potomac. There was no special occasion for the meeting, except to influence the Baltimore Convention in the selection of a candidate. To cover their real intent, they invited Mr. Lincoln to attend; and he sent the following letter in response:

"Gentlemen—Your letter inviting me to be present at a mass meeting of the loyal citizens, to be held at New York on the fourth inst., for the purpose of expressing gratitude to Lieutenant-general Grant for his signal services, was received yesterday. It is impossible for me to attend. I approve, nevertheless, whatever may tend to strengthen and sustain General Grant and the noble armies now under his direction. My previous high estimate of General Grant has been maintained and heightened by what has occurred in the remarkable campaign he is now conducting; while the magnitude and difficulty of the task before him does not prove less than I expected. He and his brave soldiers are now in the midst of their great trial; and I trust that, at your meeting, you will so shape your good words that they may turn to men and guns moving to his and their support.

"Yours truly,   A. LINCOLN."

The cordial tone of the President toward the General, effectually neutralized the object of the meeting; and, when the Baltimore Convention met, on the eighth of June, there was no name but that of the President that found adherents. Many of the delegates had come instructed to vote for him, from the conventions which sent them. Rev. Robert J. Breckinridge of Kentucky, a stern and eloquent old Unionist, was chosen temporary chairman; and Hon. William Dennison of Ohio was elected to be the permanent president of the convention. On the following day, Mr. Henry J. Raymond of New York, as chairman of the committee on resolutions, presented the platform, which was adopted with warm approval, and with entire unanimity. It pledged the convention, and those it represented, to aid the government in quelling by force of arms the rebellion then raging against its authority; approved the determination of the government not to compromise with rebels in arms; indorsed the acts and proclamations against slavery, and advocated a constitutional amendment abolishing it; returned thanks to the soldiers of the Union armies, and declared that the nation owed a permanent provision for those disabled by the war; approved of the administration of Mr. Lincoln and the acts and measures which he had adopted for the preservation of the nation against its open and secret foes; declared that the government owed protection to all its soldiers, without distinction of color; affirmed that the national faith, pledged for the redemption of the public debt, must be kept inviolate; and expressed approval of the position taken by the government that the people of the United States can never regard with indifference the attempt of any European power to overthrow by force, or to supplant by fraud, the institutions of any republican government on the Western Continent.

After the adoption of the resolutions, came the ballot for a presidential candidate. At the first ballot, every vote was given for Mr. Lincoln, except the twenty-two from Missouri which, under instructions, were given for General Grant; but the nomination was made unanimous on the motion of one of the Missouri delegates. Mr. Hamlin, the incumbent of the vice-presidential office, though an able and excellent man, was, from motives of policy, not regarded by many as the best candidate for that office; and Andrew Johnson of Tennessee received the nomination.

A single resolution in the platform, to which no allusion is made in the foregoing summary of its leading features, covertly demanded a change in the cabinet. The words, "We deem it essential to the general welfare that harmony should prevail in our national councils, and we regard as worthy of confidence and official trust those only who cordially indorse the principles proclaimed in these resolutions," were intended as an intimation that the convention would like to have the President dismiss the Postmaster-general, Montgomery Blair. The resolution was probably a concession to the Loyal Leagues, which, originally friendly to the nomination of Mr. Chase, took up the differences which were understood to exist between these two members of the cabinet, and demanded that Mr. Blair should retire. A committee consisting of John M. Ashley, John Covode and George S. Boutwell, waited upon the President, on one occasion, to urge Mr. Blair's dismissal; and on that occasion Mr. Lincoln said that, if he should be re-elected, he should probably make some changes in his cabinet—a reply which they took as an assent to their request, and so reported to the body that sent them. When the resolution in question appeared in the platform, Mr. Blair, understanding it, placed his resignation in the hands of the President, who delayed his acceptance of it until circumstances rendered the step desirable.

Washington was but a short distance from Baltimore; and Governor Dennison, the president of the convention, waited upon Mr. Lincoln, accompanied by a committee, to inform him of his nomination. After receiving the formal address of that gentleman, with a copy of the resolutions which had been adopted, Mr. Lincoln said:

"Having served four years in the depths of a great and yet unended national peril, I can view this call to a second term in nowise more flattering to myself than as an expression of the public judgment that I may better finish a difficult work, in which I have labored from the first, than could any one less severely schooled to the task. In this view, and with assured reliance on that Almighty Ruler who has so graciously sustained us thus far, and with increased gratitude to the generous people for their continued confidence, I accept the renewed trust, with its yet onerous and perplexing duties and responsibilities."

During the same day, the President was waited upon by a committee of the Union League, which came with a tender of the congratulations, and a pledge of the confidence and support, of that organization; and, in the evening, by the Ohio delegation in the convention. To both these deputations he addressed brief remarks, in the spirit of those quoted as addressed to the committee of the convention. Some days subsequently, he received the formal notification, by letter, of his nomination, to which, on the twenty-seventh of June, he replied as follows:

"Gentlemen:—Your letter of the fourteenth inst., formally notifying me that I have been nominated by the convention you represent for the Presidency of the United States, for four years from the fourth of March next, has been received. The nomination is gratefully accepted, as the resolutions of the convention, called the platform, are heartily approved. While the resolution in regard to the supplanting of republican governments upon the Western Continent is fully concurred in, there might be misunderstanding were I not to say that the position of the government in relation to the action of France in Mexico, as assumed through the State Department, and indorsed by the convention among the measures and acts of the Executive, will be faithfully maintained so long as the state of facts shall leave that position pertinent and applicable. I am especially gratified that the soldier and seaman were not forgotten by the convention, as they forever must and will be remembered by the grateful country, for whose salvation they devote their lives.

"Thanking you for the kind and complimentary terms in which you have communicated the nomination and other proceedings of the convention, I subscribe myself,

"Your obedient servant,

"ABRAHAM LINCOLN."

It was still more than two months before the assembling of the Democratic Convention, announced to be held at Chicago on the twenty-ninth of August. This convention had been deferred, with the confident expectation, if not the hope, that the events of the war would prepare the people to accept a peace policy, and leave the party free to take direct issue with the administration. During this interval, a peculiar change came over the spirit of the friends of Mr. Lincoln. Opening the campaign with perfect confidence concerning the results, a feeling of distrust and doubt crept over them; and, without any apparent cause, the thought became prevalent that a mistake had been made in the nomination. This arose partly from the consciousness that the country was really tired of a war of which they saw neither the end nor the signs of its approach; and partly from the uncertainty which prevailed concerning the action of the Democratic Convention, which was pretty sure to be based upon the results of military movements in progress, and of dubious issue. It was one of those strange and unaccountable contagions of public feeling and opinion which start, no man knows where; lead, no man knows whither; and die, at last, by no man's hand. Men did not catch it from newspapers, did not contract it from speeches, did not imbibe or absorb it in facts; but, simultaneously and universally, the friends of the administration were affected with a distrust of the future and a doubt of the wisdom of their choice.

There were still divisions in their ranks, but these were not formidable. Occasion was taken by the opposition press to magnify every mistake of the President and to condemn every doubtful measure. One Arguelles, convicted in Cuba of selling part of a cargo of negroes, illicitly landed, which, as an officer of the Spanish army, he had captured, was permitted to be taken from New York, and carried back to the island. This act—a thoroughly righteous one in the light of humanity and justice—was regarded by the opposition as a denial of the right of asylum; and a good deal of disturbance was created by it.

Early in July, Congress completed its action upon a plan of reconstruction, which it embodied in an elaborate bill. In the preparation of this bill, Henry Winter Davis of Maryland and Benjamin F. Wade of Ohio were prominently active. A good deal of time and discussion had been expended upon it, but it was passed and sent to the President less than one hour before the close of the session.   He failed to approve it, and, on the eighth of July, issued a proclamation on the subject.   In this proclamation, the President declared that he was unprepared, by a formal approval of the bill, to commit himself to any single plan of reconstruction, or to set aside the free state governments already formed in Arkansas and Louisiana on other plans.   At the same time, he was willing that the plan embodied in the bill should be recognized as one among others; and so promulgated the bill itself, as a part of his proclamation.   To the people of any rebel state who should adopt the plan provided by the bill, he pledged the executive assistance.   The action of the President in this matter exceedingly offended Messrs. Wade and Davis, who joined in a bitter manifesto against him, and published it in the New York Tribune of August fifth.   "The President," they declared, "by preventing this bill from becoming a law, holds the electoral votes of the rebel states at the dictation of his personal ambition."   Furthermore: "A more studied outrage on the legislative authority of the people, has never been perpetrated."   In its attack upon Mr. Lincoln's motives, it was an offensive paper, and pained the friends of the administration no less than it rejoiced its enemies.

Mr. Lincoln, himself, never permitted attacks of this character to trouble him.   If they were very bitter, he did not read them at all; and many men of mark who wrote things for his particular eye, failed of their object utterly by his refusal to read, or listen to, their fulminations.   After the Wade and Davis manifesto was issued, it was, on one occasion, the subject of conversation between him and a number of gentlemen who had called at the White House.   After all the gentlemen had retired, save one, who was an intimate personal friend, Mr. Lincoln turned to him, and said: "The Wade and Davis matter troubles me very little.   Indeed, I feel a good deal about it as the old man did about his cheese, when his very smart boy found, by the aid of a microscope, that it was full of maggots. 'Oh father!' exclaimed the boy, 'how can you eat that stuff? Just look in here, and see 'em wriggle!' The old man took another mouthful, and, putting his teeth into it, replied grimly: 'let 'em wriggle!' "

The evident anxiety of the people for peace was a subject of deep solicitude with the administration. Mr. Lincoln had no faith in the desire of the Richmond government for any peace which would be accepted by the loyal people of the country. It was, however, for the interest of the rebels to create a peace party in the northern states, in order to weaken the administration; and it was their policy to appear to be ready to make or receive propositions for peace. There were two things to which the administration was, in all good faith, irrevocably committed, viz: the restoration of the Union under the Constitution, and the abolition of slavery. Without being false to his oath of office and to the American people who had poured out life and treasure to save the nation, and without being faithless to an oppressed race to whom he had pledged emancipation, Mr. Lincoln could entertain no propositions for peace, and could make none, which were not based on the essential conditions of national unity and freedom to the blacks. This state of facts tied his hands; yet he was made by his enemies to appear to be averse to peace; and some of his friends, of the more timid sort, felt that, unless he could be placed in a different light before the people, his chances of re-election were slender.

On the fifth of July, one W. C. Jewett wrote a letter from Niagara Falls to Horace Greeley of New York, stating that there were, in Canada, two ambassadors of the rebel government, with full powers to negotiate a peace; and requesting that Mr. Greeley proceed to Niagara for a conference, or secure from the President a safe-conduct for them to New York. Mr. Greeley inclosed the letter to Mr. Lincoln, remarking that he thought the matter deserved attention. He also wrote: "I venture to remind you that our bleeding, bankrupt, almost dying country, longs for peace—shudders at the prospect of fresh conscriptions, of further wholesale devastations, and of new rivers of human blood; and a wide-spread conviction that the government and its supporters are not anxious for peace, and do not improve proffered opportunities to achieve it, is doing great harm now, and is morally certain, unless removed, to do far greater in the approaching elections." Mr. Greeley subjoined to his letter a plan of adjustment which he deemed proper and practicable, the first two items of which covered the restoration of the Union and the abolition of slavery. Certainly, if these were leading and essential parts of the plan, it could make no difference whether they were made conditions precedent to negotiation, or essentials in any adjustment to be procured by negotiation.

The President replied to this communication, on the ninth: "If you can find any person, anywhere, professing to have any proposition of Jefferson Davis, *in writing*, embracing the restoration of the Union and abandonment of slavery, whatever else it embraces, say to him that he may come to me with you." On the thirteenth of July, Mr. Greeley wrote to the President, stating that he had information upon which he could rely, that two persons, duly commissioned and empowered to negotiate for a peace, were not far from Niagara Falls, and were desirous to confer with the President, or such persons as he might appoint. Their names were Clement C. Clay of Alabama and Jacob Thompson of Mississippi. If these persons could be permitted to see Mr. Lincoln, they wished a safe-conduct for themselves and for George N. Saunders to Washington. In the course of the letter, Mr. Greeley said: "I am, of course, quite other than sanguine that a peace can now be made; but I am quite sure that a frank, earnest, anxious effort to terminate the war on honorable terms, would immensely strengthen the government in case of its failure, and would help us in the eyes of the civilized world." George N. Saunders wrote to Mr. Greeley on the twelfth, that he was authorized to say that Mr. Clay and Professor Holcombe of Virginia were ready, with himself, to go to Washington, provided they should have a safe-conduct. To Mr. Greeley's letter of the thirteenth, Mr. Lincoln replied on the fifteenth: "I am disappointed that you have not already reached here with those commissioners. If they would consent to come on being shown my letter to you of the ninth inst., show that and this to them; and, if they will consent to come *on the terms stated in the former*, bring them. I not only intend a sincere effort for peace, but I intend that you shall be a personal witness that it is made." This note was taken to Mr. Greeley by Major Hay, who, having been empowered by telegraph to write a safe-conduct for the commissioners, embraced in his paper the names of Messrs. Clay, Thompson, Holcombe, and Saunders. With this, Mr. Greeley started for Niagara Falls, and, on arriving there on the seventeenth, addressed to the first three of these gentlemen, at the Clifton House, on the Canada side of the river, a note, stating that he was informed that they were duly accredited from Richmond as the bearers of propositions looking to the establishment of peace; that he understood, also, that they desired to visit Washington in the fulfillment of their mission, and that they wished George N. Saunders to accompany them. If these were the facts, he declared himself authorized by the President to offer them a safe-conduct and to accompany them.

On the following day, this note was replied to by Messrs. Clay and Holcombe, who frankly acknowledged that the safe-conduct of the President had been offered under a misapprehension of facts. They were not accredited from Richmond at all, as the bearers of propositions looking to the establishment of peace. They professed, however, to be in the confidential employ of their government, and to be familiar with its wishes and opinions on the subject; and they declared that, if the circumstances disclosed in the correspondence were communicated to Richmond, they, or others, would at once be invested with the requisite authority to negotiate. It should be remembered, at this point, that these men had not been made fully acquainted with the conditions on which the President had offered them a safe-conduct. Mr. Greeley had evidently forgotten to inform them concerning the terms of Mr. Lincoln's letter of the ninth, in which he promised a safe-conduct only to those who should be duly accredited with propositions for peace, conditioned upon the restoration of the Union and the abolition of slavery. These, it must be remembered, were the original and unaltered conditions on which Mr. Lincoln had consented to receive them.

Mr. Greeley replied to Messrs. Clay and Holcombe, on the eighteenth, that the state of facts differed materially from Mr. Lincoln's understanding of them, and that he should telegraph for fresh instructions, which he did at once. On receiving the dispatch, Mr. Lincoln sent Major Hay to Niagara, with the following letter:

"EXECUTIVE MANSION, Washington, July 18th, 1864.

"TO WHOM IT MAY CONCERN:—

"Any proposition which embraces the restoration of peace, the integrity of the whole Union, and the abandonment of slavery, and which comes by and with an authority that can control the armies now at war against the United States, will be received and considered by the Executive government of the United States, and will be met on liberal terms on substantial and collateral points; and the bearer or bearers thereof shall have safe-conduct both ways.

"ABRAHAM LINCOLN."

Major Hay, on his arrival at Niagara, went with Mr. Greeley to the Clifton House, and delivered the above missive to Professor Holcombe. Then Mr. Greeley returned to New York, where he soon afterwards received the response of Messrs. Clay and Holcombe. Their letter was exactly what might have been expected. They had supposed that a safe-conduct had been offered them on the ground that they were "duly accredited from Richmond, as bearers of propositions looking to the establishment of peace;" and, when they found conditions insisted on precedent to negotiation, they could see only a "sudden and entire change in the views of the President," and a "rude withdrawal of a courteous overture for negotiation, at the moment it was likely to be accepted." It will be noticed by the reader that the President had made no

31

change whatever in his conditions from those first offered, and that the letter of Clay and Holcombe left him in a false position. Nothing appears in the correspondence, thus far published, to show that Mr. Greeley ever communicated to the commissioners the President's original conditions for a safe-conduct and an interview.

In order to place himself in a just position before the country, Mr. Lincoln applied to Mr. Greeley for permission to publish the entire correspondence, omitting certain unessential passages in Mr. Greeley's letters, which represented the country as being on the verge of destruction, intimated the possibility of a northern insurrection, and alluded to the importance of affecting favorably the North Carolina election. Mr. Greeley refused to have the correspondence published, unless these passages, which Mr. Lincoln thought would have a mischievous effect upon the public mind, should be retained. For the sake of the country and its cause, Mr. Lincoln submitted; but, determined to stand right in history, he sent a note to Henry J. Raymond, editor of the New York Times, under date of August 15, 1864, as follows:

"MY DEAR SIR:—I have proposed to Mr. Greeley that the Niagara correspondence be published, suppressing only the parts of his letters over which the red pencil is drawn in the copy which I herewith send. He declines giving his consent to the publication of his letters, unless these parts be published with the rest. I have concluded that it is better for *me* to submit, for the time, to the consequences of the false position in which I consider he has placed me, than to subject the *country* to the consequences of publishing these discouraging and injurious parts. I send you this, and the accompanying copy, not for publication, but merely to explain to you, and· that you preserve them until their proper time shall come.

"Yours truly,

"ABRAHAM LINCOLN."

So Mr. Lincoln went through the canvass with the imputation resting upon him of having pursued a vacillating course with the unaccredited and irresponsible commissioners, and of repelling negotiations for peace. All the capital that could be made against him from the materials furnished by the affair, was assiduously used by the opposition and by the rebels themselves.

The time for holding the National Democratic Convention came at last. Still the fortunes of the military campaign were undecided; and the country was groaning under efforts to furnish men for the reinforcement of the armies. But the President found aid in unexpected quarters. By the direction of that Providence in which he so implicitly believed, every treasonable and personally inimical element in the nation became his ally. Mr. Vallandigham had returned to the country before his time; and the President permitted him to remain, unmolested. He became one of the pets of his party; and, attending the Chicago Convention as a delegate, was chosen chairman of the committee on resolutions. Governor Seymour of New York, his sympathizing friend, was the president of the convention. Congressman Long of Ohio was also there, with a full representation of all those who had, from the first, opposed the war, and sympathized with the rebellion. The platform adopted was composed largely of negations, touching the policy of the administration; but one thing it distinctly demanded, viz: "a cessation of hostilities." The candidates nominated were General George B. McClellan for President, and George H. Pendleton of Ohio for Vice-President. General McClellan was nominally a war democrat, and Mr. Pendleton really a peace democrat. Both wings of the party were thus accommodated, while the platform was all that the most extreme of peace men could ask. But the convention did not dissolve; it adjourned, "subject to be called at any time and place that the executive national committee shall designate." The act was a threat, and betrayed the entertainment of possibilities and incidental purposes not entirely creditable to the patriotism of the convention. Mr. Vallandigham's tongue was busy, in and out of the convention. He was treated as a man who had suffered persecution for the sake of democratic truth. He moved that the nomination of McClellan be made unanimous. He was active in all the affairs of the occasion; and he did more than any other man to destroy the prospects of the democratic party.

The spirit manifested by the demagogues who managed this convention, was not the spirit of the people, and not the spirit of the democratic masses. The majority of the democratic party had supported the war. Many of the best officers in the army were democrats, thoroughly devoted to the destruction of the rebellion by military means. The voice of the convention was, that all that had been expended in the war, of life and treasure, should be declared a waste. The best illustration of the spirit of the convention was found in the fact that, when it was announced that Fort Morgan had surrendered, the news fell upon it like a pall. It awoke no cheers; and was so evidently unwelcome intelligence, although a great national success, that the masses of the party were disgusted.

Whatever may have been the acts, intentions and spirit of the convention, this one thing was certain: that, from the time of its adjournment, no sensible politician had any doubt of the overwhelming triumph of the administration in the election. The cloud was lifted from the republican party at once; and the democratic leaders themselves, though they relaxed no effort, confessed that they were beaten, almost from the start.

On the twenty-third of September, Mr. Blair retired from the cabinet, in consequence of an intimation from the President that his retirement would be a relief to him. It will be remembered that the Baltimore platform contained a resolution which was intended to indicate a desire on the part of the convention that Mr. Blair should leave the cabinet; but Mr. Lincoln did not, probably, have any reference to this resolution in his action. Mr. Blair had made an excellent Postmaster-general—one of the very best who had administered the affairs of his department; and it was Mr. Lincoln's policy to adhere to his friends, and especially to those who did their duty. But there was a difficulty between Mr. Blair and Henry Winter Davis of Maryland, which, in Mr. Lincoln's judgment, endangered the adoption of the free state constitution in that commonwealth. He could solve the difficulty, and help the cause, by permitting Mr. Blair, whose resignation had been in his hands for months, to retire. The President and the Secretary parted excellent friends; and Mr. Lincoln showed his good will toward the retiring officer, by appointing to his place ex-Governor William Dennison of Ohio, one of Mr. Blair's most intimate personal and family friends.

A few days before this change in the cabinet, Mr. Lincoln wrote a letter to a convention of the friends of the new constitution in Maryland, held in Baltimore on the eighteenth of September, in which he expressed his earnest solicitude for its adoption. "It needs not be a secret," said he, "and I presume it is no secret, that I wish success to this provision." (The provision extinguishing slavery). "I desire it on every consideration. I wish to see all men free. I wish the national prosperity of the already free, which I feel sure the extinction of slavery would bring." The event he so much desired was consummated by a popular vote, on the eighth and ninth of October; and the President was serenaded by the loyal Marylanders in Washington, as an expression of their satisfaction and their congratulations. Mr. Lincoln responded with a speech. An extract will show something of the subjects of public discussion at the time, as well as reveal the President's relation to them:

"Something said by the Secretary of State, in his recent speech at Auburn, has been construed by some into a threat that, if I shall be beaten at the election, I will, between then and the constitutional end of my term, do what I may be able, to ruin the government. Others regard the fact that the Chicago Convention adjourned not *sine die*, but to meet again, if called to do so by a particular individual, as the intimation of a purpose that, if their nominee shall be elected, he will at once seize control of the government. I hope the good people will permit themselves to suffer no uneasiness on either point. I am struggling to maintain the government, not to overthrow it. I am struggling specially to prevent others from overthrowing it. I, therefore, say that, if I live, I shall remain President until the fourth of next March, and that whoever shall be constitutionally elected in November shall be duly installed as President on the fourth of March; and, in the interval, I shall do my utmost that whoever is to hold the helm for the next voyage, shall start with the best possible chance of saving the ship."

The October elections indicated the inevitable result of the presidential canvass; and the successful movements of the armies confirmed the prospects of Mr. Lincoln's signal triumph. The efforts of the rebels south of the Union lines, and over the Canada boundary, to assist the peace party, and furnish capital for its operations, aided by organizations of disloyal elements within the loyal states, not only failed of their object, but helped to rally the popular feeling to the side of the administration.

An unpleasant incident of the canvass was the result of an interview between Mr. Lincoln and a committee of the opposition party in Tennessee. Andrew Johnson, the present President of the United States, was then military governor of that state; and under his sanction a convention was called, to reorganize the state, that it might take a part in the presidential election. This convention prescribed the form of an oath, that the body deemed proper for those to take who desired to vote. Governor Johnson ordered the election to be held, in accordance with the plan of the convention; and adopted its oath. The oath was one which no heartily loyal man would refuse to take, unless he should object to the following clause: "I will cordially oppose all armistices and negotiations for peace with rebels in arms, until the Constitution of the United States, and all laws and proclamations made in pursuance thereof, shall be established over all the people of every state and territory, embraced within the national Union." No man, of course, who heartily believed in the peace doctrine of the Chicago platform could take the oath; and there were evidently many men in Tennessee who would not subscribe to another clause—men who could not heartily say: "I sincerely rejoice in the triumph of the armies and navies of the United States."

Against this oath, a committee of General McClellan's friends protested; and they bore their protest to the President. Mr. Lincoln did not receive the paper good-naturedly. He undoubtedly regarded it as an attempt to get him into difficulty, and to make political capital against him. He had no

faith in the genuine loyalty of the men who would not take
the oath. He furthermore felt that it was a matter with
which he had no right to interfere, and believed it to be one
which Mr. John Lellyett, the bearer of the protest, knew he
would not undertake to control. Under these circumstances,
and in the condition of nervous and mental irritability, to
which all the latter part of his life was subject, he gave a
reply which was not at all in his usual manner, and which
pained his friends quite as much as it rejoiced his foes. The
answer, as reported by Mr. Lellyett, was: "I expect to let the
friends of George B. McClellan manage their side of this contest in their own way, and I will manage my side of it in my
way." The committee asked for an answer in writing. "Not
now," replied Mr. Lincoln. "Lay those papers down here.
I will give no other answer now. I may or may not write
something about this hereafter. I know you intend to make
a point of this. But go ahead; you have my answer."

Now this was unquestionably an undignified and injudi-
cious reply—one which the people would not receive with
any consideration of the irritable mood in which it was uttered, or the provocation, real or supposed, which inspired it.
Under date of October twenty-second, he made a reply in
writing. His conclusion was that he could have nothing to
do with the matter. The action of the convention and of
Governor Johnson was nothing which had been inspired by
the national Executive. The Governor, he believed, had the
right to favor any plan he might choose to favor, which had
been adopted by the loyal citizens of Tennessee; and the President could not see, in the plan adopted, "any menace, or violence, or coercion towards any one." If the people should
vote for president, under this plan, it would neither belong to
the President, nor yet to the military Governor of Tennessee,
to say whether the vote should be received and counted, but
to a department of the government to which, under the Constitution, it was given, to decide. So, "except to give protection against violence," he declined to have anything to do
with any presidential election. The result was the withdrawal

of the McClellan ticket in that state, and renewed charges against the President of interfering in elections, with which he had thus refused to interfere.

No headway could be made, however, against Mr. Lincoln. The issue was too plain. Yet it is but just to say that it is doubtful whether the success of the McClellan ticket would have produced an immediate armistice. Results in a military point of view were too plainly in our hands, and the country was too thoroughly committed to the war for the re-establishment of the Union, to permit so disgraceful and ruinous a proceeding. But the democratic party had consented to place itself in the position it occupied, for the sake of winning power; and, when the people saw such men as Wood, and Long, and Pendleton, and Vallandigham, all pushing the fortunes of the democratic candidate, they lost faith in the party, and determined to support the administration, its policy, and its candidates. In the meantime, Grant, Sherman and Sheridan were leading on their victorious armies, and the political voice of these armies was almost unanimous for the republican nominees.

Before taking leave of the canvass, to record its results, it is simple justice to Mr. Lincoln to place by the side of the Tennessee case, his call for five hundred thousand men, made on the eighteenth of July, to be drafted after the fifth of September, if they should not be furnished previous to that date. His friends urged that the measure would be unpopular, and that it might cost him his election. His reply to every representation of this kind was that the men were needed, that it was his duty to call for them, and that he should call for them, whatever the effect might be upon himself. Does any one believe that a man who could treat a great question like this so nobly and patriotically, would busy himself with small politics in Tennessee, or connive with any small politicians there, in a scheme for cheating patriotic men out of votes, for his own advantage?

The day of election came at last, and resulted in an overwhelming majority of votes for Abraham Lincoln. Every state that voted, except three, gave majorities for the republican candidates, and two of these three were old slave states—Kentucky and Delaware. Only New Jersey among the northern states gave its vote for McClellan. West Virginia, Tennessee, Arkansas, and Louisiana supported Mr. Lincoln. The time had come, at last, of which he had spoken in Cooper Institute, more than four years before, when the republican party had ceased to be sectional, by obtaining support in the southern states. Mr. Lincoln's clear popular majority was 411,428, in a total vote of 4,015,902, which secured 212 of the 233 votes in the electoral college.

The President might well feel gratified with this result. His policy, motives, character and achievements had received the emphatic approval of the American people. "I am thankful to God for this approval of the people," said he, on the night of his election, to a band of Pennsylvanians who had called upon him; and he added: "But, while deeply grateful for this mark of their confidence in me, if I know my heart, my gratitude is free from any taint of personal triumph. I do not impugn the motives of any one opposed to me. It is no pleasure to me to triumph over any one; but I give thanks to the Almighty for this evidence of the people's resolution to stand by free government, and the rights of humanity."

The election proved more than Mr. Lincoln's popularity; and this he understood. In subsequent remarks to the friendly political clubs of the District, he said: "It has demonstrated that a people's government can sustain a national election in the midst of a great civil war. Until now, it has not been known to the world that this was a possibility. It shows, also, how strong and sound we still are. * * * It shows, also, to the extent yet known, that we have more men now, than we had when the war began. Gold is good in its place; but living, brave and patriotic men are better than gold." To a friend he said: "Being only mortal, after all, I should have been a little mortified if I had been beaten in this canvass before the people; but that sting would have been more than compensated by the thought that the people had notified me that all my official responsibilities were soon to be lifted off my back."

The election of Mr. Lincoln destroyed the last hope of the rebellion. There was to be no change of policy; and none could know better than the rebel leaders that that policy could not be long resisted. These leaders were little inclined to make peace; and it is doubtful whether their people would have permitted them to do so. They had promised their people independence; and the latter had fought with wonderful bravery and persistency for it. There was no way but to fight on, until the inevitable defeat should come.

For many days after the result of the election was known, Mr. Lincoln was burdened with congratulations; and yet, amid these disturbances, and the cares of office, which were onerous in the extreme, he found time to write the following letter:

"EXECUTIVE MANSION, Washington, Nov. 21, 1864.

"Dear Madam:—I have been shown, in the files of the War Department, a statement of the Adjutant-general of Massachusetts, that you are the mother of five sons, who have died gloriously on the field of battle. I feel how weak and fruitless must be any words of mine which should attempt to beguile you from the grief of a loss so overwhelming. But I cannot refrain from tendering to you the consolation that may be found in the thanks of the republic they died to save. I pray that o' Heavenly Father may assuage the anguish of your bereavement, and leave you only the cherished memory of the loved and lost, and the solemn pride that must be yours to have laid so costly a sacrifice upon the altar of freedom.

"Yours very sincerely and respectfully,

"ABRAHAM LINCOLN.

"To Mrs. Bixby, Boston, Massachusetts."

From the day of the election to the close of the rebellion, the discordant political elements of the northern states subsided into silence and inaction. The election itself was attended with great dignity—almost, indeed, with solemnity. Men felt that they were deciding something more than a party question, and acted with reference to their responsibilities to

God and their country.   The masses of the democratic party were more than satisfied with the result; and such of their leaders as were thoroughly loyal undoubtedly felt that a victory to them, under all the circumstances, would have been, in many respects, a misfortune.   Among the subjects of national thanksgiving on the last Thursday in November—the day of Mr. Lincoln's appointment—certainly the result of the election was not least to be considered, or last to be remembered with devout gratitude.

CHAPTER XXVIII.

THE military operations of 1864 were of the most momentous importance. It was a year of intense activity in every
department; and, although there were great miscarriages and
serious and perplexing disasters, the grand results were such
as to show to the people of the whole country that the end
was not far off, and that that end would leave the rebellion
hopeless and helpless at the feet of the national power. Although the principal interest was attached to the operations
of the two grand armies under Grant and Sherman, there
were minor movements of subsidiary bodies, which attracted
considerable attention.

Early in February, an expedition under General Gillmore's
direction, for clearing Florida of insurgent forces, so as to enable the Union elements of the state to reorganize, resulted
in a failure. At the same time, Sherman, proceeding from
Vicksburg, with a strong infantry force, and General Smith,
starting from Memphis, with a heavy force of cavalry, undertook a joint movement for the purpose of destroying rebel
supplies and communications; but they failed in their plan
of forming a junction, though they were quite successful in
their work of destruction. Later in the month, Kilpatrick
made his bold and dashing raid upon Richmond, blowing up
the locks of the Kanawha canal, cutting railways and tele-
graphs, and penetrating within the outer defenses of the rebel
capital. In March, the disastrous Red River expedition of
General Banks occurred. Much damage was done to the

rebels, and more was received by ourselves: In April, Fort Pillow was captured from us; and here occurred one of the most shocking outrages of the war, already incidentally alluded to in these pages. Some three hundred negro troops, with women and children, were murdered in cold blood, after they had surrendered. The white officers of these troops shared their cruel fate; and the event was greeted with approval by rebel newspapers. The history of war is illustrated by no deed of blacker barbarism than this. It filled the country with horror, and inspired a universal demand for retaliation. Mr. Lincoln, who was as deeply touched as any one, promised retaliation publicly; but it was never inflicted.

Late in the spring, the western army, under Sherman, confronted Johnston at Chattanooga. The army of the Potomac, immediately under General Meade, faced Lee in Virginia. Both sides had gathered every available man for the last great trial of arms. Lieutenant-general Grant perfected his plans, and, after visiting the western army, and consulting with Sherman, he returned to the east, and took the general direction of military affairs. Everything was given into his hands; and he was supplied with all the men and material that were desired. "The particulars of your plans," said the President to him in a letter, "I neither know, nor seek to know. You are vigilant and self-reliant; and, pleased with this, I wish not to obtrude any restraints nor constraints upon you." General Grant's response to this note of Mr. Lincoln was evidently not given in ignorance of the charges which had so freely been made, by political enemies of the administration, that our generals were interfered with by the President and the Secretary of War. "From my first entrance into the volunteer service of my country to the present day," said he, "I have never had cause of complaint. * * * Indeed, since the promotion which placed me in command of all the armies, and in view of the great responsibility and importance of success, I have been astonished at the readiness with which everything asked for has been yielded, without even an explanation being asked."

Everything having been made ready, the two armies moved, at the opening of May, to the work that lay before them. On Tuesday night, May third, the army of the Potomac crossed the Rapidan; and on Thursday that series of actions was begun which will be known in history as "The Battles of the Wilderness." Thousands and tens of thousands of brave men fell on both sides; but the rebel general was obliged, from day to day, to fall back from his carefully prepared defenses, to save his communications; while Grant flanked him by a series of swift and daring swoops of his gigantic force, until Lee found himself and his army in Richmond. In cooperation with these movements of Grant's army, General Butler pushed up the James River with a large force, and secured and held City Point and Bermuda Hundred. This was his principal work; but he undertook various diversions without remarkable results.

It was not until the middle of June that the army reached the James River, and commenced the siege of Petersburgh, which was destined to ultimate in the downfall of the rebellion.

General Sherman pursued the strategy adopted by his superior. He had a larger army than Johnston, but Johnston had the advantage of strong positions and a knowledge of the country. He also moved toward his supplies, while Sherman left his behind him. The federal General flanked Johnston out of his works at Buzzard's Roost; and then, fighting and flanking, from day to day, he drove him from Dalton to Atlanta. Then Johnston was superseded by Hood, and Hood assumed the offensive. In three days of bloody battle, the new commander lost half of his army; and then he was glad to get behind the defenses of Atlanta. Here he remained more than a month, besieged. In the endeavor to escape from the toils which Sherman was weaving around him, he found himself at last thoroughly outgeneraled, and was obliged to run. Atlanta fell into our hands, on the second of September. Then Hood, a rash and desperate officer, set off to break up Sherman's communications; and, finding himself thoroughly whipped, started for a grand march to Nashville, where he hoped to find repayment for the losses and disgraces he had suffered. Sherman sent back to General Thomas, who had been left in command there, a portion of his army, and much of his material of war; and then he turned his back on Hood, for a march to the sea-coast.

This march, one of the most remarkable in the history of war, was called by the rebels a retreat. It was begun on the twelfth of November; and, leaving behind supplies and all means of communication, the gallant host started for the Atlantic. The most frantic efforts were made by the rebels to check the progress of the redoubtable army. Small forces hovered in front, in flank, and in rear, but nothing impeded its march. It was a gala-day affair, the soldiers supporting themselves upon the country through which they passed. On the eighth of December, the army arrived within twenty miles of Savannah. On the fourteenth, Fort McAllister was taken; and, on the same day, communication was opened with the federal fleet, sent to co-operate and bear supplies. The army had reached a new base; and had reached it without a single disaster. Savannah was occupied immediately, the rebel troops retreating and escaping. On the next day after Fort McAllister fell, Thomas defeated Hood in Tennessee, and sent him back, with his army cut in pieces and ruined.

In the meantime, Sheridan had whipped Early in the Shenandoah valley, in a series of brilliant engagements; and, although there had been raids of rebel cavalry across the Potomac, and panics and alarms in various quarters, the 1st of January, 1865, found the Union cause much advanced, and the rebels weakened and despondent. Sherman was at Savannah, organizing for another movement up the coast; Hood was crushed; Early's army was destroyed; Price, too, had been routed in Missouri; Canby was operating for the capture of Mobile; and Grant, with the grip of a bull-dog, held Lee in Richmond, while all these great movements in other parts of the country were in progress.

There was discord in the counsels of the rebels. They be-

gan to talk of using the negroes as soldiers.   The commanding general demanded this measure; and, at last, the singular
spectacle was exhibited of a slaveholders' rebellion, undertaken to make slavery perpetual, calling upon the slaves
themselves for help.   But the call for help came too late, even
had it been addressed to more promising sources.   Lee was
tied, and Sherman was turning his steps toward him; and
among the leaders of the rebellion there was a fearful looking-
for of fatal disasters.

Two changes occurred in Mr. Lincoln's cabinet during the
year, in addition to that already noted in the post-office department.   Edward Bates of Missouri, the Attorney-general,
left his post on the first of December, and was succeeded by
James Speed of Kentucky.   Mr. Chase, the Secretary of the
Treasury, resigned early in July.   That this resignation was
unexpected and unwelcome to Mr. Lincoln, was evident; but
it was immediately accepted.   There was probably some personal feeling on both sides, into the causes of which there is
no occasion to enter.   The matter excited Mr. Lincoln very
much—probably more than anything that concerned him personally during his administration.   He first appointed to the
vacant office Governor David Todd of Ohio; and, the appointment being declined, he named Hon. William Pitt Fessenden
of Maine.   Mr. Fessenden was a gentleman in whom the
country had full confidence; but, owing to his infirm health,
he assumed the responsibilities of the place with great reluctance, and only after such an appeal from Mr. Lincoln as he
could not resist.

On the twelfth of October, Chief Justice Taney died; and
the friends of Mr. Chase urged that gentleman at once as the
proper man to be endowed with the responsibilities of that august office.   But Mr. Chase had his enemies, like all those who
have achieved an equally prominent position.   The antagonism
between his friends and enemies was at once developed; and
Mr. Lincoln was approached with all the motives for and
against the appointment.   In this matter, Mr. Lincoln's habit
of hearing all the arguments in a case on which he had already

passed his judgment, was strikingly exhibited. Intimate
friends of Mr. Lincoln declare that there never was a time
during his administration when he did not intend to appoint
Mr. Chase to this place, if it should be made vacant by any
cause. To all arguments which related to Mr. Chase's fitness
or unfitness for the office, the President lent a ready ear; but
he was exceedingly vexed with those who appealed to his selfish resentments. There were not wanting men who tried to
arouse his prejudices, by reporting unpleasant words that Mr.
Chase was alleged to have uttered against the President;
but this gossip was always offensive, because it supposed that
he could be affected in his choice by selfish motives. To one
man who accused Mr. Chase to him of having used the patronage of his department to advance his own presidential
prospects, he simply replied: "Well, Chase would make a
pretty good president; and, so far as I am concerned, I wish
some one would take it off my hands." To another friend he
remarked that there were two considerations that controlled
him in this appointment: first, the man appointed should be an
anti-slavery man on principle; secondly, he should thoroughly
understand the financial policy of the government. Mr.
Chase's anti-slavery principles were universally acknowledged,
and the financial policy of the government was his own. So,
after a delay that gave Mr. Chase's friends and enemies time
to urge the points of their respective cases, Mr. Chase received
the appointment; and the country was no better satisfied with
this disposition of the matter than was Mr. Lincoln himself.

On the sixth of December, Mr. Lincoln sent in his annual
message to Congress, which had assembled on the fifth. The
document opened with a review of the position of foreign
governments, and our relations to those governments. The
President announced the ports of Norfolk, Fernandina and
Pensacola to have been opened by proclamation. His view
of the Arguelles case, which the opposition had made the
subject of severe criticism, he gave in the words: "For myself, I have no doubt of the power and duty of the executive,
under the law of nations, to exclude enemies of the human

32

race from an asylum in the United States. If Congress should think that proceedings in such cases lack the authority of law, or ought to be further regulated by it, I recommend that provision be made for effectually preventing foreign slave-traders from acquiring domicile and facilities for their criminal occupation in our country." Owing to raids into the states, planned in Canada by enemies of the United States harbored there, he announced that he had thought proper to give notice that, after the expiration of six months, the period conditionally stipulated in the existing arrangements with Great Britain, the United States would hold themselves at liberty to increase their naval armament upon the lakes, if they should deem it necessary to do so. Increased taxation had benefited the revenue; and the national banking system had proved to be acceptable to capitalists and the people. The naval exhibit gave a total of 671 vessels, carrying 4,610 guns, which showed an increase, during the year, of 83 vessels and 167 guns. The whole cost of the immense squadrons that had been called into existence since the beginning of the war, was more than two hundred and thirty-eight millions of dollars. One matter the President spoke of with special interest, viz: the steady expansion of population, improvement, and governmental institutions, over the new and unoccupied portions of the country, notwithstanding the civil war.

Mr. Lincoln thought fit to urge tne passage of an amendment to the Constitution, prohibiting slavery throughout the United States, notwithstanding the same Congress had killed the measure at its previous session. It may be stated here that Mr. Lincoln had contemplated this measure, and was ready for it long before Congress had come up to his position. Before even an allusion to this amendment had been publicly made, he talked about it with his friends, and was urged by one of them to become a leader in the movement. He replied that he had no ambition of that sort, but that he thought that the amendment ought to be made, and would be made. For himself, he was content to let others initiate the measure, and win the credit of it. But the matter had arrived at a new stage; and, when he saw that his influence was really necessary to its consummation, he did not hesitate to exert it.

Mr. Lincoln alluded to the lessons which had been taught by the presidential election. This election had proved the purpose of the people in the loyal states to maintain the integrity of the Union. It had proved, too, that, although the waste of war had been great, there were actually more men in the Union than when the war began. There had been, during the three years and a half of war, an increase of nearly one hundred and fifty thousand voters, without counting the soldiers who, by the laws of their respective states, were not permitted to vote. With this fact in view, it was plain that the government could maintain its contest with the rebellion indefinitely, so far as the supply of men was concerned. Mr. Lincoln closed his message by remarking that the rebels could, at any moment, have peace, by laying down their arms, and submitting to the national authority, under the Constitution. In saying this, however, he did not mean to retract anything he had said about slavery. He would not retract his Emancipation Proclamation, nor return to slavery any man free by the terms of that proclamation.

The most important measure effected by Congress at this session, was the passage of the amendment to the Constitution, abolishing slavery in all the states. It passed the House by more than the requisite two-thirds vote, having passed the Senate during the previous session. The event was hailed with great satisfaction by the friends of the administration; and only a few of the more virulent of the opposition were disaffected by it. To the President, the measure was particularly gratifying; and he took occasion to express his satisfaction to a crowd that gathered around the White House, immediately after its adoption. He said that it seemed to him to be the one thing necessary to the winding up of the whole difficulty. It completed and confirmed the work of his proclamation of emancipation. It needed only to be adopted by the votes of the states; and he appealed to his auditors to go home, and see that work faithfully accomplished.

The figures which gave the result of the presidential election showed that the country was stronger in men than it was at the beginning of the war; and, as the call for five hundred thousand men, made in July, had failed to produce all the soldiers which the war, much longer protracted, would require, the President issued a call, on the nineteenth of December, for three hundred thousand more.

A peace conference, procured by the voluntary and irresponsible agency of Mr. Francis P. Blair, was held on the steamer River Queen, in Hampton Roads, on the 3d of February, 1865, between President Lincoln and Mr. Seward, representing the government, and Messrs. Alexander H. Stephens, J. A. Campbell and R. M. T. Hunter, representing the rebel confederacy. It was an informal affair, entirely verbal in its conduct, and unproductive of results. The President consented to become a party to the interview, on representations made by General Grant, who regarded at least two of the commissioners as very sincere in their desire for peace. In the conference, these commissioners favored a postponement of the question of separation, and mutual efforts of the two governments toward some extrinsic policy for a season, so as to give time for the passions of the people to cool. The armies, meantime, were to be reduced, and the intercourse between the people of the two sections to be resumed. This the President considered as equivalent to an armistice or truce; and he informed them that he could agree to no cessation of hostilities, except on the basis of a disbandment of the insurgent forces, and the recognition of the national authority throughout all the states of the Union. He also declared it impossible to recede from his Emancipation Proclamation; and informed the Richmond gentlemen that Congress had passed the constitutional amendment, prohibiting slavery; stating, in addition, that the amendment would doubtless be perfected by the action of three-fourths of the states. There was an earnest desire for peace on both sides, without a doubt; but Mr. Lincoln could, with truth to himself and honor to his country, make peace only on certain essential conditions; while the hands of the commissioners were tied by the obstinacy which reigned in Richmond.

The reports of the conversation at this conference are very meager, necessarily; but enough has been made public to show that some of the incidents were very interesting and somewhat amusing. The Augusta (Georgia) Chronicle has published an account of the conference, which is said to have been prepared under the eye of Mr. Stephens. This account states that Mr. Lincoln declared that, in his negotiations for peace, he could not recognize another government inside of the one of which he alone was President. "That," said he, "would be doing what you so long asked Europe to do in vain, and be resigning the only thing the Union armies are fighting for." To this, Mr. Hunter replied that the recognition of Davis' power to make a treaty was the first and indispensable step to peace; and, to illustrate his point, he referred to the correspondence between King Charles the First and his Parliament, as a reliable precedent of a constitutional ruler treating with rebels. The Chronicle's account says that at this point "Mr. Lincoln's face wore that indescribable expression which generally preceded his hardest hits; and he remarked: 'Upon questions of history, I must refer you to Mr. Seward, for he is posted in such things, and I don't profess to be; but my only distinct recollection of the matter is that Charles lost his head.'"

The President told his "little story," too, on this occasion, the best version of which is given in Mr. Carpenter's Reminiscences. They were discussing the slavery question, when Mr. Hunter remarked that the slaves, always accustomed to work upon compulsion, under an overseer, would, if suddenly freed, precipitate not only themselves, but the entire society of the South, into irremediable ruin. No work would be done, but blacks and whites would starve together. The President waited for Mr. Seward to answer the argument; but, as that gentleman hesitated, he said: "Mr. Hunter, you ought to know a great deal better about this matter than I, for you have always lived under the slave system. I can only say, in reply to your statement of the case, that it reminds me of a man out in Illinois, by the name of Case, who undertook, a few years ago, to raise a very large herd of hogs. It was a great trouble to feed them; and how to get around this was a puzzle to him. At length, he hit upon the plan of planting an immense field of potatoes; and, when they were sufficiently grown, he turned the whole herd into the field, and let them have full swing, thus saving not only the labor of feeding the hogs, but that also of digging the potatoes! Charmed with his sagacity, he stood one day leaning against the fence, counting his hogs, when a neighbor came along. 'Well, well,' said he, 'Mr. Case, this is all very fine. Your hogs are doing very well just now; but you know out here in Illinois the frost comes early, and the ground freezes a foot deep. Then what are they going to do?' This was a view of the matter which Mr. Case had not taken into account. Butchering time for hogs was away on in December or January. He scratched his head, and at length stammered: 'Well, it may come pretty hard on their *snouts*, but I don't see but it will be *root hog or die!*'"

It is not supposed that Mr. Lincoln hoped for more from this conference than he did from the Niagara Falls negotiations; but he was determined to show that he was ready for peace, on the only grounds that would satisfy the loyal people of the country. The result strengthened the faith of the people in him; and the rebel President seized upon it to stir the ashes in the southern heart, in the vain hope to find fuel there which the long fire had left unconsumed.

Congress adjourned by constitutional limitation on the third of March, although the Senate was at once convened in extra session, in accordance with a proclamation of the President.

On the day of the adjournment of Congress, Mr. Lincoln's first term of office expired. Four years of bloody war had passed away—four years marked by the most marvelous changes in the spirit, position, feelings, principles and institutions of the American people. The great system of wrong, out of which the rebellion had sprung, was in rapid process of dissolution, and already beyond the reach of resuscitation. The government had passed through the severest tests, and had emerged triumphant. There was no longer doubt in the hearts of the people, and no longer contempt among the nations of the earth. Abraham Lincoln, the humble and unobtrusive citizen, the self-educated and Christian man, had been tried, and had not been found wanting. His foes no longer denied, and his friends no longer doubted, his great ability. He was, in every sense, the first citizen of the republic; and he had taken his place among the leading rulers of the world.

Mr. Lincoln was re-inaugurated into the presidential office on the fourth of March. An immense crowd was in attendance—a crowd of affectionate friends, not doubtful of the President, and not doubtful of one another and the future, as at the first inauguration. Chief Justice Chase administered the oath of office; and then Mr. Lincoln read his inaugural address—a paper whose Christian sentiments and whose reverent and pious spirit has no parallel among the state papers of the American Presidents. It showed the President still untouched by resentment, still brotherly in his feelings toward the enemies of the government, and still profoundly conscious of the overruling power of Providence in national affairs. The address was as follows:

"Fellow-Countrymen—At this second appearing to take the oath of the Presidential office, there is less occasion for an extended address than there was at the first. Then a statement somewhat in detail of a course to be pursued seemed very fitting and proper. Now, at the expiration of four years, during which public declarations have been constantly called forth on every point and phase of the great contest which still absorbs the attention and engrosses the energies of the nation, little that is new could be presented.

"The progress of our arms, upon which all else chiefly depends, is as well known to the public as to myself; and it is, I trust, reasonably satisfactory and encouraging to all. With high hope for the future, no prediction in regard to it is ventured.

"On the occasion corresponding to this four years ago, all thoughts were anxiously directed to an impending civil war. All dreaded it; all sought to avoid it. While the inaugural address was being delivered from this place, devoted altogether to saving the Union without war, insurgent agents were in the city seeking to destroy it without war—seeking to dissolve the Union and divide the effects by negotiation. Both parties deprecated war; but one of them would make war rather than let the nation survive, and the other would accept war rather than let it perish; and the war came.

"One eighth of the whole population were colored slaves, not distributed generally over the Union, but localized in the southern part of it. These slaves constituted a peculiar and powerful interest. All knew that this interest was somehow the cause of the war. To strengthen, perpetuate and extend this interest, was the object for which the insurgents would rend the Union even by war, while the government claimed no right to do more than to restrict the territorial enlargement of it.

"Neither party expected for the war the magnitude or the duration which it has already attained. Neither anticipated that the cause of the conflict might cease with, or even before, the conflict itself should cease. Each looked for an easier triumph, and a result less fundamental and astounding.

"Both read the same Bible and pray to the same God, and each invokes his aid against the other. It may seem strange that any men should dare to ask a just God's assistance in wringing their bread from the sweat of other men's faces; but let us judge not, that we be not judged. The prayers of both could not be answered. That of neither has been answered fully. The Almighty has his own purposes. 'Woe unto the world because of offences, for it must needs be that offences come: but woe to that man by whom the offence cometh.' If we shall suppose that American slavery is one of these offences, which in the providence of God must needs come, but which having continued through his appointed time, he now wills to remove, and that he gives to both North and South this terrible war as the woe due to those by whom the offence came, shall we discern therein any departure from those divine attributes which the believers in a living God always ascribe to him? Fondly do we hope, fervently do we pray, that this mighty scourge of war may soon pass away. Yet, if God wills that it continue until all the wealth piled by the bondman's two hundred and fifty years of unrequited toil shall be sunk, and until every drop of blood drawn with the lash shall be paid with another drawn with the sword; as was said three thousand years ago, so still it must be said, 'The judgments of the Lord are true and righteous altogether.'

"With malice toward none, with charity for all, with firmness in the right, as God gives us to see the right, let us strive on to finish the work we are in, to bind up the nation's wounds, to care for him who shall have borne the battle and for his widow and orphans, to do all which may achieve and cherish a just and a lasting peace among ourselves and with all nations."

On the sixth of March, Mr. Fessénden, who had never regarded himself as permanently in the office of Secretary of the Treasury, resigned; and Hugh McCulloch of Indiana was appointed to his place. Further than this, Mr. Lincoln introduced no changes into his cabinet. The people had not only indorsed Mr. Lincoln, but they had indorsed his administration. On the eleventh of March, the President issued a proclamation, in pursuance of an act of Congress, calling upon deserters to return to their posts, and promising them pardon. The proclamation called many of the wanderers back to their duty. The draft for three hundred thousand men was commenced on the fifteenth of the same month, and every necessary measure was adopted for a continuance of the war, should the constant accumulation of federal successes fail to bring the rebellion to a close.

CHAPTER XXIX.

The affairs of the rebellion were hurrying to a crisis. In January, General Sherman started northward with his hosts; and the borders of South Carolina were reached on the thirtieth. They swept through the state, a very besom of destruction—tearing up railroads, burning bridges, living on the country, and attracting large numbers of negroes to them, to learn that they were free. Columbia was occupied on the seventeenth of February, and the public property destroyed. The arteries that fed the life of Charleston were cut, and the proud city was evacuated without the cost of a life. Though threatened often, the army marched with scarcely more difficulty than they experienced in their march across Georgia. Fayetteville, North Carolina, was reached and occupied on the twelfth of March; and then communication was established with Generals Terry and Schofield at Wilmington, and the army received such supplies as were needed. Battles occurred at Averysboro and Bentonville; but still the march was resistless, and the forces gathered in front, under command of General Johnston, were driven northward as the forest leaves are driven by the wind. On the twenty-second of March, Goldsboro was occupied; and there the army remained for some days, while General Sherman visited City Point, for consultation with General Grant.

The army of Sherman was aiming at Richmond. There was no doubt of that; but Lee was held to the rebel capital by Grant, and could not get away. The grand campaign was culminating; and, on the day that Sherman entered Goldsboro, Mr. Lincoln arrived at City Point, partly to relieve himself of official cares that had made him sick, and partly to be near operations which involved momentous consequences to the country. On the twenty-fifth of March, Lee attacked and captured Fort Stedman, but was driven out of it with terrible losses; and Mr. Lincoln visited the scene on the same day, cheered by the soldiers wherever he appeared. The day had been fixed upon for a grand review, in honor of the President; but Mr. Lincoln said: "This is better than a review." On the twenty-eighth of March, a council of war was held on the steamer River Queen, at City Point, attended by the President and Generals Grant, Sherman, Sheridan, Meade, and Ord; and, soon afterwards, Sherman left to rejoin his army.

New dispositions of troops had been in progress for several days; and, on the day following the council of war, the grand movement of the army of the Potomac began. Before the morning was passed, a new line of battle had been formed, whose right was on the extreme left of the former position; and here the army commenced entrenching. A sharp little fight occurred in the afternoon, without material results. On the following day, it rained; but on Friday, Saturday, and Sunday, Grant's whole line was engaged in a series of heavy battles; and, while these were in progress, the President remained at City Point, receiving dispatches from the field, and forwarding the substance of them to the country. His first dispatch, on Saturday, reported that there had been much hard fighting that morning, in which our forces had been driven back. Later in the day, he announced that the ground had all been retaken, and that our troops were occupying the position which the rebels held in the morning. On Saturday, Sheridan and Warren met with great successes. On Sunday, the President announced "the triumphant success of our armies, after three days of hard fighting, during which the forces on both sides displayed unsurpassed valor." At half-past eight in the evening, Mr. Lincoln telegraphed to Mr. Stanton that, at half-past four in the afternoon, General Grant reported that he had taken twelve thousand prisoners, and fifty pieces of artillery. In the smoke of this great day of battle, the rebellion was overthrown. Lee, with his shattered army reduced to half of its original numbers, by the three days of fighting, evacuated Richmond. The rebel rams and wooden fleet were blown up during the night, with terrific explosions. On the north side of the James, lay General Weitzel's corps, waiting to occupy Richmond, whenever the signs should indicate the safety of an advance. On Monday morning, April third, Weitzel pushed out the Fifth Massachusetts Cavalry to reconnoiter; and they reported that no enemy was to be found. At eleven in the morning, he announced by telegraph that he entered Richmond at a quarter past eight; that the enemy had left in great haste; that he had many guns; that the city was on fire; and that the people received him with enthusiastic expressions of joy. His dispatch closed with the statement that Grant had started to cut off Lee's retreat, and that President Lincoln had gone to the front.

The day on which Richmond fell will long be remembered by the people of America, in both sections of the country. When the news was made public on Monday, the whole North was thrown into a frenzy of joyous excitement. Every bell on every public building, from the Atlantic to the Pacific, was rung for hours. Cannon answered to cannon, from mountain to mountain, and from valley to valley. Men grasped one another's hands in the streets, and wept, or embraced each other in the stress of their joyous enthusiasm. Public meetings were called, at which the deeds of the gallant heroes who had won the decisive victories were praised and cheered, and the public exultation found expression in speech and music. Nothing like it was ever seen upon the continent. The war was over. Richmond, that had so long defied the national authority and resisted the national arms, was ours. The rebel President and his associates were fugitives. Lee's army was running away, and Grant was pursuing them. The sun of peace had fairly risen. The incubus of war that had pressed upon the nation's heart for four long, weary years, was lifted; and the nation sprang to its feet, with all possible demonstrations of joyous exultation

The pursuit of Lee was relentlessly prosecuted by our victorious forces; and, after two or three battles, the rebel General was obliged to surrender his whole army, which had been reduced by his losses to less than twenty thousand men. Within a period of less than two weeks, the city of Richmond was taken, and the proud army of Virginia passed out of existence. The capture of Lee was made the occasion of another day of popular rejoicing; and the scenes and sounds that followed the capture of Richmond were repeated.

Of the feelings of Mr. Lincoln, as he sat in his tent at City Point, receiving the dispatches which informed him of the momentous movements in progress at the front, no imagination can form an exaggerated estimate. But he could not sustain the excitement of those days without relief; and he found it in a way which none but he would have adopted. Just before he arrived at City Point, a pet cat, belonging to General Grant, had presented the General with a little family of kittens. On their owner's departure, the President took them into his care; and, during all those days of battle, in the intervals while he waited for dispatches, he relieved the pressure upon his heart and brain by playing with these kittens. When Richmond had fallen, and he was about to start for the front, he took up one of the kittens, and said: "Little kitten, I must perform a last act of kindness for you, before I go. I must open your eyes." He then manipulated the closed lids as tenderly as a mother would handle her child, until he had accomplished his purpose. Then he put her down, and, as he stood enjoying her surprise at being able to see, he said sadly: "Oh that I could open the eyes of my blinded fellow-countrymen, as easily as I have those of that little creature!" The eyes of his blinded fellow-countrymen were soon opened, but alas! it involved the closing of his own!

Mr. Lincoln belied his own estimate of his physical courage, by going directly into the fallen capital, so lately swarming with armed enemies, and so crowded still with sullen rebels.

He did this apparently without a thought of danger, although the whole loyal North trembled with apprehension. He went up in a man-of-war, on the afternoon of Monday, landed at the Rocketts below the city, and with his boy "Tad" rode up the remaining mile in a boat. He entered the city in no triumphal car. No brilliant cavalcade accompanied him; but on foot, with no guard except the sailors who had rowed him up the James, he entered and passed through the streets of the fallen capital. But his presence soon became known to the grateful blacks, who pressed upon him with their thankful ejaculations and tearful blessings on every side. Better and more expressive were the hats and handkerchiefs, tossed in the air by these happy and humble people, than flags and streamers, floating from masts and house-tops. "Glory to God! Glory! Glory!" shouted the black multitude of liberated slaves. "I thank you dear Jesus, that I behold President Linkum," exclaimed a woman standing in her humble doorway, weeping in the fullness of her joy. Another, wild with delight, could do nothing but jump, and strike her hands, and shout with wild reiteration: "Bless de Lord! Bless de Lord! Bless de Lord!" At last, the streets became choked with the multitude, and soldiers were called to clear the way. A writer in the Atlantic Monthly, to whom the author is indebted for the most of these particulars, says that one old negro exclaimed: "May de good Lord bless you, President Linkum!" while he removed his hat, and the tears of joy rolled down his cheeks. "The President," the account proceeds, "removed his own hat, and bowed in silence; but it was a bow which upset the forms, laws, customs, and ceremonies of centuries. It was a death-shock to chivalry, and a mortal wound to caste."

After a visit to General Weitzel's headquarters, and a drive around the city, he returned to City Point. On Thursday, he visited the city again, accompanied by Mrs. Lincoln and the Vice-president, with others. While he was in Richmond on this occasion, he held important interviews with leading citizens, prominent among whom was Judge Campbell, one of the parties in the Hampton Roads conference. The Judge urged him to issue a proclamation; permitting the Virginia Legislature to assemble, under the representation that that body would recognize the situation, and withdraw the Virginia troops from the support of Lee. After his return to City Point, he addressed a note to General Weitzel, directing him to permit the legislature to assemble, and to protect them until they should attempt some action hostile to the United States. He was also directed to show the note to Judge Campbell, but not to make it public. The Judge sent an account of his interview and its results to the Richmond Whig; and, this having been copied into the Washington Chronicle, after Mr. Lincoln's return to the federal capital, the President was very indignant. The breach of confidence on the part of Judge Campbell, and the misrepresentations which accompanied it, quite exhausted his patience. As Lee's army had surrendered, and there was no further apology for the desire to have the legislature assemble, he revoked his permission for its convocation. It was evident, in a cabinet meeting that was held a few days afterward, that Judge Campbell's course had much embittered him. He had been inclined to trust in the personal honor of rebels with whom he had been brought in contact; but he evidently felt that his confidence had been practiced upon by Campbell; and the fact stung him to indignation, if not anger.

The order produced an unpleasant effect upon the public mind, and its revocation was received with gratification all over the North. The revocation did not come early enough, however, to save serious difficulty in other quarters; for Sherman, negotiating with Johnston, patterned his policy upon that of the President, and brought down upon himself the reprobation of the loyal press of the country—reprobation which, in extreme instances, assumed the form of direct charges of disloyalty against this gallant and most loyal soldier. But Johnston surrendered; and soon there was not an army of the rebellion that had not given itself up to our forces, or been disbanded and scattered.

The great rebellion was ended. General Grant reached Washington on the thirteenth of April, and held an interview with the President and Mr. Stanton, the result of which was the issue of an order from the War Department on the same day, or, rather, of a statement that orders would immediately be issued, to stop drafting and recruiting, to curtail purchases for arms, ammunition and supplies, to reduce the number of general and staff officers to the necessities of the service, and to remove military restrictions on trade and commerce.

The American people were floating on the high tide of joy. All were glad and happy; and, as they returned their thanks to the Giver of all good for victory and peace, they did not forget the instrument he had used in the execution of his plans. Mr. Lincoln's name was on every tongue. The patient man who had suffered the pain of a thousand deaths during the war—who had been misconstrued, maligned, and condemned by personal and party enemies, and questioned and criticised by captious friends,—was the man above all others who stood in the full sunshine of the popular affection. His motives were vindicated, his policy had been sanctioned by success, and his power had been proved. He was the acknowledged savior of his country, and the liberator of a race. He had solved the great problem of popular government; he had settled the great question of African slavery on the continent. He had won a glorious place in history; and his name had been committed to the affectionate safe-keeping of mankind.

On the evening of the eleventh of April, the White House was brilliantly illuminated; and to the immense crowd gathered around it, to express their joyous congratulations, Mr. Lincoln delivered his last public address. He said little about victory, further than briefly to express his acknowledgments to the soldiers who had fought, and the God who had prospered their arms; but, turning his eyes from the past, he regarded the future, and the new duties and perplexities which it was certain to bring. "Reconstruction" was the burden of his speech; and he explained, at length, his connection with the efforts at reconstruction which had taken place in Louisiana. The question as to whether the rebel states were out of the Union, or in it, he regarded as a "pernicious abstraction." "We all agree," said he, "that the seceded states, so called, are out of their proper practical relation with the Union; and that the sole object of the government, civil and military, in regard to those states, is to again get them into their proper practical relation." He believed the state government of Louisiana offered for that state a practicable plan of return, but he was not committed to that plan alone. The quickest way back to the old relations with the government was the best way, without any regard to any finely spun theories.

The Louisiana Legislature had ratified the Constitutional amendment abolishing slavery, and Mr. Lincoln said: "These twelve thousand persons (the loyal element of the state) are thus fully committed to the Union, and the perpetuation of freedom in the state—committed to the very things, and nearly all the things, the nation wants; and they ask the nation's recognition, and its assistance to make good this committal. Now, if we reject and spurn them, we do our utmost to disorganize and disperse them. We, in fact, say to the white man: 'You are worthless, or worse: we will neither help you nor be helped by you.' To the blacks we say: 'This cup of liberty which these your old masters, held to your lips, we will dash from you, and leave you to the chances of gathering the spilled and scattered contents in some vague and undefined when, where, and how.' "

All the President's plans considered the welfare of the black man as well as the white; and there will be no better opportunity to give his views of negro suffrage than this page will furnish. This great question, which promises to be a stone of stumbling and a rock of offence to the party which placed Mr. Lincoln in power—a stone which is certain, in the administration of God's providence, to become the head of the corner—was one which he had carefully considered, and upon which, with his respect for human rights, he could have but one opinion. In a letter to the late General Wadsworth, he once said: "You desire to know, in the event of our complete success in the field, the same being followed by loyal and cheerful submission on the part of the South, if universal amnesty should not be accompanied with universal suffrage. Since you know my private inclinations as to what terms should be granted to the South, in the contingency mentioned, I will here add that, if our success should thus be realized, followed by such desired results, *I cannot see, if universal amnesty is granted, how, under the circumstances, I can avoid exacting in return universal suffrage, or at least suffrage on the basis of intelligence and military service.*"

Thus stands Mr. Lincoln's record on this question, and thus must stand the record of every man whose love of men and whose regard for human rights are as genuine as those which moved the heart of the good President. The party which loved and supported Mr. Lincoln cannot deny the principle of universal suffrage, without denying both Mr. Lincoln and the everlasting principles of right upon which he based his action—upon which they have won all their successes. And if, for immediate advantage, in the strife for power, they so far turn their backs upon their record as to deny manhood to the African, and refuse to recognize his service in the salvation of the republic, they are sure to be defeated, as they will be certain to deserve defeat.

CHAPTER XXX.

MR. LINCOLN had reached the pinnacle of his life. By careful and painful steps he had mounted from the foot of the ladder of American society to its topmost round. He had done this by the forces of his nature and character, without adventitious aids, or favoring circumstances. He had accomplished the greatest work for his country and for mankind that had ever been committed to a mortal to perform. A great nation had been saved from wreck by his hands; a race had been disenthralled by his word and his policy; and a popular government had been established in the faith and affections of its subjects, and in the respect of the governments of the world. His enemies had been silenced, his friends had been reassured, his motives and his policy had been vindicated, and his person had come to be regarded with tender affection by tens of millions of men. Up to him were wafted the acclamations of millions of freemen. Across the ocean came appreciative and plauditory words from other continents. Benedictions were breathed upon him by multitudes of humble people whom he had enfranchised. Is it strange that the instincts of his own logical mind should forecast death as the next logical step in such a course?

Throughout all the later months and years of the war, he had freely said that he did not expect to outlast the rebellion; but in the flush of triumph,—in his large, loving, and liberal plans for the good of the people whom the fortunes of war had left at his feet,—in his dreams of the future union and harmony of the states,—he forgot this, and was hopeful and happy. He talked to his friends, his cabinet, and his family cheerfully of the future, and gratefully of the past. He had no resentment to gratify, no revenge to inflict, no malicious passion that clamored for indulgence. The thought of being able to prove to the people of the South that he owed them no ill-will, and the determination to deal with them as gently as would be for the public safety, filled his magnanimous spirit with the sweetest satisfaction.

It is hardly to be supposed that the possibility of assassination was ever long absent from his mind, during the four years of his presidency. The threats began before he left Springfield for Washington. The attempt to assassinate him was made upon the train that bore him from his home. It was repeated upon that which bore him from Cincinnati. He ran through the meshes of a conspiracy against his life at Baltimore. He was in the constant receipt of threatening letters; and these were kept in a package by themselves, appropriately labeled. He did not permit these, however, to trouble him, regarding them as only the malicious missives of bullies and cowards. He undoubtedly regarded himself as always in a dangerous position, though the fact had no tendency to make him careful of himself. He reasoned upon this, as upon other subjects, and could never 'see that anything would be gained by his death. He had no comprehension of the malice that would delight in his assassination, as a measure of revenge. He supposed that every man would require some rational purpose to be answered by so terrible a crime. "If they kill me," said he, on one occasion, "the next man will be just as bad for them; and, in a country like this, where our habits are simple, and must be, assassination is always possible, and will come if they are determined upon it." He went to and from the War Department with perfect freedom; drove out to the Soldiers' Home, his summer residence, and back at night, often in an open carriage, alone. He walked the streets of Washington at night, with only an unarmed companion, who trembled with the apprehension of the possible consequences of such an exposure. Mr. Seward, in reply to a letter from Hon. John Bigelow, the American consul in Paris, wrote under date of July 15th, 1864: "There is no doubt that, from a period anterior to the breaking out of the insurrection, plots and conspiracies for the purposes of assassination have been frequently formed and organized." Mr. Bigelow had reported to Mr. Seward a plot which had become known abroad. Mr. Seward added: "Assassination is not an American practice or habit; and one so vicious and so desperate cannot be engrafted into our political system. This conviction of mine has steadily gained strength since the civil war began. Every day's experience confirms it." Notwithstanding Mr. Seward's theory, plots were formed against his own life, as well as that of Mr. Lincoln—plots, indeed, embracing more than these two persons, and extending to nearly all the prominent men in the government and in its military service. General Grant and General Sherman were both the unconscious objects of deadly conspiracies. It is now known that, not only in the States, but in Canada and Europe, plots of this character were concocted; and it is believed that, on one occasion, the President actually took poison, in the drugs that were prescribed for him by his physician, and prepared in one of the shops of the city.

Secretary Seward, even before he came so near to death through one of these conspiracies, was compelled to give up his theory, and to acknowledge that he and the President were in positive danger.

The morning of the fourteenth of April was spent by Mr. Lincoln mainly in interviews with his friends. Among those who called was Speaker Colfax, who was about setting out upon an overland journey to the Pacific coast, a journey which has since been satisfactorily accomplished; and to him the President entrusted a verbal message to the miners, assuring them of his friendliness to their interests, and telling them that their prosperity was identified with the prosperity of the nation. General Grant, it will be remembered, was in the city; and he was invited to be present at the cabinet meeting held during the day. In public and social duties the day passed away; and in the evening Mr. Colfax came again. George Ashmun of Massachusetts also came in, and to him Mr. Lincoln gave the following little note in pencil—the last words he ever wrote:

    Allow Mr. Ashmun and friend to come in at 9 A. M. to-morrow.
                                          " A LINCOLN."

Mr. Lincoln and General Grant were the lions of the day; and the manager of Ford's theater, with a keen eye to business, had not only invited them to witness that night the representation of " Our American Cousin," but announced them both as positively to be present. The Washington papers of the fourteenth contained the following "personal notice:"

" Lieutenant-general Grant, President and Mrs. Lincoln, and ladies, will occupy the state box at Ford's theater to-night, to witness Miss Laura Keene's company in Tom Taylor's 'American Cousin.'*

General Grant did not desire to attend, and so left the city. The President was equally disinclined to the entertainment; but, as his presence and that of General Grant also had been pledged to the people, he saw that there would be great disappointment if he should fail them; and, when Mrs. Lincoln entered the President's room to inquire what decision he had arrived at, he said that he had concluded to go. He invited both Mr. Ashmun and Mr. Colfax to accompany him, but both declined, pleading other engagements; and Mr. and Mrs. Lincoln, attended to the carriage by Mr. Ashmun, left without other company, and drove directly to the house of Senator Harris, where they took in Miss Harris, a daughter of the Senator, and Major Rathbone, a son of the Senator's wife, who happened to be in at the time. The party reached the theater at twenty minutes before nine o'clock, to find the house filled in every part; and, as they passed to their seats in the private box reserved for them, the whole assembly rose and cheered them, with the most cordial enthusiasm. This

                     *Judge C. P. Daly of New York.

demonstration was intended as an expression of good-will, and as a popular congratulation on the victories that had brought the rebellion to a close. The President bowed to the audience, took his seat, and was soon afterwards absorbed in the scenes of mimic life upon the stage. Here let us leave him, to trace the movements of another person.

At half-past eleven o'clock, on the morning of the fourteenth, John Wilkes Booth, a young actor who had been openly disloyal throughout the war, visited Ford's theater, where he was informed that a box had been taken for the President and General Grant. Then he went to a stable, and engaged a high-strung mare for a saddle-ride, which he proposed to take in the middle of the afternoon. From the stable he proceeded to the Kirkwood Hotel, where he sent up to Vice-president Johnson a card, bearing the words: "I do n't wish to disturb you; are you at home?" To this, his signature was appended; and it drew from Mr. Johnson only the response that he was very busily engaged. At four o'clock, he called for the mare, and rode away, leaving her at last at a point convenient for his further purposes. In the evening, he took her from her hiding-place, and rode to the theater. Summoning one Spangler, a scene-shifter, he left the animal in his charge, to be held until he should return. Then he ascended to the dress-circle, looked in upon the stage and the audience, and gradually worked his way through the crowd packed in the rear of the dress-circle, toward the box occupied by the Presidential party. This box was at the end of the dress-circle, next the stage; and was reached by passing in the rear of the dress-circle, to a door opening first into a dark, narrow passage, and then by two doors opening from the passage. This passage was contrived so that the box might be made a double one, when occasion required, by securing facilities for a double entrance, an inside sliding partition completing the arrangement. To the entrance of this passage, Booth forced himself; and, after showing a card to the President's servant, and saying that Mr. Lincoln had sent for him, he passed into the passage, and fastened the door behind him. Presenting himself at the door of the box, he took a quick survey of the interior. He found everything favorable to his purpose; and, taking a small Derringer pistol in one hand, and a double-edged dagger in the other, he thrust his arm into the entrance, where the President, sitting in an arm-chair, presented to his full view the back and side of his head. A flash, a sharp report, a puff of smoke, and the fatal bullet had entered the President's brain. Mr. Lincoln did not stir. People thought that the report of the pistol had some connection with the play; but the awful truth was soon apparent. There was no escape for the murderer by the way through which he had reached the box; for the crowd was too great. Major Rathbone, the instant he comprehended what was done, sprang upon Booth, who, throwing him off, dropped his pistol, and struck him with his dagger, inflicting a flesh wound upon the officer's arm. Then the murderer rushed to the front of the box, parted the folds of the flag with which it was draped for the occasion, and leaped to the stage, half falling as he descended, his spurs having caught in the drapery. Then springing to his feet, he uttered with theatrical emphasis the words of the state motto of Virginia: "*Sic semper tyrannis!*" and added: "The South is avenged." Quickly turning, he rushed from the stage, striking from his path all whom he met, and, escaping at the rear of the theater, was in his saddle and away before the party around the President and the audience fully comprehended what had been done. Only a single man in the audience took in at once the meaning of the scene; and, although he undertook to follow Booth, the assassin had disappeared before he reached the door.

Mrs. Lincoln screamed, and Miss Harris called for water. The scene among the audience defies all description. Women shrieked and fainted. Men called for vengeance. The most terrible uproar prevailed. Laura Keene, the actress, begged the audience to be calm, and entered the box from the stage, bearing water and cordials. The President was entirely unconscious; and, as soon as the surgeons, who had gathered quickly to him, had ascertained the position and nature of the wound, the helpless form was borne across Tenth street to the house of a Mr. Peterson. Surgeon-general Barnes, after examination, pronounced the wound a mortal one. The words fell upon the ears of Secretary Stanton, who, bursting into tears, responded: "Oh, no! General, no, no!" Attorney-general Speed, Secretary Welles, Postmaster-general Dennison, General Meigs, Mr. McCulloch, the new Secretary of the Treasury, and Senator Sumner were gathered around the bed, the last holding one of the President's hands, and sobbing like a child. In an adjoining room, supported by her son Robert and Mrs. Senator Dixon, sat Mrs. Lincoln, bewildered and crushed by her great grief. Around the unconscious form of the President the great men of the nation bowed, and wept, watching the heaving of his breast, until, at twenty-two minutes past seven in the morning, he breathed his last.

In another part of the city, at the moment of the murder and alarm at the theater, another scene of terrible violence was enacted, which showed that one of the many conspiracies that had been organized to destroy the heads of the government was in process of execution.

A few days previously, Mr. Seward had been thrown from his carriage, and severely injured. He was still very low, and under the most careful medical and surgical treatment. A little after ten, on this fatal evening, the door-bell of his residence was rung by a man who said he came with medicine from Dr. Verdi, Mr. Seward's physician, which it was necessary for him to deliver in person. The servant who admitted him protested that no one was permitted to see Mr. Seward. The man pushed him aside, and mounted the stairs. When he was about to enter the Secretary's room, Mr. Frederick Seward, the Secretary's son, appeared, and inquired his business. He gave the same reply that he had given to the servant, when the gentleman told him that he could not enter. In return for this refusal, Mr. Frederick Seward received a stunning blow upon his forehead, with the butt of a pistol; and the man pushed on to the bedside of the Secretary, mounted the bed, and, aiming at Mr. Seward's throat, stabbed him three

times.   He would undoubtedly have killed him, had he not
been seized around the body by the nurse of Mr. Seward, a
soldier named Robinson.   While the assassin was struggling
with Robinson, Mr. Seward summoned sufficient strength to
roll himself off the bed.   The murderer, inflicting severe
wounds upon Robinson, burst away from him, rushed to the
door, forced his way down stairs, stabbing Major Augustus
Seward and one of his father's attendants on the way, and
escaped into the street.   He had stabbed no less than five
persons.   This conspirator, known afterwards to the public
by the name of Payne, was Lewis Payne Powell.

The effect of these two tragedies upon the popular feeling
in the city of Washington may possibly be imagined, but it
cannot be described.   Some cried for retaliation upon the
leaders of a rebellion that could inspire such deeds, and for
revenge even upon the helpless prisoners in our hands.   Others
were possessed by a sense of horror; others by emotions of
terror; others by an overwhelming grief; and all by a feeling
of uncertainty and insecurity.   How wide was the conspiracy?
How comprehensive was the plot?   Who were the designated
victims?   What would be the next development?   There was
no sleep in Washington that night.   A terrible solemnity took
possession of the noisy capital.   Only the military were busy.
All the drinking shops of the city were closed, the outlets of
the city were guarded, and every necessary step was taken
for the protection of the persons of the other members of the
government.

The effect of these terrible events upon the popular heart
throughout the country was touching in the extreme.   From
the sunniest hills of joy, the people went down weeping into
the darkest valleys of affliction.   The long, sad morning of the
President's death was full of the sound of tolling bells.   It
was everywhere the same.   By a common impulse the bells
from every tower in the land gave voice to the popular grief;
and from every dwelling and store and shop, from every church
and public building, the insignia of sorrow were displayed.
The markets were literally cleared of every fabric that could

be used for the drapery of mourning. Men met in the streets, and pressed each other's hands in silence, or burst into tears. The whole nation, which, the previous day, was jubilant and hopeful, was precipitated into the depths of a profound and tender woe. Millions felt that they had lost a brother, or a father, or a dear personal friend. It was a grief that brought the nation more into family sympathy than it had been since the days of the Revolution. Men came together in public meetings, to give expression to their grief. The day on which the murder was announced to the country was Saturday; and on Sunday all the churches were draped with mourning; and from every pulpit in the land came the voice of lamentation over the national loss, and of eulogy to the virtues of the good President who had been so cruelly murdered. There were men engaged in the rebellion who turned from the deed with horror. Many of these had learned something of the magnanimity of Mr. Lincoln's character; and they felt that the time would come when the South would need his friendship. These regarded his death as a great calamity; but it must seem doubtful whether those who could starve helpless prisoners, and massacre black soldiers after they had surrendered, and murder in cool blood hundreds of Union men, for no crime but affection for the government which Mr. Lincoln represented, could have been greatly shocked by his assassination. They made haste, however, to disown and denounce the deed; and pretended to regard it, not as an act of the rebellion, but as the irresponsible act of a crazed desperado.

After the death of the President, his body was removed to the White House, from which he had gone on the previous evening, under such happy circumstances. A room had been prepared for its reception; and there it was placed in a coffin, which rested upon a grand catafalque. The affection and grief of the people were manifested by offerings of flowers, with which the room was kept constantly supplied. On Monday, the seventeenth, a meeting of congressmen and others was held at the Capitol, presided over by Hon. Lafayette S.

Foster of Connecticut. A committee, of which Senator Sumner of Massachusetts was chairman, was appointed to make arrangements for the funeral; and this committee reported at an adjourned meeting, held at four o'clock in the afternoon, that they had selected as pall-bearers Messrs. Foster, Morgan, Johnson, Yates, Wade, and Conness, on the part of the Senate, and Messrs. Dawes, Coffroth, Smith, Colfax, Worthington, and Washburne, on the part of the House. They also presented the names of gentlemen, one from each state and territory of the Union, to act as a congressional committee, to accompany the remains to their final resting-place in Illinois.

Meantime, the body of the President had been embalmed; and, at ten o'clock, on Tuesday morning, the White House was thrown open, to give the people an opportunity to take their farewell of the familiar face, whose kind smile death had forever quenched. At least twenty-five thousand persons availed themselves of this liberty; and thousands more, seeing the crowd, turned back unsatisfied. Hundreds of those who pressed around the sacred dust, uttered some affectionate word, or phrase, or sentence. The rich and the poor, the white and the black, mingled their tokens of affectionate regard, and dropped side by side their tears upon the coffin. It was humanity weeping over the dust of its benefactor.

On Wednesday, the day of the funeral, all the departments were closed, all public work was suspended, flags were placed at half-mast, and the public buildings were draped with mourning. The funeral services were held in the East Room, which was occupied by the relatives of the deceased (with the exception of Mrs. Lincoln, who was too much prostrated to leave her room,) and by governmental and judicial dignitaries, and such high officials from the states as had gathered to the capital to pay their last tribute of respect to the illustrious dead. The ceremonies were conducted with great solemnity and dignity. The scriptures were read by Rev. Dr. Hale, of the Episcopal church; the opening prayer was made by Bishop Simpson, of the Methodist church; the funeral address was delivered by Rev. Dr. Gurley, of the Presbyterian church which

Mr. Lincoln and his family had attended; and the closing prayer was offered by Rev. Dr. Gray, the chaplain of the Senate, and the pastor of a Baptist church. Among those present from the states were Governors Fenton of New York, Andrew of Massachusetts, Parker of New Jersey, Brough of Ohio, Oglesby of Illinois, and Buckingham of Connecticut. Dr. Gurley's tribute was a noble one—entirely worthy of the occasion. "Probably no man since the days of Washington," said he, "was ever so deeply and firmly imbedded and enshrined in the hearts of the people as Abraham Lincoln. Nor was it a mistaken confidence and love. He deserved it; deserved it well; deserved it all. He merited it by his character, by his acts, and by the tenor and tone and spirit of his life. * * * His integrity was thorough, all-pervading, all-controlling and incorruptible." Speaking of the great national emergency in which Mr. Lincoln was called to power, he said: "He rose to the dignity and momentousness of the occasion; saw his duty as the chief magistrate of a great and imperiled people; and he determined to do his duty and his whole duty, seeking the guidance, and leaning upon the arm, of Him of whom it is written—'He giveth power to the faint, and to them that have no might he increaseth strength.' Yes, he leaned upon His arm. He recognized and received the truth that the kingdom is the Lord's."

At the close of the ceremonies in the White House, the august personages present, and various bodies of civil and military officials, joined in the procession which accompanied the sacred remains to the Capitol. It was the most impressive procession that ever passed through the grand avenue which leads from the presidential mansion to the Capitol. The avenue was cleared; and every piazza, window, veranda, and house-top, was filled with eager but mournful faces. Funereal music filled the sweet spring air; and this was the only sound, except the measured tread of feet, and the slow roll of wheels upon the pavement. This procession was so long that the head of it had begun to disperse at the Capitol, before the rear had passed the Treasury Department. As the hearse, drawn by six gray horses, reached the Capitol grounds, the bands burst forth in a requiem, and were answered by minute-guns from the fortifications. The body of the President was borne into the rotunda, where Dr. Gurley completed the religious exercises of.the occasion. Here the remains rested, exposed to public view, but guarded by soldiery, until the next day. Thousands who had had no other opportunity to take their farewell of the beloved dust thronged the Capitol all night. The pageant of the day, in many of its aspects, was never paralleled upon this continent. Nothing like it—nothing approaching it—had ever occurred in this country, if, indeed, in the world.

While these funeral services and ceremonies were in progress in Washington, similar ceremonies were observed in every part of the country. Churches were thrown open, where prayer and sermon and music united in the expression of affection for the dead, and lamentation for the national loss. Great public gatherings were held, in which the memory of the good President was celebrated in impulsive speech or studied eulogy. The whole nation suspended its business, and gave itself up to the mournful services and associations of the day. Never had such a funeral been given to a national ruler. Never had died a man who received such testimonials of universal affection and grief. A whole nation mourned its dead. One thought enthralled every heart—the thought of a great, good man—the father of his people—cruelly murdered; and all animosities were overwhelmed in the general grief. All detraction was hushed; and every heart that had done him wrong, made its amends to his memory, and won peace for itself, by awarding to him his just meed of praise.

As there was never such a funeral as this, so there was never such a procession. That which moved from the White House, on the nineteenth, was but the beginning of a pageant that displayed its marvelous numbers and its ever-varying forms, through country, and village, and city, winding across the territories of vast states, along a track of more than fifteen hundred miles. The President was to be borne back to his own people, and to be buried among the scenes of his early life. He had told the people of Springfield, Illinois, when he parted with them, more than four years before, that he owed to them all that he was. It was but right that they should have his dust.

On the twenty-first, the funeral train left Washington, amid the silent grief of thousands who had gathered to witness its departure. With the coffin which contained the remains of the President, went back to the western home the coffin which contained the dust of his beloved Willie, whose death has already been mentioned; and father and son, in the touching companionship of death, traveled together the long journey. At ten o'clock, the train reached Baltimore. The immense crowd that had assembled here to pay their last tribute of respect to the departed President, was full of its. suggestions of the change which four years had wrought upon the city. It seemed incredible that this was the city through which the living President had so lately passed, in fear of the fate which had at last overtaken him. Nothing that the ingenuity of grief could devise was left undone to make the return passage an imposing testimonial to his memory. The display of military was large; and all the ceremonies of the occasion were such as did honor, alike to the people of the city, and to the man they mourned. In the afternoon, the train moved for Harrisburg, but not until a multitude had improved the opportunity to obtain a view of the pale, dead face of their friend. On the way, new mourners were taken on; and at every considerable station people had gathered to see the solemn pageant sweep by. At York, six ladies came into the car, and deposited upon the coffin an exquisite wreath of flowers, while all who witnessed the affectionate tribute were moved to tears. Bells were tolled, and bands breathed forth their plaintive music, at every village. The funeral obsequies at Harrisburg were observed in the evening. Until midnight, the people crowded into the State Capitol, to obtain a view of the remains; and, from seven to nine on the following morning, the catafalque was surrounded by the anxious throngs that

had come in from all the country round, for the purpose.   At
this place, as at all the places on the route, there were new
pall-bearers, new processions, and new expressions of the
popular grief.   A very large procession accompanied the remains to the cars; and from Harrisburg to Philadelphia the
funeral train moved through crowds of people, assembled at
every convenient point.   For several miles before the train
reached Philadelphia, both sides of the railway were occupied
by almost continuous lines of men, women, and children, who
stood with uncovered heads as the train passed them.

Philadelphia was draped with mourning, to give a fitting
reception to the honored dead.   The streets were filled with
people, long before the funeral train arrived; and cannon
thundered forth the announcement of its coming.   All that
ingenuity, aided by abundant means, could do, to make the
fresh pageant a worthy one, was done.   A new hearse had
been built, and this was drawn by eight splendid black horses,
in silver-mounted harnesses.   The procession itself was composed of eleven divisions, and was one of the most remarkable,
in every respect, with which the remains of the President
were honored during their long passage to their resting-place.
What place more fit for the brief sojourn of these remains
than Independence Hall, intimately associated, as it was,
with the principles which the sleeping patriot had faithfully
defended, and still echoing to the ear of sorrowing affection
with the sound of his living voice?   To this hall he was borne,
amid the tears of a vast multitude.   The hall was literally
filled with the most exquisite flowers.   From ten o'clock until
midnight, the people had the opportunity to view the remains
of their beloved chief magistrate.   Then the doors were
closed; but hundreds remained around the building all night,
that they might be first in the morning.   The following day
was Sunday, and from six o'clock in the morning until one
o'clock on Monday morning, during which the remains were
exposed to view, a dense, unbroken stream of men, women,
and children, pressed into and out of the building.   The Philadelphia Inquirer, in its report of the occasion, said: "Never

before in the history of our city was such a dense mass of humanity huddled together. Hundreds of persons were seriously injured, from being pressed in the mob; and many fainting females were extricated by the police and military, and conveyed to places of security." After a person was once in the line, it took from four to five hours to reach the hall. At one o'clock, on Monday morning, the procession recommenced its march, bearing the body to Kensington Station, which was left at four, for the passage to New York. Bells were tolled, mottoes were displayed, minute-guns were fired, and the people were gathered at the various stations along the entire passage through New Jersey. It seemed as if the whole state had come to the railroad line, simply to witness the passage of the funeral train.

It is bewildering to read the accounts of the ceremonies at New York, and impracticable to reproduce them. The passage of the beloved remains into and through the great city, and the interval of their brief rest while they lay in state in the City Hall, were marked at every stage by some new and impressive expression of the public grief. Minute-guns, tolling bells, requiems by choirs of singers, dirges by bands of musicians, military and civic displays, suspended business, draped flags, and shrouded private and public buildings,— all mingled their testimony to the universal sorrow, and the common wish to do justice and honor to a hallowed memory. Every street and avenue around the City Hall was filled with people. The first line formed for viewing the remains was three quarters of a mile long, and reached far up the Bowery. From the moment when the coffin-lid was removed, until nearly noon on the following day, through all the long night, the people pressed into the hall, caught a hasty glimpse of the beloved features, and then retired; until it was estimated that one hundred and fifty thousand persons had gained their object, while it was evident that twice that number had failed to win the patiently awaited vision. The military procession which accompanied the remains to the depot of the Hudson River Railroad was the most remarkable ever wit-

34

nessed in the city, numbering fully fifteen thousand troops. The carriages in the procession were filled with federal and state dignitaries, and representatives of foreign governments in full court costume; and the line of the procession was thronged from the beginning to the end by crowding multitudes of spectators. The New York Herald's report says: "The people, with tearful eyes, under the shadow of the great affliction, watched patiently and unmurmuringly the moving of the honored dead and the mournful procession, and silently breathed over them the most heartfelt and fervent prayers. * * * Such an occasion, such a crowd, and such a day, New York may never see again."

At a quarter past four, on the afternoon of the twenty-fifth, the train which bore the funeral party from New York left the station, drawn by the "Union," the same locomotive that brought Mr. Lincoln to New York, on his passage to Washington, more than four years previously. The train passed to Albany without stopping, except at Poughkeepsie, where a delegation from the city government of Albany was taken on board; but the people were gathered at every point to witness the passage. Mottoes were displayed, draped flags floated everywhere, and all along the route stood the silent crowds, with heads uncovered, as the train which bore the martyred President swept by. It was nearly midnight when Albany was reached; and it was not until one o'clock, on the morning of the twenty-sixth, that the removal of the coffin-lid exposed, in the State Capitol, the white face that so many were anxious to see. From that time until two o'clock in the afternoon, there was a constant throng, the line reaching four deep from the State House to the foot of State street. It was estimated that there were sixty thousand people in the streets of Albany. Here was another great procession; and, at four o'clock in the afternoon, the train started for Buffalo. Throughout the entire range of large and beautiful towns which the Central Railroad threads in its passage from Albany to Buffalo, the same demonstrations of grief and respect were witnessed which had thus far distinguished the homeward journey of the dead President. The reporter of the New York Tribune wrote that "a funeral in each house in Central New York would hardly have added solemnity to the day."

At seven o'clock on the morning of the twenty-seventh, the funeral train reached Buffalo; and the sacred remains were taken to St. James' Hall, where, from half-past nine until eight o'clock in the evening of the next day, they were visited by an immense throng of persons. Buffalo had already paid its tribute to Mr. Lincoln's memory by a large procession on the day of the funeral ceremonies at Washington, and omitted the usual pageant on this occasion; but a fine military escort, accompanied by a crowd of citizens, conducted the remains to the depot in the evening, which was left by the funeral train at ten o'clock, for the pursuit of the journey to Cleveland. The demonstrations of the popular grief which had been witnessed throughout the journey, were repeated at every station along the route. Not only men, but women and children were up and wakeful all night, to catch a glimpse of the car which bore the precious dust of the beloved ruler; and, whenever the train stopped, flowers were brought in and deposited upon the coffin. At Cleveland, great preparations were made to receive the President's remains and the funeral party, with befitting honors. A building for the deposit of the coffin was erected in the park, that the people might have easy access to it. The city was crowded at an early hour, on Friday morning; and on every hand were displayed the symbols of mourning. At seven o'clock, the train arrived at the Union depot, amid a salute of artillery; and from this point it was taken back to the Euclid Street station of the Cleveland and Pittsburg Railroad, whence the procession moved—the most imposing pageant that this beautiful city on the lake had ever created or witnessed. Bishop McIlvaine, of the diocese of Ohio, read the Episcopal burial service on the opening of the coffin, and offered prayer; after which the long procession filed through the pavilion, and caught a last glimpse of the honored dead. All day long, through falling rain, the crowd, unabated in numbers, pressed through the little building. At ten o'clock at night, one hundred thousand people had viewed the remains; and then the gates were shut. Soon afterwards, the coffin was taken from its beautiful resting-place; and, at twelve o'clock, the funeral party was again in progress, on the way to Columbus, the capital of the state.

But why repeat the same story again, and again? Why say more than that at Columbus and Indianapolis and Chicago, as well as at all the intermediate places, men did what they could, and all that they could, to honor him who had died in their service—who had been murdered for his truth to them and to freedom? It was a most remarkable exhibition of the popular feeling, and is unparalleled in history. There was nothing empty, nothing fictitious about it. There was never a sincerer tribute of affection rendered to a man than this. It was a costly one, but men rendered it gladly, and hesitated no more at the cost than if they were expressing their grief over the lost members of their own homes.

It seemed almost like profanation of the sleeping President's rest, to bear him so far, and expose him so much; but the people demanded it, and would take no denial. All parties, all sects—friends and foes alike—mingled in their affectionate tributes of honor and sorrow.

When the remains of the President reached Chicago, they were at home. They were in the State in which he had spent the most of his life; and the people grasped him with almost a selfish sense of ownership. He was theirs. Only a short distance from the spot, lay his old antagonist, Douglas, in his last sleep. The party champions were once more near each other, upon their favorite soil; but their eloquent lips were silent—silent with an eloquence surpassing sound, in the proclamation of mighty changes in the nation, and the suggestions of mutability and mortality among men. One more journey, and the weary form would rest. The people of Chicago honored the dead President with emotions that few thus far had experienced. Mr. Lincoln had been loved and admired by the people of Illinois, long before the rest of the nation knew anything about him. His face and voice had been familiar to them for many years; and they had introduced him to the country and to immortality. He had walked through the portals of the new city into a fame as wide as the world. "He comes back to us," said the Chicago Tribune, "his work finished, the republic vindicated, its enemies overthrown and suing for peace. * * * He left us, asking that the prayers of the people might be offered to Almighty God for wisdom and help to see the right path and pursue it. Those prayers were answered. He accomplished his work, and now the prayers of the people ascend for help, to bear the great affliction which has fallen upon them. Slain as no other man has been slain, cut down while interposing his great charity and mercy between the wrath of the people and guilty traitors, the people of Chicago tenderly receive the sacred ashes, with bowed heads and streaming eyes."

The remains reached Springfield on the morning of May third. Throughout the long ride of two hundred miles, over the continuous prairie that lies between Chicago and Springfield, there had transpired the most affecting demonstrations of the popular grief. Mottoes, flags, minute-guns, immense gatherings of the people, music, flowers, and copious tears, testified the universal sorrow. But in Springfield lived the heartiest mourners. Here were his intimate and life-long personal friends; and they received the dust of their murdered neighbor and fellow-citizen with a tenderness of which the people of no other community were capable. The President was forgotten in the companion and friend, endeared to them by a thousand ties. The State House, the Lincoln residence, and every store, public building, and dwelling, were draped heavily with mourning—a manifestation of the public sorrow which remained for weeks and months after it had disappeared from all other places that had been passed in the long procession. For twenty-four hours, or until ten o'clock on the morning of May fourth, the people pressed into the State House, to gain a last glimpse of their departed friend. Through all the long night of the third, the steady tramp of thousands was heard, winding up the stair-case that led to the Representatives' Chamber, and passing out again. Silently, patiently, sorrowfully, the unfailing procession moved; and it did not stop until the coffin-lid was shut down, no more to be opened. The procession which conducted the remains to their final resting-place, in a tomb prepared for them at Oak Ridge Cemetery, a beautiful spot about two miles from the city, was under the immediate charge of Major-general Joseph Hooker. The town was thronged; and every train that arrived augmented the crowd. A large choir of two hundred and fifty singers sang the familiar hymn, beginning with the words,

"Children of the Heavenly King,"

as the coffin was borne out to the hearse; and amid the sounds of solemn dirges and minute-guns the mournful procession moved. The cemetery was occupied by a vast multitude, before the procession arrived; and from hill and tree they looked tearfully on, while the coffin which contained the dust of their friend was consigned to its sepulcher. By the side of it was placed the coffin of "little Willie;" while the living sons, Robert and Thomas, standing by the tomb, were objects of an affectionate interest only equaled by the deep sorrow for their own and their country's loss. Rev. A. Hale of Springfield opened the religious exercises with prayer; a hymn written for the occasion was sung; selections from Scripture, and Mr. Lincoln's last Inaugural were read; and Bishop Simpson, a favorite of Mr. Lincoln while living, delivered an eloquent address. Requiems and dirges, sung and played, completed the exercises of the occasion, closing with a benediction by Rev. Dr. Gurley of Washington.

The address of Bishop Simpson, able, affectionate, and excellent as it was, contained nothing more notable than the quotation that the speaker made from one of Mr. Lincoln's speeches, uttered in 1859, in which, speaking of the slave power, he said: "Broken by it I, too, may be, bow to it, I never will. The probability that we may fail in the struggle, ought not to deter us from the support of a cause which I deem to be just; and it shall not deter me. If ever I feel the soul within me elevate and expand to those dimensions not wholly unworthy of its Almighty Architect, it is when I contemplate the cause of my country, deserted by all the world besides, and I, standing up boldly and alone, and hurling defiance at her victorious oppressors. Here, without contemplating consequences, before high Heaven and in the face of the world, I swear eternal fidelity to the just cause, as I deem it, of the land of my life, my liberty and my love." No inspiration finer than this breathes in any of Mr. Lincoln's utterances. It almost seems as if an intimation of his life and death were given to him at the moment—as if a glimpse into his own and his country's future had been vouchsafed to his excited vision.

The crowd slowly separated; the citizens moved back to their homes; those who had accompanied the precious remains—at last resting, and in safe and affectionate keeping— from Washington and points along the route, took their departure by the out-going trains; the guard paced their little round before the tomb, where through the grate the large and the little coffin lay in the dim light; and the people of Springfield were left to their grief and their glory.

There, surrounded by the sweetest scenes of nature, his tomb a shrine, his name the watchword of liberty, his fame in the affectionate keeping of mankind, his memory hallowed by martyrdom for the humane and Christian principles to which his life was devoted, the weary patriot rests. His sun went down suddenly, and whelmed the country in a darkness which was felt by every heart; but far up the clouds sprang soon the golden twilight, flooding the heavens with radiance, and illuminating every uncovered brow with the hope of a fair to-morrow. The aching head, the shattered nerves, the anxious heart, the weary frame, are all at rest; and the noble spirit that informed them, bows reverently and humbly in the presence of Him in whom it trusted, and to whose work it devoted the troubled years of its earthly life.

The death of Mr. Lincoln wrought a great change in the feelings of all the representatives of foreign opinion, not only toward him, but toward the country and its cause; and many were the testimonials that came in every ship, of foreign sympathy with the nation in its bereavement, and with those whose family life had been so cruelly dissolved by the deed of the assassin. The British Queen wrote to Mrs. Lincoln a letter of condolence, with her own hand. All the foreign governments took occasion to express their horror at the crime which had deprived the nation of its head, and their sympathy with the people thus suddenly and violently bereft. The London Times, which had always been unjust to Mr. Lincoln, said: "It would be unjust not to acknowledge that Mr. Lincoln was a man who could not, under any circumstances, have been easily replaced." Further on in its article, it confessed that "Englishmen learned to respect a man who showed the best characteristics of their race, in his respect for what is good in the past, acting in unison with a recognition of what was made necessary by the events of passing history." The London Star said: "It can never be forgotten, while history is read, that the hands of southern partisans have been reddened by the foulest assassin-plot the world has ever known; that they have been treacherously dipped in the blood of one of the best citizens and purest patriots to whom the land of Washington gave birth." The London Spectator spoke of Mr. Lincoln as "the noblest President whom America has had since the time of Washington;" and "certainly the best, if not the ablest, man ruling over any country in the civilized world." The London Saturday Review said: "During the arduous experience of four years, Mr. Lincoln constantly rose in general estimation, by calmness of temper, by an intuitively logical appreciation of the character of the conflict, and by undisputed sincerity." The Economist said: "The murder of Mr. Lincoln is a very great and very lamentable event—perhaps the greatest and most lamentable which has occurred since the *Coup d'etat*, if not since Waterloo. It affects directly and immensely the welfare of the three most powerful countries in the world,—America, France and England,—and it affects them all for evil." Goldwin Smith, in

Macmillan's Magazine, said: "He (Mr. Lincoln) professed to wait on events, or, rather, on the manifestations of the moral forces around him, wherein, with a mind sobered by responsibility and unclouded by selfishness, he earnestly endeavored to read the will of God, which, having read it, he patiently followed to the best of his power. In him, his nation has lost, not a king, or a prophet,—not a creative moulder of its destinies, or an inspired unfolder of its future,—but simply a sensible interpreter, and a wise, temperate, honest executor of its own better mind."

Even these expressions of the British press do not indicate the popular feeling with which the English people received the announcement of Mr. Lincoln's assassination. The excitement which filled the public mind, on the reception of the startling tidings, in all the great cities and considerable towns of England, was only equaled by that which swept over those of our own country. It was hard to tell whether horror at the crime or grief for its victim was the predominant emotion of the British people. Men who applauded the deed, were kicked out of assemblies in London, as they were in New York. The dignified Mr. Mason, the rebel commissioner, was boldly condemned for an attempt to extenuate the crime on the ground that it was a natural incident of civil war.

At home, the change of feeling was hardly less marked and gratifying. Presses that had done Mr. Lincoln injustice throughout his whole career, made haste to lay their tribute of respectful praise upon his bier. Men who had cursed him, joined tearfully in the processions which attended his long journey homeward. Even from the depths of the dead rebellion, there came honest lamentations, and sincere praises. The eyes of his "blinded fellow countrymen," which he so ardently desired to open, were unsealed at last, to behold, in the man they had so long regarded with hatred or contempt, the friend they had always possessed, and the benefactor they sorely needed, but had lost forever.

Andrew Johnson, the Vice-president, became, under the provisions of the Constitution, the President of the United States, by taking the oath of office, on the morning of the murder. The people who had battled for the Constitution and the laws so long, did not dream of a resort to any other course. The speculations of a portion of the foreign press, concerning this event, showed how unworthy and inadequate still was the estimate of the American people and their institutions. There was not a hand lifted, or a word uttered, to question or dispute the step which installed a new President over the republic; and there was not, in a single American heart, a doubt as to the result. There was no panic, no excitement, no danger, no disaster; but the country kept to its groove, and felt no jar as it slid into the new administration.

The world could not conceal Mr. Lincoln's murderer. It had no waste so wide, no cavern so deep, as to give him a safe hiding-place. That was evident to everybody; and would have been foreseen by himself, had he not been stultified by his greed for blood. Large rewards were offered for his apprehension, and military and police were quickly on the alert. After a few days of doubt, it became evident that Booth, with a companion, had passed over the Navy Yard Bridge, which crosses the eastern branch of the Potomac. It was known that the assassin had been in the habit of spending much time in Charles County, Maryland, and had been in correspondence with the disloyal people there. It afterwards appeared that Booth, accompanied by David C. Harold, rode all night after the commission of the murder; and that near Bogantown he called on one Dr. Mudd, to have his leg dressed, which had been fractured by his leap upon the stage, at the time he committed the murder. The detectives, reaching this region, and hearing that Dr. Mudd had received the visit of two suspicious strangers, arrested him and all his family. From this point, Booth and his accomplice were tracked toward the Potomac. The ruffians were undoubtedly aided in their progress by disloyal citizens, for the officers were frequently not more than an hour behind them. Although gunboats were patrolling the river, the murderer and his accomplice crossed the Potomac under cover of darkness. It was soon afterwards ascertained where they had crossed, and the cavalry started in pursuit. The men were found at last in a barn belonging to William Garratt. The building was surrounded, and Booth was called upon to surrender himself. He flatly refused to do so. Harold was ready to surrender, but Booth cursed him for a coward; and declared to Colonel Baker, at the head of the force, that he would not be taken alive. The barn was fired, and Booth attempted to extinguish the flame, but failed. Harold then gave himself up, while the murderer remained, displaying all the qualities of the hardened desperado. Sergeant Boston Corbett, moved by a sudden impulse, drew up his pistol, and fired upon Booth, who was seen standing in the barn, with a revolver in each hand; and planted a ball in his neck, which passed entirely through his head. He died within less than three hours, sending to his mother a message to the effect that he had died for his country, and exhibiting no penitence whatever for the terrible deed he had committed. He was shot on the twenty-sixth of April, twelve days after the murder. His body was taken back to Washington, and was buried, no one save those to whom the task of sepulture was assigned having any knowledge of its place of burial. Harold was committed to prison to await his trial.

John Wilkes Booth was the son of the famous actor, Junius Brutus Booth, and had attained some celebrity in his father's profession. He was an exceedingly handsome man; but he had been notoriously and grossly profligate and immoral in his habits. Still, his gifts and his beauty had made him a favorite in certain nominally respectable social circles. His sympathy with the rebellion was well understood in Washington, but he was never regarded as a dangerous man. That he committed the crime which cost him his life from any romantic love of the South, or from any desire to avenge the South for fancied wrongs, is not probable. The deed seems to have been the offspring of a morbid desire for immortality. He had given frequent hints, in his conversation, of the miserable passion which possessed him; and there is no doubt that he had worked himself into a belief that he should rid the world of a tyrant by murdering the President, and thus link his name with a startling deed which, in the future, would be admired as a glorious act of heroism. Certainly his deed was one of wonderful boldness; and the bravery which he exhibited at his capture was worthy of a better cause and a better man.

Fortunately, no fatal wounds were inflicted upon Mr. Seward in Payne's attempt upon his life, or upon any of those who were subjects of violence at that ruffian's hands. The Secretary and his son, Mr. Frederick Seward, were desperately wounded; but, under skillful surgical care, they entirely recovered. Payne was arrested, and, with his fellow conspirators—David E. Harold (who was captured with Booth,) George A. Atzerodt, Michael O'Laughlin, Edward Spangler (who held Booth's horse at the theater, and aided his escape,) Samuel Arnold, Mary E. Surratt and Dr. Samuel Mudd— was tried by a military commission. The conspiracy contemplated not only the murder of Mr. Lincoln and Mr. Seward, but that of Vice-president Johnson and Lieutenant-general Grant. Booth alone accomplished his task. Payne made a desperate effort,—such as only a man of his great physical strength could make; but failed. Atzerodt, to whose hands the murder of the Vice-president was committed, was not. competent, morally or physically, to the task he undertook; while General Grant escaped the projected attempt upon his life by leaving the city. Harold, Atzerodt, Payne and Mrs. Surratt, the latter of whom aided and abetted the plot, were sentenced to be hanged; and they suffered the penalty of their crimes on the seventh day of July. Dr. Mudd, Samuel Arnold, and Michael O'Laughlin were sentenced to hard labor for life, and were consigned to the Dry Tortugas. Edward Spangler accompanied them, sentenced to hard labor for six years.

The writer cannot bid farewell to the reader, and to the illustrious subject of this biography, without a closing tribute to a character unique in history, and an administration that stands alone in the annals of the nation. We have seen one of the humblest of American citizens struggling through personal trials and national turmoils, into the light of universal fame, and an assured immortality of renown. We have seen him become the object of warm and devoted affection to a whole nation. We have witnessed such manifestations of grief at his loss as the death of no ruler has called forth, within the memory of man. We have seen a great popular government, poisoned in every department by the virus of treason, and blindly and feebly tottering to its death, restored to health and soundness through the beneficent ministry of this true man, who left it with vigor in its veins, irresistible strength in its arms, the fire of exultation and hope in its eyes, and with such power and majesty in its step, that the earth shook beneath its stately goings. We have seen four millions of African bondmen who, groaning in helpless slavery when he received the crown of power, became freemen by his word before death struck that crown from his brow. We have seen the enemies of his country vanquished and suing for pardon; and the sneering nations of the world, whose incontinent contempt and spite were poured in upon him during the first years of his administration, becoming first silent, then respectful, and then unstinted in their admiration and approbation.

These marvelous changes in public feeling, and the revolutions imbodied in these wonderful results, were not the work of a mighty genius, sitting above the nation, and ordering its affairs. That Mr. Lincoln was much more than an ordinary man, in intellectual power, is sufficiently evident; but it was not by intellectual power that he wrought out the grand results of his life. These were rather the work of the heart, than the head. With no wish to depreciate the motives or undervalue the names of Mr. Lincoln's predecessors in office, it may be declared that never, in the history of the government, have the affairs of that office been administered with such di-

rect reference to the will of God, and the everlasting principles of righteousness and justice, as they were during his
administration. It was eminently a Christian administration—
one which, in its policy and acts, expressed the convictions of
a Christian people. Standing above the loose morality of
party politics, standing above the maxims and conventional-
isms of statesmanship, leaving aside all the indirections and
insincerities of diplomacy, trusting the people, leaning upon
the people, inspired by the people, who in their Christian
homes and Christian sanctuaries gave it their confidence, this
administration of Abraham Lincoln stands out in history as
the finest exhibition of a Christian democracy the world has
ever seen. The power of a true-hearted Christian man, in
perfect sympathy with a true-hearted Christian people, was
Mr. Lincoln's power. Open on one side of his nature to all
descending influences from Him to whom he prayed, and open
on the other to all ascending influences from the people whom
he served, he aimed simply to do his duty, to God and men.
Acting rightly, he acted greatly. While he took care of
deeds, fashioned by a purely ideal standard, God took care of
results. Moderate, frank, truthful, gentle, forgiving, loving,
just, Mr. Lincoln will always be remembered as eminently a
Christian President; and the almost immeasurably great results which he had the privilege of achieving, were due to the
fact that he was a Christian President.

Conscience, and not expediency, not temporary advantage,
not popular applause, not the love of power, was the ruling and guiding motive of his life. He was conscientious
in his devotion to the Constitution and the laws. In this
he was in advance of his people, and in advance of a multitude of his own friends. With every constitutional right,
he dealt tenderly and carefully, while taunted by his own
friends with subserviency to an institution which, in his inmost soul, he hated. His respect for law was as profound
and sincere as his respect for God and his will. Uninfluenced
by popular clamor, and unbent by his own humane and Christian desire to see all men free, he did not speak the word of

emancipation until his duty to the Constitution which he had sworn to protect and defend demanded it. There is no doubt that, if he could have saved the country without destroying slavery, he would have done it, and done it against the most ardent wishes of his heart, through his regard for the Constitution which protected the inhuman institution, and the oath by which he had been invested with power. It was not slowness, nor coldness, nor indifference, that delayed the emancipation of the slaves. It was loyal, devoted, self-denying virtue.

Mr. Lincoln was conscientious in his patience. He knew and felt the weakness of human nature, and appreciated the force of education in moulding character and opinion. Hence, he was patient with his enemies, and equally patient with equally unreasonable friends. No hasty act of his administration can be traced to his impatience. When such an act was performed, and was followed by its inevitable consequences of evil, it originated in the impatience of those whom he could not control. His steps were taken with the deliberateness of destiny; and, as these steps are retraced by the historian, he can compare them to nothing but those leisurely and irresistible proceedings by which the Great Father in whom the good President trusted had wrought out his will in creation and Providence. Step by step, hand in hand with events, he worked and waited patiently, for the great consummation to which all the efforts of his life were devoted. Maligned, misunderstood, abused, cursed, his motives the foot-balls of malice and envy and pride and foolishness, he waited patiently for history to vindicate him, and permitted no smarting sense of personal injustice to divert him from his duty to his country.

He was conscientious in his regard for human rights. His opposition to slavery, and his love of the African, were no mere matters of policy, or means for winning power. He had a tender, brotherly regard for every human being; and the thought of oppression was a torment to him. There was nothing that moved him to such indignation as a wrong committed against the helpless ones of his own kind. He believed that negroes were men, endowed by their Creator with the rights of men; and, thus believing, there was no manly privilege which he enjoyed, that he would not have been glad to see conferred upon them. Hence, had he lived, he would logically have numbered himself among those who will agitate the right of universal loyal suffrage until that right shall be secured to every loyal man living under the American flag.

In Mr. Lincoln's life and character, the American people have received a benefaction not less in permanent importance and value, than in the revolution in opinion and policy by which he introduced them to a new national life. He has given them a statesman without a statesman's craftiness, a politician without a politician's meannesses, a great man without a great man's vices, a philanthropist without a philanthropist's impracticable dreams, a Christian without pretensions, a ruler without the pride of place and power, an ambitious man without selfishness, and a successful man without vanity. On the basis of such a manhood as this, all the coming generations of the nation will not fail to build high and beautiful ideals of human excellence, whose attractive power shall raise to a nobler level the moral sense and moral character of the nation. This true manhood—simple, unpretending, sympathetic with all humanity, and reverent toward God—is among the noblest of the nation's treasures; and through it, God has breathed, and will continue to breathe, into the nation, the elevating and purifying power of his own divine life.

Humble child of the backwoods—boatman, ax-man, hired laborer, clerk, surveyor, captain, legislator, lawyer, debater, orator, politician, statesman, President, savior of the republic, emancipator of a race, true Christian, true man—we receive thy life and its immeasurably great results, as the choicest gifts that a mortal has ever bestowed upon us; grateful to thee for thy truth to thyself, to us, and to God; and grateful to that ministry of Providence and grace which endowed thee so richly, and bestowed thee upon the nation and mankind.

INDEX